W9-BKB-738

An
American
History
SECOND EDITION

SECOND EDITION

Volume I to 1877

Rebecca Brooks Gruver

**Hunter College of the
City University of New York**

ADDISON-WESLEY PUBLISHING COMPANY

*Reading, Massachusetts ▪ Menlo Park, California
London ▪ Amsterdam
Don Mills, Ontario ▪ Sydney*

 Printed in the United States of America. Published simultaneously in Canada. Library of Congress Catalog Card No. 75-14794.

ISBN 0-201-02739-9
EFGHIJKLM-DO-7987

To my mentor
Armin Rappaport

Preface

This second edition of *An American History* is a substantive and comprehensive revision. As all new editions should, this revision has benefited from use, from the opportunity to evaluate and reconsider content and coverage, and particularly from the constructive—sometimes critical but always helpful—comments of students and teachers.

The entire text has been rewritten. Still evident are characteristics of the original edition generally applauded by students and teachers alike, such as the use of clear and familiar language and the coherence of presentation. At the same time, we have expanded the development of some ideas and themes and updated the research and historiography. We also focus on tracing more clearly the historical origins of complex problems and influential movements and developments and on integrating new material on the lives of minorities, working people, and women. A completely new chapter brings the coverage of events up through President Ford's first year in office and adds considerably to our treatment of more recent events. There are many new illustrations, the maps have been improved, and a number of charts have been added to give some statistical depth to the book's coverage.

The revised text also incorporates, where relevant, a consideration of what the author believes to be the significant and enduring ideals of American history: individual freedom, equality of opportunity, and a humanitarian concern for the less fortunate and oppressed in society. These ideals have not always been expressed with any uniformity, nor have they always worked harmoniously with each other. But our nation's history does demonstrate the uneven efforts of a diverse population to give expression to their ideals and to come to terms with the gap between their ideals and reality.

Thirteen brief feature articles, each telling a story with particular interest for young Americans in the 1970s, add a further new dimension to the text's coverage. *New Worlds* (p. 68), for example, speculates on the relevance of our first colonists' experience to future colonists' attempts to settle other planets. *Written with a Sunbeam: Women in the American Revolution* (p. 140) describes the contribution a number of American women made to the Revolutionary War effort. *Early Television: Creating a National Neighborhood* (p. 854) discusses the way television has created a new kind of shared national experience. And *The American History of Yap* (p. 953) describes life-style changes on a small Pacific island since it became a United States protectorate. There is a complete list of special features on p. x of the Contents.

While improving the original edition, we have also been careful to retain the features that students and teachers most liked. The essays on interpretive controversies remain and have been brought up to date. And the contrasting opinions of people who have been involved in some of our country's major events also remain, although in a more abbreviated form. Both students and teachers appreciate material that suggests the role of controversy in shaping past events as well as the way we look at the past.

The second edition remains a comprehensive treatment of the American past. While there is broad and incisive coverage of political and diplomatic events, equal attention is also given to the evolution of the American economy from a simple agrarian society to its present position of industrial leadership. The development of business enterprise is presented in such a way as to show its influence on other important sectors of the economy, such as labor and agriculture. The impact of the country's ethnic diversity and racial problems has also been described in some detail. And finally, the social and intellectual history of the nation has been given broad coverage.

For those who are interested in supplementary teaching aids, the *Study Guide and Workbook*, *Instructor's Manual*, and *Test Items Book* have also been comprehensively revised for the second edition. The *Study Guide and Workbook* contains many new questions, including a large number that help the student understand some of the more conceptual aspects of American history. The *Instructor's Manual* has new behavioral objectives for each chapter, and many of the Resources for Discussion have been changed to include some of the latest scholarship. Finally, the *Test Items Book* includes many new questions demanding that the student show a more substantive understanding of the material.

ACKNOWLEDGMENTS

I would like to extend my special appreciation to Joan Labby, Project Editor, for her unflagging dedication to the highest standards of accuracy and clarity of expression. I would also like to express my gratitude to the following people, whose help was invaluable in improving the second edition: Marlou Belyea, Alex Bloom, Jim Bradley, Marilyn Clawson, Armand Choquette, Michael J. Crawford, Richard O. Curry (University of Connecticut), Eleanor Weber Dickman, Charles Farkas, Mary Pat Fisher, Ellen Fitzpatrick, Sam Hurst, Nancy Jones, David Labby, Michele Schurgin Lachman, Cristin Lindstrom, Jessica Lipnack, Thomas McDaid (Columbia University), Sabra Wakefield Morton, Thomas B. Nickel, Meredith Nightingale, Kim Phillips (University of Connecticut), Thomas M. Preisser (Sinclair Community College), Frederick Simon, Jeffrey Stamps, Judith Wallace, Frank White, Charles E. Wynes (University of Georgia), and Howard Zavin (Hunter College).

R.B.G.

New York
January 1976

Contents

The French arrive in Florida. Engraved in 1591 from a painting by Jacques le Moyne, an artist who accompanied the French expedition to Florida in 1564. ▶

1

The Meeting of Two Worlds

The French landed on the shore of this river and were met by a number of Indians, who received them with kindness and in the friendliest spirit. The natives were anxious to prove with deeds how well they meant; some of them gave their own garments, made of skins, to the French commander, and they offered to take him to their chief. When they came before him, the chief was sitting upon boughs of palm and laurel and did not rise; but he presented our commander with a large skin decorated with pictures of wild animals.

Jacques le Moyne, 1564

People began migrating westward from Asia into the Americas before the dawn of recorded history. Estimates of the first arrivals vary from 12,000 to 35,000 years ago, but most experts agree that these first immigrants came across the Bering Strait. They were probably able to come on foot, traveling across a land bridge which connected Siberia with Alaska. According to current theories, this land bridge was submerged at the end of the last Ice Age, about 10,000 years ago. At this time, all overland passage came to a halt.

Some anthropologists believe that later travelers sailed to the Americas across the Pacific. One group is thought to have come from present-day Japan to the coast of Ecuador in about 3000 B.C., bringing pottery and perhaps domesticated cotton. Still later, some of the first Asians who sailed to the Polynesian islands may have come further east, arriving in the Western Hemisphere between A.D. 500 and 1000.

By the fifteenth century there were millions of people in the Americas, and they had organized themselves into many different political units. Some of the civilizations were primitive, but others were among the most advanced cultures in the world.

The Aztecs of Mexico

One of the most advanced Indian cultures was that of the Aztecs who rose to power in central Mexico in the fifteenth century. When a Spanish army of conquest led by Hernando Cortez arrived in 1519, they found a flourishing civilization of over five million people. The Aztecs presided over a loosely administered empire. For the most part, other tribes living in territories controlled by the Aztecs were left alone as long as they paid tribute and traded on favorable terms.

The Aztecs inherited much of their technical know-how from the Mayas, an earlier Central American civilization. Thanks to these remarkable predecessors, the Aztecs possessed a system of hieroglyphic writing and astronomical knowledge so precise that their priests were able to predict eclipses and devise an accurate calendar. They were also advanced in other arts and sciences, including mathematics, pottery, sculpture, and architecture. The Aztec capital, Tenochtitlan, covered about eight square miles of the area that is now Mexico City. It had about sixty thousand citizens, and was built around a pyramid 200 feet high. To support a city of this size, the Aztecs had to use sophisticated agricultural techniques, such as irrigation and terracing. However, neither they nor any of the other tribes of the New World had discovered the wheel and its uses. Because horses did not exist in the Western Hemisphere until they were introduced by the Europeans, most transport depended on human beings or boats.

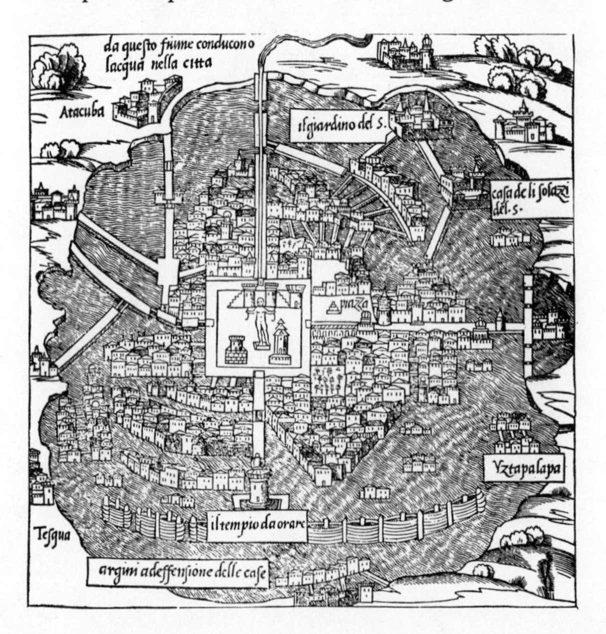

Mexico City in 1528. ▶

The Incas of Peru

When the Spanish conquistadores arrived in Peru in the sixteenth century, they also found an advanced civilization there. The rulers of this area were the Incas, who controlled a vast empire of seven million people that extended some 2000 miles along the Pacific coast of South America. The Incas had possessed an advanced culture, equal in complexity to any of the civilizations of Europe or Asia, since about 200 B.C.

Like the Aztecs, the Incas were sophisticated in the area of agriculture. They built extensive aqueducts and irrigation systems, and enriched their crops with fertilizer. They were the originators of many edible plants, including the white potato. Textile weaving was another achievement of South American culture. Llama and alpaca wools were woven, embroidered, and braided into fabrics. The material was then ornamented with designs dyed as many as 190 different hues on a single piece of cloth.

Politically, the Inca civilization was dominated by the emperor and his family. All property was owned by the government or the state religious organization. Every aspect of life, from public health to the transportation of food from one end of the empire to the other, was controlled by the ruling family which presided over its holdings with great ceremony. Surrounded by numerous wives and servants, Inca rulers wore gold and silver and were carried about on litters.

To maintain their authority over conquered areas, the Incas used harsh and dictatorial methods, including forcibly uprooting troublemakers and moving them elsewhere. The Inca language, customs, and religion were imposed on the entire empire, and the historical traditions of subjugated peoples were obliterated. The totalitarianism of the Inca empire helps explain their defeat by the Spanish conquistadores. Once the head was overthrown, administration broke down rapidly throughout the whole empire.

The Indians of North America

Most anthropologists believe that of the fifteen to twenty million Indians in the Western Hemisphere at the time of Columbus' arrival, only about one million were living in what is now the United States and Canada. There were many important differences among all the tribes scattered over this immense area, but a few generalizations can be made. The Indians of North America tended to be less technologically advanced than the Aztecs or the Incas. Their forms of political organization were also very different from their neighbors to the south, as were their religious practices. For example, most North American Indians believed in a Great Spirit which pervaded the universe, and were more likely to practice healing ceremonies than the rites of human sacrifice and self-torture used by some of the Mexican and South American tribes.

Of all the Indian cultures of the United States, perhaps the most advanced in Western terms when the Europeans arrived were the tribes of the American Southwest—the Hopis, the Zunis, and the Pueblos. These Indians were peace-loving, farming people. They lived in stone or adobe (dried mud) homes which almost had the look of modern apartments. Built into cliff walls or at the top of steep plateaus, some of the structures were four stories high and looked down upon spacious streets and squares. Collectively, these tribes are known as the Pueblo people, after the Spanish word *pueblo*, meaning town. So community-minded were the Pueblos that wealth was divided equally among all residents. No distinctions of possessions, work, or prestige were allowed among the members of any village.

Indian town of Secota in Virginia. 1590.

As was the case with most Indian cultures, Pueblo life was dominated by religion. The men of the village devoted as much as half their time to various rituals, often performed with brilliantly colored prayer sticks and feathered masks. The different ceremonies had many purposes, such as healing the sick, bringing rain during periods of drought, and establishing peace and harmony.

To the northeast of the Pueblos, in the great heartland of the United States, lived the Plains Indians. Before the coming of the Europeans, these tribes were primarily agricultural, growing corn and gathering wild rice. Hunting was very difficult, for it had to be done on foot until the first horses were brought to the New World.

One misconception about the Plains Indians and other North American tribes concerns the amount of power attributed to their village chieftains. Chiefs did earn their power by displaying courage and wisdom, but they were only able to advise their followers, not control them. Few Europeans ever understood how limited the chiefs' authority really was, and this led to serious misunderstandings. Frequently a group of settlers would reach agreement with a chief. Then, when the chief was not able to persuade the rest of the tribe to go along with him, the settlers would interpret it as a treacherous breach of faith.

Still further east, along the Mississippi River, lived a highly developed tribe called the Natchez. The Natchez were ruled by an absolute monarch, believed by his followers to be descended from the sun. Like the Inca emperors, he received total power, and was both a religious and a political leader. When he died, his wife and servants were also killed so that they could continue to serve him in the next world. The Natchez, like other tribes east of the Mississippi, built huge burial mounds for the dead which were also frequently used as platforms for temples. Like the other tribes of southeastern America, the Natchez survived from a combination of farming, hunting, and fishing. Food was abundant, and they dined on such exotic fare as bear ribs and root jelly. Two dishes invented by these Indians were destined to become part of later American Southern cooking: hominy and corn bread.

Other important tribes of the Southeast—the Creeks, Chickasaws, Choctaws, and Cherokees—had living patterns quite similar to those of the woodland Indians of the Northeast. One important difference, though, was their lack of intertribal cooperation. Southeastern Indians were often persuaded by colonists to attack other tribes which had allied themselves with rival European groups.

The Iroquois, Algonquin, and Siouan families were the major tribes of the Northeast woodlands. The first group to be encountered by the English in North America were the Algonquins. They were relatively peaceful, and since they were thinly settled along the East Coast, they allowed some "breathing room" for the new settlers. The Iroquois were more warlike and had a shrewd grasp of politics. In the sixteenth century, or possibly even earlier, five Iroquois tribes banded together into a powerful league which became the strongest political force in North America. Their confederation had a central governing council chosen by the most important women of the tribal clans. Unfortunately for these tribes, the League supported the English during the American Revolution, and most of their members were exiled to Canada after the war.

Many of the struggles between these Eastern Indians and the Europeans stemmed from their different concepts of private property. The hunting territories of the tribes of the Eastern seaboard were always used in common by all members of the tribe. The Indians were usually willing to share the land with the colonists, and when they "sold" it, they thought that they were merely leasing hunting rights. The newcomers, however, believed that they had acquired complete possession. The concept of complete possession was unknown to the Indians, and this repeatedly led to bitter misunderstandings.

NORTH AMERICAN INDIAN TRIBES

Indian Contributions to European Culture

The original inhabitants of North, Central, and South America had a deep influence on the Europeans, and they made many important contributions which are still part of our lives today. One of the most vital ways the Indians helped the newcomers was by showing them a range of foods which Europeans had never known before. The most valuable was maize, or Indian corn, which became the staple food of many parts of the world. Indian farmers began to cultivate wild corn thousands of years ago, and eventually, after much trial and error, plump yellow maize was developed. Easy and economical to grow, corn was an enormous help to the early colonists. Other foods first found in the Americas were squash, white and sweet potatoes, many varieties of beans, peanuts, peppers, vanilla, tomatoes, pumpkins, avocados, pineapples, and cacao (the plant from which chocolate is processed).

The Indian way of life has also had an important impact on Western thought. Some colonists were impressed and influenced, for instance, by the democratic practices they found among various tribes of North America. At a time when many Europeans had known only absolute monarchy as a form of government, some types of Indian political organization suggested exciting new possibilities. Moreover, the individual freedom and reverence for nature so characteristic of Indian life helped to create the utopian image of the noble savage for a philosopher such as Rousseau.

Indian art and literature are other areas which have had an important influence on later Western civilization. Indian jewelry has always been popular, as have Indian folklore and mythology. Many utilitarian objects which have come into wide use were also designed by the Indians, including canoes, snowshoes, sleds, parkas, moccasins, and hammocks.

Exploration

It is still not known why the famous Viking captain Leif Ericson set out from Greenland in about A.D. 1000. He sailed west until his ships reached Labrador and Nova Scotia, but there are no signs that the Vikings were interested in colonizing the territories he discovered. Soon, these mysterious lands lying in the West were all but forgotten by the people of Europe. The next known transatlantic voyages would not take place for almost five hundred years. Until that time, the New World would be remembered only in legends and folktales.

It was the Spanish who led the way in the next phase of exploration and discovery of the Americas. However, they owed a large debt to earlier Portuguese advances in the techniques of navigation. The figure most responsible for

Ships preparing to leave for the New World from Lisbon, Portugal.

Portugal's contributions was Prince Henry the Navigator. Equipped with the knowledge of the best experts of the time, Prince Henry's captains sailed along the west coast of Africa, discovering the Azores, the Madeiras, and the Canary Islands. Their goal was to reach the Orient and establish a regular trade in spices, highly prized in the days before refrigeration. By 1488 another Portuguese captain, Bartholomeu Dias, had made it almost halfway to India by sailing to the southern tip of Africa and the beginning of the Indian Ocean.

It was these Portuguese triumphs, plus new technical developments, which encouraged explorers of other nations. The introduction of the magnetic compass also made navigation much safer and easier for long voyages, as did improvements in the design of oceangoing vessels.

COLUMBUS

Christopher Columbus, the son of a poor wool weaver, was born in 1451 in the Italian town of Genoa. He began sailing at a young age, and dreamed of the day when he would lead an expedition across the Atlantic to reach the Orient. Since Portugal was the European country most interested in exploration at this time, he first proposed his voyage to the king of Portugal. A committee of scholars considered the scheme and decided that Columbus had underestimated the distance he would have to travel. Their assessment was correct, for many of Columbus' calculations were in error. No one suspected, though, that something might lie between Europe and Asia.

Fortunately, Columbus was not willing to give up easily. He next approached the rulers

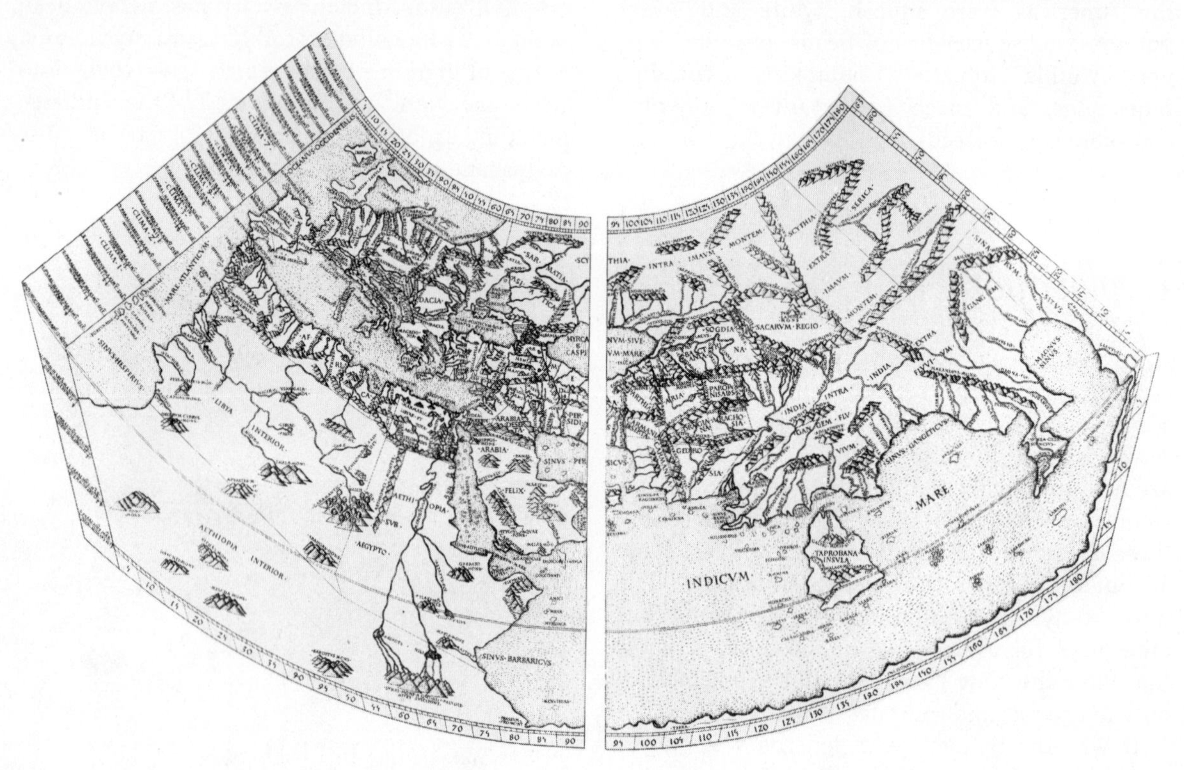

▲ *This map, published in Rome in 1490, shows China directly west of Europe—an error which led Columbus to believe he could reach India by sailing west from Spain.*

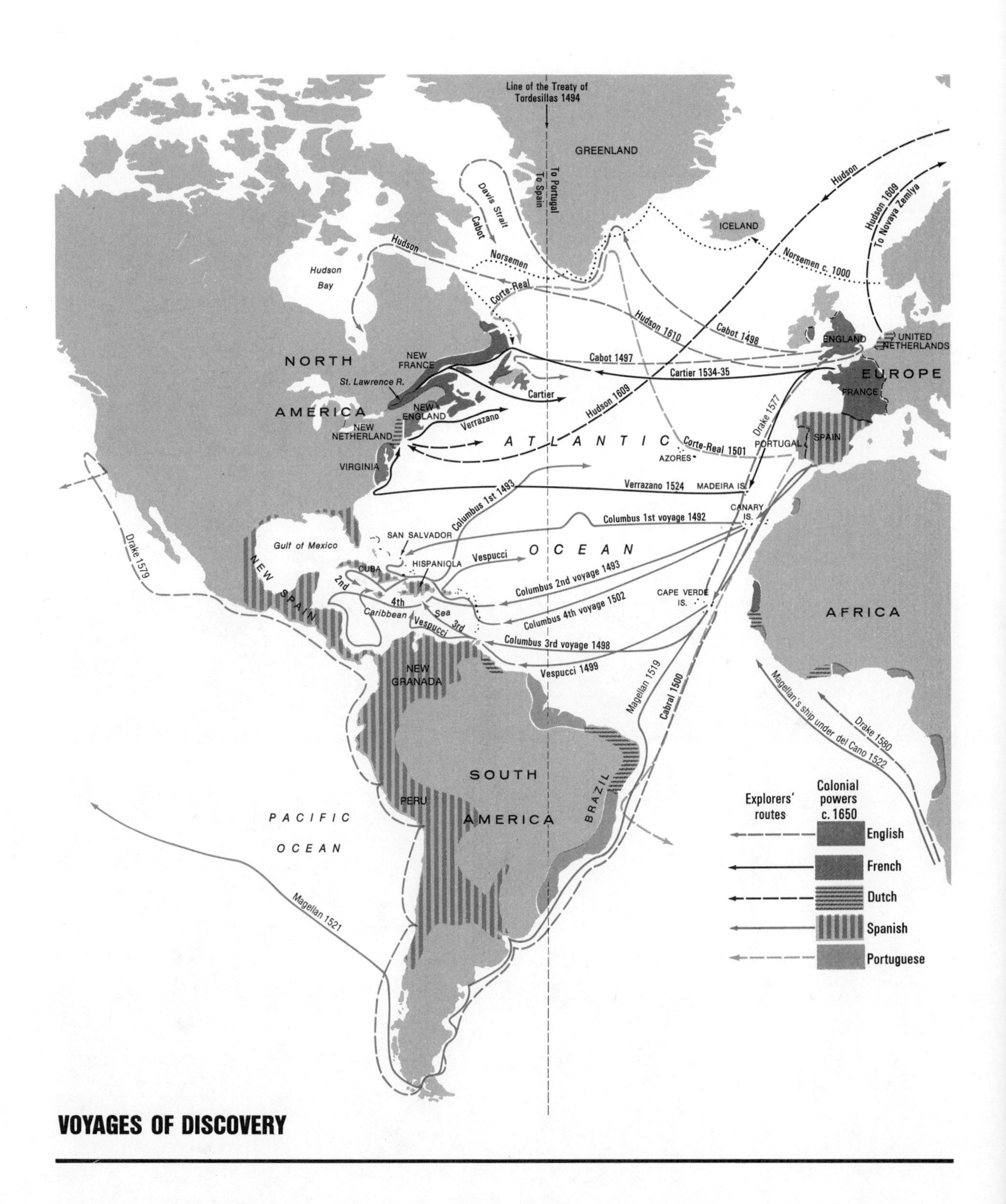

VOYAGES OF DISCOVERY

The first New World explorers returned to their native countries with strong images of the land and native life they had seen on their travels. All the pictures below and opposite were published with early accounts of New World explorations, but some are more true to life than others. Below, top: "Wild Life in New Spain," published in 1615, is a view of Mexico as described by a Spanish explorer. Below, bottom: "Pictorial Account of Columbus' Second Voyage," published in 1621, is a fanciful image of a milk-and-honey paradise peopled with friendly, frolicking natives. Both of these images are slightly romanticized. The narrative and pictures on the opposite page are a good deal closer to reality. The narrative was written by Arthur Barlowe, captain of one of the ships Sir Walter Raleigh sent to Roanoke Island, Virginia, in 1584. The two engravings were copied from paintings made by John White, an artist who visited the Roanoke colony between 1585 and 1587. The engravings were published in 1590—the first eyewitness pictures of life in the New World.

"We surveyed the land and found the shores sandy and low toward the water's edge and so overgrown with grapes that the surging waves flowed over them. The grapes grew everywhere, on the sand; on the green soil of the hills, over the plains; climbing on every little shrub and toward the tops of high cedars. I do not think such plenty could be found in any other place in the world—and I have seen those parts of Europe where grapes grow most abundantly. The difference was so great that one could scarcely believe it.

The island has many large forests overrun with deer, rabbits, hares, and woodfowl in great abundance, even in midsummer. The woods are not barren and fruitless like those in Bohemia, Moscovia, or Hercynia, but are thick with the highest and reddest cedars in the world, far better than the cedars of the Azores, of the Indies, or of Lebanon. Pine, cypress, sassafras, and the lentisk, or gum tree, all grow there, as well as the tree whose bark is black cinnamon, which Master Winter brought back from the Straits of Magellan; and there are many other trees of excellent quality and fine fragrance."

of Spain, Queen Isabella and King Ferdinand. After four years of arguing his case, Columbus finally received the Queen's approval for a journey across the Atlantic. He was assigned three ships, a crew of ninety men and boys, and a budget equal to about $14,000.

Columbus set sail from Spain on August 3, 1492. He stopped briefly at the Canary Islands and began the long Atlantic crossing early that September. To gauge direction, Columbus relied on a compass, for he was not aware of how to navigate by using the stars. There was one minor mutiny aboard the *Santa Maria* during the long voyage. But the mutiny was quickly put down and nothing else of note took place. Finally, after sailing more than 3000 miles in thirty-three days, a lookout on the *Pinta* sighted one of the Bahama Islands at 2:00 A.M. on October 12, 1492. This was the first bit of land discovered by the Spanish in the New World. Columbus named it San Salvador, but it is now called Watlings Island.

Columbus later wrote these first impressions to his patrons, Isabella and Ferdinand:

> In order that we might win good friendship, because I knew that they were a people who could better be freed and converted to our Holy Faith by love than by force, I gave to some of them red caps and to some glass beads, which they hung on their necks, and many other things of slight value, in which they took much pleasure; they remained so much our friends that it was a marvel; and later they came swimming to the ships' boats in which we were, and brought us parrots and cotton thread in skeins and darts and many other things. . . . They ought to be good servants and of good skill, for I see that they repeat very quickly all that is said to them; and I believe that they would easily be made Christians, because it seemed to me that they belonged to no religion.

This pleasant encounter between people of two different worlds was not typical of what was soon to come. Within a few years the Spanish would exterminate or enslave millions of inhabitants of this New World, plundering their land for gold.

THE ADMIRAL'S DELUSIONS

Columbus was so eager to believe that he had landed in Asia that he ignored all evidence to the contrary. Every day he and his men encountered things never before seen by European travelers, even in the Orient. Columbus and his crew saw people using hammocks and were very impressed by their comfort and simplicity. In Cuba they saw Indians smoking cigars called *tobacos*; soon thousands of Europeans would be smoking this new plant, too. On a later voyage they saw their first cannibals, and on another they met a strange Central American tribe who turned their backs when they spoke and lived on pineapple wine and sardines. But none of these extraordinary findings could convince Columbus that this New World was not the fabled Orient.

Although many other Europeans gradually came to suspect that Columbus had discovered a whole new continent, he himself never realized it. He was certain that by sailing west he had simply charted a new way of reaching the East. His four voyages between 1492 and 1504 took him to Cuba, Haiti, many small Caribbean islands, and parts of Central and South America. Of all these places, the only one which he admitted *might* be a new discovery was South America. This, he thought, was probably the Garden of Eden.

Today, the fact that many people still call natives of the Americas "Indians," and refer to the Caribbean islands as "the West Indies," is a reminder of Columbus' mistake. The full extent of his error was not known until 1521, when the Spanish captain Ferdinand Magellan headed an expedition which sailed around the world for the first time. Magellan himself died in the Philippines, but his crew came back with clear reports that indicated the true size of the globe.

SPANISH SETTLEMENTS

In 1493 Columbus made his second voyage to the Americas, leading a fleet of seventeen ships and some 1500 colonists who laid the foundations for Spain's New World empire. Within a few years Spanish ships were regularly crossing the Atlantic. They carried colonists and their supplies to the New World, then brought cargoes of gold and silver back to Europe. These expeditions were motivated by two equally strong impulses: religious idealism and desire for wealth. Since Queen Isabella intended to use the riches she was acquiring for religious deeds, the two motives were closely related. Isabella was an extremely pious ruler who relished the idea that all the inhabitants of "the Indies" could be converted to Catholicism and saved.

However, most of the Spanish conquistadores were more interested in territorial control than in religious ideals. Almost every year a new territory was added to the Spanish domains, and once a region was secured its people and riches were exploited without scruple. Some of the most famous Spanish explorers included:

1. Columbus himself, whose principal discoveries were the islands of Cuba, Puerto Rico, and Santo Domingo.

2. Amerigo Vespucci, a Florentine sailing for Spain who traveled along the northern coast of South America and around the Caribbean in 1498. His glowing account of the voyage led a German geographer to publish a map of the area labeled with the Latinized form of Amerigo's name: America.

3. Ponce de Leon, who sailed along the east coast of Florida in 1512, becoming the first European to set foot in what is now the United States.

4. Vasco Núñez de Balboa, who traveled through the jungles of Panama to the Pacific Ocean in 1513.

5. Hernando Cortes, who landed in Mexico in 1519 and conquered the entire Aztec empire within two years.

6. Francisco Pizarro, who overcame the Incas of Peru in the 1530s.

Why did the mighty Aztec and Inca empires fall so easily to the small bands of Spanish adventurers? First, the conquistadores had tremendous courage and discipline, were mounted on horses, and used powerful weapons. Gunpowder was unknown to the Indians. Second, both the Aztecs and the Incas had religious legends about white-skinned gods, and they feared the newcomers as "men from Heaven." Third, both the Aztec and Inca rulers had been in power for only a short time. Neither one commanded a great deal of popular support among the people. Cortes took advantage of this situation by imprisoning the Aztec monarch, Montezuma, and then ruling through him. According to a Spanish account of 1519, titled *The Pleasant History of the Conquest of the West Indies:*

> There was never Greek nor Roman, nor any other nation since the names of Kings was ordained, did give the like enterprise as Hernando Cortes did, in taking Montezuma prisoner in his own house, being a most mighty King in a most strong fort among infinite people, Cortes having but 450 companions.

Outraged by Cortes' plundering of Aztec treasures and by the heavy Spanish taxes, the people rose up and killed their own king. This uprising gave Cortes an excuse to complete his conquest of Mexico. Later, other Spaniards carved out huge estates for themselves and conscripted Indian laborers to work the fields. This was not for Cortes, though, who stated openly, "I came to get gold, not to till the soil like a peasant."

Pizarro followed much the same strategy in his conquest of Peru. After hearing rumors of great wealth in the Inca capital of Cuzco, Pizarro made friendly overtures to the Inca ruler, Atahualpa. When Atahualpa then came to the

Spanish camp with a small group of unarmed men, Pizarro's soldiers opened fire and easily captured the ruler. The booty they gained from Inca temples and treasuries soon exceeded all the riches taken from Mexico.

Treaty of Tordesillas

Realizing the economic potential of the New World, Isabella and Ferdinand were anxious to guarantee exclusive possession of the territory for Spain. First they attempted to gain papal support for such a monopoly. In 1493 Pope Alexander VI obliged by granting to Spain all lands west of a north–south line through the Atlantic Ocean (38 degrees longitude). At the same time Portugal was presented with all lands ruled by non-Christians lying to the east of this line. In effect, the Pope's decision handed the Western Hemisphere to Spain, and Africa and Asia to Portugal. The Portuguese, however, were not entirely satisfied with the arrangement. So, in 1494 Portugal and Spain agreed to the new Treaty of Tordesillas, shifting the line eight degrees further west. This new line sliced off the eastern bulge of South America, giving Brazil to the Portuguese.

WEALTH FROM THE NEW WORLD

Before the end of the sixteenth century, gold and silver from Mexico and Peru were contributing thirty million dollars annually to the European economy. By law, one-fifth of that sum went into the royal coffers. In terms of mineral wealth, the Potosí silver mines of Bolivia were the single most fabulous discovery in the New World. At one time Potosí was the richest mining city in the entire world. Its population of 120,000 was larger than any city of Europe except London and Paris. Aided by technological advances in the extraction of ores in the late 1500s, Spanish miners were able to ship more than ten million ounces of silver per year from Potosí and other mines back to Europe.

The wealth of Spain was further enriched by cattle hides and crops of tobacco and sugar from the colonies. The revenues from these products eventually surpassed even the gold and silver in value. The Spanish monarchs granted the conquistadores the right to draw tribute from the Indians. This tribute took the form of cheap labor. In return for this right, the conquistadores would promise to protect the natives, and Spanish missionaries could convert them to

Spanish conquistadores and their Indian bearers.

Christianity. Since the natives were considered royal subjects, they could not legally be made into slaves, but it was a simple matter for the conquistadores to take advantage of their "rights" and reduce the Indians to serfdom.

In addition to being cruelly exploited, the native population was severely reduced by epidemics of European diseases against which the Indians had no immunity. When this occurred, the Spanish turned to the use of imported slave labor. Dutch and Portuguese traders brought Africans who were enslaved to serve in the fields of the Caribbean and parts of South America.

SPANISH COLONIAL GOVERNMENT

Although several European powers were expanding their influence throughout the world at this time, Spanish America was the first important colonial possession. Portugal, the other nation with an overseas empire in the sixteenth century, established trading posts in India, the East Indies, and along the African coast. Spain, by contrast, sent thousands of her nationals to live in the New World. The Spanish method of colonial control was the first European attempt to run the political affairs of a faraway territory.

The overriding goal was strong royal domination. Very little self-government was allowed, for native-born leaders might end in separatism. The complex hierarchy of officials began in Spain, where the Council of the Indies was the principal body for administering colonial policy. Beneath this council were the Spanish viceroys, actually ruling in the New World. The two main ones, based in Lima and Mexico City, were responsible for governing huge territories. The domain of these viceroys was, in turn, divided into ten audiencias or courts of appeal. These bodies watched the viceroys carefully, advised them, and reported to Spain on their conduct. They could also hear appeals against the viceroys' decisions. At the local level, landed oligarchies ran the town councils and purchased their offices from the Crown for life.

Competition for America

Spain's new sources of wealth did not go unnoticed by the other European powers. Early in the sixteenth century, France, the Netherlands, and England were ready to join the race for overseas empires. Nationalism was on the rise in western Europe, and a contest for imperial power, wealth, and prestige was inevitable.

FRENCH EXPLORATIONS AND COLONIZATION

In 1521 Magellan's crew completed their trip around the world, establishing the fact that the Americas were a huge landmass blocking the way to the Orient. This discovery led geographers to imagine that a Northwest Passage might be found through the continent, a shortcut to the East. So in 1524 King Francis I of France sent an Italian navigator named Giovanni da Verrazano on one of the first expeditions aimed at locating this Northwest Passage. Verrazano sailed along most of the Atlantic coast of North America, from Nova Scotia to North Carolina, but failed to find a route to Asia.

Undaunted, Francis I next dispatched Jacques Cartier on a series of voyages in 1534, 1535, and 1541. This time the quest was not so much for the Northwest Passage as for gold and diamonds, which the French expected to find in a mysterious northern kingdom called Saguenay. Although Cartier sailed up the St. Lawrence as far as present-day Montreal, the fabled kingdom of Saguenay was not to be found. In fact, the only successes the French had in their search for riches during this period occurred when they raided Spanish galleons carrying gold and silver back to Europe. French ships became such a threat that Spain was forced to build a fort at St. Augustine, Florida to guard the entrance to the Caribbean. This outpost was established in 1565, becoming the first European settlement in what is now the United States.

In the second half of the sixteenth century, French internal conflicts put a temporary halt to their colonial ambitions. Their next expedition to the New World was not launched until 1603, when Samuel de Champlain led another French voyage up the St. Lawrence River. In 1608 Champlain's men built a fort at Quebec, establishing the first permanent French settlement in North America.

The French government had very serious plans for its New World possessions. It wanted to create a New France, which would be an ideal feudal society. Stability would be ensured by keeping the vast majority of the people legally tied to the land. Acceptable behavior was carefully laid out for each segment of the population, Protestants were banned, even styles of clothing were to be regulated. The chosen landlords, or seigneurs, had the right to demand feudal oaths of loyalty from their tenants, as well as to hold private court and to have a monopoly on all milling. The peasants who settled in New France were supposed to clear the land, pay rent, give free labor to the landlord, and take no part in the lucrative fur trade.

This "ideal" system was never successfully implemented. Because labor was scarce, tenants were able to refuse most of the obligations forced upon them. The government soon found that discipline had to be considerably relaxed simply in order to attract settlers. Contrary to royal instructions, about one-third of the sparse adult male population of New France was engaged in the fur trade by the 1680s.

After 1660 New France came under stronger control from the French government. A royal governor was sent out to organize military protection for the colony, and an official called an intendant was put in charge of administering justice and overseeing economic development. French explorers, traders, and priests gained control over much of eastern Canada, the Great Lakes area, and the Mississippi Valley region by the late seventeenth century, but French settlements were never much more than sparsely populated trading centers.

DUTCH EXPLOITS

Like the early French voyages, the first Dutch expeditions to the New World were aimed at finding the elusive Northwest Passage. In 1609, eighty-five years after Verrazano's unsuccessful mission, the Dutch sent an Englishman named Henry Hudson to find the westward sea route to the East. For his efforts, Hudson had a river and a large Canadian bay named after him, but neither one turned out to be the Northwest Passage.

After this initial failure, the Dutch settled down to something more productive—raiding and trading. Early in the seventeenth century they looted so many Spanish ships for gold and silver that Spanish shipping was virtually destroyed. As Spain's control over the Caribbean began to wane, the Dutch moved in and took over some of the key islands. For a while they also occupied hundreds of miles of the coast of Brazil. These outposts served the Dutch as convenient centers for selling the slaves they bought from Portuguese traders in Africa.

Although they had a population of only two million in the middle of the 1600s, the Dutch were the most successful merchants in the world. Their trading network spread like a web all over the globe. Aggressive and practical, many Dutch merchants became extremely wealthy despite the fact that the Netherlands was tiny and had no natural resources. They were the middlemen, buying spices, cotton, and tea in the Orient, and sugar, tobacco, and furs in America for sale in Europe. They were so successful that the center of European trade shifted from the Mediterranean to the Atlantic. Amsterdam, the center of

Early Amsterdam.

Dutch commerce, commanded access to the Baltic Sea, the Rhine River, and the English Channel. Thus it became the nerve center of the world's shipping routes.

ENGLISH VOYAGES

Like other Europeans, the English first came to the shores of the New World in search of the Northwest Passage. In 1497, five years after Columbus' first voyage, John Cabot sailed to the mouth of the St. Lawrence River. Much later, Martin Frobisher, John Davis, and a series of other English captains sailed throughout the Arctic area in an effort to find the passage. English explorers were actually still searching for the great shortcut as late as 1746, only thirty years before the Declaration of Independence. None of these early English ventures had any lasting results.

The European Background

What drove Europeans to leave their native lands and explore unknown parts of the globe? Why did some of them stay in the New World and create colonies? This surge of activity was part of a complex process of tremendous change which had been building in Europe for centuries. Because these changes—economic, political, and religious—were to shape the destiny of the New World, they deserve a close look.

THE COMMERCIAL REVOLUTION

Colonization of the New World took place only when economic conditions in Europe made it possible. Before Columbus made his voyages, there was little interest in colonizing far-off territories. The excitement which began in 1492 can be explained in part by long-term economic changes in Europe between the eleventh and fifteenth centuries.

In A.D. 1000, when Leif Ericson was exploring the northern coastal areas of Canada, Europe was divided into countless small duchies, principalities, and estates. The chief economic unit was the manor, a virtually self-supporting community ruled by an hereditary nobility. All the food or labor required to sustain the manor was supplied by its inhabitants. These serfs, or servants, were dominated by their local lord, for they were permanently attached to his property. They were in bondage to the soil and were never permitted to leave the manor. In return for a guarantee of personal safety, much of the serf's time was devoted to serving the lord of the manor. This meant plowing and tilling his fields several months per year, repairing his castle, and fighting as foot soldiers in the periodic battles with neighboring lords.

The dominant role of the manor in European life began to change slowly about the time of the Crusades, between 1095 and 1291. The Crusades were an attempt by the Christian Church of western Europe to recover Palestine from the Moslems, and to liberate Middle Eastern Christians from Islamic authority. The efforts were ultimately unsuccessful, but most modern historians believe that the Crusades helped transform the entire European way of life by increasing commercial activity.

As a result of the Crusades, the small amount of trade between the towns of southern Italy and the eastern Mediterranean was enlarged to include Venice, Genoa, and other port cities in the western Mediterranean. This pattern continued until the early fifteenth century, when Portugal began seeking other routes to the Orient and the Middle East to break the monopoly held by Italian merchants. Further incentive for discovering an alternate route to the East was provided by the fall of Constantinople to the Turks in 1541.

Since the exchange of goods took place mainly in towns, these trading centers grew larger and more influential partly as a result of the increase in commercial activity during the Crusades. In addition, to raise funds for the long voyage to the Holy Land, feudal knights often sold towns the right to incorporate. For a large fee, townsfolk were able to buy from their ruling baron or bishop a charter granting them the right to levy taxes, enroll a militia, and name their own officials. The growth of cities in turn encouraged the expansion of commerce. Nobles, eager to buy the new products, raised money by selling freedom to their serfs. More and more of these freed serfs moved into the towns, thus increasing their population. An increase in town dwellers meant more craftsmen to produce goods for trade, heightening the demand for manufactured goods and for luxury items from the eastern Mediterranean.

Merchants

Before the Crusades, goods were usually exchanged through the barter method. Trade took place on a small-scale, local basis because it was costly and dangerous to transport goods over any significant distance. Only a few luxury items such as carpets from Turkey, dyes from the Middle East, and silks and glass from Syria, were ever carried from faraway regions.

During and after the Crusades, however, long-distance trade became safer and cheaper. Money in the form of gold and silver coins also began to come into widespread use, providing the means for more people to pay for goods without relying on the barter system. As trade between towns, countries, and even continents increased, the merchant became an increasingly important figure. Emphasis was slowly shifting from small groups of craftsmen making goods for local consumption, to production for distant markets.

During the fifteenth century the merchant class continued to gain in importance. The new sea routes to the Orient and the Americas that were pioneered at the end of the century brought a great upsurge in trade, especially in such bulk commodities as lumber, rice, tea, and sugar. Heavy industries such as shipbuilding and cannon manufacture were also stimulated by colonization. This intercontinental trade, as well as trade within Europe, enlarged the role of the middleman. The merchant of this period often functioned as a banker and a manufacturer too. If they did not make the goods they were selling, they frequently financed the production of the goods.

These successful European merchants affected the development of America in at least two direct ways. First, the merchants had made international trade into such a vital part of the European economy that the New World was almost a necessity, since it offered new raw materials as well as a potentially large, new market. Second, the rise of the merchant class gave some European countries the means to finance the expensive colonization of the New World. As described in the next chapter, the first English colonies were backed financially by merchants, not by the government. Private companies, operating with the approval of the Crown, were the sponsors of the first settlers in North America.

Laborers

Another important force in colonizing the New World was the large number of discontented laborers who were willing to leave the Old World. As merchants steadily improved their position in European society, the gap between the wealthy middle class and the impoverished laborers widened year by year. One reason was the great inflation of the sixteenth and seventeenth centuries, caused in part by the importation of vast amounts of precious metal from the Spanish colonies in America. There were other causes for the inflation too, including a tremendous population boom, the development of banking facilities and commercial paper which expanded credit, and the dissipation of natural resources wasted in war. The result of all this was that prices rose, while wages lagged far behind. In 1560 workers in Spain, France, Germany, and England had fifty percent less purchasing power than their grandparents had had a hundred years earlier.

In addition to the effects of inflation, the decline of the guild system made laborers look to the New World as a source of economic opportunity. In the twelfth and thirteenth centuries any worker could rise from apprenticeship to journeyman status, and eventually become a master craftsman. But by the sixteenth century the possibilities for upward mobility declined. Master craftsmen tended to hand their positions down to their sons, so that journeymen had little hope of ever improving their status.

Some workers responded to these labor problems by trying to organize unions and wage strikes. However, in almost every case they were suppressed, or industrialists simply agreed never to hire the troublemakers. Thus many laborers learned that the only way to get some share of the New World's wealth was to actually go there. It meant leaving Europe to face unknown hazards, but it also meant new economic opportunities.

THE RISE OF NATIONAL MONARCHIES

In the feudal period each lord had almost absolute control over his lands and his subjects. He could start wars, collect taxes, and administer laws any way he saw fit. Throughout Europe, the kings were actually quite dependent on these powerful nobles in order to accomplish anything significant. It was only in the fifteenth century that the kings of western Europe were able to reverse this situation.

In Spain royal power was established by first uniting the nation geographically. During most of the 1400s, the country was divided into three separate realms which all came together only six months before Columbus sailed in 1492. Ferdinand and Isabella joined two of the kingdoms through their marriage, and the third was added when their army conquered the Moslem territories in the South. Even with this consolidation there were still limitations to centralized royal authority. One problem was that people in different regions of Spain spoke languages so dissimilar that they could not understand each other. Another drawback was the great difference in temperament and motivation between Isabella and Ferdinand. She was an extremely devout Catholic, while he was only vaguely religious and far more interested in international political intrigue.

Despite these conflicts Ferdinand and Isabella became very powerful figures, partly because of the wealth reaching them from their New World possessions. Their heirs continued to control the Spanish throne and to gain many important royal prerogatives. The right to tax supplied funds to send expeditions to the Americas. The right to maintain an army gave the monarchy the military strength needed to protect colonies. And the right to make laws established royal authority over trade between Spain and the faraway territories.

The French monarchy had the aid of the growing middle class in the development of its base of power. It was a natural alliance, with the merchants supplying the wealth and the king offering protection for trade as well as administrative and military appointments. The French nobility feared this centralizing tendency as a threat to its own influence, but the lords were gradually forced to give up the power of taxation over their lands until it became the exclusive right of the king. Nobles were willing to surrender this privilege only in exchange for their own immunity from taxation. Since noblemen and clergy were exempt, the tax burden fell partly on the middle class, but mostly on the peasants.

The tax revenues were necessary to support royal armies. Before the fifteenth and sixteenth centuries, European kings had seldom maintained professional armed forces. In this time of intense national competition, though, the French king built a permanent military composed mainly of paid soldiers. Soon, Spain and other powers were forced to follow suit.

The French monarchy also strengthened its control of the state by limiting the power of the Catholic Church in nonreligious matters. Church authority over official appointments was ended and the large outflow of gold and silver from France to the Vatican was restricted. At the same time, the number of royal officers greatly increased. This new bureaucracy saw to it that the king's will was enforced in every town, bishopric, and feudal estate throughout France.

Some similar tactics were employed in England, but there were important differences too. Unlike France, where only part of the population was taxed, England taxed all of its citizens. In return for their money, nobles and wealthy merchants gained the right to have a voice in government. The English Parliament became a strong national force, able to check royal authority through its control of taxation. Another distinction was the voluntary basis on which local justices of the peace served in England. Their amateur status made them less dependent on royal favors. Because of their economic independence, the king could not easily force many of his public servants to execute laws to which they objected. Even so, the English monarchs had extensive powers. By outlawing private armies, and bringing the rising middle class into their councils, they limited the strength of the great nobles. By taking over the authority of the church courts, they broke the independent basis of religious power. And by confiscating church lands, they enriched their own treasury. By and large English monarchs concentrated on domestic policy in the sixteenth century, ensuring that the royal will was effectively enforced in every corner of the land.

Thus, the rulers of France and Spain were on their way to becoming absolute rulers, and the English throne was on the way to becoming a constitutional monarchy. All three were stronger than ever before, well able to sponsor the competition for empire.

THE PROTESTANT REFORMATION

Columbus regarded all of his successful voyages as triumphs for Christendom, rather than as strictly personal accomplishments. In 1493 the Pope was powerful enough to assign whole continents to the nations he favored, by drawing the line of demarcation between Spanish and Portuguese territory. In the next century, though, many parts of Europe would break away from the Catholic Church in violent disputes over religious and political issues. This upheaval, an essential part of the background for the colonization of North America, began with one man's protest against the basic doctrines of the Catholic Church.

Martin Luther

Luther was a sixteenth-century German monk, gifted with an eloquent pen and driven by powerful religious convictions. Initially, he did not intend to break with the Catholic Church. Deeply troubled by the thought of his own sinfulness, he was simply seeking a way to find peace of mind by obtaining the grace of God. This search led him to a study of the Scriptures, where he found a solution in the idea that absolute faith in God's love was all one needed. His concept became known as "justification by faith," and it brought Luther into open conflict with the papacy.

Luther was offended by what he saw as the Church's effort to sell the grace of God in the form of papal letters called *indulgences.* According to Catholic theology, the Church had the power to dispense the excess grace which had been accumulated by Christ, Mary, and the saints. An indulgence represented some portion of this additional grace, and it could be distributed to individuals to reduce the time spent in purgatory before entering heaven. In theory, priests were not able to sell indulgences, but at this period in history Catholics were strongly urged to make a cash offering after receiving one.

To Luther, the acquisition of an indulgence did not prove that a person had absolute faith in God's love. He abhorred the entire practice and in 1517 posted his famous Ninety-five Theses on the church door in Wittenberg, Ger-

Martin Luther preaching. At right, popes, and monks, and cardinals in the mouth of Hell, at left, salvation.

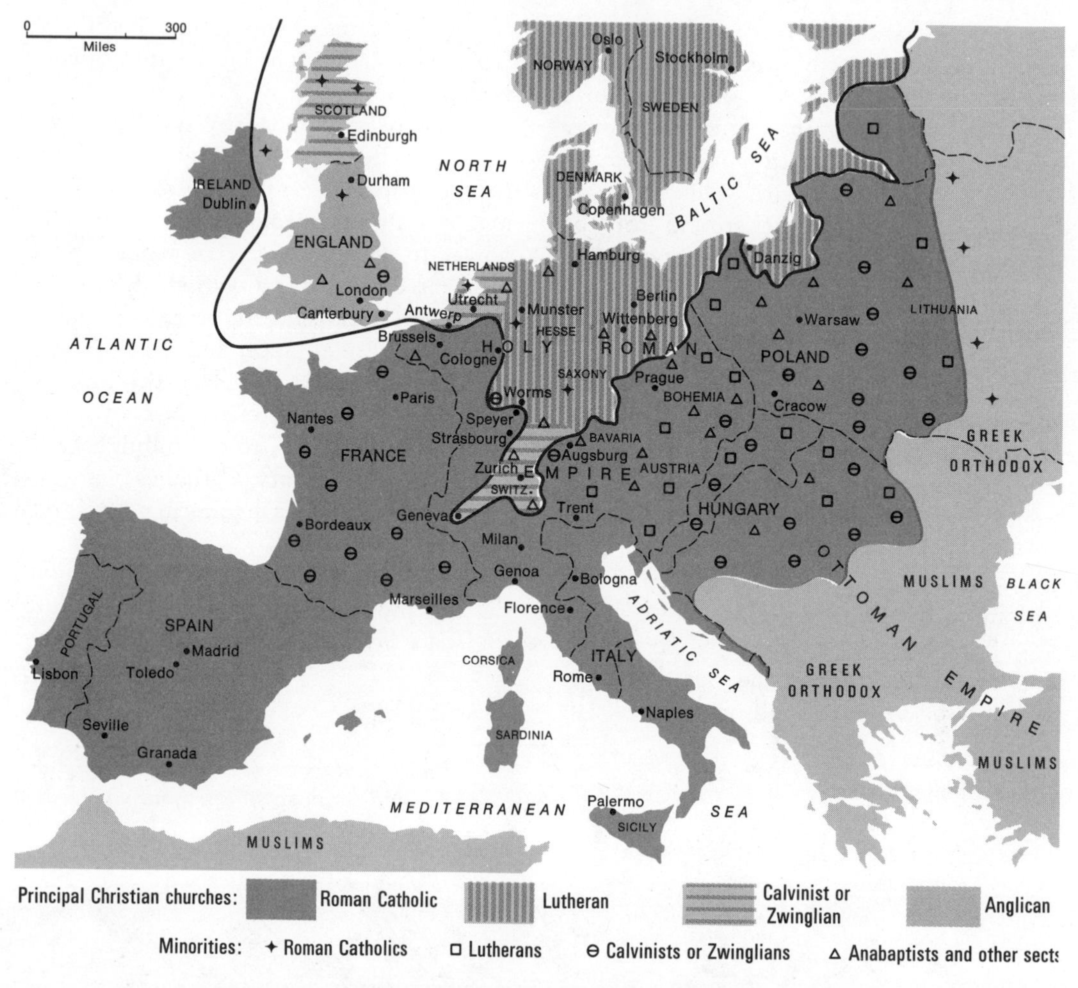

RELIGIOUS GROUPS · SIXTEENTH CENTURY EUROPE

many, where he taught at the university. His aim was to provoke scholarly debate on the issue. Instead, he received a stern rebuke from the Pope for his questioning attitude.

Not willing to accept the papal rebuke, Luther immediately began publicly questioning other aspects of orthodox theology. Soon his opinions were spreading all over Germany, aided by the recently invented printing press. The essence of his beliefs was that in all matters of religion, the final authority was not the Pope or a church council, but the Bible itself. Feeling that all Christians should be able to read the Scriptures and rely on their guidance alone, he translated the New Testament into his native language, German. To Luther, every Christian was a priest, for in the eyes of God there were no distinctions among true believers. Moreover, he challenged the age-old Catholic doctrine that there were seven sacraments, relying on scriptural passages to show that Jesus Christ had recognized only two: baptism and communion.

John Calvin

John Calvin was eight years old when Luther tacked the famous Theses to the church door in Wittenberg. He came to agree with the basic ideas of the great German leader, especially with the idea of the overriding importance of the Bible. But there are two significant areas of different emphasis in Calvinism, and these differences were to have a profound impact on the religious life of those communities in the New World settled by Calvinists.

Calvin's beliefs emphasized the doctrine of predestination. According to the doctrine, God, being omniscient, had always known which human beings would be saved and which would not. No matter what an individual did during a lifetime, it would have no effect. Salvation or damnation had been predestined by God since the dawn of creation. The only sign of election to heaven was to be found in the moral quality of an individual's life on earth. If it was spotlessly pure, the person was probably one of the "elect." As a consequence of this belief, Calvin's followers were known for tirelessly examining their own actions and their neighbors', searching for any moral corruption.

Calvin's politics also differed from Luther's. Whereas Luther was willing to allow local German rulers to administer church affairs, Calvin believed the church should govern the state. Ideally every community would be concerned only with carrying out God's will and all affairs would be conducted according to principles drawn from the Bible. Calvin put this theory into practice when he became the leader of the Swiss city of Geneva, attempting to turn it into a model of the pure Christian community.

Another aspect of Calvin's theology is its intense individualism and its respect for material success. Calvin taught that diligence in one's occupation, which often brought success, was a sign of possessing saving grace. In *The Protestant Ethic and the Spirit of Capitalism,* the famous German sociologist Max Weber argues that this Calvinist belief encouraged many values that were essential to modern capitalism. Other historians have disagreed with this interpretation, pointing out that Calvinism was popular in economically backward areas such as Scotland, as well as among wealthy merchants. But even though there are exceptions, the fact remains that Calvinism had a strong appeal to the growing middle class of Europe, partially because it justified many of their ambitions. And it was this middle class which invested heavily in the great colonial ventures of the sixteenth and seventeenth centuries.

THE REFORMATION IN ENGLAND

England's break with the Catholic Church began as a political contest over the personal goals of King Henry VIII. Real disagreement over religious doctrines did take place eventually, but at first the conflict was strictly a matter of perpetuating Tudor family power.

The essential problem was in the king's desire to divorce his wife, Catherine of Aragon, and marry Anne Boleyn, all in order to produce a legitimate male heir to the throne. Henry did seek the Pope's permission to take this step, but an official papal annulment was not granted. But he was determined to remarry anyway, with or without the Pope's consent, and by 1534 Henry had persuaded Parliament to abolish all ties between Rome and England. Under the Act of Supremacy, Parliament established the Church of England and made Henry its supreme authority. England had established a national Catholic Church. In the next few years, Henry seized all lands belonging to Catholic bishops and monasteries, parceling much of them out to his followers. This maneuver strengthened his support among the new landed middle class, many of whom were also wealthy businessmen.

Eventually Henry obtained the son he sought, but only after beheading Anne Boleyn and remarrying once again. He saw that England was moving toward the Protestant outlook and had his son Edward raised as a Protestant. His son ascended the throne as Edward VII when Henry died in 1547. Edward died after reigning for only six years, though, and the crown passed to his Catholic half-sister, Mary, the daughter of Catherine of Aragon. Catholicism was briefly restored in England during Mary's reign. Many subjects who refused to accept her faith either fled in exile to the Continent or were burned at the stake, earning her the epithet "Bloody" Mary. On the Continent, about eight hundred of these exiles absorbed the ideas of Calvinism in Frankfort, Strasbourg, Zurich, and Geneva.

At the end of Mary's five-year reign, Elizabeth, the second child of Henry VIII, came to power. Many of the former exiles were then able to return, filled with far more radical ideas than had been formerly associated with English Protestantism.

Elizabeth I was a brilliant ruler who brought England to a peak of power, wealth, glory, and national pride. During her long reign, England defeated the Spanish Armada, became a world trade center, and produced the greatest playwright of any age, William Shakespeare. In the area of religion, Elizabeth was responsible for stabilizing the Church of England and giving it essentially its present form. The Thirty-nine Articles, approved by the queen in 1571, outlined basic Protestant doctrine but retained many Catholic rituals for the Church of England. Most Calvinists, however, were not satisfied with this compromise position. Although they were divided among themselves, all Calvinists agreed that the Church had to be "purified" of all remnants of Catholicism. They became known as Puritans because they insisted that any customs and rituals not founded on the Scriptures corrupted the Church of England, no matter how many concessions were made. Ac-

Separatists leaving for the New World. ▼

cording to the Puritans, centuries of laws, literature, ceremonies, and papal rulings had to be set aside. Most Puritans were willing to try to reform Anglicanism from within.

The Separatists, however, were a more radical group of English Puritans who believed that the Church was completely beyond repair. Religious extremists, they wanted a total break with the established church in order to start their own true form of worship.

The Puritans would soon become some of the first English settlers in the New World. They brought with them to America the same religious zeal and determination which had characterized their movement since Elizabethan times. Many of the habits of the early settlers in the New England area stemmed directly from the ideas of John Calvin as absorbed by the English before and during the reign of Queen Elizabeth I.

England: The Mother Country

As discussed earlier, the first English voyage to the New World took place in 1497 when John Cabot sailed to the mouth of the St. Lawrence River. But it was not until 1607, over one hundred years later, that the first permanent English settlement was established in America. English rulers were too preoccupied with their own problems to initiate successful attempts at overseas colonization. Part of the reason for the delay was the instability of the Tudor throne and the turmoil caused by the break with Rome. Another factor, during the reign of Elizabeth, was the availability of far easier profits through privateering. The defeat of the "Invincible Armada" in 1588 ended fear of Spain, opening the door for much successful plundering, and efforts to establish a North American colony in the 1580s received little support. The attacks on Spanish commerce did not stop until 1604, when a peace treaty with the Spanish put a damper on English piracy. From that point on, profits had to be generated in other ways, and colonization efforts soon took over from the pirate captains.

Because of the enormous changes which took place in the mother country, the century-long delay had an enormous effect on the type of colonies eventually established. The sixteenth century saw the rise of nationalism in western Europe, the birth of modern capitalism, and the foundation of Protestantism. Out of the English version of this experience, the North American colonies would become a nation, not simply a chain of independent commonwealths. They would also be dominated by the capitalist form of economics and the Protestant form of worship.

A HERITAGE OF REPRESENTATIVE GOVERNMENT

Many of the later American political institutions were patterned after practices that had deep roots in English history. As early as 1215 some of the great nobles and churchmen of England presented the king with a document known as the Magna Carta. Against his will, it compelled him to rule with their "common counsel." In 1265 members of the middle class joined with these two groups to form the first Parliament, although its original character was very different from its present character. Its power grew steadily and in the middle of the fourteenth century it was formally separated into two houses, the hereditary House of Lords and the elected House of Commons.

By the sixteenth century Tudor monarchs were relying on the sanction of Parliament for most major decisions. However the Stuart family, which came to the throne in 1603,

A Heritage of Representation in Government

"12. No scutage or aid shall be imposed on our kingdom, unless by common counsel of our kingdom, except for ransoming our person, for making of our oldest son a knight, and for once marrying our eldest daughter, and for these purposes there shall not be levied more than a reasonable aid. . . .

14. And for obtaining the common counsel of the kingdom, a rent, the assessment of an aid (except in the three cases aforesaid) or of a scutage, we will cause to be summoned the arshbishops, bishops, abbots, earls and greater barons severally by our letters; and we will moreover cause to be summoned generally through our sheriffs and bailiffs, all others who hold of us in chief, . . .

38. No Bailiff for the future shall, upon his own unsupported complaint, put anyone to his "law," without credible witnesses brought for this purpose.

39. No freeman shall be taken or imprisoned or disseised, or exiled or in any way destroyed, nor will we go upon him nor send upon him, except by the lawful judgment of his peers or by the law of the land.

40. To no one will we sell, to no one will we refuse or delay, right or justice."

Magna Carta,
1215

The Divine Right of Kings

"Kings are justly called Gods, for that they exercise a manner or resemblance of Divine power upon earth: For if you will consider the Attributes of God, you shall see how they agree in the person of a King. God hath power to create, or destroy, make, or unmake at his pleasure, to give life, or send death, to judge all, and to be judged nor accomptable to none; To raise low things, and to make high things low at his pleasure, and to God are both soule and body due. And the like power have Kings: They make and unmake their subjects: they have power of raising and casting downe, of life and death; judges over all their subjects, and in all causes and yet accomptable to none but God onely. . . ."

**The Political Works of James I,
1609**

claimed to rule by "divine right" with no parliamentary restrictions. Whenever the first of the Stuarts, James I, was unable to get the House of Commons to provide him with the tax money he wanted, he was so furious that he dissolved the session. His son, Charles I, faced an even more rebellious Parliament, which he also dissolved several times.

The greatest power of the House of Commons was its control of England's purse strings. This power was reaffirmed in 1628 when Charles I accepted the Petition of Right, claiming that "no man hereafter be compelled to make or yield any gift, loan, benevolence, tax, or such like charge, without common consent by Act of Parliament." In practice this meant that a king might dissolve or ignore Parliament, but if money was needed he would eventually have to reconvene it. The Petition of Right was also an important forerunner of the idea that "taxation without representation is tyranny," one of the earliest slogans of the American Revolution.

Now Charles I tried to reign without Parliament. From 1629–1640 he not only defied the Petition of Right but tried to stamp out the Puritan influence in the Anglican Church. However, when his efforts to force his religious views on Scotland failed, he was forced to call Parliament to obtain revenue for his army. Because the king was unwilling to allow Parliament to completely control taxation and to regulate the Church, a Parliamentary session took steps to raise its own army in May 1641. Subsequently, the two armies met in the English Civil War, the king was imprisoned, and to the horror of Europe finally beheaded in 1649.

A HERITAGE OF CAPITALISM

While representative government developed very gradually in America, the influence of capitalism was easily noticeable from the beginning. The first American colonies were financed by private enterprise through a new economic institution called the joint-stock company. Where the government or wealthy individuals had once been the only source of money for colonization, this new concept involved smaller contributions from a great many investors. Since each shareholder bought only a small share of the company, the risk was not so great in any one enterprise. Due to this Dutch financial innovation adopted by the English, colonization became an attractive source of investment. Backed by these joint-stock companies, the English immigrants brought with them the new capitalistic spirit of the early seventeenth century, rather than the old economic concepts of medieval times.

Of course the economic changes of the sixteenth century were not advantageous to all members of English society. For instance, the enclosure of grazing land for the growing sheepherding industry ruined many small farmers and drove them into the cities. Urban overpopulation then became a serious problem as bands of unemployed people began wandering around ter-

The "Tree of Classes" progresses from peasants and laborers at the base of the tree, to laborers, merchants, kings, and popes.

rorizing the wealthier citizens. As difficult as it may have been, in some ways it was necessary for the successful colonization of America, for these homeless vagabonds made up a large percentage of those who came to the New World. Others who left England in search of new economic opportunities were the second sons of country gentry who could not inherit their father's wealth, since by the laws of primogeniture and entail all property had to go to the eldest son. There were even a few nobles who emigrated, pushed aside by the rise of the new merchant class.

A HERITAGE OF PROTESTANTISM

Many colonists came to the New World for religious reasons. Ever since Henry VIII, Catholics and extreme Protestants alike had found England a hostile environment for their beliefs. Under the Stuarts, the situation became even worse. James I and Charles I were both very harsh on all who dissented from the middle road of the Church of England, opposing any attempt at reform.

From 1629 to 1640 non-Anglicans were so badly persecuted that many of them fled the country in the so-called Great Migration. Some moved to the Netherlands, which tolerated a variety of Protestant sects. But life in Holland was not satisfactory, and in 1620 a group called the Pilgrims left on the *Mayflower* for America, where they founded Plymouth Colony. Ten years later they were followed by the Puritans, who established Massachusetts Bay Colony.

Thus many of the first colonists in America were carriers of powerful new ideas. The strong religious, political, and economic concepts developed in Europe were stored in the minds of these travelers, driven across the Atlantic Ocean, and transplanted on another continent. Because of this process, it was almost inevitable that the American colonies would be primarily Protestant, that political life would be based on English institutions, and that the economy would be capitalistic in form.

Readings

GENERAL WORKS

Brebner, J. B., *The Explorers of North America, 1492–1806.* New York: Macmillan, 1933.

Cheyney, E. P., *The Dawn of a New Era.* New York: Harper & Row, 1936 (Paper: Harper Torch Books, 1962).

Debo, Angie, *A History of the Indians of the United States.* Norman, Okla.: University of Oklahoma Press, 1970.

Driver, Harold E., *Indians of North America.* Chicago: University of Chicago Press, 1961 (Paper, 1964).

Ferguson, Wallace K., *Europe in Transition, 1300–1520.* Boston: Houghton Mifflin, 1962.

Gibson, Charles, *Spain in America.* New York: Harper & Row, 1966.

Josephy, Alvin M., Jr., *Indian Heritage of America.* New York: Bantam Books, 1969. (Paper)

McNeill, William H., *The Rise of the West.* Chicago: University of Chicago Press, 1963.

Nowell, Charles E., *The Great Discoveries and the First Colonial Empires.* Ithaca, N.Y.: Cornell University Press, 1954.

Washburn, Wilcomb E., *The Indian in America.* New York: Harper & Row, 1975.

Wright, Louis B., *Gold, Glory & the Gospel: The Adventurous Lives & Times of the Renaissance Explorers.* New York: Atheneum Publishers, 1970.

SPECIAL STUDIES

Bindoff, S. T., *Tudor England.* Baltimore, Md.: Penguin, 1950.

Boxer, C. R., *The Dutch Seaborne Empire: 1600–1800.* New York: Knopf, 1965.

Bridenbaugh, Carl, *Vexed and Troubled Englishmen, 1590–1642.* New York: Oxford University Press, 1968.

Coe, Michael D., *Mexico.* New York: Praeger, 1962.

Hemming, John, *The Conquest of the Incas.* New York: Harcourt Brace Jovanovich, 1970.

Jones, Gwyn, *A History of the Vikings.* New York: Oxford University Press, 1968.

Mattingly, Garrett, *The Armada.* Boston: Houghton Mifflin, 1959 (Paper: Sentry Edition, 1962).

Morison, Samuel E., *The European Discovery of America: The Northern Voyages.* New York: Oxford University Press, 1971.

Morison, Samuel E., *The European Discovery of America: The Southern Voyages.* New York: Oxford University Press, 1974.

Parkman, Francis, *Pioneers of France in the New World.* Boston: Little, Brown, 1900.

Powicke, F. Maurice, *The Reformation in England.* New York: Oxford University Press, 1961.

Prescott, William H., *Prescott's Histories: The Rise and Decline of the Spanish Empire.* Edited by Irwin R. Blacker. New York: Viking, 1963.

Rowse, A. L., *The England of Elizabeth.* New York: Macmillan, 1961.

Simpson, Alan, *Puritanism in Old and New England.* Chicago: University of Chicago Press, 1955 (Paper: Phoenix Books, 1961).

Weber, Max, *The Protestant Ethic and the Spirit of Capitalism.* New York: Scribner's, 1958.

PRIMARY SOURCES

Bainton, Roland, *The Age of the Reformation.* New York: D. Van Nostrand, 1956.

Diaz del Castillo, Bernal, *The Discovery and Conquest of Mexico.* Edited by Genaro Garcia. Translated by A. P. Maudslay. New York: Farrar, Straus & Cudahy, 1956 (Paper: Farrar, Straus and Giroux, 1965).

Komroff, Manuel (Ed.), *The Travels of Marco Polo.* New York: Random House, 1953.

Leon-Portilla, M., *The Broken Spears: The Aztec Account of the Conquest of Mexico.* Boston: Beacon Press, 1962.

Viereck, Philip (Ed.), *The New Land.* New York: John Day, 1967.

BIOGRAPHIES

Bainton, Roland, *Here I Stand.* New York: Abingdon, 1950 (Paper: New American Library, 1955).

Hackett, Francis, *The Personal History of Henry VIII.* New York: Modern Library, 1945.

Morison, S. E., *Admiral of the Ocean Sea.* Boston: Atlantic Monthly-Little, Brown, 1942.

Neale, J. E., *Queen Elizabeth.* London: Jonathan Cape, 1935 (Paper: Doubleday Anchor, 1957).

Rowse, A. L., *Sir Walter Raleigh: His Family and Private Life.* New York: Harper & Row, 1964.

Williamson, J. A., *Sir Francis Drake.* New York: Macmillan, 1962.

HISTORICAL NOVELS

Cather, Willa, *Shadows on the Rock.* New York: Knopf, 1931.

Forester, C. S., *To the Indies.* Boston: Little, Brown, 1940.

Hugo, Victor, *Notre Dame de Paris.* New York: Modern Library, 1941.

Kingsley, Charles, *Westward Ho!* New York: Airmont, 1968.

Scott, Walter, *Kenilworth.* New York: Airmont, 1968.

Scott, Walter, *Quentin Durward.* New American Library, 1963.

Shellabarger, Samuel, *Captain from Castile.* Boston: Little, Brown, 1945.

Shute, Nevil, *An Old Captivity.* New York: W. Morrow, 1940.

RELATED RESOURCES

Bushnell, G. H. S., *The First Americans*. New York: McGraw-Hill, 1968.

Lehner, Ernst and Johanna. *How They Saw the New World,* Gerard L. Alexander, ed. New York: Tudor, 1966.

New York in 1670, just before the English seized it from the Dutch. ▶

2

Colonizing the New World

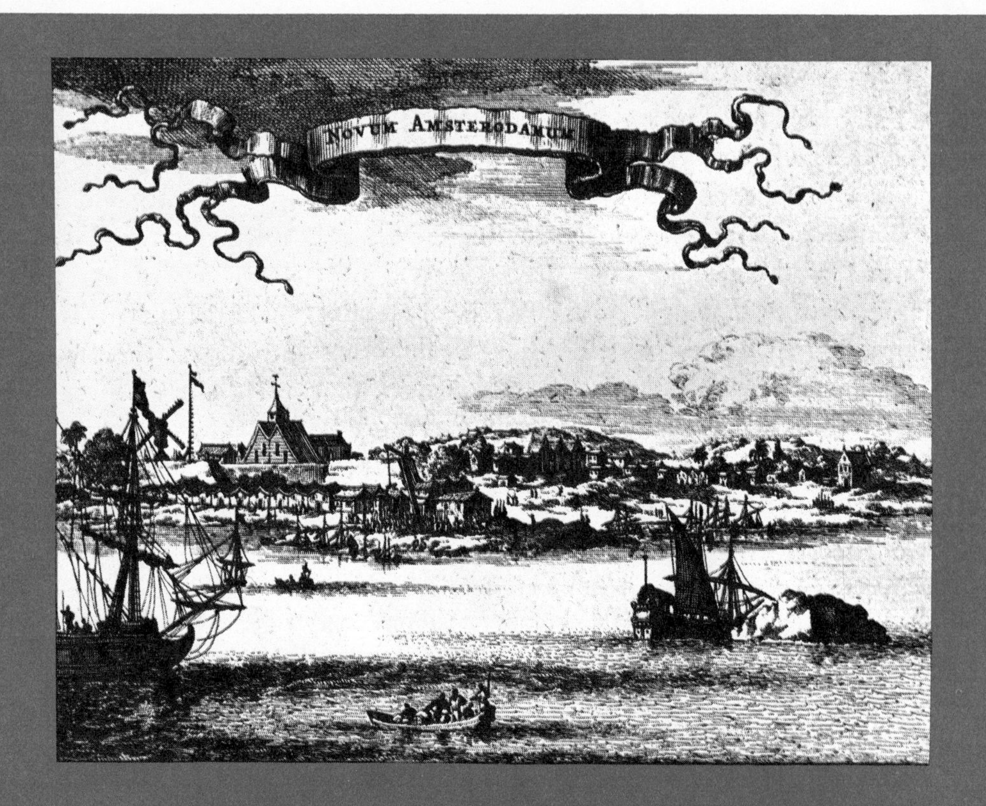

The mildnesse of the aire, the fertilitie of the soile, and the situation of the rivers are so propitious to the nature and use of man as no place is more convenient for pleasure, profit, and mans sustenance. . . . The waters, Isles, and shoales, are full of safe harbours for ships of warre or marchandize, for boats of all sortes, for transportation or fishing, etc. The Bay and rivers have much marchandable fish and places for Salt coats, building of ships, making of iron, etc.

Captain John Smith,
Narratives of Early Virginia

The English arrive at Roanoke, Virginia in 1585.

Those who made the long and hazardous ocean voyage to the New World in the seventeenth century were looking for something they could not find in Europe. Soldiers of fortune came to find wealth. Poor farmers came to improve their position. Religious dissenters came to find a place where they could live and worship freely. Few had the remotest notion of what life would be like in this unknown place. Would their new home be wintry or tropical? Would it offer them lush vegetation and rivers of gold, or barren land and poverty? Were the native Americans noble savages or cruel pagans? Future colonists could only guess at the answers to such questions.

At the beginning of the seventeenth century England had no colonies anywhere in the world. In the 1580s Sir Humphrey Gilbert and Sir Walter Raleigh had both tried to establish colonies in America. But their efforts had ended in disaster. In fact, Raleigh's last colony on Roanoke Island vanished without a trace, leaving a mystery which has never been solved.

These early failures were warning signs. Colonizing the New World would be a difficult and often frightening undertaking. In some cases the barest essentials of life would have to be eked out of a grudging land and a stable, organized society developed slowly.

Considering all this, it is almost miraculous that a quarter of a million settlers had established themselves in twenty English colonies in the New World by the end of the seventeenth century.

Beginnings on the Chesapeake

In 1604 the English king, James I, signed a peace treaty with Spain which brought his people twenty years of security. The nation prospered and the colonization effort, abandoned since the earlier failures, was able to begin again.

The king himself had little interest in the merchants or in their colonizing projects, but his Privy Council had plenty. They were intrigued by every aspect of navigation, colonization, and business. In fact, many members of this influential group of royal advisors had invested in the joint-stock companies that financed the first American colonies.

In 1606 two joint-stock companies petitioned the king for a charter to settle Virginia (the name the English gave to the entire Atlantic seaboard from Maine to Florida). The king granted their petitions, giving the Virginia Company of Plymouth the northern half (38–45 degrees) and the Virginia Company of London the southern half (34–41 degrees). The area from 38–41 degrees was open to colonization by either company.

A FALSE START IN MAINE

The Plymouth Company's activities were short-lived. After sending two ships to explore the coast, the company dispatched 120 men in the *Gift of God* and the *Mary and John*. The party landed on August 7, 1607 at the mouth of the Kennebec River in the present state of Maine. They chose a place for their settlement, or "plantation," a short distance upriver, and spent the next two months building a fort and trying to establish friendly relations with the Indians. Unfortunately, the president of the plantation, George Popham, turned out to lack the qualities of leadership the situation demanded. As one contemporary said, he was "fearful to offend or contest with others that will or do oppose him." When the colonists began quarreling among themselves, Popham was unable to hold them together. As a result, the Indians soon lost all respect for their new neighbors and refused to trade with them.

Lacking a strong leader, fragmented by bickering, and short on food and supplies, the settlers were badly demoralized. But their troubles were not over. A bitter cold Maine winter shattered their hopes of a tropical climate, several important members of the expedition died, and a fire destroyed their storehouse and other buildings. The colonists packed their belongings and returned to England.

JAMESTOWN IS SETTLED

The London Company plantation met with even greater hardship, but endured to become the first successful colony. The cost of success, however, was staggering: four-fifths of the colonists who came to Jamestown between 1607 and 1624 died, and the company spent roughly seven million dollars without ever turning a profit. In 1624 the company lost its charter and the king took control of the colony.

In December 1606 the *Susan Constant*, the *Godspeed*, and the *Discovery* set sail from England with 144 colonists, all men. When they arrived in Virginia four months later, thirty-nine men had died at sea and Captain John Smith, the military officer for the settlement, had been put in the brig for mutinous grumblings. During the trip over no one knew who would be governing the settlement. The company had sent along a sealed steel box containing the names of seven colonists who were also shareholders. The box was to be opened upon arrival in the New World and the seven investors were to take charge of the colony. When the box was opened one of the investors turned out to be none other than John Smith. Taking advantage of the powers granted them by the charter, the other members removed Smith from the resident council. But Smith later proved to be a hard man to suppress.

The expedition, which had been organized for financial purposes, had three main responsibilities: to discover a passage to China through the mainland of North America, to trade with the Indians, and to mine gold, copper, and iron. But first they had to establish a fort in which to live. This they did—on a site some thirty miles up the James River where they would be hidden from roving Spanish ships. While one group started to build the fort, another set out to find the route to China.

The colony was in trouble from the beginning. The site they had chosen for their fort turned out to be swampy and a source of malaria. It was also far from any source of fresh water. The explorers were unable to find a passage to China. And within days of the group's arrival, a band of Indians attacked the fort, wounding seventeen men and killing one boy.

To make matters worse, the colony had no effective government. James I had retained the right to send instructions to the resident council in Virginia through a London Company council in England. The resident council lacked the authority to originate orders or to enforce those sent from England.

The settlers, almost half of them English gentlemen unused to physical labor, were there to turn a quick profit. With single-minded zeal they chose to mine the gold of Virginia rather than to provide for the coming winter. "No talk, no hope, nor work," wrote Captain John Smith in despair, "but dig gold, wash gold, refine gold, load gold." In the end Virginia's "gold" turned out to be a commonplace mineral called iron pyrite.

By the autumn of 1607, half the settlers had died. Those who had dug enthusiastically for gold turned their energies to digging graves. As winter set in, more and more people perished from disease and starvation. One colonist described how three or four men might die in a single night: "In the morning their bodies trailed out of their cabins like dogs to be buried." Only the help of the Indians enabled a few to survive. As one early settler wrote:

> It pleased God, after a while, to send those people which were our mortal enemies to relieve us with victuals, as bread, corn, fish and flesh in great plenty, which was the setting up of our feeble men, otherwise we had all perished. Also, we were frequented by diverse kings in the country, bringing us store of provision to our great comfort.

With no relief in sight, decorum declined: even the president of the council was once charged with raiding the hen house and drinking too much of the communal brandy. In January 1608, when a ship finally arrived from England bringing supplies and 120 new settlers, there were only 38 colonists left to receive them.

The Jamestown settlers never knew quite what to expect from the neighboring Indian tribes. If they were attacked one day, they were often befriended the next. When they arrived in Virginia a local chief, Powhatan, was trying to bring about 30 tribes (some 9000 people) into an empire under his leadership. Powhatan soon realized that the English might be able to help him discipline unruly tribes in his confederation and subdue hostile alien tribes. The Indians were also interested in the settlers' weapons; their own technology had never produced anything as deadly as a gun.

Clearly, the English interested Powhatan more than they threatened his way of life. However, once the settlers were drawn into the political struggles of warring Indian tribes, they ran the risks to which such involvement exposed them.

In any event, it is possible that without the Indians' help the Jamestown settlement might not have lasted any longer than the ill-fated plantation in Maine. The Indians not only brought the settlers food when they might have perished without it, but also taught them many of the skills they needed to survive in their new environment: how to clear the forests for farm-

"How they till the soil and plant." Virginia Indians observed in 1564.

land and how to grow new crops such as corn and yams.

Jamestown's early years

The winter of 1608–09 was much better: only twelve people died and the colony began to prosper. This was due to the leadership of the indomitable John Smith, who was elected president of the resident council in September. Smith called a halt to the search for gold and saw to it that buildings were repaired, crops planted, livestock nurtured, and slackers punished. If a rough-and-ready "adventurer" (as the settlers were called) swore too much, Smith had a glass of water poured down the offender's sleeve. He established peaceful relations with the Indians and is rumored to have asked to marry Powhatan's daughter, the princess Pocahontas. There are many versions of this episode. The most famous tells how she saved Smith by warning him of an Indian plot against his life. His critics started rumors that Smith wanted to marry Pocahontas and make himself emperor of Virginia. In any event, reports of Smith's harsh rule and rumors of his "plans" reached the London Company. He was sent back to England for trial.

Although he was removed from office, Smith had demonstrated the importance of strong leadership. When the king granted a new charter in 1609 it called for an all-powerful administrator and reduced the council's role to an advisory one.

The new charter also included a provision to encourage emigration. Settlers could exchange seven years of unpaid labor on the company lands for free passage over. Those who took advantage of this option were called indentured servants. Settlers who paid their own way over received one share of stock in the enterprise. All agreed to work for the company until 1616, when the profits would be divided equally and every shareholder would receive a bonus of 100 acres.

This plan sounded so promising that 600 people signed up. The trip was financed by a

An early woodcut illustrates a popular myth about Captain John Smith and the Indian princess, Pocahontas. Smith is held on the floor by Indian braves while Pocahontas begs her father, Chief Powhatan, for Smith's life. According to the myth, the princess wins the argument and *Smith as well.*

national lottery held in England. Losers were consoled in verse:

> Let no man think that he shall lose,
> Though he no prize possess.
> His substance to Virginia goes,
> Which God no doubt will bless. . . .

In May 1609, nine ships left England bound for Jamestown. In addition to the new settlers, this great fleet carried Sir Thomas Gates who was to serve as the colony's interim governor until the real governor could get there. During a terrible storm at sea, one of the ships was lost and Gates's ship was wrecked on one of the Bermuda Islands. Meanwhile the rest of the fleet arrived in Jamestown.

Finding their numbers increased some five times and finding themselves deprived of leadership, the colonists suffered badly through the next winter. When Gates finally arrived in May 1610, he was appalled to find a settlement "which appeared rather as a ruins of some antient fortification, than that any people living might now inhabit it."

This was Jamestown's "starving time." Food had been so scarce that the settlers had been reduced to eating dogs, cats, rats, snakes, and boiled shoes. One man even killed his wife, "powdered" (salted), and ate her, "for which he was executed, as he well deserved," as one colonist wrote. He added with grim humor, "Whether she was better roasted, boiled or carbonadoed, I know not, but of such a dish as powdered wife I never heard of."

Back in England, the company hired preachers to silence reports of starvation and cannibalism. One overzealous minister praised Virginia's "abundance of mulberries, minerals, rubies, pearls, gems, grapes, deer fowl" and "ashes for soap." Alas, there were no such riches in Virginia.

When the colony's governor finally arrived a few weeks after Gates, he managed to restore some order and organize repairs to the town. However, he could do nothing about the colonists' terrible weakness to disease. He himself finally became so ill that he had to return to England in March 1611.

But the worst was almost over. Jamestown's second governor, a stern Puritan by the name of Thomas Dale, arrived in May 1611 and it was not long before he had managed to restore order.

The House of Burgesses

During Dale's forceful governorship and that of his successor, life in Jamestown took a turn for the better. John Rolfe's agricultural experiments with tobacco enabled the colonists to develop a profitable export. By 1617 Jamestown was able to ship 20,000 pounds of tobacco to England. Another boon was the arrival of a group of

Tobacco plantation.

The Reality of Virginia

"This was that time, which still to this day we called the starving time; it were too vile to say, and scarce to be believed, what we endured: but the occasion was our own, for want of providence industry and government, and not the barrenness and defect of the Country, as is generally supposed; for till then in three years, for the numbers were landed us, we had never from England provision sufficient for six months, though it seemed by the bills of loading sufficient was sent us, such a glutton is the Sea, and such good fellows the Mariners; we as little tasted of the great proportion sent us, as they of our want and miseries. . . ."

Captain John Smith,
The Generall Historie of Virginia, 1624:
The Fourth Booke

The Pilgrim's Trial

"But here I cannot but stay and make a pause, and stand half amazed at this poor people's present condition; and so I think will the reader too, when he well considers the same. Being thus passed the vast ocean, and a sea of troubles before in their preparation . . . they had now no friends to welcome them, nor inns to entertain or refresh their weatherbeaten bodies, no houses or much less towns to repair to, to seek for succor. . . . And for the season it was winter, and they that know the winters of that country know them to be sharp and violent, & subject to cruel & fierce storms, dangerous to travel to known places, much more to search an unknown coast. Besides, what could they see but a hideous & desolate wilderness, full of wild beasts & wild men? and what multitudes there might be of them they knew not. . . ."

**William Bradford,
Of Plymouth Plantation,
The Pilgrims in America, 1604–1646**

women in 1620. Ninety young women, whom the company guaranteed to be "pure and spotless," came over to be the colonists' wives. The cost of one wife: 120 pounds of tobacco!

The colony's prosperity created a demand for more economic and political freedom. In 1619 a new charter was issued. Once again the company was allowed to transport settlers in exchange for seven years of indentured servitude. Those who paid their own way over were given fifty acres of land, plus fifty more acres for every person they brought with them. This land was called a headright and the person receiving it was obliged to pay a yearly quitrent (land tax) of one shilling for every fifty acres of land. The new charter also assured the settlers of all the legal rights of English citizens.

There was also a major innovation in the charter: the colonists were given permission to elect representatives to an assembly, called the House of Burgesses. On July 30, 1619 Virginians met in the first representative assembly of the New World. The representatives had the authority to make laws for the entire colony, and to ratify all directives sent by the London Company. This strong provision for self-government was the work of the company treasurer, Sir Edwin Sandys. Sandys was known for his tolerance and learning, as well as for his opposition to any extension of the king's power.

Jamestown becomes a royal colony

Sandys had other new plans for the colony, too. Under his direction the company began to sell private plantations to small groups which settled in semi-independent villages, each of which had two representatives in the House of Burgesses. He also convinced the company to send, at its own expense, tradespeople and artisans (glassblowers, ironmongers, shipbuilders) so that the colony could diversify its business interests and protect itself against a possible tobacco crop failure. In his enthusiasm to stimulate emigration, however, Sandys overlooked a few details: he lured more than 3500 settlers to Virginia without making sure the colony had enough food, housing, and supplies to support the new arrivals. Three years later, all but about 900 had died of disease or starvation.

A heavy blow followed on March 22, 1622. The Indians, alarmed by the English advancement on their lands, massacred some 347 settlers, including John Rolfe. The attack was well planned in advance. All through the week before the massacre, the Indians were especially friendly, bringing the settlers gifts of food and breakfasting with them. Then, on the appointed morning, when they were eating and trading at the English settlements, they suddenly rose up and slaughtered their hosts. The colonists responded in kind. They invited 250 Indians to a peace conference, gave them poisoned wine to drink, and killed every one of their guests.

The colony's future was beginning to look pretty uncertain. In spite of the increasing export of tobacco, the company still had not seen a return on its investment and was near bankruptcy. In 1623 a royal commission investigated the company's management of the colony and, in 1624, a court revoked the company's privileges. The colony was handed over to the king and his Privy Council.

The king was having trouble with Parliament and was not about to encourage independence among his subjects on the other side of the Atlantic. So, he dissolved the House of Burgesses, appointed a royal governor, and sent him off to Virginia. The governor had instructions from the king and absolute authority to govern the colony. However it soon became apparent that he could not govern effectively without an appointed council of local property holders.

This development threatened to undo all the progress the colonists had made toward self-government. However, the royal governor and his council soon learned that it was easier to govern with the colonists' cooperation than without it. So, in 1629 the governor invited a group of former representatives to come together and begin to function informally as a representative assembly. This body had almost as much power as the House of Burgesses had before. In 1639 the king's instructions contained formal recognition of the Burgesses' law-making powers.

The Jamestown colony may have seemed a disaster at the outset: 4600 settlers perished trying to establish the plantation and the company's shareholders never realized the profits they had expected. But an enduring settlement was built. Farms began to flourish. Children were born and raised in the New World. The Indian threat gradually diminished. From 1629 on, some form of representative government was functioning again in the House of Burgesses. The first steps had been taken toward establishing an English frontier in the New World.

MARYLAND: A PROPRIETARY GRANT

Virginia was organized by businessmen for the sole purpose of making a profit. Maryland, on the other hand, was settled by Lord Calvert as a refuge for persecuted Catholics like himself.

George Calvert was not born into the nobility, nor into the Catholic faith. He was educated at Oxford and, by knowing the right people and working hard, eventually became secretary of state in the king's Privy Council. Like other members of the Privy Council, Calvert was intrigued by schemes for settling the New World. He was one of the commissioners who had supported turning Virginia into a royal colony.

It was during his years of service to the throne that Calvert converted to Roman Catholicism. This was an unpopular move in a country dominated by Protestants and it also made him useless to the government. His dealings with Catholic countries such as Spain were immediately suspect. And, since Catholics could not take the Oath of Supremacy recognizing the monarch as supreme head of both church and state, he was technically disloyal to the Crown.

Calvert stepped down from power but remained a royal favorite. The king personally excused him from taking the Oath of Supremacy and made him a noble, with the title of Baron Baltimore of Baltimore (an estate in Ireland).

In 1623 Calvert's request for an area to colonize was granted, and he received a charter for a huge tract of land on Newfoundland. Soon afterward he set out to govern the small settlement of Catholics already there. Finding it too cold and too exposed to French raids, he applied to Charles I for an estate in a warmer climate. The king granted him land on the Chesapeake Bay north of Virginia and named it after his wife, Queen Henrietta Maria.

George Calvert died before he actually received the charter. When the document was finally fixed with the king's seal in 1632, the colony went to George's son Cecil, the second Lord Baltimore. In November 1633, two Jesuit priests, seventeen gentlemen, their wives and children, and about two hundred other settlers set sail on the *Ark* and the *Dove*. At the head of the enterprise was Cecil's brother, Leonard Calvert.

The Calvert brothers were intelligent administrators who learned the lessons of the Jamestown settlement. The site they chose for their first town (St. Mary's) had an excellent harbor and plenty of fresh water, and they were careful to obtain the land by trading with the friendly local Indians. The settlers planted vegetable gardens right away and had the Indians teach them how to cultivate corn. When ambitious farmers wanted to devote their fields to that profitable export, tobacco, the governor copied a Virginia law and insisted that they also cultivate at least two acres of corn.

A feudal estate

The royal charter that created Maryland was a throwback to the Middle Ages. In theory, at least, Maryland was completely subject to the will of its proprietor, Lord Baltimore. He owned all of the colony's ten million acres, and was free to make laws, appoint officials, try criminals, bequeath titles, and tax trade almost without restriction. In fact, Lord Baltimore theoretically had more power in his colony than the king could exercise in England. All he had to do in return was promise the king one-fifth of all the gold and silver discovered in Maryland and two Indian arrowheads a year.

In some respects the Baltimores did reproduce a medieval social structure: gentlemen who brought five other people with them were allowed to establish manors of 2000 acres. Those who qualified were usually Baltimore's close friends and fellow Catholics. Other male settlers (called freeholders) were given 100 acres of land plus another 100 acres for a wife and each servant, and 50 acres for each child over sixteen. Manor lords could also dispense land to freeholders. This unequal granting of land created social class distinctions based on the size of a person's property holdings. The lords of manors (the colony's Catholic elite) enjoyed the same rights and privileges the nobles enjoyed in England, while the freeholders lacked all such privileges. Both manor lords and freeholders had to pay the proprietor a quitrent, or land tax.

The medieval pattern of life never took a strong hold in Maryland, however, partly because of the people who came to settle the colony and partly because of the wisdom of the proprietor.

Religious Toleration. Despite the Calverts' land policies, Protestants outnumbered Catholics from the start. Lord Baltimore tried to maintain order by demanding "no scandal or offense to be given to any of the Protestants." But the situation could not be contained by such a mild measure. In 1649 under a Protestant lieutenant governor, an official Toleration Act banning all religious insults was passed. Catholics were forbidden to call Protestants heretics and Protestants were not allowed to scream popish priest at Catholics. More important, the law provided that anyone who admitted belief in Jesus Christ would not be molested on religious grounds. This act was an important step toward the religious freedom that would ultimately become a fundamental civil liberty in the United States.

Representative Government. Representative government took hold gradually in Maryland, helping to prevent the development of full-blown feudalism. Lord Baltimore's charter had guaranteed him and his heirs control over the colony's government, with the "advice, assent, and approbation of freemen." Three years after the colony was settled the governor convened an assembly in order to receive this assent. The members, however, balked at being asked merely to endorse laws that were handed down to them. Like members of Parliament back in England, they wanted the right to initiate legislation. They also demanded immunity from arrest for any rebellious remarks they might make during a session. This set a precedent for the concept of congressional immunity later incorporated into the United States Constitution.

Although Lord Baltimore rejected in principle the assembly's right to draft laws of its own, he soon discovered that he would have to bow to the people's will if he wanted his statutes approved. Before long, the people's representatives were suggesting legislation and rewriting most of the proprietor's proposals. By 1650 Maryland had a strong legislature. Like Virginia, Maryland's government now consisted of a governor, an appointed council of local property holders, and a representative assembly (called the House of Commons) made up of two elected officials from each of the local counties. The only difference was that in Virginia the governor and council were appointed by the king, while in Maryland they were appointed by the proprietor, Lord Baltimore.

Life in the Chesapeake Bay Area

Although Virginia was a royal colony after 1624 and Maryland was the personal property of the Calverts, life was essentially the same in the two Chesapeake Bay settlements. This was partly because of the nature of the bay area.

Chesapeake Bay is nearly 200 miles long and 22 miles wide, and it is fed by hundreds of rivers and creeks. This vast system of waterways produced a distinct kind of life. Tobacco farmers had to be able to get their crops to a harbor for shipment to England and the bay area's rivers and creeks were just what they needed: their plantations never had to be more than a few hundred feet from water. Farmers who lived along the smaller rivers and creeks could ship their tobacco in canoes to Jamestown or St. Mary's, while those who lived along the deep rivers could load their crops directly onto oceangoing vessels.

This pattern of settlement made the bay area extremely hard to administer. As one English official put it, "How is it possible to govern a people so dispersed?" In the early years this problem was exaggerated by the kind of people who came to settle the area. Many of Virginia's first colonists were so-called undesirables. As early as 1618 the city of London had sent 100 homeless children, and the following year 100 "fellons and other desperate villanes" were shipped over. By the middle of the century, however, most of Virginia's 40,000 white settlers were English freemen, indentured servants, and apprentices. Most of the freemen had originally come over under some form of indenture.

Slaves and indentured servants of African descent were part of the Chesapeake Bay population as early as 1619. By 1661 Virginia had legalized slavery as the status for all people of African descent and by 1670 there were some 2000 black Africans and West Indians in the colony. In the early years of settlement, however, most farms were small or medium sized and were worked by their owners and a few indentured servants. Only in the next century would the use of slave labor become extensive enough to support the growth of huge plantations and a leisured class of white property owners.

FREEMEN, INDENTURED SERVANTS, AND WOMEN

So many people who came to America were looking to improve their lot in life that few wanted to work for someone else. On the other hand, those who could not afford to get here any other way were often willing to exchange a term of service for the chance to better themselves afterwards. People who came over as indentured servants worked for whoever paid their fare: the company, the Crown, or a private citizen.

The amount of land a colonist received under the headright system depended on the number of people (or heads) they brought with them. The more land they received, the more help they needed cultivating it. This was a major source of employment for indentured servants. The tobacco economy of Virginia and Maryland was built on the labor of gangs of indentured servants which were gradually replaced by black slaves only in the late seventeenth century and after.

Settlers who received land under the headright system did not actually own the land. It was licensed to them on the condition that they cultivate it, live on it in some sort of house, and pay the Crown or the proprietor a small quitrent or tax for the privilege. Even though the quitrent was often as little as one shilling per year for fifty acres of land, many farmers refused to pay. It has been estimated that by the time of the Revolution only half the quitrents were being paid.

Indentured servants were not allowed to hold land until they had completed their term of service under their indenture. Their other rights were also limited since they were considered to be their master's dependents. They could be bought and sold, rented out, and inherited. They could only engage in trade with their master's consent. They could sue and be sued, but not vote. They were subject to corporal punishment, but could petition the courts against abuse. They could not marry without the consent of their master.

Once their term of service was over, they were free to seek their own fortune and were supposed to receive fifty acres of land. Their employer usually gave them a new suit of clothes and some agricultural equipment. Some who did not receive land tried to save enough money to buy their own farm while others "squatted" on unclaimed land and farmed it. Squatters sometimes ran into legal trouble if someone else wanted to buy the land. But they eventually began claiming the right to buy the land from the legal owner without paying for the improvements they had made. If they were dispossessed, they often moved on, found a new piece of land, and farmed it.

Indentured servitude was common everywhere except New England. More than half of all those who came to the colonies in the eighteenth century came as indentured servants, and about one-fourth were women.

A free woman's position in colonial society was not much different from an indentured servant's. They were also dependents: of their husband if they were married, of their father if they were not. Their husband or father controlled their earnings and their property if they had any. In the case of legal separation, the

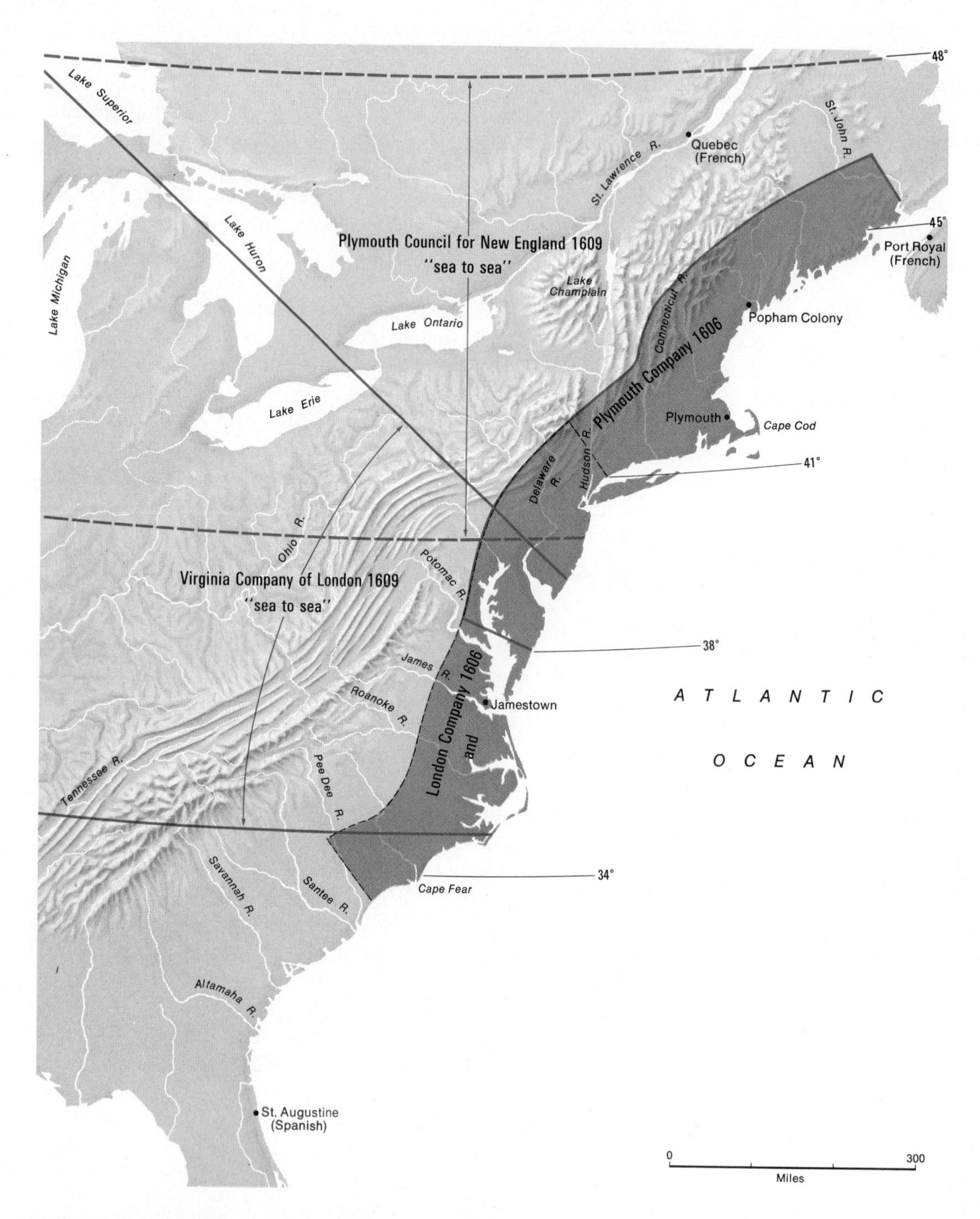

EARLY COLONIAL LAND GRANTS · 1606 TO 1620

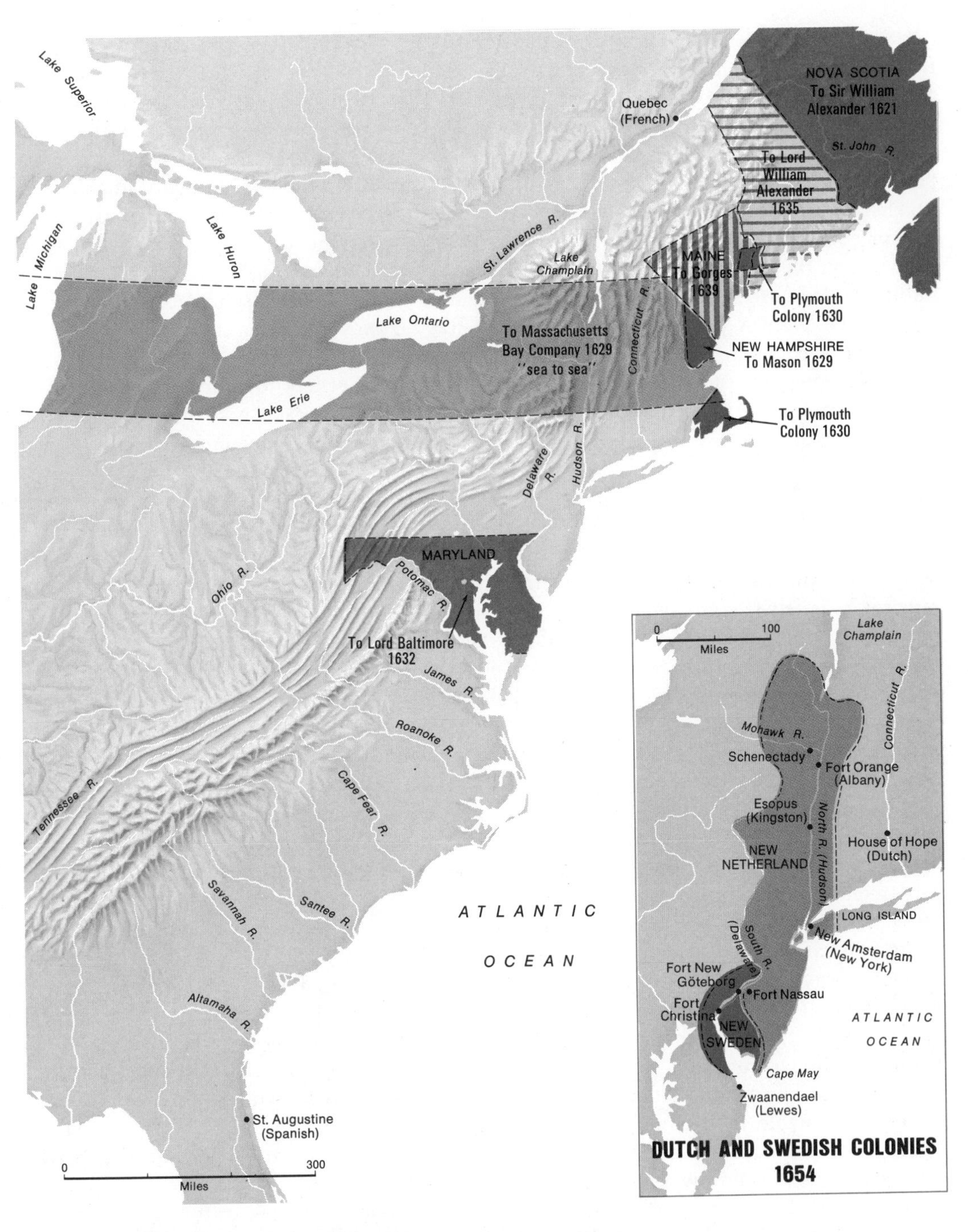

EARLY COLONIAL LAND GRANTS • 1620 TO 1639

husband retained legal rights to the children of the marriage. And divorces were granted in only the most extreme cases. Women could not sign contracts, vote, or marry without their father's consent. They were also subject to corporal punishment.

There were, however, a few acres of endeavor in which women occasionally were engaged on their own. Some were seamstresses, milliners, or house servants. There were women innkeepers, women printers, and even women who managed stores or newspapers. Often these were widows carrying on their husband's business, but sometimes they were simply enterprising women.

BACON'S REBELLION

In 1644, twenty-two years after the massacre at Jamestown, the Indians rose again. White reprisal was swift and the Indians sued for peace after their chief had been captured and killed. The peace settlement was based on a policy of segregation. A line was established: the settlers agreed not to enter Indian territory and the Indians agreed not to trespass on white territory. The policy lasted three years.

As the settlers' numbers increased, so did their demand for new land. In 1649 the government gave in to white pressure and allowed settlement on the Indian side of the line. In 1653 a new solution was tried. Indians were settled on farms in an attempt to convert them to white ways. This experiment was acknowledged a failure in 1663. In 1675 new hostilities erupted when the Susquehannocks began foraging into white territory.

Why were the white settlers and the native Americans unable to live peacefully as neighbors? The two cultures' opposing concepts of land use and ownership were one serious barrier to mutual understanding. Also, in their great yearning for new land to settle, the colonists found it easy to take what they wanted and to justify their conduct on the grounds that they were spreading a superior civilization.

To make matters worse, frontier settlers were not happy with the government's use of forts to protect them from Indian attack: it was a simple enough matter for the Indians to go around the forts. The settlers felt exposed and, in their fear, were often unable to distinguish between hostile and peaceful tribes.

As the colonists pushed deeper and deeper into Indian territory, these tensions increased.

By 1670 Virginia's frontier was fifty miles from Jamestown, just far enough to destroy the sense of common interests that had bound the first settlers together. Two groups of elites had emerged, each with its own special interests to protect. The county leaders (especially those from the frontier) wanted the government to open up new territories for settlement and to take a more aggressive stance against the Indians. The governor's faction, on the other hand, was enjoying a profitable monopoly of the fur trade and hardly wanted to stir up troubles with the Indians. Nor did they want to increase the county elite's wealth and power.

There was a third element in this power struggle: the ordinary colonists who resented both groups. As far as they were concerned, Governor Berkeley had failed to protect them against the Indians and their local leaders came no closer to representing their interests than the governor's elite did.

In 1676 a newly arrived frontier farmer named Nathaniel Bacon led a rebellion against Berkeley and the government. Backed by older, established frontier planters Bacon massacred two neighboring Indian tribes. Berkeley labeled him a rebel and ordered him to stop. Bacon's response was to rally 500 men and march on Jamestown. The frightened governor and the House of Burgesses were forced to grant the rebel's request for an army with which to continue fighting the Indians. The House also passed a series of measures—dubbed Bacon's laws—decreasing the governor's power and removing the property qualification for voting.

But when Bacon returned to the frontier, Berkeley again branded him a rebel. Furious,

Bacon marched back to Jamestown and burned it down. And then, suddenly, in October the rebellion collapsed when Bacon died of dysentery. The governor executed twenty of Bacon's followers before the king's commissioners arrived to remove him from office.

When the brief but turbulent episode was over, England tightened her control over the Chesapeake Bay colonies by increasing the authority of the royal governors. This initiated a long period of controversy between the Virginians and their governors.

The Founding of New England

Religion played only a minor role in the settlement of the Chesapeake Bay area. Even though Maryland was designed as a refuge for persecuted Catholics, Lord Baltimore and his heirs never tried to create an exclusively Catholic settlement. In Virginia the Church of England was receiving government support by the 1640s and all non-Anglicans were required to "depart the colony with all convenience." Yet the religious establishment was never strong in Virginia. Control of church matters was in the hands of the important lay members of the church, known as the vestry. The vestry even chose the minister and, when no minister was available, read the service themselves.

The religious history of New England, however, was quite different.

THE PLYMOUTH COLONY

The first English settlers in New England were backed by merchants, but they came for religious reasons. This combination of religious and economic motivation had figured in previous efforts to colonize the New World. The Spanish had conquered Central and South America in order to gain gold as well as converts. But the Pilgrims were more modest: they wanted to repay the merchants who had financed their voyage but, most of all, they wanted to practice their religion without being persecuted for it.

The Pilgrims were a group of Calvinists who wanted to break away from the Church of England. Thus they became known as Separatists. The sect had originated among a group of well-to-do farmers in the town of Scrooby in northern England. The Separatists were so badly treated by the other people in Scrooby that they eventually fled to Holland which was known for its tolerance. There they settled in the town of Leyden.

But life in The Netherlands was not what the Separatists were looking for. Most were farmers who found city life strange and unnatural. Their children were growing up speaking Dutch and some were even drifting away from their parents' faith. Furthermore, there was a constant threat from Catholic Spain which was trying to conquer Holland. The Separatists wanted land of their own. They wanted to live by farming, maintain English customs and the English language, and practice their religion free from persecution.

America sounded like just what they were looking for. Before making the voyage, however, they had to obtain permission from the English government and backing from English merchants. The king made them promise to remain loyal to him personally and he, in return, promised to leave them alone as long as "they carried themselves peaceably." In 1620 the London Company of Virginia granted the Pilgrims a patent, permitting them to settle in Virginia. A hardware dealer named Thomas Weston and several of his fellow merchants formed a joint-stock company to finance the venture. The company made an agreement with

the Pilgrims that, in return for free passage over, the colonists would divide all profits equally with the merchants after seven years. The company's financial affairs were to be managed by officers residing both in London and in the New World.

Thirty-five Separatists, some from Leyden and some from London, sailed from England in August 1620. They set out in two ships, the *Speedwell* and the *Mayflower*, but the first ship soon sprang a leak, and both had to turn back. Finally, in September the *Mayflower* set sail again. This time there were 102 passengers, only a third of them Pilgrims. The majority were "strangers," as the Pilgrims called those of other faiths. Among the strangers were John Alden, who sympathized with the persecuted Pilgrims, and Captain Miles Standish, who helped prevent a mutiny when they sighted the cold, rocky coast of New England where they expected to see the warm, rich coast of Virginia.

Finding themselves outside the jurisdiction of the London Company and their patent useless, the Pilgrims feared that the strangers (some of whom, according to the Pilgrim leader and historian, William Bradford, were an "undesirable lot") would "use their own liberty" and run wild. To prevent chaos, the Pilgrims drew up the famous Mayflower Compact, a document scarcely 200 words long. The forty-one men who signed it agreed that they were forming a "body politic" and that they would obey whatever laws the group passed. The compact was not a constitution. It was a temporary measure until the Pilgrims could obtain a patent from the rightful owners of New England.

The area of New England was now under the jurisdiction of a company of aristocrats called the Council of New England. They were led by Sir Ferdinando Gorges, who had won a royal charter replacing the one originally granted to the Virginia Company of Plymouth.

◀ *The Pilgrims landing at Plymouth.*

The Council of New England had done little about its vast holdings, except to discuss how the land would someday be divided into feudal estates. The unexpected arrival of the Pilgrims was not at all what Gorges and his associates had had in mind. Still, on June 1, 1621, they issued a patent to the firm that represented Thomas Weston's merchants and the Pilgrims.

In the meantime, on December 21, 1620, the Pilgrims had landed at Plymouth. Never did an enterprise face more difficulties. By spring, half the settlers had died. A friendly Indian named Squanto saved the rest from starvation by teaching them how to fish and plant corn. Sometime in October 1621, they gathered to thank God for their first harvest. They had little else to cheer them. When the *Mayflower* returned to Plymouth the following November, it brought thirty-five more mouths to feed and no supplies at all. Six years after their arrival they had only one cow for every six people and one goat to every three. By the 1640s they still had only one plow. The region produced scarcely any useful commodities other than furs, lumber, and fish.

The London merchants soon realized they would never make a return on their investment. So, on November 15, 1626, they sold their stock to the Pilgrims. This transaction placed the tiny, impoverished community under an enormous debt that took seventeen years to pay off.

Plymouth's first governor was William Bradford who governed with absolute authority for more than thirty years. As the colony gradually became self-supporting, new towns were added and the problems of government grew increasingly complex. In 1636 the first system of laws that originated in the colonies was passed. The Great Fundamentals created a representative government in which each town elected two deputies to a unicameral (one-house) legisla-

Reproduction of an early dwelling at Plymouth, Massachusetts.

ture that sat with the governor and the governor's assistants.

The settlers never managed to obtain a charter from the king and their patent from the Council of New England was a vague document that said nothing about establishing a civil government. So in 1691, when Plymouth and its related villages were absorbed into the flourishing colony that had grown up around the city of Boston, there was little they could do about it.

THE MASSACHUSETTS BAY COLONY

Ten years after the Pilgrims landed, another group of Protestant dissenters, the Puritans, crossed the Atlantic to New England. Seven hundred settlers, including many well-to-do merchants, arrived in a great fleet of eleven ships, four of which carried livestock and supplies.

Like the Pilgrims these newcomers were Calvinists who despised the "popish practices" which they felt infected the Church of England, and they came to the New World to build a self-governing community of saints. Unlike the Pilgrims, however, they remained loyal to the Church, wanting only to reform it. Also unlike the Pilgrims, the Puritans wanted to completely escape the authority of the King of England. They had an unshakable conviction that God would favor their migration. "We doubt not but God will be with us," one Puritan wrote, "and if God be with us, who can be against us?"

The Puritans had common sense to equal their spiritual confidence. They had set sail in the spring so that they would be able to plant a crop before winter set in. They carried a large supply of limes with them on the voyage to prevent an outbreak of scurvy. When they landed at Salem, they were met by 400 settlers who had come over in two groups (in 1628 and 1629) to prepare the way for them. Most important, the Puritans established from the outset the right to rule themselves.

Charles I granted the Puritans a royal charter which formed them into a joint-stock company called the Massachusetts Bay Company. The charter gave twenty-six investors the right to the land which lay approximately between the Merrimac and the Charles rivers, the area between what is now Boston and the state of New Hampshire. In most respects this charter resembled earlier ones. But there was one crucial difference: there was no provision insisting that either the charter or company headquarters remain in England.

This was the first time in history that the headquarters of a joint-stock company moved to the colonies with the settlers. The Puritans realized that if they took the charter and some of the investors with them to America, they would be a legally independent and self-governing body politic, free from interference by royal governors and English officials. They could make their own laws, decide on their own taxes, establish their own school system, administer their own justice and, most important, determine their own religious life.

The 1630 migration was unlike any earlier English movement of settlers. The Puritans, united in religious purpose and well financed, carried with them all of the governmental machinery they would need to rule themselves in the New World. When John Winthrop, the first governor of the company, stepped off the *Jewel*, he carried the charter with him into the New World. The Puritan dream of founding an independent City of God had finally been realized.

Soon after landing the Puritans decided that Salem would not do as their holy city, for the simple reason that "it pleased them not," as one wrote in a letter. Many settled in Boston, while others settled in the towns of Charlestown, Medford, Watertown, Roxbury, and Dorchester. New England was settled in towns, unlike Virginia and Maryland. This was partly because the Puritans were trying to reproduce the existing order as they knew it. But they also felt safer in numbers and town living made it easier for them to practice their religion.

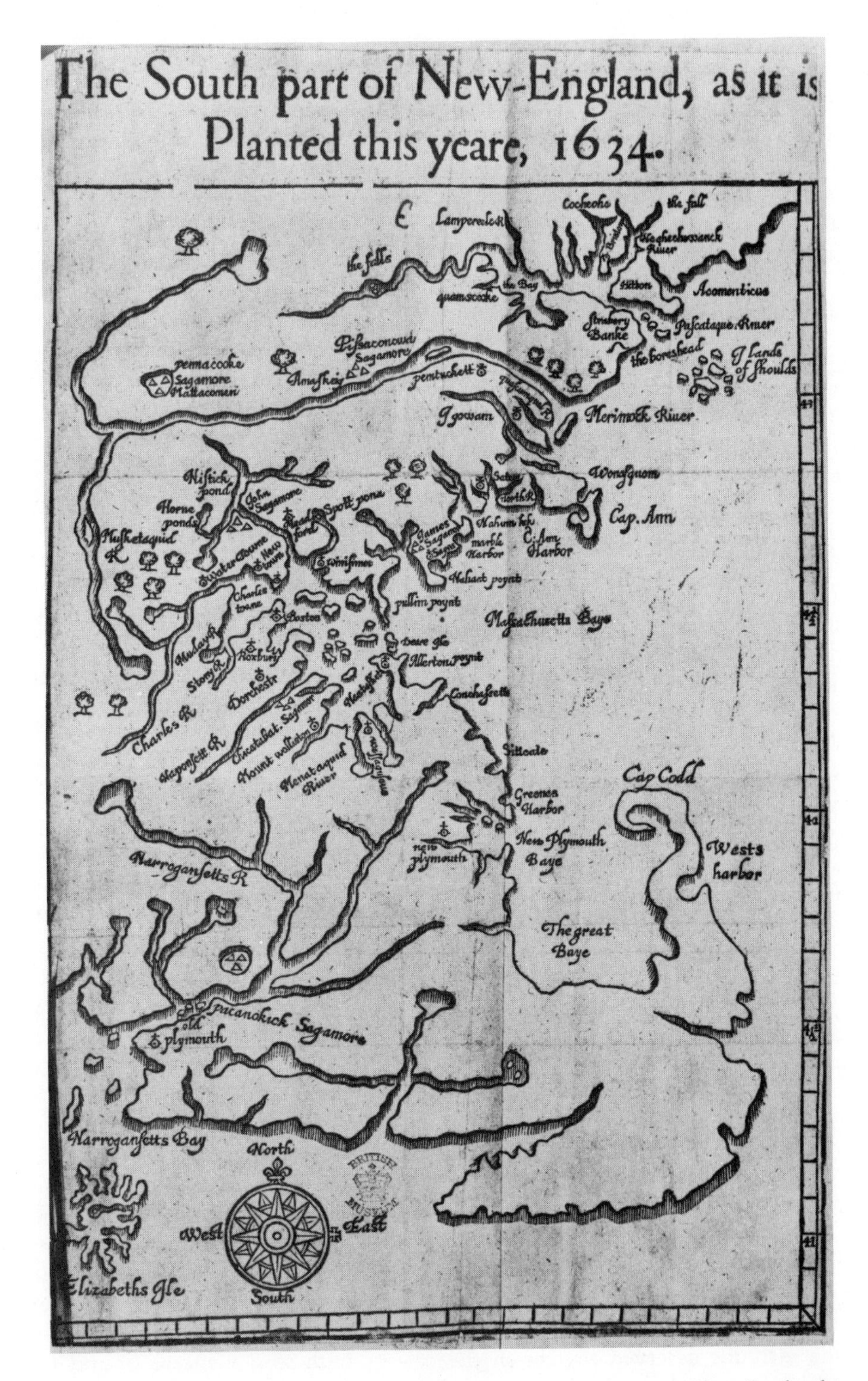

A map of New England in 1634.

Even with the precautions they had taken against hunger, nearly 200 people died from starvation the first winter. But fresh supplies arrived in February and by the middle of 1631 more Puritans had arrived, bringing with them guns, saws, and window glass. Except for their first difficult winter, the Puritans never suffered the horrors of Jamestown or Plymouth.

The Great Migration

Over the next decade, fifteen to twenty thousand more Puritans escaped to New England, while many more fled to English colonies in the West Indies. This was the Great Migration, that resulted from Charles I's bitter struggles with Parliament. The king had dissolved Parliament in 1629, crushing Puritan hopes of church and state reform. To make matters worse, the king was increasingly impatient with all nonconformists. Puritan ministers were turned out of their churches. Puritan books were burned. Government officials who happened to be Puritans felt the weight of royal displeasure.

Political and religious oppression was matched by economic decline. Prices and unemployment rose. Rents for farmland were fixed by law and disgruntled landlords (including a large number of Puritan country squires) watched their property losing its value every day. They concluded that a mighty disaster was about to demolish the entire country, that evil and corruption were stalking the land. As John Winthrop wrote, it was better to "avoid the plague when it is foreseen than to tarry till it should overtake us."

A Puritan government

The Puritan leaders were determined to keep Old World vices out of the New World. In order to ensure that their colony would remain as pure as humanly possible, they designed a strong government modeled closely after their religious ideals. Their's was not a democracy. Only the virtuous deserved a voice in the colony's affairs. So, only male church members were given the right to vote. This requirement violated the Massachusetts Bay Company charter, but the Puritan leaders were intent on preventing the colony from losing its religious character.

Becoming a church member was no easy matter. Candidates first had to demonstrate that they had been touched by God's grace and that the true meaning of being a Christian had been revealed to them. A congregation could reject applicants for such crimes as "rash carriage and speeches savoring of self-confidence," or for being "too much addicted to the world," or for charging too much for grain. While this theology may have seemed harsh and exclusive to later generations of Americans, it was an expression of the Puritans' heartfelt desire to carry out God's glory in a settlement dedicated to Him. Their sense of purpose gave them courage in their new and often hostile environment.

Shortly after arriving in the New World the administrators turned their trading company/colony into a commonwealth. Originally Governor Winthrop, his lieutenant governor, and a handful of other stockholders held absolute power. Only stockholders were "freemen," that is, voting members. But there were more than a hundred adult men, all Puritans of good standing, who did not hold stock and therefore could not vote. These men eventually persuaded Winthrop and his aides to extend the status of freeman to all adult male church members. The governor, the lieutenant governor, and the governor's assistants still governed the colony.

It required renewed effort on the part of the freemen to bring about real self-government in the Massachusetts Bay Colony. At first the freemen could elect only the governor's assistants. But in 1632 they gained the right to elect the governor. And in 1634, after seeing that the company charter provided for an assembly, the towns gained the right to elect two deputies each to a General Court. These deputies were elected annually by the freemen.

As the years passed, the governor's rule was more and more restricted by the citizens. At first the deputies had no authority to enforce their decisions against the will of the governor and his assistants. But in 1644 an argument over a pig changed all this. A poor widow and a rich moneylender got into an argument over who owned a plain white sow. The governor's assistants (called magistrates) favored the moneylender, while most of the people's deputies supported the widow. The magistrates had the right to veto all decisions made by the deputies. But the deputies suddenly challenged this power by demanding an equal voice. Governor Winthrop, alarmed by the demand, pointed out that if the magistrates lost their right to veto the deputies' actions, the colony would degenerate into a democracy and, according to the Holy Scriptures, "there is no such government in Israel."

The deputies stood fast, and in 1644 the General Court was divided into two houses. The upper house consisted of the governor and the magistrates, and the lower house consisted of the deputies. Each house had to approve the proposals the other made. Thus, because of a pig, Massachusetts ultimately gained a bicameral (two-house) legislature. This destroyed one of the original features of the Puritan commonwealth—government by magistrates acting as the spokesmen of God.

A few years later the people outflanked Governor Winthrop on another issue of great importance to him. Winthrop had always feared that a written body of statutes might give their enemies in England evidence against the colony. He also believed that the only laws that should ever be written down were those that appeared in the Bible. For these reasons the governor had always been against any effort to codify the laws of the commonwealth. But the people were unwilling to let Winthrop continue governing as a self-appointed spokesman for God and the Divine Will. In 1641 the deputies pushed a Body of Liberties, which included a provision for trial by jury, through the General Court. Then, in 1648, the Liberties were expanded into The Laws and Liberties, which lessened punishments for criminals and debtors, and simplified and strengthened the court system. The Laws and Liberties also established specific punishments for specific crimes. These measures put an end to what remained of the governor's arbitrary authority.

While only male church members could vote for deputies of the General Court, nonfreemen could vote in their town meeting and hold local offices such as "hog reeve," fire warden, or "fense mender." The town meetings became an important instrument for direct participation in government, and even now in many small New England communities, the townspeople vote directly on local issues.

RHODE ISLAND

Massachusetts was a commonwealth whose laws were based on the Puritan interpretation of the Scriptures. Citizens of the commonwealth could thus be assured of living good, religious lives. All citizens were required to attend church, although some were deemed unworthy of being church members. Ministers' salaries came out of public taxes. And only church members and property owners were allowed to vote.

Nowadays it is hard to appreciate how seriously the Puritans took the smallest points of religious doctrine. And yet, Rhode Island was founded solely as a result of a theological argument.

In 1631 an intelligent and pious young minister named Roger Williams came to New England. Like the Pilgrims, Williams was a Separatist who believed that the Church of England was beyond redemption. He soon found himself at odds with the Puritan majority. Although the Puritans desperately wanted to reform the Church, they still regarded it as their sacred mother and they allowed New Englanders to attend Anglican services whenever they visited England.

Williams considered even this loose bond unacceptable: he demanded a complete break. He even refused a job in a Boston church because he would have had to minister to non-Separatists. Williams argued that the law requiring everyone to attend church brought unregenerate sinners into houses of worship and he could find no precedent in the Scriptures for such a practice. As far as he was concerned, only those who were regenerate, who had been "born again" into God's love, should be allowed to attend church services.

Politically, young Williams was even more of a troublemaker. He felt that the king of England's claim to America was unsound. The English neither owned the land, nor had they discovered it. Properly speaking, the land belonged to the Indians, and he felt the English should have bought it from them. In fact, the Puritans had paid the Indians whenever they took cultivated land, but they had regarded undeveloped land as free for the taking.

Williams attacked the Massachusetts Bay government on another score as well. Why should people pay taxes to support ministers? What right did the General Court and the governor have to legislate on religious questions? In what biblical passage did the Puritans find words to justify such high-handed procedures?

Williams' outspoken doubts about the Puritan commonwealth threatened to disrupt the colony. But he was so well liked that the magistrates tried time and again to persuade him to change his views or, at least, to stop promoting them so noisily. He ignored this friendly advice and the magistrates banished him in 1635.

The magistrates planned to ship Williams back to England, but he took matters into his own hands, fled south with a few followers, and settled a new colony: Providence, Rhode Island. Rhode Island broke with the Church of England and forbade the civil government to interfere with religious matters.

Williams had long tormented himself over the question of who had been redeemed. The only way he could resolve his doubts was to decide that it was unclear which was the true religion and that all groups should be allowed to seek wisdom in their own fashion. For the first time in America genuine religious freedom was practiced.

Another dissenter from the Puritan way of life, Anne Hutchinson, was banished from Massachusetts at about the same time as Williams. Anne Hutchinson and her family came to Massachusetts Bay from England in 1634. They settled in Boston and she began holding weekly prayer meetings for women where she also discussed religious matters. Her meetings were so popular that she soon had a large following of men and women. Anne Hutchinson's thinking was quite different from that of the established Puritan majority. She believed that good works and moral behavior had nothing to do with salvation. Quite the contrary: God might reveal His divine truths to a sinner and keep an upright person in darkness forever. According to Anne Hutchinson, neither church attendance, prayer, moral behavior, nor even the clergy, were necessary for salvation. All laws of society were useless in this most important pursuit.

To the Puritans this was nothing short of heresy. As far as they were concerned, people could be saved only by receiving a revelation. And only people who lived exemplary lives—attending the Puritan church and conforming to its practices—could receive such a revelation.

Anne Hutchinson got into trouble when her followers became so numerous that they were able to vote Governor John Winthrop out of office and replace him with a Hutchinsonian. But the Puritan establishment pulled itself together and, by the barest majority, managed to put Winthrop back into office the following year. In 1637 the General Court banished the leaders of the Hutchinsonian party and, later, Anne and her family as well. They fled to Rhode Island and founded Portsmouth. In 1643 Anne Hutchinson and twelve members of her family were killed by Indians.

In 1640, when Roger Williams applied for a charter, Charles I had been forced to recall his overwhelmingly Puritan Parliament. The charter was granted in 1644. It provided for a governor with assistants, and an assembly based on representation from the towns. In this it resembled the Massachusetts Bay government. But there was one notable difference. In Rhode Island the right to vote was not limited to church members.

CONNECTICUT, NEW HAMPSHIRE, AND MAINE

Other Puritan colonies sprang up in other parts of New England. But these were not always the result of a religious quarrel. Some congregations started new settlements because they found life in Boston or other older towns either too strict, or too wicked (Boston, after all, had two taverns).

In 1636 Thomas Hooker, a minister from Newtown, led his congregation to the Connecticut Valley and established Hartford, Springfield, and two other towns there. Hooker's group was looking for better land as well as a less oppressive religious atmosphere. They modeled their colony after Massachusetts, but followed Rhode Island's lead in not restricting the right to vote to church members. In 1639 the Fundamental Orders of Connecticut, the first written constitution of the New World, was drafted. The Orders left voter qualifications up to the individual towns.

In 1638 John Davenport and Theophilus Eaton established New Haven, a strict little religious colony, south of Hartford. Hartford and New Haven later banded together as Connecticut. In 1662, after the Stuarts had been restored to the throne, these colonies obtained a charter from the English government. The following year the Rhode Island towns were also recognized by the Crown when they received a second charter. Connecticut and Rhode Island retained their charters, under which they elected all their officials, throughout the colonial period.

In their search for new land, Massachusetts Bay colonists went north as well as south. In the 1640s and 1650s Massachusetts incorporated these northern settlements under its jurisdiction. In 1679 the British government separated the colony of New Hampshire from Massachusetts and made it a royal colony. In 1820 Maine became a separate state in the American union.

New England's economy depended originally on farming and on unlimited trade in lumber and fur. But by the middle of the seventeenth century commerce had replaced agriculture, and fishing became a new source of wealth. The Puritan settlers never found a single commodity which could make them as wealthy as tobacco made the Virginians or sugar made the West Indians. However, this proved to be a blessing in disguise. It forced the people of New England to make commerce their business and to diversify their economy.

INDIAN RELATIONS

Despite the religious conflicts which separated the New England colonies, they all shared a need for protection against Indian attack. It was around this problem that The Confederation of the United Colonies of New England was created in 1643. The confederation, the first instance of cooperation among any of the American colonies, consisted of Massachusetts Bay, Connecticut, New Haven, and Plymouth. Rhode Island was never allowed to join, since Massachusetts always hoped to uproot the heretics settled there.

The Puritans in New England usually treated the native tribes fairly. They were careful about offering the Indians something in exchange for the cultivated land they took, and felt that Indian claims to undeveloped land were weak since the Indians used these lands only intermittently as game preserves. In addition, the

Indians were often given the right to hunt, trap, and fish on these lands, and these rights were written into the deeds.

The Indians are also known to have received justice in the Puritans' courts, sometimes even sitting on juries in cases involving other Indians. One case is known of three English servants who were executed by the courts for murdering an Indian.

However, the Pequot War is an outstanding exception to this record. In 1637 Massachusetts and Connecticut, together with their Indian allies, all but completely wiped out the Pequot tribe of southern Connecticut. This war provided the impetus for the formation of the New England Confederation.

The Pequot War was followed by almost forty years of peace between the colonists and the native Americans. The peace was broken in 1675 when a Wampanoag chieftain known as King Philip initiated hostilities against settlers in Massachusetts. King Philip charged the settlers with acquiring Indian lands by devious means such as unjust arbitration of land disputes and getting Indians drunk in order to buy their lands cheap. There is little evidence to support such claims and it seems likely that King Philip's real grievance was against the increasing numbers of Indians "selling out" to the European culture. It is a fact that the Puritans tried to convert the Indians and that by 1675 they had succeeded with about 1000. John Eliot, the Apostle to the Indians, had even gone so far as to establish fourteen so-called praying towns where converted Indians could live Christian lives in a Christian environment.

Some 500 colonists and at least 1000 Indians were killed in King Philip's War. Many captured warriors were sent as slaves to the West Indies. Peace returned to the area and the New England Confederation fell into disuse.

The Proprietary Grants

While Virginia and New England were originally settled by joint-stock companies, the rest of the Atlantic seaboard was parceled out by the English kings to their relatives or favorites. Maryland had been the first of these proprietary grants and, after the Stuart Restoration in 1660, there were more.

NEW YORK

In 1664 Charles II bestowed the area between New England and the Chesapeake Bay settlements on his brother, the Duke of York. England's commercial rival, The Netherlands, had already laid claim to part of this land. In 1624 they had established a fur-trading outpost at Albany, and in 1626 the Dutch West India Company had made their now-famous deal for Manhattan Island. The Dutch had plans for America. They wanted to settle the entire Hudson Valley with immense feudal estates called patroonships. But their plans were never popular and only one Dutch estate, Rensselaerswyck, was ever successfully established in the area.

By the middle of the century the Dutch and the English were involved in an intense rivalry for control of sea trade. And so even though the Dutch were never especially dedicated to colonizing the Hudson Valley, they did want to hold onto New Amsterdam, their settlement on Manhattan Island. New Amsterdam was an excellent base from which to raid gold-bearing Spanish galleons and to compete with English merchant vessels for the increasingly profitable colonial trade. The Hudson River Valley also had the advantage of being the main entrance to the fur-trading regions of the interior.

The English saw these advantages too. By the 1670s Great Britain's navy had reduced Dutch sea power and driven the Dutch out of

North America. In April 1664 an English officer leading four ships seized the unprepared Dutch colony of 10,000 people on Manhattan without a fight.

New York was a cosmopolitan city from the very beginning. When New Amsterdam surrendered to the English, eighteen languages were already being spoken there and so many religious sects prevailed that one governor wrote:

> Here be not many of the Church of England; few Roman Catholics; abundance of Quakers . . . Singing Quakers, Ranting Quakers; Sabbatarians; Antisabbatarians; some Anabaptists; some independents; some Jews; in short, of all sorts and opinions there are some, and the most part of none at all. . . . The most prevailing opinion is that of the Dutch Calvinists.

So sophisticated were New Amsterdam's rich young ladies that they followed the latest Paris fashions and spoke several languages. The Dutch had provided a few schools, a fire patrol, and a small police force. By 1680 the colony of New York (as the English renamed it) had some thirty taverns doing a thriving business and rents were considered outrageously high.

Yet, the colony's economic and political development lagged behind New England's. While some grain and cattle were exported, New Yorkers were slow to exploit the advantages of their farmlands and their superb harbor at the mouth of the Hudson. And it was not until the end of the century that the colony finally received a representative government of its own. Up to that time, it was ruled by a governor and a council appointed by the proprietor.

NEW JERSEY

Three other English colonies were carved out of the land under the Duke of York's jurisdiction: New Jersey, Pennsylvania, and Delaware. Immediately after receiving his grant the Duke of York gave part of it to two of his friends: Sir George Carteret and John, Lord Berkeley. Lord Berkeley named the territory New Jersey as a compliment to Carteret who had once been governor of the Isle of Jersey. In 1676 the territory was divided into two sections. Lord Berkeley sold his half (which was now called West Jersey) to a group of Quakers. Carteret inherited a settlement of Puritans with his half (now called East Jersey). In 1702 the king of England officially rejoined the two halves, restored the name New Jersey, and made the territory a royal colony, sharing New York's governor until 1738.

PENNSYLVANIA AND DELAWARE

Like New England, Pennsylvania was settled by a religious sect that was looking for a place to live according to religious beliefs that were unpopular at home in England. The proprietor of the new colony was William Penn, the son of a wealthy English admiral.

Penn was destined to be a great gentleman —rich, powerful, and a close friend of the king. As a young man he was friendly with the future King Charles II and with Charles' brother the Duke of York. He was educated at Oxford and then sent on a luxurious two-year grand tour of the European continent.

In 1666, while he was managing his father's estates in Ireland, Penn became interested in the Society of Friends, or Quakers. (The term Quaker had been coined by enemies of the sect because the Friends spoke so much about trembling before God.) Quakerism was one of the nearly two hundred obscure sects that emerged in England during the mid-seventeenth century. While the others had vanished almost as quickly as they had appeared, the Society of Friends endured.

The Quakers

The Society of Friends was founded by George Fox. In 1646, after experiencing a revelation, Fox began to preach a form of Christian mysticism. Somewhat like Anne Hutchinson, Fox believed that people could communicate directly with God, without the help of clergymen and church services. Fox preached that every human being had a spark of divinity. All a person had to do to experience God's presence was learn to detect this inner light. Reading the Bible was not essential. Divine wisdom could be found within one's heart as well as in the Bible. Fox's religion was an emotional, even an irrational, pursuit.

Such notions seemed wild and wicked to Anglicans and Puritans alike. And the Quakers' strange public behavior incensed them even more. Believing that all people were created equal by God (since all possessed the inner light), the Friends refused to doff their caps to nobles or bow to the king. They also refused to use the polite form *you,* addressing everyone with the familiar form *thee,* which seemed shockingly disrepectful to most seventeenth-century English people. To make matters worse, the Quakers refused to pay taxes for the support of the Church of England and its clergy, and claimed exemption from military service because they were opposed to war.

The Quakers' religious services, which rejected all forms and ceremonies, were illegal in England, but the Quakers continued to hold them anyway. When they were threatened with arrest they refused to resist or to pay their fines. More than 8000 Friends were thrown in prison between 1660 and 1685. William Penn himself spent two years in jail.

In America they fared little better at first: Quakerism was illegal in Virginia and in 1660 two Friends were lashed and then banished from that colony. In New England, the Quakers were as intolerant of the Puritans as the Puritans were of the Friends. But the Puritans had the advantage of being in the majority. The Quakers felt called upon to demonstrate against the Puritans, anyway. They would break bottles in churches to symbolize the emptiness of the services, or burst noisily into a Puritan church and hysterically denounce the minister. Quaker women even walked naked through New England streets to register their protest. Such outrageous acts aroused the Puritans' fury. They reacted by fining people for reading Quaker tracts, banishing Quakers as witches, branding and whipping Quakers, driving red-hot irons through their tongues, and even trying to sell Quaker children as slaves to sugar farmers in the West Indies. Half a dozen noisy Quaker adults were hanged for their demonstrations.

William Penn

Although many Friends seemed almost to take pleasure in their martyrdom, William Penn longed for a refuge for his fellow Quakers. In 1681 he received a grant from his old friend, Charles II, for territory north of Maryland. Penn's father, the admiral, had once lent Charles a great sum of money which the king had never repaid. Although the king seldom felt the need to repay his debts, he used this debt as an excuse for helping his persecuted Quaker friend. Charles may have had his own best interest at heart, too. It seems that he urged Penn to settle the new territory as quickly as possible. As Penn wrote later, "The government at home was glad to be rid of us at so cheap a rate as a little parchment to be practiced in a desert three thousand miles off. . . ."

Penn wanted to call the colony New Wales, but an influential Welshman indignantly objected. Penn's next suggestion was Sylvania (land of woods). His own name was immediately prefixed and, much as Penn objected to it, it stuck. The chief port on the Delaware River he named Philadelphia, which means brotherly love in Greek. In this new land, Penn, like the Puritans before him, hoped to create an ideal Christian community.

Penn was sure that Quakerism would thrive and attract believers in this new environment. In fact, he was so sure of success that he made religious freedom for all who believed in God

William Penn makes a peace treaty with the Indians. ▶

John Winthrop on Liberty

"There is a twofold liberty, natural (I mean as our nature is now corrupt) and civil or federal. The first is common to man with beasts and other creatures. . . . The other kind of liberty I call civil or federal, it may also be termed moral, in reference to the covenant between God and man, in the moral law, and the politic covenants and constitutions, amongst men themselves. This liberty is the proper end and object of authority, and cannot subsist without it. . . . If you stand for your natural corrupt liberties, and will do what is good in your own eyes, you will not endure the least weight of authority, but will murmur, and oppose, and be always striving to shake off that yoke; but if you will be satisfied to enjoy such civil and lawful liberties, such as Christ allows you, then will you quietly and cheerfully submit unto that authority which is set over you, in all the administration of it, for your good."

John Winthrop's Journal,
History of New England, 1630–1649

William Penn on Liberty and Property

"In England the Law is both the measure and the bound of every Subject's duty and allegiance, each man having a fixed Fundamental Right born with him, as to freedom of his person and property in his estate, which he cannot be deprived of, but either by his consent, or some crime, for which the law has imposed such a penalty or forfeiture . . .

This original happy Frame of Government is truly and properly called an Englishman's Liberty, a Privilege not exempt from the law, but to be freed in person and estate from arbitrary violence and oppression. . . ."

**William Penn,
The Excellent Privileges of Liberty and Property, 1687**

one of the cornerstones of his "holy experiment." This prompted one Anglican clergyman to exclaim: "Africa never more abounded with New Monsters than Pennsylvania does with New Sects." Religious freedom was matched by civil freedom and together they formed what Penn called Soul Liberty.

Because of their concern for humanity the Friends formed committees to help the poor, the Indians, and the slaves. The friendship they extended to the Indians resulted in seventy-five years of peace between the two cultures.

In 1682 Penn drew up the Frame of Government as the basic structure for the colony's government. Penn gave himself the authority to choose the governor, but also provided for a bicameral (two-house) legislature whose members would be elected by the freemen of the colony. All male citizens who owned a small amount of land or paid taxes were freemen. The Council (the upper house) had the right to initiate all legislation; the Assembly (the lower house) could only approve or disapprove the bills handed down to it. The members of the Assembly attacked this discrepancy from the beginning. They finally won the right to initiate legislation when Penn lost his charter for a few years (1692–1696). When he regained his colony he found that the only restriction on an otherwise all-powerful legislature was the governor's power to veto legislation. Being a wise administrator, Penn accepted this new order.

The Charter of Liberties, enacted in 1701, confirmed the legislature's power. In addition to restricting the governor's privileges and creating a unicameral legislature, the Charter gave three counties their own representative assembly. These three counties later became the colony of Delaware but the governor of Pennsylvania continued to administer them until the Revolution.

Not only was Penn a wise legislator, he was a gifted publicist, too. He wrote promotional brochures about the advantages of the colony and circulated them throughout Europe. By 1684 fifty shiploads of settlers had come to Pennsylvania from England, Wales, Holland, Germany, and Ireland.

Pennsylvania harvest scene.

So practical, enterprising, and understanding was Penn that his colony thrived almost immediately. Only eight years after Pennsylvania was founded, 20,000 settlers lived there and they were producing large quantities of wheat, flour, beef, and pork. Philadelphia became a prosperous commercial center.

Penn himself, however, did not prosper. His tenants rebelled against paying the rents they owed him, and a dishonest agent made his financial problems even more severe. In 1701 Penn was sent to a debtor's prison where he died in 1718.

THE CAROLINAS

In 1663 Sir George Carteret, John, Lord Berkeley, and six other aristocrats received a grant to Carolina, the territory lying between the colony of Virginia and the Spanish outpost of St. Augustine in Florida. The English hoped that by colonizing this area they could prevent the Spanish from advancing any farther into North America. They also wanted to take advantage of the colony's warm climate to produce commodities they could not produce in England—silk, in particular.

Carolina's proprietors did not want to go to the expense of bringing colonists over from England. They hoped to populate their lands with settlers who were already in the New World. But this policy was never a great success. The Puritans, in particular, were reluctant to move, since they would have to live with people who did not share their religious notions. Lord Berkeley did manage to persuade a few Virginians to migrate south, but they found nothing there that they could not get on better terms in Virginia, so few other Virginians followed their example. When North Carolina became a separate colony in 1691, only four or five thousand settlers lived there, and most of them were barely making a living from farming tobacco and corn, and raising livestock.

Despite the proprietors' reluctance to sponsor immigrants, many of the people who settled in the Carolinas came from overseas. The first group came from Barbados and Jamaica. These West Indian islands had originally been colonized by poor English farmers, but over the years the small landholders were driven out as great sugar-growing estates were consolidated and English yeomen were replaced by African slaves. By 1666 some 800 white settlers from the West Indies had tried to establish themselves near Cape Fear in South Carolina. But they were soon discouraged by frequent storms and by the apparently barren soil. Most of them moved on to North Carolina, Virginia, and New England, while some even returned to Barbados.

All hope of populating the Carolinas seemed doomed. But then in 1669 Sir Anthony Ashley Cooper, one of the proprietors, brought over three shiploads of colonists from England. By 1672 there were 200 colonists in South Carolina, and in the 1680s they were joined by a small group of French Protestants and Scots. The principal city, Charles Town (soon called Charleston) was built at the junction of two rivers which the immodest proprietor had named after himself, the Ashley and the Cooper.

The proprietors wanted the government of their colony to encourage the development of an ordered society. So Ashley Cooper and his confidential secretary, the philosopher John Locke, drew up The Fundamental Constitutions of Carolina. The latest political theories held that a just and stable society was one in which a noble leisured class was balanced by a larger class of independent freeholders. The Fundamental Constitutions therefore provided that forty percent of the colony's land would be reserved for nobility and the rest would be distributed to freeholders. The nobility was to be both

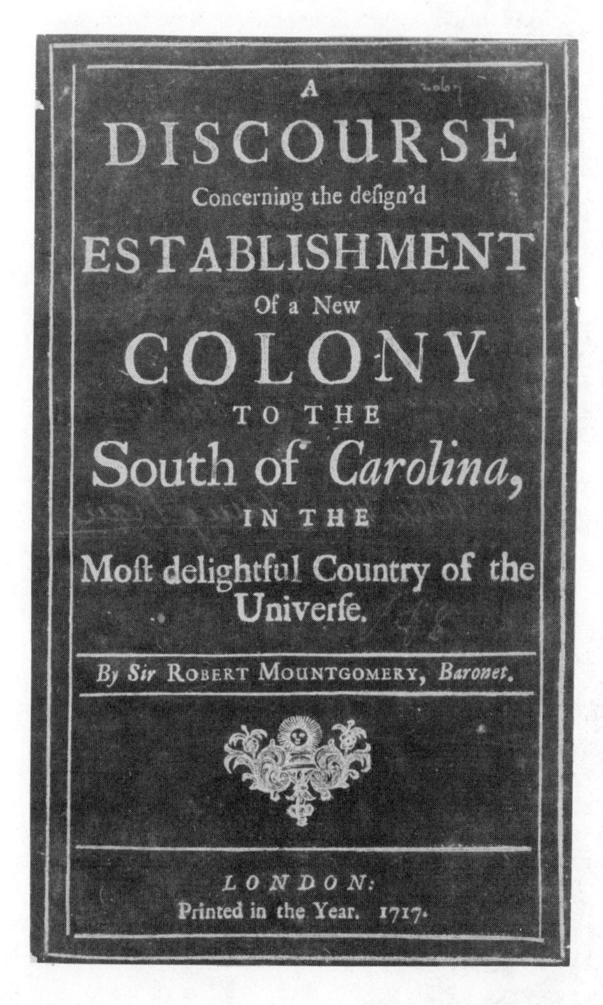
A
DISCOURSE
Concerning the deſign'd
ESTABLISHMENT
Of a New
COLONY
TO THE
South of *Carolina*,
IN THE
Moſt delightful Country of the Univerſe.

By *Sir* ROBERT MOUNTGOMERY, *Baronet*.

LONDON:
Printed in the Year. 1717.

An advertisement that describes the wonders of colonial life in the New World.

titled and hereditary. The Constitutions also provided for distributing the land in a grid pattern of surveyed lots.

The size of a man's property holdings determined the rank he could hold in the government. The government consisted of the familiar pattern of an appointed governor and a bicameral legislature. The upper house, representing the nobility, reserved the right to introduce legislation. Gradually, however, the Constitutions were liberalized. As in the other colonies, the lower house fought for and slowly won more power. By the end of the century the Constitutions had faded from practice.

After 1664 North Carolina had its own government, though it did not become a separate colony until 1691. There never had been much to bind the two areas of Carolina together. Most of North Carolina's population had settled around Albemarle Sound, the colony's northernmost region. They were poor, fiercely individualistic farmers who raised vegetables, tobacco, livestock, and made naval stores. Economically they were a satellite of Virginia, since most of their imports and exports moved through the Norfolk area. South Carolina's population, on the other hand, was orderly, conservative, aristocratic, and cosmopolitan. Their economy was based on the export of rice and deerskins and their own distinct trade patterns emerged from this economic base. Both Carolinas were made royal colonies in the 1720s in response to settlers' repeated complaints that their proprietors were not helping them against the Spanish and the Indians.

GEORGIA

In 1732 George II created a new colony on the southern border of South Carolina. The king wanted the colony (which he named after

Savannah, Georgia in 1734. ▼

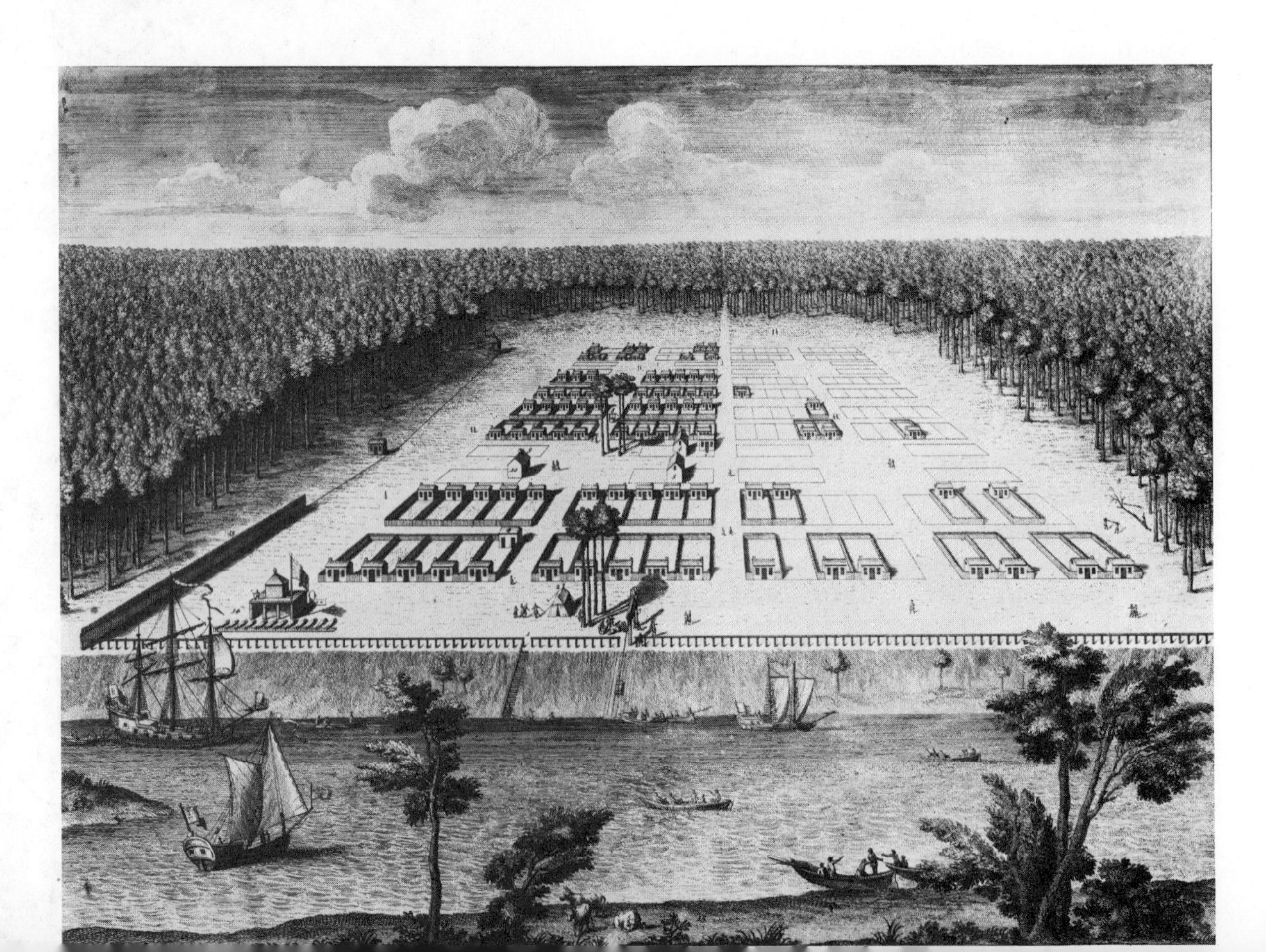

himself) to be another military outpost against the Spanish in Florida. However the group of English philanthropists led by General James Oglethorpe to whom he granted the colony had nobler hopes: they wanted Georgia to be a refuge for debtors languishing in English prisons.

Georgia's administration reflected the idealism of its trustees. No one was to be allowed to become extremely wealthy: farmers could own no more than 500 acres; slavery was prohibited, as were rum and brandy. However, the mixed group of Scots, Welsh, Germans, and English who came to Georgia did not accept these restrictions gracefully. In 1742, as a result of their protests, the law against rum was repealed and in 1750 slavery became legal, along with the right to dispose of land as an individual wished. The 500-acre limit was also lifted. Georgia was not prosperous, however, and in 1751 the colony was turned over to the Crown.

The proprietary colonies of the Carolinas and Georgia never had a strong sectional character. Unlike New England, where the English Puritan majority gave the region a distinct unity, the three southern colonies had a much more diverse population. Except for a few Virginians who had drifted down into North Carolina, most Carolinians came directly from England, France, or the West Indies. Georgia was populated by an even greater mixture of nationalities.

The Development of an Empire

During the first half of the seventeenth century the English government took little interest in its American colonies. The constant disputes between the monarchy and Parliament focused attention on matters close to home. During the 1650s, however, the political situation changed, and England began to think more about regulating her colonies in the New World.

The power struggle between the king and Parliament was muted after 1649 when Charles I was beheaded. In 1653 Oliver Cromwell became Lord Protector of England, and this office replaced the monarchy until 1660 when the Stuarts returned to the throne. Cromwell's protectorate and the reign of Charles II which followed ushered in a period of internal stability which encouraged the government to take a more forceful approach toward the English colonies.

We have already seen one aspect of this approach: uncolonized areas of the Atlantic seaboard (and even some areas settled by the Dutch) were parceled out to royal favorites. Another aspect was a series of navigation acts which regulated colonial trade for the profit of England. The acts had far-reaching effects on relations between the mother country and her New World colonies.

THE MERCANTILIST THEORY

In the sixteenth century economists began to argue that trade should not be allowed to follow its own course. To the contrary, governments should regulate commerce in order to end their economic dependence on other nations. Gold and silver were considered the only true measure of wealth. The more gold and silver a country had, the richer it was. Therefore a nation's economic goal should be to increase its own supplies of precious metals.

One of the main reasons Spain colonized the New World was to add to its supply of gold bullion. England, France, and The Netherlands colonized for the same reason, but were not as lucky as Spain: their colonies did not yield great quantities of precious metals. They therefore concluded that the best thing for them to do was to export more than they imported. Foreign countries that bought from them would have to pay in bullion.

Interpreting mercantilism

What effect did the strong mercantilist regulations have on colonial trade? Historians have long debated the question. In the 1830s George Bancroft, a prominent American historian, wrote a *History of the United States.* Bancroft pictured British mercantilism as a cold-blooded plan to exploit the colonies' natural resources and stunt their economies. He even argued that American resentment over the navigation acts was one of the principal causes of the Revolution.

Fifty years later, George L. Beer and Charles M. Andrews took quite a different tack. They contended that the navigation acts had done more to protect American industries and encourage American shipping than to dampen the colonial economy. True, certain minor industries had been forbidden in order to prevent competition with English industries. But this was a small price to pay for guaranteeing other markets—and occasionally even monopolies—in England. Furthermore, the acts guaranteed the colonials a part in the British Empire's lucrative sea trade with the rest of the world. Beer and Andrews also rejected the possibility that the navigation acts had played an important role in precipitating the American Revolution, as did L. A. Harper's important study of the navigation acts during the New Deal era.

In the late 1930s, the (then) Marxist historian Louis M. Hacker described the navigation acts as an attempt by one capitalist state to suppress another. According to Hacker, the colonies had to throw off the restrictions in order to fulfill their own capitalistic destiny.

In the 1950s Oliver M. Dickerson examined seventeenth- and eighteenth-century pamphlets, newspapers, and essays, and found that the colonists rarely objected to the navigation acts until 1763, when the British began to exploit the colonies.

The relevant evidence is enormous and insufficient at the same time. While thousands of contemporary writings remain, shipping and trade figures are incomplete. At this time it seems unlikely that more data will be uncovered. Future interpretations will probably depend upon more sophisticated analysis of the information we already have and on the biases of the historians themselves.

England saw her American colonies as a useful part of this system. England's industry needed many raw materials that would not grow in her climate: hemp for ships' ropes, indigo for the manufacture of dyes, and tobacco, for example. If England bought these crops from foreign countries, she would have to use her own supply of gold to pay for them. According to mercantilist theory, she would be draining her wealth away.

But if England could buy these crops from her own colonies, her gold would remain within the British Empire. Her situation could even be improved if the colonies bought goods manufactured in the mother country. America had vast natural resources, but few people to consume them; England had limited resources and a large population. If America could be made to exchange its resources for English goods, British wealth would be recycled back to British coffers.

Besides accumulating as much hard cash as possible, this system would protect native industry and agriculture from competition and encourage the growth of English shipping.

THE NAVIGATION LAWS

Under Cromwell Parliament passed the first of a series of navigation acts. These acts were designed to encourage England's merchant marine and to prevent English gold from being wasted on foreign shippers. The first navigation act was passed in 1651. It provided (1) that all goods bought in England could be transported to the colonies only in English ships; and (2) that foreign goods could be brought to England only in English vessels or in ships from the product's country of origin. This act was aimed at the Dutch who produced few goods themselves but whose shipowners were busy acting as agents in world trade.

In 1660 Charles II ascended the throne. Despite the reaction against Cromwell's regime, Charles and his Parliament continued and expanded Cromwell's trade policies. The first navigation act had allowed the colonies to continue trading directly with European countries. In 1660 a second navigation act was passed which severely limited colonial trade with Europe. Now, all goods bound for the colonies had to be shipped on English or colonial vessels and the master of the ship and most of the sailors had to be either English or English colonials. In addition, the colonies were forbidden to sell certain articles directly to the Continent. These so-called enumerated articles (which included sugar, tobacco, and cotton) had to be shipped to England. Europeans had to go to England to buy them and had to pay English duties on them, too.

In 1663 still another law was passed. Now, all European goods bound for America had to be brought first to England and then loaded onto English vessels for shipment to the colonies. Only salt, slaves, and wine were excepted from this necessity.

English officials soon discovered they had left a loophole in their navigation acts. The colonies were still allowed to trade freely among themselves. So colonial shippers carrying enumerated articles would simply tell the customs officials that they were headed for another colony, when they were actually smuggling these goods into European ports. To close this loophole, another navigation act was passed in 1673. Now, American captains had to pay export duties when they left port. To collect these duties, customs officials were to be stationed in all important colonial ports.

The navigation acts were enlarged in the following decades, mainly by modifying the list of enumerated articles. This allowed England to control the manufacture as well as the trade of certain colonial products. These included certain colonial textiles (1699), rice (1704), naval stores (1705), copper and furs (1721), and American-made hats (1732). The Iron Act of 1750 made it illegal to build new iron mills for manufacturing products from iron and removed English import duties on pig and bar iron.

Enforcing the Navigation Acts

To administer the navigation acts, the English took a tougher, more direct approach to governing the colonies. In 1675 the Lords of Trade, a committee of Charles II's Privy Council, was created to enforce the acts and oversee all aspects of colonial rule. One of its first acts was to send an agent to New England. This agent, Edward Randolph, was charged with investigating reports of smuggling and other evasions of the navigation acts. Randolph hated the colonists as much as they hated him and his report condemned almost every aspect of life in Massachusetts. He reported that French ships were entering New England ports in open violation of the navigation acts and that colonial merchants were cooperating with them. He made other charges, too: that public officers were neglecting to take oaths of allegiance to the king, the the Church of England was virtually nonexistent in New England, and that Massachusetts had annexed Maine and New Hampshire without royal permission and against the will of the people in those colonies.

The Dominion of New England. Alarmed by Randolph's reports, the Lords of Trade annulled the Massachusetts Bay Company's charter in 1684 and those of Connecticut and Rhode Island two years later. When James II became king in 1865, one of his first acts was to join New England, New York, and New Jersey together into a single administrative district. The area, called the Dominion of New England, was to be ruled from Boston by a royal governor.

On December 20, 1686, Sir Edmund Andros, the first and only Dominion governor, sailed into Boston harbor aboard the *Kingfisher.* Three hours after his arrival, he antagonized the Puritans by holding an Anglican service. That was only the first of many grievances he inflicted upon them. But what the colonials resented most about Andros was that he possessed dictatorial powers. James II had seen to it that there was no provision for a representative assembly in the Dominion's constitution. A council of officials appointed by the king was the only limit on the royal governor's authority. The governor and his advisors could make laws, dispense justice, and levy taxes as they saw fit —without the consent of those they governed.

Andros enraged merchants by imposing a heavy duty on imported rum, brandy, and wine. Then he infuriated landowners by levying a direct tax on real estate. By 1688 he had questioned the validity of all New England land titles and told all property owners that they had to obtain new patents from the king. He dedicated himself to enforcing the navigation acts and had offenders tried by judges expert in maritime law, rather than by juries.

Andros' measures spelled the end of the old Puritan dominance over New England. Their religion was no longer the exclusive faith of the province. Their rights to their land, to trial by jury, to representative government—all were in jeopardy. The Puritans had come to America to rule themselves in a completely independent community. Now they were reduced to being dependents of the Crown.

THE GLORIOUS REVOLUTION

James II made two foolish mistakes which led to his abdication in 1688. In the first place, he tried to return to the concept of an absolute monarchy. This angered Parliament, which was determined not to lose the prerogatives it had consolidated over the last century. In the second place, James tried to reestablish the Roman Catholic church. This alarmed his overwhelmingly Protestant subjects. James became so unpopular that a number of prominent Englishmen boldly invited Prince William of Orange, James' Protestant Dutch son-in-law, to come to England and seize the throne. The expected revolution turned out to be nothing more than a peaceful and triumphant procession. James II fled the country and Parliament crowned the foreign prince as William III and—in order to maintain a link with English monarchs—crowned James's daughter, Mary, as coruler.

In exchange for the crown William agreed to abide by a Bill of Rights drawn up by Parliament. The bill denied the king the right to suspend laws, levy taxes, or maintain a standing army without the consent of Parliament. In an effort to end religious strife, Parliament also passed the Toleration Act in 1689, permitting all Protestants to worship openly. The Glorious Revolution, which brought William III to power, established once and for all that Parliament, not the king, was the ultimate source of authority in England.

As word of James II's abdication spread, several colonies carried out small rebellions of their own. In Massachusetts they threw the royal governor, Andros, in prison. Connecticut, Plymouth, and Rhode Island began to rule themselves again. In New York, a wealthy merchant named Jacob Leisler ousted Andros' assistant and governed the colony for almost two years in the name of the new king. He was backed by his own militia. When William's royal governor finally arrived, Leisler resisted briefly. The royal governor denounced him as a traitor and had him hanged. In Maryland, John Coode led a Protestant revolt against the government in order to prevent Lord Baltimore from making Maryland a Catholic colony. Coode ruled Maryland until 1691.

THE ENGLISH SYSTEM

The Glorious Revolution was a turning point in America's colonial history. Britain never again tried to form larger administrative units by combining individual colonies. Nor did royal governors try to rule without a colonial legislature. On the other hand, the Glorious Revolution was not the end of British interference in colonial affairs. Far from it.

By the end of the seventeenth century the colonies had undergone a transformation. Most of the colonies founded by joint-stock companies or by proprietors had come under royal jurisdiction. And the freewheeling smugglers who had once ignored British regulations were hemmed in on all sides by a battery of laws and an army of customs officials.

Massachusetts received a new charter in 1691. The new charter enlarged the colony's territory by adding Plymouth and Maine, but restricted the colonists' political power. From now on Massachusetts governors would be appointed by the English king and all laws passed by the assembly would be subject to review in England. Massachusetts was also forced to drop the religious qualification from the right to vote. This had the positive effect of allowing more people to take part in the political process.

Maryland became a royal colony in 1692 and then reverted back to the Baltimores in 1715. New Jersey became a royal colony in 1702, South Carolina in 1721, and North Carolina in 1729.

These developments strengthened the authority of the royal governors. In theory, and to some extent in practice, British monarchs retained direct control over America. The king appointed governors as well as most of the upper houses of the colonial legislatures. In the eighteenth century, English kings vetoed one out of every twenty laws passed by colonial assemblies. The royal governors actively promoted the Anglican faith. Vice-admiralty courts and royal judges without juries often tried people who were involved in maritime disputes. The number of colonial goods that could be shipped to England was increased, but new restrictions prevented the colonists from trading with any other foreign country. In addition, fewer and fewer of these items could be exported from the colonies at all, not even to England where they would compete with English goods.

Despite these limitations, the new order did have some advantages. Dutch shippers and other commercial rivals were no longer allowed to interfere with colonial trade. This guaranteed American merchants a place in Britain's thriving commerce. And Parliament's religious toleration act put a stop to the most outrageous attacks on Quakers, Catholics, and other dissenters.

Although royal control was occasionally oppressive, in many ways it simplified regulations and promoted harmony among the various colonies. And even with the British restrictions, widespread smuggling was still possible. For the moment, at least, most colonials were willing to accept the demands of belonging to a mighty empire in order to also take advantage of the rewards.

Readings

GENERAL WORKS

Adams, James T., *The Founding of New England.* Boston: Atlantic Monthly Press, 1921 (Paper: Atlantic Monthly-Little, Brown, 1965).

Andrews, Charles M., *The Colonial Period of American History.* New Haven: Yale University Press, 1964.

Craven, Wesley F., *The Southern Colonies in the Seventeenth Century.* Baton Rouge, La.: Louisiana State University Press, 1949.

Craven, Wesley F., *Colonies in Transition.* New York: Harper & Row, 1968 (Paper: Harper & Row).

Langdon, George, *Pilgrim Colony: A History of New Plymouth, 1620–1691.* New Haven: Yale University Press, 1966.

Parkman, Francis, *Pioneers of France in the New World.* Boston: Little, Brown, 1900.

Pomfret, John E. & Shumway, Floyd M., *Founding the American Colonies.* New York: Harper & Row, 1970.

Tolles, Frederick B., *Meeting House and Counting House: The Quaker Merchants of Colonial Philadelphia 1682–1763.* Chapel Hill, N.C.: University of North Carolina Press, 1948 (Paper: W. W. Norton, 1963).

Wertenbaker, T. J., *The Middle Colonies.* New York: Scribner's, 1938.

Wertenbaker, T. J., *The Old South.* New York: Scribner's, 1942.

Wertenbaker, T. J., *The Puritan Oligarchy.* New York: Scribner's, 1947 (Paper, 1970).

SPECIAL STUDIES

Bailyn, Bernard, *The New England Merchants in the Seventeenth Century.* Cambridge: Harvard University Press, 1955 (Paper: Harper & Row Torchbook, 1964).

Battis, Emery, *Saints and Sectaries: Anne Hutchinson and the Antinomian Controversy in the Massachusetts Bay Colony.* North Carolina: University of North Carolina Press, 1962.

Crane, V. W., *The Southern Frontier, 1670–1732.* Ann Arbor: University of Michigan Press, 1956.

Demos, John, *Little Commonwealth: Family Life in Plymouth Colony.* New York: Oxford University Press, 1971. (Paper)

Demos, John, *Little Commonwealth: Family Life in Plymouth Colony.* New York: Oxford University Press, 1970.

Harper, L. A., *The English Navigation Laws.* New York: Octagon Books, 1964.

Morgan, Edmund S., *The Puritan Family.* New York: Harper Torchbook, 1966.

Morison, Samuel E., *Builders of the Bay Colony.* Boston: Houghton Mifflin, 1964.

Morison, Samuel E., *The Intellectual Life of Colonial New England.* New York: New York University Press, 1956 (Paper: Cornell University Press, 1960).

Smith, Abbot E., *Colonists in Bondage: White Servitude and Convict Labor in America 1607–1776.* Chapel Hill, N.C.: University of North Carolina Press, 1947.

Vaughan, Alden T., *New England Frontier, Puritans and Indians 1620–1675.* Boston: Little, Brown, 1965.

Washburn, Wilcomb E., *The Governor and the Rebel: A History of Bacon's Rebellion in Virginia.* Chapel Hill, N.C.: University of North Carolina Press, 1967.

Wright, Louis B., *The First Gentlemen of Virginia.* San Marino, Calif.: The Huntington Library, 1940 (Paper: University Press of Virginia, 1964).

PRIMARY SOURCES

Beverly, Robert, *The History and Present State of Virginia,* Louis B. Wright (Ed.). Charlottesville, Va.: University Press of Virginia, 1968.

Bradford, William, *Of Plymouth Plantation,* Samuel E. Morison (Ed.). New York: Knopf, 1952.

Hawke, David F., *Captain John Smith's History of Virginia.* New York: Bobbs-Merrill Co., 1970. (Paper)

Miller, Perry and Thomas H. Johnson (Eds.), *The Puritans: A Source Book of Their Writings.* New York: Harper & Row Torchbooks, 1969.

Morton, Thomas, *The New English Canaan,* Charles F. Adams (Ed.). New York: B. Franklin, 1966.

Percy, George. *Observations Gathered Out of a Discourse of the Plantation of the Southern Colony of Virginia by the English, 1606.* Charlottesville, Va.: University Press of Virginia, 1967.

Tolles, Frederick B. and E. G. Alderfer (Eds.), *The Witness of William Penn.* New York: Macmillan, 1957.

Winthrop, John, *Winthrop's Journal,* James K. Hosmer (Ed.). New York: Scribner's, 1908.

BIOGRAPHIES

Barbour, Philip, *Pocahontas and Her World.* Boston: Houghton Mifflin, 1970.

Barbour, Philip L., *The Three Worlds of Captain John Smith.* Boston: Houghton Mifflin, 1964.

Miller, Perry, *Roger Williams: His Contribution to the American Tradition.* New York: Atheneum, 1962.

Morgan, Edmund S., *The Puritan Dilemma: The Story of John Winthrop.* Boston: Little, Brown, 1958.

Peare, Catherine O., *William Penn.* New York: Holt, Rinehart and Winston, 1958 (Paper: University of Michigan, Ann Arbor Books, 1966).

Vaughan, Alden, *American Genesis: Captain John Smith and the Founding of Virginia.* Boston: Little, Brown & Co., 1975.

Winslow, Ola E., *Master Roger Williams.* New York: Macmillan, 1957.

HISTORICAL NOVELS

Barth, John, *The Sot-Weed Factor.* New York: Grosset & Dunlap, 1964.

Cannon, Le Grand, Jr., *Come Home at Even.* New York: Holt, 1951.

Forbes, Esther, *Paradise.* New York: Harcourt, Brace, 1937.

Hawthorne, Nathaniel, *The Scarlet Letter.* New York: New American Library, 1970.

Johnston, Mary, *To Have and to Hold.* New York: McGraw-Hill, 1953.

New Worlds

America was known as the New World to the colonists who settled here in the seventeenth century. And to the people of that time, this continent must indeed have seemed like a different planet.

The voyage across the Atlantic Ocean took seven times longer than a modern astronaut's round trip to the moon. And when they arrived, most of the colonists knew less about America than modern astronauts know about Venus or Mars. Colonization was truly a step into the unknown.

In the twentieth century, the entire earth has been almost completely explored and settled. It seems that the era of colonization is at an end. But is it? This feature examines the possibility that modern humanity may again take up the colonizing spirit—this time in outer space.

The device is an imaginary letter from a "professor of American history" to the "director of NASA's Task Force on the Colonization of Mars." Remember, this is a letter that has not *yet* been written. . . .

April 3, 197_

Ms. Anita Seira
National Aeronautics and
Space Administration
Task Force on the
Colonization of Mars
400 Maryland Avenue, SW
Washington, D.C.

Dear Ms. Seira:

Thank you for your inquiry of March 1. It is gratifying to know that my studies of the past are valuable to people who are so concerned with the future.

To answer your question specifically: Yes, I think there are some parallels between the colonization of America and your own plans to colonize the planet Mars. I also agree with you that your group could learn much by studying our ancestors' efforts, since like them you will be exploring a truly "new world."

I won't take up your time by describing the conditions which led to American colonization, nor by analyzing the policies followed by the early colonists. Such information is available in any good history book. (I would recommend Rebecca Brooks Gruver, *An American History*).

Instead, I would prefer to make a series of recommendations based on my own studies of the American experience. Then, after your staff has had a chance to review my suggestions, we might meet in Washington to discuss the matter in greater detail.

First let me say that your work must begin with comprehensive research into conditions on the planet Mars. Our ancestors didn't pay much at-

tention to that sort of thing, and they wasted precious time digging for gold that wasn't there or searching for passages to the East Indies that didn't exist. Many of them died because of their ignorance, and if you want your colonists to avoid the same fate, do your homework *before* blasting off to Mars!

Once you know what you are doing, you had better raise enough money to do it right. The Virginia Company, which settled Jamestown, tried to start up a new country on less than a million dollars. Before they went bankrupt, they had lost about seven million, $1.40 for every man, woman, and child living in England at that time. Starting colonies has always been a risky business, and no matter how complete your research, Mars is bound to spring surprises on you. When that happens, you had better have enough money to buy your way out of trouble. So if Congress won't give you enough funds to colonize Mars properly, don't colonize it at all.

Similar considerations lead me to recommend against relying on a private corporation to fund your venture. A profit-making corporation has to show results quickly, otherwise it can't raise more money from its stockholders. The Virginia Company was constantly pestering the Jamestown settlers to turn a profit, and these demands put unnecessary pressures on the whole enterprise. Your colony on Mars may take a long time to get on its feet; don't add impatient investors to its troubles.

On the other hand, you should encourage the colonists to become self-sufficient as soon as possible. Otherwise, they will become accustomed to supplies and support from home and won't be able to survive on their own. The Jamestown settlers almost starved in their early years because they depended on England to feed them. The Massachusetts Bay Company colonists planted a crop as soon as they arrived, and were self-sufficient within a few years. I urgently hope that you will figure out a way to grow food on Mars and make self-sufficiency the first priority of the new colony.

Now, your most difficult job will be persuading your superiors that the colonists should be granted political independence as soon as they leave the Earth. It is natural for bureaucrats to try to control everything from a distance if they can, but this is usually disastrous. For example, the Virginia Company's officers sat comfortably in London trying to make all the decisions while the Jamestown colonists struggled along in America doing all the work. As you might

Columbus discovers a new world.

imagine, this arrangement proved unsatisfactory and contributed to the company's downfall.

The organizers of the Massachusetts Bay Company again showed more wisdom. They were the first joint-stock company to travel "lock, stock, and barrel" to the New World with the colonists. This arrangement worked well for a while. But in the late seventeenth century Britain forced Massachusetts to become more subservient to Royal authority and in the eighteenth century she tried to reassert strong imperial control over all the colonies. The resulting disagreements led straight to the Revolution.

So I suggest that if your task force cannot agree that the purpose of your work is to create an *independent* new society, you would do all of us a favor by abandoning the project. A war of liberation fought by the settlers of Mars against the people of Earth is a very unpleasant prospect, don't you think?

Assuming you have done all your research, raised plenty of money, and agreed on the purpose of the project, we come to another difficult question: Who should go? I raise this question because it would be very easy for you to make the same mistakes the Virginia Company made. You see, England in the seventeenth century shared many of our present-day social problems such as unemployment, inflation, overpopulation, crime in the streets, and revolt against established authority. Unfortunately, many intellectuals of the time saw colonization as a solution to those problems. The English poet John Donne, referring to

Apollo 15 Commander Scott on the Moon.

this problem, said colonization would "redeem many a wretch from the jaws of death . . . sweep your streets, and wash your doors from idle persons . . . and employ them."

The Virginia Company was delighted with this idea. Criminals, poor people, and unemployed soldiers would work for low wages in the New World, increasing company profits while serving their country. However, such men (and they were mostly men) did not make stable citizens of the New World, and the Virginia Company was soon forced to impose a form of martial law to keep order in the colony.

By contrast, the Massachusetts Bay Colony was composed of people who wanted to leave England for more exalted reasons than to escape prison. These Puritans were a community of believers united by a common determination: to build a new society where they would be free to pursue their own unique "lifestyle." They brought farmers, skilled workers, and entire families to America—20,000 people in thirteen years. And they succeeded.

On the basis of this comparison, I would advise you against attempting to solve Earth's problems by exporting them to Mars. You should find colonists like the Puritans—intelligent, educated, but also a bit radical, and anxious to build a new life far from home. (Frankly, I would recommend that you recruit my son as soon as possible.)

Finally, I urge that you cancel this project if you cannot formulate a humane policy for dealing with native cultures which might now inhabit Mars. No one involved with the

American colonial movement, including the Puritans, ever found a way to live in peace with the native Americans. Consequently, we all but completely destroyed a wonderful culture which had so very much to offer us. If we human beings are not yet mature enough to treat alien cultures with equality and respect, we should stay on the Earth and leave Mars to the Martians.

I hope that this information will be useful to you. I am also attaching a couple of items which your group may find interesting. I look forward to meeting with you and your staff in the near future. In the meantime, I wish you luck in carrying out your considerable responsibilities.

Yours very truly,

James J. Arret

James J. Arret
Professor of American History
Massachusetts State College
Boston, Mass.

Attachment One: Overpopulation as a Reason for Colonization

Then: "We read that the bees, when they grow to be too many in their own hive at home, are wont to be led out by their captains to swarm abroad and seek themselves a new dwelling place . . . if we would behold . . . how all our prisons are pestered and filled with able men to serve their country, which for small robberies are daily hanged up in great numbers . . . we would hasten and further . . . the deducting of some colonies of our superfluous people into those temperate and fertile parts of America. . . ."

Richard Hakluyt,
Preface from *Divers Voyages touching the Discovery of America,* 1582

Now: "Continuation of recent trends in human activity through the end of the twentieth century are likely to cause the quality of life of most humans to deteriorate. . . . Choices that will become more restricted on a finite and crowded planet can be tested in the extended environment of space. . . . Whether sufficiently large numbers of people may choose to emigrate from the earth to such worlds [space stations] as to have a major effect on the earth's population is uncertain. . . ."

Theodore Taylor,
"Strategies for the Future", *Saturday Review/World,* December 14, 1974

Attachment Two: The Costs of Colonization

*Partial Budget of the Virginia Company (1606–1623)**

The General Stock	£52,862
Joint Stock for a Magazine (1616–17)**	7,000
Joint Stock for a Fishing Voyage (1618)	1,800
Joint Stock for a Fishing Voyage (1620)	1,000
Joint Stock for a Magazine (1620)	1,000
Joint Stock for Apparel (1621)	1,800
Joint Stock for a Glass Furnace (1621)	1,000
Joint Stock for Transporting 100 Maids (1621)	800
Joint Stock for a Trade in Furs (1621)	900
Joint Stock to Transport Shipwrights (1621)	1,000
Joint Stock for "Bringing Home Tobacco" (1622)	8,000
Magazines for Relief of the Colony (1623)	727
Total	£77,889

* Virginia Company budget from W. R. Scott, *Joint Stock Companies to 1720* (Cambridge, England, Cambridge University Press, 1910).

** A "magazine" was a separate company formed primarily for the purpose of handling shipping of supplies and products to and from the colony.

Both the Massachusetts Bay and Virginia companies spent a total of about £200,000 on their two enterprises. The Massachusetts Bay Company succeeded in planting about 20,000 colonists at that amount, or about £10 per colonist. At a rate of $5.00 to the pound (as it was calculated in those days), this works out to $50.00 per colonist. The Virginia Company succeeded in planting fewer than 1,000 colonists.

Opposite:
This painting shows a plantation mansion surrounded by the slave quarters, barns, laundry buildings, kitchen, and grist mill. Crops were stored in a warehouse on the waterfront so that they could be easily transferred to oceangoing ships.

3

Shaping an Identity

After a foreigner from any part of Europe is arrived, and become a citizen; let him devoutly listen to the voice of our great parent, which says to him, "Welcome to my shores, distressed European; bless the hour in which thou didst see my verdant fields, my fair navigable rivers, and my green mountains!—If thou wilt work, I have bread for thee; if thou wilt be honest, sober, and industrious, I have greater rewards to confer on thee—ease and independence."

St. John de Crèvecoeur,
Letters from an American Farmer, 1782

During the seventeenth and eighteenth centuries, the American colonies gradually developed their own distinct identity. Economic and cultural characteristics originally transplanted from Europe slowly evolved into new forms, each of them uniquely American.

The exceptional class structure of the colonies was one factor which helped create new styles of life. About five percent of the free population was regarded as part of an upper class, or aristocracy. This segment included the wealthy planters, merchants, lawyers, and clergy of the Anglican and Congregational churches. Another seventy percent, the vast majority of free Americans, was the eighteenth-century equivalent of a middle class. They were either yeoman farmers who owned their own land, or skilled craftsmen and small businessmen living in the towns. The other twenty-five percent were poor farmers, indentured servants, tenants on great estates, or day laborers. With some effort, many of these people were also able to enter the middle class. A poor peasantry never existed on a large scale in colonial America. With the important exception of blacks, who made up about twenty percent of the total population, there was no large, oppressed lower class, making the standard of living of free Americans the highest in the world at the time of the Revolution.

The mixed ancestry of the colonies was another influence which tended to make America quite different from any of its European parents. Much of the free population was of English descent, but by 1765 about thirty percent of the colonists came from a non-English background. The impact of the frontier, and the development of religious toleration and representative government also characterized colonial life and even surpassed the English model. To be sure, colonial Americans generally thought of themselves as part of the British Empire—yet they lived in a different world. The distinctions would eventually grow sharper and finally lead to a violent break with the mother country.

At the same time, the individual colonies were in some ways as different from each other as they were from Europe. In order to understand the varieties of life style in the New World, it is necessary to focus on the economic and social systems of the three major colonial regions.

The Southern Colonies

During the first half of the seventeenth century, the Southern economy was characterized by yeoman farmers working their own modest landholdings. Until late in the century, small farms were much more common than large plantations. Near the end of the century this situation changed markedly. Southern society was becoming frozen, and a new sort of aristocracy was asserting control over the region's economic and political life.

THE PLANTATION SYSTEM

The main reason for the rise of the plantation system lay in the type of export crops grown in the South: tobacco, rice, and indigo. All three were enumerated articles which, under the navigation acts, had to be shipped to England. On the one hand, the privileged place of these products on the British market encouraged the expansion of their production. But on the other hand, the customs duties collected there cut into the income of the planters back in the colonies. Strict enforcement of the navigation acts in the late seventeenth century narrowed the profit margin for all enumerated articles. This tended to hurt small farmers the most, keeping them continually in debt.

Tobacco had become the major export of Virginia, and later Maryland, after America was granted a monopoly of the English market in 1617. Production went from 2500 pounds in

1616 to 30 million pounds in the late 1600s, and finally to over 100 million pounds per year at the time of the Revolution. The colonial tobacco crop was so abundant that the supply exceeded England's demand, causing prices to drop rapidly in the late seventeenth century. This further encouraged the development of a plantation system, since the only tobacco growers who could make a reasonable profit were the ones who owned vast estates where huge crops could be produced.

The plantation owners enjoyed another important advantage in the tobacco business. Tobacco wore out the soil rapidly, stripping it of valuable minerals within a decade or two. Small farmers had no choice but to keep planting and replanting until their land was exhausted of its nutrients. Large landholders, on the other hand, could afford to rotate crops, letting some fields lie fallow every year. And even if they allowed parts of their land to become totally depleted, the owners of large plantations had the luxury of simply putting new acreage under cultivation.

THE INTRODUCTION OF SLAVERY

It was impossible to force European immigrants into slavery. Most of them came to the New World by their own consent, seeking more freedom than they had had in Europe, not less. A few Indians were enslaved, but they proved difficult to capture in large numbers. The Indians were skilled warriors familiar with the geography of America, and it was hard to hunt them down. So colonial farmers began looking more and more to the importation of workers from the continent of Africa, thinking they could hold them in bondage permanently to meet the labor needs. These people were completely unprepared by their African cultural background for the onslaught of slavers. And once they were bound and carried away to a new continent, many of them were initially too shocked psychologically to offer strong resistance.

A French slave ship. ▼

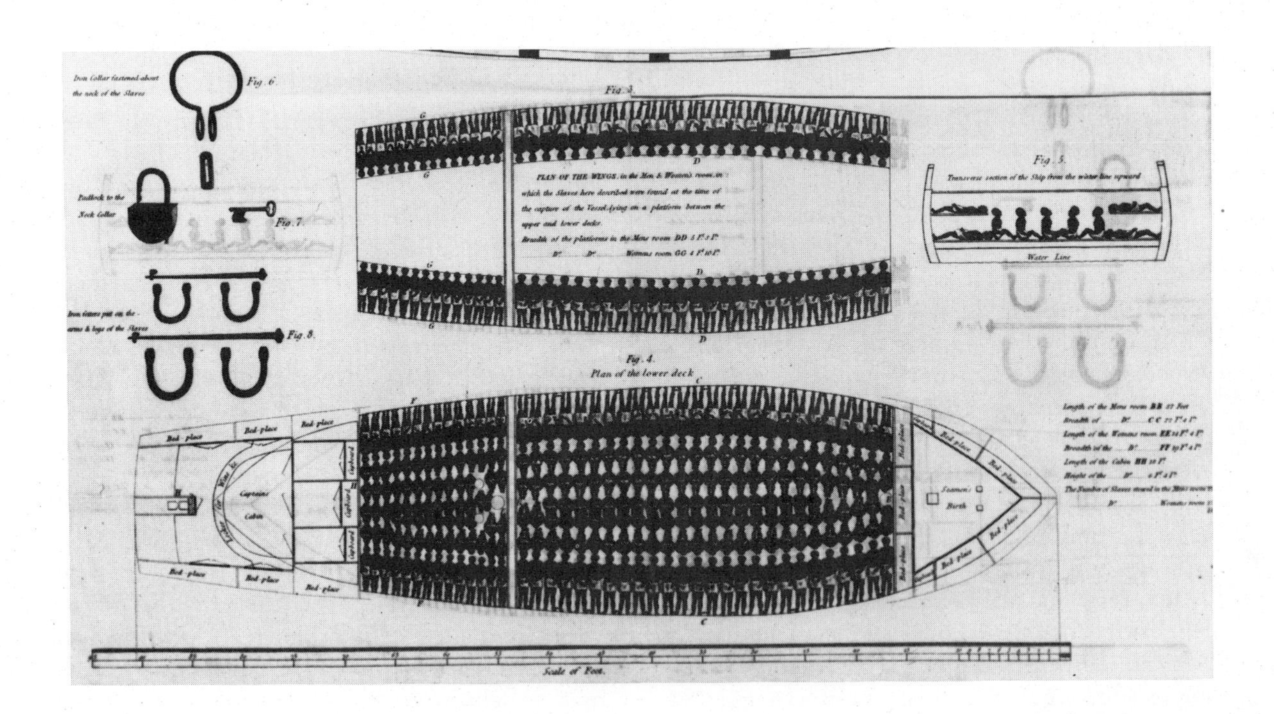

The Portuguese had begun the slave trade as early as 1441 and dominated it for almost two hundred years. Gradually the Dutch, French, and English also began to take part in the business. After 1713 England was powerful enough to assert its own monopoly over the slave trade.

European slave traders all operated in the same way. The trade was carried on from ships or from trading centers established along the west coast of Africa, and corral areas were built in which slaves were held until a full shipload was collected. The slaves were actually captured by other Africans, mostly leaders of coastal tribes who raided villages in the interior for the Europeans. Captives were then exchanged at the trading center for firearms, liquor, or trinkets.

Next came the hot, miserable "middle passage," lasting about fifty days. The slaves were branded, packed tightly into ships, and dispatched off to the Western Hemisphere. One out of every eight slaves usually died on the voyage, and the danger of suicide was high. There are also circumstantial records of some fifty-five black mutinies during the years 1699 to 1845 and references to many others, so not all Africans submitted docilely to their enslavement.

Blacks were first used as slave labor in the West Indies and South America, primarily to grow sugar on plantations. By 1655 Jamaica was the chief slave market of the Western world. The first cargo of Africans appeared in the North American colonies at Jamestown, Virginia in 1619, brought by Dutch traders.

At first the legal status of Africans in the American colonies was not clear. Some may have been considered slaves from the beginning, but others were considered indentured servants and were allowed to gain their freedom. Only gradually, as the plantation system replaced small-scale farming, did the custom of holding black workers for life become a widespread practice. After 1660 most of the colonies passed laws legalizing the status of slavery for those of African descent, and by 1700 slavery was a major source of labor for the Southern colonies. In 1756, blacks made up forty-one percent of Virginia's population and twenty-nine percent of Maryland's. Slavery was not legalized in Georgia until 1750, but by 1775 the black population there outnumbered the free white population.

Of course, slavery was not confined to the South. Although slaves were never a large portion of the population in New England or the Middle colonies, there were slaves throughout America. The one New England colony in which slaves were numerous was Rhode Island. There, merchants played an active role in the slave trade, often bringing blacks they were unable to sell in the South home to Newport.

In general, Northern slave codes were far milder than those of the South. Northern slaves, for instance, had the right to a jury trial, the right to sue, and the right to testify in court. Many also were able to obtain some education and religious instruction. In the South slaves could not testify against whites, nor were their marriages legally recognized. Also, if a Southern slave died while being submitted to physical discipline, it was not considered manslaughter.

A SLAVE ECONOMY

The institution of slavery was an essential part of the Southern system of large-scale staple production for profit. Unlike an indentured servant, a slave worked for life. This was important because after their work term was over, indentured servants were free to set up their own small farms. Bound to a lifetime of service, slaves offered no such competition. Slaves could also be forced into exhausting, unhealthy work which no free person would do. It was only necessary that a slave survive for six or seven years in order to return the owner's investment.

Rice was cultivated in South Carolina and Georgia exclusively by slaves because of the horrible working conditions involved. Rice was grown in low-lying coastal areas or near rivers where the fields could be flooded. Slaves had to work in humid swampy areas, frequently exposing themselves to malaria.

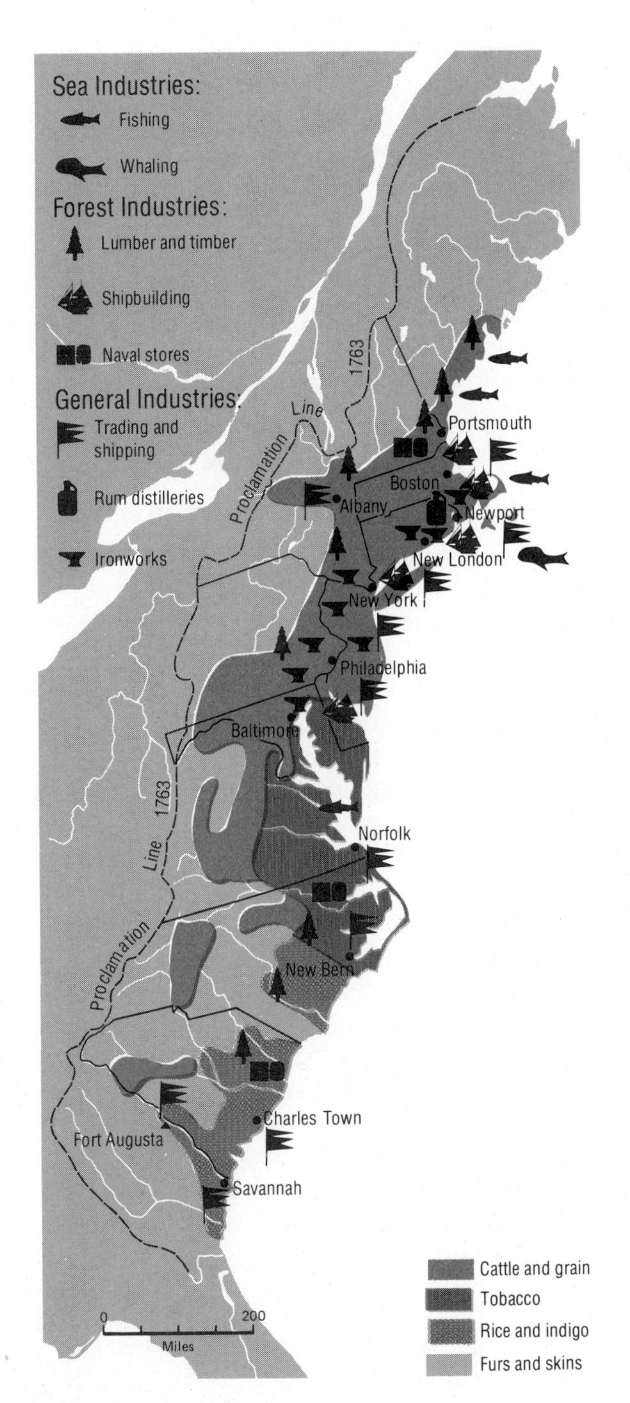

COLONIAL ECONOMY

One recent explanation as to why slavery in the American South took these brutal forms is that there were no traditional institutions in the region to modify it. European feudalism provided certain immunities for laborers in the Old World, but these did not apply in America. The blacks were of no concern to the Crown, which was primarily interested in its customs revenues. Finally, the colonial governments and churches were not strong enough in North America to have any real control over what the plantation owners claimed was their private property under the law.

AFRICAN CULTURE

Europeans have generally assumed that their own culture was infinitely superior to anything ever produced in West Africa. It is now known, however, that unique and sophisticated civilizations flourished there as early as A.D. 700. In the fourteenth century, many Arab travelers wrote about the great wealth, learning, and humane social order attained by various African states.

The great kingdoms of Ghana, Mali, and Songhai, unknown to European historians until modern times, dominated life in the Niger River valley from 700–1600. These states were complex confederations of tribes governed by a king, a council of ministers, and royal representatives assigned to the tribal villages. While the villages themselves frequently had political autonomy, the king was normally the final judge in questions of justice.

The social and economic life of these kingdoms, and of the smaller coastal kingdoms directly involved in the slave trade, was equally complex. The extended family unit was very important. Individual families often held slaves, and some kingdoms permitted the practice of polygamy. Religious life included the worship of ancestors and nature as well as the practice of magic. The Moslem faith was an important influence by the eleventh century, but the West Africans knew nothing of Christianity until the slave traders introduced it in the sixteenth century. Based on agriculture, cattle raising, mining,

◀ *Armed rebel of Guiana, 1772–1777.*

TO BE SOLD on board the Ship *Bance-Yſland*, on tueſday the 6th of *May* next, at *Aſhley-Ferry*; a choice cargo of about 250 fine healthy

NEGROES,

juſt arrived from the Windward & Rice Coaſt. —The utmoſt care has already been taken, and ſhall be continued, to keep them free from the leaſt danger of being infected with the SMALL-POX, no boat having been on board, and all other communication with people from *Charles-Town* prevented.

Auſtin, Laurens, & Appleby.

N. B. Full one Half of the above Negroes have had the SMALL-POX in their own Country.

and craftsmanship, the West African economies were also characterized by much commercial activity. Gold from the Niger Valley, for instance, was traded for textiles and salt with Arab merchants in the north.

The remains of these civilizations also clearly indicate how artistic the people were. In addition to their beautiful pottery and religious objects, they built and decorated huge temples. Their artisans were extremely skilled at working in bronze, silver, copper, and gold. While most of our knowledge of the culture of the area remains in folktales and poems, at the height of West African civilization there was a university at Timbuktu with a library of thousands of books.

Despite the oppressive conditions of slave life, blacks were able to transport some of their heritage to the New World. Because of the isolation of the black communities, Africanisms survived in the Gullah dialect of slaves living on the coastal islands off Georgia and South Carolina. Their music, dances, and folklore have become a part of American culture. However, direct carryovers from Africa are more easily observed in Latin America and the Caribbean, where mortality rates were so high that the constant influx of new slaves kept awareness of former practices alive.

SOUTHERN ARISTOCRACY

Although small landowners and tenant farmers predominated in the South, the elegant life style of the minority of plantation owners set the tone of Southern life. Many of these rural aristocrats came originally from families of humble English background and laid the foundations of their fortunes in the 1600s when the rapid accumulation of wealth was still possible. In America it was not so much inherited wealth which determined one's place on the social scale as it was the successful acquisition of wealth. In the seventeenth century, a Southern colonist with moderate capital had a good chance of increasing it through landholdings. However, by the eighteenth century, less than five percent of the newcomers were becoming landowners.

The aristocratic life style was modeled closely after that of the English country gentleman. Within the huge mansions most of the expensive furnishings were imported from England. English manners and English dress were copied; English manuals even dictated the proper forms of behavior.

Southern plantation owners often entertained each other on their magnificent estates. Balls frequently ran for days, and visits could easily stretch into month-long stays. Horseracing and cockfights engaged the gentlemen, while the ladies played cards or performed in musicals. Hospitality was lavish, and all the socializing inevitably led to matchmaking. By the time of the Revolution, most of the great planters were related by marriage.

The plantation owners were also the chief political leaders in Southern society. Wealth and power were both based on the amount of land a person owned. In Virginia, Maryland, North Carolina, and Georgia, land ownership was a requirement for voting. In South Carolina, voters had to have either land or money. Many colonists took the concept of a graded society for granted, and the "lessers" readily deferred to their "betters." This allowed a small group of well-to-do planters to dominate electoral politics with very little effort. Out of custom and necessity the active electorate regularly chose the same men to represent them in their assemblies year after year.

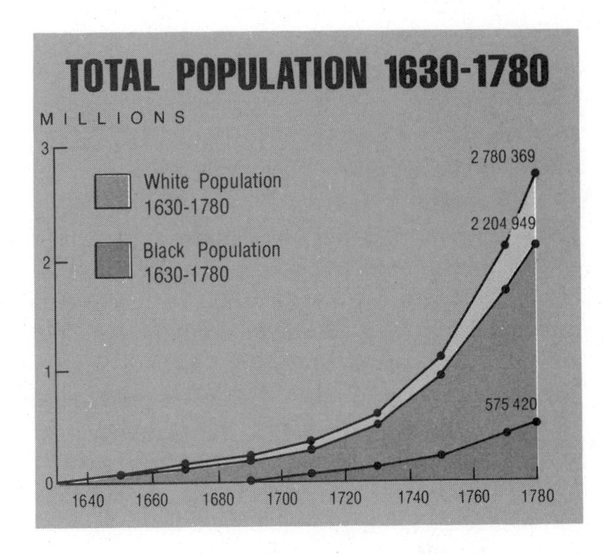

Politics at the local level was also dominated by the aristocracy. Justices of the peace, sheriffs, and judges were all county officials appointed by the governor of the colony. He would naturally restrict his consideration to his own upper-class acquaintances. Subdivisions of the counties, known as parishes, were initially controlled by officials elected by members of the parish church. By the later part of the seventeenth century, these positions had also become hereditary in the wealthiest families in each parish.

Because Southern life was rural, the only city of consequence during the early plantation days was Charleston, South Carolina. In the summer months wealthy planters and their families generally left the country for a stay in this cool, seaside town. And Charleston was well prepared to cater to their tastes. Huge banquets were held at the major taverns, and traveling shows were scheduled for the summer season. Merchants of all sorts were also on hand, as well as London fashion designers, tailors, and craftsmen to show the latest English styles.

The Middle Colonies

Between Maryland and New England lay the four Middle colonies: Delaware, New York, Pennsylvania, and New Jersey. In the early years they were primarily farming areas, and corn was usually the first crop a newcomer cultivated. Corn was easy to grow, required little attention, provided abundant nourishment, and served as fodder for livestock. After a farmer began to prosper in the Middle colonies, land was generally turned over to the production of grain crops such as wheat, barley, and oats.

During the eighteenth century the Middle colonies became the breadbasket of America. Huge wheat surpluses were shipped out of the ports of Philadelphia and New York to New England and the West Indies. Meat products were also exported from these areas in the 1700s, finding markets in southern Europe, while horses raised in the Middle colonies were sold in New England and in the American South. This intercolonial trade had two primary effects: it increased specialization and it helped tie the colonies together. Each area was gradually able to market what it could produce most efficiently because it could rely on the other colonies to supply what it lacked.

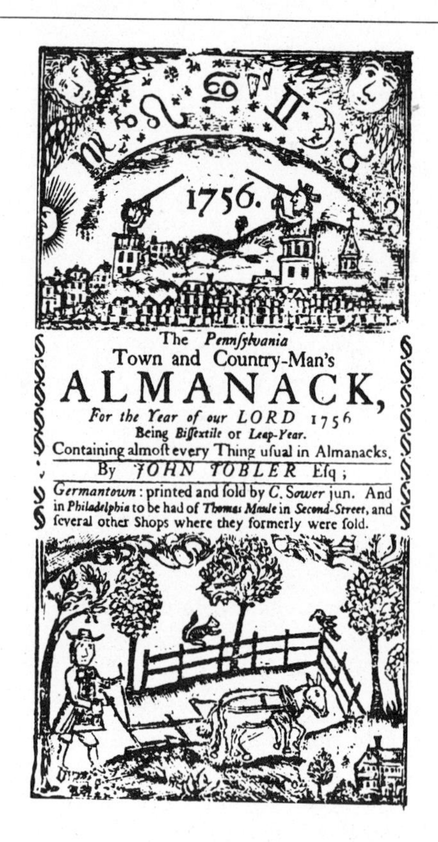

1756.

The Pennſylvania
Town and Country-Man's
ALMANACK,
For the Year of our LORD 1756
Being Biſſextile or Leap-Year.
Containing almoſt every Thing uſual in Almanacks.
By JOHN TOBLER Eſq;
Germantown: printed and ſold by C. Sower jun. And in Philadelphia to be had of Thomas Maule in Second-Street, and ſeveral other Shops where they formerly were ſold.

Philadelphia, the "City of Brotherly Love," 1754. ▼

LAND SPECULATION

Thousands of people in the Middle colonies, no matter how honest or how poor, were consumed by land fever. As one New York observer commented:

> An unaccountable thirst for large tracts of land without the design of cultivation hath prevailed over the inhabitants of this and the neighboring provinces with a singular rage. Patents have been lavishly granted (to give it no worse term) upon the pretense of fair Indian purchases, some of which the Indians have alleged were never made but forged. . . . They say that the surveyors have frequently run patents vastly beyond even the pretended conditions or limits of sale.

As in the South, land in the Middle colonies was distributed by the headright system which demanded that all the land a person claimed had to be cleared, planted, and lived on. In Pennsylvania and New Jersey the system worked smoothly, but in New York it broke down and became a cover for dishonest speculation and corruption. Through political cronyism, huge estates were granted, even though the legal limit was 2000 acres.

Land speculators in New York sometimes resold their enormous holdings, but more often they rented out small parcels to tenant farmers. The terms of the rental could include additional obligations reminiscent of feudalism. For instance, land might be leased for ten bushels of wheat, "four fat hens," and a few days' work on the landlord's own property. The landlords also reserved all milling and mineral rights for themselves, and sometimes even established private court systems on their property.

IMMIGRATION

The Middle colonies tended to absorb most of the non-English immigrants to the New World, especially in the late seventeenth and early eighteenth centuries. The South had an ample supply of slave labor with which the immigrants could not compete, and Puritan intolerance and exclusivity tended to discourage newcomers to New England.

In 1700 the population of America was about 250,000. By the 1760s it had increased to almost 2,000,000, about one-third of whom had been born abroad. Most of the newest arrivals were from non-English backgrounds, but they were hardly the first such immigrants to America. When the British annexed New York in 1664, they had inherited a settlement originally established by the Dutch. Danes, Finns, and Swedes had settled in the Delaware Valley in the seventeenth century, and in 1683 William Penn persuaded a group of Germans to come to Pennsylvania, where they founded Germantown, north of Philadelphia. So the eighteenth-century non-English immigrants were part of a well-established tradition.

The early arrivals were a trickle compared to the deluge that flooded America after 1713, however. Impoverished by wars on the Continent and hounded by religious persecution, thousands of Germans were among the immigrants of the early eighteenth century. Some of them went to New York at first, but when reports of the restrictions on landholding were printed in German newspapers, German immigrants began to avoid that colony. This helps to explain why New York's population increased very slowly during the 1700s.

Almost half of the Germans who came to the colonies eventually settled in Pennsylvania, where they became known as the Pennsylvania Dutch. The name *Dutch* was an English mispronunciation of the German word for German, *Deutsch*. Pennsylvania attracted the immigrants because it promised almost complete religious freedom, a generous land policy, and soil that was so similar to Germany's that newcomers could farm the same way they had in Europe.

A minority of the Germans were members of strict religious sects such as the Mennonites (Amish), Moravians, and Dunkards, who wished

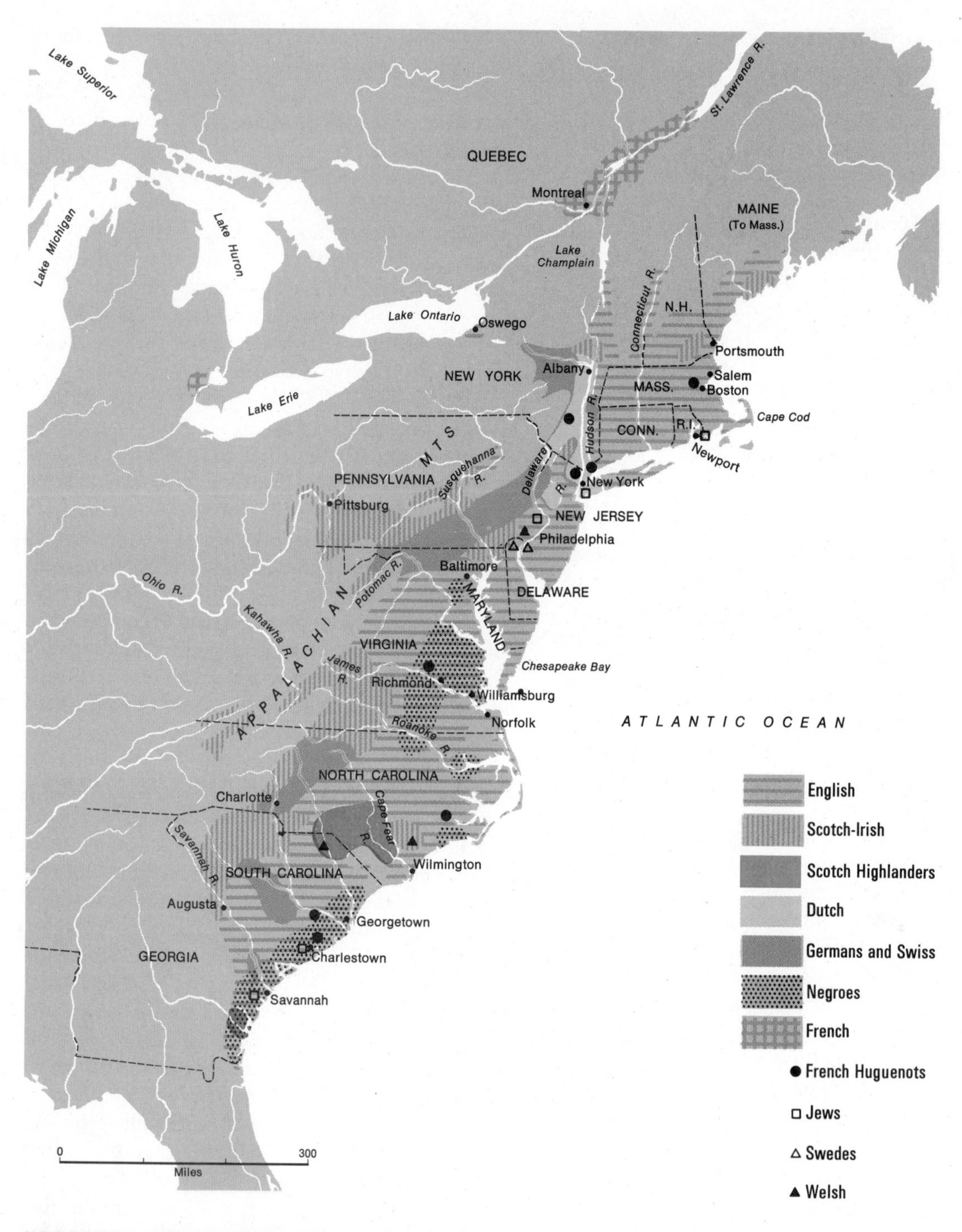

COLONIAL SETTLEMENT BY NATIONALITIES • 1770

to avoid contact with the rest of the world. The vast majority, however, quickly threw themselves into commerce and politics. Many were craftsmen whose skill far surpassed the abilities of most Anglo-American settlers. It was partly because of these German immigrants that Philadelphia was the largest and richest city in the colonies by the time of the Revolution.

Another substantial wave of immigrants in the early 1700s came from Ireland. A few were of pure Irish ancestry, but most were Presbyterian Scots who had moved to northern Ireland early in the seventeenth century. They became known as the Scotch-Irish, and they left the British Isles following a series of economic and political disasters. First, Parliament outlawed the importation of Irish beef and wool into England, and in 1704 it barred Presbyterians from holding public office. Then in 1714 a horrible drought struck northern Ireland. Four years of bad crops followed, and in 1717 landlords of Irish properties doubled or trebled their rents.

Life in Urban America

"[Philadelphia] must certainly be the object of every one's wonder and admiration. It is situated upon a tongue of land, a few miles above the confluence of the Deleware and Schuilkill; and contains about 3,000 houses, and 18 or 20,000 inhabitants. It is built north and south upon the banks of the Delaware; and is nearly two miles in length, and three quarters of one in breadth. The streets are laid out with great regularity in parallel lines, intersected by others at right angles, and are handsomely built: on each side there is a pavement of broad stones for foot passangers; and in most of them a causeway in the middle for carriages. Upon dark nights it is well lighted, and watched by a patrole: there are many fair houses and public edifices in it. . . . The city is in a very flourishing state, and inhabited by merchants, artists, tradesmen, and persons of all occupations. There is a public market held twice a week, upon Wednesday and Saturday, almost equal to that of Leadenhall; and a tolerable one every day besides. The streets are crowded with people, and the river with vessels."

Andrew Burnaby,
Travels through the Middle Settlements in North America in the years 1759 and 1760

The Small Farmer

"None of my ancestors, on either side, were either rich or great, but had the character of honesty and industry, by which they lived in credit among their neighbors, free from real want, and above the frowns of the world. . . . Meat, bread and milk was the ordinary food of all my acquaintance. I suppose the *richer sort* might make use of *those* and other luxuries, but to such people I had no access. We were accustomed to look upon, what were called *gentle folks*, as beings of a superior order. For my part, I was quite shy of *them*, and kept off at a humble distance. A *periwig*, in those days, was a distinguishing badge of *gentle folk*—and when I saw a man riding the road, near our house, with a wig on, it would so alarm my fears, and give me such a disagreeable feeling, that, I dare say, I would run off, as for my life. Such ideas of the difference between *gentle* and *simple*, were, I believe, universal among all of my rank and age. . . ."

Devereux Jarratt,
The Life of the Reverend Devereux Jarratt, 1794

This was the final blow and thousands of Scotch-Irish began to leave for America.

At first they headed for New England, but the Puritans gave them a cold reception. One Puritan minister saw the new arrivals as "formidable attempts of Satan and his Sons to unsettle us." Soon, like the Germans, they moved into Pennsylvania. From there they slowly pushed west to the Appalachian Mountains and into the Southern uplands, becoming America's most rugged frontier people.

COUNTIES

In Europe farmers generally lived in villages. In America, with the exception of New England, farms were scattered far apart and separated by vast forested areas. Since there were few towns, farmers in the Middle colonies carried on their civic duties through much larger, looser governmental units: counties. This was a practice similar to that of the Southern colonies.

About once a month, farmers would ride to the county courthouse to vote, take part in drills of the local militia, or pursue legal business. Once a year those who met the property qualification also elected representatives to sit in the colonial assembly. The county courthouse was the site where births, deaths, and marriages were registered; wills and deeds were recorded; and licenses were issued for various businesses. The county judges were important regional authorities who had much to say about an area's growth and development through their power to permit the building of new roads or the opening of new ferry lines.

The New England Colonies

Of the three main regions along the Atlantic coast, New England was the most closely knit. By the middle of the eighteenth century the region had a population of 500,000, very little of which was drawn from the more recent waves of immigration. During the entire pre-Revolutionary era, New England remained predominantly Puritan in religious outlook and English in ethnic background. Of course there were significant differences among the various offshoots of Calvinism which sometimes led to sharp disputes. Nevertheless, the area still possessed a more unified regional character than any other part of America.

Similarities of religious and national background were only part of New England's distinctive personality. Another factor which promoted regional unity was the method by which unsettled land was distributed. Unlike the areas which had a great deal of land speculation or illegal squatting by settlers, in New England the process was orderly, legal, and community-minded. Virgin lands were granted not to individuals but to groups of settlers. This meant that new immigrants to the area were automatically organized into towns. A group usually received a five-square-mile tract to settle a town. Near the center of the tract the citizens erected a village around a town square. Here all the farmers and their families lived in a true community, with a church and a school. The land around the village was divided into farms, pastures, and woodlands. Farms were parceled out to each family, but pastures and timberlands were held in common by the village.

The pattern of organization based on towns encouraged a lively participation in local government affairs. All adult male members of the township were able to vote on municipal issues, but citizen involvement went well beyond the ballot. At some time in his life, almost every New England townsman held a local public office. In fact, interest in local politics was so intense that the average New Englander tended to neglect the larger colonial issues. These matters were left to the elected representatives in the colonial assembly. Merchants, lawyers, and prosperous farmers usually received these positions, and the same individuals were usually reelected over and over again.

FAMILY LIFE

A typical seventeenth-century New England household consisted of a husband and wife, their children, at least one aged grandparent, and often servants or apprentices. It was rare for an extended family to live under one roof, and married siblings seldom shared the same home. As soon as a person was betrothed, plans for a new house began.

New England courtships were apparently initiated by the young people themselves, but parental consent was required when the couple became serious. After marriage, a man was usually given land, cattle, tools, and a house, or the promise of help in building one. A bride was given movable property: furniture, clothing, or money.

New research has also shown that the average age at marriage was higher than it is today, and that parents were frequently able to use land ownership to control their children. Families were large, with an average of seven or eight children surviving to adulthood. With such a large second generation needing land, marriage depended on the parent's willingness to supply it. The majority of fathers continued to own the land they gave their sons, releasing full possession only at their death. Since the average adult life expectancy was well over sixty-five, most sons were under parental control for a large portion of their lives. They could not sell out and leave, because they had no title to the land on which they lived.

CRAFTS AND TRADE

Despite the efforts of New England farmers, the region could not grow enough food to fill its own needs. The ground was too rocky, the growing season too short, and the amount of arable land too small. Throughout the eighteenth century, the area had no large staple crop nor any important mineral resources — and yet New England prospered.

Its wealth was based on the energy of its merchants, craftsmen, and fishermen. Even small towns could support the skilled laborers it needed, such as carpenters, tailors, weavers, and blacksmiths. Some villages built their fortunes by specializing on one craft in particular. In the 1760s, for instance, 80,000 pairs of shoes a year were being manufactured in Lynn, Massachusetts. Working people were paid considerably higher wages than laborers in England, and their importance to the region's economy helped keep the working class in a relatively comfortable position.

The success of New England manufacturing was matched by its commercial ventures. In the seventeenth century the Northern colonies were indisputably the masters of America's trade. Later their dominance was threatened by New York and Pennsylvania, but New England merchants always controlled a large part of colonial shipping. At the time of the Revolution, they owned about one thousand oceangoing vessels.

To a large extent New England's commerce was built on what has been called the triangular trade, with New England itself, the West Indies, and Africa as the three corners. Part of New England's contribution to the trade stemmed from its fishing industry, which directly or indirectly involved some 7500 people. Great catches were dried and shipped to southern Europe and the West Indies. In the Caribbean the fish were exchanged for molasses which would be converted into rum back in the New England distilleries. Next, the rum was transported to the west coast of Africa where it was traded for

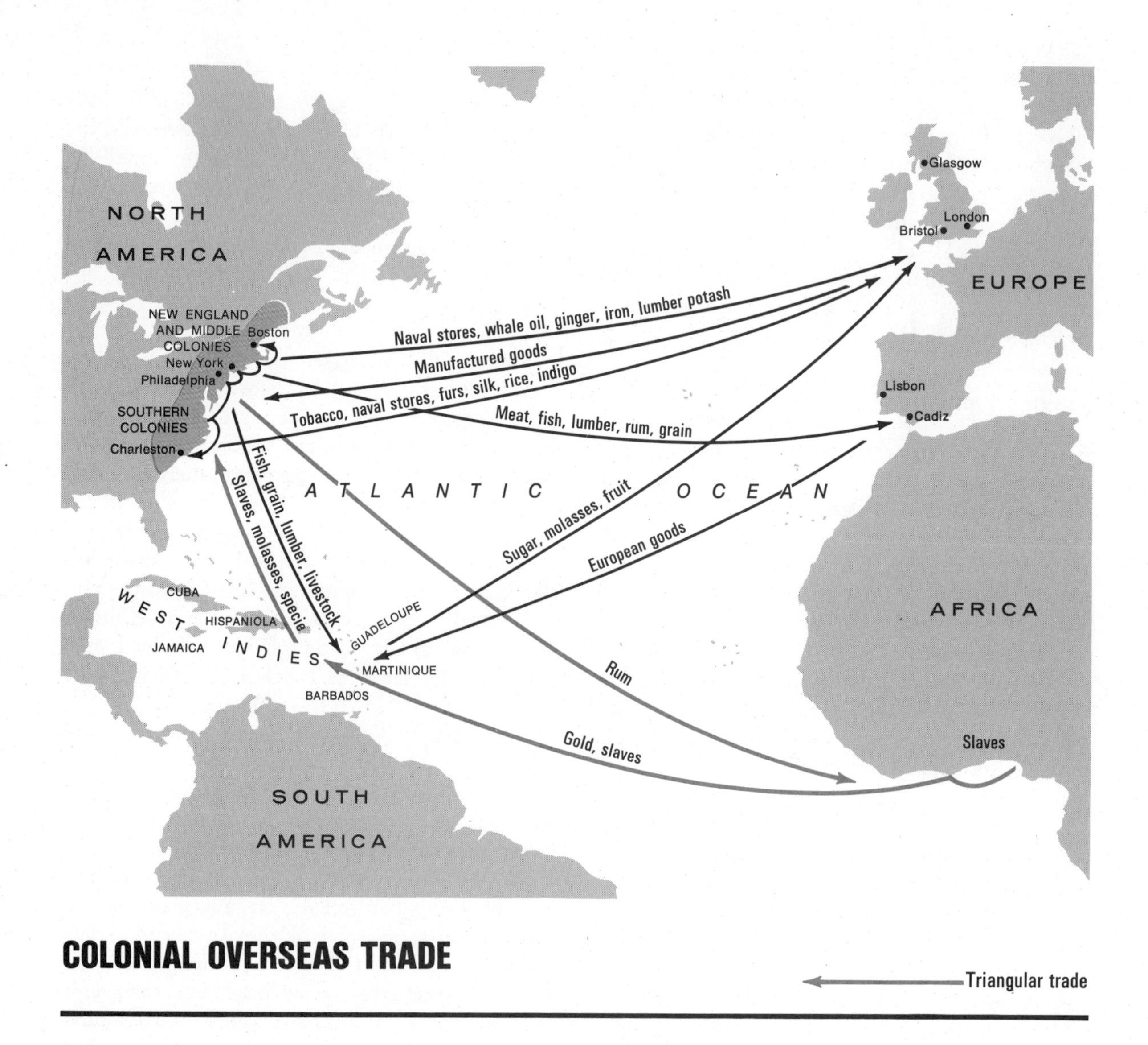

COLONIAL OVERSEAS TRADE

slaves, ivory, or gold dust. Finally, the slaves were taken to the West Indies and sold to plantation owners. With the profits, more molasses was purchased. The triangular trade was not a neat, precise pattern, since few ships ever followed an exact New England–West Indies–Africa route. There were many criss-crossings back and forth across the ocean, with New England vessels often stopping off in southern Europe or England.

THE CITIES

Thriving commerce created thriving cities, and the most important city in New England was Boston. By 1722 Boston had a dozen major shipyards, forty-two principal streets, three thousand houses, and sixteen thousand citizens. Most of these citizens owned some property, although the number of urban poor did grow steadily throughout the eighteenth century. Distinctions also existed within the propertied class itself, and these differences tended to become more pronounced during the 1700s. At the end of the seventeenth century, anyone with a little cash to invest held shares in New England's shipping ventures. This widespread ownership of mercantile wealth resulted in the creation of a large middle class. But as Boston's wealth increased, economic specialization began to occur. It soon became unnecessary to rely on the less affluent citizens for commercial investment, and by the Revolution the ownership of shipping was concentrated among a relatively small number of entrepreneurs. Property owners were clearly differentiated between a large body of shopkeepers, artisans, and laborers and a much smaller group with extensive commercial investments. Still, Boston was prosperous enough to offer a living in trades and crafts of every variety. In addition to necessary occupations such as carpentry, bricklaying, and leather-tanning, the city could support the services of America's finest goldsmiths, silversmiths, and clockmakers.

Despite the strictness of Puritan morality, Boston was much like any city in England. The Puritan ban against frivolous amusement was strong enough to ensure that no plays or concerts were performed in the city, but several merchants were rich enough to afford coaches, fine houses, and expensive furniture. Boston also had more than a thousand blacks in bondage during the eighteenth century. Women who were shopping or gentlemen conducting business were carried about in sedan chairs or carriages, often accompanied by slaves. An English traveler described how the well-to-do Bostonians diverted themselves:

> For their domestic amusements, every afternoon, after drinking tea, the gentlemen and ladies walk the Mall, and from thence adjourn to one another's houses to spend the evening. . . . But, notwithstanding plays and such like diversions do not obtain here, they don't seem to be dispirited nor moped for want of them; for both the ladies and gentlemen dress and appear as gay, in common, as courtiers in England on a coronation or birthday. And the ladies here visit, drink tea, and indulge every little piece of gentility, to the height of the mode; and neglect the affairs of their families with as good a grace as the finest ladies in London.

In the area of fashion, Boston sophistication often conflicted with Puritan self-denial. In the seventeenth century, for instance, gentlemen began to wear wigs costing as much as $250. Then, when hundreds of settlers were killed in the Indian attacks of 1676, many stern preachers attributed the disaster to God's anger over the "elect" making such displays of themselves.

Even with its air of wealth and luxury, however, Boston had many problems. By the 1740s, its growth rate was falling behind that of Newport, Philadelphia, and New York. Portsmouth, Rhode Island began to take over much of the shipbuilding industry, and Newport's shipowners (who controlled half of America's slave trade) diverted a great deal of business away from Boston.

Like other cities Boston was also experiencing new kinds of urban problems. The construction of an underground drainage system was supervised by city officials and paid for by private citizens. The city government also found it necessary to build jails, pay doctors to visit the city's poor families, and organize a public fire department. The department consisted of six engines and twenty men, who were helped after 1717 by the first volunteer fire company in the colonies. Called the Boston Fire Society, the group had twenty gentlemen members. Each member brought two buckets to the fire, as well as two large bags in which to carry away valuable goods to prevent looting. Similar volunteer associations sprang up in other cities and became a familiar feature of colonial life.

The Frontier

Although America's five main cities — Newport, Boston, Philadelphia, New York, and Charleston — seemed like transplanted English communities, America was unlike any place in Europe. It was different partly because of its odd regional and ethnic mixtures, but also because many of its inhabitants were constantly confronting the wilderness.

One famous American historian, Frederick Jackson Turner, considered the continuing presence of the frontier as *the most* decisive factor in the formation of the American character. In 1893, Turner wrote:

> American social development has been continually beginning over again on the frontier. This perennial rebirth, this fecundity of American life, this expansion westward with its new opportunities, its continuous touch with the simplicity of primitive society, furnish the forces dominating American character. . . . Thus the advance of the frontier has meant a steady movement away from the influence of Europe, a steady growth of independence on American lines.

Today many historians contend that Turner has overemphasized the importance of the frontier. Some stress the persistence of the English and European political and cultural heritage as the most important factor in shaping American life. Others have claimed that the cities contributed as much as the wilderness to the creation of a uniquely American way of living.

A strong case can be made that the development of life in the New World was influenced significantly by the immense wilderness of the continent. Because most frontier settlers lived such isolated lives, families had to rely on themselves for practical and spiritual needs. They built their own furniture, raised most of their own food, and made most of their own clothes. Parents taught their children how to read, write, and do simple arithmetic since there were few schools in colonial America outside of New England and the eastern settlements in other colonies.

The needs of frontier life also made for large families. Parents frequently had ten or twelve children because a great deal of help was needed for work on the farm. As soon as a boy reached seven years of age, he was helping his father in the field. Little girls attended their mother in the kitchen or at the sewing table as soon as they were old enough to follow instructions. Women often labored in the fields beside the men. Throughout the eighteenth century America suffered from a great labor shortage, which accounted for the large families, the importation of slaves, and the encouragement of immigration.

However, numerous children were rarely a permanent solution to the labor problems of a frontier family. Unlike England, where a son usually brought his wife to live with his parents, frontier America offered too much free land to keep the young at home. Newlyweds usually got their own farms early in life. Servants were as hard to keep as grown children. In England, a maid or butler generally served a family for life, but in America the labor shortage forced families to pay servants three or four times as much as the normal wages in London. Most hired help were able to amass enough money to start farms of their own.

The wilderness also hindered the preservation of many other traditional English institutions. For instance, Virginians who tried to import the English sport of fox-hunting during the colonial period soon had to abandon the pastime. Whenever there was a hunt, the fox simply disappeared into the forest. Many other more important upper-class customs were just as difficult to transplant from the Old World to the New World. Peasants could no longer be kept as menial laborers on a lord's estate. As

Pioneers clearing the wilderness.

we have seen, several attempts to start manorial estates in the colonies never went beyond the planning stages. Only in New York were there tenant farmers with feudal obligations to their landlords. So much cheap land was available, and labor was so scarce and highly paid, that few would plow another's fields for very long. The constant movement of people into new territories tended to erode old class distinctions. Permanent differences of rank were replaced on the frontier by social distinctions based on a family's qualities, including such intangibles as strength of will and self-control.

In addition to the social effects of the frontier, the geography of the continent influenced the way the New World was settled. Inland settlements were somewhat impractical since land travel was difficult over any great distance. The Dutch, for instance, founded Albany 150 miles up the Hudson River immediately after arriving in New York. But almost 100 years passed before other towns were established only a few miles inland from the river or the Atlantic Coast. Roads were expensive to build and maintain. As late as 1723 Benjamin Franklin preferred going from Boston to Philadelphia by taking a boat down the coast to New York and up the Delaware River, rather than traveling by road.

Conflicts Among the Colonies

We have seen that the colonies were spread out along the Atlantic seaboard; that with the exception of New England, most farmers were isolated from each other; and that it was tedious and slow to travel overland. These three factors — distance, isolation, and poor transportation — tended to make each colony a distinct entity. Colonists had little sense of belonging to any larger group. In fact, the term *American* was seldom used. Thomas Jefferson himself usually referred to "my country, Virginia," and people in New York and Pennsylvania generally felt a closer allegiance to England than to the other colonies. Southerners would speculate on the New England character as though they were studying foreigners.

Here, for example, is a list Jefferson once drew up comparing the people of the North to the people of the South:

In the North they are	In the South they are
cool	fiery
sober	voluptuary
laborious	indolent
independent	unsteady
jealous of their own liberties, and just to those of others	zealous for their own liberties but trampling on those of others
interested	generous
chicaning	candid
superstitious and hypocritical in their religion	without attachment or pretensions to any religion but that of the heart

In general, aristocrats of the Chesapeake country disliked the plain manners and democratic ways of New England, while John Adams of

Massachusetts prided himself and his "countrymen" on their "purer English blood, less mixed with Scotch, Irish, Dutch, French, Danish, Swedish, etc. than any other."

As a result of these and other differences there was little cooperation among the colonies. Maryland tried to undersell Virginia in the tobacco trade. New York, New Jersey, Virginia, and Pennsylvania all refused to help New England during a series of French-provoked Indian attacks in 1703. Only five years later did New York finally offer any aid to the beleaguered New Englanders, and it did so because some New Yorkers realized that they might gain control of the western fur trade if New France and her Indian allies were crushed. Border disputes were also a frequent occurrence between colonies. The settlers of the Carolinas and Georgia, for instance, had several bitter quarrels over trading rights with the Cherokees and Chickasaws.

EASTERN AND WESTERN CONFLICTS

The sharpest disagreements, however, were felt between the eastern and western regions within each colony. Although the frontier in colonial times was seldom more than 100 miles inland, the distance was sufficient to generate hostility. People living in the back country faced different problems and had different needs from those who lived in the more settled areas. Westerners wanted the government to spend money on new roads and strong fortifications against the Indians. Usually the pioneers were poorer than the town dwellers and resented the high prices on goods and the high rates of interest on loans set by eastern merchants.

In many colonies these conflicts were intensified by differences in national origin. The great immigration of the first half of the eighteenth century brought thousands of Germans and Scotch-Irish to Pennsylvania. These rugged frontier people pushed into the back country of Virginia in the 1730s, the Carolinas in the next two decades, and Georgia in the 1760s. Unlike the wealthier Anglicans living in Charleston or Jamestown, the newcomers were usually Presbyterians or German Pietists. Often the judges, sheriffs, and other officials of English background appointed to administer the new counties frankly despised the Germans and the Scotch-Irish. This led them to serve only the interests of the governor and the eastern clique of well-to-do merchants and large plantation owners.

One sort of political injustice was the control exercised by the seaboard counties over each colony's assembly, which denied fair representation to the back country. In 1760, for example, Lancaster County in western Pennsylvania had twice as many people as Bucks County in the east, but Bucks had twice as many representatives. In Virginia and the Carolinas, discrimination against the frontier was even more unfair. At the time of the Revolution, the older counties there still elected two-thirds of the members of the assembly.

In the decades immediately before the American Revolution, an observer might have predicted that a war between easterners and westerners was more likely than a united colonial effort against England. Tempers flared in frontier counties and rhetoric became heated. One frontiersman denounced the eastern ruling class as "cursed hungry Caterpillars, that will eat out the very Bowels of our Commonwealth, if they are not pulled down from their Nests in a very short time." In North Carolina a group of small farmers in the west decided to actually "pull down the Caterpillars" in order to end political corruption. In 1771 some two thousand frontiersmen banded together and engaged in a battle with the governor's militia. The Regulators, as the westerners called themselves, were defeated, but their resentment against corrupt officials, high taxes, and underrepresentation continued.

INDIAN WARFARE

The greatest source of contention between east and west was the question of how to handle relations with the Indians. From about 1660 to 1760 powerful tribes kept the colonists from penetrating too far west by controlling the Appalachian Mountains. These tribes included the Iroquois in the North and the Cherokees in the South. To the north of the colonies lay New France, which also had claims to land in the Ohio Valley. The Indians maintained their power for nearly a century by playing one group of colonists off against the other. They were willing to trade with the white settlers, but not to permit encroachments into their own territories.

Nevertheless squatters did gradually manage to take over Indian lands, driving away game that was essential to the native Americans' survival. Deadly clashes took place almost daily, and authorities did nothing to stop the conflicts. Leaders in both England and America seemed to feel that it was the price that had to be paid in order to reach the long-range goal of destroying French control in the North and Spanish dominance south of Georgia.

In the last chapter we saw that Nathaniel Bacon raised an illegal army in western Virginia to fight the Indians. Bacon's Rebellion finally

A cartoon of the Paxton Boys' march on Philadelphia. ▼

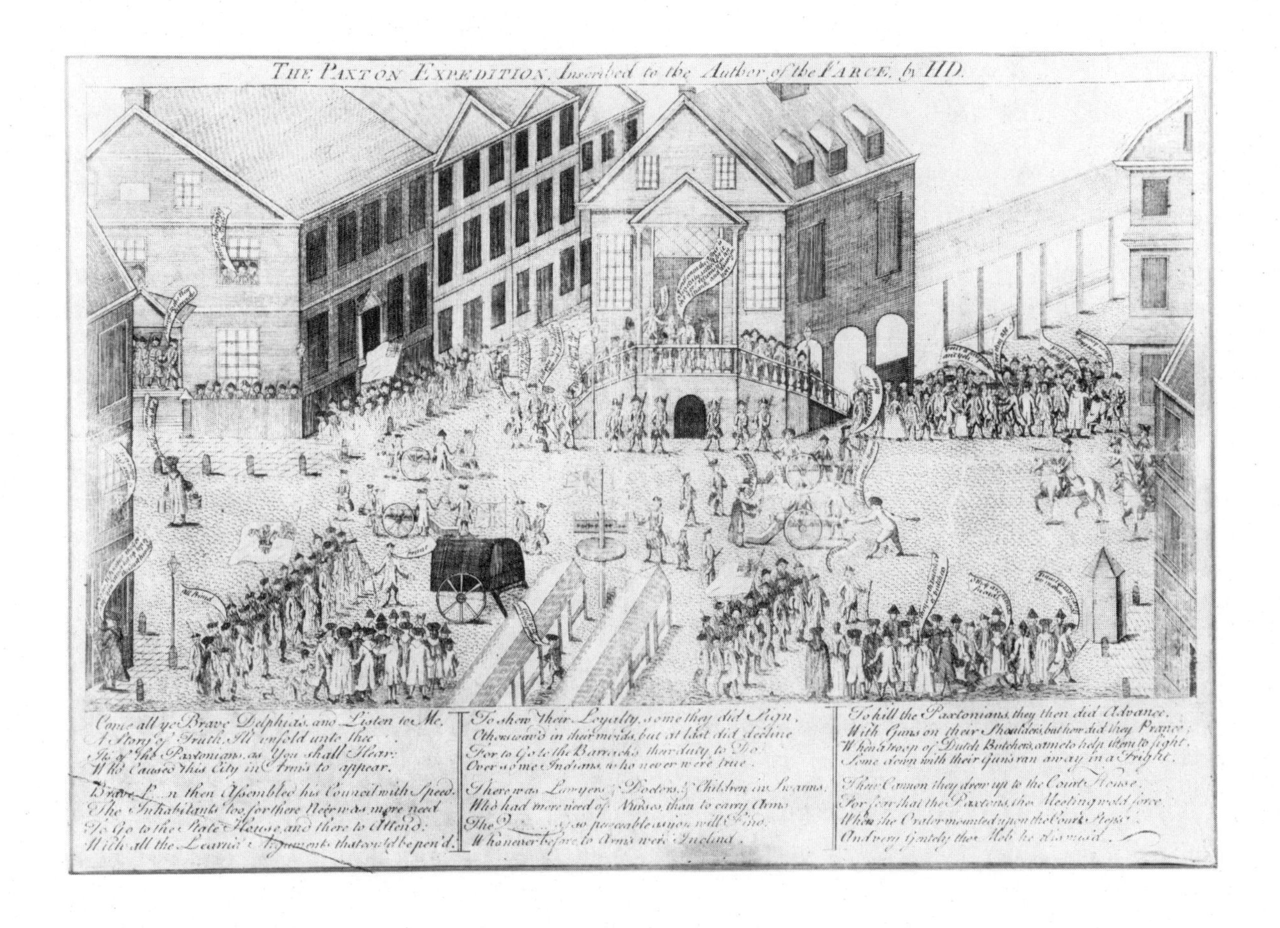

ended in an attack on Jamestown itself, as bitter frontier farmers showered their rage on the colonial administration.

In the eighteenth century, a similar uprising took place in Pennsylvania. In 1763, a band of Scotch-Irish from the western townships of Paxton and Donegal killed twenty peaceful Conestoga Indians in revenge for raids carried out by another tribe. Excited by their action, the Paxton Boys decided to march on the capital in an effort to force the governor to send troops against the Indians. The Quakers in Philadelphia were pacifists and had maintained peaceful relations with the Indians for decades. To them, Scotch-Irish fierceness seemed more of a problem than the Indians had ever been. Attempting to use reason, Benjamin Franklin and four others were delegated to negotiate with the Paxton Boys. Ten miles outside the city, Franklin made peace with the mob. He was forced to promise a bounty for Indian scalps, and in private he referred to the frontiersmen as "Christian white savages."

Thus, colonial life often differed in the east and west as much as the colonies themselves differed from Europe. Tensions between the seaboard and the frontier mounted throughout most of the eighteenth century, and it took a strong common cause—the Revolution—to relax them even partially.

The Impact of Religion

There were several striking facts about religion in colonial America. First, the colonies were overwhelmingly Protestant. At the time of the Revolution there were about 25,000 Catholics and 2,000 Jews out of a total population of about 2.5 million. Second, although there were numerous denominations in existence, many of the colonists attended no church at all. By the middle of the eighteenth century, the percentage of nonchurchgoers was greater in the colonies than in any European country. The main reason that there were so many nonprofessing Christians, as they were called, is that large areas of the country were too poor or too sparsely settled to support a church. In 1701, for example, the Carolinas had a population of about 12,000, but no ministers from the Church of England. As late as 1729 a Virginian wrote about the capital of North Carolina: "I believe this is the only Metropolis in the Christian or Mahometan World, where there is neither Church, Chappel, Mosque, Synagogue, or any other place of Public Worship of any Sect or Religion whatsoever."

ANGLICANS IN THE SOUTH

The Church of England, sometimes called the Anglican Church, was by no means the strongest religious institution in the colonies. In 1775 there were 668 Congregational (Puritan) churches in America, 588 Presbyterian churches, and only 495 Anglican places of worship. The Baptists were next with 494, and then the Quakers with 310.

The Church of England failed to gain genuine support in many places where it might have been expected to flourish. By 1758 it was the established religion from Maryland to Georgia, but many Southerners resented their obligation to pay the salaries of Anglican ministers even though they swore allegiance to the church. The Anglican position in the South was further weakened by the fact that an American bishop was never appointed for the colonies. The Bishop of London, who was in charge of America, never once crossed the Atlantic to visit his charges. Moreover, in the Anglican faith a minister could only be ordained by a bishop. Ordination meant sailing to London, and few prospective ministers made the trip. As a consequence, many colonial preachers were not "real" ministers at all, and colonial congregations felt free to hire and fire them as they pleased. Services were frequently conducted by laymen who gave the Anglican service a tone which was almost Puritan.

Along the frontier the Anglican Church made an even smaller impression. Most of the back country was populated by Scotch-Irish Presbyterians, Welsh Baptists, and Germans of a variety of sects. Occasionally Anglican ministers did travel into pioneer settlements, but their welcome was not always warm. One such clergyman reported that a group of Presbyterians "hired a band of rude fellows to come to service who brought with them fifty-seven dogs (for I counted them), which in time of service they set fighting and I was obliged to stop." The disturbance stopped only when the minister concluded by thanking the "fifty-seven Presbyterians" for attending his sermon.

PURITANS IN THE NORTH

The Bible commonwealth established by the Puritans in Massachusetts was a strong fortress in the seventeenth century. The founders of the colony had come to America partly to search for religious freedom, but once they secured it, they were not at all eager to extend it to others. As Richard Mather wrote in 1643:

> The discipline appointed by Jesus Christ for his churches is not arbitrary, that one church may set up and practice one form, and another another form, as each one shall please, but is one and the same for all churches. . . . And if that discipline which we here practice, be (as we are persuaded of it) the same which Christ hath appointed, and therefore unalterable, we see not how another can be lawful.

Convinced that they had recreated in America a society which bore close resemblance to the original community of Christ and his followers, the Puritans were determined to exclude all heretics. Seventeenth-century laws allowed for whipping, branding, and executing non-Puritans under certain circumstances. Under these laws four Quakers met death in Massachusetts in 1659 and 1660.

On the other hand, Puritans were not as prudish as they have sometimes been pictured. They were not opposed to liquor or sex. Wine

WEDNESDAY, *January* 1. 1701.
A little before Break-a-Day, at *Boſton* of the *Maſſachuſets*.

ONCE more! Our GOD, vouchſafe to Shine:
Tame Th[illegible] the Rigour of our Clime.
Make haſte with thy Impartial Light,
And terminate this long dark Night.

Let the tranſplanted **Engliſh** Vine
Spread further ſtill : ſtill Call it Thine.
Prune it with Skill : for yield it can
More Fruit to Thee the Huſbandman.

Give the poor **Indians** Eyes to ſee
The Light of Life : and ſet them free ;
That they Religion may profeſs,
Denying all Ungodlineſs.

From hard'ned **Jews** the Vail remove,
Let them, their Martyr'd JESUS love ;
And Homage unto Him afford,
Becauſe He is their Rightfull LORD.

So falſe Religions ſhall decay,
And Darkneſs fly before bright Day :
So Men ſhall GOD in CHRIST adore ;
And worſhip Idols vain, no more.

So **Aſia**, and **Africa**,
Europa, with **America** ;
All Four, in Conſort join'd, ſhall Sing
New Songs of Praiſe to CHRIST our KING.

Puritan poem by Samuel Sewall, judge in the witchcraft trials.

was something that God had provided for the purpose of pleasure, and sexual enjoyment between husband and wife was also completely permissible. Sexual intercourse outside of marriage was forbidden, but even here the Puritans were willing to make allowances for the weakness of human nature. The laws were enforced with patience and understanding, and the emphasis was on prevention rather than punishment. The methods used to prevent various transgressions would be seen today as serious invasions of personal liberty, but in general the Puritans were not the narrow-minded bigots which they are too often believed to have been.

Whereas the Anglican Church in the South was a pale imitation of the mother church in England, the Puritan commonwealth was an unprecedented experiment. It has been argued that the Puritans had come not only to establish a religious refuge, but also to set up a joint church and civil partnership which would serve as a model for England. When the Protectorate was formed in England in 1653, it was hoped that Cromwell would follow the Puritan example. When he did not, the mission in the New World seemed to have failed. After the monarchy was restored in 1660, the New England Puritans underwent a serious identity crisis. No longer able to pursue the goal of reforming the Old World, they were forced to look for some meaning in their own society. But in turning inward, the Puritans came to believe that they had failed to live up to the high standards of a people who were God's elect. Their sermons began to warn that God would avenge the wrongdoings of a chosen people, and all the Puritan sins were listed. These sermons served as token payments for their sins, allowing the Puritans to go about the business of adapting to the environment, expanding the frontier, and undertaking commercial ventures.

Moreover, by the middle of the seventeenth century, the Puritan establishment's control of the colony's population was evaporating. Many were going to church as a mere ritual, observing only the outward appearance of moral life. Few children of church members were able to prove that they had experienced the religious conversion necessary for church membership, so that Puritan domination was threatened by a lack of members from the younger generation. Consequently, in 1662 the colony's leaders felt compelled to change the requirements for joining the church. They adopted the so-called Half-way Covenant, which automatically permitted the children of any church member to be baptized. The result was a half-way membership, entitling the recipients to have their own children baptized. Full membership, though, was still reserved for those who had experienced a religious conversion and only they could receive communion.

The Half-way Covenant muted dissent within the colony for a while, but in 1699 hostility against old-line Puritanism rose to the surface. A group of well-to-do merchants broke away from the Boston congregation and started the Brattle Street Church. The members of the new congregation gave their emphatic approval to the Half-way Covenant. They also insisted that baptism could not be denied to any child, and argued that anyone who attended and contributed to a church was entitled to help select the minister, even if that person was not a full church member. Conservatives in the community tried to stop the spread of such reform measures, but the efforts were of no avail.

Witchcraft trials

Meanwhile the Puritan ruling class suffered other blows that weakened its hold over the colony. Its control was curbed by the charter of 1691, which made Massachusetts a royal colony, and its respected position was further undermined by the hysteria and remorse generated by the infamous Salem witchcraft trials.

By the early 1690s many Puritans were certain that God had abandoned them as his chosen people. They felt that they had failed to live up to the standards of orthodox Calvinism and they were ready to interpret all their misfortunes as signs of divine wrath. To the Puritans the development of a frenzy over the presumed presence of witches in the little village of Salem, Massachusetts seemed to be just such a sign.

The episode began when a few young girls, overexcited by voodoo stories they had heard from a West Indian woman, started shouting at odd moments and twitching nervously for no apparent reason. A doctor was summoned, and he announced that the girls were under a witch's spell. Next the girls pointed out their tormentors, mostly older women against whom they may have felt some resentment. Soon a witch-hunt was launched and spread rapidly to neighboring areas, including Boston itself.

The trials began in June 1692 and continued into 1693. They were not normal trials, based on evidence testified to by witnesses. Instead, "spectral" evidence was used, evidence consisting of voices or apparitions which had supposedly affected the young girls. One reason that the trials were able to continue at all was that the Puritan clergy refused to intervene in the strange proceedings. They may have felt that the outbreak of emotion would serve to strengthen their authority in the colony. In fact many members of the clergy encouraged the people to believe in witches and demons in the period leading up to the trial. In 1689, for example, one of Boston's most eloquent and respected theologians, Cotton Mather, published a widely-read tract on the subject of witchcraft. It dealt with a case in the 1680s in which the children of a Boston Puritan had, according to Mather, really been bewitched. On the other hand, the modern historian John Demos has argued that the accusers in Salem Village were "projecting" their feelings of aggression onto older, eccentric members of the village.

Whatever the explanation for the girls' behavior, by September 1692, 20 "witches" had been executed and 150 suspects were in jail, awaiting their fate. At first, most officials kept silent, but gradually a few brave souls stepped forward to speak out against the executions. The

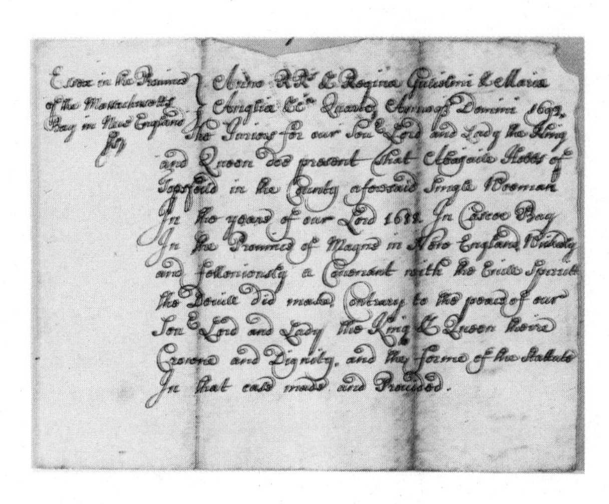

Essex in the Province
of the Massachusetts
Bay in New England
ss//

Anno RRs & Reginae Gulielmi & Mariae
Angliae &c Quarto Annoq Domini 1692.
The Juriors for our Sov'r Lord and Lady the King
and Queen doe present That Abigaile Hobbs of
Topsfield in the County aforesaid Single Woman
In the yeare of our Lord 1688. In Casco Bay
In the Province of Maine in New England Wickedly
and felloniously a Covenant with the Evill Spiritt
the Devill did make Contrary to the peace of our
Sov'r Lord and Lady the King & Queen theire
Crowne and Dignity, and the forme of the Statute
In that case made and Provided.

A court indictment against Abigail Hobbs for "covenanting with the Devil." Evidence such as this was enough to sentence a person to hang.

governor, Lord Phips, finally lost patience when his own wife was accused of being a witch. He ordered all the suspects released, and several of the girls who had made the original accusations confessed that they had lied.

Although he had warned the court not to accept the evidence presented by "witches," Cotton Mather guiltily admonished himself for not "appearing with vigor to stop the proceedings of the judges when the inexplicable storm from the invisible world assaulted the country." It was an embarrassing affair for the Puritan hierarchy, and it cost them much public respect.

THE GREAT AWAKENING

The early decades of the eighteenth century were marked by a widespread apathy toward religion in general. Shocked by this attitude, many colonial ministers were prompted to begin a great crusade aimed at gaining new converts and reinspiring their congregations.

As early as 1725 a Dutch Reformed minister in New Jersey named Theodore Frelinghusen was delivering highly-emotional sermons to his congregation, insisting on faith rather than reason as a means to salvation. In New England,

Skepticism of the Great Awakening

"For is it reasonable to think that the *Divine SPIRIT* in dealing with Men in a Way of Grace, and in Order to make them good Christians, would give their *Passions* the *chief* Sway over them? Would not this be to invert their Frame? To place the Dominion in those Powers, which were made to be kept in Subjection? And would the alwise GOD introduce such a State of Things in the human Mind? Can this be the Effect of the *Out-pouring* of his SPIRIT? It ought not to be supposed. One of the most *essential* Things necessary in the *new-forming* Men, is the Reduction of their *Passions* to a proper Regimen. . . ."

Charles Chauncy,
Seasonable Thoughts on the State of
Religion in Massachusetts, 1742

Awe of the Great Awakening

"A considerable Number convened every Sabbath to hear these Sermons [written by Rev. George Whitefield], instead of going to Church, and frequently on Week Days. The Concern of some was so passionate and violent, that they could not avoid crying out, weeping bitterly, etc. and that when such Indications of religious Concern were so strange and ridiculous, that they could not be occasioned by Example or Sympathy, and the Affectation of them would have been so unprofitable an Instance of Hypocrisy, that none could be tempted to it. My Dwelling-House at length was too small to contain the People; whereupon we determined to build a Meeting-House. . . ."

Samuel Davies,
The State of Religion among
the Protestant Dissenters in Virginia, 1751

the most outstanding preacher of this period was Jonathan Edwards. In the 1730s, Edwards used violent, highly-charged rhetoric to remind his parishioners of the horrors and suffering waiting in hell for all sinners. His sermons appealed strictly to the emotions as he urged people to surrender themselves dramatically to God's mercy. The most important figure in the entire Great Awakening, however, was an English revivalist named George Whitefield. Whitefield made his first speaking tour of the colonies in 1739 and quickly became the best known preacher of his generation in America.

Whitefield drew such large crowds in every town he visited that the meetings were almost always held outside the church. One of his sermons outside of Philadelphia attracted ten thousand people, a huge attendance for that period. Aside from his great speaking ability, Whitefield excited his audiences with his level of emotional intensity. Other roaming preachers soon began to imitate his style, and many of them were also able to whip up mass hysteria wherever they went. Zealous men and women would frequently burst into tears and exhibit the most extraordinary behavior at these revival meetings. After experiencing shattering visions of the divine light, they would promise to change their ways and reform their lives. As one observer noted:

> Some would stand in the pulpit exhorting, some in the body of the seats, some in the pews, and some up in the gallery; and oftentimes, several of them would speak together; so that some praying, some exhorting, and testifying, some singing, some screaming, some crying, some laughing, and some scolding, made the most amazing confusion that ever was heard.

Evaluating Puritanism

Historians have disagreed sharply in their interpretations of the Puritan influence on American culture. Some have said that the Puritans obstructed freedom of thought and religion, while others have maintained that they established the foundations of American democracy. Sometimes these opposing viewpoints say a great deal about the personal outlook of the historians themselves, since students of the past often frame their interpretations according to the needs of the present.

For instance, most nineteenth century historians seemed to idolize certain Puritan personalities. John Gorham Palfrey, a descendant of the Puritans, found little to condemn in his own forefathers. He regarded John Winthrop in particular as a genius for his part in establishing the idea of self-government.

By the twentieth century, however, an anti-Puritan attitude had developed among historians. In the 1920s critics such as H. L. Mencken saw certain narrow-minded ideas of his own day as a cultural result of the Puritan outlook. In addition, three scholars of this period—James Truslow Adams, Vernon L. Parrington, and Thomas J. Wertenbaker—were all strongly affected by the economic and social inequities of their day. In looking for similar situations in earlier American history, they found the roots of some of these modern ills in the Puritan past. This led them to condemn the early Puritan leaders for their oppressive control over peoples' lives.

In the 1930s, the outlook shifted once again. A group of historians, including Samuel Eliot Morison, Perry Miller, and Clifford K. Shipton, began to draw a more sympathetic portrait of the Puritans, emphasizing their intellectual sophistication. Morison in particular praised the Puritan qualities of self-discipline and energy, which enabled them to carry European culture to the wilderness of America. While other colonists often degenerated into half-savagery in their struggles with the new land, he wrote, the Puritans were able to found Harvard College only a few years after arriving in Boston. Morison also pointed out that the Puritans created a public elementary school system; printed, imported, and read a great many books; and were in touch with most European scientific and artistic developments.

Yet another group of historians, called the neoconservative school, added a new interpretation after World War II. Writing at a time when America's security seemed threatened by the Cold War and subversion from within, historians such as Daniel Boorstin claimed that institutions founded by the practical-minded Puritans were still strong and viable. The neoconservatives emphasized the Puritans' pragmatic approach to problem-solving as a uniquely American characteristic.

One final point of view, represented by Darrett B. Rutman, argues that Puritanism has been overemphasized as a concept for understanding New England and American history. According to Rutman, the early settlers in New England were most concerned with personal economic gain and did not subordinate their own interests to the overall schemes envisioned by the Puritan leaders. Many facets of New England thought and character were also not uniquely Puritan, he claims, but merely reflected people's former way of life in England.

Regardless of the emotional excesses of the Great Awakening, it had far-reaching consequences. Traveling evangelists assured their listeners that salvation had nothing to do with education and even criticized local ministers for being too well educated. Several denominations split into two groups: a conservative wing and a "new side" which called for spiritual democracy. The wave of revivalism produced strong tendencies toward anti-intellectualism, and many congregations fired their ministers simply for being too learned. One of the newer factions, later known as the Methodists, gained large numbers of followers in the back country of America where disenchantment with the Anglican Church was high.

As the first truly intercolonial movement, the Great Awakening also had political and social side effects. As the Church of England weakened, so did respect for British authority, especially in Virginia. The growth of membership in the dissenting churches also prepared the way for the separation of church and state. The Anglicans in the South and the Puritans in New England had political as well as religious authority. When these two established churches could no longer claim the allegiance of a majority of the settlers, it became difficult to obtain financial support and their power gradually decreased.

Attitudes of racial intolerance may also have been softened during the Great Awakening through the doctrine of the sinfulness of all people and the Methodist and Quaker emphasis on universal salvation. The Quakers, in fact, were the first religious denomination to attack slavery as being opposed to the will of God.

One concrete result of the Great Awakening was the establishment of many new religious seminaries to carry on the spirit of the revival. The most famous of these were the College of New Jersey, which later became Princeton (Presbyterian); Queen's College, which later became Rutgers (Dutch Reformed); the College of Rhode Island, which later became Brown (Baptist); and Dartmouth (Congregational).

The Secular Mind

While the ordinary people of America were experiencing an epidemic of revivalism, the intellectual elite was embracing a new religion of its own: the cult of reason. For the rich, educated, and influential minority, a new way of looking at the world was being developed in the eighteenth century, the philosophy of the Enlightenment. Puritan theology had seen people as essentially evil creatures dependent on the mercy of God. The philosophy of the Enlightenment, on the other hand, taught that reason was the most important human faculty, and that through reason life could be progressively improved.

THE ENLIGHTENMENT

In England the two leading figures of the Enlightenment were Sir Isaac Newton and John Locke. Building on his own mathematical discoveries as well as on the experiments of such earlier scientists as Copernicus and Galileo, Newton published his *Principia Mathematica* in 1687. In it he explained how his mathematical calculations proved that the universe was controlled by the law of gravity. Ever since the Greek and Roman periods, scientists had sought to define the overriding order and harmony of nature in exact terms. Now Newton had explained it with precise simplicity: every particle of matter is subject to gravitational force. The far-reaching implications of this seemingly simple discovery were expressed by Newton's contemporary, Alexander Pope: "Nature and Nature's laws lay hid in the night. God said: 'Let Newton be,' and all was light." Newton had created a new view of the universe, and everything began to seem possible for human reason.

Generations of philosophers before him had attempted to explain the workings of the universe by turning to Aristotle or the holy scriptures. Instead of returning to these sources, Newton used the scientific method of arriving at conclusions through investigation, experimentation, and rational analysis of specific data. The success of this method in helping to illuminate one aspect of life was grounds for great expectations. Hopefully, human reason could discover the laws relating to other areas as well, including politics, morality, and religion.

Accepting the implications of Newton's work, John Locke published his *Essay on Human Understanding* in 1690. In this treatise he argued that the human mind was not already filled at birth with sin or any definite ideas. On the contrary, he claimed, it was like a blank slate, an empty page. Children coming into the world were totally receptive to the experiences which would eventually fill their minds. All knowledge came through the senses, from observation and experiment, according to Locke.

This was a very radical new theory, and the *Essay* struck many Americans as a strong argument against original sin and predestination. At the same time it seemed to point out the need for serious scientific study of the senses. If sensory impressions were the only means for gaining knowledge, it would be important to see how reliable they were.

Locke was also very interested in politics. He wrote two further treatises on government which were his versions of a rational model for civil rule guided by reason. According to his political theory, people were born free under the natural law of the universe and endowed with the natural rights of life, liberty, and property. But a disorganized society could prevent people from enjoying their rights, for people could be violent and selfish as well as rational. This meant that individual freedom could be limited by aggressive neighbors. Locke believed that reason could potentially overcome this danger, though. By forming an agreement or contract among themselves, people could protect their rights by establishing a government.

To Locke, England's parliamentary government appeared to be the most rational political system. Thus his political philosophy called for a government of laws, with divided powers and majority rule. There would be executive, legislative, and judicial branches, each having the power to prevent the other two from creating a tyranny. Locke believed, however, that a representative legislature based on the popular will should be the most important branch since its laws would be passed by majority decision and would apply equally to all citizens.

But if the government did not operate to protect the natural rights, was there a remedy? Yes, said Locke. Under some circumstances the people should take back the power they had delegated under the contract. In other words, he believed that government was an artificial creation. If people were dissatisfied with it, they could modify it, by revolution if necessary. Thus, John Locke's political ideas offered strong support for the right to revolt against established authority.

For many educated Americans, Locke's theory of government had the same clarity as Newton's explanation of the laws of the universe. In both theories, God had created a grand design before retiring quietly. God did not intervene in people's lives. According to this concept, God was like a clockmaker who built and wound a perfect machine, then sat back and watched it tick. The scientist and political philosopher only needed to study nature in order to see God's great plan.

This nonreligious faith in human potential, sometimes called Deism, stood in startling contrast to the beliefs fostered in the same period by the Great Awakening. For the religious revivalists, God was a personal deity intensely involved in everyone's fate. God could sweep sinners off to heaven or hurl them screaming into hell. While Enlightenment philosophers pictured God as utterly indifferent once the universe had been set in motion, the revivalists saw him as a stern father, passionately concerned over the deeds of his wayward children. Yet both movements stressed religious freedom, separation of church and state, educational improvements, and reliance on experience rather than traditional authority.

At first the ideas of the Enlightenment appealed mostly to the social and intellectual elite of the cities. By the time of the Revolution, however, many of these ideas had filtered down to the masses. Although many people had never heard of Newton or Locke, the idea that government could be made to serve human needs was becoming familiar to the public at large. Religious denominations such as the Baptists, Methodists, and Quakers also preached that people were perfectible. The need for scientific investigation was not at all strange to frontier Americans, who had learned long before about the importance of practical experimentation. Ultimately, when the English government began enacting laws which seemed unjust and tyrannical, the American people felt justified in rebelling. They did not feel that they were breaking the law. Rather, they saw themselves as conforming to the natural law of the universe, as outlined by John Locke.

EDUCATION

Many colonists had been concerned about education since the early seventeenth century, and the Enlightenment created a great deal of momentum for starting schools. Of the three major regions in America, New England had always given the most encouragement to education. Puritan theology required each individual to be able to read and interpret the Bible and make independent religious judgments. In 1636, only six years after they arrived in Massachusetts, the Puritans founded a college. It began with one house, one professor, one acre of land, and the revenues from the local ferry service. When a Bostonian named John Harvard died in 1638 leaving 400 books and half of his money to the college, the Board of Overseers decided to name their school after him. Harvard was orginally built to train new ministers, but the college was not limited to religious instruction. In 1738 John Winthrop (great-grandson of the colony's first governor) began to teach mathematics and science at Harvard. John Locke's *Essay on Human Understanding* was part of Harvard's curriculum as early as 1742.

The other New England colonies followed the Massachusetts example, if somewhat slowly. A Puritan-supported college was established in Connecticut in 1701 and permanently located at New Haven in 1716. Two years later it was named Yale College to honor Elihu Yale, a major benefactor. Rhode Island College was started in Providence in 1764 by a group of Baptists who felt the need to educate clergy for their own denomination. In 1804 it was renamed Brown University.

Elementary education also played a prominent part in New England life. In 1647 the Massachusetts assembly ordered all towns of at least fifty families to hire a reading instructor for the children. It also required that the instructor be paid out of public funds. Although school attendance was not compulsory, learning to read was. If parents did not want to send their children to school, they had to teach them at home. Some of the schools were free and some demanded a small tuition, but children of the poor could attend any of them without paying. All of the New England grammar schools were created by the government and none were run by religious groups such as the Puritans.

In the Middle colonies, the level of education was slightly lower. There were no public school systems in existence, although fourteen private schools were thriving in New York by 1762. In addition, various religious denominations had founded elementary schools in Pennsylvania and New Jersey to educate their children. In the religious enthusiasm spurred by the Great Awakening, though, several important colleges were established in the Middle colonies. The Quakers and the Scotch-Irish had already started church schools of their own in Pennsylvania, and sectarian rivalries prompted several denominations to found colleges of their own. The Presbyterians started the College of New Jersey (Princeton, 1746); Dutch Reformed revivalists

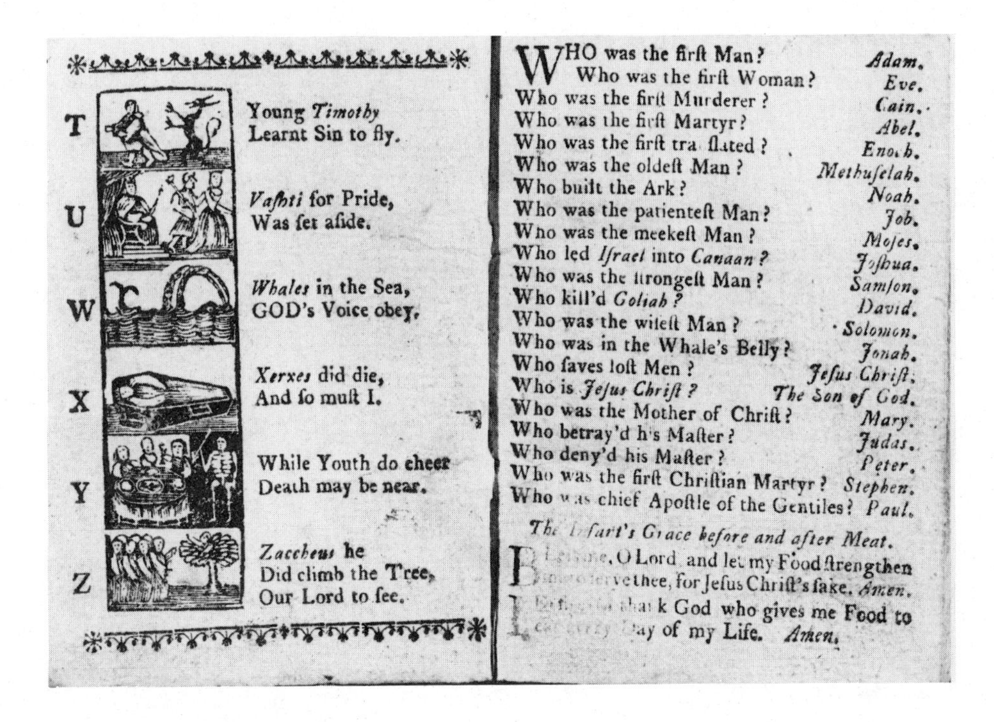

T — Young *Timothy*
Learnt Sin to fly.

U — *Vaſhti* for Pride,
Was ſet aſide.

W — *Whales* in the Sea,
GOD's Voice obey.

X — *Xerxes* did die,
And ſo muſt I.

Y — While Youth do cheer
Death may be near.

Z — *Zaccheus* he
Did climb the Tree,
Our Lord to ſee.

WHO was the firſt Man? *Adam.*
Who was the firſt Woman? *Eve.*
Who was the firſt Murderer? *Cain.*
Who was the firſt Martyr? *Abel.*
Who was the firſt tranſlated? *Enoch.*
Who was the oldeſt Man? *Methuſelah.*
Who built the Ark? *Noah.*
Who was the patienteſt Man? *Job.*
Who was the meekeſt Man? *Moſes.*
Who led *Iſrael* into *Canaan*? *Joſhua.*
Who was the ſtrongeſt Man? *Samſon.*
Who kill'd *Goliah*? *David.*
Who was the wiſeſt Man? *Solomon.*
Who was in the Whale's Belly? *Jonah.*
Who ſaves loſt Men? *Jeſus Chriſt.*
Who is *Jeſus Chriſt*? *The Son of God.*
Who was the Mother of Chriſt? *Mary.*
Who betray'd his Maſter? *Judas.*
Who deny'd his Maſter? *Peter.*
Who was the firſt Chriſtian Martyr? *Stephen.*
Who was chief Apoſtle of the Gentiles? *Paul.*

The [illegible]fant's Grace before and after Meat.

B[illegible], O Lord and let my Food ſtrengthen [illegible]ve thee, for Jeſus Chriſt's ſake. *Amen.*

I[illegible] thank God who gives me Food to [illegible] Day of my Life. *Amen.*

Pages from The New England Primer, *1767.* ▲

founded Rutgers (1766); and Anglicans and Presbyterians worked together in the founding of King's College (Columbia, 1754) and the College of Philadelphia (University of Pennsylvania, 1755).

The South lagged behind the other two regions in both elementary schools and colleges. Virginia was the first Southern colony to attempt to start a college, but its plans were thwarted by the Indian massacre of 1622. In 1693 the first Southern college, William and Mary, was founded at Williamsburg, Virginia. Grammar schools did not exist in the South, and wealthy planters had to hire private tutors for their children. Sometimes a few neighboring families would band together and hire one tutor to instruct all their youngsters. Thomas Jefferson learned Latin and Greek at such an improvised elementary school. Women and blacks of both sexes seldom received any education at all, and most backwoods farmers could neither read nor write. At the end of the seventeenth century, only fifty-five percent of the white men in Virginia could sign their own names, whereas at least ninety percent of New England's men could demonstrate at least that much literacy. The South's lack of adequate schooling did seem advantageous to one man, though. In 1671 Governor Berkeley of Virginia thanked God that "there are no free schools nor printing in Virginia . . . for learning has brought disobedience, and heresy, and sects into the world, and printing has divulged them, and libels against the best government. God keep us from both!"

Historians are often tempted to picture the colonial period as one of unbroken progress. In the field of education, however, the facts belie this interpretation. Although there were more schools in the colonies in the eighteenth century than there were in the seventeenth, they had definitely become less effective. In fact, the national rate of illiteracy was on the rise in the years before the Revolution. Third and fourth generation Americans may have been better adapted than their parents to life in the wilderness, but fewer were able to read. Those who were in school were receiving an inferior education.

Although pre-Revolutionary schools were not very good, at least they were freer than their European counterparts. Most American colleges were founded by a particular religious denomination, but none were tightly controlled by any sect. Men of various denominations sat on the board of directors in each college and students of different faiths were admitted to every school.

Most universities were very traditional in the courses they offered. As in European schools, students learned Latin, Greek, Hebrew, rhetoric, and moral philosophy. Few courses prepared graduates for actual professional careers other than the ministry, and only twenty-five percent of all college graduates followed this career. For example, if a young man wanted to enter the field of law, he had to apprentice himself to an established lawyer and read law books on his own. Consequently, the highly specialized professional distinctions of England disappeared. Technical legal training was hardly necessary where the need existed only for general legal services. While American lawyers were less learned in the law than English professionals, practical legal knowledge was readily available to any literate layman.

The medical profession also became less specialized in America. Government regulation of doctors hardly existed, causing fine distinctions between medical occupations to break down. American doctors became general practitioners, and the absence of many trained doctors produced the need for a diffusion of practical medical knowledge among laymen. Of the 3500 doctors in America on the eve of the Revolution, only 200 held medical degrees, and these they had earned abroad.

SCIENTIFIC ADVANCES

A number of people in the colonial period reflected the growing interest in natural science and improved medical techniques which developed from the philosophy of the Enlightenment. Most of the outstanding scientists in colonial America were amateurs. Few of them were connected with universities, and many had not even attended college. Botany and zoology were two of the fields in which America's early scientists excelled. Perhaps the leading naturalist of the colonial period was Dr. Alexander Garden of South Carolina, for whom the gardenia is named. Garden was famous throughout Europe for his genius in classifying plants. Other well-known American botanists included John Bartram, who collected and catalogued plants from Florida to the Great Lakes, and Dr. John Mitchell of Virginia, who discovered twenty-two new classes of plants.

An outstanding contribution in the field of medicine was made in 1721 by the Puritan minister, Cotton Mather. It involved the technique of inoculation and was applied in the fight against smallpox, the most deadly disease of colonial times. Mather happened to read in an English medical journal that the people of Turkey used inoculation. This reminded him that his slave, Onesimus, had once told him that in Africa he was given "something of the smallpox" in order to "forever preserve him from it." A storm of controversy broke out in Boston when Mather began injecting live smallpox germs into his fellow citizens, but a lowered casualty rate in the next epidemic proved the value of this practice. Mather thus made one of America's greatest contributions to medical technique prior to the nineteenth century.

America's most prominent scientific genius during the colonial period, however, was Benjamin Franklin. Franklin was passionately devoted to science and convinced that the universe was governed by knowable laws. His intense curiosity about every aspect of his environment led him to many practical inventions: the Franklin stove, bifocal spectacles, the lightning rod, and the grocery store's long arm (a pole with a movable clamp for fetching objects from high shelves). His famous experiment with a kite and a metal key during a

Benjamin Franklin performing his famous lightning experiment with a key and a kite.

thunder and lightning storm gave the first definite proof that electricity was a force which coursed freely through nature. After Franklin's discovery, physicists attempting to explain any natural phenomenon had to take into account the role of electricity.

DEVELOPMENT OF THE ARTS

Libraries, literature, and newspapers

Some of the best writers of the colonial period were ministers, and religious literature composed the bulk of colonial reading matter. John Wise of Massachusetts wrote a rousing defense of Puritanism in his book, *The Churches' Quarrel Exposed* (1710). As one critic has remarked, "No other American author of the colonial time is the equal of John Wise in the union of great breadth of power and thought with great splendor of style." The energetic Cotton Mather, in addition to his treatise on witchcraft, authored a church history of New England. Jonathan Edwards, mentioned earlier for his role in the Great Awakening, was also a writer of some note. The leading historian of New England was Thomas Hutchinson, whose *History of the Colony of Massachusetts* is generally considered straightforward and scrupulously fair.

New England also had a number of fine poets, including Michael Wigglesworth, Anne Bradstreet, and Edward Taylor. Wigglesworth, who graduated from Harvard in 1651, is famous for the sincerity and deeply religious feeling of his poetry. It was written not for a leisured class of literary devotees, but as a device for teaching ordinary people. His most artistic poem was "God's Controversy with New England," written in 1662. This poem describes God's punishments in store for New England because of its failure to keep faith with him as a chosen people. Samuel Eliot Morison called Anne Bradstreet "the greatest American poetess before Emily Dickinson." Her first poems were highly imitative, but a second volume published after her death was more original and expressive of her personal feelings. Unlike Wigglesworth, her religious poetry was written not to instruct but to express her own emotions. The works of Edward Taylor, minister of the First Congregational Church of Westfield, only became known when they were published after his death. Taylor drew from his observations of normal community life, to write poems that were a series of meditations before administering or partaking of the Lord's Supper.

Benjamin Franklin was probably the most prolific of all the colonial writers. His *Poor Richard's Almanack*, a collection of pithy sayings, is still admired today, as is his autobiography. But even Franklin could not make a living as a writer. In fact, no American writer was able to be supported on literary earnings alone during this period.

Many towns established public libraries during the pre-Revolutionary era. As might be expected, most of the volumes dealt with religious subjects, but every collection also contained works on science, history, medicine, and farming. A few individuals were able to amass impressive private libraries at a time when books were so scarce and costly that most were owned by churches and schools. Cotton Mather owned 3000 books and William Byrd II of Virginia had 4000. Most educated people, however, seldom owned more than 100 volumes.

America's first successful newspaper, the *Boston Newsletter,* was started in 1704. By 1763, twenty-three newspapers were being printed in the colonies. Most articles concerned news from other colonies, England, and other European nations, rather than local affairs. The colonists already had a general idea of what was happening at home, but they were starved for information from the mother country. In 1729 Franklin took over the *Pennsylvania Gazette* and made some lively innovations, such as the inclusion of poems, literary essays, and cartoons. These ideas were later copied by other colonial newspapers.

Freedom of the press received a major boost in the famous Peter Zenger case. Zenger was tried in New York in 1733 for publishing articles which the governor of the colony claimed were libelous. He was finally acquitted on the grounds that the articles were true, even though they were highly critical of the colony's executive. This case set an important precedent for the publication of controversial articles, paving the way for freedom of the press and its protection by the First Amendment to the United States Constitution.

The visual arts

American painters, furniture makers, and architects were quite dependent on English models and styles. The English Georgian style was imitated by the architect Christopher Wren in church spires and the main building of William and Mary College. Other American architectural design was mainly the work of amateurs, such as Jefferson's plan for Monticello.

John Singleton Copley painted this famous portrait of Paul Revere around 1770.

Painting in colonial America focused on the portrait. One of the most famous painters of the period, John Singleton Copley, had a new, characteristically American approach: he showed his subjects working. When Copley did a portrait of the silversmith Paul Revere, he placed Revere at his workbench wearing workclothes. In England, a painter would have posed him in his Sunday best to give the impression that he was really a country squire. But in his portrait of Revere, Copley expressed an American pride in manual labor.

In Philadelphia, craftsmen turned out beautiful objects fashioned from brass, copper, and wood. Joseph Richardson produced some of the most expertly crafted silver pieces in the world. Furniture makers made delicate but sturdy Windsor chairs and cabinets in the Philadelphia Chippendale style. Like the prevailing architectural design, this type of furniture was borrowed directly from England.

As we have seen colonial America was fundamentally a hybrid culture. There were sharp regional differences, as well as important similarities which bound the colonies together. Although certain basic traditions clearly reflected the Old World heritage, other aspects of colonial life were quite unique, born of the experience of settling in a new land. In some ways, America was a mature culture well before the Revolution. It had its own political structures, religious movements, educational systems, and even booming cities. But in other ways, colonial America was very dependent on the countries of Europe, especially England. In the decades before the Revolution, many possible futures could have been predicted for the American experiment, but few of those visions would have included a violent break with the mother country.

Readings

GENERAL WORKS

Boorstin, D. J., *The Americans: The Colonial Experience.* New York: Random House, 1958.

Bridenbaugh, Carl, *Myths and Realities: Societies of the Colonial South.* New Orleans: Louisiana State University Press, 1952 (Paper: Atheneum, 1963).

Cremin, Lawrence A., *American Education: The Colonial Experience, 1607–1783.* New York: Harper & Row, 1970. (Paper)

Gipson, L. H., *The British Empire Before the American Revolution,* Vols. 1–11. New York: Knopf, 1936–1965.

Hofstadter, Richard, *America at 1750: A Social History.* New York: Alfred A. Knopf, 1971. (Paper)

Jones, H. M., *O Strange New World: American Culture—The Formative Years.* New York: Viking, 1964.

Mead, S. E., *The Lively Experiment: The Shaping of Christianity in America.* New York: Harper & Row, 1963.

Morison, S. E. (Ed.), *The Parkman Reader.* Boston: Little, Brown, 1955.

Parrington, V. L., *The Colonial Mind. Main Currents in American Thought,* Vol. 1. New York: Harcourt Brace Jovanovich, 1927.

Rossiter, Clinton, *Seedtime of the Republic: The Origin of the American Tradition of Political Liberty.* New York: Harcourt Brace Jovanovich, 1953.

Stearns, Raymond P., *Science in the British Colonies of America.* Illinois: University Illinois Press, 1970.

Ver Steeg, C. L., *The Formative Years: 1607–1763.* New York: Hill & Wang, 1964.

Wright, L. B., *The Cultural Life of the American Colonies: 1607–1763.* New York: Harper & Row, 1957.

SPECIAL STUDIES

Bridenbaugh, Carl, *Cities in the Wilderness: The First Century of Urban Life in America, 1625–1742,* New York: Putnam's, 1964.

Bridenbaugh, Carl, and Jessica Bridenbaugh, *Rebels and Gentlemen: Philadelphia in the Age of Franklin.* New York: Oxford University Press, 1965.

Degler, C. N., *Neither Black nor White: Slavery and Race Relations in Brazil and the United States.* New York: Macmillan Publishing Co., 1971. (Paper)

Hansen, M. L., *Atlantic Migration, 1607–1860: A History of the Continuing Settlement of America,* A. M. Schlesinger (Ed.). Cambridge, Mass.: Harvard University Press, 1940 (Paper: Harper & Row, 1964).

Heimert, Alan E., *Religion and the American Mind: From the Great Awakening to the Revolution.* Cambridge, MA: Harvard University Press, 1966.

Jordan, Winthrop D., *White Over Black.* Chapel Hill, N.C.: University of North Carolina Press, 1968 (Paper: Penguin, 1969).

Klein, Herbert S., *Slavery in the Americas: A Comparative Study of Virginia and Cuba.* Illinois: University of Chicago Press, 1967. (Paper)

Smith, A. E., *Colonists in Bondage: White Servitude and Convict Labor in America, 1607–1776.* Chapel Hill, N.C.: University of North Carolina Press, 1947.

Starkey, M. L., *The Devil in Massachusetts: A Modern Inquiry into the Salem Witch Trials.* New York: Knopf, 1949 (Paper: Doubleday, 1969).

Sydnor, C. S., *Gentlemen Freeholders: Political Practices in Washington's Virginia.* Chapel Hill, N.C.: University of North Carolina Press, 1952.

Wertenbaker, Thomas J., *The Old South.* New York: Scribner's, 1942.

Wood, Peter H., *Black Majority: Negroes in Colonial South Carolina from 1670—Through the Stono Rebellion.* New York: Alfred A. Knopf, 1974.

PRIMARY SOURCES

Bruchey, Stuart (Ed.), *The Colonial Merchant.* New York: Harcourt Brace Jovanovich, 1965.

Colden, Cadwallader, *History of the Five Indian Nations.* Ithaca, N.Y.: Cornell University Press, 1958.

Franklin, Benjamin, *Autobiography.* New York: Simon & Schuster, 1970.

Heimert, Alan E., & Miller, Perry (Eds.), *Great Awakening: Documents Illustrating the Crisis and its Consequences.* New York: Bobbs-Merrill Co., 1967. (Paper)

Riley, E. M. (Ed.), *The Journal of John Harrower: An Indentured Servant in the Colony of Virginia, 1773–1776.* Holt, Rinehart & Winston, 1964.

Sewall, Samuel, *Diary of Samuel Sewall.* New York: Putnam's, 1967.

BIOGRAPHIES

Crane, V. W., *Benjamin Franklin and a Rising People.* Boston: Little, Brown, 1954.

Ketcham, Ralph, *Benjamin Franklin.* New York: Simon & Schuster, 1965.

McLoughlin, William G. (Ed.), *Isaac Backus and the American Patriotic Tradition.* Boston: Little, Brown, 1967.

Marambaud, Pierre L., *William Byrd of Westover.* Virginia: University Press of Virginia, 1971.

Van Doren, C. C., *Benjamin Franklin.* New York: Viking, 1964.

Winslow, O. E., *Jonathan Edwards, 1703–1758: A Biography.* New York: Macmillan, 1940.

HISTORICAL NOVELS

Cooper, James F., *The Deerslayer.* New York: Macmillan, 1962.

Cooper, James F., *The Last of the Mohicans.* New York: Airmont, 1964.

Cooper, James F., *The Pathfinder.* New York: Airmont, 1964.

Cooper, James F., *The Pioneers.* New York: Airmont, 1964.

Johnston, Mary, *Audrey.* Boston: Houghton Mifflin, 1902.

Simms, William Gilmore, *The Yemassee.* Boston: Houghton Mifflin, 1961.

Opposite:
The Boston Massacre as engraved by Paul Revere.

4

Prelude to Independence

If we inquire into the business of a king, we shall find that in some countries they may have none; and after sauntering away their lives without pleasure to themselves or advantage to the nation, withdraw from the scene, and leave their successors to tread the same idle round. . . . In England a king hath little more to do than to make war and give away places; which, in plain terms, is to empoverish the nation and set it together by the ears. A pretty business indeed for a man to be allowed eight hundred thousand sterling a year for, and worshipped into the bargain! Of more worth is one honest man to society, and in the sight of God, than all the crowned ruffians that ever lived.

Thomas Paine, *Common Sense*, 1776

Between 1690 and 1776 Americans increasingly felt the need to decide for themselves how to relate to their New World environment and to each other. But the British government had too much at stake to give them this much self-determination. Although few people on either side of the Atlantic would have predicted a permanent break between Britain and her American possessions, the events that unfolded in these crucial years led logically and irrevocably toward such a break.

Eighteenth-Century Politics

By the middle of the eighteenth century all of the thirteen original colonies had been founded. Eight of them were royal colonies whose governments were tied closely to the British government. The five remaining colonies governed themselves, more or less. Maryland and Pennsylvania were proprietary colonies whose proprietors (or owners) appointed their governors. Pennsylvania's governor served also as the governor of Delaware. All three colonies had representative assemblies whose members were elected by the freemen.

Connecticut and Rhode Island were charter colonies with virtual independence in internal affairs. In these colonies the governors and members of the council and assembly were elected by the freemen.

THE GOVERNOR

In the eight royal colonies, the governors were direct representatives of the Crown. At first they enjoyed many of a king's privileges. But as the king's powers had been gradually limited by Parliament in the seventeenth century, so the royal governors' powers were increasingly curtailed by the colonial legislatures in the eighteenth century.

Every royal governor came to the New World with two documents from the king: his commission and his instructions. The commission was a public document that established the form of government the colony was to have: a Crown-appointed governor and council, and an elected assembly. The instructions were secret orders the governor was to follow for regulating trade, promoting religion, and sponsoring laws in his colony. The secrecy of these instructions put the royal governors in an awkward position. They were deeply involved in every aspect of colonial life and yet they could not disclose their instructions to the people.

The governors granted land and appointed judges, justices of the peace, and many other minor officials. They also served as commanders-in-chief of the colonial militias. But the British government gradually withdrew some of their powers of appointment and of land distribution. Their military powers were also diminished in the eighteenth century: first, when the colonial assemblies passed legislation restricting them and later when the colonial troops were outnumbered by royal troops led by British commanders based in the colonies.

THE GOVERNOR'S COUNCIL

In the royal colonies twelve men were usually appointed to act as the governor's council. These councilmen were supposedly chosen by the Board of Trade in England, but in practice the Board merely confirmed the governors' recommendations. Massachusetts was an exception. There, the council was elected by the assembly.

The governor's council had three basic functions: (1) It was the governor's chief advisory body. The governor could not summon the assembly, appoint judges, or issue paper money without the council's consent; (2) The council was the upper house of the legislature, equivalent to the House of Lords in Parliament. In this capacity, the council had the final say about how all financial legislation was worded and had an equal vote in the passing of all other laws; (3) The council acted as the highest court in each colony, much like the United States Supreme Court today. In other words, the governor's council had executive, legislative, and judicial functions.

By the first half of the eighteenth century, the council was beginning to lose its power. Authorities in England started to bypass the council and deal directly with the governor. Laws became so complex that the councilmen no longer had the time or training to serve effectively as a supreme court. And, most important, the lower houses of the colonial legislatures were slowly and steadily eroding the council's law-making powers.

THE ASSEMBLY

The lower house of a colonial legislature was called an assembly. Colonial assemblies modeled themselves after Parliament's House of Commons. They copied Commons' procedures and, like the Commons, believed their authority came from the people they represented.

Assemblymen were elected directly by the freemen of the colony. Freemen had to be white, male, at least twenty-one years old, and own a certain amount of land or cash. Each colony had its own requirements about the amount of land or cash a freeman had to own. But since land was relatively easy to acquire, the percentage of men eligible to vote in America was much larger than it was in England.

Even though colonial assemblies were more representative than Britain's House of Commons, few provided equal representation. There were two main reasons for this. First, the smaller, less populated seaboard counties usually had more representatives in their assembly than the larger, more populated interior counties. In South Carolina the interior counties had no representation at all. New England was the only exception. All New England towns had equal representation in their assemblies.

Second, most assemblymen came from the wealthy families in their colony. This was partly because certain colonies had stiffer property qualifications for officeholders than for voters. But it was also because eighteenth-century colonial society was firmly based on the principle of deference. People believed that men of merit (and merit was often associated with wealth and social position) ought to govern and use their talents for the benefit of all. They also believed that only a man of means would be able to resist bribes and had enough of a stake in the community to be a responsible legislator. It is not particularly surprising that the colonists thought this way. After all, they came to this country from Europe, where only the wealthy ever had power.

There was yet another reason the wealthy were consistently returned to power. They were more likely to be literate than the other colonists. One-quarter of all colonists could not read and one-fifth of those who could read did not speak English. Furthermore, in most colonies a man voted out loud in front of his fellow citizens. The less affluent often found it in their best interest to vote for a rich neighbor upon whom they depended for many small favors.

The question of authority

At first the authority of most colonial assemblies extended only to Indian relations, the militia, and the local courts. But by 1720 the assemblies had won the right to propose legislation and the sole right to initiate money bills. This second right was particularly important: it gave assemblymen the power of the purse. Unless they designated funds for the governor's salary, he would not be paid. Unless they voted funds for a military expedition or a road-building program, wars could not be fought and roads could not be constructed.

One View of Royal Authority

"You ask me, if we have not reason to fear we shall soon be reduced to a worse situation than that of the colonies of France, Spain, or Holland. I may safely affirm that we have not; that we have no reason to fear any evils from a submission to the authority of parliament, equal to what we must feel from its authority being disputed, from an uncertain rule of law and government. . . . What can be expected more, from any authority than when the unfitness of a measure is discovered, to make it void? When, upon the united representations and complaints of the American colonies, any acts have appeared to parliament to be unsalutary, have there not been repeated instances of the repeal of such acts? We cannot expect these instances should be carried so far as to be equivalent to a disavowal, or relinquishment of the right itself. . . ."

Alden T. Vanghan (Ed.),
Chronicles of the American Revolution,
published 1822

A Different View of Royal Authority

"Here then, let my countrymen, ROUSE yourselves, and behold the ruin hanging over their heads. If they ONCE admit, that Great-Britain *for the purpose of levying money on us only,* may lay duties upon her exportations to us, she then will have nothing to do, but to lay those duties on the articles which she prohibits us to manufacture—and the tragedy of American liberty is finished. We have been prohibited from procuring manufactures, in all cases, any where but from Great-Britain. . . . We have been prohibited, in some cases, from manufacturing for ourselves. . . . If Great-Britain can order us to come to her for necessaries we want, and can order us to pay what taxes she pleases before we take them away, or when we have them here, we are as abject slaves . . . ."

**John Dickinson,
Letters from a Farmer in Pennsylvania,
1767–1768**

Because they depended on the assemblies for their salaries, the governors often hesitated to veto the laws the assemblies passed. However, the authorities in England did find themselves at odds with the colonial assemblies on more than one occasion. This was largely because the English authorities looked upon the colonial assemblies as subordinate agencies of the Crown, with no real authority of their own—a view that conflicted seriously with the colonists'.

The assemblies' conflicts with the English authorities tended to be confusing since no one knew who was really in charge of colonial affairs. The king had certain claims over the colonies since most of them were *royal* colonies. But in 1714 a German monarch, George I of Hanover, came to the throne. He and his successor, George II, left the management of colonial affairs to their ministers, although all decisions required the consent of the Crown. For its part Parliament insisted that it had the right to control colonial affairs through the Cabinet, its advisors to the Crown. But the king frequently disputed their claims. Finally, the agency with the strongest actual control over colonial administration was the Board of Trade. By 1730 all colonies except Rhode Island and Connecticut (the charter colonies) had to submit their laws to the Board of Trade for review. If the Board recommended that a law be rejected (or "disallowed"), the Privy Council disallowed it. But the Board acted slowly and years sometimes went by before it reviewed a law.

In other words, the lines of authority and communication between England and the colonies were complex. If a colony wanted to object to an imperial measure, to whom did it object? To the king? The House of Commons? A particular Cabinet member? Or the Board of Trade? Colonial politicians never could answer these questions with any certainty.

The Wars For Empire

North America was frequently the arena in which the four imperial European powers (England, France, Spain, and The Netherlands) came to blows. In the sixteenth century France and Spain fought over Florida. Spain, weakened by the defeat of her Armada in 1588, barely managed to hold onto Florida. In 1670 Spain was forced to recognize British control of the Atlantic seaboard. In the seventeenth century England expelled the Dutch from New Amsterdam and, by the 1680s, eliminated Dutch competition for colonial trade. So by the end of the century Spain and Holland had been effectively eliminated from the contest for North America.

That left only England and France in the struggle to dominate North America. France held Canada and the Ohio and Mississippi valleys, and England occupied the Atlantic seaboard. French and English colonials constantly wrangled over fishing rights off of Maine, Newfoundland, and Nova Scotia. To add to these tensions, both sides made alliances with the Indians in the fur-rich areas in their territories. The French allied themselves with the Algonquin Indians and the Huron Indians in Canada, and the English made agreement with the Iroquois tribes in New York.

As the two powers competed with each other for domination in Europe, their wars constantly spilled over into other parts of the world, including North America.

THREE FRENCH AND ENGLISH WARS

Between 1689 and 1697 the first of a series of French–English conflicts spread to the New World. In Europe it was called the War of the League of Augsburg. In America it was called King William's War. The war was Britain's attempt, with Holland's help, to curb Louis XIV's power. Although the major campaigns took place in Europe, there were a number of frontier incidents along the New York–New England borders. The French took Schenectady, New York and a few villages in New England; New Englanders held Port Royal in Nova Scotia for a short time. Both sides had the help of their Indian allies. The situation was indecisive and the peace settlement that ended the war restored all captured territories to their original owners.

The second French–English war broke out five years later. In Europe it was called the War of the Spanish Succession because England, Holland, and Austria were trying to prevent the grandson of Louis XIV from "succeeding" to the throne of Spain. In America it was called Queen Anne's War, after the reigning English monarch. This time the Abenaki Indians, goaded on by their French allies, attacked Deerfield, Massachusetts and spilled a great deal of English blood. New Englanders marched north to recapture Port Royal in Nova Scotia. When the war ended in 1713, France surrendered Nova Scotia, Newfoundland, and Hudson's Bay to

English ships lay siege to the French fort at Louisbourg in Nova Scotia during King George's War.

Britain, and the powerful Iroquois Indians allied themselves more closely with England.

There were no wars for the next thirty years, so the two powers used the time to strengthen their positions in the New World. France built Fort Toulouse on the border of South Carolina and made a compact with Spain for mutual aid in case of attack. Both powers strengthened their fortifications around the Great Lakes and in upper New York.

The third French–English clash to spread to America lasted from 1744 to 1748. In Europe it was called the War of the Austrian Succession, and in America King George's War. Once again, tribes allied with the French crossed the St. Lawrence River and attacked English settlements. And once again, a force from New England marched north. This time the New Englanders seized Louisbourg on Cape Breton Island, a strategic French fortress that protected the mouth of the St. Lawrence. This was a serious blow to France. It seriously weakened French control of Canada and the American territories beyond the Appalachian Mountains. France regained the fortress in the Peace of Aix-la-Chapelle in 1748, but to do so had to surrender French conquests in the Austrian Netherlands. Now the French were so worried about their future power in America that they completely refortified Louisbourg and began building a line of forts along the Appalachian Mountains. The people of Massachusetts, Connecticut, Virginia, Pennsylvania, and New York were all looking hungrily toward the Ohio Valley, and France was determined to keep the English colonials out.

THE ALBANY CONGRESS

Many Europeans believed that a showdown between France and England was coming. In 1758 a French minister wrote:

> The King believes . . . that it is possessions in America that will in the future form the balance of power in Europe, and, that if the English invade that part of the world, as it appears they have the intention of doing, it will result that England will usurp the commerce

of the nations, and that she alone will remain rich in Europe.

In this long struggle, which nation would finally control North America? English colonials outnumbered French settlers more than twenty to one. In the English colonies along the Atlantic coast, towns, farms, and scattered industry flourished; while in the French colonies, concentrated around Quebec and Montreal on the St. Lawrence River, only a few soldier-settlers and fur trappers were scattered. Yet the French had certain advantages. Although outnumbered, they had a much larger and more carefully trained army. They were also backed by strong Indian allies, and had built a line of forts in the Ohio Valley to prevent the British from advancing into French territory.

Britain, not about to be outdone, began shoring up her position against the French. The first item of business was to improve relations with the Iroquois Confederacy. The confederacy had been complaining that New York fur traders were bypassing the Iroquois and dealing directly with other tribes under Iroquois control. They also complained that speculators from the English colonies had been invading Iroquois lands. The British, fearing that the Iroquois might desert England and join forces with France, decided to attend to these grievances.

In 1753 the Board of Trade in England ordered the colonists to meet with the Iroquois at Albany, New York. In June, 150 Iroquois leaders gathered at Albany where they were met by 23 delegates from New Hampshire, Massachusetts, Connecticut, Rhode Island, Pennsylvania, Maryland, and New York. After much pomp and ceremony, the Indians left with thirty wagonloads of guns, scarlet coats, axes, scissors, silver buttons, and other presents. Despite their gifts, however, the colonials never got a specific promise of Indian aid in the event of another war with France. The Albany Congress was off to a poor start.

Not only did the colonial representatives fail to obtain a promise from the Iroquois, but they also failed to establish an alliance among themselves. Pennsylvania's representative, Benjamin Franklin, had presented the colonial delegates with a plan of union calling for a "general government . . . under which the government of each colony may retain its present constitution." Each colony in the federation would send delegates to a grand council that would handle Indian affairs, dispose of lands in the Ohio Valley, govern frontier territories beyond the boundaries of the present colonies, and levy taxes for an intercolonial army.

The delegates to the Albany Congress took Franklin's plan back to their colonial assemblies, and every single assembly rejected it. None of the colonies were willing to hand over to a federation the right to levy taxes. And the colonies that were competing with each other over unclaimed land in the Ohio Valley were not at all pleased with the idea of federation.

"Everyone cries, a union is necessary," Franklin wrote to a friend, "but when they come to the manner and form of the union, their weak noodles are perfectly distracted." In England, Franklin added, the proposal was "judged to have too much of the *democratic.*" Britain

Benjamin Franklin's rendition of his proposal to the Albany Congress that the colonies either unite together or die.

looked with suspicion on any measure that might unify the colonies and threaten its own domination.

The first colonial attempt to join forces had come to nothing.

THE FRENCH AND INDIAN WAR

The Ohio Valley was a bone of contention between the British and French as well as among the colonies. But it was the colonists' desire for more land to expand into that sparked the next French–English confrontation in America.

In 1748 the Loyal Land Company, a group of land speculators from Virginia, obtained a grant of 800,000 acres in the area. In 1749, the Ohio Company, another Virginia corporation, obtained a grant of 200,000 acres. Companies in Pennsylvania and Connecticut also had claims to the unsettled territory. When an Ohio Company fur trader named George Crohgan set up a post at Pickawillany in Ohio, the French regarded it as an invasion of their territory. In June 1752, a French force attacked the post, wiping it out and capturing five English colonials.

Assuming he had rid the Ohio Valley of the British, the new French governor of Canada, the Marquis Duquesne, was very pleased. The following year, to make certain the British stayed out, the Marquis constructed a line of forts in western Pennsylvania: Fort Presque Isle (present-day Erie), Fort Le Boeuf (Waterford), and Fort Venango (Franklin).

The new Lieutenant Governor of Virginia, Robert Dinwiddie, was not so pleased, however. He had instructions to protect the interests of the Ohio Company, and he also happened to own a few shares in the enterprise. Dinwiddie sent a twenty-one-year-old Virginia surveyor named George Washington to inform the French that they were trespassing on property claimed by Virginia. Washington and six other men arrived at Fort Le Boeuf on December 11, 1753. They were treated with perfect French hospitality—and then rebuffed. As Washington later interpreted the situation, the French announced "it was their absolute design to take possession of the Ohio, and by G—— they would do it." In fact, the French had coolly announced their intention of building yet another fort in the Ohio Valley, at the point where the Monongahela and Allegheny rivers join to form the Ohio (present-day Pittsburgh).

Dinwiddie, determined to beat the French to this strategic site, sent a small work force to build a fort there. Then, in the spring of 1754, he sent Washington and two small companies of soldiers out to protect the work force. But it was too late: the French had already driven the Virginians out and had begun to erect their own fort (which they named Duquesne).

The war begins

Washington, full of enthusiasm but completely inexperienced in military strategy, was leading his men through the mountains southeast of Pittsburgh when he heard that the Virginians had been driven out. On May 28, 1754 he attacked a small group of French scouts, killing ten and taking twenty-one prisoners. Then, realizing that he was outnumbered, Washington retreated. He set up a camp at Great Meadows (near present-day Uniontown, Pennsylvania) which he aptly named Fort Necessity. A few weeks later, 500 French soldiers and 400 Indians attacked the fort. After nine hours of battle, Washington and his men surrendered. The French let them go after tricking Washington (who could not read French) into signing a document in which he "confessed" that he had "assassinated" the leader of the French scouts on May 28.

This minor event had far-reaching consequences. It sparked a conflict known in Europe as the Seven Years' War and in America as the French and Indian War.

Early French victories

Governor Dinwiddie appealed to England for help. And, even though she was still officially

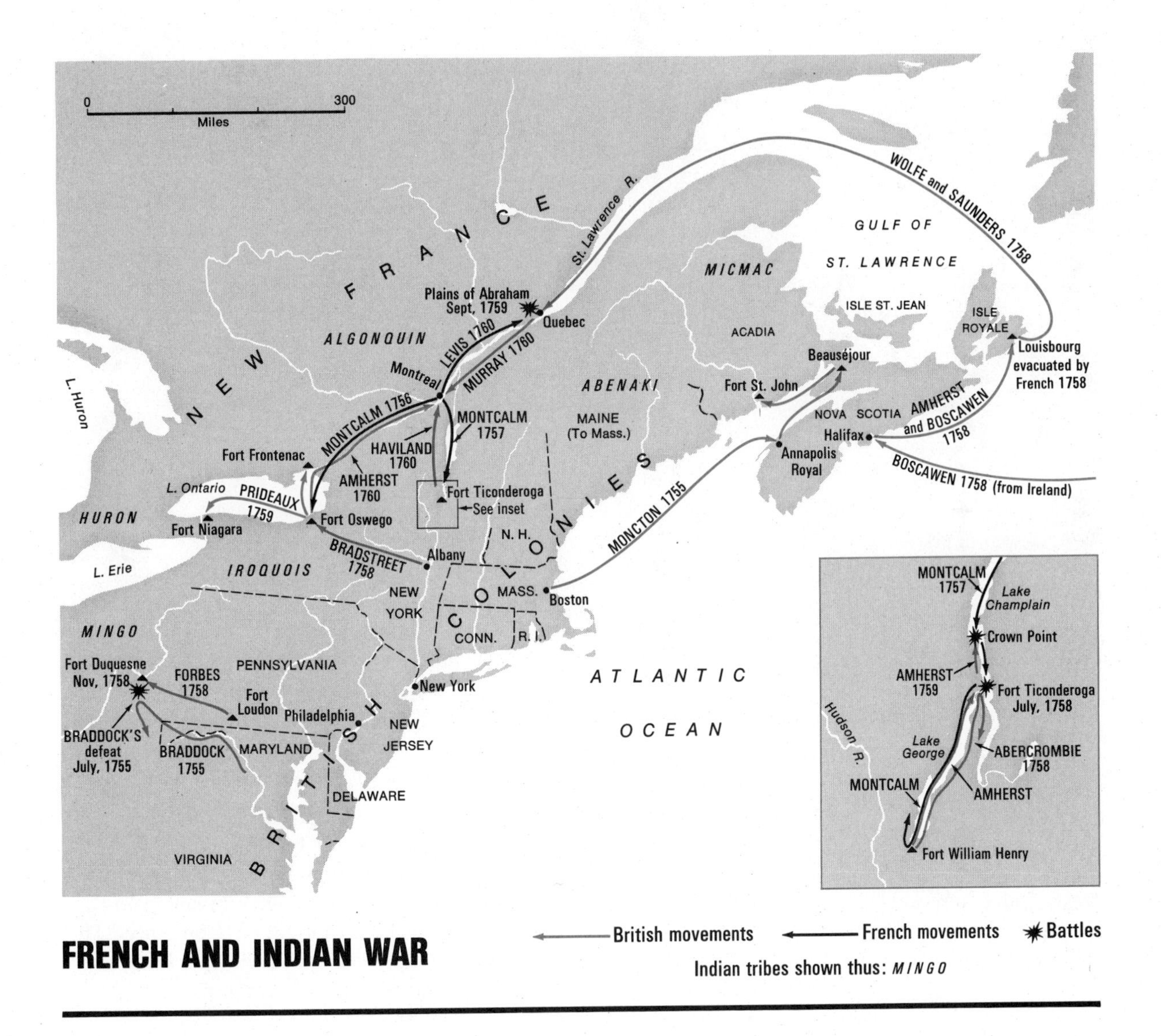

FRENCH AND INDIAN WAR

at peace with France, England sent General Edward Braddock and two regiments of regulars to the New World.

When he arrived in Virginia Braddock expected to swell his ranks with American volunteers and Indian allies. But he was sharply disappointed: only 8 Indians and 1200 colonials were willing to march with him into the Ohio Valley. Furthermore, New York, Pennsylvania, and Virginia voted only paltry sums of money to finance the venture. When Braddock set off into the wilderness he was understandably disgruntled.

As the English troops forded a stream near Fort Duquesne, the French, though greatly outnumbered, attacked. The young English officer in charge ordered a retreat, but the retreating first wave of English soldiers collided with a second wave that was rushing forward to aid them. In the resulting melee, Englishmen fired

An English battle plan for the capture of Fort William Henry on Lake George.

on Englishmen, while the French and their Indian allies picked off their victims one by one. George Washington had two horses shot out from under him and Braddock lost five mounts. By the end of the disastrous skirmish, Braddock had lost 976 men and was himself fatally wounded.

Following Braddock's defeat Britain offered to accept the Allegheny Mountains as the permanent boundary between British and French colonial possessions if France gave Britain control of Nova Scotia. France refused. Britain declared war and immediately captured Fort Beausejour in the strategic Bay of Fundy, between New Brunswick and Nova Scotia.

The first three years went badly for the English. The French were more familiar with the wilderness west of the mountains, they had more and stronger Indian allies, and they were able to make more efficient war preparations. Furthermore, the colonists did not rush to help the British war effort. New England was reluctant because she thought Virginia was exaggerating the danger of a French invasion to further the interests of the Ohio Company. The only colony that was badly hit by French attacks was Pennsylvania, and the pacifist Quakers who were still in control there opposed any military venture whatsoever.

Meanwhile, the Indians were so impressed with the French victory over Braddock that every tribe north of the Ohio River, except for those in the Iroquois Confederacy, transferred its loyalty to New France. As the war intensified the British were repelled in attempts to capture Fort Niagara and Crown Point on Lake Champlain. In 1756 the French Commander, the Marquis de Montcalm, captured Fort Oswego on Lake Ontario as well as nearby Fort Bull and in 1757 he took Fort William Henry on

Lake George. The war was going so badly for Britain that the Earl of Chesterfield felt moved to write: "The French are masters to do what they please in America. We are no longer a nation. I never yet saw so dreadful a project."

William Pitt

The tide of events was turned when William Pitt, a military and political genius, took control of the English war effort. Pitt came to power in 1758, declaring: "I believe that I can save this nation and that no one else can."

Pitt spared no expense. First he sent the British navy to blockade the coast of France. Then he sent numerous English regiments and adequate supplies to America, and promised to pay the colonies whatever it cost to fight the French. Pitt had no patience with mediocre and incompetent officers no matter how many years they had served the Crown. He sent new, younger commanding officers to lead the English and colonial forces.

Pitt's new armies soon gained the upper hand. In July 1758, Brigadier General James Wolfe and Major General Jeffrey Amherst took the fortress at Louisbourg. This ended once and for all French control of the Atlantic fishing grounds and the mouth of the St. Lawrence. The victory inspired great bonfire celebrations in London, Philadelphia, Boston, and New York. Fort Frontenac, at the other end of the St. Lawrence, fell a month later. Soon after, the French gave up Fort Duquesne, which the British renamed Fort Pitt.

In the fall of 1759 James Wolfe, now considered the most brilliant of all English generals, captured Quebec. Quebec was protected by a high rock cliff facing the river and was generally considered to be completely safe from attack. But Wolfe managed to find an undefended route up the stone precipice. One night he put his men on boats and floated them silently to the base of the path. At dawn the French saw 5000 British redcoats lined up for battle on the Plains of Abraham beside their fort. Both Wolfe and the Marquis de Montcalm died in the ensuing struggle, but the English won the day. In 1760 Montreal fell to the English. The Seven

The capture of the French city of Quebec by the English in 1759.

Years' War would be fought for three more years in Europe, India, and the Caribbean, but in America it had come to an end.

Effects of the war

In 1763 the Treaty of Paris, which ended the conflict, radically reshaped the map of America. Britain received all lands north of the Great Lakes (Canada) and all lands east of the Mississippi River, including Florida. Spain had fought on France's side and had lost Florida to the British during the war. As a reward for her help, France gave Spain all lands west of the Mississippi. Of its once vast holdings in America, France retained only two islands in the Caribbean, Guadeloupe and Martinique, and two tiny islands in the St. Lawrence, as well as the fishing rights off Newfoundland.

In the previous American wars colonial forces had fought with little English help. But British money and British soldiers were responsible for victory in the French and Indian War. The colonial assemblies had contributed small amounts to the effort, but the English repaid most of this money. Colonial soldiers had fought poorly compared with trained English troops. One English officer had described the Americans as "broken innkeepers, horse jockeys and Indian traders."

The English victory was so impressive that the colonials felt a sudden surge of pride in belonging to the British Empire. Some Englishmen feared that the Americans might turn their thoughts to independence now that the French had been driven out of Canada, but Benjamin Franklin expressed the view of many colonials when he remarked that a union among the colonies "is not merely improbable, it is impossible." Franklin then added: "When I say such a union is impossible, I mean without the most grievous tyranny and oppression."

Britain's New Empire

Victory proved to be an expensive prize. England's financial burden increased with the size of her American possessions. In fact, her possessions in North America cost five times more to administer after the war than they had before.

Victory brought new administrative problems, too. The imperial machinery for governing the thirteen colonies could no longer cope with the demands of an expanding population. Conflicting claims to the Ohio Valley had to be settled now that the territory was secured, and Canada and Florida had to be given some form of government.

In addition, English politics had become so complex that the government was almost completely unable to deal with these new problems. George III had come to the throne in 1760 with the idea of increasing the powers of the monarchy. Since he needed help in this effort, he campaigned actively in British elections for men who agreed with his ideas. Those of his candidates who were elected to Parliament were known as the king's friends. To complicate matters there were three important Whig factions, each with differing outlooks, but all opposed to increasing the power of the Crown. One faction was led by George Grenville, the second by William Pitt, and the third called itself the Rockingham Whigs. As these three groups rose and fell from power in the House of Commons between 1763 and 1770, British policy toward the American colonies went through many changes.

THE PROCLAMATION OF 1763

British relations with the Indians, always tense, deteriorated seriously after the war. Most of the tribes had allied themselves with the French,

NORTH AMERICA • 1713

NORTH AMERICA • 1763

hoping that a French victory would stop the westward migration of English colonists. After the last English victories in the war, an Ottawa chief named Pontiac made a desperate attempt to stem English expansion. In the summer of 1763 the Ottawas and their allies attacked the line of English forts and trading posts around the Great Lakes and along the Appalachian Mountains.

Pontiac's Rebellion failed, but the British were anxious to avoid stirring the Indians up any further. Therefore, they issued the Proclamation of 1763, prohibiting settlers from crossing the Appalachians or purchasing Indian lands. No white people, whether settlers, land speculators, or fur traders, were to be admitted to the new lands in the West. Colonists who had been planning to migrate west were advised to go either to Quebec or to Florida. These two new colonies were to be given a representative government similar to that in the thirteen original colonies.

The Proclamation enraged the colonists. Some had already migrated to Kentucky. Dozens of land development companies had plans to develop the Ohio Valley. George Washington, for one, announced that he had no intention of conforming to the Proclamation, saying, "Any person . . . who neglects the present opportunity of hunting out good lands, and in some measure marking and distinguishing them for his own (in order to keep others from settling them), will never regain it." Washington promptly sent an agent to protect his claims.

The Proclamation was meant to be a temporary measure, but the British continued to enforce it year after year. Trying to keep settlers out of the Ohio Valley was the easiest way to avoid confrontations with the Indians. But the colonists chafed under the restrictions. The Virginians, in particular, were badly in need of new farmlands. Tobacco farming had depleted their soil, crops were smaller, and erosion was eating away the topsoil.

Opposition became so fierce that in 1768 the British began revising the restrictions bit by bit. First they made a treaty with the Cherokees that extended the western boundary of Virginia. Then they made a treaty with the Creeks that enlarged the territory of South Carolina and Georgia. A third British treaty, with the Iroquois, added land to New York.

But these small gains did not appease the colonists' hunger for more land. In 1769 Daniel Boone defied the Proclamation and began exploring the land north of the Ohio River. In 1775 he led the first group of settlers into the Midwest.

The British had intended the Proclamation not only to stop Indian uprisings but also to keep the colonists inside the area controlled by the British government. They feared that once the colonists slipped beyond the Appalachians, it would be impossible to govern them.

THE CURRENCY AND SUGAR ACTS

Britain's next move was to extract more money from the colonies. Because of the French and Indian War British taxpayers were paying as much as one-fifth of their income to the government. Now officials estimated that 10,000 British troops would have to be permanently stationed in America to protect the colonies from Indian raids. The British public resented paying for these troops and insisted that the Americans assume a major part of the burden.

When George Grenville became Britain's chancellor of the exchequer in April 1763, he persuaded Parliament to pass several pieces of legislation to deal with these problems. Already angered by restrictions against settling the Ohio Valley, the colonists responded vocally at first and then with physical violence.

In April 1764 Grenville persuaded Parliament to pass the Currency Act which, together with a similar act of 1751, forbade all colonies from issuing paper money as legal tender. This meant that creditors no longer had to accept paper money in payment of debts. English businessmen had become increasingly uneasy over American paper money. As Southern lands were worn out by tobacco farming, producing smaller and smaller crops, Virginia plantation owners refused to reduce their standard of living. As a consequence, they ran up huge debts with British merchants and ship owners. Jefferson once remarked that these debts "had become hereditary from father to son, for many generations, so that the planters were a species of property annexed to certain mercantile houses in London." Since American paper money was usually worth less than its face value, English merchants wanted to be paid in gold or silver, not in American paper currency.

The Currency Act imposed a real hardship on the American economy as a whole. It became more expensive not only to repay English debts, but to engage in any trade at all. The colonies had little gold and silver of their own and it was against the law to export bullion from England into the colonies. Forbidden to issue paper money as legal tender, and deprived of hard cash, the colonists found it increasingly difficult to conduct business.

At the same time that it passed the Currency Act, Parliament also passed the Sugar Act, imposing import duties on certain commodities coming into the colonies. The Sugar Act infuriated the colonists even more than the Currency Act. Previous British duties and taxes had been designed to regulate trade within the empire and to keep profits from trickling into foreign pockets. Customs regulations had favored colonists who traded with England and penalized those who dealt with foreign countries. Grenville's new duties, however, were quite a different matter: they were designed specifically to raise revenue for the British government.

In 1733 the British government had imposed a duty on molasses imported from French islands in the Caribbean, but colonial ship owners had usually been able to bribe customs officials and avoid paying the duty. Grenville recognized that the old duty had been too high, so he cut it in half. And then, to make sure the new law would produce the needed revenues, he added sugar, indigo, coffee, wine, and woven cloth to the foreign molasses. He also made it more difficult to engage in smuggling: ship owners were required to fill out lengthy documents whenever they sailed into or out of an American port. As further discouragement smugglers could be tried by an admiralty court in Nova Scotia where a Crown-appointed judge alone heard the case, rather than in a common law court where juries of fellow colonists would inevitably treat offenders leniently. Furthermore, defendants would be presumed guilty until proven innocent—the exact opposite of traditional English legal practice.

THE STAMP AND QUARTERING ACTS

The colonists, badly shaken by the indirect taxation of the Sugar Act, rebelled openly when Parliament tried to impose direct taxation the very next year. In February 1765, Grenville asked Parliament to levy a stamp tax requiring colonists to pay a tax every time they registered a legal document (such as wills and deeds to property). The stamp tax would also apply to newspapers, pamphlets, almanacs, and even to

"View of the Year 1765," Paul Revere's comment on the Stamp Act. ▼

playing cards and sets of dice. Again, tax dodgers would be tried by a royal judge in an admiralty court.

The Stamp Act became law on March 22, 1765 and was due to go into effect the following November. A few days later Parliament passed the Quartering Act requiring colonial cities to provide royal troops with living accommodations in public inns, alehouses, empty buildings, or barns and to furnish them with candles, firewood, blankets, salt, and liquor.

The colonial response

Grenville's acts had an immediate impact on the colonies. The Currency Act made it difficult to do business. The Sugar Act, with its strict provisions for collecting molasses duties, threatened to destroy New England's rum distillers. English sugar-producing islands could not provide them with enough molasses, and molasses from the French Islands was terribly expensive because of the added duties. But the Stamp Act was the worst blow of all. As far as the colonists were concerned it not only deprived them of their money, it deprived them of their liberties as well.

The colonial response was swift and completely unexpected in England. Those most affected were the colonies' articulate groups, the lawyers, clergy, and merchants. Protest meetings, speeches, and pamphlets abounded. In New York, Boston, and other cities, groups calling themselves Sons of Liberty formed to resist the Stamp Act "to the last extremity." Mainly made up of small businessmen, artisans, and laborers, the Sons of Liberty acted at first in secret. But soon they were demonstrating in open protest. In 1765 violent eruptions were frequent: stamp collectors were bullied into resigning and all public officials who had anything to do with the stamps were harassed. Professionals and businessmen who seemed inclined to go along with the law were also intimidated. In Massachusetts the governor's house was overrun and many valuable items destroyed. Later the Sons of Liberty organized more disciplined actions such as writing letters to the papers.

Most colonists believed that the Stamp Act violated their rights, as English citizens, to be taxed only by their elected representatives. Clearly, the Stamp Act raised the question of how the colonial assemblies were related to Parliament. The colonists probably would not have welcomed any plan of taxation. But they particularly disliked the Stamp Act because they had been given no voice in its passage into law.

The right to control taxation had been one of the chief issues between Parliament and the monarchy in the seventeenth century. Parliament knew that whoever controlled the purse strings controlled the country, and it had been determined to have that power for itself. Parliament won its fight when William III signed the Bill of Rights after the Glorious Revolution of 1688. In securing the power of taxation to Parliament, the Bill of Rights embodied John Locke's theory that only the people's chosen representatives had the right to dispose of the people's property, whether that property was land or money. This principle of no taxation without representation was the cornerstone of English liberty.

The colonists assumed that this principle extended to them, at least in legislation providing revenue for the needs of the individual colonies. Parliament, however, thought otherwise. It was jealous of the powers it had finally established in the Glorious Revolution, and it was not prepared to admit that a colonial legislature had as much power to legislate for its own people as Parliament had to legislate for England. The colonial legislatures existed only by the generosity of the mother country. They had no real authority unless delegated by Parliament.

Grenville tried to pacify the colonists. He agreed that they should be taxed only by their own representatives and maintained that every member of Parliament *was* such a representative. Even though they did not actually elect any members to Parliament, the colonists had

The Supremacy of Parliament from the Declaratory Act

"Be it declared . . . . That the said colonies and plantations in *America* have been, are, and of right ought to be, subordinate unto, and dependent upon the imperial crown and parliament of *Great Britain;* and that the King's majesty, by and with the advice and consent of the lords spiritual and temporal, and commons of *Great Britain,* in parliament assembled, had, hath, and of right ought to have, full power and authority to make laws and statutes of sufficient force and validity to bind the colonies and people of *America,* subjects of the crown of *Great Britain,* in all cases whatsoever. . . ."

Declaratory Act,
1766

Samuel Adams Questions Parliament's Right to Legislate for the Colonies

"It is an essential, unalterable right in nature, engrafted into the British constitution, as a fundamental law, and ever held sacred and irrevocable by the subjects within the realm, that what a man has honestly acquired is absolutely his own, which he may freely give, but cannot be taken from him without his consent; that the American subjects may, therefore, exclusive of any consideration of charter rights, with a decent firmness, adapted to the character of free men and subjects, assert this natural and constitutional right.

It is, moreover, their humble opinion, which they express with the greatest deference to the wisdom of the Parliament, that the Acts made there, imposing duties on the people of this province, with the sole and express purpose of raising a revenue, are infringements of their natural and constitutional rights; because, as they are not represented in the British Parliament, his Majesty's commons in Britain, by those Acts, grant their property without their consent."

**Works of Samuel Adams,
1768**

virtual representation. After all, every member of Parliament represented the whole empire, not merely the district from which he was elected. Grenville's logic was not acceptable to the colonists. Their own assemblymen had to live in the colonial district they represented and they did not believe that the members of Parliament in England could represent them. They also knew that, even if they could elect members to Parliament, their representatives would be greatly outnumbered by the English members. In addition, the colonists were painfully aware that admiralty courts were being used to deny them the traditional English right to trial by jury.

The Stamp Act Congress

"One single act of Parliament set the people a'thinking in six months more than they had done in their whole lives before," wrote James

Otis, the leader of the Massachusetts assembly. Suddenly colonists everywhere were questioning British policies in a way that probably would not have occurred to them before the Stamp Act crisis. The assemblies of New York and Virginia sent petitions to England objecting to the Sugar Act. By the time the Stamp Act was passed, every colonial assembly was hotly debating what action it should take.

In June 1765 Massachusetts called for the first intercolonial assembly ever to be summoned by the colonists themselves. This assembly, the Stamp Act Congress, met in New York City the following October. Nine colonies were represented. The only reason Virginia, Georgia, and North Carolina were not represented was that their royal governors had strictly forbidden it.

After going through the formality of avowing "all due subordination" to Parliament, the representatives set about drafting a joint statement. They resolved "that the people in these colonies are not and from their local circumstances cannot be, represented in the House of Commons in Great Britain; that the only representatives of the people of these colonies are persons chosen by themselves, and that no taxes ever have been, or can be constitutionally imposed on them, but by their respective legislatures." They then petitioned the king and Parliament to repeal the Sugar and Stamp acts and to abolish the admiralty courts.

Months before, the colonies had been so suspicious of each other that they had been unable to cooperate in even the smallest venture. Now, however, there was a new spirit of unity in America. Merchants in every colony agreed to stop importing British goods, hoping that a total embargo would throw England into a depression. The boycott never really extended farther south than Philadelphia, but it was an important first step toward economic cooperation. A South Carolina representative to the Stamp Act Congress sounded a new note when he declared that "there ought to be no New England man, no New Yorker known on this continent, but all of us Americans."

The Stamp Act went into force in November, but colonial mobs so thoroughly intimidated the royal officials that no one tried to sell a single stamp. In fact, not one stamp was ever issued in America. Hundreds of merchants in every port suspended business and when they opened their shops again in late December, they ignored the Stamp Act with a unanimity never before witnessed in America. To a large extent this was the work of the Sons of Liberty who had stepped up their activities and had learned to focus them where they would have the greatest effect.

Repeal of the Stamp Act

By July 1765 the king had lost confidence in Grenville and had asked the Rockingham Whigs to form a new government. By August 1765, news of the American reaction had reached Britain. The new government was besieged by merchants' petitions calling for repeal of the Stamp Act. The king supported repeal to back the Rockingham faction and prevent the return of Grenville, whom he disliked. Pitt also supported repeal, even going so far as to say: "I rejoice that America has resisted."

In March 1766, before it officially received the petition of the Stamp Act Congress, Parliament repealed both the Stamp and the Sugar acts. Only a onepenny duty remained, on sugar. When the news reached the colonies, there was much rejoicing—even though the Americans learned that on the same day the Stamp Act was repealed a Declaratory Act had been passed. In this act Parliament clearly asserted its right to "make laws and statutes of sufficient force and validity to bind the colonies and people of America . . . in all cases whatsoever." Parliament had stated its supreme control over the empire in the clearest possible terms. And the colonists waited to see whether the British government would try to enforce such a position.

"The Repeal, or the Funeral Procession, of Miss Americ-Stamp," an English cartoon published in 1766.

THE TOWNSHEND ACTS

American political thinkers had objected to the Stamp Act on the grounds that it was a *direct* tax—taxes collected on items at the time they were sold in America. Benjamin Franklin went so far as to inform Parliament that the colonists objected only to direct taxes and not to indirect taxes—taxes collected at the ports before the goods entered the country. Although this sounded like an exercise in theory, the members of Parliament finally persuaded themselves that the easiest way for them to get money from the colonies would be to levy a new series of indirect taxes.

The duties were proposed in June 1767 by Charles Townshend, the new chancellor of the exchequer and a man of so frivolous a reputation that the public nicknamed him "Champagne Charlie." The Townshend Acts taxed glass, lead, paints, paper, and tea—all products that, under the navigation acts, Americans could import only from England. The duties had to be paid in gold and silver, and they were to be used to pay the salaries of royal officials.

Even more upsetting than the new duties was the establishment of a Board of Customs Commissioners, with headquarters in Boston. These officials could use the hated writs of assistance (general search warrants) to search for smuggled goods. New admiralty courts were established in four major American ports. And the salaries of the new customs commissioners were to be paid out of fines collected from shippers convicted in the admiralty courts. This last provision led quickly and inevitably to corruption. In addition, officials were to receive one-third of the total value of every ship and cargo caught violating any British mercantile law. The final blow came when Parliament suspended the New York assembly for refusing to obey the Quartering Act, a move which seemed a direct attack on colonial self-government.

Franklin had convinced the members of Parliament that Americans objected only to direct taxes. But the truth of the matter was that Americans did not want any kind of new taxes. So now the colonists had to invent a distinction between the supposedly acceptable indirect taxes and the unacceptable Townshend duties. John Dickinson, a lawyer who wrote a series of *Letters from a Farmer in Pennsylvania,* came up with one of the most widely-accepted arguments. He maintained that it was legal for Parliament to use indirect taxation to regulate trade (as in the navigation acts), but not to raise revenue (which was the purpose of the Townshend Acts).

Demonstrations against the Townshend duties were peaceful since organizers did not want to alienate moderates and conservatives from the effort to repeal the acts. Merchants throughout the colonies worked out an effective boycott of the British goods listed in the acts. People made their own clothes, and paper and paint were manufactured in the colonies. The boycott did not affect England right away, but the slowdown in trade with her most important possession gradually had its influence on Britain's parliamentary leadership.

From Discord to Disunion

England was again surprised by America's reaction to the Townshend Acts. Even many Americans were amazed by the growing unity in resisting British revenue measures. Throughout the French and Indian War the colonies had continued to compete with each other over rival territorial claims. The only connection they had been willing to admit was that they were all subjects of the same king. But the Townshend duties struck many people as another in a series of British attempts to interfere with American self-government, and Americans began to think of cooperative efforts to bring about their repeal. They knew that individually they could do little to resist Parliament, but that united they posed a considerable threat.

At the time of the Stamp Act crisis a small group of people in each of the colonies had begun to take a stand against British policy. They were the first to sense that the Stamp Act had political as well as economic implications for America's future. The activities of this small patriot group led to widespread organized resistance and eventually to the Revolution. Ultimately, they were able to win the support of one-third to two-fifths of the moderate and conservative colonists, first in their demand for redress of grievances and finally for complete independence. In a single decade the patriots engineered one of the greatest shifts of public opinion in world history, turning the colonies from loyalty to the mother country to disloyalty. Although the majority of Americans probably never supported the break, a large percentage did and these included many of the economic, social, and political leaders of colonial America.

In New England the battle against Parliament was led by James Otis, Samuel Adams, and John Adams. These three were supported behind the scenes by many merchants, and even some clergy of the Congregational Church. Otis was a lawyer and a flamboyant, energetic speaker, whose effectiveness was diminished by lapses into emotional illness. Samuel and John Adams were cousins. At first, Samuel had the greatest influence on events. He whipped the public into a fury against the mother country by leaping on every British insult and mistake, and distorting, or to use his own word, "improving," it. "We cannot make events," Sam Adams once remarked, "our business is wisely to improve them." He was also the greatest force behind the formation of the Sons of Liberty. John Adams was much more sober, but in his quiet, dignified way he helped step up the growing hostility against Parliament.

There were also important patriot leaders in the South. In Virginia the fiery Patrick Henry and the wealthy planter Richard Henry Lee were outspoken in their attacks on British policy. In 1767 Thomas Jefferson was still a young law student. But his training in political philosophy and his interest in Locke's arguments about people's natural rights were preparing him to emerge very soon as one of the most articulate advocates of American independence. In South Carolina the formidable Christopher Gadsden worked tirelessly for the patriot cause.

TROUBLE IN MASSACHUSETTS

In 1768 the Massachusetts assembly sent a circular letter written by Samuel Adams to the other colonial legislatures. The circular letter complained about the Townshend duties and asserted Americans' rights as British subjects to have taxes levied by their elected representatives. Meanwhile intelligent people all over America were debating the question of how much power Parliament should have over the colonies.

Back in England Lord North, the new chancellor of the exchequer and a favorite of the king, could scarcely be made to understand that a problem existed. The debate over colonial rights was crucial and Lord North should have handled it with tact and diplomacy, but he treated it as mere insubordination. The secretary of state, Lord Hillsborough, ordered the Massachusetts assembly to withdraw its circular letter immediately. Then, while the king's other advisors were considering a "kind and lenient" circular letter of their own, Hillsborough took matters into his own hands. He instructed the royal governors to dissolve their assemblies if the dangerous document from Massachusetts was not rejected.

The Massachusetts assembly voted ninety-two to seventeen against withdrawing the letter. Governor Bernard dissolved the assembly as ordered. In September 1768, two regiments of royal troops were billeted in Boston in case of violence against British officials.

An unofficial Massachusetts convention met a few days later. Sam Adams tried to rouse it to take strong action, but the delegates refused. Instead, they issued a statement resolving that "as Englishmen they have an aversion to an unnecessary standing army, which they look upon as dangerous to their civil liberty." For the time being, the British troops were received without trouble.

Violence did finally break out—a year and a half later. On March 5, 1770, a band of unemployed laborers attacked a British sentry at the Boston customhouse. The officer on duty tried to reason with the mob, but it continued to pelt the soldiers with oyster shells and snowballs. In the confusion, someone shouted, "Fire!" The British fired. Five of the rioters were killed and six were wounded. The first man killed was Crispus Attucks, an unemployed black seaman. Sam Adams and James Otis blew this street brawl up into a "massacre" for propaganda purposes, but John Adams defended the British soldiers against a murder indictment and all but two were acquitted.

By one of those strange coincidences of history, on the day of the Boston Massacre, Parliament repealed every one of the Townshend duties except the one on tea. The colonial boycott of British goods had had its effect. Lord North, who was now chief minister, thought it was important to keep the tea tax, if only to prove that Parliament *did* have the right to tax the colonies. Although more than half of the members of Parliament believed the tea duty would only stir up more trouble, they let North have his way.

A PERIOD OF PEACE

The Sons of Liberty tried, unsuccessfully, to hold out for a continued embargo of all English goods until the tea tax was withdrawn. But most Americans were so pleased by the repeal of the other duties that colonial merchants soon began trading with England again. The Townshend Acts had benefited no one: Americans had had to do without many goods, British manufacturers had watched with dismay as American industries began to make the goods under embargo, and Parliament received very little revenue from the customs officers.

From 1770 to 1773, Americans paid the small duties on tea and foreign molasses without much grumbling. Business was better than it had been in years and all but a handful of colonials seemed to lose interest in questions of who had the right to tax whom.

Once the colonists stopped quarreling with England, however, they began quarreling with each other—a fact which did not make the British unhappy. New England Anglicans asked the Church of England to send a bishop to America. This proposal infuriated Southern Anglicans who enjoyed running their own congregations, and it infuriated non-Anglicans everywhere.

Squabbles over lands in the West were renewed. Connecticut invaded northeastern Pennsylvania where it set up a county of its own. Pennsylvanians and Virginians renewed their disputes over lands in the Ohio Valley, even though the Proclamation of 1763 was still in effect. In the Southern colonies, tensions between frontiersmen and the East Coast establishment surfaced again.

However, the patriots were ardently at work all this time. Sam Adams and his colleagues publicized every British mistake and insult. While Adams realized that existing institutions such as town meetings, assemblies, county courts, churches, local and colonial clubs, and newspapers were useful vehicles for protest, he wanted to find a new way to reach people. So in 1772 he formed a committee of correspondence to draw up a list of grievances and persuaded the other towns in Massachusetts to form similar committees. Within three months, eighty more committees had been formed in Massachusetts, all exchanging written complaints against the English. Other New England colonies joined the growing movement and eventually there was at least one committee in every colony, except Pennsylvania and North Carolina.

One subject the committees found to complain about was a new plan for paying the governor of Massachusetts. Until now the governor's salary had been paid by the assembly, an arrangement which ensured the colonists a certain amount of control over their royal rulers. After June 1772, however, the governor was to be paid directly by the Crown. As one committee put it, this "exposed the province to a despotic administration of government." The Crown soon took over responsibility for paying Superior Court judges as well.

An even more inflammatory issue developed around an incident involving a British warship. The *Gaspee* had been lent to the customs service to suppress smuggling in New England. The ship's captain had been harassing farmers and fishermen who traded in the Narragansett Bay, and when the *Gaspee* ran aground in pursuit of a smuggler, local citizens boarded her at night, wounded the captain, and burned the ship.

The British government's reaction to this outrage was surprisingly mild. But Americans everywhere heard a false rumor that the suspects in the *Gaspee* affair would be taken to England for trial. The right to be tried in one's own district was among the oldest privileges of English justice. The rumor so incensed the Virginia House of Burgesses that it set up correspondence committees all over the colony. By mid-1773 all of New England and South Carolina had agreed to correspond with the committees in Virginia. An underground news system had been set up which kept alive suspicion of British policy and laid the groundwork for union.

THE BOSTON TEA PARTY

The *Gaspee* affair had been the colonists' fault and Americans had overreacted to it. The event that brought on the final crisis, however, was a grave miscalculation on England's part, a mistake compounded by British arrogance and ignorance.

For almost 175 years the British East India Company had had a monopoly over all trade between India and the rest of the British Empire. The company had prospered enormously, but in the 1770s it fell on hard times and was faced with bankruptcy. In addition, the English market was glutted with tea and the company still had some seventeen million pounds of Indian tea stored in its warehouses.

Lord North came up with what he considered a brilliant scheme for disposing of the tea and saving the East India Company. To implement it he guided the Tea Act of 1773 quickly through Parliament. The Tea Act provided that the government would withdraw its usual import duties on all tea brought *into* England. Moreover, it allowed the company to export tea directly to America without going through English or American wholesalers. This new arrangement would bring the price of East India Company tea down, well below the cost of Dutch tea which Americans had been drinking illegally for years.

The plan pleased everyone—except the colonists, who felt they were being denied freedom of choice. If Parliament could eliminate American tea wholesalers, who could stop it from destroying other colonial wholesalers? Then the East India Company added insult to injury: they allowed only those merchants who had ignored or opposed the embargo against English goods to be their agents in America. Americans began to worry that if the Tea Act went into effect, England would start setting up monopolies for wine, spices, cloth—all goods, in fact—and the monopoly would favor those merchants who could pass a loyalty test.

"The Bostonian's Paying the Excise-Man, or Tarring & Feathering." An English cartoon published in 1774.

American opposition to the Tea Act was almost unanimous. The committees of correspondence had done their work well. In Charleston the tea was unloaded but immediately locked in public warehouses, where it remained unopened until after the Declaration of Independence. In New York and Philadelphia ship's captains never even tried to unload their tea. East India Company agents were harassed in every port.

In Boston the governor was determined to land the tea, collect the duty, and proceed normally, despite the abnormal tensions in the town.

On the night of December 16, 1773, between thirty and sixty men boarded three ships in the harbor. They were lightly disguised as Indians in war paint and feathers. As a cheering crowd watched from the wharf, they dumped forty-five tons of tea, worth nearly £10,000, into the harbor.

Lord North was appalled. He had devised the Tea Act to *please* the colonists, but now he realized there was no way to deal with these "haughty American republicans." The king announced: "We must master them or totally leave them to themselves and treat them as aliens."

Initial American reaction was equally critical. Most colonists thought the Boston Tea Party was a shameful affair, "calculated to introduce anarchy, confusion and bloodshed among the people." But the Boston Tea Party brought to a head the conflict over British authority. The patriots had committed violence in the hope of rallying popular support at home against British rule and to see what measures, if any, Britain would take in reply.

They did not have long to wait for their answer.

THE INTOLERABLE ACTS

To punish the Bostonians Lord North steered four measures through Parliament. Americans promptly dubbed them "the intolerable acts." The Boston Port Bill closed Boston's harbor to all shipping until the citizens compensated the East India Company for the tea and paid the required duty. Boston was stunned by the choice it now faced: starvation and poverty or bowing to the will of an unyielding English government.

The Boston Committee of Correspondence began furiously penning letters to other committees throughout the colonies. When the news reached Virginia, Thomas Jefferson proposed that June 1 be declared a day of mourning for the "heavy calamity which threatens destruction to our civil rights, and the evils of civil war." Jefferson's proposal was adopted and on June 1 flags hung at half mast and church bells tolled in every colony. Americans who had recently denounced Boston for staging the tea party now rushed to the city's aid. Charleston sent rice. Philadelphia dispatched 1000 barrels of flour.

Meanwhile Parliament was passing three other "intolerable" acts. The Massachusetts Government Act revised Massachusetts' charter. From now on the governor's council (which was also the upper house of the legislature) would be appointed by the king, as in the other royal colonies. If the governor saw fit, he could ban town meetings, except once a year when local officers were elected. The colony had started out as virtually self-governing. Now it had a governor appointed and paid by the king, judges on the royal payroll, and a council chosen by the king.

The Administration of Justice Act provided that any government or customs official charged with committing violence in the course of suppressing a riot or other disturbance could be tried in England, rather than by an American jury.

Finally, a new Quartering Act ordered local authorities to provide housing whenever troops were needed to put down disturbances in towns that had no barracks.

An unrelated piece of legislation, the Quebec Act, was also passed at this time. At the end of the French and Indian War the British government had tried to establish representative government in Canada. The Quebec Act extended the colony's territory south to the Ohio River and West to the Mississippi, and it gave the whole colony a permanent government, without a representative assembly. It also made the Catholic Church the region's established faith, supported by tax money.

The Quebec Act was Parliament's attempt to give French-speaking residents a government similar to the one they had enjoyed under France, but Americans viewed it as an attempt to extend despotic rule in the colonies. Protestants also objected to the establishment of Catholicism so close to their borders. Land speculators with claims in the Ohio Valley were infuriated that those rich lands had been given to Quebec. And all were disturbed that Quebec would be ruled by an autocratic governor. This seemed a terrible threat to their own struggle for self-government.

The intolerable acts brought the crisis between England and her North American colonies to the point of no return. The imperialists who were in power in Parliament wanted no compromise with the colonists. For a century and a half Americans had regarded themselves as loyal English citizens and as recently as 1763 had felt nothing but goodwill toward the king. Now the patriots, who were even considering independence, were gradually getting the upper hand.

As far as the British were concerned, the Americans were insubordinate and ignorant of the responsibilities of empire. They had lived with few taxes and great freedom, far from the bureaucratic and financial complexities of London. Now that they were more populous and richer, the time had come for them to submit to taxation.

Most Americans were willing to let Parliament make laws relating to imperial matters such as foreign policy and international trade. They were not willing to surrender their rights as free people to participate in deciding matters of internal policy. But Parliament stubbornly insisted on treating the colonial governments as subordinate agencies in an imperial system: agencies which it could destroy at will.

Assemblies had been suspended and trial by jury set aside. British troops had been stationed on American soil in peacetime. American territorial aspirations in the Ohio Valley had been constantly frustrated. American merchants were bullied by corrupt customs officials and American overseas trade undermined. Most insulting of all, the Declaratory Act had spelled out in no uncertain terms Parliament's claims to be able to do anything it chose in America, without consulting Americans. Parliament finally pushed this dubious privilege to the limit in the intolerable acts.

The colonies, frustrated beyond endurance, called for an intercolonial congress to meet in September 1774.

THE FIRST CONTINENTAL CONGRESS

Every colony except Georgia sent representatives to the First Continental Congress. The delegates met in Carpenters' Hall in Philadelphia. The patriots were there in strength: Sam and John Adams, Patrick Henry, Richard Henry Lee, and Christopher Gadsden were all delegates to the Congress. Moderates and conservatives were also there: George Washington, Payton Randolph, Joseph Galloway, John Dickinson, and John Jay were also delegates.

The patriots were determined to push their convictions. They worked tirelessly to win the moderates and conservatives to their point of view. Joseph Galloway balefully observed that Sam Adams "eats little, sleeps little, thinks much, and is most decisive and indefatigable in the pursuit of his objects."

The patriots won the day. The conservative Galloway proposed a revised system of colonial government. His plan included a grand council that would share power with Parliament on colonial matters and a president-general with the right to veto all acts of Parliament affecting the colonies. The Congress voted six to five against Galloway's plan after unanimously adopting a much more radical plan advanced by Sam Adams of Massachusetts. Adams' plan, already adopted in Massachusetts as the Suffolk Resolves, called on the colonies to raise troops and suspend all trade with Great Britain. However, to conciliate the moderates a new petition of colonial grievances was sent to the British government.

The Congress also established what they called a Continental Association to manage a new trade embargo. The Continental Association was charged with setting up committees at town, county, and provincial levels of government to enforce a total embargo on all British trade. The committees were also supposed to encourage frugality, publish the names of all who violated the agreement, and check all customs entries. These committees soon fell into the hands of the revolutionary elements in each colony, who enforced the boycott rigorously and often violently in the first few months.

The Continental Association was vital to the growing revolutionary movement, not because it ever had much of an effect on Britain but because of its effect on colonial opinion. Moderates and conservatives found they had to take sides. Washington, for example, supported the policy of resistance while Joseph Galloway eventually sided with Britain. America was almost ready for independence. As John Adams later wrote of the First Continental Congress and its effect, "The revolution was complete, in the minds of the people, and the Union of the colonies, before the war commenced."

Parliament's response was to pass two more measures. The first act, passed to conciliate the colonies, allowed each colony to tax itself and then hand the money over to England. The second act forbade New England fishermen to fish off Newfoundland and extended the navigation acts to cover all commerce. Now New England could trade only with Britain, no matter what goods were bought or sold. Britain also stopped exporting British weapons and ammunition to America in anticipation of a possible armed conflict.

The mother country did not have long to wait. Violence actually began on April 19, 1775 when General Gage, the governor of Massachusetts, sent 700 soldiers to confiscate a supply of weapons stored at Concord by the colonial militia. When the commanding officer, Major John Pitcairn, arrived at the town of Lexington, he found the colonial militia ready to stop him. No one knows who fired the first shot, but when the smoke cleared British redcoats had killed eight Americans and wounded ten.

Pitcairn hurried on to Concord and took a few supplies (most of the munitions had already been spirited away by the militia). Two colonial and three British soldiers died in that encounter. But on the way back to Boston, Pitcairn was surprised by real danger. Summoned by riders like Paul Revere, who had galloped across the countryside calling for resistance, 4000 Americans lined the Boston road and fired on the British regulars from behind rocks and trees. By the time Pitcairn limped back to Boston, 73 of his men had been killed and 174 wounded. That night the colonial militia laid siege to the city.

The Battle of Lexington.

Grant Wood's painting of the Midnight Ride of Paul Revere.

The Second Continental Congress

From 1774 to 1775 royal control over the colonies crumbled rapidly. Most of the governors fled for their lives to British warships while colonial assemblies continued to meet without British authorization. Caution was the keynote, however, and mob rule never took over. The assemblies raised troops and issued paper money, preparing for the conflict they thought was inevitable.

In May 1775, only a month after the battles of Lexington and Concord, the Second Continental Congress assembled in Philadelphia. The streets of the town were festooned with banners proclaiming "Liberty or Death" and an escort of soldiers led a solemn parade the day the New England delegation arrived.

A brilliant assembly of the colonies' most gifted men gathered at the statehouse. Some of them had attended the first Congress: Sam and John Adams were the most notable. Among the new faces were Thomas Jefferson, the quiet, very tall, shy Virginian. Jefferson had just published *A Summary View of the Rights of British America*, in which he had stated that "kings are the servants, not the proprietors of the people." Benjamin Franklin was there, having just returned from England. George Washington came in the blue uniform of the Virginia militia. The president of the Congress was John Hancock, Boston's richest merchant who, according to rumor, had been one of the "Indians" at the Boston Tea Party.

The Second Continental Congress was expected to make some important decisions. It began by dealing boldly with the military crisis in Massachusetts. The militia surrounding Boston were formed into a continental army and George Washington was appointed commander-in-chief.

BUNKER HILL

Washington left to join his troops on June 23, six days after the worst battle of the entire Revolution had already been fought. On June 17 the patriots had seized Bunker Hill and

Interpreting the Revolution

Why did the Continental Congress finally declare American independence? What motives inspired the delegates? What were the true reasons for the rupture and what did the colonists hope to accomplish? American historians since the Revolution have answered these questions in different ways.

Throughout most of the nineteenth century, American historians took the words of the Founding Fathers literally. The Revolution had been fought for life, liberty, the pursuit of happiness, and as a blow against tyranny. The outstanding advocate of this patriotic point of view was George Bancroft who wrote a ten-volume *History of the United States* that was published from the 1830s to the 1870s. Writing at a time when America was being torn apart by civil war, Bancroft summoned up a nostalgic image of the past: a nation united, a country guided by the purity of its ideals.

Bancroft's morally uplifting interpretation began to be discarded in the 1890s. Relations with Britain had improved to such an extent that many American historians were enthusiastic admirers of the English. George L. Beer, Charles M. Andrews, and Lawrence H. Gipson were the main exponents of this imperial school of historians.

Beer studied Britain's mercantilist policies and concluded that, far from restricting the American economy, they had helped it prosper. Andrews and Gipson both claimed that the navigation acts were enlightened, liberal pieces of legislation.

Andrews concluded that the Revolution had been fought because Americans were demanding more and more freedom at the very time that England was moving to tighten her imperial grip: "On the one side was the immutable, stereotyped system of the mother country, based on precedent and tradition and designed to keep things comfortably as they were; on the other, a vital dynamic organism, containing the seeds of a great nation, its forces untried, still to be proved."

In the early twentieth century a new school of historians emerged. Called the progressive school, it was deeply influenced by the growing socialist movement in America, the ideas of Marx, and the general social unrest of the period. The progressive historians viewed the revolutionary movement as a class struggle that had economic origins. Some of the flavor of their writing is reflected in the titles of their books: *An Economic Interpretation of the Constitution* by Charles A. Beard, *The Colonial Merchants and the American Revolution* by Arthur M. Schlesinger, and *The American Revolution Considered as a Social Movement* by J. Franklin Jameson.

Beard felt that during the nation's early years the conflict between the haves and the have-nots within America was as important as the conflict between England and America. Schlesinger argued that the revolutionary movement had been started by rich merchants who were losing money as a result of Britain's economic policies after the French and Indian War. After the Declaration of Independence, however, the rich were more afraid of their poor compatriots than of England, and their revolutionary ardor cooled considerably. Jameson concentrated on democratic advances made during the Revolution. Property qualifications for voting were lowered, the vast estates of Tories (those who remained loyal to the Crown) were confiscated and distributed to poor farmers, and lands that had been controlled by England were opened to the mass of Americans.

After World War II American historians tended to reflect the conservative climate in the nation. Robert E. Brown and Daniel J. Boorstin are the best known of these neoconservatives. This new school of historians challenged the progressives' theory that colonial America had been undemocratic. In *Middle-Class Democracy and the Revolution in Massachusetts, 1691–1780* Brown set out to demonstrate that in Massachusetts, at least, the vast majority of men owned enough property to vote. The Revolution was not a radical movement for social reform, but a conservative movement for restoring the good old days before the French and Indian War. In the *Genius of American Politics* Boorstin also argued that the colonists rebelled in order to preserve the status quo. The English were the radicals, because it was they who wanted to change the existing order.

More recently, Bernard Bailyn has looked at the Revolution as a period in intellectual history. In his *Pamphlets of American Revolution* Bailyn interpreted the Revolution as the logical outcome of a developing political theory. Bailyn read scores of colonial writers and showed the importance of those ideas that came from English common law, Enlightenment philosophers, and New England Puritanism. American revolutionary thought held that the hunger for power was a natural but corrupting lust that government had to control lest it infringe on the people's liberties. After 1763 the colonists believed that the British government was deliberately trying to deprive its subjects in England and America of their liberty. In taking up arms, Bailyn concluded, Americans were motivated out of love for the rights of English citizens, which by 1776 had been expanded into the concept of universal human rights.

Recent historians have focused their attention on the role of the common people in the Revolution. Pauline Maier has compared the traditional role of colonial mobs to the riots that broke out in prerevolutionary crises. Mobs were not necessarily illegitimate. If they represented the whole population, then it is possible that they reflected the common consensus aroused to uphold the law or to resist arbitrary power. Jesse Lemisch points to the evidence of increasing class stratification and reemphasizes class conflict in revolutionary America. He also criticizes Bailyn for disregarding the beliefs of the common people. Lemisch argues that Bailyn ignored a body of political thought which was majoritarian and democratic. He has begun to fill the gap in our knowledge of what the common people were thinking through his study of American seamen during the Revolution.

Breed's Hill in Charlestown and were preparing to pound Boston with artillery. General Gage ordered his men to retake the hills—and they did, at a terrible cost. More than a thousand English troops fell while the patriots lost only about four hundred men. Even though the British recaptured Breed's Hill, Americans counted the so-called Battle of Bunker Hill an American victory.

Meanwhile, the Congress in Philadelphia was trying to find the right approach to the growing crisis. On July 5 it sent George III the Olive Branch Petition. The Petition denounced Parliament and begged the king to free the colonies from its incompetent management. The very next day Congress issued a Declaration of Causes of Taking-up Arms. The Declaration announced to the world that "the arms we have been compelled by our enemies to assume, we will, in defiance of every hazard . . . employ for the preservation of our liberties; being with one mind resolved to die Freemen rather than live Slaves." A secret committee of correspondence was created to write to America's friends abroad for support. Congress also: ordered an attack on Canada; created officials to deal with the Indians; authorized the outfitting of a navy; and urged the colonies to appoint committees of safety to direct local military operations against the English.

Despite these decisive moves the Congress hesitated to take the final step and officially declare independence. The colonists had always considered themselves English first and Americans second. English liberties were all that they had been clamoring for.

The terrible word *traitor*—and the knowledge of what happened to unsuccessful traitors—weighed heavily on the delegates' minds. Upper-class Americans feared that a revolution might drive America's native aristocracy out along with the English. Once the mob was unleashed, who knew how violent it might become? Finally, no colony in the history of the modern world had ever rebelled against its mother country.

By late 1775 events had moved swiftly beyond the control of the moderates. On November 9 Congress learned that George III had refused to read the Olive Branch Petition and that he had dispatched 20,000 troops to the New World. He had also declared every member of the Congress a traitor. The moderates saw that if captured they would be hanged no matter what position they now took. In addition the soldiers on their way to America were not ordinary English troops, but paid German mercenaries. The colonists believed that these Hessians would ravage the land, making no distinction between those who remained loyal to the king and those in rebellion. Mercenaries would take whatever they could get from whomever they could overpower.

The final incentive for an open break came in January 1776 when Thomas Paine published his pamphlet *Common Sense.* All America was aroused. Some 150,000 copies were sold in a few months. Paine, an Englishman who had been living in America for only a year, called George III a "royal brute" and declared, "Of more worth is one honest man to society and in the sight of God than all the crowned ruffians who ever lived." Respect for the king had been bred into most Americans almost as strongly as respect for God, but suddenly here was an eloquent argument for abolishing royalty and establishing a republican government. British society, Paine firmly announced, was corrupt and it was corrupting America. These ideas struck most Americans as very much the essence of common sense. Revolutionaries who had whispered the same sentiments in the dark now discussed them openly.

THE DECLARATION OF INDEPENDENCE

Paine's passionate attack unleashed American patriotism and spurred the Continental Congress to action. In March the Congress directed American ships to raid British vessels. In April it opened American ports to foreign shipping. In May it asked the colonial assemblies to establish new state governments.

On July 2, 1776, the Congress adopted a resolution that had been introduced a month earlier by Richard Henry Lee. The first sentence read:

> That these United Colonies are, and of right ought to be, free and independent states, that they are absolved from all allegiance to the British crown, and that all political connection between them and the state of Great Britain is, and ought to be, totally dissolved.

Early in June a committee had been chosen to draw up a document justifying American independence to the world. The committee members were Thomas Jefferson, Benjamin Franklin, John Adams, Robert Livingston of New York, and Roger Sherman of Connecticut. Jefferson was the chairman and was responsible for the document's wording. He had tried to get Adams to write it, but Adams considered Jefferson the better writer.

When the statement was read to the Congress every colony approved it, except New York, which abstained. Since no negative votes had been recorded, Congress spent the next two days editing the text and cutting it by about a third. On the fourth of July "The Unanimous Declaration of the Thirteen United States of America" was sent to the printer. When it was read to the public four days later, a crowd tore the king's coat of arms down from the door of the statehouse and that night abandoned itself to great demonstrations of joy.

The Declaration had two parts. The first and most important part justified a people's right to rebel against a government that denied them their natural rights. In this section, Jefferson paraphrased the words of the Enlightenment philosopher John Locke: "Men being . . . all free, equal and independent, no one can be put out of his estate and subjected to the political power of another without his consent." Jefferson had also been influenced by Locke's assertion that "absolute monarchs are but men." When John Adams, who rather envied Jefferson, accused him of having mouthed commonplaces, Jefferson modestly replied: "I did not consider it any part of my charge to invent new ideas, but to place before mankind the common sense of the subject, in terms so plain and firm as to command their assent. It was intended to be an expression of the American mind."

"The Manner in which the American Colonies Declared themselves Independent of the King of England," English cartoon.

Indeed, most of Jefferson's educated contemporaries were familiar with the sentiments expressed in this first section. They had read the works of John Locke and the dozens of sermons and pamphlets on the foundations of government written in the past hundred years.

The second part of the Declaration listed the crimes the Americans accused the English king of committing against the colonies. Here Jefferson accused the king of dissolving the colonial assemblies whenever they opposed the king's invasion of the colonists' rights; of putting off elections of public officials; of paying judges directly instead of allowing colonial assemblies to determine their salaries; and of keeping "among us in times of peace standing armies, without the consent of our legislatures." He also accused the king of "cutting off our trade with all parts of the world"; of "imposing taxes on us without our consent"—and of many other "injuries and usurpations."

Jefferson did not mention Parliament by name at all in the Declaration, referring to it only once indirectly. Even though it was Parliament's attempt to impose taxes and other legislation on the colonies that had created the crisis leading to the Declaration, George III was singled out as the tyrant and he alone was held responsible for British oppression.

The Declaration showed Jefferson's keen flair for propaganda. After all, it was directed as much to the people of the world as it was to Americans. The people of Spain, France, Prussia, were not likely to understand complex references to the British parliamentary system, but they would understand accusations against a tyrannical king. In addition Jefferson would hardly want to attack the representative branch of the British government when the Revolution had come about to preserve the sanctity of representative institutions.

Readings

GENERAL WORKS

Andrews, Charles M., *The Colonial Background of the American Revolution.* New Haven: Yale University Press, 1961.

Bancroft, George, *History of the United States of America from the Discovery of the Continent,* Vols. I–VI. Chicago: University of Chicago Press, 1966.

Greene, Jack P. (Ed.), *The Reinterpretation of the American Revolution: 1763–1789.* New York: Harper & Row, 1968. (Paper)

Jensen, Merrill, *The Founding of a Nation: A History of the American Revolution, 1763–1776.* New York: Oxford University Press, 1968.

Knollenberg, Bernhard, *Origin of the American Revolution: 1759–1766.* New York: Macmillan, 1965.

Leder, Lawrence, *Liberty & Authority: Early American Political Ideology, 1689–1763.* New York: Quadrangle, 1968.

Main, Jackson T., *The Social Structure of Revolutionary America.* New Jersey: Princeton University Press, 1965. (Paper)

Miller, John C., *Origins of the American Revolution.* Boston: Little, Brown, 1943.

Miller, John C., *Triumph of Freedom: 1775–1783.* Boston: Little, Brown & Co., 1948. (Paper)

Miller, John C., *Triumph of Freedom, 1775–1783.* Boston: Little, Brown, 1948.

Morgan, Edmund S., *Birth of the Republic, 1763–1789.* Chicago: University of Chicago Press, 1956.

Peckham, Howard H., *The Colonial Wars, 1689–1762.* Chicago: University of Chicago Press, 1963.

SPECIAL STUDIES

Bailyn, Bernard, *Ideological Origins of the American Revolution.* Cambridge: Harvard University Press, 1967.

Becker, Carl L., *The Declaration of Independence: A Study in the History of Political Ideas.* New York: Harcourt Brace Jovanovich, 1922.

Brown, Robert E., *Middle Class Democracy and the Revolution in Massachusetts, 1691–1780.* Ithaca, N.Y.: Cornell University Press, 1955.

Green, Jack P., *The Quest for Power: The Lower Houses of Assembly in the Southern Royal Colonies, 1689–1776.* Chapel Hill, N.C.: University of North Carolina Press, 1963.

Labaree, Benjamin W., *The Boston Tea Party.* Oxford: Oxford University Press, 1964.

Maier, Pauline, *From Resistance to Revolution: Colonial Radicals & the Development of American Opposition to Britain, 1765–1776.* New York: Alfred A. Knopf, 1972.

Maier, Pauline, *From Resistance to Revolution: Colonial Radicals & the Development of American Opposition to Britain, 1765–1776.* New York: Random House. (Paper)

Morgan, Edmund S., and Helen M. Morgan, *The Stamp Act Crisis: Prologue to Revolution.* Chapel Hill, N.C.: University of North Carolina Press, 1953 (Paper: Collier Books, 1963).

Schlesinger, Arthur M., *The Colonial Merchants and the American Revolution.* New York: Atheneum, 1968.

Zobel, Hiller B., *Boston Massacre.* New York: W. W. Norton & Co., 1971. (Paper—1970)

PRIMARY SOURCES

Commager, Henry S., and Richard B. Morris (Eds.), *The Spirit of Seventy-Six: The Story of the American Revolution As Told by Participants,* Vols. I–II. New York: Harper & Row, 1967.

Morgan, Edmund S., *Prologue to Revolution: Sources and Documents on the Stamp Act Crisis.* Chapel Hill, N.C.: University of North Carolina Press, 1959.

Oliver, Peter, *Peter Oliver's Origin and Progress of the American Revolution: A Tory View,* Douglas Adair (Ed.). Calif.: Stanford University Press, 1961.

Paine, Thomas, *Common Sense* and *Crisis.* New York: Doubleday, 1970.

BIOGRAPHIES

Bailyn, Bernard, *The Ordeal of Thomas Hutchinson.* Cambridge, MA.: Harvard University Press, 1974.

Beeman, Richard R., *Patrick Henry: A Biography.* New York: McGraw-Hill, 1974.

Chinard, Gilbert, *Honest John Adams.* Boston: Little, Brown, 1933.

Crane, Verner W., *Benjamin Franklin and a Rising People,* Oscar Handlin (Ed.). Boston: Little, Brown, 1954.

Cunliffe, Marcus, *George Washington: Man and Monument.* Boston: Little, Brown, 1958.

Forbes, Esther, *Paul Revere and the World He Lived In.* Boston: Houghton Mifflin, 1942.

Hawke, David F., *Paine.* New York: Harper & Row, 1974.

Malone, Dumas, *Jefferson and His Time: Jefferson the Virginian,* Vol. I. Boston: Little, Brown, 1948.

Miller, John C., *Sam Adams: Pioneer in Propaganda.* Boston: Little, Brown, 1936.

HISTORICAL NOVELS

Cannon, Legrand, Jr., *Look to the Mountain.* New York: Holt, Rinehart and Winston, 1942.

Churchill, Winston, *Richard Carvel.* New York: Macmillan, 1914.

Forbes, Esther, *Johnny Tremain.* New York: Dell, 1969.

Gordon, Caroline, *Green Centuries.* New York: Scribner's, 1941.

Roberts, Kenneth, *Arundel* (1944), *Lydia Bailey* (1947), *Northwest Passage, Oliver Wiswell* (1940), *Rabble in Arms* (1947). New York: Doubleday (Paper: Fawcett, 1970).

Written with a Sunbeam

Women in the American Revolution

Yes, I am a rebel!
My brothers are rebels!
And our dog Trip
is a rebel, too!

With these few words, Isabella Ferguson of South Carolina summed up the sentiments of colonial women who had chosen to stand against the British in the American Revolution.

Everywhere throughout the colonies, women were "making the revolution" in the 1770s. As consumers, women helped carry out the effective boycott of tea, spices, fabrics, and other British imports. As spies, women traveled across British lines to warn American troops of impending attack. As soldiers, women took up arms and contributed to American political victories. As writers, women produced political satire, debated forms of government, and reported on the growing revolution. As fund-raisers, munitions manufacturers, farmers, tavern-keepers, seamstresses, doctors, morticians, and publishers, women paid the bills, made the bullets, grew the food, housed the troops, sewed the uniforms, ran the hospitals, buried the dead, and kept the presses rolling.

Who were these Founding Mothers and where is their history to be found?

Elizabeth Ellet set out to answer these questions half a century after the Revolution. Her three-volume work, *Women of the American Revolution,* was first published in 1850 and has become the classic work of the period. Her thoughts on the role of women in the Revolution were contained in her introduction:

> It is almost impossible now to appreciate the vast influence of woman's patriotism upon the destinies of the infant republic... History can do it no justice; for history deals with the workings of the head, rather than the heart.

Yet a considerable history of women revolutionaries has survived in addition to Ellet's work. This body of knowledge is contained primarily in the private writings of women who took part in the struggle. In particular, the work of two women has been preserved almost in its entirety, while fragments of other women's lives have been retained both on paper and by oral tradition. The recent growth of interest in the history of American women is bringing this information to the attention of historians.

Despite the fact that formal education was not available to women and that they were not allowed to vote or hold office, two Massachusetts women distinguished themselves as political thinkers: Abigail Smith Adams, who took the penname of Portia, and Mercy Otis Warren, who was known to her correspondents as Philomela, and to her biographer as the First Lady of the Revolution.

Reared under similar circumstances, the two women became friends at an early age. Their friendship spanned many years,

A British cartoon satirizing American women's support of the Revolutionary effort. Published in 1775. ▶

as both lived into their eighties. Their thoughtful correspondence in which each developed her own political ideas is one of the origins of the Revolutionary Committees of Correspondence.

As the twentieth-century historian Mary Sumner Benson points out in her study, *Women in Eighteenth Century America,* Abigail Adams was a person of considerable political foresight. By late 1773 she was predicting that civil war within the British Empire would be the likely outcome of the colonists' protests. Two years later she was urging separation from England and had begun to develop her ideas on the form of the new government.

On March 31, 1776, "Portia" wrote the letter which distinguished her as America's first suffragist, indirectly seeking the vote for her sex. She implored her husband to:

> Remember the Ladies, and be more generous and favourable to them than your ancestors. Do not put such unlimited power into the hands of the Husbands. Remember all Men would be tyrants if they could. If particular care and attention is not paid to the Laidies we are determined to foment a Rebelion, and will not hold ourselves bound by any laws in which we have no voice, or Representation.

Traditionally, history fails to mention Abigail Adams's political contributions but does record her for one other distinction. She was the only woman in American history to have been both wife and mother to American presidents. John Adams, who followed Washington to the presidency, was her husband; John Quincy Adams, the nation's sixth president, was her son.

While the Adams family's place in history has been secured, Mercy Otis Warren's clan has often been ignored. However, both the Otises and the Warrens were leaders in fighting the Revolution and in forming the new government. Mercy Otis Warren herself occupied a unique role as the Revolution's foremost political satirist, dramatist, and (later) historian.

Though her plays were never performed, her reputation spread rapidly and her works were widely published. Her first play about the British appeared in the March 1772 issue of the magazine the *Massachusetts Spy*.

As the Revolution progressed, "Philomela's" work became bolder in language. Her caricatures of the Tories became increasingly transparent. In 1775 she published *The Group,* which grew to be her most popular work, probably because its characters were immediately recognizable to the audience of the day. The members of the British government were portrayed as Brigadier Hate-All, Hum Humbug, and Crusty Crowbar.

After the new government came into effect under the Constitution, Mercy Otis Warren turned to prose. Using her pen to attack the Federalists, she strongly opposed their idea of a strong centralized government. In her opinion, such a government encouraged its officials to act like royalty. Her strong commitment to this belief caused a severe rift in her friendship with the Adamses, who were now among the leading Federalists. It was not until many years later that their friendship was renewed.

In her later years, Mercy Otis Warren completed her most significant but little recognized work, the three-part *History of the Rise, Progress and Termination of the American Revolution.* If publication had not been delayed due to the unpopularity of her political beliefs, this work would have been the first complete history of the American struggle.

THE SENTIMENTS of an
AMERICAN WOMAN.

ON the commencement of actual war, the Women of America manifeſted a firm reſolution to contribute as much as could depend on them, to the deliverance of their country. Animated by the pureſt patriotiſm, they are ſenſible of ſorrow at this day, in not offering more than barren wiſhes for the ſucceſs of ſo glorious a Revolution. They aſpire to render themſelves more really uſeful; and this ſentiment is univerſal from the north to the ſouth of the Thirteen United States. Our ambition is kindled by the ſame of thoſe heroines of antiquity, who have rendered their ſex illuſtrious, and have proved to the univerſe, that, if the weakneſs of our Conſtitution, if opinion and manners did not forbid us to march to glory by the ſame paths as the Men, we ſhould at leaſt equal, and ſometimes ſurpaſs them in our love for the public good. I glory in all that which my ſex has done great and commendable. I call to mind with enthuſiaſm and with admiration, all thoſe acts of courage, of conſtancy and patriotiſm, which hiſtory has tranſmitted to us: The people favoured by Heaven, preſerved from deſtruction by the virtues, the zeal and the reſolution of Deborah, of Judith, of Eſther! The fortitude of the mother of the Macchabees, in giving up her ſons to die before her eyes: Rome ſaved from the fury of a victorious enemy by the efforts of Volumnia, and other Roman Ladies: So many famous ſieges where the Women have been ſeen forgeting the weakneſs of their ſex, building new walls, digging trenches with their feeble hands, furniſhing arms to their defenders, they themſelves darting the miſſile weapons on the enemy, reſigning the ornaments of their apparel, and their fortune, to fill the public treaſury, and to haſten the deliverance of their country; burying themſelves under its ruins; throwing themſelves into the flames rather than ſubmit to the diſgrace of humiliation before a proud enemy.

Born for liberty, diſdaining to bear the irons of a tyrannic Government, we aſſociate ourſelves to the grandeur of thoſe Sovereigns, cheriſhed and revered, who have held with ſo much ſplendour the ſcepter of the greateſt States, The Batildas, the Elizabeths, the Maries, the Catharines, who have extended the empire of liberty, and contented to reign by ſweetneſs and juſtice, have broken the chains of ſlavery, forged by tyrants in the times of ignorance and barbarity. The Spaniſh Women, do they not make, at this moment, the moſt patriotic ſacrifices, to encreaſe the means of victory in the hands of their Sovereign. He is a friend to the French Nation. They are our allies. We call to mind, doubly intereſted, that it was a French Maid who kindled up amongſt her fellow-citizens, the flame of patriotiſm buried under long misfortunes: It was the Maid of Orleans who drove from the kingdom of France the anceſtors of thoſe ſame Britiſh, whoſe odious yoke we have juſt ſhaken off; and whom it is neceſſary that we drive from this Continent.

But I muſt limit myſelf to the recollection of this ſmall number of atchievements. Who knows if perſons diſpoſed to cenſure, and ſometimes too ſeverely with regard to us, may not diſapprove our appearing acquainted even with the actions of which our ſex boaſts? We are at leaſt certain, that he cannot be a good citizen who will not applaud our efforts for the relief of the armies which defend our lives, our poſſeſſions, our liberty? The ſituation of our ſoldiery has been repreſented to me; the evils inſeparable from war, and the firm and generous ſpirit which has enabled them to ſupport theſe. But it has been ſaid, that they may apprehend, that, in the courſe of a long war, the view of their diſtreſſes may be loſt, and their ſervices be forgotten. Forgotten! never; I can anſwer in the name of all my ſex. Brave Americans, your diſintereſtedneſs, your courage, and your conſtancy will always be dear to America, as long as ſhe ſhall preſerve her virtue.

We know that at a diſtance from the theatre of war, if we enjoy any tranquility, it is the fruit of your watchings, your labours, your dangers. If I live happy in the midſt of my family; if my huſband cultivates his field, and reaps his harveſt in peace; if, ſurrounded with my children, I myſelf nouriſh the youngeſt, and preſs it to my boſom, without being affraid of ſeeing myſelf ſeparated from it, by a ferocious enemy; if the houſe in which we dwell; if our barns, our orchards are ſafe at the preſent time from the hands of thoſe incendiaries, it is to you that we owe it. And ſhall we heſitate to evidence to you our gratitude? Shall we heſitate to wear a cloathing more ſimple; hair dreſſed leſs elegant, while at the price of this ſmall privation, we ſhall deſerve your benedictions. Who, amongſt us, will not renounce with the higheſt pleaſure, thoſe vain ornaments, when ſhe ſhall conſider that the valiant defenders of America will be able to draw ſome advantage from the money which ſhe may have laid out in theſe; that they will be better defended from the rigours of the ſeaſons, that after their painful toils, they will receive ſome extraordinary and unexpected relief; that theſe preſents will perhaps be valued by them at a greater price, when they will have it in their power to ſay: *This is the offering of the Ladies.* The time is arrived to diſplay the ſame ſentiments which animated us at the beginning of the Revolution, when we renounced the uſe of teas, however agreeable to our taſte, rather than receive them from our perſecutors; when we made it appear to them that we placed former neceſſaries in the rank of ſuperfluities, when our liberty was intereſted; when our republican and laborious hands ſpun the flax, prepared the linen intended for the uſe of our ſoldiers; when exiles and fugitives we ſupported with courage all the evils which are the concomitants of war. Let us not loſe a moment; let us be engaged to offer the homage of our gratitude at the altar of military valour, and you, our brave deliverers, while mercenary ſlaves combat to cauſe you to ſhare with them, the irons with which they are loaded, receive with a free hand our offering, the pureſt which can be preſented to your virtue,

BY AN AMERICAN WOMAN.

Other women wore the mantle of soldier, an aspect of revolutionary activity which was almost exclusively reserved for men. Deborah Samson, a young schoolteacher from Massachusetts, outfitted herself in men's clothing, and at the age of nineteen, enlisted in the Army under the assumed name of Robert Shurtliffe. Her disguise was so successful that she managed to serve for three years without being discovered and even spent time at West Point. Eventually a severe attack of fever forced her to see a doctor while on duty in Philadelphia. He discovered that Robert was in fact Deborah and, with her knowledge, wrote a letter to her commanding officer at West Point who gave her an honorable discharge at the age of twenty-three.

More typical was the case of Mary Ludwig Hays who, like many women, lived with her soldier-husband in camp. During the intense June heat of the Battle of Monmouth, she hauled water to the weary men who called out as she approached, "Here comes Molly with her pitcher." As the day wore on, the chant was shortened to "Molly Pitcher," and so she was known for the rest of her life.

But hauling water was not her only contribution to the battle. When her husband fell stricken at his gun, she took his place behind his cannon and fired round after round. Some historians have written that on the following day Washington commissioned her as a sergeant.

The most celebrated military heroine of all was the legendary Nancy Morgan Hart. In what may have been one of the most incredible feats of the struggle, she single-handedly captured five Tories who had come to her house demanding a meal. Thinking quickly, she got them drunk, then grabbed one of their rifles and killed one, wounded another, and trained the gun on the rest while her daughter went to get additional help.

Yet another group of women provided intelligence to American troops at critical moments. Lydia Darrah, a Philadelphia Quaker, overheard the plans of British officers who were staying at her house to attack at Whitemarsh the following morning. Later that night, she slipped out, crossed through British lines, and warned the American troops. When the British arrived the next morning, the rebel army was ready and waiting.

At the age of twenty-two, Deborah Champion rode from New London, Connecticut, to Boston, Massachusetts, with an urgent message for Washington. According to a letter which she wrote to a friend describing the adventure, she was stopped only once by the British who quickly released her, saying, "Well, you are only an old woman anyway."

Jane Thomas, an accomplished horsewoman from the South, undertook a similar journey, riding sixty miles to warn the Americans at Cedar Springs, South Carolina, of a planned British attack.

Still other women labored at equally important though rarely mentioned work. Two Rhode Island women, Dorcas Matteson and Anne Aldrich, reportedly "labored in fields, making hay, harvesting corn, hoeing potatoes and in many other ways doing the work of their absent husbands."

Like many other women who chose to contribute their wealth to the cause, Mary Draper of Dedham, Massachusetts, melted down her pewter heirlooms and made them into bullets. According to Mary Beard's history, *America Through Women's Eyes:*

> Colonial women could fire guns and make munitions. 'Handy Betsy the Blacksmith' was the peer of the most skilled in her work on cannon and other arms. Mrs. Proctor of Salem, who owned a tool factory at the opening of the war, was a boon to Joseph Swain placed in charge of collecting a rebel arsenal.

Esther Reed formed the Philadelphia Relief Association to raise funds for the army in 1780. Elizabeth Peck Perkins, a Boston businesswoman, subscribed $1000 to this effort.

Not that all the women involved in the Revolution were very wealthy. Other women, concerned with simply feeding and clothing their families, reacted spontaneously to injustices which affected their everyday lives.

While much has been written of the Boston Tea Party, little has been said of what might be called the Boston Coffee Party. As reported by Abigail Adams, on July 31, 1777, a group of 100 women took matters into their own hands when a Tory merchant refused to sell them coffee at a reasonable price:

> ... one of them [the women] seized him by his neck and tossed him into the cart. Upon his finding no quarter, he delivered the keys, when they tipped up the cart and discharged him, then opened the warehouse, hoisted out the coffee themselves, put into the trucks and drove off ... A large concourse of men stood amazed, silent spectators of the whole transaction ...

Even more women contributed to the revolutionary effort in ways which history has not recorded. Their names may be anonymous but their thoughts have often survived, as in the letter of this, now nameless, Philadelphia woman. She, as much as anyone, summarized the revolutionary spirit of the American woman:

> ... I know this—that as free I can die but once, but as a slave I shall not be worthy of life. I have the pleasure to assure you that these are the sentiments of all my sister Americans. They have sacrificed assemblies, parties of pleasure, tea drinking and finery, to that great spirit of patriotism that actuates all degrees of people throughout this extensive continent ... You say you are no politician. Oh sir, it requires no Machiavellian head to discover this tyranny and oppression. It is written with a sunbeam.

Suggested Reading

Anthony, Katharine, *First Lady of the Revolution* (New York: Doubleday & Co., 1958). The biography of Mercy Otis Warren.

Beard, Mary R. (Ed.), *America Through Women's Eyes* (New York: Macmillan Company, 1933). A compilation of the writings of "women with the devil in them," as the author put it.

Benson, Mary Sumner, *Women in Eighteenth Century America* (New York: Columbia University Press, 1935). The role of women in the cultural, political, social, legal, and economic life of the eighteenth century.

Ellet, Elizabeth F., *Women of the American Revolution* (Philadelphia: George W. Jacobs & Co., 1900). First-hand, detailed impressions and anecdotes of the domestic life of women in the American Revolution.

James, Edward T., and James, Janet Wilson (Eds.), *Notable American Women 1607–1950, A Biographical Dictionary* (Cambridge, Massachusetts: Harvard University Press, 1971). An encyclopedia of detailed biographical information about "notable" women in American history.

Whitney, Janet, *Abigail Adams* (Boston: Little, Brown and Co., 1947). The biography of Abigail Smith Adams.

A British cartoon depicting an American rifleman as wounded, sick, and feebleminded. The words on his cap echo the words of Patrick Henry: "Give me liberty or give me death."

(The Metropolitan Museum of Art, Bequest of Charles Allen Munn, 1924.)

5

The Emergence of a Nation

We hold these truths to be self-evident, that all men are created equal, that they are endowed by their Creator with certain unalienable rights, that among these are life, liberty, and the pursuit of happiness. That to secure these rights, governments are instituted among men, deriving their just powers from the consent of the governed; that whenever any form of government becomes destructive of these ends, it is the right of the people to alter or to abolish it. . . .

The Declaration of Independence, 1776

America launched its bid for independence with high ideals. But in its struggle to free itself from England, its treatment of British sympathizers, its dealings with other countries, and its search for a structure of its own, the young nation soon began to accommodate its brave words to the realities of its shaky situation.

The Revolutionary War

Unlike most other nations embarking on a war for independence, America was fighting for its rights before it had a national government. There was the Continental Congress, but it had the authority neither to pass binding legislation nor to tax. America had no army, no navy, no real government, and a population of only 2.5 million people. Britain, in contrast, was a mighty power of 10 million people with a highly trained army and the world's best navy.

America faced not only an impressive enemy abroad but also opposition from within. One-fifth to one-third of the population were Tories (or Loyalists) who sympathized with the English and 30,000 to 50,000 of these people actually fought on a regular basis for the king.

British sympathizers came from all classes and all of the states. Tory strength was highest in the Middle states, the Carolinas, and Georgia, and weakest in New England, Virginia, and Maryland. Officeholders under the Crown, Anglican clergymen, and some planters and merchants remained loyal to the king. In addition, many middle- and lower-class farmers from the Middle and Southern states became Tories, perhaps trying to avoid violence. Many probably did not understand what the Revolution was about. Some may have feared the colonial aristocracy even more than they feared the British government.

Whatever their reasons for siding with the English, Tories were forced by the states to take loyalty oaths. Death for those who failed was rare, but imprisonment frequent. Tory property was confiscated by the revolutionaries on a scale comparable to that of the French Revolution.

Stripped of their civil liberties and their political rights, about 100,000 Loyalists eventually left America. Some returned to England with the retreating British army. Many lower-class Tories fled to Canada.

In addition to those Americans who were actively opposed to the Revolution, one-third to two-fifths of the population remained uninterested or unmoved by the break with England. Many such Americans simply refused to take part one way or another in the war effort.

RAISING AN ARMY

Before the Continental Congress could concern itself with establishing an American government, it needed to make certain there would be a nation to govern. The colonists had to create an effective army to drive out the British.

Bunker Hill had demonstrated that American patriots were not always as ineffective in battle as the British liked to think they were. However, the men encamped around Boston were a hastily assembled gathering of outraged citizens, not a disciplined army. When the Continental Congress appointed George Washington commander in chief of the colonial troops, it was in order that he weld such scattered units into an efficient fighting instrument. He took command at Cambridge on July 3, 1775.

One of Washington's first tasks was to choose a capable staff. Although the demands of self-defense and food gathering had put firearms in nearly everyone's hands, few Americans had professional military training. The local militias had elected their own officers, but

popularity proved to be no guide to strategic skill. So when Washington took over he dismissed many of the unfit officers and appointed his own. Fortunately he was aided by a few officers from abroad, such as the Polish Count Casimir Pulaski, the French Marquis de Lafayette, and the Prussian Baron Friedrich von Steuben who was particularly helpful in drilling raw recruits.

Washington's problems were further aggravated by the volunteer nature of the army. The Continental Congress had no power to draft soldiers or to requisition supplies. Food, arms, and housing for the troops were supposed to be furnished by the states, but supplies were always inadequate.

Most enlisted men were farmers and could not afford to be away from their fields for long. They were willing to serve a few months but just when they were beginning to learn how to follow orders and fire a musket, they had to go home to harvest the crops. Although some 400,000 Americans took up arms at one time or another during the eight years of the war, Washington never had more than 17,000 men serving under him at any one time. For all his tact and eloquence, he could never count on keeping more than about 5000 regular troops in the Continental Army. Wherever he went he had to call on the local militia for back-up help. To avoid spreading his few, ill-supplied regulars too thin, he seldom sought direct engagements with the British forces.

FINANCING THE WAR

In addition to military deficiencies, the country also suffered from financial deficiencies. The Revolution was really fought against taxation, yet Congress had to come up with money to finance the rebellion. Congress invented three solutions to its financial problems: it borrowed about eight million dollars from American citizens through the sale of national bonds and another eight million from foreign governments; it collected some 5.5 million dollars from state governments; and it issued more than 240 million dollars' worth of paper money. America had always been short of hard money and the paper the Congress issued had little backing in gold or silver. To make matters worse, wealthy Tories fled with most of the existing supply.

The individual states also issued their own paper money. Soon there were fourteen different currencies in circulation. As more and more

A 36-shilling note issued by the Massachusetts Bay Colony in 1775.

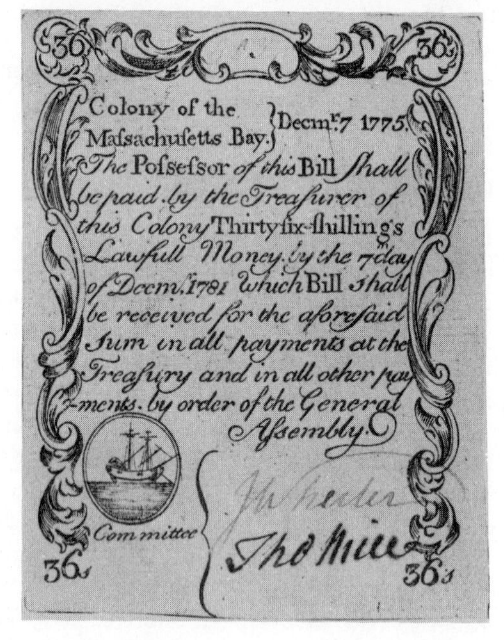

paper notes were printed, the buying power of the different currencies fell well below face value. This led to an inflation which was worsened by profiteering American entrepreneurs who kept hiking the price of war supplies.

Because of America's money problems serving the army was a terrible economic burden for most soldiers. Officers had to pay most of their own expenses. Ordinary soldiers were paid very low salaries in nearly worthless paper money. Only the 20,000 sailors who aided the war effort as privateers were well paid. Local ship owners who were instructed by the states to raid English vessels were so successful that they cost the king 2,000 ships and 12,000 British sailors.

STRATEGIC ADVANTAGES

Although America had serious military and financial problems, she also had certain strategic advantages. Britain was 3000 miles away. In past wars the colonies had been able to supply British troops with food and ammunition, but now most supplies had to be shipped across the Atlantic. In addition, no single American city was so central, so crucially important, that by taking it Britain could win the war. In the French and Indian War Britain had won Canada by conquering Quebec and Montreal. But in the Revolutionary War the English had to spread their forces over the length of the Atlantic coastline and into the interior at selected points. Most of this vast territory was not accessible by road, for few roads existed. As one English officer said, the lack of roads "absolutely prevented us this whole war from going fifteen miles from a navigable river."

Under these circumstances the Americans seemed able to prolong the war indefinitely. To prevent the superior British forces from putting down the Revolution, the rebels merely had to keep symbolic resistance alive. Though ill trained, ill equipped, and few in number, the Americans had learned about sneak attacks, ambushes in the woods, and fighting in all kinds of weather from the Indians. They could use these guerrilla tactics to continually harass the professional British soldiers, who persisted in fighting according to the formalized open battlefield rules of European warfare.

Another American advantage was that the war had little support from the people of England. Few British politicians had any enthusiasm for what they considered a civil war in the empire. Britain was still staggering under the debts it had accumulated from other recent wars. And powerful enemies on the Continent were eager for another opportunity to humble her. Should British forces be fighting a costly war thousands of miles away against people who, after all, were mostly English in origin, when these forces might suddenly be needed against French or Spanish attack at home? To many Englishmen the answer was clearly "No."

FIRST CONFLICTS WITH THE BRITISH

Boston was the first major theater of the war. The Battle of Bunker Hill had been fought in June 1775. After being dislodged from Breed's Hill the American troops, now under Washington, fortified Dorchester Heights which overlooked the city from the south. Washington set up fifty-nine cannons and mortars that had been dragged across the country from Fort Ticonderoga, captured by Ethan Allen and Benedict Arnold in May 1775. Rather than risk another battle as bloody as Bunker Hill, the English commander, General William Howe, withdrew his forces from the city. Accompanied by 1000 Boston Tories, they sailed to Halifax, Nova Scotia. Thus abandoned, Boston was occupied by Washington on March 17, 1776.

In the South everything seemed to favor the Americans during the opening months of the war. On February 27, 1776, 1000 patriots defeated a Tory army at the Battle of Moore's Creek Bridge in North Carolina. Four months later the British tried to sail into Charleston, South Carolina, but they were unable to get

Fort Ticonderoga, New York. ▼

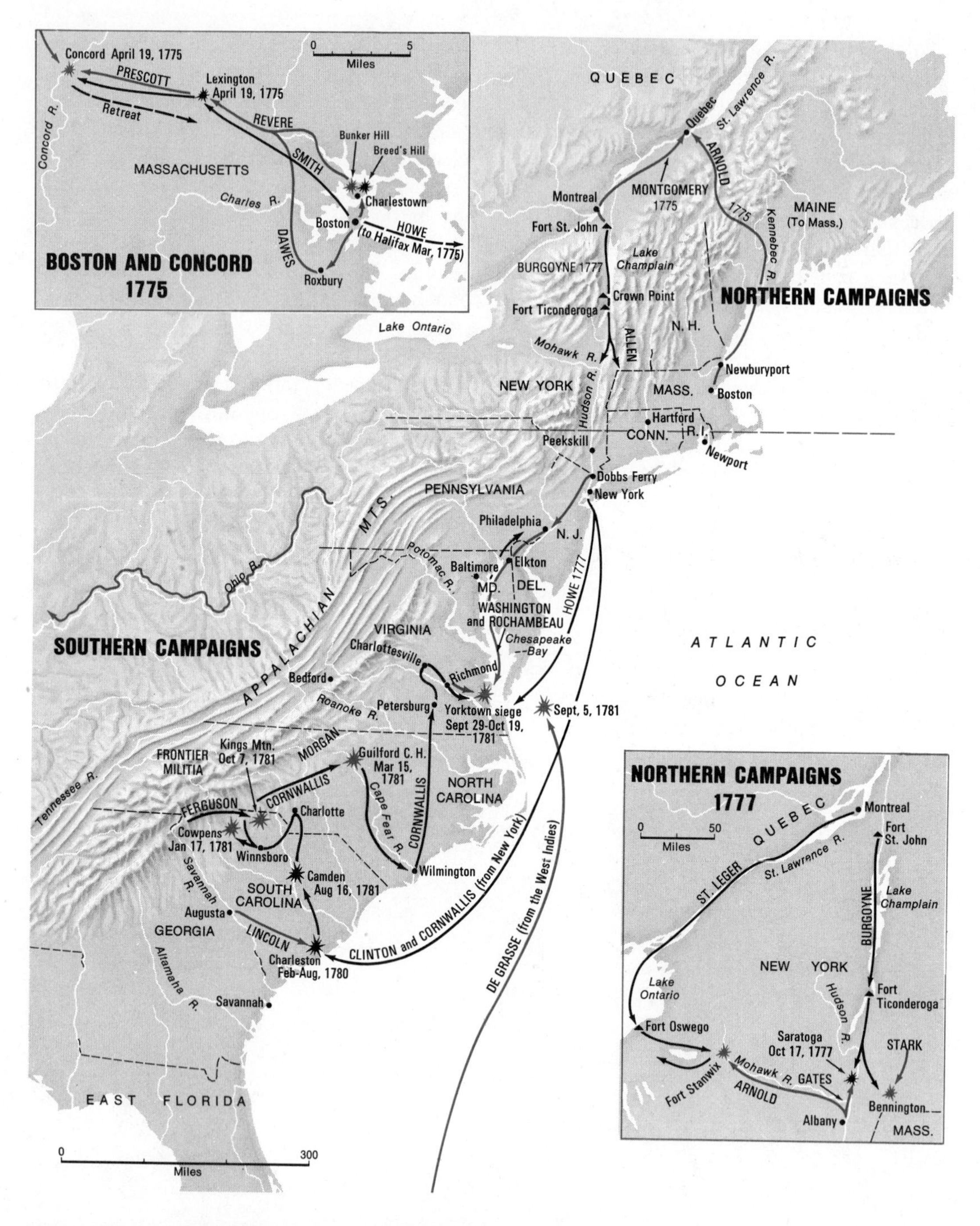

MILITARY CAMPAIGNS OF THE REVOLUTION

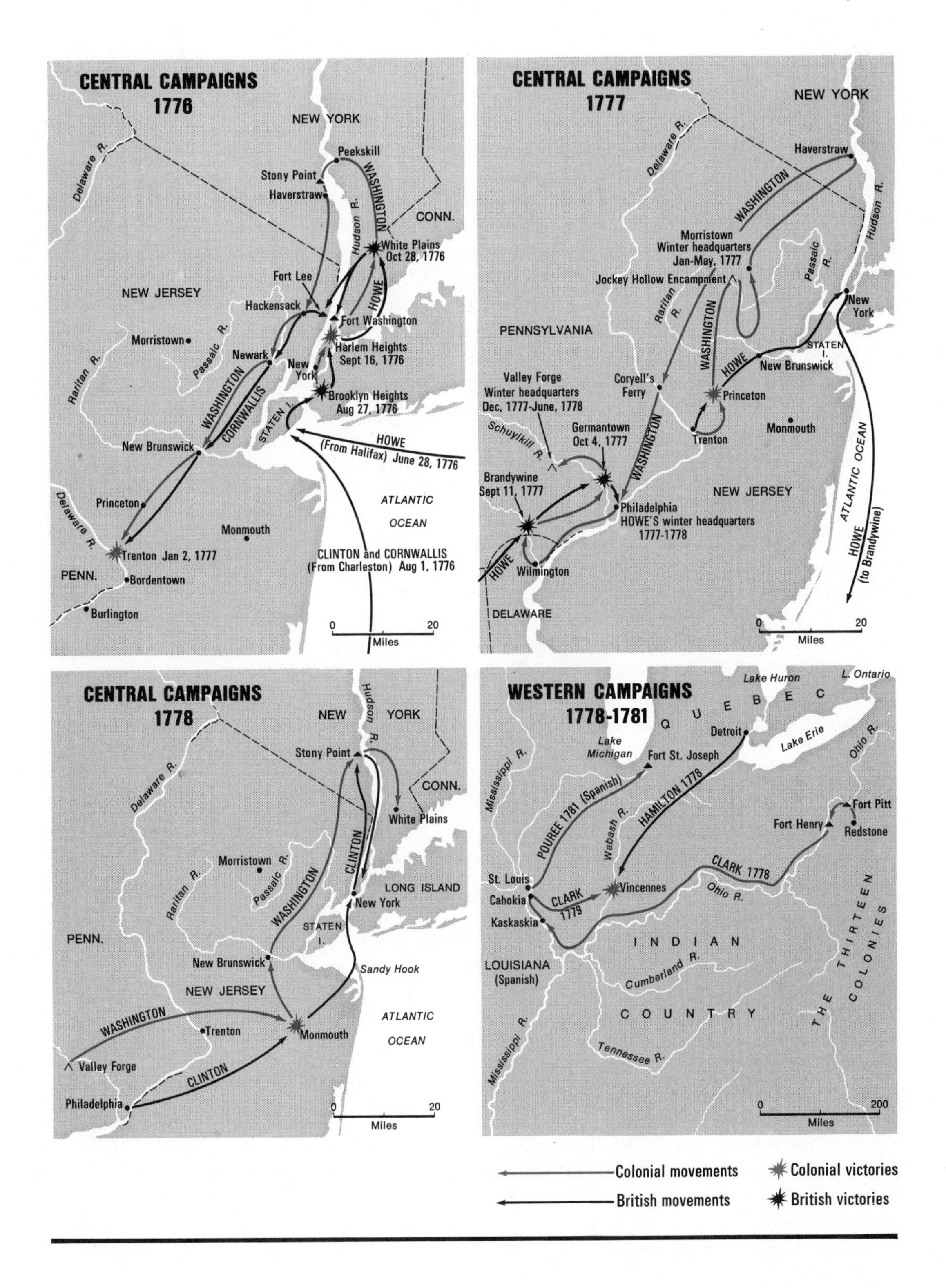
CENTRAL CAMPAIGNS
1776
NEW YORK
Delaware R.
Peekskill
Stony Point
Haverstraw
WASHINGTON
Hudson R.
CONN.
White Plains
Oct 28, 1776
Fort Lee
NEW JERSEY
Hackensack
HOWE
Fort Washington
Morristown
Passaic R.
Newark
Harlem Heights
Sept 16, 1776
New York
Raritan R.
Brooklyn Heights
Aug 27, 1776
WASHINGTON
CORNWALLIS
STATEN I.
HOWE
(From Halifax) June 28, 1776
New Brunswick
Princeton
ATLANTIC
OCEAN
Delaware R.
Monmouth
Trenton Jan 2, 1777
CLINTON and CORNWALLIS
(From Charleston) Aug 1, 1776
PENN.
Bordentown
Burlington
0
20
Miles
CENTRAL CAMPAIGNS
1777
NEW YORK
Delaware R.
Haverstraw
WASHINGTON
Hudson R.
Morristown
Winter headquarters
Jan-May, 1777
Passaic R.
Jockey Hollow Encampment
New York
Raritan R.
PENNSYLVANIA
WASHINGTON
STATEN I.
HOWE
New Brunswick
Valley Forge
Winter headquarters
Dec, 1777-June, 1778
Coryell's
Ferry
Princeton
Schuylkill R.
Germantown
Oct 4, 1777
WASHINGTON
Trenton
Monmouth
ATLANTIC OCEAN
Brandywine
Sept 11, 1777
NEW JERSEY
Philadelphia
HOWE'S winter headquarters
1777-1778
HOWE
(to Brandywine)
HOWE
Wilmington
DELAWARE
0
20
Miles
CENTRAL CAMPAIGNS
1778
NEW
YORK
Hudson R.
Stony Point
Delaware R.
CONN.
White Plains
Morristown
Raritan R.
Passaic R.
WASHINGTON
CLINTON
LONG ISLAND
New York
PENN.
STATEN I.
New Brunswick
Sandy Hook
NEW JERSEY
WASHINGTON
ATLANTIC
Trenton
Monmouth
OCEAN
Valley Forge
CLINTON
Philadelphia
0
20
Miles
WESTERN CAMPAIGNS
1778-1781
Lake Huron
L. Ontario
QUEBEC
Detroit
Lake Michigan
Fort St. Joseph
Lake Erie
Mississippi R.
Ohio R.
POUREE 1781 (Spanish)
HAMILTON 1778
Wabash R.
Fort Pitt
Fort Henry
Redstone
CLARK 1778
St. Louis
Cahokia
Vincennes
CLARK 1779
Ohio R.
Kaskaskia
THE THIRTEEN COLONIES
INDIAN
LOUISIANA
(Spanish)
Cumberland R.
COUNTRY
Mississippi R.
Tennessee R.
0
200
Miles
Colonial movements
British movements
Colonial victories
British victories

past a fortress that guarded the harbor on Sullivan's Island. The fort was built of spongy palmetto logs and dirt which literally absorbed cannonballs. Even a tremendous barrage from British ships could not destroy it. After a ten-hour duel the English gave up and left.

In Canada the Americans were not as successful. The American General Richard Montgomery did capture Montreal, but he and Benedict Arnold failed to take Quebec. Arnold's troops fought bravely, but they were greatly weakened by a long march through Maine, during one point of which they were reduced to living on boiled candles and roasted moccasins. After the defeat at Quebec Americans had to give up the hope that Canada would become the fourteenth state.

The British campaign against New York City

Temporarily turned back in Boston and the South, the British devised a plan to split the states in half by seizing New York City. Besides occupying a key position, New York had a large Tory population. To capture the city the British put together the largest invasion force of the eighteenth century: 34,000 troops, 10,000 sailors, 400 transport vessels, and 30 warships. General William Howe was again in command of the British land forces, a large part of which he had brought with him from Nova Scotia. His brother, Admiral Richard Howe, led the naval contingent.

Washington arrived before the British and fortified Brooklyn Heights. He thought that because these bluffs overlooked the East River and the island of Manhattan they would serve as a strategic vantage point, much as Dorchester Heights had dominated Boston. Washington, however, had only 20,000 men and he himself was relatively inexperienced as a commander.

General Howe arrived with his soldiers on July 2, 1776, and camped on Staten Island. Ten days later Admiral Howe arrived with his impressive fleet. They then sent Washington a letter asking him to submit peacefully to the superior English force. Washington refused to open the letter, which was addressed to "George Washington, Esq. etc., etc.," since it did not recognize his rank as general.

Unable to awe the Continental Army into submission, General Howe attacked one of Washington's divisions on Long Island. The battered American army managed to retreat to Manhattan. Howe again offered to confer with the rebels on ending the war. Congress replied by sending Benjamin Franklin, John Adams, and Edward Rutledge to speak with the British commanders.

The conference was a failure. After dining on "good claret, good bread, cold ham, tongues and mutton," Admiral Howe said sentimentally that "he felt for America as a brother, and, if America should fall, he should feel and lament it like the loss of a brother." To which Benjamin Franklin tartly replied: "My lord, we will do our utmost endeavours to save your lordship that mortification." The Americans made it clear that they would accept nothing less than independence.

In the next encounter, however, Washington's soldiers did not fulfill Franklin's promise. Howe attacked Manhattan and chased Washington off the island and north to White Plains. Once more defeated Washington fled to New Jersey. Washington was so discouraged that he admitted, "I think the game is pretty near up." However, in an effort to prevent complete defeat, he switched to a new strategy: "We should on all occasions avoid a general action or put anything to the risk, unless compelled by a necessity, into which we ought never to be drawn."

Trenton and Princeton

In December 1776 General Howe drove Washington out of New Jersey and across the Delaware River into Pennsylvania. But rather than dealing the badly weakened American army a final death blow at this point, Howe suspended operations for the winter, as was customary. Set-

A few days after his success at Trenton Washington attacked the British at Princeton.

tling his troops in winter quarters in Jersey, Howe returned to New York.

Washington, already discouraged by his own defeats, was further disheartened when he learned that the British had captured Newport, Rhode Island on December 8. In less than three months the enemy had gained control of New York City and most of New Jersey. Washington's army had dwindled to fewer than 8,000 men, and at the beginning of the year most of them would finish their terms of service.

Washington decided on a drastic move. On a wintry Christmas night he crossed the Delaware River with his men, marched them nine miles to Trenton, and attacked. The enemy, hibernating in its winter camp, never suspected Washington would depart from the traditional winter recess. In forty-five minutes the Americans captured 1000 of Howe's hired Hessian soldiers and killed their colonel.

Buoyed by this success, Washington attacked Princeton a few days later. By a brilliant bit of strategy he outmaneuvered the British and drove them back to New Brunswick. Neither the victory at Trenton nor the one at Princeton was decisive, but both helped boost American morale, badly in need of encouragement since the defeat in New York.

The Battle of Saratoga

A decisive American victory finally did take place during the summer and fall campaign of 1777. Pursuing their strategy of divide and conquer, the British now planned to seize Albany, New York. With Albany as well as New York City they would control the Hudson, split the colonies, isolate New England, and gain access to the back country beyond the Appalachian Mountains.

General John Burgoyne masterminded a three-pronged British attack on the town. From the south, General Howe would lead his forces up the Hudson from New York City. From the west, Lieutenant-Colonel Barry St. Leger would set out from Fort Oswego on Lake Ontario. And from the north, Burgoyne himself would descend from Canada and join the other two forces in Albany.

Nothing worked out as it had been planned. General Howe was playing a cat-and-mouse game with Washington in New Jersey and put off his departure for a long time. He finally decided to attack Philadelphia before fulfilling his part of the Albany strategy. This he did, severely trouncing Washington at the Battle of Brandywine before capturing Philadelphia. Washington retaliated in October at Germantown, Pennsylvania, almost defeating Howe who still had not set out to meet Burgoyne.

St. Leger was also slow to move his forces. When at last he left Fort Oswego and started heading east toward Albany, he was battered all along the way by the Americans. He had gone only a third of the way to Albany when he was attacked by Benedict Arnold at Fort Stanwix. Arnold cleverly negotiated with St. Leger's Indian allies, convincing them to desert the British. Deprived of his large supporting force, St. Leger beat a hasty retreat back to Fort Oswego.

Meanwhile Burgoyne was moving clumsily down to Albany, never suspecting that his associates would not be there to greet him. Burgoyne, known as "Gentleman Johnny," had to march at a snail's pace. He led a force of 7000 men, accompanied by 1000 women. Moreover, he dragged along fifty-two cannons and a huge baggage train, including thirty carts devoted to his personal luggage. This slow-moving caravan made an easy target. In Vermont the local militia, known as the Green Mountain Boys, fell on a foraging party of 700 of Burgoyne's redcoats and destroyed them. When the reduced British army reached Saratoga, it met with American forces and fortifications of unexpected strength. Burgoyne attacked the Americans on September 19 and again on October 7. Both times he was turned back and suffered very heavy losses. On October 17, 1777, Burgoyne had no choice but to surrender his entire army of some 5700 men.

The American victory astounded the British. General Howe, who had entered and occupied Philadelphia without a struggle, submitted his resignation when he received the staggering news. A captured British officer declared: "The courage and obstinacy with which the Ameri-

General Howe as the British lion takes Philadelphia and the colonial leaders flee. Below, a verse ridicules colonial efforts to break from England. English cartoon published in 1777.

cans fought were the astonishment of everyone, and we now become fully convinced they are not that contemptible enemy we had hitherto imagined them, incapable of standing a regular engagement. . . ."

Burgoyne's surrender did not seriously reduce the superiority of the British forces in troops and supplies. The most important result of the American victory was that it persuaded France to become an open ally of America.

THE FRENCH ALLIANCE

The news of Saratoga prompted not only France but also Britain to take a new course of action. Lord North foresaw that the American victory would probably mean a Franco-American alliance and he took immediate steps to end the war. He proposed to Parliament a series of concessions that would guarantee the Americans virtual home rule. If necessary, all of the acts Parliament passed after 1763 would be repealed. The British would pledge that the Americans would never be taxed.

Parliament, however, delayed acting on the proposals. When they were finally approved and sent to the Continental Congress, they were too late to prevent the much-feared alliance with France. The Americans had already accepted the French offer to recognize their independence.

Secret French aid

According to popular myth the French rushed to aid the Americans because they loved freedom and democracy. The idea of a republic in the New World did appeal to many French aristocrats and intellectuals. To the French Foreign Office, however, the prospective alliance was a well-calculated strategic move against Britain's influence in the world. After the Seven Years' War, Britain had become the most powerful—and most arrogant—nation in the Western world. As Benjamin Franklin wrote, "Every nation in Europe wishes to see Britain humbled, having all in their turns been offended by her insolence. . . ." But the French were at first reluctant to help the Americans directly. They feared that an open alliance would lead to another war with England.

The Continental Congress had sent Silas Deane and Arthur Lee to Paris seeking France's help months before independence was declared. Both agents made themselves ridiculous in the sophisticated French capital. Deane pretended to be a figure of great mystery, wrote in invisible ink, and vowed to speak only French in order to fool the English. This behavior led the French foreign minister, the Comte de Vergennes, to remark: "He must be the most silent man in France, for I defy him to say six consecutive words in French." Lee was equally eager to play the secret agent, but he inadvertently managed to hire six British spies as aides.

Such bungling was not sufficient, however, to prevent the French from helping America secretly. Vergennes' policy was influenced by a remarkably versatile Frenchman named Pierre Augustin Caron de Beaumarchais. Beaumarchais was famous as the author of two popular, and dangerously democratic, comedies: *The Barber of Seville* and *The Marriage of Figaro.* With the permission and financial backing of King Louis XVI, Beaumarchais set up a fake private concern, Roderique Hortalez et Compagnie, through which war supplies were secretly channeled into America. In the first two and one-half years of the war, fourteen ships operated by Hortalez et Compagnie sailed back and forth across the Atlantic. Among other things they supplied ninety percent of the gunpowder the Americans used during the war.

The French treaty

Five months after the Declaration of Independence, Congress sent Benjamin Franklin to Paris to encourage the French to openly acknowledge their support for America. Congress could not have made a better choice. When Franklin arrived in France in December 1776, he was sev-

◀ *When he was seventy years old Benjamin Franklin was sent to France to secure support for the Revolution. His visit was a great personal, as well as diplomatic, success.*

enty years old but still vigorous. An experienced diplomat, he was world-famous for his experiments with electricity, and a great showman. Knowing that the French regarded all Americans as simple, homespun pioneers, Franklin accommodated their fantasies by doffing his wig and donning a fur cap. The cap and its wearer were the sensation of Paris. Ladies piled their hair up into "caps," the *coiffure à la Franklin.* The great man sat for dozens of portraits, and Parisians paid good money for a vantage point to watch him walking through the streets.

But for all of Franklin's charm and celebrity, it was news of the American victory at Saratoga that made France decide to declare itself an ally. Even then the French government was technically not free to make a move without the approval of Spain. The two nations had signed a compact agreeing to act together in all decisions that might lead to war. Although Spain had cooperated with France in aiding America through Rodrique Hortalez et Compagnie, they were against an alliance with the revolutionaries. Spain had colonies of its own in the New World and feared that the spirit of rebellion might spread from North to South America. Finally, thinking that America might succumb to England's peace offers, France decided to act on its own.

On February 6, 1778, Franklin, Deane, and Lee signed two pacts with the Comte de Vergennes. The first was a treaty of commerce in which France officially recognized North American independence. The second treaty was an alliance which established three points: both nations would fight until American independence had been won; neither France nor America would sign a peace treaty with Britain without the formal consent of the other; and each country would respect the other's American holdings "mutually from the present time and forever against all other powers."

Americans had already been forced to compromise their ideals of independence. In order to free themselves from British oppression, they had to link their fortunes with those of France in an alliance which was to be perpetual.

THREE MORE YEARS OF WAR

The French alliance, though immensely encouraging, did not end the war. In fact Washington still had to endure his worst trial: the winter of 1777–1778 at Valley Forge. While General Howe and the British occupying forces wintered comfortably in Philadelphia, Washington and his men endured terrible suffering only twenty miles away. One officer wrote: "All my men except eighteen are unfit for duty for want of shoes, stockings and shirts, breeches and coats. . . . We are becoming exceedingly lousy." An army surgeon summarized the desperate situation in these terse words:

> Poor food—hard lodging—cold weather—fatigue—nasty clothes—nasty cookery—vomit half my time—smoked out of my senses—the Devil's in't—I can't endure it. Why are we sent here to starve and freeze?

Almost 2000 of Washington's men deserted to the British. The Continental Congress threatened to replace the commander in chief with the "hero" of Saratoga, Horatio Gates, a man who actually had little to do with the victory. The local Pennsylvania farmers sold their crops to the highest bidder, which was usually the British. General Howe probably could have wiped out Washington's dispirited forces with one quick blow, but he had already submitted his resignation and refused to stir himself from the comfort of Philadelphia.

Despite American misfortunes in the East, Virginian recruits under George Rogers Clark had some success in the West. Clark was never able to take Detroit, nor did his victories at the river towns of Kaskaskia, Cahokia, and Vincennes give the Americans complete control of the Ohio and Illinois country. But he succeeded in removing British-sponsored Indian pressure from the areas of Kentucky and West Virginia.

The battlefield moves south

When General Henry Clinton took command from Howe in May 1778, British spirits were at a low ebb. France had just entered the war, and America had refused a peace offer including complete self-government within the British Empire. In search of a morale-building, surefire victory, the British looked southward. Optimistic reports led them to believe that the South was a stronghold of Tory sympathizers who would spontaneously rise up and throw in their lot with the British. Therefore General Clinton received orders to move the British army to New York, where he was to devise a strategy for overrunning the South. However, on his march to New York, Clinton was attacked by Washington at Monmouth Court House. Although Washington did not gain a clear victory, his army's good showing cheered Americans.

Monmouth was the last major battle in the North. From there the war shifted to South Carolina and Georgia. The Americans hoped to stop the transfer of British troops from New York to Savannah with the help of the French Navy, since Congress had let the American navy dwindle to seven ships. The expected aid was slow in coming, however. The French Vice-Admiral Comte d'Estaing arrived in the spring of 1778 with seventeen French ships and 4000 troops, but he failed to act decisively. In November he sailed south for a warm winter in the French West Indies.

Once the French Navy was out of sight, Clinton sent General Archibald Campbell and 3500 British troops to Savannah, Georgia. After six days the city fell, and the British soon controlled the entire state.

A year later Clinton came down from New York to personally conduct a new attack on Charleston. After three months the most important city of the South capitulated on May 12, 1780. The British took 5000 prisoners, including three generals. The rest of South Carolina surrendered soon after. Clinton returned to New York in high spirits. Convinced that total victory was now in sight, he left behind 8000 men under the command of General Charles Cornwallis.

The situation was so alarming that Congress again turned to the "hero" of Saratoga, Horatio Gates. Against Washington's objections, they directed him to take charge of American operations in the South. Washington's low opinion of Gates was soon justified. On August 16, 1780, near Camden, South Carolina, Gates launched a surprise attack on the British and then fled the moment the battle seemed to be going against him. Gates' entire force surrendered. Within a four-month period Britain had thus captured two sizable American armies, each as large as the one she had lost at Saratoga. Georgia and South Carolina were firmly in British hands.

In the North Washington's men were living on such meager rations, even during the summer of 1780, that he had to cut down his army to a scant 1000 men for fear a larger number would face starvation. "I have almost ceased to hope," Washington commented gloomily. Then, as the final blow, he learned that Benedict Arnold, his ablest general—possibly the best general to fight in the Revolution on either side—had gone over to the British side.

From this low point American fortunes finally began to rise in the fall of 1780. In October the commander of a 1200-man Tory force was killed along with many of his men by frontier patriots at King's Mountain, North Carolina. Now that the disgraced Horatio Gates had retired, Washington appointed his own protégé, Nathanael Greene, to head American operations in the South. Under Greene hit-and-run American forces won several battles against Cornwallis, the most notable at Cowpens, North Carolina, on January 16, 1781. At the Battle of Guilford Courthouse in North Carolina, the following March, Greene was forced to retreat after inflicting heavy casualties. But Cornwallis had lost so many men that he now abandoned the state and moved into Virginia.

The Battle of Yorktown

In the spring and summer of 1781, American troops led by another Washington protégé, General Lafayette, and aided by forces under Von Steuben, harassed Cornwallis in Virginia and drove him to Yorktown on the coast.

Throughout the war the British had always felt safe on the coast, relying on their vastly superior navy to provide them with supplies and a cover of cannon fire. They had learned that once they moved inland, they could win specific battles but never hold territory for long. America was simply too vast, its roads too poor, and its citizens too rebellious to control through might alone.

In August 1781 Washington was stationed outside British-held New York City, still waiting for help from the French Navy. When he learned that the new French Admiral, the Comte de Grasse, was sailing north from the West Indies with thirty ships and 3000 marines, Washington gave up ideas for a New York campaign. He immediately ordered Lafayette to keep Cornwallis penned up in Yorktown until he arrived in Virginia.

Cornwallis surrendering to Washington, a contemporary English engraving.

On September 5 De Grasse attacked and crippled the British navy in Chesapeake Bay, thus preparing the way for an assault on Yorktown. On September 28 Washington laid siege to Yorktown with the aid of 7000 French troops. Three weeks later Cornwallis surrendered his entire force. Seven thousand English soldiers, most of them drunk, handed over their weapons to the Americans while a band played "The World Turned Upside Down."

It was October 19, four years and two days after "Gentleman Johnny" Burgoyne's defeat at Saratoga.

PEACE NEGOTIATIONS

When Lord North heard about the defeat at Yorktown he exclaimed, "Oh, God! It is all over." Britain immediately began to extend peace feelers. Washington had expected the war to continue, but Britain was experiencing serious defeats elsewhere at the hands of other enemies. Spain had captured Pensacola, Florida, in May 1781, and would soon take Minorca in the Mediterranean. France had seized several key British islands in the Caribbean. In Africa and Asia the British were also meeting reverses. The English national debt had doubled in seven years. Overwhelmed by these reverses, Lord North resigned in March 1782. A new ministry headed by Lord Rockingham decided to try to negotiate a peace settlement with the Americans.

A settlement would involve not only America, Britain, and France, but also Spain and Holland, who had both joined in the war against England. Hence the negotiations in Paris tended to be complicated and at times confusing. The Continental Congress instructed its representatives in Paris to conform in all matters to French advice. Some congressmen had been bribed by the French government; the others naively believed that the French felt nothing but sincere interest in the problems and future of the new nation. France did indeed favor an independent America, but one that was weak and confined to the territory east of the Appalachians.

The American delegation in Paris included Benjamin Franklin, John Jay, and John Adams. Franklin carried the burden of the peace negotiations until the summer of 1782, when he was joined by John Jay. Adams, who was in The Netherlands negotiating a much-needed loan for the American government, did not arrive in Paris until October.

Jay was a man of great dignity and reserve who had been president of the Continental Congress before embarking on a diplomatic career. Before coming to Paris, he had been neglected and insulted for two and one-half years as American minister to Spain. Jay came to Paris determined to redeem his own and his country's honor. Becoming suspicious of French motives, he ignored congressional instructions and rejected the guidance of the French minister.

When Franklin became ill in August of 1782, Jay carried on the negotiations alone for several weeks. He learned that the French were making an undercover trip to London, possibly to deal secretly with the British. He also knew that both Spain and France were determined that America should gain as few concessions as possible from Britain and be kept out of the western territories. Convinced that America's allies were now as dangerous as her enemy, Jay told Franklin that they would be wise to ignore French advice. Franklin was at first cool to Jay's suggestion that they make the best agreement they could on their own. But when Adams arrived in Paris and agreed with Jay, Franklin changed his mind. Although they knew the unethical implications of their action, they conferred with the British secretly.

As a result a preliminary treaty was signed by the Americans and the British in November 1782. The formal treaty was then signed by France as well, as stipulated in the Franco-American alliance.

The treaty

Franklin had at first tried to persuade the British to cede Canada to America, but the British refused. Britain, however, fully recognized American independence and made generous territorial concessions. The new country received all lands lying between the Great Lakes and the northern border of Florida, and all territory between the Atlantic Coast and the Mississippi River (Florida and the Gulf Coast had been retaken by Spain during the war). The treaty also recognized the right of both nations to navigate the Mississippi River from its source to its mouth. This provision would cause great future difficulty since Spain, which was not a party to the treaty, controlled the mouth of the river. The British promised to withdraw their troops from American soil as soon as possible and even granted the Americans liberal fishing rights off Newfoundland.

In return America made a half-hearted promise to "earnestly recommend" that the states compensate Tories for property confiscated during the war. Negotiators on both sides knew that the "earnest recommendation" would be largely ignored by the various state governments. America also agreed to pay pre-Revolutionary War debts owed to British merchants. This clause, too, proved difficult to implement.

Although the unilateral action of the American delegation freed France from a series of impossible obligations to Spain, the French foreign minister was flabbergasted when he learned of the treaty and its provisions. He wrote to Franklin:

> I am at a loss, sir, to explain your conduct and that of your colleagues on this occasion . . . You are wise and discreet, sir; you perfectly understand what is due to propriety; you have all your life performed your duties. I pray you to consider how you propose to fulfill those which are due to the King?

Off the record, however, Vergennes communicated his admiration of American diplomatic finesse and his amazement at British generosity.

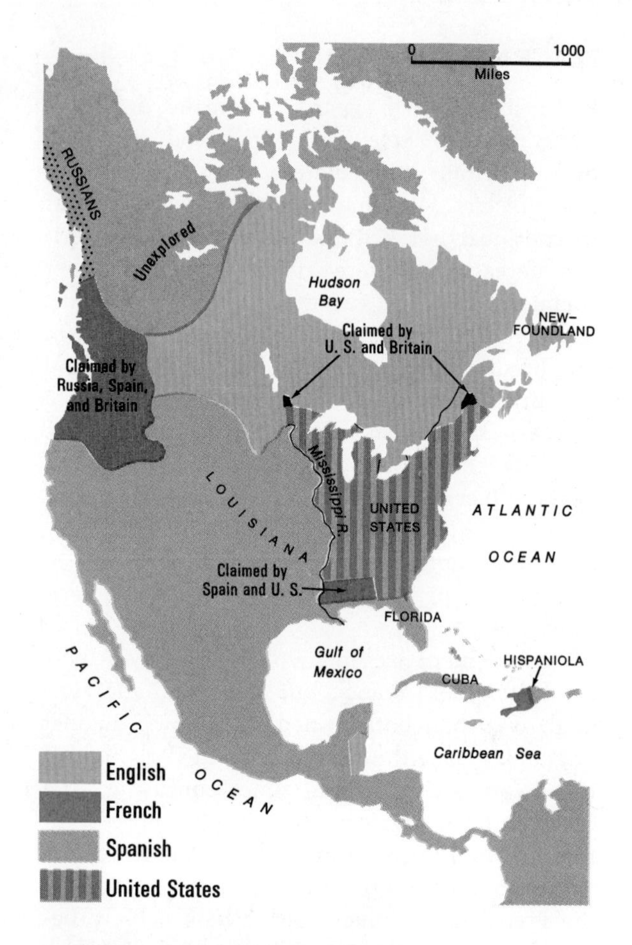

NORTH AMERICA • 1783

Creating a Nation

During the Revolutionary War the new American states had been slowly developing new governmental forms. One of the most remarkable aspects of the war, in fact, was the generally peaceful and legal way that the colonies became states.

A written constitution struck Americans as essential. They believed that they had been governed for too long under the unwritten British Constitution. The very vagueness of the British system of rule had made it flexible, an advantage under changing social conditions. But unscrupulous politicians could easily interpret it to serve their own ends. Americans were determined to have their rights stated in black and white and their government's functions clearly

An early Fourth of July.

defined. In forming their new state constitutions, they used as guides their written charters and compacts, Enlightenment philosophy, the English Bill of Rights, and their own long experience with self-government.

Each state established itself as a republic and in May 1776 the Continental Congress recognized the states as independent. By the end of 1777 ten states had turned their colonial charters into state constitutions. Only Pennsylvania had called a constitutional convention to write a new document. In the other nine states the assemblies had simply written and approved the new constitutions themselves, without submitting the documents to the people.

Massachusetts broke with this practice. In 1780 it selected delegates to a special convention to form a new state constitution which would then be presented to the voters. The people of Massachusetts believed that only a popular vote for the constitution could secure a firm basis for the government. If the assembly were free to create a constitution without referring to the people, then what could prevent that assembly from changing, corrupting, or abolishing the constitution at will? Popular ratification became an essential part of the process of forming new state constitutions and eventually of the United States Constitution.

The framers of the state constitutions wanted to preserve what they already had—republican government, government based on popular will and the rule of law. They had no desire to make a sharp break with the past. Despite some innovations, the patterns of colonial government were usually retained. As a result the new state constitutions were all very much alike.

In most cases the new constitutions tried to enhance legislative power at the expense of the executive branch. The idea of a strong governor who could veto legislation was rejected. Royal governors had possessed this privilege, and Americans were not about to put so much power again into one man's hands. In New York and Massachusetts the governor retained the power of veto, but that veto could be overridden by the legislature. Pennsylvania so disliked executive power that it abolished the office of governor altogether and replaced it with a twelve-member council.

The lower house of the colonial legislatures had been the branch of government closest to the people, since its members were usually elected every year. In their new constitutions most states strengthened the powers of the lower house and retained the annual election of assembly members. In most states, judges were to be appointed by the legislatures.

However, most constitutions did make important innovations in four general categories:

1. All states provided a bill of rights, guaranteeing protection of life, liberty, and property; the right to trial by jury; moderate bail and humane punishment; rotation in office; free elections; and freedom of speech, assembly, and religion. These ideas were drawn directly from English constitutional tradition.

2. The requirements for the right to vote were eased slightly. Most states maintained some property qualifications but they were lower than in the colonial period. Yet, "The rich having been used to govern, seem to think it their right," wrote a citizen of New Jersey, adding that the poor, "having hitherto had little or no hand in government, seem to think it does not belong to them to have any." For at least one old-fashioned Virginia farmer the Revolution had brought about too much equality. He protested, "There is more *leveling* than ought to be." No state extended the right to vote to all adult men or to any women.

3. A provision for amendment was written into all the new constitutions. Guided by Enlightenment philosophy, which stressed the experimental nature of government, the framers of these documents tried to make them flexible enough to be changed here and there if time proved them faulty.

4. The new constitutions tried to deal with long-standing conflicts between the older and more-established East Coast counties and the western frontier regions. The coastal regions had consistently denied full representation in the colonial assemblies to the western regions. In Pennsylvania, where the more democratic element from the western region was quite influential, the new constitution came close to equalizing representation from all counties. But nowhere in the Middle or Southern states was representation perfectly fair. The eastern counties were still overrepresented.

SOCIAL REFORMS

The Revolution relaxed class distinctions among Americans and fanned a philosophical idealism which encouraged social change. Most of the new constitutions established limited social reforms or confirmed those which already existed. Some of the innovations indicated a growing awareness of an ideal expressed in the Declaration: "All men are created equal."

Slavery

During the eighteenth century slavery had increasingly become part of American life, particularly in the South. Few people, except the Quakers, had questioned its morality. During the Revolution, however, some white men fighting for their own freedom from the British began to see the injustice in the graver denial of liberty to black people. In many states both the English and the Americans promised to free slaves who fought alongside them.

The idealism of the revolutionary era also fostered the beginnings of an antislavery movement. By the end of the Revolution, all the states except Georgia and South Carolina had passed legislation against the slave trade. Antislavery societies were active from Virginia to Massachusetts by 1792. Some of them called for deporting free blacks from the country. North of Maryland the abolition of the slave trade soon led to the gradual abolition of slavery itself. The first article of the Massachusetts Constitution, "All men are born free and equal," inspired one slave to sue for his freedom. He won his case, automatically freeing all other slaves in the state. The other Northern states provided by law for the gradual abolition of slavery by the beginning of the nineteenth century. In the South, where most whites considered slavery a benevolent institution, progress lagged far behind. But in 1782 Virginia did pass a law permitting owners to free their slaves. Ten thousand Southern slaves had been given their freedom by 1790.

The status of women

The Enlightenment ideas encouraged by the Revolution stimulated some thought about the natural rights of women. Under frontier conditions they worked as hard as men and distinguished themselves in professions ranging from teaching and health services to real estate and printing. During the labor shortages created by the war many American women worked outside their homes. After the war there was some agitation for broader education for women. But although many opportunities, including the right to vote, were denied them, the subordinate legal position of women and the denial of their right to vote did not become vital issues until the westward and industrial expansion of the first half of the nineteenth century affected the whole social structure of the country.

The decline of the aristocracy

The 100,000 Tories who left the country created a great change in property ownership. Many of those who fled were from the colonial aristocracy. Considering that there were twenty-four Tory emigrants per thousand persons in America, their departure significantly decreased the number of wealthy Americans. Behind them, they left landed estates which were confiscated by state governments, broken into smaller units, and sold to farmers. Land redistribution in many cases was drastic. For example, 311 people eventually moved onto the former estate of the Phillips family in New York.

Some token steps were also taken to increase opportunities to own land. Feudal laws derived from medieval England were discarded. These included primogeniture (by which a man's oldest son had to inherit all his property), entail (by which a man could prevent his land holdings from being broken up by dictating in advance the succession of heirs to his property), and quitrents (the small sums landowners paid for the use of their land).

In the republican spirit of the new states, it became illegal for citizens to accept titles of nobility from foreign nations. Suspected attempts to establish a native aristocracy aroused equal opposition. When officers of the Continental Army formed the Society of the Cincinnati in 1783, naming it after a Roman farmer who had gone to war to protect the ancient republic, they were severely criticized for creating an elite organization and particularly for making membership in the charitable club hereditary.

Religion

The American Revolution also weakened the ties between church and state, leading to a total separation that would be a basic part of American life. When the Declaration of Independence was adopted most of the colonies had an established church (that is, one supported with tax money levied within the individual colonies). In the South and in the lower counties of New York, the Church of England was established; in New England it was the Congregational Church. During the Revolutionary War the Church of England stopped receiving state support, and its many Loyalist ministers fled to England. Under their new constitutions the New England states continued to support an established religion, but taxpayers could specify to which Protestant church they wanted their money to go. The American Methodist Church was growing fast, with a system of circuit riders traveling to preach in rural communities. In the absence of permanent preachers, local lay groups gathered weekly to strengthen each other's faith by testimony, admonition, prayer, and joint Bible study. The Baptist Church grew, too, on a wave of revivalist fervor.

The new state constitutions guaranteed religious freedom in their bills of rights, but this meant the freedom to belong to any Protestant church, not necessarily the freedom to belong to no church at all. For instance, all states required that their elected officials take a religious oath.

Virginia was the first state to abolish all such religious restrictions. Its legislature adopted a statute written by Thomas Jefferson which stated "no man shall be compelled to frequent or support any religious worship, place, or ministry whatsoever," since "Almighty God hath created the mind free." By 1800 all but three states had followed Virginia in separating church and state by law. Only Massachusetts, Connecticut, and New Hampshire maintained a state-supported church into the early nineteenth century. In addition rationalism gained in popularity, and by the beginning of the nineteenth century church membership had dropped to only one out of every ten or twenty Americans.

Education

Five state constitutions paid lip service to the idea of publicly supported education, but by 1800 none of the states had actually implemented such a plan. In fact, town-supported schools actually declined in number and were usually replaced by private academies. Efforts to reform school curricula by replacing the study of Greek and Latin with more practical courses met with only limited success. The classics remained requirements for admission to every university. After the war the number of colleges in the United States doubled. By 1789 there were eighteen schools of higher learning, with at least one in almost every state. College names were changed in a show of American patriotism: King's College became Columbia, and Queen's College became Rutgers.

AMERICAN NATIONALISM

The states came together in an unusual process. Most peoples that have fought for independence have experienced a strong sense of nationalism first and then gone to war to secure their national freedom. In America the process was reversed. As one historian has said, "Our nation was the child, not the father, of our revolution."

After the Revolution most Americans still felt that their first loyalty was to their own state. However, a new sense of being American was developing. The members of the Continental Congress, uprooted from their homes in the various colonies, left behind some of their provincial concerns. In Philadelphia they worked together for the welfare of the entire nation. They drew up the Declaration of Independence in the name of the people of the united colonies. The literature of the period from 1764 to 1780 was full of self-conscious statements about American culture and the American past. The flag of thirteen stars and thirteen stripes adopted in June 1777 gave the American people a visible symbol of their unity.

The war itself had done much to promote a spirit of nationalism. Patriots had fought for American liberty, not for the freedom of Connecticut or New York, and the struggle had often taken them far from their home states. A common enemy had made Americans realize that they had a common cause. British soldiers' and officers' disdain for Americans intensified the feeling of separateness from England.

Practical considerations also brought the states together. Now that the United States could no longer depend on Britain for manufactured goods, American industries had to increase their output and cooperate with each other. Increased trade between states showed American merchants that they had common interests. Similarly, Americans recognized the folly of having thirteen separate postal systems, or thirteen separate ministries of foreign affairs. A central post office, a centralized diplomacy, a single government that could declare war, deal with the Indians, establish weights and measures, and settle disputes between the states or on the high seas was increasingly seen as a necessity.

Finally, Americans of every state felt pride in their great national leaders, especially Benjamin Franklin, Thomas Jefferson, and George Washington. Franklin's *Poor Richard's Almanack* was read by many Americans and the French considered him an even greater scientific genius than Newton. His skill in handling the intricate diplomacy of the revolutionary era crowned him with new laurels when he was already seventy. In Europe Franklin was regarded as an American, not as a Pennsylvanian, and he was regarded in the same way by his fellow citizens. Jefferson, the author of the Declaration of Independence, was also becoming a figure of national prominence, and Washington was undoubtedly the greatest American in the eyes of his contemporaries. As a military strategist, a courageous general, and a model of personal integrity and solid republican virtues, Washington was the symbol of the new nation's aspirations.

CREATING A NATIONAL GOVERNMENT

Despite widespread feelings of nationalism, Americans were quite wary about uniting their sovereign states. People who had just revolted against an overly centralized government could hardly find it easy to give similar power to another central government. Many Americans also doubted whether a republican form of government was suitable for a country as large as the United States. Montesquieu, an eighteenth-century French philosopher widely read in America, maintained that a large territory could not be organized as a republic; it could be ruled only by a despot. Indeed, history provided few examples of successful large republics. The republics of ancient Greece had been city-states; Rome had abandoned republicanism after it became an immense empire; the republic of Switzerland was a tiny country, broken up into still smaller districts. In a large nation, the argument ran, the legislature would inevitably sit in a capital far from the electorate, thus growing out of touch with the will of the voters.

Nevertheless, most educated Americans recognized that thirteen independent states could not survive in a world dominated by such powers as Britain, Spain, and France. In an effort to establish a basis for a national government, Congress decided to define its powers in a constitution. A committee presented a first-draft Articles of Confederation to Congress eight days after the Declaration of Independence was sent to the printer. Busy trying to run a war, Congress bickered over the document for a year. Four more years passed before all the states ratified the revised version.

Finally adopted in 1781, the Articles of Confederation were much weaker than the Constitution which would replace it in 1787. But under the circumstances the creation of any kind of permanent centralized authority was quite an achievement.

The Articles of Confederation

The way states would be represented in a new legislature was a major stumbling block. As things stood representatives to the Congress were elected annually by their state legislatures. Each state had one vote in congressional decisions. Small states such as Rhode Island thus wielded the same power as very large states such as Pennsylvania and Virginia. The large states had agreed to this arrangement only as a temporary, wartime measure. When the first draft of the Articles of Confederation proposed to make it permanent, a vehement debate erupted that lasted almost a year. Finally, the rule of one state, one vote was accepted, when it was further stipulated that every major measure had to pass by a two-thirds majority of the states. Thus the interests of every region (the North, the Middle states, and the South) would be protected.

The controversial first draft framed by John Dickinson attempted to establish a stronger national government than most members of Congress found acceptable. After the Articles were revised, however, federal power was severely limited. The union was to be barely more than a "league of friendship" between the states. Each state would retain "its sovereignty, freedom, and independence, and every Power, Jurisdiction and right" not delegated to Congress in the Articles. It was so natural for Americans to think of their states as independent units that no one, not even the author of the Articles, referred to the United States in the singular. People invariably said, "The United States *are* winning the war."

The Articles provided for a federal system of government but left the most important powers to the states. Congress was given no power to regulate trade (which meant it could not impose a tariff) or to levy internal taxes. Its lack of power to impose taxes was a crucial decision, for it weakened the power of Congress considerably. In addition, the country was to have no chief executive or national court system. A one-house congress would direct the league of thirteen nations. It would have the power to ask the states for revenue, regulate foreign affairs, send and receive ambassadors, make treaties, declare war and conclude peace, establish a post office, regulate the coinage, and control Indian affairs. All other powers were left to the states.

Problems of ratification

Ratification of the Articles was a long and difficult process. The main obstacle blocking the required approval by all the states was the question of what to do with the huge territory beyond the Appalachian Mountains, the western lands. The Proclamation of 1763 had kept most Americans out of this territory. But the measure had not kept land speculators from staking out prospective claims, or seven states from demanding vast tracts. Six of these "landed" states (Massachusetts, Connecticut, Virginia, the Carolinas, and Georgia) based their claims on their royal charters. These documents had granted them all territories to the west—in fact, to the Pacific Ocean. The rather shadowy claims of the seventh landed state, New York, were based on the argument that since New York governed the Iroquois Indians, it should also govern their lands.

The remaining six "landless" states had fixed western boundaries. They wanted Congress itself to take charge of the western lands, canceling the claims of the landed states. It seemed to them that the western lands should be a national area accessible to the citizens of all thirteen states.

These territorial disputes were bitter. Even during the Revolutionary War, Virginia and Pennsylvania bickered over the Ohio Valley; Connecticut and Pennsylvania both wanted the Wyoming Valley. Three of the landless states—Pennsylvania, New Jersey, and Maryland—had entered into the fray by purchasing territory in the Ohio Valley from the Indians.

Now Maryland, speaking for the six states with fixed boundaries, refused to ratify the Articles of Confederation until the seven landed states renounced their claims to the western lands. Maryland argued that if the landed states received territories in the west, they could sell the land and use the profits to free their own citizens from paying taxes. Citizens of the landless states would all flock to the landed states, attracted by the prospect of paying few or no taxes.

The deadlock was finally broken when New York, and then Virginia, gave up their western claims. Patriots in Virginia, led by James Madison, preferred giving up the Ohio Valley to standing in the way of a union of the thirteen states. Eventually all the landed states surrendered their claims to Congress.

After learning that Virginia had yielded, Maryland finally ratified the Articles of Confederation on March 1, 1781. The Articles immediately went into effect, and the first union of the independent states took place the day after Maryland's ratification. A nation of sorts had been born.

The Confederation Period

The years 1781 to 1789 made it clear that the government of the new nation had little power. Many Americans soon felt that a weak national government was not the best way to protect the individual freedom and equal opportunity they desired.

Under the Articles Congress could pass resolutions but it had no way of putting them into effect. The states frequently ignored the resolutions as well as federal requests for funds. Congress had no power to impose taxes or tariffs. The delegates to Congress had little opportunity to exercise their abilities because their terms were so short. A delegate was elected for only one year at a time and could not be reelected for more than three years in every six. The older leaders of Congress during the Revolution—Patrick Henry, Thomas Jefferson, Benjamin Franklin, John Adams, Samuel Adams, John Hancock—had all left government service. Their places were taken by younger, less experienced men.

In order to pass any legislation the Articles of Confederation required that at least seven states had to support it. To make decisions about war and peace or to vote appropriations, nine states had to support it. During the first four months of 1784, Congress had a nine-state quorum on only three days. The frequent lack of such quorums continually interrupted the work of Congress, especially since there was no executive branch to provide continuity. Congress created the departments of war, foreign affairs, and finance to help fill this gap. The three department heads assumed some executive responsibility, but these appointive posts were not always filled. For example, after the first secretary of war resigned in 1783, the position remained vacant for two years.

Geographical as well as political uncertainties also handicapped Congress. There was no permanent capital. In 1783 a mutiny among the militia in Philadelphia frightened Congress away from that city and the delegates wandered about like gypsies, from Princeton to Annapolis, to Trenton, and finally to New York.

Worst of all, Congress was impoverished. Throughout the 1780s Congress received only one-fourth of the revenue it requested from the states. The dismal situation of the Confederation Congress prompted John Jay, now secretary for foreign affairs, to write in a gloomy letter to Washington on June 27, 1786:

> Our affairs seem to lead to some crisis, some revolution—something that I cannot foresee or conjecture. I am uneasy and apprehensive; more so than during the war. Then we had a fixed object, and though the means and time of obtaining it were often problematical, yet I did firmly believe we should ultimately succeed, because I was convinced that justice was with us. The case now is altered; we are going and doing wrong, and therefore I look forward to evils and calamities, but without being able to guess at the instrument, nature, or measure of them.

FOREIGN AFFAIRS

The absence of unity among the states (which continued to behave like independent countries during the Confederation period) and the lack of power in the central government made it extremely difficult to carry on diplomatic relations with foreign powers. The impoverished, ineffective, fragmented new country was scorned abroad. A best-selling pamphlet in England stated:

> It will not be an easy matter to bring the American states to act as a nation. They were not to be feared as such by us . . . . We might as well dread the effect of combinations among the German as among the American states.

John Adams and Thomas Jefferson—the American ministers to London and Paris, respectively—suffered daily from the humiliations imposed upon them. Adams complained that the British treated him with "dry decency and cold civility." He confessed, "No step that I can take, no language I can hold will do any good, or indeed much harm." Jefferson echoed the lament: "We are the lowest and most obscure of the whole diplomatic tribe."

John Adams was the American minister to London during the Confederation Period.

Problems with the English

There were several causes of friction between America and Great Britain during the 1780s. One problem was mutual treaty violations. In the peace treaty of 1783 which ended the Revolution, Congress had pledged that British creditors would meet with "no lawful impediment" in collecting the millions of dollars owed them by individual Americans. However, when English creditors tried to get their money, American debtors flatly refused. "If we are now to pay the debts due to British merchants," asked George Mason of Virginia, "what have we been fighting for all this while?" Years later the United States government finally paid its citizens' debts in a lump sum to Great Britain.

Tories met with similar difficulties. The peace treaty had promised that American authorities would protect Loyalists against the vengeance of patriots and agreed to "recommend" that the states make sure that confiscated Tory property would be restored to its owners. This article was not honored. Years later Britain itself finally awarded 5000 American Tories more than three million pounds to help cover their losses.

Britain violated the treaty by refusing to turn over the forts it held on American soil along the Great Lakes. Canadian merchants had urged the British to hold onto the forts in order to continue the profitable fur trade with the Indians as long as possible. England also worried that the Indians in the area, left to the mercy of American frontier farmers, might turn on the Canadians in revenge for the British departure.

The Continental Congress, as in all its diplomatic ventures of this period, was helpless. It was unable to protect the Tories or to drive the English out of American territory. Knowing that Congress was weak, England used American violations of the treaty as a pretext for retaining the Great Lakes forts. The British announced that they would give up the posts only when Loyalist properties were restored and English merchants had been paid.

Another lingering controversy developed with Britain over Vermont. Both New Hampshire and New York had squabbled over the land between the Connecticut River and Lake Champlain. In 1777, however, the people of Vermont created their own independent government. They even went so far as to promise England their neutrality during the war in exchange for British diplomatic recognition. After the war, Vermont's most important leaders—the three Allen brothers, Ethan, Levi, and Ira—considered making such an agreement again. They hinted that they might reunite with the mother country and attach Vermont to Canada. British intrigue with Vermont continued until 1791, when Vermont finally chose to become the fourteenth state in the American union.

Problems with the Spanish

After the war England and Spain still exercised strong influence over more than half of America's territory. Britain dominated the Northwest from its forts along the Great Lakes, and Spain retained control over the Southwest through its possession of New Orleans and the lower Mississippi River.

Although Britain had granted America all land north of Florida, south of the Great Lakes, and east of the Mississippi River, as well as the right to navigate the Mississippi, Spain had not been a party to the peace treaty. Now Spain claimed the entire Southwest from the Gulf of Mexico to the Ohio River. But by 1785 some 50,000 Americans had settled in the areas which would become Tennessee and Kentucky and they could hardly afford to haul their produce by land over the Alleghenies to markets in the East. The only economical way to transport their goods was by boat, down the Mississippi to the Gulf of Mexico before heading east. Spain, recognizing this necessity, attempted to drive out unwelcome Americans by announcing in 1784 that henceforth the river would be closed to all foreigners.

Spain further harassed settlers by arming the Indian tribes of the Southwest for periodical raids on American villages. At the same time, however, she offered western settlers land, religious toleration, and even the use of the Mississippi at low rates if they would swear allegiance to Spain.

Spain's tactics made many American settlers in the territories of Tennessee and Kentucky consider breaking off all ties with the ineffective Confederation government, declaring their independence, and negotiating directly with Spain for more favorable trading conditions. As early as 1775 Daniel Boone had rejected the prospect of statehood for Kentucky, declaring it "entirely against the voice of the people at large." In the 1780s the people of Tennessee began to listen with interest to Spanish offers. In 1784 George Washington, after journeying hundreds of miles through the back country, reported: "The western settlers . . . stand as it were on a pivot. The touch of a feather would turn them any way."

Spain tried to drive a deeper wedge into the union of American states by encouraging a conflict of interests between the Northeast and the South and Southwest. Merchants in New England had little use for the western settlers, whom they regarded as boors and ruffians. What concerned New England more was the trade with Spain. During the war Spain had permitted Americans to trade with her empire to a limited degree. Now American business was hungry for a larger part of that profitable market. Accordingly, the Spanish envoy, Don Diego de Gardoqui, made an offer to Secretary for Foreign Affairs John Jay. Americans, Gardoqui said, would be invited to expand their trade with Spain if the United States would abandon use of the Mississippi River for twenty-five years.

John Jay—and the merchants of Boston, Newport, Philadelphia, and New York—were willing to make a treaty on such a basis. According to rumor, Gardoqui had persuaded Jay to ignore his instructions from Congress, which were to demand the right to navigate the entire Mississippi River. The charming Spaniard, it was said, had managed to ingratiate himself with Mrs. Jay, who had a great hold over her husband. Such attentions were, in fact, part of Gardoqui's official instructions from Madrid. He wrote to the Spanish foreign office: "Notwithstanding my age, I am acting the gallant and accompanying Madame to the official entertainments and dances, because she likes it and I will do everything which appeals to me for the King's best interest."

Jay's decision to ignore his instructions, however, was based on his belief that commerce with Spain was more in the interest of America at that time than the use of the Mississippi River. As he told Congress, the river would be an American possession in due time. All the United States had to do was wait perhaps twenty to twenty-five years until it was strong enough, and then seize the waterway. In the meantime, why not grasp the benefits of a favorable trading agreement with Spain?

When Jay proposed a treaty meeting Gardoqui's terms, the Southern delegates in Congress and the whole Southwest erupted in rage. "The prohibition of the navigation of the Mississippi," wrote one indignant pioneer, "has astonished the whole western country. To sell us and make us vassals of the merciless Spaniards is a grievance not to be borne." The settlers were so furious that Jay had to abandon his talks with Gardoqui.

In 1788, Spain did finally grant Americans the right to navigate the Mississippi (although they had to pay high duties for the privilege). But settlers in the West long remembered with bitterness the East Coast's plan to exchange free passage through the Mississippi for trade concessions with Spain, in defiance of the wishes of Congress.

THE WESTERN LANDS

Opposition to British and Spanish control of the area between the Appalachian Mountains and the Mississippi River, as well as the westward movement of Americans, finally pushed the Confederation Congress toward its most important accomplishment—the creation of a policy for orderly westward expansion. Legislation passed from 1785 to 1787 pertaining to the Old Northwest (the area above the Ohio River) was later applied to the rest of the country as settlers continued to move across the continent.

Although the vast northwest tract of land America received in the peace of 1783 was rich and promising, it was almost entirely inhabited by Indian tribes, French traders, and British soldiers. None of the area's inhabitants wanted Americans to enter their wooded paradise, but by 1785 Congress was already laying plans for the invasion.

When Virginia ceded to Congress its claims to the Northwest, the state had stipulated that the territory "shall be formed into distinct republican states, which shall become members of the Federal Union, and have the same rights of sovereignty, freedom, and independence of the other States." Under the Land Ordinance of 1785, and the more important Northwest Ordinance of 1787, Congress set up a system under which these goals could be realized.

The Land Ordinance of 1785 provided for surveying the Northwest into six-mile-square townships. Each township was to be further subdivided into thirty-six sections. Purchasers could buy no less than one section (640 acres) at the price of a dollar an acre. Since $640 was

WESTERN EMIGRATION.

JOURNAL

OF

DOCTOR JEREMIAH SMIPLETON'S

TOUR TO OHIO.

CONTAINING

An account of the numerous difficulties, Hair-breadth Escapes, Mortifications and Privations, which the DOCTOR and his family experienced on their Journey from Maine, to the 'Land of Promise,' and during a residence of three years in that highly extolled country.

BY H. TRUMBULL.

Nulli Fides Frontis.

BOSTON--PRINTED BY S. SEWALL.

Two early views of pioneering in Ohio. The glowing account appeared in a 1799 advertisement offering Ohio land for sale. The sad tale, on the other hand, appeared in Doctor Jeremia Smipleton's Tour to Ohio, *an anti-emigration tract published in Boston in 1819. The truth probably lay somewhere in between.*

"No Part of North America will require less Encouragement for the Production of Naval Stores, and raw Materials for Manufactories in Europe, and for supplying the West-India Islands with Lumber, Provisions, &c. than the Country of the Ohio; and for the following Reasons: —1st. The Lands are excellent, the Climate temperate, the Grapes, Silk-Worms and Mulberry-Trees, abound every where. Hemp, Hops, and Rye grow spontaneously in the Vallies and low Lands; Lead and Iron Ore are found in Plenty in the Hills; Salt Springs are innumerable, and no Soil is better adapted to the Culture of Tobacco, Flax and Cotton, than that of the Ohio. —2dly. The Country is well-watered by several navigable Rivers communicating with each other. —3dly. The River Ohio is, at all Seasons of the Year, navigable for large Boats, like West Country Barges, rowed by four or five Men, and from the Month of February to April large Ships may be built on the Ohio and sent to Sea, laden with Hemp, Iron, Flax, Silk, Tobacco, Cotton, Pot-Ash, Beef, Flour, Corn, Ship-Plank, &c."

"You will, on your arrival there, be obliged to sleep in a hollow tree, or build yourself a log hut, for here are no carpenters—kill and dress your own game, for here are no butchers—clothe yourself in skins, when your stock of apparel is worn out, for here are no factories, shoemakers, tailors, hatters or tanners—and pound your own corn, for you may travel in this wild wilderness many miles, without discovering the sign of a mill—in short, nothing can be obtained here without costing more for the transportation than the original price of any article you may want. As to *society,* if you wish to converse in any human language out of your family, you must go twenty or thirty miles to your next door neighbor, with your axe instead of staff—for you must cut your way thither, for want of roads—and perhaps, after all, find him almost as hoggish as the 'swines in your pens' or the more numerous class of the inhabitants of Ohio, the wildcat, panther, etc. who frequently associate with our tame animals to their sorrow, and sometimes with young children to our mourning:—and fags I'd rather be a hog-reeve in good New-England than hold any office in this back woods country, where the inhabitants walk on all fours, with the exception of a few double headed fools. Take my advice, therefore, Scruple, and put off your journey, til you think a little further on the subject.

steep for a pioneer farming family, this provision attracted few customers. In later years the price and minimum number of acres was lowered. In the meantime speculators bought up large tracts of land illegally at lower prices and then resold small pieces of it to farmers. Many farmers simply settled on a tract of land in the hope that when it was eventually surveyed and put up for sale, they would have the first opportunity to buy it.

According to the Northwest Ordinance of 1787, the entire Northwest Territory was to be carved into no more than five and no less than three states. These states were to provide public elementary education and be free forever from the institution of slavery. The first stage of

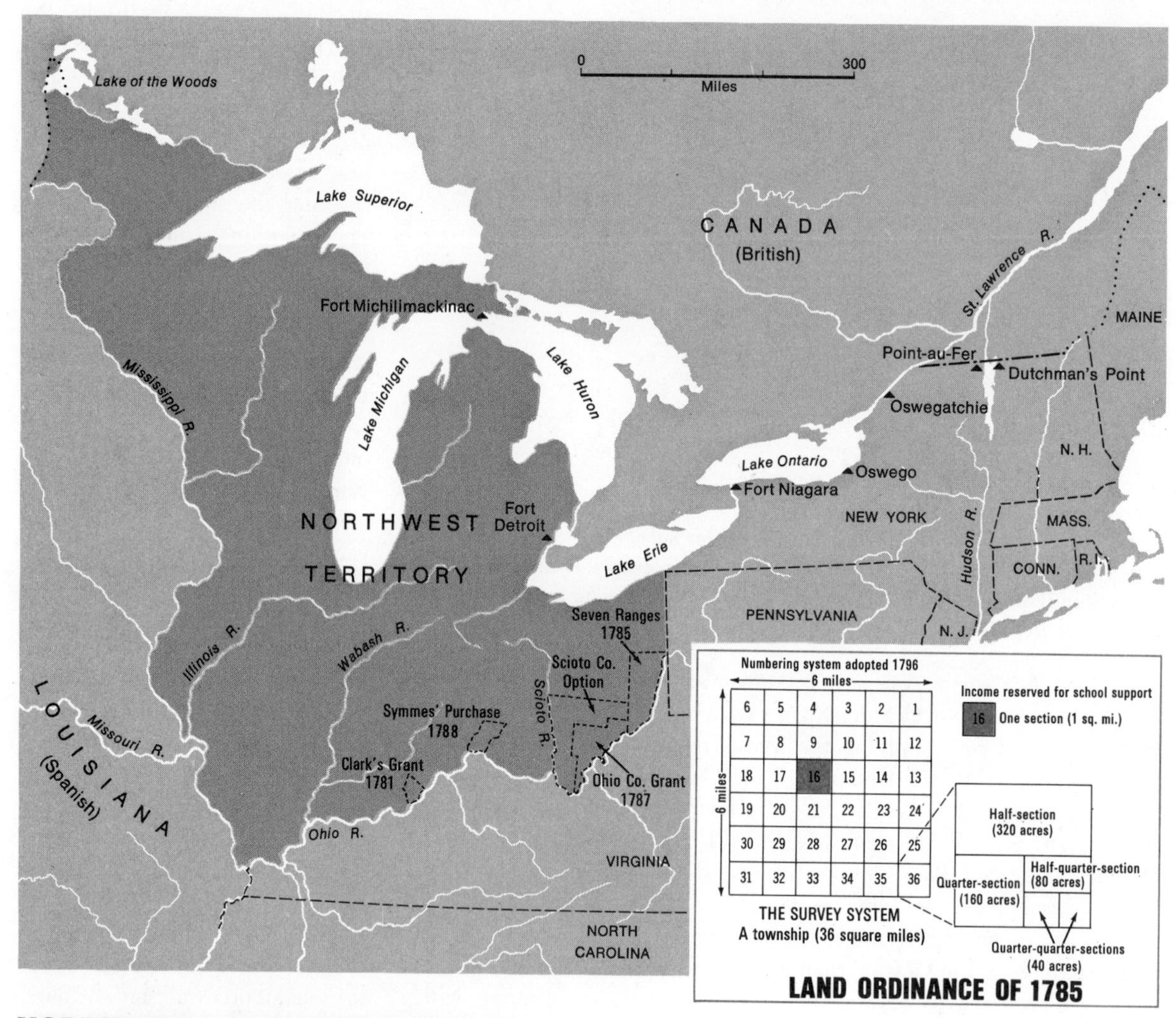

NORTHWEST ORDINANCE OF 1787

 Northwest Territory (acquired 1781; organized 1787)

▲ British posts after 1783

territorial government would consist of a governor, a secretary, and three judges, all appointed by Congress. When 5000 male inhabitants over twenty years of age had settled in the territory, the second stage of territorial government would begin. Property owners with fifty acres or more could elect the lower house of a legislature of their own; the upper house, a five-person legislative council, would be appointed by Congress. The joint body would enact laws for the region that would be subject only to the governor's veto. Moreover, the assembly would send a nonvoting delegate to Congress. When the territory had 60,000 inhabitants the third phase of government would begin. It could be admitted into the Union "on an equal footing with the original states in all respects whatever," as soon as it formed a state constitution similar to the ones in the original thirteen states. When Ohio became a state in the Union in 1803, its Senators may not have had the prestige of those from Massachusetts or Virginia, but their votes counted for just as much.

The Ordinance established the basic procedures by which most new territories would become states as the nation advanced to the Pacific. It solved America's problem of how to dispose of its landed empire and prevented its pioneers from losing their political rights as they moved west. The first British empire had foundered on the question of imperial control versus home rule, but the new nation had found a way to avoid the same mistake. In the territorial phases the Confederation Congress followed the British procedure of an appointed governor and council, and an elected assembly. But it wisely decided against a policy of indefinite colonial status for the newly settled areas.

ECONOMIC PROBLEMS

The Confederation Congress inherited a terrible economic situation. In 1781, when Robert Morris became head of the newly created Department of Finance, the government's credit was collapsing, the army was suffering from lack of food and uniforms, and the Continental dollar was almost worthless. Morris managed to hold off these problems for a few years, with help from the privately controlled Bank of North America. He obtained foreign loans to restore America's credit, improved the method for supplying the army, and checked the devaluation of paper money by backing it with borrowed gold. But despite Morris's efforts, the war and its aftermath disrupted foreign trade and created a depression which badly weakened public confidence in the Confederation government. The instability of the American economy became the overriding issue of the 1780s.

America had always had an unfavorable balance of trade. But while it was still part of the British Empire this imbalance had been a family matter. In the first few years after the Revolutionary War, America imported three times more from Britain than it exported. This drained almost every ounce of American silver and gold into Britain's coffers. Moreover, Britain set high tariff walls around its empire. America could import only a few raw materials from Britain in its own ships. No American manufactured goods could be taken into Britain. In addition, America was cut off from the West Indies trade except by smuggling or using British ships. The shipping industry, halted by the British blockade during the war, was crippled once more as American vessels were prevented from returning to familiar trading areas. These losses were only slightly offset by new markets that American merchants were desperately trying to establish. Trade with France and Holland provided some relief. American merchants also turned profits in far-off China by selling sea otter skins they had purchased from the Pacific Northwest Indians.

The continuing unfavorable balance of trade prevented the stabilization of the American economy, made prices drop as much as twenty-five percent, caused numerous bankruptcies, and eventually undermined the currency. The obvious solution was for Congress to set up tariffs that would protect native manufacturers, but the Articles of Confederation had specifically denied Congress this power. Some states individually passed laws to discourage imports, but these were piecemeal measures that often backfired. One observer said of the New Hampshire tariff law: "It was a blow aimed at Britain but wounds us and our friends."

Seeing the need for a national tariff system, eleven states agreed to give Congress that power as early as 1781. The Articles of Confederation, however, required that any amendment would have to receive the unanimous consent of the states. The amendment was defeated by a slim margin as was a similar one a few years later. The nation's economy demanded central control, but the existing governmental machinery was incapable of imposing it.

The lack of foreign trade further strained a domestic economy already in a state of confusion. During the war years, Congress had resorted to printing more and more paper money to meet its operating expenses. Because no gold existed in a national treasury to back the paper, the Continental dollar was almost worthless by 1781.

After the war the Congress was saddled with a domestic debt of approximately forty-two million dollars and a foreign debt of about twelve million (actually very low compared to today's national debt). Congress had to rely on the states for the needed funds. Because only about one-fourth of the requested sum was honored, the debts could not be paid. Faith in the government's ability to meet its obligations declined. In 1783 Robert Morris resigned the treasury post in disgust.

The states had their own war debts to meet and some of them also needed money to repair war damage. As a result they also continued to print paper money as they had during the war. Soon paper currency dropped sharply in purchasing power, for there was no gold in state treasuries either. To restore credit the states began imposing heavy taxes on their citizens; some severely restricted the issuance of new paper currency. In the postwar years Massachusetts farmers handed over about one-third of their income in state taxes.

Popular unrest

The postwar depression hit merchants in the cities first. However, about ninety percent of the population was farmers, and they were only gradually affected by hard times. During the war, and even for a few years after, farmers made money selling their produce at very high prices to both the British and American armies. However, by 1785 the British army had been withdrawn and the American army disbanded. The farmers' market shrank and so did their income. At the same time state legislatures raised taxes. During the war debtors, who were usually farmers, could pay their creditors in easily available, devalued paper money. But now they were called upon to pay their debts and high taxes on a sharply reduced income.

Nonetheless this depression was not as damaging as some modern historians have stated. Virginia farmers were soon selling more tobacco than before the war. By 1790 the export of American farm produce had doubled over its prewar level. Banks were paying handsome dividends to their investors. Many workers were needed for building new roads, canals, bridges, and houses. Cities were growing rapidly. In fact, the depression that followed the French and Indian War may well have been worse.

Trouble in Rhode Island

The postwar depression, however, was serious enough to many people. Throughout the country, debtor farmers were begging their state governments for relief. They were making three demands: stay laws (which would give debtors a period of grace before they had to resume paying their loans), tender laws (which would allow them to pay their debts in produce), and more paper money (which would again devalue the currency and favor those with large debts).

In 1785 and 1786 seven of the state governments yielded to these demands. In South Carolina, New York, and Pennsylvania, where paper money was issued with care, the new currency held its value. In other states, however, devaluation soon set in. In Georgia state dollars lost seventy-five percent of their value in one year. In Rhode Island a new issue of paper money prompted a minor crisis. Creditors distrusted the new notes and refused to accept them. Finally, in a move to force acceptance of the new money, the Rhode Island assembly (which was controlled by debtor farmers) passed a law fining creditors for declining payment in paper dollars. In a test case trying the constitutionality of the law, the Rhode Island Supreme Court refused to rule on the matter. The law was subsequently repealed.

An episode from Shays' Rebellion in 1786.

SHAYS' REBELLION

During the Confederation period the political leadership of most states was a conservative one that demanded order in society. These leaders were nervous about signs of unrest anywhere in the nation. In 1786, when a group of Massachusetts farmers rose in protest, they were convinced that the collapse of authority was at hand in America. Hard times, tight money, and heavy taxes had sent many bankrupt Massachusetts farmers to debtors' prison and caused more to lose their land. The state legislature was controlled by wealthy merchants from the Atlantic coast, partly because other areas were too poor to send delegates to Boston. There were even times in some counties when nobody could meet the property qualifications for serving in the state government.

Oppressed and underrepresented, about a thousand farmers in the west rebelled. They were led in a haphazard way by Captain Daniel Shays, a veteran of the Revolutionary War. Weary of fruitlessly petitioning an unresponsive legislature to pass stay laws and issue paper money, the rebels took the law into their own hands. Shays' ragged forces attacked the civil courts where hundreds of mortgage foreclosure cases were scheduled. When the rebels menaced federal arsenals, state troops put down the disturbances. By the end of February 1787, Captain Shays had fled the state and his "army" had vanished.

Thomas Jefferson pointed out that it had only been "a *little rebellion*." But George Washington, who feared mob violence, dramatically exclaimed, "What, gracious God, is man! That there should be such inconsistency and perfidiousness in his conduct? We are fast verging to anarchy and confusion!" Perhaps the usually taciturn general was overreacting. Nonetheless, when Massachusetts appealed to Congress to quell the rebellion, Congress had been powerless to help. Washington's horror of the Massachusetts mob was equaled only by his disgust with Congress. He described it as "a half-starved, limping government, always moving upon crutches and tottering at every step."

Many Americans now felt that the time had come to give the Confederation government more power. American representatives were being insulted in foreign capitals; American manufacturers were suffering from foreign competition; American settlers west of the Appalachians were threatened by the British, the Spanish, and the Indians; and American goods were barred from British ports. Worst of all, the country was in a depression. Although conditions took a turn for the better by 1786, they were still bad enough to cause outbreaks of violence. Against each of these grave national problems, Congress was powerless to take action. Many delegates in Congress had for a long time wanted a stronger central government. They believed the opportunity to obtain it was now at hand.

Readings

GENERAL WORKS

Alden, John R., *The American Revolution, 1775–1783.* New York: Harper & Row, 1954.

Burnett, Edmund C., *The Continental Congress.* New York: Macmillan, 1941 (Paper: W. W. Norton, 1964).

Davis, David B., *The Problem of Slavery in an Age of Revolution, 1770–1823.* New York: Cornell University Press, 1975.

Douglas, Elisha P., *Rebels and Democrats.* Chapel Hill, N.C.: University of North Carolina Press, 1955.

Jensen, Merrill, *The Articles of Confederation: An Interpretation of the Social-Constitutional History of the American Revolution, 1774–1781.* Madison, Wis.: University of Wisconsin Press, 1940.

Jensen, Merrill, *The New Nation.* New York: Knopf, 1950.

Main, Jackson T., *The Sovereign States, 1775–1783.* New York: Franklin Watts 1973. (Paper)

Morris, Richard B., *The American Revolution Reconsidered.* New York: Harper & Row, 1967.

Nagel, Paul C., *One Nation Indivisible: The Union in American Thought, 1776–1861.* New York: Oxford University Press, 1964.

Nettels, Curtis P., *The Emergence of a National Economy, 1775–1815.* New York: Holt, Rinehart & Winston, 1969.

Nye, Russel B., *The Cultural Life of the New Nation, 1776–1830.* New York: Harper & Row, 1960.

Peckham, Howard H., *The War for Independence. A Military History.* Chicago: University of Chicago Press, 1958.

Wood, Gordon S., *Creation of the American Republic, 1776–1787.* Chapel Hill, N.C.: University of North Carolina Press, 1969.

SPECIAL STUDIES

Bemis, Samuel F., *The Diplomacy of the American Revolution (Foundations of American Diplomacy, 1775–1823).* New York: Appleton-Century-Crofts, 1935 (Paper: Indiana University Press, 1957).

Jameson, J. Franklin, *The American Revolution Considered as a Social Movement.* Princeton, N.J.: Princeton University Press, 1926 (Paper, 1967).

Main, Jackson T., *The Antifederalists: Critics of the Constitution: 1781–1788.* Chapel Hill, N.C.: University of North Carolina Press, 1970.

Morris, R. B., *Peacemakers: The Great Powers and American Independence.* New York: Harper & Row. (Paper)

Nelson, William H., *The American Tory.* New York: Oxford University Press, 1962 (Paper: Beacon Press, 1964).

Starkey, Marion L., *A Little Rebellion.* New York: Knopf, 1955.

Zilversmit, Arthur, *The First Emancipation: The Abolition of Slavery in the North.* Chicago: University of Chicago Press, 1967.

PRIMARY SOURCES

de Crèvecoeur, J. Hector, *Letters from an American Farmer*. New York: Dutton, 1969.

Kenyon, Cecelia M. (Ed.), *Antifederalists*. New York: Bobbs-Merrill Co., 1966. (Paper)

Taylor, Robert J. (Ed.), *Massachusetts, Colony to Commonwealth: Documents on the Formation of Its Constitution, 1775–1780*. North Carolina: University of North Carolina Press, 1961. (Paper)

BIOGRAPHIES

Brant, Irving, *James Madison: Father of the Constitution, 1787–1800*, Vol. II. Indianapolis: Bobbs-Merrill, 1950.

Flexner, James T., *George Washington in the American Revolution, 1775–1783*. Boston: Little, Brown, 1968.

Mitchell, Broadus, *Alexander Hamilton*, Vol. II. New York: Macmillan, 1957.

Tyler, Moses C., *Patrick Henry*. Ithaca, N.Y.: Cornell University Press, 1962.

Van Doren, Carl C., *Benjamin Franklin*. New York: Viking, 1964.

HISTORICAL NOVELS

Bellamy, Edward, *The Duke of Stockbridge: A Romance of Shays' Rebellion*. Cambridge: Harvard University Press, 1962.

Boyd, James, *Drums*. New York: Scribner's, 1968.

Brown, Charles B., *Ormond*, Ernest Marchand (Ed.). Darien, Conn.: Hafner, 1969.

Cooper, James Fenimore, *The Spy*. New York: Oxford University Press, 1968.

Edmonds, Walter D., *Drums Along the Mohawk*. Boston: Atlantic Monthly Press–Little, Brown, 1969.

Lancaster, Bruce, *Guns of Burgoyne*. New York: Stokes, 1939.

Simms, W. Gilmore, *The Partisan: A Romance of the Revolution*. New York: AMS Press, 1969.

Dark Eagle: The Rise and Fall of Benedict Arnold

The Dark Eagle will soar aloft to the sun . . . Yet when he soars highest his fall is most certain. When his wings brush the sky then the arrow will pierce his heart . . .

CHIEF NATANIS TO BENEDICT ARNOLD
NEAR QUEBEC, AUTUMN, 1775

Most Americans know that General Benedict Arnold plotted to betray the United States during the Revolutionary War, thus linking his name for all time with that terrible word *traitor*. Few realize, however, that Arnold was also one of the nation's first authentic heroes. From 1775 to 1777 his battlefield successes stood unequalled in either the British or American armies, and he has since been compared with great generals from Hannibal to George Patton. One of Arnold's biographers goes so far as to call him "easily the outstanding battlefield officer of the Revolution."

Benedict Arnold lived two full lives in only a few years, and history's characterization of him as a traitor obscures his true contribution to the Revolutionary War. Even his treachery worked to the advantage of the American cause, shocking and uniting the country at a time of deep division and defeatism. As hero *and* as traitor, Arnold was one of those Americans most responsible for the war's success.

His career as a hero was full of extraordinary feats. Two years after he volunteered for service in the Continental Army, Arnold had (among other things) captured Fort Ticonderoga in upstate New York, led a march through several hundred miles of Canadian wilderness in a bold attack on Quebec, built a small fleet from scratch on Lake Champlain and defended the colonies from a naval invasion, and played the dominant role in General Horatio Gates' defeat of General John Burgoyne at Saratoga, New York.

Arnold seemed to have a knack for participating in crucial battles, and his reputation grew accordingly. The capture of Ticonderoga, for example, was the first major American offensive of the war and gave the rebels control of the northern sections of the war zone throughout the conflict. While the assault on Quebec failed, it proved that the Americans could take the conflict to their enemies. Arnold's conduct inspired admiration in friend and foe alike. Lord George Germaine, secretary of state for the colonies, lamented that the British had narrowly failed to capture Arnold, calling him "the most enterprising man among the rebels." And George Washington wrote to Congress in 1777, "Surely a more active, a more spirited, and sensible officer fills no department of your army."

Contemporary historians flatly credit Arnold with

The Engagement on Lake Champlain. ▲

saving the country on at least two occasions. The naval historian, Alfred Thayer Mahan, asserted that the Americans' great victory at Saratoga in 1777 was "due to the invaluable year of delay secured to them . . . by their little navy on Lake Champlain, created by the indomitable energy . . . of the traitor, Benedict Arnold." Willard M. Wallace, a leading student of Arnold's career, said that Arnold "was acclaimed by many as the real hero of the successful Saratoga campaign that brought to the side of the struggling republic the kingdom of France, without whose help the war could not have been won."

The Dark Eagle's wings had indeed brushed the sky, but in his ascent Arnold himself had released the arrow that would one day pierce his heart. From Ticonderoga to Saratoga, Arnold's audacity, courage, and enterprise often turned his enemies into admirers. But his sensitivity, egotism, and arrogance often turned his friends into bitter enemies.

Arnold had quarreled with Ethan Allen over the command at Saratoga, and two of Allen's subordinates became Arnold's lifelong enemies. On the march to Quebec, he strongly reprimanded one of his officers, who retaliated by leading a near-mutiny of junior officers before the very walls of the city. Only after the most strenuous of efforts was Arnold able to persuade his officers to attack their objective. On his return to America, Arnold was accused of illegally plundering Montreal merchants to secure provisions for his retreating army and of misusing the funds Congress had provided for his expedition. Arnold only managed to become the hero of the decisive battle of Saratoga by seizing his horse and dashing into battle against the orders of his commanding officer, General Horatio Gates.

By the end of 1777 Arnold was a hero with many detractors, and had been or would be investigated by the Massachusetts Provincial Congress, the Board of War, the Continental Congress, the Treasury, and a military court-martial. He had been severely wounded in the right leg both at Quebec and at Saratoga and would not be fit for a battlefield command for months, if ever. Arnold's new life was about to begin.

In the spring of 1778, Washington appointed Arnold military governor of Philadelphia. The assignment was meant to be an honor, but it proved to be Arnold's undoing. A man who disliked politics, he found himself at the very center of American politics. Philadelphia served as the capital both for the Continental Congress and for the Pennsylvania Council. Within a week of taking office, Arnold found himself caught in the middle of disagreements between military and civilian authorities, power struggles between state and national officials, and disputes between Patriots and Loyalists.

At the same time, investigations into his finances continued (stemming from charges regarding the Canadian expedition), and almost from the first day of his new assignment, the Pennsylvania Council urged examinations of Arnold's conduct in office. Members of the Council suspected him of being a Tory sympathizer and of using his public office for private gain. Both charges may well have been true: he did marry the daughter of one of the more prominent Loyalists in the city, and there is some evidence that he took advantage of his office to supplement his own income.

Ultimately, the Council brought eight charges against him, and these were reviewed by a court-martial appointed by Washington. Only two of the charges were found to have any substance, and the sentence was relatively light—a public rebuke from Arnold's commander-in-chief, General Washington. But for a person like Arnold, the sentence was extremely painful. At the same time, the Treasury decided that Arnold owed a substantial amount of money to Congress.

Whether Arnold was really a Loyalist sympathizer, or whether the events just described turned him against his country, we cannot know, but we do know that in May of 1779 he opened secret negotiations with the British. His contact was Major John André, twenty-nine-year-old adjutant general and director of intelligence for Sir Henry Clinton, British commander in New York City. By May of 1780 both sides had defined their bargaining positions. André wanted Arnold to secure command of the fort at West Point and then to devise a way of surrendering it to the British. Arnold wanted 20,000 pounds, an equivalent rank in the British Army, and compensation for personal property losses suffered as a result of his actions.

Through a series of complex maneuvers, Arnold did persuade Washington to give him command of West Point, the last major rebel stronghold, which controlled the strategic Hudson River Valley. He took over his new post in late summer, 1780.

Within a month, Arnold and André managed to rendezvous at midnight on the shores of the Hudson, with the British Man-of-War, *Vulture*, standing by. They believed this meeting would consummate an agreement that would end the rebellion and make heroes of them both. But, through an extraordinary sequence of events, the plot failed. Unable to complete their negotiations that night, Arnold and André retired to a Loyalist sympathizer's home nearby. While they were eating breakfast, they were horrified to hear cannon fire and then to see the *Vulture* sailing away, under attack by an American shore battery.

André was forced to attempt his return to British lines via a far more dangerous and roundabout land route to Tarrytown. Foolishly, he accepted from Arnold a set of detailed plans of the West Point garrison and hid them in his socks. One of Arnold's accomplices then led André to within a few miles of British lines and mysteriously disappeared. Left to find his way alone, André made it to the bridge at Tarrytown, where he was stopped and searched by rebel sympathizers. They were inclined to rob and release him, until they found the plans in his socks. They concluded that André must be a spy.

The plot unravelled rapidly after André's capture and arrest by American authorities. Arnold barely escaped capture by dashing his horse down the steep rocky cliffs of the Hudson and forcing his bargemen to row him to the *Vulture*. By yet another extraordinary coincidence, General Washington himself arrived at Arnold's home for breakfast only moments after the escape and was one of the first Americans to learn of the treachery.

The plot was foiled, André was hanged, and Arnold finished out the war in the British Army. His transformation from hero to traitor was swift and complete. As Washington now said, Arnold had "lost all sense of honor and shame." The *New Jersey Gazette* called him "that most abandoned and infamous traitor," and he was burned in effigy throughout the colonies. His father's tombstone was even defaced because it bore the traitor's name, Benedict Arnold.

Any curious person will, of course, ask why it all happened. What led Arnold to betray a cause he had

served so honorably and so well? There is evidence to support a number of motives, both noble and mercenary. Arnold always needed money, and the 20,000 pounds he was offered certainly played its part. His ego may well have grown larger than his patriotism, and the continued attacks on his reputation could have convinced him that only the British

Benedict Arnold persuades John André to conceal the plans of West Point in his socks. ▲

A two-faced effigy of Benedict Arnold was driven through Philadelphia in September 1780. ▼

could really appreciate his talents. There is even a case to be made for Arnold believing that his was a truly patriotic act. At the time of the plot, inflation was ravaging the Continental dollar, mutiny stalked the Continental Army, and ineptitude plagued the Continental Congress. More than a few Americans wondered whether ending the war might not be the path of real patriotism.

Arnold's failure as a traitor seems (from hindsight) to have been as essential to the American victory as were his previous successes on the battlefield. In fact, while no one has suggested that Arnold was a double agent—serving the American cause by pretending to serve the British—he could not have done more for the rebel cause if that had been his intention. Consider the fact that the loss of Major André not only deprived Sir Henry Clinton of a fine young officer but also effectively destroyed the British intelligence network André had created and commanded. Consider further that at a time of division and declining morale, "the treason shocked the country into a semblance of unity," in Wallace's words. The rebellion was neither so popular nor the rebels in so great a majority that being a Loyalist represented treason. After Arnold's defection, however, "to be a Tory in politics was to be an enemy."

Suggested Reading

Bakeless, John, *Turncoats, Traitors, and Heroes* (Philadelphia: J. B. Lippincott Company, 1959). Good background on intelligence networks and spy rings during the Revolutionary War.

Lengyel, Cornel, *I, Benedict Arnold* (Garden City: Doubleday and Company, Inc., 1960). Well-written account of Arnold's career from his assignment to Philadelphia until the failure of the treason plot.

Mayo, Bernard, *Myths and Men* (Athens, Georgia: University of Georgia Press, 1959). Excellent analysis of how historians create myths around their subjects. Patrick Henry, George Washington, and Thomas Jefferson are treated.

Van Doren, Carl, *Secret History of the American Revolution* (New York: Viking Press, 1941). Detailed account of several conspiracies and plots drawn from original British documents and sources.

Wallace, Willard M., *Traitorous Hero: The Life and Fortunes of Benedict Arnold* (New York: Harper and Brothers, 1954). Complete biography of Arnold, sympathetic but balanced.

6

Founding a New Government

[James Wilson] contended strenuously for drawing the most numerous branch of the Legislature immediately from the people. He was for raising the federal pyramid to a considerable altitude, and for that reason wished to give it as broad a basis as possible. No government could long subsist without the confidence of the people. In a republican Government this confidence was peculiarly essential. He also thought it wrong to increase the weight of the State Legislatures by making them the electors of the national Legislature. All interference between the general and local Governments should be obviated as much as possible. On examination it would be found that the opposition of States to federal measures had proceeded much more from the Officers of the States, than from the people at large.

The Records of the Federal Convention of 1787

Amos Doolittle's engraving shows George Washington and John Adams being inaugurated on the balcony of Federal Hall in New York City.

When dissatisfaction erupted into the violence of Shays' Rebellion, some people saw the short-lived outbreak as a warning of further violence and social upheaval. Mortgage foreclosures were driving farmers off their property, and times were so hard that the jails in some areas were overflowing with debtors. The ever-worsening depression made many citizens question the value of a national government that could neither regulate commerce nor levy taxes. Many Americans had come to feel that their government should be somehow strengthened without diminishing individual freedom and opportunity. But how could this best be done?

Some felt that a central government for all the states was impossible and a plan was advanced for dividing the country into three separate nations. This abortive effort was described by a concerned citizen: "Some of our enlightened men who begin to despair of a more complete union of the states in Congress have secretly proposed an Eastern, Middle, and Southern Confederacy, to be united by an alliance, offensive and defensive."

Most influential people throughout the country favored a stronger central government. Two minor conventions that were assembled to consider interstate problems paved the way for the Convention of 1787. There, delegates from all the states gathered to revise the Articles of Confederation and ended up creating the United States Constitution.

The first of the interstate meetings was held in 1785, as representatives from Virginia and Maryland discussed their rivalry over the navigation of certain waterways. The second meeting was held in 1786 in Annapolis, Maryland, when five states got together to talk about commercial problems affecting the entire country. This convention brought together two staunch nationalists: James Madison of Virginia and Alexander Hamilton of New York. Together they successfully urged the other delegates to ask the state governments and the Confederation Congress to endorse a national meeting of delegates from all the states. The purpose of the proposed convention, as Madison put it, would be to consider how "to devise such further provisions as shall appear to them necessary to render the Constitution of the Federal government adequate to the exigencies of the Union."

The Constitutional Convention

The Constitutional Convention was held in Philadelphia. Representatives attended from all the states except Rhode Island. They met from May 25 to September 17, 1787, and in those four months they created the new Constitution.

Who were these delegates? Of the fifty-five men who attended, most were well-to-do. Only one, William Few of Georgia, represented the average farmer. Most of the delegates were college educated in a day when attending a university was unusual even for the wealthy. The most common profession among them was law. Benjamin Franklin, at eighty-one, was by far the oldest member of the convention. The average age was forty-two. Five representatives were in their twenties, and many more were in their early thirties. Despite the youthfulness of the gathering, many delegates had been active in the Revolution. Well over half of the members had also attended the Continental Congress and had held important political positions in their states at one time or another.

With few exceptions, these "Founding Fathers" were the best men America had for the job. Four had already achieved widespread fame. They were the revered George Washington, unanimously elected president of the convention; James Madison, a brilliant young Virginian who

"George Washington addressing the Constitutional Convention" by J.B. Stearns.

had already been working for several years to strengthen the federal government; New York's Alexander Hamilton, the group's most ardent advocate of a strong centralized government; and Benjamin Franklin, the sage of the convention. There were also a number of prominent men who did *not* attend. These were men such as John Adams, the minister to England; Thomas Jefferson, the minister to France; and John Jay, the secretary for foreign affairs.

Despite their disagreements on specific issues at the convention, the delegates were united on a number of basic ideas. Like most educated Americans they were commonly influenced by the Enlightenment idea that human beings could govern themselves if they could devise controls for their strong aggressive tendencies. Moved by this notion and by the conditions in the country, most of the delegates agreed that the Articles should be strengthened, or even scrapped.

The delegates were generally predisposed to the nationalist position. In fact, many of those who later opposed the new Constitution deliberately declined to attend the convention. There was a large group in the country that looked with disfavor on strengthening the national government; but this group tended not to be outspoken. Patrick Henry was an exception: he underlined his boycott of the convention by commenting, "I smell a rat."

The delegates were united in the opinion that a new government should be created which had its own source of income as well as control over foreign affairs and commerce. They also agreed that the government should have three branches —executive, legislative, and judicial—in order to avoid concentrating power in the hands of one person or one group. The delegates further agreed that the states should retain some of their former powers, that the central government should be responsible to each citizen, and that the citizens should participate in the election of representatives to the new government.

The convention in Philadelphia had originally been called to revise the existing Articles of Confederation. But on May 30 the delegates, urged on by the contingent from Virginia, voted to forge an entirely new constitution. With remarkable unanimity the delegates quickly approved additional powers for the new government. They gave the national government the right to levy taxes, regulate interstate and foreign commerce, and to raise and maintain an army and navy. At the same time they deprived the states of the right to coin money, make treaties, or tax imports and exports without the consent of Congress.

These major issues aroused little debate, but three other questions led to weeks of controversy which nearly destroyed the Constitutional Convention. The conflicting interests of the large states and small ones, the North and the South, states with Western land and those without, and manufacturing/commercial regions and agricultural regions were finally dealt with by compromise.

CONTROVERSY AND COMPROMISE

The problem of representation almost deadlocked the convention. The trouble appeared as early as the third day, when Edmund Randolph presented a plan for a new government which had been drafted by his fellow Virginian, James Madison. This "Virginia Plan" called for a national government with three branches: legislative, executive, and judicial. The legislative branch would be the most important arm of the government for it would elect both the executive and the judicial departments. The legislature itself would be composed of two houses, a lower house elected by the people, and an upper house chosen by the lower house. Seats would be distributed according to each state's population. The more populous states would have more representatives in *both* houses. This differed from the Articles, which provided for a one-house Congress and which gave one vote to each state, no matter how small or how large.

The method of apportioning representatives on the basis of population alone brought an immediate protest from the smaller and less populous states. With no room to expand, they were afraid that states with unsettled land would grow in population and thus overbalance them in representation.

The smaller states banded together to present their own views in a proposal introduced by William Paterson of New Jersey. The "New Jersey Plan" essentially called for a continuation of the old form of government, a Congress of one house in which each state would have one vote. Representatives would continue to be elected by the state legislatures, not by the people. But the New Jersey Plan did offer three innovations: first, Congress would have the power to tax; second, Congress could regulate trade; and third, the government would have an executive branch with authority placed in several individuals chosen by the Congress.

Many of the delegates thought the New Jersey Plan would work because it was simply a slight revision of the old form of government. In addition, the plan drew attention to the smaller states' fear of being continually outvoted by the more populous states if congressional representation were based on the number of citizens in each state.

On July 2 a committee was appointed to review the question of representation. Three days later it presented a compromise, devised by Benjamin Franklin. Congress would have two houses. In the lower house (the House of Representatives) the states would be represented according to population. This part of the proposal pleased the larger states. In the upper house (the Senate) each state would have two representatives, regardless of its size. This part of the plan pleased Connecticut, New Jersey, Delaware, Maryland, and North Carolina—most of them small and/or without Western lands—and they united behind it. Despite the provision for proportional representation in the lower house, the large states were not satisfied. Pennsylvania, Virginia, South Carolina, and Georgia voted against the compromise. But the Massachusetts delegation split its vote, and Franklin's proposal passed by the narrow margin of five votes to four.

Franklin's plan, called the Great Compromise,

Benjamin Franklin addressing James Madison at the Constitutional Convention.

brought about an important change in attitude. The smaller states were now ready to accept a stronger federal government because the protection of their interests had been ensured. The representation compromise thereby paved the way for discarding the Articles of Confederation and creating a federal government with true power to act.

Once the convention had decided the question of representation in the legislature a new question arose: Who would be counted? Southerners wanted their slaves counted as part of their population (although they had no intention of allowing the slaves to vote). Northerners agreed in essence but then insisted that slaves also be counted in deciding each state's share of direct federal taxes, to be figured on the basis of population. Southerners objected to this stipulation since they had no desire to pay a heavier load of taxes than was strictly necessary. Once again Franklin's committee worked out a compromise: three-fifths of the South's slaves would be counted for *both* purposes.

The North and South were divided on several other questions, all related to the power to be granted the federal government in regulating

◀ *Northern harbor and counting house.*

Southern tobacco plantation. ▼

commerce. The conflicting viewpoints reflected the different sources of income in the two regions. The North made a large part of its money from commerce. The region therefore wanted the federal government to be able to make protective commercial regulations, and to use a low tariff on imports as a source of revenue. The South, on the other hand, stood to gain nothing from such tariffs. The region made its money by exporting staple produce like tobacco and rice, and it feared that a government with the power to regulate commerce might legislate high export duties on such items. To guard against such legislation, the South demanded that all acts regulating commerce be passed by a two-thirds majority in Congress. And since Southerners were worried that Congress might try to put an end to the slave trade, they also demanded assurance that no such interference would occur.

Once again the convention found a solution in compromise. The North made several concessions: the Constitution provided that the government would never levy export taxes, that the slave trade could continue for twenty more years, and that the states would return fugitive slaves to their owners. In return, the South made a concession of its own: Congress could pass acts regulating commerce with a simple majority vote.

THE NEW CONSTITUTION

On September 17, 1787, thirty-nine of the original fifty-five delegates signed the new Constitution. It incorporated many aspects of the various state constitutions and of the Virginia and New Jersey plans, and introduced a few new provisions as well.

One of the most significant innovations was the office of the president. There was no precedent in America for a chief executive for the whole country. Under English rule there had never been one governor with authority over all the colonies, nor had the Articles of Confederation provided for a chief executive. After much debate the convention created the office of the president with the power to veto legislation, negotiate treaties, and to be commander in chief of the army and navy.

The presidency was to be a powerful office, but almost every one of its powers would be limited to a certain extent by the legislature. The president's veto could be overruled by a two-thirds majority of Congress; the country's treaties had to be approved by two-thirds of the Senate, the president would have control of the armed forces, but only Congress could set aside funds to support the military and only Congress could declare war. Congress could even impeach the chief executive for "Treason, Bribery, or other high Crimes and Misdemeanors." This concept of checks and balances was borrowed from English constitutional tradition and from the Massachusetts Constitution, written by John Adams.

The new Constitution also brought the federal government closer to the citizenry. Under the Articles of Confederation the people had no direct contact with the government. The representatives had been selected by the state legislatures. Under the new Constitution, however, voters would directly elect members to the House of Representatives and the popularly elected legislature of each state would select its two senators (a practice changed in 1913 by the Seventeenth Amendment which established the direct popular election of senators). Voters would also indirectly participate in the selection of the president.

Most of the delegates to the Constitutional Convention were quite suspicious of too much popular control of government. They feared that a popularly elected president might turn out to be a demagogue who thought mainly of pleasing crowds. On the other hand, the strong nationalists wanted an independent executive, one who would not be dependent on the legislature for election. The question was, if the president were neither popularly elected nor selected by the legislature, how would the office be filled?

The electoral college was devised as a compromise between these two customary ways of electing officials. Each state would have the same number of delegates to the electoral college as it had representatives and senators in Congress. The way these electors would be chosen was up to the individual state legislatures. They could be popularly elected, for instance, or they could be chosen by the state legislature itself. Each elector would vote for two people. The candidate with the most votes would be president; the one with the second largest number would be vice-president. If no two individuals received a clear majority, then the election would be determined by the House of Representatives (something that has happened only twice in American history).

Finally, the delegates made the Constitution and federal laws and treaties "the supreme Law of the Land." The specific powers given to the federal government were listed in Article I, Section 8. Powers not delegated to the national government and not forbidden to states (in Article I, Section 10) remained in state hands. This left the states with the power to levy taxes, maintain a police force, control education, and regulate working conditions. Article VI also made the state courts responsible for carrying out federal law.

Since the Constitution contained compromises and wording which could be interpreted in various ways, no member of the convention was completely satisfied with it. Yet most probably agreed with Benjamin Franklin when he said to Washington: "I consent, Sir, to this Constitution, because I expect no better, and because I am not sure that it is not the best. The opinions I have had of its errors, I sacrifice to the public good."

Ratification

Even after the Constitution had been signed by the delegates the document was still a mere piece of paper. It went through months of public debate before it became the "supreme law of the land," as it proclaimed itself.

The framers of the Constitution were realistic enough to expect opposition to the proposed changes, so they devised two means to simplify ratification. First, they provided that the Constitution should not be referred to the state legislatures for approval, but rather to popularly elected conventions in every state. Since under the new government the power of the states would be reduced, state legislatures had a vested interest in defeating it. Representatives chosen directly by the people would be likely to treat the Constitution far more favorably. Moreover, popular ratification would authenticate the Constitution's opening words: "We the people of the United States . . . ." Massachusetts had provided the model for this process when it held a popularly elected convention to approve its state constitution.

Second, the delegates further simplified the process by defining ratification as approval by at least nine of the states. They thus dispensed with the requirement of unanimous ratification, even though the Articles of Confederation had specifically stated that they could be revised only by unanimous vote of the states. Rhode Island had not even sent a delegate to Philadelphia, and it was known that in some states powerful forces opposed a strong central government. The convention provided insurance against opposition from these quarters.

FEDERALISTS VERSUS ANTIFEDERALISTS

Those who championed the new Constitution called themselves "Federalists" and labeled the document's enemies "Antifederalists." No clear-cut geographic or economic differences can fully account for their divisions over ratification. Many Federalists were wealthy, well-educated people from urban and rural areas, while many Antifederalists were yeoman farmers. Yet this type of analysis is not nearly as enlightening as an analysis of the economic differences between the small and large states.

Support for the Constitution was strongest in the small states, which liked the provision giving them as much influence in the upper house as the larger states. The small states also recognized that a stronger federal government could protect their economic interests—even their very existence—from competition with the larger states. Several of the large states, on the other hand, did not believe they needed the economic support or political protection of a strong federal government.

In addition, many people still felt their first loyalty was to their state government, and feared that under the new system the states would be downgraded. Antifederalists also raised an outcry over the broad powers the new Constitution gave to the federal government. Finally, the document did not include a bill of rights. Many Antifederalists seized upon this omission as clear proof that the new federal government would be tyrannical. Never before had one person possessed as much power over

Opposition to Ratification

"The writer of these essays has clearly proven, that the president is a King to all intents and purposes, and at the same time one of the most dangerous kind too—*an elective King*, the commander-in-chief of a standing army, etc. and to these add, that he has a negative over the proceedings of both branches of the legislature: and to complete his uncontrouled sway, he is neither restrained nor assisted by a *privy council*, which is a novelty in government. I challenge the politicians of the whole continent to find in any period of history a monarch more absolute.

Who is so base as not to burn with resentment against the conspirators, who have dared to establish such a tyrant over his life, his liberty and property? . . ."

"Philadelphiensis Letter,"
The Antifederalist, 1788

Support for Ratification

"The constitution of the executive department of the proposed government, claims next our attention. . . .

Here the writers against the Constitution seem to have taken pains to signalize their talent of misrepresentation. . . . The authorities of a magistrate, in few instances greater, in some instances less, than those of a governor of New York, have been magnified into more than royal prerogatives. He has been decorated with attributes superior in dignity and splendor to those of a king of Great Britain. . . .

It is impossible not to bestow the imputation of deliberate imposture and deception upon the gross pretence of a similitude between a king of Great Britain and a magistrate of the character marked out for that of the President of the United States. . . ."

"Paper Number 67,"
***The Federalist*, 1788**

the country as that given the president. Such authority, argued the Antifederalists, might lead the president to become a king.

Under the Constitution the federal government, as well as the states, would have the right to tax. Antifederalists worried that the poor would be bled dry by tax collectors. They even went so far as to claim that the Constitution was the handiwork of the nation's wealthy who simply wanted more personal power. As Amos Singletary, a Massachusetts farmer, put it:

> These lawyers, and men of learning, and moneyed men, that talk so finely, and gloss over matters so smoothly, to make us poor, illiterate people swallow down the pill, expect to get into Congress themselves; they expect to be managers of this Constitution, and get the power and all the money into their own hands, and then they will swallow up all of us little folks, like the great leviathan . . . yes, just as the whale swallowed up Jonah. This is what I am afraid of.

The Antifederalists also raised the old argument of eighteenth-century political thinkers, that a republican form of government could not rule a country as large as the United States. Congress would sit in a city far from many of its constituents and would lose touch with their interests. There would be so many special interest groups clamoring for legislation favorable to themselves that Congress would act in a way that pleased no one.

Interpreting the Founding Fathers

Throughout the nineteenth century American historians generally viewed the Founding Fathers as enlightened statesmen struggling against people with no vision of the nation's great future destiny. In 1913, however, historian Charles Beard published *An Economic Interpretation of the Constitution of the United States.* Beard claimed that the Constitution was "an economic document drawn with superb skill by men whose property interests were immediately at stake." Beard's suggestion was that the Founding Fathers' attitudes had been shaped by their economic interests, not that they had worked cynically for their own interests. He did find, however, that most of the Founding Fathers held United States public securities and therefore stood to gain if the national credit were strengthened. More than any other historian, Beard succeeded in demoting the Philadelphia delegates from their status as "demigods" (Jefferson's own word for them).

After decades of acceptance Beard's thesis came under increasing attack by the 1950s. In *Charles Beard and the Constitution* (1956) Robert E. Brown attacked virtually every important statement in Beard's work. "There was absolutely no correlation between the delegates' property holdings and the way they behaved on the question of a constitution. Farmers as a class were by no means chronically debtors; many were creditors and many others were both. The supporters of Shays' Rebellion . . . were certainly not united against the Constitution."

Forrest McDonald's *We the People* (1958) was a major attempt to shake off Beard's analysis of Federalists and Antifederalists. McDonald demonstrated that there was no split between landed wealth (supposedly Antifederalist) and monied wealth (supposedly Federalist). He replaced Beard's intercolonial property interests with new categories: specific economic interests in specific places. "The states where ratification was achieved most readily were those that were convinced for one reason or another, that they could not survive and prosper as independent entities; those holding out the longest were the ones most convinced that they could go it alone."

If the Founding Fathers linked government and property, it may have been more a reflection of their interest in John Locke's Enlightenment thinking than an indication of their own self-interest. According to Locke, one of the main purposes of government was the protection of property. Human freedom could be defined and measured only by the amount of protection the government afforded to private property. But the Founders went beyond Locke. The security of property was only part of their larger dream. They envisioned a nation that offered and protected individual and political liberty and economic opportunity. If a stronger central government could achieve this, many Founders believed, the republic would fulfill its great destiny.

Jackson Turner Main, in *The Antifederalists: Critics of the Constitutions, 1781–1788* (1961) has shown, however, that as a group Federalists were wealthier than the Antifederalists. They tended to dominate the towns and rich agricultural areas in each state. And in some states they occupied slightly higher social positions than the Antifederalists.

If the Founders were not moved primarily by personal economic considerations, were they then acting out of sheer idealism? Stanley Elkins and Eric McKitrick, in "The Founding Fathers: The Young Men of the Revolution" (*Political Science Quarterly* **LXXVI**, June 1961), examined the nine leading Federalists and nine leading Antifederalists and came up with some observations that throw a different light on the possible motivations of these men.

The Federalist leaders were ten to twelve years younger, on the average, than the Antifederalists. Most of the Federalists saw their careers launched by the Revolution. The political futures of these younger men came to depend on the national activity. They viewed any effort to limit the scope of national concerns as a powerful personal challenge.

On the other hand, the careers of the Antifederalists were state-centered and rested on events preceding 1776. They apparently found it difficult to think in national terms. According to Cecelia M. Kenyon in "Men of Little Faith: The Antifederalists on the Nature of Representative Government," *William and Mary Quarterly*, 3rd Ser. XII (January 1955), "Their minds could not embrace the concept of a national interest which they themselves might share and which could transcend their own parochial concerns. Republican government that went beyond the compass of state boundaries was something they could not imagine."

THE STATE CONVENTIONS

In the popular elections of delegates to state ratifying conventions, the Federalists had the advantage. Nearly everyone agreed that the Articles needed some revision. The Federalists had a positive program and it was well known that the respected Washington and Franklin favored ratification.

The Antifederalists had no common program. They usually did not know each other and had not organized their opposition. People who lived in the most remote areas were likely to see no need for a strong central government. But they were also most likely to find it difficult to get to a polling place. Three-quarters of those who were eligible to vote failed to do so, mostly out of apathy, and this worked in favor of adoption. Those who did turn out tended to favor the Constitution.

As noted, the Federalists could count on strong support from the small states, which were generally delighted by the protections granted them in the Constitution, and from the Southern states, which had been wooed by several compromises. The Federalists knew, however, that if any one of the four large states —Massachusetts, Pennsylvania, New York, and Virginia—failed to ratify the Constitution, the new government might not survive.

In general, the first states to ratify were those whose experience as independent states had been the least successful; they did not hesitate to admit that they could not make it on their own. As expected, the small state of Delaware ratified first, voting unanimously for the Constitution on December 7, 1787. By June 21, 1788, Pennsylvania, New Jersey, Georgia, Connecticut, Massachusetts, Maryland, South Carolina, and New Hampshire had voted for the Constitution, in some cases only after strenuous debate and close votes. The nine-state requirement for adoption had been met, but there was still concern about what the four other states would do.

North Carolina and Rhode Island were still holding out, but most attention was focused on the two remaining large states, Virginia and New York. Many in these crucial states felt that because they were economically self-sufficient they did not need a federal government to protect their interests. Many of the delegates to their ratifying convention also feared a powerful federal government.

Washington wrote: "A few short weeks will determine the political fate of America." He pointed out that in Virginia the Antifederalists were using "every art that could inflame the passions or touch the interest of men." George Mason argued that the federal government would destroy the sovereignty of Virginia, saying: "These two concurrent powers cannot exist long together; the one will destroy the other: the general government being paramount to, and in every respect more powerful than the state government, the latter must give way to the former." Mason finally conceded, however, that he would vote for ratification if a bill of rights were added to the Constitution.

Patrick Henry, on the other hand, was not willing to make a single concession. Deeply loyal to Virginia, he seized upon the opening words of the Constitution as proof that it would undermine the states: "The question turns, sir, on that poor little thing—the expression, We, the *people*, instead of the *states*, of America." Henry played on the deepest fears of those Antifederalists who apparently had little faith in human nature. He warned against putting so much power into the hands of the masses: "Your President may easily become your king. Your Senate is so imperfectly constructed that your dearest rights may be sacrificed by what may be a small minority; and a very small minority may continue forever unchangeably this government, although horridly defective." From the Antifederalists' pessimistic view of human nature, the protection of liberty could not be entrusted to some remote authority. It would be safer to leave it in the hands of the states.

Virginia finally ratified by a slim majority, largely because the state's governor, Edmund Randolph, dramatically switched his loyalties to

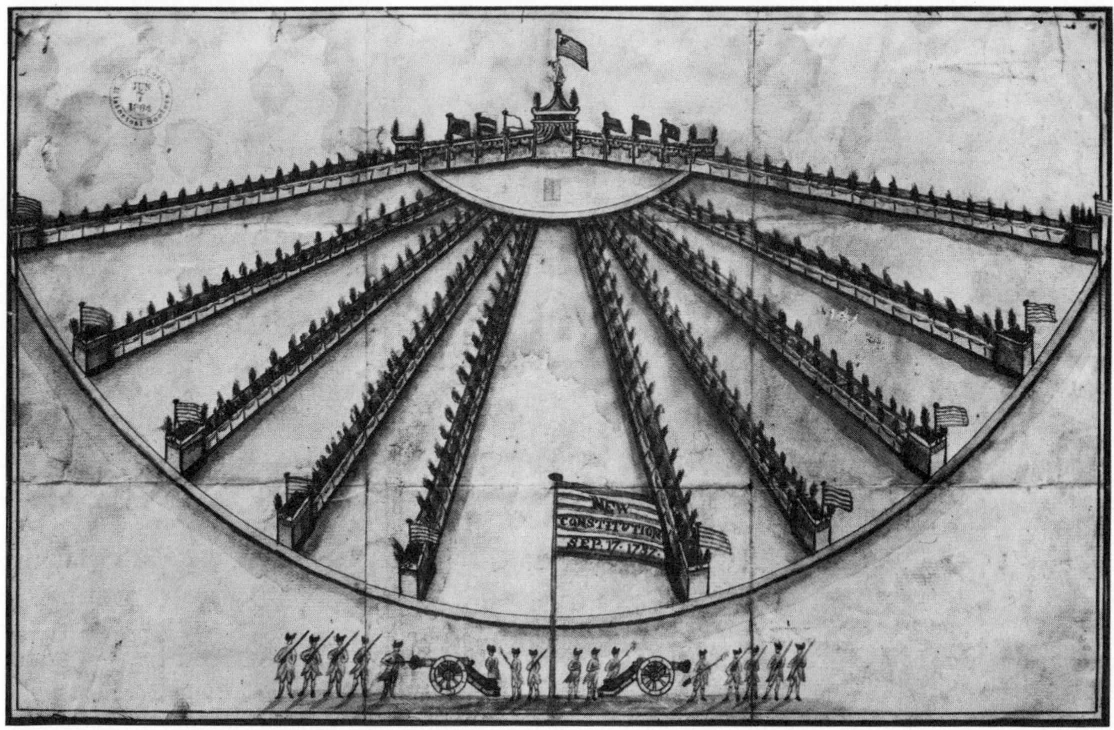

New Yorkers held a parade and a banquet attended by 6000 people to celebrate the ratification of the Constitution. The float in the top picture honors Alexander Hamilton who played a key role in obtaining the state's ratification. It fired a thirteen-gun salute when it passed Washington and his cabinet.

the Constitution at the last minute, declaring: "I am a friend to the Union." He had been persuaded by Madison that a bill of rights would be enacted under the new government.

Madison and Hamilton arranged for the news of Virginia's ratification to be sped by couriers to New York. New York was sharply divided on the question, with the Antifederalists having an overwhelming majority. In general, New York City favored ratification while the upstate delegates, led by Governor Clinton, opposed it. The state was enjoying extraordinary prosperity. Its revenues from import duties had jumped from $95,000 in 1784 to $450,000 in 1785. The state government's financial position was so strong that Clinton's faction felt New York could go it alone without the help of a strong central government.

In order to plead the cause of the Constitution John Jay and Alexander Hamilton of New York and James Madison of Virginia produced *The Federalist,* a series of brilliant newspaper articles. Although some members of the New York ratification convention were probably influenced by these essays, most were probably swayed far more by the news that nine states, and now Virginia, had ratified. In addition, the delegates from New York City vowed to take the city into the Union on its own if the convention did not ratify the document. In July 1788, New York adopted the Constitution by the narrow margin of thirty votes to twenty-seven.

The two remaining states entered the Union only after the new government was already in operation. North Carolina held out until November 1789. Rhode Island finally ratified in May 1790, after Congress threatened to deal with the obstinate little state as a foreign power.

The New Government

Early in 1789 the states began choosing their representatives to the first legislature under the new Constitution. There were to be many familiar faces: forty-four members of the First Congress had taken part in the Constitutional Convention.

The new Congress was supposed to convene on March 4, 1789, in New York's City Hall, which had just been luxuriously remodeled by a French architect. But travel in America was still difficult and the House of Representatives did not gather until a month later, causing a congressman from Boston to moan: "The people will forget the new government before it is born." However, by April 6 the Senate, too, had formed a quorum. When the two houses examined the electoral college ballots for president, no one was greatly surprised at the results: Washington had been unanimously elected president and John Adams (just back from his post as minister to England), vice-president.

Washington made a triumphal journey from his Virginia plantation, Mount Vernon, to New York City. Everywhere parades and cheering crowds greeted the revered "Father of His Country." Washington himself recognized that his new office carried awesome responsibilities. Everything he did in his first months in office would be taken as an omen of things to come. As he said, "There is scarcely an action, the motive of which may not be subject to a double interpretation. There is scarcely any part of my conduct which may not hereafter be drawn into precedent."

The vice-president, John Adams, was, according to Benjamin Franklin, "always an honest man, often a wise one, but sometimes, and in some things, absolutely out of his senses." Adams quickly became involved with the question of how to address the president. The simple title of president seemed to him ridiculous. "What will the common people of foreign countries, what will the soldiers and sailors say, 'George Washington, President of the United States'? They will despise him to *all eternity*." Called merely "the President," he might be confused with the president of a cricket club, Adams argued. He would have preferred "His Highness the President of the United States and Protector of Their Liberties." This question occupied the Senate's time for three weeks. Nothing came of it except that the rather stout Adams earned himself the unofficial title, "His Rotundity."

WASHINGTON AS PRESIDENT

Stern, dignified, and austere, Washington was an impressive first president who deliberated carefully (some felt *too* carefully) before making a decision. Since Washington was well aware that many Antifederalists feared that the president might become a tyrant, he took great care never to overstep his bounds. For example, he took literally the constitutional stipulation that the president must make treaties with "the advice and consent" of the Senate. When negotiations with certain Indian tribes were pending, Washington personally went to the Senate, took the vice-president's chair, and asked the senators for their advice. Intimidated by Washington's presence and unprepared for his sudden demand for advice, the senators hemmed and hawed. Finally they came up with the suggestion that the proposals should be studied by a committee of five. Washington stood up angrily, exclaiming: "This defeats every purpose of my coming here," and left abruptly. From then on his communications with the Senate on treaty negotiations took the form of written messages.

Washington laid to rest public fears that he would overstep his constitutional powers, yet he was in no way a man of the people. He had no interest in being considered a king, but he continued to live in the same aristocratic manner he had enjoyed at Mount Vernon. He traveled in a magnificent coach drawn by six cream-colored horses. His mansion in Manhattan was staffed with twenty-one uniformed servants. His birthday was the most important event of the social season. Like the king of England in Parliament, Washington delivered his State of the Union speech to Congress personally and then insisted that the members of both houses attend him to his mansion. He regularly held receptions for dignitaries; Mrs. Washington did the same for their wives. Madison complained that the "satellites and sycophants which surrounded him had wound up the ceremonials of the government to such a pitch of stateliness which nothing but his personal character could have supported, and which no character after him could ever maintain."

A cabinet of advisers

The Constitution did not specifically mention that the president would have advisers, but executive departments to aid the president had been provided for. One of the first acts of the new Congress was to create two new offices, those of attorney general and postmaster general. Congress also provided for the continuation of the three departments created under the Articles, the departments of state (formerly called foreign affairs), war, and treasury. Since power over money appeared to be a tool for corruption, some members of Congress tried to weaken the post of secretary of the treasury by dividing it among three men. But James Madison's arguments for efficiency in financial affairs won out.

To head the departments Washington appointed men he considered most highly qualified for the posts. He asked Thomas Jefferson to head the State Department, and Alexander Hamilton, the Treasury Department. As his secretary of war, he selected Henry Knox, a man of large girth (300 pounds worth) and a reputation as a marksman earned during the Revolution. Edmund Randolph, a personal friend of Washington's, was given the post of attorney general.

Washington's failure to obtain the Senate's advice on the matter of the Indian treaty made him turn increasingly to the heads of his executive departments for counsel. Thus began the institution of the cabinet, which was holding regular meetings by 1793. Washington was a skilled administrator, leaving the work of the individual departments to those in charge while overseeing all government activities himself. He asked for the opinions of all department heads on important questions, a practice which occasionally aroused controversy within the administration. But he never hesitated to make the final decisions and to take responsibility for them. He was industrious, prompt, systematic, and exacting.

Relations with Congress

The President did not, however, play a positive leadership role in relations with the Congress. He became so wary of treading on the toes of Congress that he believed the president should never propose or even appear to favor pieces of legislation while they were being debated. He also believed that he should never use his veto power unless a proposed bill was, in his opinion, unconstitutional.

Because Washington took little or no initiative in guiding the Congress, Madison, Hamilton, and (later) Jefferson filled the vacuum. Madison and Hamilton had been the prime movers behind the ratification of the Constitution. Now they were the two most dominant figures, besides Washington, in the first years of the Federalist era.

Madison was elected to the House and quickly became its leading member, as well as a close personal adviser to the president. Hamilton's greatest contribution to the new nation was his keen understanding of the intricacies of high finance. As secretary of the treasury he not only advised the House on financial matters but often even drafted the bills he wanted. He was a man of enormous energy and vast powers of persuasion, and many representatives constantly deferred to his genius. Jefferson, who became secretary of state in 1790, had little official contact with Congress. But he nevertheless made his presence felt. His close friendship with Madison gradually gave him considerable influence.

THE FIRST CONGRESS LEGISLATES

In addition to setting up the executive departments the First Congress passed legislation creating a federal judiciary and the national Bill of Rights.

On the subject of establishing the important third arm of government, the Constitution had merely stated: "The judicial power of the United States shall be vested in one Supreme Court, and in such inferior courts as the Congress may from time to time ordain and establish."

In September 1789, Congress passed the important Judiciary Act, setting up thirteen federal district courts and three circuit courts of appeal. It set the number of Supreme Court justices at six, and Washington appointed John Jay as chief justice. The act provided that cases dealing with the Constitution, federal laws, or treaties could be appealed from the state courts to the federal court system. This, in effect, ensured that the final authority on any federal matter would be the highest federal court—the Supreme Court. Thus, the doctrine of judicial review, not mentioned in the Constitution, received strong support in one of the first acts of Congress.

The framers of the Constitution had decided to omit a bill of rights for several reasons. First, the Articles of Confederation had not contained such a bill. Second, the Constitution had not superseded the bills of rights that were included in almost every state constitution. Third, the new federal government had been instituted by the people themselves through their representatives. Why should the people need a guarantee of their liberties in a document they themselves had ratified? Finally, some of the framers of the Constitution had feared that a specific list of rights might be interpreted as excluding those rights that were not specifically mentioned.

Nevertheless, the Antifederalists had cited the omission of a bill of rights from the new Constitution as a reason for not ratifying it. Even while the First Congress was meeting, New York and Virginia called for a second constitutional convention to write a new document from an extreme states' rights point of view.

In order to stop such disruptive moves and to honor the promises that Federalists had made to several ratifying conventions, Madison proposed a bill of rights as one of the first orders of business in the new Congress. "If we can make the Constitution better in the opinion of those who are opposed to it without weakening its frame, or abridging its usefulness in the judgment of those who are attached to it," Madison said, "we act the part of wise and liberal men to make such alterations as shall produce that effect."

Madison drew up twelve amendments listing guaranteed liberties, condensing the first eight from a list of forty suggested by the Virginia ratifying convention. Only ten of them were ratified. Passed by Congress on September 25, 1789, and by three-fourths of the states by 1791, the Bill of Rights was added to the Constitution as its first ten amendments. These amendments guaranteed the freedom of speech, religion, peaceful assembly, and the press; the right to bear arms; freedom from unreasonable search; no general search warrants; and the right to the protection of certain legal procedures known as the due process of law. The ninth and tenth amendments promised that the federal government would not assume any powers not accorded it in the Constitution, an assurance that all other rights belonged to the states and the people.

HAMILTON'S FISCAL POLICY

The new national government's most pressing need was to establish a sound economic policy. The first government had not had the power to tax, and it had failed to support itself or impose its authority on the country. Now a second government had been born and had been given the right to raise revenue. Would Americans submit to federal customs officers and tax collectors? Could Americans learn, as Washington wrote, "to distinguish between oppression and the necessary exercise of lawful authority"?

Washington had foreseen that the new government would have a hard time establishing its authority. In order to gain respect for the ability of the United States to remedy its financial situation, he had appointed the brilliant New York lawyer, Alexander Hamilton, as the first secretary of the treasury. In this post Hamilton headed what became by far the largest department in the new administration. Under his control the treasury had thirty clerks and almost one thousand customhouse officers and internal revenue agents in its employ. The State Department had only four clerks, and the Department of War only three.

Hamilton's political thought was characterized by the notion that the national interest was morally higher than the private interests of individuals. He felt that one should sacrifice one's own interests for the public good. In addition he had a pessimistic view of human nature which led him to believe in the necessity of a strong central government. But, although he believed it was human nature to be selfish, he had more faith in the upper class than in the masses. The wealthy, he thought, were less prone to act out of greed and self-interest. They were less likely to force changes which would be, in his opinion, incompatible with good government. Thus he tended to associate good government and the national interest with the interests of the rich and wellborn.

Hamilton himself had not been born into the monied class. He was born out of wedlock in the British West Indies, and was a self-made man. He had risen to prominence in his adopted country by marrying into a weathy family and by making good use of his own natural talents and zeal. His fiscal policies aimed at tying the upper class to the national government, sometimes to the exclusion of the interests of the other classes.

By Hammer & Hand all Arts do Stand

New York No. 196

These are to Certify that [illegible] was by a Majority of Votes regularly admitted a Member of the New York Mechanick Society at a Meeting held the [illegible] day of May A.D. 1791 Given under my hand and the Seal of the Society this 3rd day of [illegible] Annoque Domini 1791

[illegible] Chairman.

[illegible] Sec.

A 1791 certificate of membership in the "New York Mechanick Society," an early labor organization for manually skilled workers.

A sound economy was essential to Hamilton's concept of an orderly government. He considered a nation's economy sound when its budget was balanced and it could pay its debts. In order to reach these two goals he called for an expansion of the commercial and manufacturing sectors and for allowing the predominant agricultural interest to continue developing on its own. Eventually, he reasoned, all areas of the American economy would be equally strong and interdependent. The United States would then be almost self-sufficient, no longer dependent on other countries for its economic needs.

To accomplish this Hamilton tried to establish a tie between the commercial and manufacturing interests and the government through economic policies designed to please the business community. From an economic standpoint Hamilton's fiscal program was a brilliant success. However, it turned out to be so one-sided that it gradually alienated the agricultural element, which represented over ninety percent of the population at that time. Thus Hamilton's program led in the long run to political disaster for its supporters.

The national debt

America had a foreign debt of over $11 million. The new government also owed approximately $42 million to those of its own citizens who had either bought bonds to support the Revolutionary War, or who had fought in the war and received bonds instead of pay. By 1790, however, few of these bonds were still in the hands of their original owners. Their value had declined over the previous ten years as it seemed increasingly unlikely that the government would ever redeem them. Speculators, mainly the commercial interests on the Eastern seaboard, had gradually bought up most of the certificates at a fraction of their original price.

In his *Report on Public Credit* presented to Congress in January 1790, Hamilton recommended that these certificates be paid in full. To fund the national debt, he proposed to withdraw the old certificates and to replace them with new certificates of government indebtedness. These new certificates could then be paid off very slowly. The plan was not to pay off the total national debt immediately—which the government did not have the means to do—but to establish American credit by showing the ability to pay at least a small amount each year.

Hamilton's bold plan created an uproar. The chief opponent of the plan was Madison, Hamilton's old political ally. Madison believed that some method of establishing American credit should be found, but he objected to Hamilton's scheme for two reasons. First, Madison was a Southerner; four-fifths of the national debt was owed to Northerners. If the entire country were taxed equally to redeem the certificates, the payment would amount to a massive transfer of money from Southern pockets to Northern ones. Second, Madison objected on ethical grounds. He felt no hesitation in paying the soldiers and citizens who had bought the certificates *originally*. The soldiers, after all, had served in the army and received the certificates as pay, while the citizens had taken a risk in order to help finance the Revolutionary War. But Madison vehemently objected to paying the speculators, some of whom had bought the certificates only quite recently at about a quarter of their original price.

Hamilton defended his proposal as firmly as Madison opposed it. First, he pointed out that if the government distinguished between one sort of certificate holder and another, America's credit would remain shaky. Foreign and native investors would hardly be likely to trust a government that did not pay *all* its debts, no matter to whom they were owed. Second, Hamilton believed that the well-to-do speculators who owned most of the certificates (many of them members of Congress) were the only people in America who "thought continentally." The rest of the citizens, "the community at large," was provincial in its outlook and still felt that its first loyalty was to the states. Little support for a strong federal government could be won from these people. Therefore the government should court the well-to-do, for only through their support could the new government succeed and the country expand in the areas Hamilton thought necessary: commerce and manufacturing.

Hamilton won his way. The entire national debt was funded. This action undeniably benefited speculators, but it also had the desired effect of restoring the national credit. Henceforth, citizens and foreign bankers were not afraid to invest in the United States.

In the struggle Madison had lost prestige in Congress, and he was no longer its undisputed master. Now Hamilton became increasingly influential in the House of Representatives. His victory also endeared him to the monied class in the nation. Although Hamilton had not personally profited from funding the national debt, he had allowed news of his plan to leak to friends in high places. These confidants immediately bought up all available shares for considerably less than their face value, putting them in a position to reap enormous profits under the new program.

The state debts

The second part of Hamilton's proposals to Congress called for the government to assume an additional obligation: repayment of the debt that each state had incurred during the Revolutionary War. Hamilton thought this plan would enhance the federal government's prestige. He believed that the states' creditors would become increasingly attached to the national government, and that the influence of the states would gradually wither away.

The heated controversy over assumption (as this part of Hamilton's plan was called) deadlocked Congress for nearly six months. In general, members of Congress approved of the plan if their own state still had large unpaid wartime debts, but disapproved if their state's debts had been paid off. Many quite legitimately feared the possibility that assumption would enhance the prestige and credit of the federal government at the expense of the states.

The outcry against assumption was particularly strident in Virginia. Virginia had already paid a large share of its debts and felt that it should not have to assist states that were less prompt in discharging their obligations. Virginia senator George Mason declared that Hamilton had "done us more injury than Great Britain and all her fleets and armies." Patrick Henry called the plan unconstitutional. He had long predicted that the new federal government was up to no good. Now his fellow Virginians honored him as a vindicated prophet.

The controversy was finally resolved in July 1790. Hamilton agreed that the states which had already paid a large part of their debts would receive a partial reimbursement in the form of an outright grant of money. More important, Hamilton made a deal with Madison and Jefferson. The two Virginians had both opposed Hamilton's plan, but they agreed to support it in return for his promise that the national capital would be moved, after a temporary ten-year stay in Philadelphia, to the banks of the Potomac River.

Jefferson later regretted this compromise. But at the time he thought conceding to Hamilton on the matter of assumption was not too high a price to pay for placing the nation's capital in Virginia. He anticipated that such a move would benefit the South by attracting people and business to the region, making it easier for Southern legislators to get to Congress, and improving the chances that Southerners would be appointed to government positions.

The national bank

Hamilton's financial plans for the new government did not stop at funding the national debt and assuming the states' wartime debts. He now proposed that Congress charter a national bank. The Bank of the United States would be funded by a $10 million dollar investment. Some of this money would come from the government, but most of it would come from private individuals. Most of the private investment could be in certificates of government indebtedness. Only a small amount of the total investment would consist of gold and silver.

Hamilton argued that a national bank was necessary for a variety of purposes: it would serve as a safe depository for government funds; it would facilitate the collection of taxes; and it would issue a uniform national currency to aid American economic expansion. In addition, a national bank would greatly benefit the well-to-do by providing them with easy credit and a safe place to invest their money.

Although Hamilton's policies seemed to be driving a wedge between the wealthy business people (most Northerners) and the rest of the nation, the president had reservations of a different sort about the bank. Washington profoundly respected Hamilton's financial genius, but he was concerned that the proposed national bank might be unconstitutional. This possibility was suggested to him by Madison, who opposed the national bank.

Although the bill authorizing the Bank of the United States had already passed in the House of Representatives, the president decided to ask Jefferson for his opinion. The secretary of state also opposed the bank. He cited the Tenth Amendment, which states that "all powers not delegated to the United States by the Constitution . . . are reserved to the states, or the people." Jefferson argued that establishing a national bank was clearly *not* a power delegated to the federal government. Although the last clause of Article I, Section 8 of the Constitution allowed the Congress to "make all Laws which shall be necessary and proper for carrying into Execution the foregoing Powers," Jef-

A 1799 engraving of the first Bank of the United States.

ferson could not see that a national bank was "necessary" in the sense of being absolutely essential to the operation of the government. If Congress started expanding its powers without authority, the states would rise up in anger, he reasoned, and soon Congress would "take possession of a boundless field of power, no longer susceptible to any definition."

Jefferson, Madison, and others of their persuasion came to be known as "strict constructionists." They believed the federal government should exercise only those powers which were explicitly given it by the Constitution.

Hamilton replied to this argument by submitting his own *Opinion on the Constitutionality of the Bank* on February 23, 1791. He favored a broad, or loose, construction of the Constitution. As he himself put it, "the powers contained in a constitution of government, especially those which concern the general administration of the affairs of a country, its finances, trade, defense etc., ought to be construed liberally in advancement of the public good. . . ." Hamilton insisted that the right to set up a bank was implied in the "necessary and proper" clause since "a bank has a natural relation to the power of collecting taxes—to that of providing for the common defense," all of them "powers vested by the Constitution in the government." Therefore the bank was wholly in accord with the Constitution. According to Hamilton, "necessary" did not have to mean what was absolutely essential, but only what was convenient. One of his motives for creating the bank was to test the "necessary and proper" clause and to create a precedent for expanding the power of the federal government. Washington was convinced by Hamilton's argument and signed the bank bill.

The positions taken by Jefferson and Hamilton on the bank bill have been echoed by political figures in America ever since. Whether they have argued for a strict or a loose interpretation of the Constitution has more often depended on which argument has best suited their interests and those of their constituents at the time than on any abstract belief in whether the citizenry's best interests were served by extending or limiting the powers of government.

Economic growth

In 1790 the House had asked Hamilton to draw up a plan that would encourage American manufacturers and make the United States independent of other nations, particularly in its production of military supplies. After studying world economic conditions Hamilton submitted his *Report on Manufactures* in December 1791. He pointed out that other countries were setting up increasingly restrictive mercantilist systems. The United States, he argued, could only follow suit by adopting a closed economic system of its own. To protect fledgling American manufacturers Hamilton proposed to construct a system of tariffs, subsidies, and "bounties" (or awards), for new industries.

His proposition aroused much controversy. The South, which had little industry and was primarily agricultural, resented the plan. Southern farmers would gain nothing from higher tariffs; they would simply have to pay higher prices on manufactured goods. Most Northern merchants joined Southerners in opposing Hamilton's plan. They feared high tariffs would discourage trade.

Hamilton's report was not implemented, although many of his suggestions were incorporated into the Tariff Act of 1792. All of his proposed bounties were discarded, except one to encourage the fishing industry. As Hamilton learned, the United States was not yet ready to become a great manufacturing center. It was still predominantly agricultural and would remain so for some time.

FIRST SIGNS OF POLITICAL TENSION

Hamilton's fiscal policies, his admiration of the rich, his distrust of the common people, and his clear preference for the North over the South earned him the political enmity of both Madison and Jefferson. Whereas Hamilton disliked the state governments, Jefferson and Madison were both convinced that a too-powerful federal government was a real threat to liberty. Jefferson and his backers claimed that Hamilton was leading a royalist plot to overthrow republicanism in America and to replace it with a monarchy.

In return, Hamilton called Jefferson "the most intriguing man in the United States," a man who was "cautious and sly, wrapped up in impenetrable silence and mystery." Hamilton threw his support behind John Fenno, the publisher of a Philadelphia newspaper called the *Gazette of the United States.* Hamilton gave him many treasury printing contracts and outright loans. Out of "gratitude," Fenno praised Hamilton as the greatest American statesman next to Washington. For his part, Jefferson subsidized Philip Freneau, a well-known poet of the Revolution, by giving him an honorary paid post in the State Department. In 1791 Freneau set up a rival newspaper, the *National Gazette,* which heralded Jefferson as "the Colossus of Liberty" and attacked Hamilton and his policies. Fenno retaliated by characterizing Jefferson as an atheist and a foe of orderly government and the Constitution.

Washington tried to stand above the quarrel between his cabinet members, although it greatly disturbed him. In their rivalry, Jefferson and Hamilton had begun to accumulate followers. The Founding Fathers had hoped that America would not have political parties, which they equated with the bitter factions prevalent in eighteenth-century England and in some of the colonies before the Revolution.

Washington disliked the developing political controversy and longed to return to the peace of his beloved Mount Vernon. He was prepared to retire in the spring of 1792, but Hamilton, Jefferson, and Madison convinced him to serve another term. They believed that the new government would collapse without him. Washington reluctantly accepted, and he and John

Adams were reelected in the fall. Washington persuaded Hamilton and Jefferson to maintain at least an outward show of mutual respect. However, the fierce antagonism that would eventually split Americans into the first political parties subsided only temporarily.

THE FRENCH REVOLUTION

The ever-widening gulf between Jefferson and Hamilton also showed up in their disagreements over American foreign policy.

Jefferson's main goal, as secretary of state, was to establish true American independence. The only alliance the United States had was with France. Although Jefferson had a strong personal attachment to France because of his years there as minister, his primary interest in maintaining the friendship was strategic. France did not menace the country's western borders, as did Spain at the mouth of the Mississippi and England around the Great Lakes. In fact France might help the United States expel these two powers. Jefferson wanted to establish American sovereignty to the Mississippi River and at the same time keep the country out of European quarrels.

Hamilton's foreign policy goals, on the other hand, were based on protecting American credit. He therefore convinced Congress not to pass measures (favored by Jefferson and Madison) which would have cut off all trade with Great Britain until she negotiated a favorable commercial treaty with the United States. Hamilton was against such a policy. After all, the main sources of revenue for the hard-pressed United States Treasury were tariffs on British goods imported into the country. In this case, the foreign policy favored by the secretary of state, was subordinated to the needs of the treasury.

Hamilton and Jefferson clashed again as developments in France brought the Franco-American Alliance into question. The French Revolution began in 1789 and in 1791 a French republic was proclaimed. At first Americans of every political persuasion greeted the news enthusiastically. America's Revolutionary War ally was now following the example of the United States and freeing herself from the yoke of royal tyranny. The Marquis de Lafayette later sent Washington the key to the Bastille, a prison in Paris where the Bourbon kings had imprisoned their political enemies. Washington declared the key "a token of victory gained by liberty over despotism."

But by the fall of 1792 the first phase of the French Revolution, relatively moderate and middle-class in character, had come to an end. The second and much more violent phase of the great upheaval was under way. France, now under the control of a party anxious to spread the doctrines of the Revolution throughout Europe, was at war with Austria and Prussia. Internally, the constitutional monarchy of 1791 was overthrown by the combined forces of the war party, the workers, and the peasantry. Unrest and fear swept the land, and the government resorted to the guillotine to restore order. France's "reign of terror" had begun. In January 1793, King Louis XVI was beheaded.

American conservatives began to fear that these violent attacks on property, religion, and those in authority might spread to the shores of the United States. While Hamilton, Washington, and their followers were horrified by the French excesses, Jefferson remained steadfast in his approval of the goals of the French Revolution. He deplored the beheadings but announced: "The liberty of the whole earth was depending on the issue of the contest and . . . rather than it should have failed, I would have seen half the earth devastated."

American neutrality

Following the beheading of the French king, Great Britain formed an alliance with Holland, Prussia, Austria (and, later, Spain) to stop what they considered a threat to European civilization. On February 1, 1793, these powers declared war on France.

News of the international war refocused the

debate in America from the merits of the French Revolution to the question of whether the United States should become involved in the conflict. The Franco-American Alliance of 1778 required the United States to defend French possessions, such as the French West Indies, against the enemies of France. Would France demand that the United States fulfill this obligation?

Hamilton watched with horror as France's "war of all peoples against all kings" progressed. If America were drawn into the conflict, Hamilton would find himself siding with a country whose policies were the very opposite of everything he believed in. What was more, the war would reach into the American treasury. He argued that the Treaty of 1778 was no longer valid, since it had been made with the French monarch and not with the government now in power. The United States must renounce the treaty, proclaim its neutrality, and refuse to receive a minister from the revolutionary government.

Jefferson, who had served as America's first minister to France, admired French civilization and particularly the spirit of French democracy. He strongly disagreed with Hamilton. Although Jefferson recognized that it would be foolhardy for the United States to enter a war against Great Britain, he urged Washington not to declare American neutrality without congressional support. He further argued that the United States should not renounce the Alliance of 1778 unless American security was directly endangered. The agreement had been made with the French people, not a specific government. It was therefore important for America to set a precedent of living up to its international commitments.

Washington finally compromised and accepted the counsel of both his advisers. He proclaimed American neutrality on April 22, 1793, but without using the word *neutrality*. At the same time the United States did not renounce the French Alliance, nor did it refuse to receive the French minister to the United States, Citizen Edmond Genêt.

Citizen Genêt

While France had decided not to press the United States to defend her West Indian islands, she did wish to use American ports for launching attacks on British merchant ships. In April 1793, the young French minister, Edmond Genêt, arrived in Charleston, South Carolina, a stronghold of pro-French sentiment. Genêt was a hot-blooded idealist who was determined to throw diplomatic caution to the wind and take any risk to aid his country. Violating American law, he commissioned fourteen Charleston ship captains as privateers for the French. They managed to capture about eighty British ships without the sanction of the United States government. Moving on to Philadelphia, Genêt also planned an abortive expedition against Louisiana led by the Revolutionary War hero, George Rogers Clark.

Deeply displeased, President Washington warned Genêt to stop his illegal activities. But Genêt was unperturbed, having enjoyed a triumphant march from Charleston to Philadelphia. Everywhere, the Frenchman had been met with adoration. In Philadelphia he founded a Democratic Society, dedicated to upholding the cause of France. Soon more than forty other such clubs sprang up across the country. Encouraged by so much popular support, Genêt decided to appeal to public opinion and ignore the president.

Genêt's actions antagonized the whole administration. Washington was furious. Hamilton was convinced that unless Genêt was stopped Federalist heads would soon be rolling in Philadelphia. Even the pro-French Jefferson lost patience. He described the reckless Genêt as "all imagination, no judgment, passionate, disrespectful and even indecent towards the President." Jefferson knew that while the majority of Americans might be pro-French, they certainly did not want to enter the war on France's side. Washington demanded that the French government recall the impudent Genêt back to Paris.

The government that had dispatched Genêt, however, no longer existed. Genêt had repre-

This Federalist cartoon exaggerates Jefferson's pro-French attitude and Washington's anxieties over the state of affairs following the French Revolution. The French are shown attacking from the left. Washington is trying to advance to meet them but Citizen Genêt, Albert Gallatin, and Thomas Jefferson are trying to restrain him.

sented a political faction called the Girondists. They had been overturned by a new, even more radical group, the Jacobins, who declared that Genêt's actions were "criminal maneuvers." The frightened young man recognized that a return to France might mean the loss of his head. He begged Washington to grant him asylum in America. Washington relented. A few months later the attractive hothead married the daughter of Governor Clinton of New York and retired to a quiet farm.

British aggression

In the meantime, British criticism of Genêt's actions had led the president to ask Congress for legislation that would help keep America out of the war. A Neutrality Act passed by Congress in June 1794 specifically prohibited foreign powers from recruiting soldiers in the United States and banned belligerents from engaging in warfare in American coastal waters.

Nonetheless, England and France did seize about six hundred American ships in international waters between 1793 and 1794. The provocation for these seizures was quite simple: France captured American vessels headed for England, and England took American ships sailing for France. France, whose ships had been virtually swept from the seas by the powerful British navy, hoped to use American merchantmen to bring urgently needed supplies to her home and colonial ports. The French had previously kept her colonial ports closed to foreign trade and Americans hoped to profit by supplying both the belligerents with American products. But both European powers were determined to obstruct American trade with the enemy.

But the British had the most powerful navy in the world. They invoked the Rule of 1756, which declared that commerce prohibited in time of peace would not be allowed to neutrals in time of war. The British disagreed with the American definition of contraband. Since the Revolutionary War the United States had insisted that only arms and ammunition should be considered contraband, while the British insisted that anything (food, for example) that might conceivably aid the French war effort was contraband and therefore subject to seizure. British warships seized some two hundred and fifty American vessels that were trying to trade with the French West Indies and confiscated

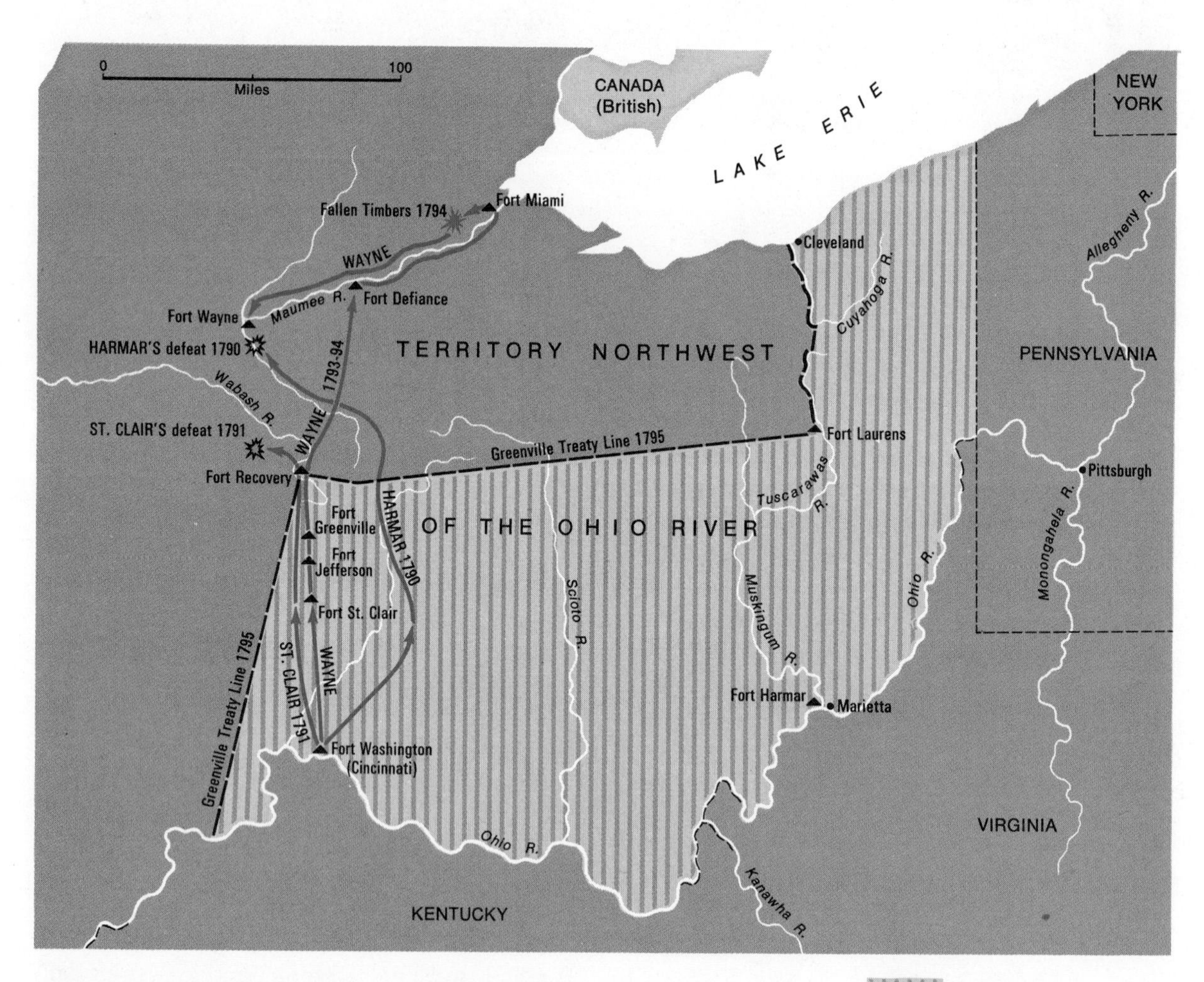

INDIAN WARS IN THE NORTHWEST • 1790 TO 1794

Indian lands ceded in 1795
American victory
Indian victory

their cargoes. The British navy also forced (impressed) many American sailors into its service.

On top of inflaming anti-British feelings by its seizures and impressments, England was helping the Northwest Indians resist American encroachment on Indian lands. The United States had obtained the entire Northwest from England in the Treaty of 1783, but as yet few American settlers had been able to enter the territory. Washington sent Arthur St. Clair in 1791 to crush the Miamis of Ohio. But the Indians, encouraged by the British, had routed St. Clair.

In February 1794 Major General Anthony Wayne (known as "Mad Anthony" for his fierce leadership in the Revolution) prepared to enter the Northwest to enforce the government's claim to the area. At the same time the British governor of Canada gave the Indians supplies to fight the Americans. To make matters worse, the British still had one thousand redcoats stationed in the Northwest, and England was actually beginning to build a new fort in the Ohio country.

War between the United States and Great Britain was a real and immediate danger. American public opinion was inflamed over British conduct, and even Hamilton, the Anglophile, characterized England's aggressive acts on the high seas as "atrocious." Jefferson's followers in Congress secured a temporary embargo on trade with England in early 1794. Hamilton was alarmed and persuaded the president to send a special negotiator to London to prevent outright war between the two countries. After receiving congressional approval in April 1794, Washington sent Chief Justice John Jay to England with instructions to: get the British out of the Northwest, force England to pay for American ships that had been seized, urge Britain to accept America's rights as a neutral, and negotiate a new commercial treaty with Britain.

Jay's treaty

After months of discussion, Jay and the British foreign minister, Lord Grenville, worked out a treaty that was not popular in either country. The British regarded it as too generous to the United States, and most Americans considered it a national disgrace.

The British war effort was doing well at this time, and English spies reported that America was pitifully unprepared for a full-scale war. Moreover, Lord Grenville knew that the United States could not afford a war with England. The United States depended on the duties collected on imported British goods for most of its revenue. War with England would put a stop to the imports and bring the United States close to bankruptcy.

Equally bolstering to English confidence was the retirement of Jefferson, the friend of France and enemy of Britain. Exhausted by his long quarrel with Hamilton, Jefferson quit his post as secretary of state in December 1793. His resignation left Hamilton's control over American diplomacy stronger than ever. Hamilton was so indiscreet as to communicate to George Hammond, the British minister in America: "I have always preferred a connection with you to that of any other country, *we think in English*, and have a similarity of prejudices and predilections." Hamilton also revealed that Washington had decided not to arm American merchant ships to prevent seizure by England, as neutrals Denmark and Sweden were doing. It is quite unlikely, however, that this information, or any other that Hamilton could have given, would have changed the final outcome of the negotiation. Britain did not want war with the United States, but neither did it want to make concessions which would weaken the English war effort against France.

When Jay signed the Treaty of London on November 19, 1794, the United States gained only some of its demands. The British agreed to evacuate their forts in the Northwest within two years. A commercial treaty opened additional trade with the British. It also granted American merchants the right to trade freely with the British East Indies and, with certain limitations, with the British West Indies. The waterways of the American continent were to be open to both countries. The British promised to compensate American shipowners for vessels recently seized in the West Indies.

These gains were all Jay was able to squeeze out of England. He had no success in convincing the English to respect American rights as a neutral power on the high seas. And he ended up accepting the English definition of contraband, to include not only provisions but also naval stores (such as turpentine and tar). Jay also failed to convince the British to give up the infuriating practice of impressment.

Of all the articles of the treaty, the one pertaining to American participation in the British West Indian trade was the most controversial. Ever since the Revolution, Britain had excluded Americans from the lucrative trade with the British West Indies, once so important to the American economy. One of Jay's primary goals had been to convince the British to reopen this trade. Britain responded with a plan that was so hedged with restrictions that the American public regarded it as an insult. For example, American ships trading in the West Indies could not weigh more than seventy tons, and they could only carry their cargoes back to the United States. These terms would deny American merchants a part in the world trade of such valuable Caribbean produce as molasses, coffee, cocoa, sugar, and cotton.

When the terms of Jay's treaty leaked out, the American people were indignant. They nicknamed the unfortunate emissary "Sir John Jay." Washington observed that a cry went up against the treaty "like that against a mad dog." To large numbers of Americans acceptance of the treaty seemed a humiliation, but rejection might mean war with England. Washington stifled his pride and submitted the treaty to the Senate. The Senate immediately threw out the annoying provisions for trade with the British West Indies, and, after much debate, ratified the rest on June 24, 1795, by a bare two-thirds majority.

Agreeing to the treaty was one of the most unpopular moves of Washington's career. But as events turned out, it was one of the wisest. Feeling against the treaty was still so strong a year after it was ratified that in April 1796, when the House voted on the appropriation of money to implement its provisions, it passed by only three votes. Probably only the brilliant oratory of the Federalist Fisher Ames convinced a sufficient number of representatives to pass the measure.

Despite such violent reactions, the treaty could be credited with three accomplishments: it probably kept the country out of a war which it could ill afford and had little hope of winning; it allowed America to continue making immense profits as a neutral nation trading with the two great belligerents, France and England; and it finally cleared the way for American expansion into the Ohio Valley. After the British withdrew their troops and support, the Northwest Indians ceded most of the Ohio country to the American government. They signed the Treaty of Fort Greenville a month and a half after Jay's treaty was signed.

In hindsight, Jay's treaty was not a disaster, considering the weakness of the United States. The British could have refused to negotiate at all. The treaty rankled not because better terms were really possible, but because it secured from the hated former mother country so much less than the American people thought they should have obtained.

Pinckney's treaty

Jay's treaty was unpopular, but it helped prepare the groundwork for a treaty with Spain that was an unqualified success. Spain had withdrawn from its alliance with Britain and had made peace with France. For this desertion, she expected British reprisals. What Spain especially feared was a joint British-American attack against her possessions in America: Florida and the Gulf Coast. She may have feared that the Americans and English had formed a secret military alliance along with Jay's treaty. Moreover, Spain was bankrupt and knew she could no longer hope to hold back American expansion in the Mississippi Valley.

New Orleans in 1804.

As a result, Spain tried to placate the United States by signing a treaty with Thomas Pinckney, a special American envoy to Madrid. Pinckney's treaty granted everything America had previously wanted: free navigation of the Mississippi "in its whole length from its source to the ocean"; free use of the port of New Orleans for three years, after which time a new, mutually satisfactory arrangement would be made; and Spanish acceptance of the thirty-first parallel as America's southern boundary. Spain gave up its claims over the disputed areas of the Southwest and even promised to discourage Indian attacks on American settlements. For its part, the United States only pledged to try to pacify the Indians in the area, but made no further commitments.

The Senate accepted Pinckney's treaty unanimously on March 3, 1796. The treaty removed the possibility that Kentucky and Tennessee, which had become states in 1792 and 1796, might secede from the Union and annex themselves to Spain. Americans in those states desperately needed to transport their farm produce down the Mississippi. As long as Spain had kept the river closed to American citizens, farmers in the Southwest had considered changing their citizenship. But the Mississippi was now open to trade.

American sovereignty over the Northwest and the Southwest was finally achieved through Jay's treaty and Pinckney's treaty. The promise of the Treaty of Paris of 1783 had at last been fulfilled.

THE WHISKEY REBELLION

While Jay was negotiating in London, the Washington administration faced unrest on the domestic front. In several Western areas there were eruptions of open rebellion against the federal goverment over an excise tax on liquor.

Seeking to raise money for the assumption of the states' debts, Hamilton had recognized that tariffs on commerce could not be raised any higher without encouraging smuggling and evasion. The necessary money had to come from somewhere else. Hamilton's solution to this problem was to levy an excise tax on several domestic products, of which whiskey was the most prominent. He had engineered the tax through Congress in 1791. Not only would it create new revenues, but it would also enhance federal power, he thought, by demonstrating to backcountry farmers that they were living under a federal government with the power to tax them.

Alexander Hamilton on the Whiskey Rebellion

"In compliance with your requisitions, I have the honor to submit my opinion as to the course which it will be advisable for the President to pursue, in regard to the armed opposition recently given in the four western counties of Pennsylvania to the execution of the laws of the United States laying duties upon spirits distilled within the United States, and upon stills . . .

A competent force of militia should be called forth and employed to suppress the insurrection, and support the civil authority in effectuating obedience to the laws and punishment of offenders.

It appears to me that the very existence of government demands this course, and that a duty of the highest nature urges the Chief Magistrate to pursue it. The Constitution and laws of the United States contemplate and provide for it. . . ."

Letter from Hamilton to Washington, August 1794

Thomas Jefferson on the Whiskey Rebellion

"The excise law is an infernal one. The first error was to admit it by the Constitution; the 2d, to act on that admission; the 3d and last will be, to make it the instrument of dismembering the Union, and setting us all afloat to chuse which part of it we will adhere to. The information of our militia, returned from the Westward, is uniform, that tho the people there let them pass quietly, they were objects of their laughter, not of their fear; that 1,000 men could have cut off their whole force in a thousand places of the Alleganey; that their detestation of the excise law is universal, and has now associated to it a detestation of the government; and that separation which perhaps was a very distant and problematical event, is now near, and certain, and determined in the mind of every man."

Letter from Jefferson to Madison, December 1794

Whiskey was a very important product in the West. While the Mississippi River was closed to American traffic, whiskey was the only form in which grain could be transported cheaply overland. Whiskey was also used instead of money in exchange for other goods.

Hamilton's excise taxes were high, as much as twenty-five cents on every dollar. Western farmers began to protest in 1792, but managed to hold their anger in check until the summer of 1794, when rioting broke out in western Pennsylvania. Government agents were terrorized, federal court proceedings were interrupted, and the federal inspector for western Pennsylvania was forced to surrender to an unruly mob and his house was burned.

A contest had developed that tested the authority of the new federal government. Shays' Rebellion had been one of the immediate causes for abandoning the Articles of Confederation and ratifying the Constitution. Now that a second popular revolt had broken out, would the federal government be able to suppress it?

Washington, after calls for compliance with the law, acted boldly to put down this Whiskey Rebellion. He called out a force of some thirteen thousand militiamen and put Alexander Hamilton in charge of the troops. Despite Hamilton's ability, this was a political mistake since he was loathed by Western farmers. The secretary of the treasury was determined to see to it personally that the law and order he had done so much to establish would survive this test. He even welcomed this opportunity for a confrontation that would demonstrate the power of the federal government. But to his dismay, the whiskey rebels fled out of sight at the approach of such a large army. Only a few prisoners were taken, and only two were accused of high treason. Washington pardoned both of them, considering one a "simpleton," the other "insane."

Hamilton and Jefferson, by now open political enemies, had quite different reactions to the Whiskey Rebellion. Jefferson scoffed, "An insurrection was announced and proclaimed and armed against, but could never be found." He believed that the proper method of ridding the country of the problems of the excise tax was to repeal the tax. Hamilton, on the other hand, announced that the government had gained "reputation and strength" by the display of military force. He seemed satisfied that the forces of anarchy had been dispelled.

The Rise of Political Parties

The large coalitions of ideological and economic interests we call political parties originated in the United States in the 1790s. Before this there had been factions and family cliques similar to those in British politics. But under the new American government there was a need for organizations which could bring more order to political life by appealing to a large, national electorate. These new political organizations channeled political differences into verbal confrontations and prevented them from breaking up the Union. They also helped bind together similar interests in all parts of the country and brought issues before the public in a coherent way. Political parties were a practical innovation to help resolve problems in a pluralistic society.

By the middle of the 1790s the political life of the United States was dominated by Jefferson and Hamilton. Although Jefferson retired from his post as secretary of state in 1793 and Hamilton left his position as secretary of the treasury in January 1795, both men continued to exert strong influence over their followers. Jefferson's backers called themselves Democratic Republicans. Hamilton's followers and the backers of the more moderate John Adams were known as Federalists—a slightly different group from those who had supported ratifying the Constitution, who had also called themselves Federalists.

Jefferson's main complaint against the Federalists was that they constantly wanted to strengthen the federal government at the expense of the states and of individual liberty. In the exaggerated rhetoric of the period Jefferson charged the Federalists with conspiring to convert America into a monarchy. Hamilton himself outlined his differences with Jefferson in a remarkably dispassionate summary:

> "One side appears to believe there is a serious plot to overturn the state governments, and substitute a monarchy to the present republican system. The other side firmly believes there is a serious plot to overturn the general government and elevate the separate powers of the states upon its ruins. Both sides may be wrong. . . ."

Jefferson, the gentleman farmer, also distrusted Hamilton's efforts to make manufacturing and urban life more important than farming. According to Jefferson, "those who labor in the earth are the chosen people of God," whereas "the mobs of great cities" were like sores sapping "the strength of the human body." He felt that America could remain morally pure and true to its traditional virtues only so long as it remained rural.

Jeffersonians and Federalists also had different views on the potential of the human race. Jefferson acknowledged that human nature consisted of both worthy and unworthy instincts. But he had much more faith than the Federalists in the possibility of improvement through education and experience. Whereas the Federalists believed that "those who own the country ought to run it," Jefferson wanted eventually to extend the vote to every white male and do away with all property qualifications (although he did believe that universal education had to come before universal suffrage).

Hamilton's leading followers were the elite of the Revolutionary era. Having already achieved prominence, they viewed any challenge to government authority as an attack on an order of which they were a part. The Jeffersonians, on the other hand, were mostly newcomers to politics who felt that they had been left out of the inner circles of power. It was perhaps natural that they should regard strong national government as a means of protecting a native aristocracy, counter to the trends and ideals of American life. The Federalists' aristocratic bias predisposed them to admire Great Britain and its obvious class distinctions. Correspondingly, the Jeffersonians' democratic prejudices led them to admire the French Revolution and its attacks on entrenched power.

The Federalists and the Jeffersonians were not comparable to twentieth-century political parties. They were not as highly structured, nor had they evolved to the point of having national committees or conventions. On the other hand, there were state and local committees, and by 1796 a Democratic Republican caucus in Congress was nominating candidates. They were the first true parties in America in that they both followed a clearly formulated set of ideas and sought to administer the government for the benefit of distinct economic interests which were national in scope.

The Federalists generally represented the merchants, shipowners, and financiers of the Northeast, as well as a decreasing number of prosperous Northern farmers and tidewater planters in the South. The Democratic Republicans represented many artisans and workers in the towns, as well as the small farmers all over the country. They were gradually joined by the wealthy agricultural interests, who were increasingly alienated by Hamilton's programs. His fiscal policies (such as funding, assumption, the enactment of the whiskey excise, and the founding of a national bank) had favored the Northeast, and in general worked against the economic interests of the South and West.

THE ELECTION OF 1796

When Washington decided to step down from office in 1796 the nation faced its first real presidential contest. Washington, unanimously chosen to his office, had always imagined that he was above political parties. But since he had favored Hamilton's program, most Americans thought of him as a Federalist. In fact, most Jeffersonians considered Washington's Farewell Address, which called for an end to partisanship in domestic affairs and warned against permanent entangling alliances in foreign relations, as a partisan statement.

The Democratic Republicans had a congressional caucus which put forward Jefferson, their acknowledged leader, as their candidate to succeed Washington. Jefferson was aided by the organizational work of James Madison and James Monroe, another Virginia planter, as well as by state and county committees. Only Genêt's misadvised activities seemed, for a short time, to slow the party's steady growth. Hamilton's policies, the Whiskey Rebellion, and above all the unpopularity of Jay's treaty, solidified support for Jefferson's candidacy.

The leading Federalist politicians, on the

other hand, passed over their too-controversial leader, Hamilton, as a candidate for president. They decided to back Washington's vice-president, John Adams, as his logical successor. Thomas Pinckney, negotiator of the Spanish treaty, was nominated as vice-president.

Rejected as a candidate by his own party, Hamilton certainly did not want to see his old enemy, Jefferson, in office either. But he also did not want Adams as the second president. Adams, being strong-willed, was not likely to follow Hamilton's advice. In addition, Adams had at one time been an intimate friend of Jefferson's. Hamilton therefore preferred the more pliable Pinckney. He intrigued to round up the support of all the Northern electors for Pinckney so that the South Carolinian might become president with Adams as vice-president.

The scheme, however, backfired, mainly because Hamilton was too indiscreet to nurse a secret plan into full success. Adams was elected president with seventy-one electoral votes. Because Jefferson had received the second highest number of votes (only three less than Adams), he became vice-president. Adams carried New England, and New York, New Jersey, and Delaware. Jefferson's support came from Pennsylvania and the South and West.

THE ADAMS ADMINISTRATION

Adams' political philosophy was more moderate than Hamilton's and actually represented the thinking of a larger proportion of the Federalist voters. Adams shared Hamilton's view of human nature. However, he believed that a government based on the separation of powers and checks and balances would curb the human weaknesses characteristic of all classes in society. Adams lacked Hamilton's skill at organization, and so he never mobilized his supporters or dominated his party. Because of his farming background and his concern with achieving a balanced government, he was somewhat distrustful of granting excessive power to the monied group to which Hamilton catered. Adams favored the expansion of commerce but, unlike Hamilton, did not approve of land speculation or the expansion of bank credit. He did favor widespread ownership of land as the basis of social stability and believed a country's true wealth was based on rising land values. Like Jefferson, he believed the only true aristocracy was one of education and talent, not money. However, as a conservative he did not believe that life would become progressively more enlightened and happy for the mass of humanity.

In order to dispel the Democratic Republicans' fear that the Federalists intended to turn America into a monarchy, Adams made it clear in his inaugural address that he was, and always would be, loyal to the principle of republicanism, the central political philosophy of the Revolutionary era. Republican newspapers praised Adams' "incorruptible integrity," and Jefferson hailed the "talents and integrity" of the new president. Political partisanship seemed to be declining.

Party feeling was not to be so easily smothered, however. Madison urged Jefferson to remember the long-term ambitions of the Democratic Republicans. Federalist leaders discouraged Adams from sending Jefferson's ally, Madison, as an envoy to France. Then Adams had to break with Jefferson after a letter came to public attention in which the vice-president seemed to criticize George Washington. The president had to concede that his administration could not rise above the party battles that had begun during Washington's term.

Adams inherited not only the factionalism of the previous administration, but Washington's cabinet as well: Oliver Wolcott as secretary of the treasury, James McHenry as secretary of war, and Timothy Pickering as secretary of state. All three were mediocre administrators, and all three received constant instruction from Hamilton, now practicing law in New York.

To make matters worse, Adams devoted only part of his energies to the business of running a nation. He spent much of his time at home in

Quincy, Massachusetts, because of his wife's illness. Since he was not a politician by inclination, Adams never tried to develop a program or mobilize his supporters in Congress to direct the Federalist party to a more moderate course than it was taking under Hamilton's guidance.

CONFLICT WITH FRANCE

During Adams' presidency the French, in their efforts to defeat England, continued to attack American shipping. The French were angry because the United States, while claiming to be neutral or even an ally, consistently seemed to be favoring Britain. Jay's treaty, in particular, struck the French as a gift from America to England and a violation of the spirit of the Franco-American Alliance of 1778.

The French, quite rightly, blamed this pro-British bias on the Federalists. Consequently, in 1796 the new French minister to America tried to engineer a Federalist defeat by threatening to break off Franco-American relations if Adams won the election. When Adams did win France carried out her threat: she captured several American vessels bound for England, refused to receive the American minister, and announced that from then on France would treat American commerce the same way Great Britain was treating it.

To persuade the French to abandon these tactics, Adams sent a three-man commission to Paris. The American mission failed completely. The French foreign minister, Talleyrand, offered a humiliating proposal through a matching trio of French agents. These agents, referred to as X, Y, and Z, suggested to the Americans that a bargain could be worked out between the two nations. France would begin official negotiations with the American commission in return for a

huge bribe (Talleyrand's personal fortune had been depleted by the Revolution and he hoped to replenish it at America's expense). The French also demanded an apology from the president for remarks criticizing the French Revolution, as well as a large loan. "No, no, not a sixpence," declared Commissioner Charles Pinckney.

Adams decided that France's demands should be exposed to the American public. He released the commissioners' reports, and Pinckney's mild retort was quickly magnified into the overblown slogan, "Millions for defense, but not one cent for tribute!" Some Federalists, who feared the French Revolution and sympathized with Britain, seized upon the news as a pretext for demanding war with France.

The Jeffersonians, until now strongly pro-French, at first refused to believe Adams. They demanded to see the commission's papers, to which Adams willingly agreed. The documents substantiated France's guilt. Then, Jeffersonians joined Federalists, and both agreed to repudiate America's treaties with France, suspend all trade with France, establish a navy department, and authorize attacks by American vessels on French warships and privateers.

Washington was prevailed upon to come out of retirement and command the army. Hamilton, delighted at this turn of affairs, was made second in command at the old general's request. For the next two years France and America waged an undeclared war on the high seas.

The French were anxious to avoid a full-fledged war with the United States. Napoleon's campaign in North Africa was stalled by the British. Moreover, Napoleon feared that French naval attacks on the United States might provoke an Anglo-American alliance. He therefore ordered Talleyrand to reverse French policy. Talleyrand, after all, had only wanted to humiliate the United States and line his own pockets.

◀ *In this 1799 cartoon a multi-headed monster (Talleyrand) demands money from the American delegates at knifepoint.*

When he saw what a tempest he had stirred up, he quickly backed down. One of Adams' ministers in Europe reported that France was daily becoming more conciliatory. Talleyrand humbly assured the president's son, John Quincy Adams, that an American envoy to Paris would "undoubtedly be received with the respect due to the representative of a free, independent and powerful nation."

Meanwhile the Hamiltonian wing of the president's own party was clamoring for a declaration of war. And the members of Adams' cabinet, who were all under Hamilton's influence, echoed the cry. Adams, however, recognized that declaring war against France would cancel out the advantages of neutrality. He felt that there were no legitimate grounds for declaring such a war and that peace was always preferable to an unnecessary war.

Putting patriotism over popularity with his party, Adams appointed a new three-man commission to deal with France. The commission reached a compromise in the Convention of 1800: the United States was formally released from the encumbering Alliance of 1778 and agreed, in return, to stop demanding French payment for the losses to American commerce.

THE ALIEN AND SEDITION ACTS

On the domestic front the furor aroused by the XYZ Affair gave the Federalists an opportunity to try to silence political opposition. In June and July 1798 Congress passed several laws known collectively as the Alien and Sedition Acts. The Naturalization Act increased from five to fourteen years the period a foreigner had to live in America before qualifying for citizenship. Two Alien Acts empowered the president to expel aliens in time of peace or of war if it was believed necessary for American security.

The most controversial law was the Sedition Act. This act made it illegal not only to instigate a conspiracy against the government, but also to publish or even utter any "false, scandalous and malicious" criticism of the government or its top officials. This was the first time an administration in power had tried to curb the freedom of expression of those opposed to its policies.

The Federalists used the Sedition Act to silence some of Jefferson's followers. Ten Republicans, mostly newspaper editors, were convicted under the law. For example, three editors who favored Jefferson's policies were each given stiff fines and jail sentences.

Madison and Jefferson responded immediately with what are known as the Virginia and Kentucky Resolutions. They declared the Alien and Sedition Acts to be flagrant violations of the First Amendment guarantee of freedom of speech and press. Madison's resolutions condemning the acts were presented to the Virginia assembly. Jefferson sent a somewhat more extreme statement to the Kentucky legislature. He went so far as to propose that it was the right of a majority of state legislatures to nullify a federal law which they felt was unconstitutional. Jefferson based his argument on his belief that the Constitution was a compact among the states. The states had never given up their sovereignty, and they therefore had an "equal right," to judge the constitutionality of laws passed by the federal government.

Jefferson's theory was not put to a test at the time because the other state legislatures either disagreed with or ignored the Virginia and Kentucky Resolutions. However, his ideas proved to be a dangerous legacy for the future.

THE ELECTION OF 1800

As the war scare waned, so did Federalist popularity. Although the public respected Adams for his peaceful stand, many Americans now viewed the Federalist party as a warmongering group. The undeclared war against France had led to new taxes and an increase in the national debt.

In addition, the split between Adams and Hamilton over whether or not to declare war had weakened Federalist unity. The Alien and Sedition Acts and the raising of a standing army drove moderate Federalists into an alliance with the Jeffersonians. New York moved into the Jeffersonian camp in an alliance with Virginia. The Federalist party declined further as wealthy farmers joined the small farmers in the Democratic Republican party.

Jefferson's vigorous party attracted many young, energetic politicians and many young voters, while the older Federalists sank back into what historian John C. Miller has called "opulent apathy." Wealthy and satisfied, leading Federalists refused to run for political office; they preferred their luxurious privacy to the glare of public life. Washington, the most respected Federalist, died in December 1799.

The presidential contest in 1800, again between Adams and Jefferson, was very close. But when the electoral votes were counted the Democratic Republicans had won. They had won, but it was still not clear who was to be the new president. Once again the electoral college system presented problems. According to the Constitution the candidate receiving the most votes would be president and the runner-up would be vice-president. But for the first time Republican electors, voting strictly according to party loyalties, had returned as many votes for Jefferson as for his running mate, Aaron Burr. The two men had received seventy-three votes each. The Constitution provided that in such cases the House of Representatives would choose between the two candidates. But a new deadlock occurred in the House. Through thirty-five ballots neither Jefferson nor Burr was able to win a clear majority. The Federalists, who detested Jefferson, preferred to vote for the elegant, urbane, and pliable Burr.

Several factors created a swing to Jefferson on the thirty-sixth ballot. Hamilton disliked Burr, whom he viewed as "the most unfit and dangerous man of the community," even more than he disliked Jefferson. Hamilton therefore did all he could to defeat the former New York senator. In addition, Jefferson's backers gave reassurances to Federalist delegations. Maryland and Vermont finally changed their votes to

Jefferson and he was elected on February 17, 1801, with ten votes to Burr's four. Delaware and South Carolina cast blank ballots rather than support Jefferson. To prevent such a dangerous deadlock from happening again Congress drafted the Twelfth Amendment, providing for the president and vice-president to be elected by separate ballots.

Many Federalists were still horrified at the outcome of the election. In the congressional elections they had lost about forty seats in the House of Representatives, leaving it with a sound Democratic Republican majority. Jefferson, this wild-eyed atheist—this revolutionary, this enemy of stable, centralized government—was president. Federalist preachers had predicted that if Jefferson were elected, the United States must expect "the just vengeance of insulted heaven." That hour had come and Federalists awaited the holocaust which would destroy constitutional government.

FEDERALIST ACCOMPLISHMENTS

On March 4, 1801 Jefferson was sworn in at the new national capital, the city of Washington on the banks of the Potomac. Government officials exchanged the comforts of Philadelphia for the mud, mosquitoes, and crowded boardinghouses of the half-built city. In this uncomfortable atmosphere Jefferson delivered his Inaugural Address.

The Federalist era had ended. The party's accomplishments were great and enduring. The Federalists had strengthened the national government and rescued its finances. They had implemented the Constitution and demonstrated that large republican governments could be both stable and beneficial to the public welfare. They had brought about official harmony between the United States and Great Britain, established American sovereignty to the Mississippi River, and, in general, maintained American neutrality in the European war. As some Federalists viewed their legacy, they had "found America disunited, poor, insolvent, weak, discontented and wretched." And they had left the country "united, wealthy, respectable, strong, happy, and prosperous."

Why had the once dominant Federalists lost the election of 1800? Perhaps chiefly because of their aristocratic prejudices. As Noah Webster put it, "they have attempted to resist the force of current public opinion, instead of falling into the current with a view to direct it. In this they have manifested more integrity than address."

After its defeat in 1800 the Federalist party slowly waned as a national force. Historian Paul Goodman accounts for its decline by pointing to the newness of political parties in America. The first parties were fragile associations without deep roots, fixed loyalties, or entrenched organization. Furthermore, their leaders did not consider themselves professional politicians, but statesmen called from their regular occupations to serve their country. When defeat came they returned to their normal callings. They had not yet experienced the cyclical return of parties to power: their defeat seemed final. The party did not die out completely, however. David Fisher has shown that a younger generation of Federalists built elaborate party organizations in a number of different states after 1800. But this effort to revive the party ultimately failed to reestablish it as a national force.

More to the point, the Federalist outlook was not in tune with the forces shaping the future direction of the republic. Most Americans were not interested in having a strong central government guide their political and economic activities. The advocates of such a government had been a vocal minority with superior leadership qualities. The majority of Americans believed that the meaning of the American experiment lay in the ever-widening opportunity for each individual to participate in political life and to take advantage of unrestricted economic opportunity. They wanted to achieve these goals on their own or through their state legislatures. It was the Jeffersonians, not the Federalists, who sponsored these ideals.

Readings

GENERAL WORKS

Chambers, William N., *Political Parties in a New Nation.* New York: Oxford University Press, 1963.

Charles, Joseph, *The Origins of the American Party System.* Williamsburg, Va.: Institute of Early American History and Culture, 1956.

Cunningham, Noble E., Jr., *The Jeffersonian Republicans.* Chapel Hill, N.C.: University of North Carolina Press, 1957.

Dauer, Manning J., *The Adams Federalists.* Baltimore: Johns Hopkins Press, 1953.

Hofstadter, Richard, *The Idea of a Party System: The Rise of Legitimate Opposition in the United States, 1780–1840.* Berkeley, Calif.: University of California Press, 1969.

Koch, Adrienne, *Jefferson and Madison: The Great Collaboration.* New York: Knopf, 1950.

Miller, John C., *The Federalist Era.* New York: Harper & Row, 1960.

Nichols, Roy F., *The Invention of the American Political Parties: A Study of Political Improvisation.* New York: Free Press, 1967. (Paper) 1972.

Schachner, Nathan, *The Founding Fathers.* New York: Putnam, 1954.

SPECIAL STUDIES

Baldwin, Leland D., *Whiskey Rebels: The Story of a Frontier Uprising.* Pittsburgh: University of Pittsburgh Press, 1939.

Bemis, Samuel F., *Jay's Treaty.* New Haven: Yale University Press, 1962.

Bemis, Samuel F., *Pinckney's Treaty.* New Haven: Yale University Press, 1960.

Cooke, Jacob E. (Ed.), *Alexander Hamilton: A Profile.* New York: Hill & Wang, 1967.

DeConde, Alexander, *Entangling Alliance: Politics and Diplomacy Under George Washington,* Durham, N.C.: Duke University Press, 1958.

DeConde, Alexander, *The Quasi-War.* New York: Scribner's, 1966.

Gilbert, Felix, *The Beginnings of American Foreign Policy: To the Farewell Address.* Princeton, N.J.: Princeton University Press, 1961.

Kurtz, Stephen G., *The Presidency of John Adams.* Philadelphia: University of Pennsylvania Press, 1957.

McDonald, Forrest, *We the People: The Economic Origins of the Constitution.* Chicago: University of Chicago Press, 1958. (Paper: 1958)

Perkins, Bradford, *The First Rapprochement: England and the United States.* Berkeley, Calif.: University of California Press, 1967.

Rossiter, Clinton L., *Seventeen Eighty-Seven: The Grand Convention.* New York: New American Library, 1968. (Paper)

Rutland, Robert A., *Birth of the Bill of Rights, 1776–1791.* New York: Macmillan Publishing Co., 1962. (Paper) Chapel Hill: University of North Carolina Press, 1955.

Smith, James Morton, *Freedom's Fetters: The Alien and Sedition Laws and American Civil Liberties.* New York: Cornell University Press, 1956. (Paper)

PRIMARY SOURCES

Commager, Henry S. (Ed.), *Selections from the Federalist.* New York: Appleton-Century-Crofts, 1949.

Maclay, William, *The Journal of William Maclay.* New York: Boni, 1927.

BIOGRAPHIES

Brant, Irving, *James Madison,* Vols. I–VI. Indianapolis: Bobbs-Merrill, 1970.

Chinard, Gilbert, *Honest John Adams.* Boston: Little, Brown, 1933.

Flexner, James T., *George Washington: Anguish and Farewell.* Boston: Little, Brown, 1972.

Flexner, James T., *George Washington and the New Nation, 1783–1793.* Boston: Little, Brown, 1970.

Malone, Dumas, *Jefferson and the Ordeal of Liberty.* Boston: Little, Brown, 1969.

Malone, Dumas, *Jefferson and the Rights of Man.* Boston: Little, Brown, 1951.

Miller, John C., *Alexander Hamilton: Portrait in Paradox.* New York: Harper Torchbooks, 1959.

Monaghan, Frank, *John Jay.* Indianapolis: Bobbs-Merrill, 1935.

Peterson, Merrill D., *Thomas Jefferson & the New Nation: A Biography.* New York: Oxford University Press, 1970.

Walters, Raymond, Jr., *Albert Gallatin.* New York: Macmillan, 1957.

Native American Democracy

When white people first crossed the great water, they came to our country like naked babies washed up on the rocks. We Indian people took pity on them. We fed them and helped them build their shelters because we saw that they would die if we did not help them. We saw that there was plenty of room for everyone on our Mother, the Earth, and we wanted life to be good for our white brothers. When we had taught the white people how to find food and shelter, we taught them about how to have good government. They were not happy being ruled by kings, so we showed them the good way our Creator, the Great Spirit, taught us to live as equals.

Iroquois leader, 1974

Democracy was not a new concept brought to America by Europeans. Traditional native Americans and recent historians agree that a number of Indian tribes practiced democracy for centuries before white people came to America. Many whites enthusiastically studied Indian governments and used native American concepts in creating the United States government.

Hundreds of Indian nations lived in what is now the United States. Although every nation was uniquely different from every other nation, most shared certain values. These included individual freedom, government through the consent of the governed, dedication to the welfare of the nation, respect for the variety of people and their visions, and reverence for the environment and for all living things.

Many colonials were deeply impressed with the ways of Indian people. Whereas settlers from the European continent were accustomed to the absolute authority of a monarch, native Americans believed that no human being had the right to tell another what to do. For the most part, Indian chiefs were the servants of their people and could do nothing without their support.

News of native American political and philosophical life reached Europe, where it influenced Locke, Montesquieu, Rousseau, Voltaire, and other great philosophers. In America, many of those who framed the Constitution were thoroughly familiar with native American political systems. Of particular interest was the most powerful and highly developed native American government north of Mexico, the League of the Great Peace.

Under the League of the Great Peace (which the British called the Five Nations Confederacy), five powerful Iroquois-speaking nations with a long history of conflict renounced warfare among themselves and formed a peaceful alliance. This league of Indian nations was based on the concept of states within a state which we have come to call federalism. Originally, it included the Mohawk, Oneida, Onondaga, Cayuga, and Seneca nations. The stronghold of the League of the Great Peace was the heart of what is now New York State. The Mohawks, or People of the Flint, occupied the Mohawk River area; the Oneidas, or Standing Stone People, were settled around Oneida Lake; the Onondagas, or People of the Hills, lived along Onondaga Creek; the Cayugas, or Great Pipe People, were settled along Cayuga Lake; and the

Senecas, or People of the Great Mountain, lived along Canandaigua Lake. It is said that between fifty and sixty nations have been included at one time or another in the League of the Great Peace.

It is not possible to state exactly when the Iroquois formed the League of the Great Peace. Some say the League was developed in the fifteenth or sixteenth century, while others say it began several centuries earlier. At any rate, it is agreed that the League began when two great statesmen, known as the Peacemaker and the Lawgiver, persuaded the five warring nations to join together under one constitution, the Great Law of Peace. The newly united Iroquois people compared themselves to one longhouse in which there were five fireplaces, but all who lived within were of one family.

This government of the League of the Great Peace was a natural extension of the political system which had been practiced by the individual Iroquois nations for centuries. It continues to this day. Under the Iroquois system all people have a voice in the government, which operates by consensus in open council. The chiefs do not have the authority to carry out any decisions with which the people do not agree.

Women have a unique role in the Iroquois political system. Their task of bringing forth the future generations is considered to be the most important responsibility of the nation. Because of their experience observing and carefully nurturing potential leaders from infancy, it is the women who appoint and remove chiefs. But here again, no decisions can be made without the approval of the people.

To hold the office of chief is a reward for public service. The word for chief means, among other things, "one of the nice people," "support in the Longhouse," and "he who eats last." The Great Law of Peace carefully outlines the qualifications of the chiefs of the League. It says that they are to be unselfish, immune to anger and criticism, peaceful, and of goodwill. Their minds are to be "filled with a yearning for the welfare of the people." * They are to be patient, unselfish, and receptive to good advice. The Great Law instructs that the chiefs should "look and listen for the welfare of the whole people, and always have in view not only the present, but also the coming generations, even those whose faces are yet beneath the surface of the ground—the unborn of the future Nation." The power of the chiefs is in their ability to reason, to persuade, and to maintain the respect of the people. They are usually poor, as they traditionally share their wealth with their people.

It is not possible to begin to understand the democracy of the Iroquois without first attempting to develop some insight into their basic traditional values. As with most other native Americans, the principle which is at the basis of Iroquois belief is respect—respect for one another and all other creatures, respect for the ways of nature, respect for the earth, and respect for the Creator. According to this tradition, when an Iroquois man takes a tree for firewood, he first speaks to the trees in the forest and apologizes for taking the life of one of their brothers. He then gives thanks to the trees for allowing him to take

* This and all future quotes from the Great Law of Peace by permission of Akwesasne Notes, Mohawk Nation at Akwesasne via Rooseveltown, New York.

Iroquois in Council. Engraved around 1712.

▲ *"Scenes about a Seneca bark lodge" by Jesse Cornplanter, Seneca artist. Scene depicts traditional Iroquois life. Women pound corn into meal and prepare it over the fire. The lodge, or longhouse, was often much longer, over one hundred feet, and lodged several families.*

one of them to keep his people warm. Similarly, when a woman harvests the corn, beans, and squash, she gives thanks to her mother, the earth, for providing food for her people. She celebrates the spirits of the crops in dance and ceremony.

Respect is deeply spiritual and is part of every aspect of Iroquois life. It follows from respect for one's people that food, shelter, and clothing are available equally to all, since all are seen to be equally deserving. Respect permeates all activities and institutions and makes possible a smoothly functioning society in which each individual is valued and agreement in council can be attained. The fundamental importance of respect was recognized in the development of the Great Law of Peace, which instructs that every session of the Grand Council begin with an expression of gratitude to the statesmen gathered in Council and a statement and offering of thanks to the earth, waters, food and medicine plants, forests, animals, winds, thunder, sun, moon, and the Creator.

When the League of the Great Peace was established, individual nations continued to decide local issues. The League deals only with matters which are crucially important to all members. These have included major alliances and wars, internal disputes between member nations, sale of territory, and relations with outsiders. The League also serves as an information center for the sharing of news and opinion. The Great

▲
"Raising the slain hero" by Jesse Cornplanter. The animal "people" toward whom the slain Iroquois hero has shown respect and friendship come to his aid and bring him back to life.

Law of Peace states that nations of the League are ". . . completely united and enfolded together, united into one head, one body and one mind." The long-range aim of the League is to bring peace to all the world. It is a spiritual union as well as a political one.

The Great Law calls for fifty statesmen, or chiefs, to sit on the Grand Council of the League of the Great Peace. Though some nations seat more chiefs than others, there is an equal distribution of power because each nation has only one voice, and all units are equal. Operations of the government are based on agreement in Council. Once a decision is reached, it is final, and all nations are bound to it.

In sessions of the Grand Council, the Mohawk and Seneca chiefs function together as one body, the Older Brothers, similar to the upper house of Congress, the Senate. All questions go to them first. When they have discussed and unanimously passed on an issue, they report their decision to the Oneida and Cayuga chiefs, who also function together as one body, the Younger Brothers, similar to the lower house of Congress, the House of Representatives. Their decision is then referred to the Onondagas chiefs for final judgment and ratification. The Onondaga confirm the decision when the two bodies are in agreement and offer a compromise or table the issue when the two bodies are in disagreement. When the Onondagas disagree with both of the two bodies, the question is again considered by the two sides and if they reach the same decision as before, the Onondagas are compelled to confirm their decision.

In 1851 Lewis Henry Morgan, noted student of the Iroquois, stated that "it would be difficult to describe any political society, in which there was less of oppression and discontent, more of individual independence and boundless freedom."

Some historians believe that the Great Law of Peace influenced colonial Americans in their efforts to form a national union. For example, both Thomas Jefferson and Benjamin Franklin studied the political system of the League of the Great Peace. In 1744, when a council was held between the colonies of Pennsylvania and Connecticut and the League, one of the chiefs of the League suggested that an organization patterned after the League of the Great Peace might be advisable for the American colonies. The Iroquois saw that the common speech and interests of the colonies were sufficient basis for such a union.

At the Albany Congress of 1754, where a union of the colonies was formally proposed for the first time, Benjamin Franklin said that it would be strange if the Iroquois ". . . should be capable of forming a scheme for such a union and be able to execute it in such a fashion that it has subsisted for ages and appears indissoluble; and yet that a like union should be impracticable for ten or a dozen English colonies. . . ." Franklin utilized the Great Law of Peace in his contribution to the Albany Plan of Union, and the framers of the Articles of Confederation also studied it.

Our history tells us that the League of the Great Peace was at the height of its power from the time of early white settlement to the Revolution. From that point on, white expansion reduced the territories of the nations of the League, which at one time included much of the land east of the Mississippi River. While the League was at the height of its power, the English, Dutch, and French all solicited and threatened it. Many people believed that it was the League's aid to the British which decided the outcome of the French and Indian War.

Lewis Henry Morgan stated that the League of the Great Peace "never even approximated dissolution from internal disorders." Four hundred years of white influence has, however, considerably weakened it. Nonetheless, the League has continued functioning with vigor in the twentieth century. On every Iroquois reservation but one, there is a Longhouse, or meeting place for League members. (There are Iroquois reservations in Ontario, Quebec, and New York.) Many Iroquois people still follow the Great Law of Peace and the Councils continue to meet as they have for centuries. In order that "the strength of the union be preserved," the chiefs have maintained the wisdom of the Great Law, "to be firm so that if a tree should fall upon your joined hands, it shall not separate or weaken your hold."

Suggested Reading

Collier, John, *Indians of the Americas* (New York: Mentor, 1947). A sensitive, comprehensive overview of native American history.

Mohawk Nation at Akwesasne (People of the Longhouse), *Akwesasne Notes* (Mohawk Nation at Akwesasne via Rooseveltown, New York). Native American newspaper and resource center for the distribution of books, pamphlets, and newspapers by and about native Americans.

Morgan, Lewis Henry, *League of the Iroquois* (New York: Sage and Brothers, 1851). The classic study of the Five Nations Confederacy.

White Roots of Peace, *The Great Law of Peace of the Longhouse People*. (Mohawk Nation at Akwesasne via Rooseveltown, New York, 1973). Translation of the Great Law of Peace.

Wilson, Edmund, *Apologies to the Iroquois* (New York: Farrar, Straus and Giroux, 1970). Study of contemporary Iroquois life and history.

▶

Opposite: The USS *Constitution* ("Old Ironsides") confronts and destroys HMS *Guerriere* at the beginning of the War of 1812. (The Granger Collection, New York.)

7

The Jeffersonians in Power

I know, indeed, that some honest men fear that a republican government can not be strong, that this Government is not strong enough; but would the honest patriot, in the full tide of successful experiment, abandon a government which has so far kept us free and firm on the theoretic and visionary fear that this Government, the world's best hope, may by possibility want energy to preserve itself? I trust not. I believe this, on the contrary, the strongest Government on earth. I believe it the only one where every man, at the call of the law, would fly to the standard of the law, and would meet invasions of the public order as his own personal concern. Sometimes it is said that man can not be trusted with the government of himself. Can he, then, be trusted with the government of others? Or have we found angels in the forms of kings to govern him? Let history answer this question.

Thomas Jefferson,
The First Inaugural Address, 1801

The election of the Jeffersonians in 1800 brought into power the party which embodied the spirit of American nationalism. It proved that most voters did not favor a strong central government and did not want federal direction of the economy. Jefferson's victory also represented a protest by the agricultural sector against the tremendous influence which commercial and banking interests had on national politics. In hindsight, the election could be considered a victory for the concept that a responsible political opposition had the right not only to exist, but to assume power when it obtained majority support. It showed, contrary to Federalist fears, that the Jeffersonians did not plan to overthrow the Constitution or the government established under it. Jefferson's victory meant an unqualified commitment to republican government. In fact, the modern political party system came into being with this election. At a time of war and repression in Europe, the majority of adult white American men had voted in free elections for government by the party of their choice. The Jeffersonians assumed power in 1801, if not without unyielding opposition from extreme Federalists, at least without bloodshed.

Domestic Changes

Jefferson's tendency toward democratic beliefs was demonstrated by his style of living. The Federalist presidents, Washington and Adams, had been formal and lofty. Jefferson, with his casual, unpretentious style, was just the opposite. Although he was a landowning member of the Virginia gentry, he was egalitarian in his dealings with others. At social functions he purposely ignored the customary rules of precedence by allowing his guests to sit wherever they wanted, instead of placing the most important dignitaries at the head of the table. At times he even served dinner himself from a dumbwaiter. These changes in etiquette were a deliberate shift in diplomatic protocol, and they irritated the British and Spanish ministers so much that they both began to boycott White House banquets. Jefferson explained his behavior by saying, "The principle of society with us is the equal rights of all. . . . Nobody shall be above you, nor you above anybody, *pell mell* is our law."

Under this studied casualness, however, was a poised and refined mind. Jefferson was a lawyer; he was also an expert in the science of agriculture. He owned the country's best library, and his 6500 volumes later became the nucleus of the Library of Congress. Jefferson was also an accomplished linguist. He had mastered Greek and Latin before he was eighteen, could read French and Italian, and had studied some forty American Indian languages. His writing style was a model of clarity and eloquence and he wrote prolifically. Between 1760 and 1826 he produced fifty thousand pieces of writing, one of the richest literary legacies in human history.

Jefferson was known for his "sunny aspect." Some critics even regarded him as overly optimistic about human potential. But other observers also noticed in him an underlying current of cynicism, coldness, and even bitterness. This side of his personality may have been the result of family tragedies. He had six children, four of whom died between 1772 and 1782. In 1782 his wife also died. At that point, Jefferson threw himself into politics, giving it the same commitment of his energies he had once devoted to such pursuits as architectural design, horticulture, birdwatching, and mastering the violin.

THE INAUGURATION

Jefferson was probably the most skilled statesman of his day. Federalists feared that once he became president, he would immediately undermine all established institutions. Instead he made every attempt to reconcile the opposition to his presidency. The Federalists' fears were completely groundless for Jefferson had always been a politician who hated controversy. Throughout his whole career he had tried to create as little bitterness as possible as he pursued his vision of the public good. In truth, Jefferson was a moderate and compromising person who stood for popular politics and the agrarian point of view.

In his Inaugural Address Jefferson, never a good speaker, talked in such a whisper that his words were heard by only two or three people sitting quite close to him. After the ceremony printed copies of the speech were distributed and the public was able to read his calm, reasonable statements: "... every difference of opinion is not a difference of principle. We are all republicans; we are all federalists." He also declared that "the minority possess their equal rights, which equal law must protect, and to violate would mean oppression."

Jefferson's Inaugural Address reflected popular demands while at the same time assuring his political enemies that he would be fair-minded. Like Washington in his Farewell Address, Jefferson warned the nation against entering into "entangling alliances" with European powers, alliances that might lead America into foreign wars. He emphasized his desire to limit the responsibilities of the federal government and to support the state governments and their rights. In Jefferson's view domestic concerns belonged in state hands. The federal government would function to keep order, preserve personal freedom, and reduce the national debt. In addition, the new president promised to stimulate and protect both agriculture and its "handmaid," commerce.

OLD AND NEW POLICIES

Jefferson regarded his coming to power as "the Revolution of 1800." He believed that the people of America had, as in 1776, demonstrated their virtue by overthowing corrupt rulers. His administration, however, did not make many changes in the actual policies established by his predecessors. Federalist policy had centered on Hamilton's economic program: the funding of the national debt, the assumption of the states' Revolutionary War debts, and the founding of the first national bank. Jefferson had fought each of these policies while secretary of state. But as president he retained all of them, on the advice of Albert Gallatin, his secretary of the treasury. Hamilton's economic framework was left virtually intact because it worked. With the Federalists out of power Jefferson also saw little danger that the system would be used as a tool of corruption. Consequently, funding and assumption both went ahead as before. The Bank of the United States continued to operate until 1811, when its charter expired. Many Federalists were suspicious of this cautious, reasonable behavior, attributing it cynically to his "immoderate thirst for popularity." One Federalist diehard said, "In dress, conversation and demeanor, he studiously sought and displayed the arts of a low demagogue seeking gratification of the democracy on whose voices and votes he laid the foundation of his power."

Some parts of the Federalist legacy were changed, though. Jefferson had bitterly opposed the Alien and Sedition Acts of the Adams administration, so when the Alien Act expired in 1801 the new Democratic Republican administration refused to renew it. When the Sedition Act expired in the same year Jefferson freed all citizens who had been imprisoned under it and refunded their fines. Finally, the residence requirement for citizenship which Adams had raised to fourteen years was now returned to the original five-year period.

Jefferson also turned his attention to a promise he had made in his Inaugural Address: frugal management of the nation's economy. He and Gallatin had a clear-cut policy regarding public finance. They both believed that the United States should pay off the national debt as quickly as possible. On this subject, Jefferson had once remarked, "We can pay off his [Hamilton's] debt, but we cannot get rid off his financial system." By keeping within a strict budget Gallatin was able to shrink the national debt during Jefferson's eight years in office from $83 million to $57 million. All federal bonds were thus paid off by 1807.

Jefferson's second great economic goal was for the United States to pay its own way through tariffs, revenues from land sales, and postal services. Tariff duties would bring in the most income, and Jefferson thought these duties would fall mostly on the rich. Accordingly, the Congress repealed all excise taxes, including the hated whiskey tax. In order to cut back on federal expenses Jefferson reduced the army from four thousand officers and enlisted men to twenty-five hundred. He also decreased the navy's annual appropriation from $3.5 million to $1 million in 1802 by selling a few ocean-going vessels and halting the construction of others. Other savings were made by closing the United States legations in Berlin and The Hague, leaving American ministers in only three European cities: Madrid, Paris, and London.

The effect of these measures was to bring America close to Jefferson's ideal of a nation of citizens "managing their own affairs in their own way and for their own use, unembarrassed by too much regulation, unoppressed by fiscal extractions."

WAR ON THE JUDICIARY

When Jefferson assumed power he was free to appoint men of his own party to important political offices. At first he adopted the moderate attitude that Federalist officeholders would be removed only if they had been appointed after the election or if they had been found guilty of misconduct. But the continued hostility of the Federalists, along with pressure from Democratic Republicans who wished to see men of their own party in office, caused Jefferson to take a more partisan approach to the problem. He envisioned a policy by which members of both parties would hold offices according to the percentage of the total population which supported each party. If this policy of "due proportion" had been carried out, the Jeffersonians would have held two-thirds to three-quarters of the available posts. But the plan was not completely successful. By July 1803, 130 of the 316 offices within the president's domain were still held by Federalists. Jefferson had managed to force out 146 incumbents, almost one-half the offices under his control.

Congress was also controlled by Jefferson's party. In the House of Representatives, Democratic Republicans outnumbered Federalists sixty-nine to thirty-six. In the Senate, the margin was eighteen to thirteen.

Thus the only remaining Federalist stronghold was the judicial branch of the government. In the final days of the Adams administration the departing Congress had quickly passed the Judiciary Act of 1801. This law did institute some badly needed reforms, but it also served to reinforce Federalist domination of the courts. Adams made a number of last-minute judicial appointments during his final night in office, and the new judges were immediately dubbed "midnight justices." Adams had also appointed John Marshall of Virginia, a devout Federalist whom Jefferson loathed, to the position of chief justice of the Supreme Court.

Jefferson and the new Congress immediately attacked the Judiciary Act, which they saw as a Federalist attempt to maintain control of at least one branch of the federal government. Once they repealed the act, Jefferson believed, all of Adams' midnight justices would be automatically removed from office. In 1802 the Democratic Republicans passed their own Judiciary Act, which enlarged the number of lower federal courts without creating any new judicial positions.

In abolishing Adams' appointments, however, the Jeffersonians had performed an act whose legality was in doubt. Since the Constitution guaranteed that federal judges "shall hold their offices during good behavior," the new act could be challenged as unconstitutional. Did the Constitution permit the executive and legislative branches to control the judiciary by eliminating jobs in this way? In theory it was the role of the Supreme Court to declare a law void, but up to this point the Court had never reviewed the constitutionality of any law. On the other hand, many Americans doubted that the Supreme Court had the power to review legislation at all.

Chief Justice Marshall made his position clear in the famous case of *Marbury* v. *Madison*. William Marbury was among the very last of Adams' midnight appointees. His commission to serve as justice of the peace in the District of Columbia had been signed by Adams on March 2, 1801. Marbury was confirmed by the Senate on the next day, but the papers were not delivered to him before Jefferson took office on March 4. Informed that his appointment was ineffective, Marbury petitioned the Supreme Court to issue a writ ordering the new secretary of state, James Madison, to deliver the vital commission to him.

Chief Justice Marshall was now in a very difficult position. He knew that issuing the writ (called a *mandamus*) would bring about open warfare between the executive and judicial branches. The writ would probably be ignored and the Court would have no means of forcing Madison to comply. If this occurred, the Court would lose prestige. But Marshall also knew that a failure to act at all would be an admission that the Court was afraid to challenge the president. Caught between these two unacceptable alternatives, Marshall finally decided to pursue a third course. He began by lecturing the administration, saying that Marbury had a legal right to his commission. However, he argued that Marbury's request had been based on a clause in the Judiciary Act of 1789 by which Congress granted the Supreme Court the right to issue a writ of *mandamus*. According to Marshall's interpretation of Article III, Section 2 of the Constitution, Congress had no right to delegate such authority to the Court in this type of case. The clause in the Judiciary Act was therefore unconstitutional.

Because he turned down Marbury's request for the writ, Marshall seemed to be handing a victory to Jefferson and Madison. Yet at the same time he was maintaining the Court's right to judge the constitutionality of laws passed by Congress. Although Marbury's appointment had been sacrificed, Marshall had established an important precedent—the Supreme Court could use its power to invalidate federal laws which conflicted with the Constitution. With due respect, a colleague remarked of Marshall, "His head is one of the best organized of anyone I have known."

Jefferson had been cleverly outmaneuvered by Marshall, but the president soon tried another tack to drive out Federalist judges. On Jefferson's orders the House began impeachment proceedings against a New Hampshire district judge named John Pickering, charging him with "high crimes and misdemeanors." Once the Senate received the case, it quickly voted to remove Pickering from office. Pickering, however, was considered almost insane, for he had been delivering drunken harangues from his bench for the previous three years. Since an insane person cannot be tried on such charges, the impeachment proceedings were of doubtful legality.

The Democratic Republicans next sought a more clear-cut precedent for their impeacement strategy. Only one hour after Pickering was convicted by the Senate, the House impeached another Federalist, Supreme Court Justice Samuel Chase. Chase was a wholehearted supporter of the Sedition Act as well as a staunch opponent of Jefferson and the Democratic Republicans. Once he had lectured a grand jury for hours on the evils of the Jefferson administration, insisting that it would bring on a "mob-acracy, the worst of all possible governments." Although Jefferson himself used every effort to remove Chase, the Senate was unable to convict him. A simple majority was prepared to find him guilty of "high crimes and misdemeanors," but the necessary two-thirds majority could not be obtained. Chase was thus able to return triumphantly to the bench. Most Senators agreed that Chase had not maintained the dignity expected of a Supreme Court justice, but even many firm Jeffersonians could not be convinced that his conduct was really criminal.

In some ways, Chase's acquittal was fortunate. At the outset, Jefferson's attack on the judiciary was an attempt to establish a broad interpretation of the grounds for impeachment. Part of his initial goal was to make the courts more directly responsible to the people. But if Chase had been convicted, Jefferson might have been tempted to continue the war against all Federalist judges, and the courts might have lost their independence. In his anger, Jefferson had come perilously close to suppressing political opposition. During his eight years in office Jefferson did have the opportunity to appoint three Jeffersonians to the Supreme Court.

The Westward Movement

The outstanding achievement of Jefferson's presidency was probably the acquisition of the Louisiana Territory in 1803. The Louisiana Purchase was one of the most fabulous real estate bargains in history, enabling the United States to increase its territory by 140 percent at a cost of only $15 million.

In 1800 nearly one million American settlers were living in the vast area between the Appalachian Mountains and the Mississippi River. The territories of Kentucky and Tennessee had become states in the 1790s, and in 1803 Ohio was the first state to be carved out of the Northwest Territory. Seeking to encourage even more settlers to enter the Western lands, Jefferson urged Congress to pass new land acts which would lower the price and the minimum acreage of individual farms. His efforts were successful. By 1804 the requirements had been so reduced that a person could gain title to 160 acres for a small down payment. In 1806 Congress further encouraged settlement by authorizing the construction of the National Road, which ultimately extended across the Appalachian Mountains and into Illinois.

Even if roads were built carefully, overland transportation still was not cheap, quick, or efficient enough for Western farmers with produce to ship to East Coast markets. The Westerners needed water transportation, which meant free access to the Mississippi River and its tributaries. After 1763 this access had been blocked by Spain. At the end of the Seven Years' War, France had ceded the immense territory of Louisiana to the Spanish. From the port of New Orleans, Spain was able to control the mouth of the Mississippi and prevent Americans from using the harbor. Pinckney's Treaty of 1795 finally eliminated this barrier by allowing Americans to deposit their cargoes on the wharves of New Orleans and then reload them onto ocean-going vessels.

Access to the port was not enough, though, for Jefferson had visions of owning New Orleans outright. In fact, he imagined that some day the United States would own all the territory between the Mississippi River and the Pacific Ocean. America would be one enormous, freedom-loving republic, an "empire for liberty." Despite such dreams, Jefferson did not hurry to take New Orleans from the Spanish by force. He knew that Spain was a weak nation, powerless to obstruct American navigation of the Mississippi indefinitely.

THE LOUISIANA PURCHASE

Jefferson's patient frame of mind did not last long. Just before he assumed office in 1800, Spain agreed to return the Louisiana Territory (but not the Floridas) to France. In exchange, Napoleon promised Spain that he would not sell the land to a third power. He also offered to create a handsome little Italian kingdom for one of the Spanish dukes. Eventually, he broke both promises.

From the French point of view, the reacquisition of Louisiana turned around the official policy it had followed since 1763. Napoleon was apparently ready for a new attempt at extending France's empire in the Western Hemisphere. According to this new scheme the territory of Louisiana, with its fertile soil, was to be used to produce food for the French West Indian sugar islands. Spain was willing to give up the territory because the effort to hold it had grown too costly. The Spanish also believed Napoleon's assurances that French settlers would be a reliable buffer between Spain's other New World possessions and the aggressive Americans to the east.

Before Louisiana was formally transferred to France in 1802, the Spanish official at New Orleans proclaimed that the right of Americans to deposit their cargoes on the city's wharves was suspended. Pinckney's treaty had stipulated that this right would exist for only three years.

Americans were deeply distressed by this turn of events. Spanish possession of the Mississippi had not been a serious threat, for Spain was a declining power. But France was the strongest country in Europe. French ownership of the strategic port of New Orleans placed an important lifeline in the powerful grip of Napoleon. If the Spanish closing of the harbor to Americans was any indication of coming French policy, the United States faced a crisis.

Jefferson wrote to Robert R. Livingston, the American minister in France, that there was "on the globe one single spot, the possessor of which is our natural and habitual enemy. It is New Orleans, through which the produce of three-

West Indian sugar plantation.

eighths of our territory must pass to market. . . . France placing herself in that door, assumes to us the attitude of defiance." If France gained possession of New Orleans, the United States would have no choice, Jefferson thought, but to ally herself with Britain. "The day that France takes possession of New Orleans," he wrote, we must "marry ourselves to the British fleet and nation."

But Jefferson wanted neither war nor foreign alliances. He envisioned America as a peaceful agrarian state and he dreaded the prospect of an exhausting and expensive war. Consequently, Jefferson obtained an appropriation of $2 million from Congress and instructed Livingston in May 1802 to try to buy New Orleans and West Florida. Livingston discussed the sale with Talleyrand, Napoleon's foreign minister, but made little headway. So in December 1802

Jefferson took a bolder position. He appointed James Monroe as a special envoy to France, with instructions to offer $10 million for New Orleans and the Floridas.

Two days before Monroe arrived in Paris, Napoleon reversed his policy. He suddenly offered to sell not only New Orleans, but the entire territory of Louisiana! No one is quite certain why he made this incredible proposal since few French documents dealing with the matter have been preserved. But it seems likely that Napoleon was having second thoughts about extending the French empire in the Western Hemisphere. In the late 1790s France had lost control of the Caribbean island of Santo Domingo (today divided into the nations of Haiti and the Dominican Republic) when slaves there rebelled under their brilliant general, Toussaint L'Ouverture. Hoping to retake the island, Napoleon sent his brother-in-law with a force of thirty thousand French soldiers to the Caribbean. The effort was unsuccessful. The Santo Domingans outfought the French, and those they did not defeat were vanquished by yellow fever.

There was also another reason for Napoleon's offer. Napoleon was a skilled military man who realized that Britain's superior navy would beat the French in any contest over North American territory. Moreover, since 1799 the chief goal of French New World diplomacy had been to prevent an alliance between America and Britain at the least cost to France. The sale of Louisiana would win the friendship of the United States and keep her from joining forces with the British. Instead of costing money, this strategy would actually enrich the French treasury.

On April 30, 1803 Livingston and Monroe agreed to a price of $15 million. A little over $11 million was paid in United States bonds, which Napoleon immediately sold to Dutch and English bankers for ready cash. The rest was obtained from funds in the United States Treasury and from money borrowed by Gallatin.

In return for this small sum the United States gained millions of acres of land with vaguely defined boundaries. The agreement merely described the territory as the same area formerly possessed by Spain. The United States also inherited a population of two hundred thousand Spanish, French, and Indians and agreed to grant them citizenship and religious freedom.

IMPACT OF THE PURCHASE

Most Americans rejoiced over the Louisiana Purchase. The United States was able to pay one-quarter of the price in cash, and the remainder without having to introduce any new internal taxes. Jeffersonians called the purchase a great diplomatic victory, and Westerners were very relieved to have the Mississippi River securely in American hands. Only a few unrelenting Federalists raised any objections at all. They argued that France did not have the right to sell Louisiana in the first place since Spain had ceded the territory on condition that it never be sold to a third power. They also believed that the president had exceeded his powers in buying the new land. Democratic Republicans countered by reminding the Federalists that they had once called for America to go to war to take New Orleans, while now they were objecting to a purchase of far greater territory at much less expense. The real worry behind the Federalist complaints, however, was that the rural interest in this vast region would someday overwhelm the commercial demands of New England.

Jefferson did take some of the Federalist objections seriously, though. As an ardent expansionist, he could foresee great possibilities in a landed empire stretching all the way to the Rockies and inhabited by free farmers. Yet he also believed in a strict interpretation of the Constitution, and the document did not provide specifically for the acquisition of new territory. Jefferson knew that if he tried to secure a constitutional amendment before making the purchase he would risk losing the deal. So he finally decided that the territory could be acquired under the treaty-making power in Article II of the Constitution. In later years Jefferson justi-

The Louisiana Purchase: The Executive View

"This treaty must of course be laid before both Houses, because both have important functions to exercise respecting it. They, I presume, will see their duty to their country in ratifying and paying for it, so as to secure a good which would otherwise probably be never again in their power. But I suppose they must then appeal to *the nation* for an additional article to the Constitution, approving and confirming an act which the nation had not previously authorized. The Constitution has made no provision for our holding foreign territory, still less for incorporating foreign nations into our Union. The Executive, in seizing the fugitive occurrence which so much advances the good of their country, have done an act beyond the Constitution. The Legislature, in casting behind them metaphysical subtleties and risking themselves like faithful servants, must ratify and pay for it, and throw themselves on their country for doing for them unauthorized what we know they would have done for themselves had they been in a situation to do it."

Thomas Jefferson, Letter to John Breckinridge, 1803

The Louisiana Purchase: The Legislative View

"I have no doubt but we can obtain territory either by conquest or compact, and hold it, even all Louisiana, and a thousand times more, if you please, without violating the Constitution. We can hold territory; but to admit the inhabitants into the Union, to make citizens of them, and States, by treaty, we cannot constitutionally do; and no subsequent act of legislation, or even ordinary amendment to our Constitution, can legalize such measures. If done at all, they must be done by universal consent of all the States or partners to our political association. And this universal consent I am positive can never be obtained to such a pernicious measure as the admission of Louisiana, of a world, and such a world, into our Union. This would be absorbing the Northern States, and rendering them as insignificant in the Union as they ought to be, if, by their own consent, the measure should be adopted."

Uriah Tracy,
Annals of Congress, 1803

fied his action in these words: "Strict observance to the written laws is doubtless *one* of the high duties of a good citizen, but it is not the *highest.* The laws of necessity, of self-preservation, of saving our country when in danger, are of a higher obligation."

EXPLORATION

Jefferson's great interest in natural science led him to quickly dispatch a team of explorers into the vast Louisiana Territory. Early in 1803 Congress appropriated $2500 to support an expedition headed by Meriwether Lewis and William Clark. Lewis, an experienced wilderness explorer, was Jefferson's private secretary, and Clark was the younger brother of Revolutionary War hero George Rogers Clark.

Jefferson issued copious instructions to the team, ordering them to note "the soil and face of the country," "mineral productions of every kind, but particularly metals," as well as animal remains of extinct species, and meteorological information. Much of this data was expected, of

LOUISIANA PURCHASE AND WESTERN EXPLORATION • 1803 TO 1819

course, to be of practical value. Lewis and Clark were to find a usable route to the Pacific, learn the territory's geography, study Indian trade possibilities, and determine how to develop the fur trade.

Lewis and Clark left St. Louis in May 1804 with about forty-five men. The explorers followed the Missouri River up to North Dakota, where they spent the winter. In April 1805 they pushed farther west after shipping nine boxes

(Top) A fanciful sketch from the first published account of the Lewis and Clark expedition showing a member of the party treed by a bear. (Bottom) Clark's own sketch of a canoe used by the Northwest coast Indians.

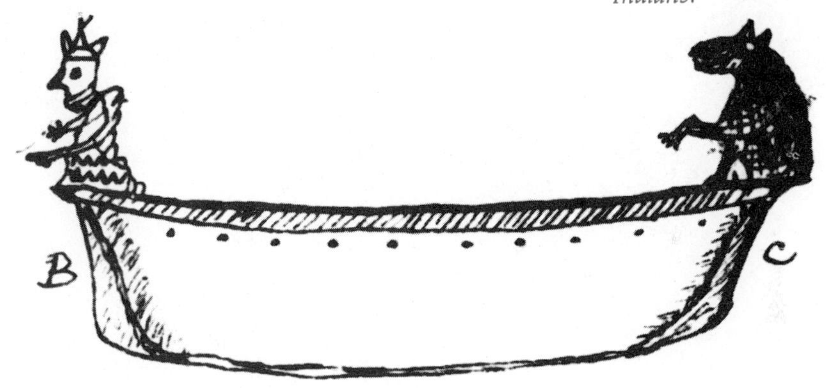

full of specimens and curios back to the eager president. They were guided by a French Canadian and his Indian wife Sacajawea (which meant "Canoe Launcher," not "Bird Women" as some writers have mistakenly called her). Passing over the Continental Divide in southwestern Montana, the expedition descended to the Pacific by the Columbia River. They reached the ocean in November 1805, and carved on a tree, "By land from the U. States in 1804 & 5." After spending the winter there, they returned to St. Louis in September 1806. Because of Lewis' tragic suicide, the only records immediately available to the public were the journal of one of the members of the team (1807), a fake account (1809), and a synthetic journal pieced together from actual events (1814). The full Lewis and Clark records were not published until 1904. The greatest scientific achievement of the expedition was a map released in 1814. Jefferson, however, was pleased to receive many specimens of wildlife, including two grizzly bear cubs which lived for some time in a stone pit on the White House lawn.

Other explorers also began charting the West as traders and new settlers slowly moved into

On Thanksgiving Day, 1806, Lt. Zebulon Pike first viewed the mountain which now bears his name. Shown here are Pike's own drawing of this famous peak, a photograph taken from the same view, and Pike's own description of the day's events.

27th November, Thursday.—Arose hungry, dry, and extremely sore, from the inequality of the rocks, on which we had lain all night, but were amply compensated for toil by the sublimity of the prospects below. The unbounded prairie was overhung with clouds, which appeared like the ocean in a storm; wave piled on wave and foaming, whilst the sky was perfectly clear where we were. Commenced our march up the mountain, and in about one hour arrived at the summit of this chain: here we found the snow middle deep; no sign of beast or bird inhabiting this region. The thermometer which stood at 9° above 0 [+ 52° Fahr.] at the foot of the mountain, here fell to 4° below 0 [+ 23° Fahr.]. The summit of the Grand Peak, which was entirely bare of vegetation and covered with snow, now appeared at the distance of 15 or 16 miles from us, and as high again as what we had ascended, and would have taken a whole day's march to have arrived at its base, when I believe no human being could have ascended to its pinical. This with the condition of my soldiers who had only light overalls on, and no stockings, and every way ill provided to endure the inclemency of the region; the bad prospect of killing anything to subsist on, with the further detention of two or three days, which it must occasion, determined us to return. The clouds from below had now ascended the mountain and entirely enveloped the summit on which rests eternal snows. We descended by a long deep ravine with much less difficulty than contemplated. Found all our baggage safe, but the provisions all destroyed. It began to snow, and we sought shelter under the side of a projecting rock, where we, all four, made a meal on one partridge, and a piece of deer's ribs, the ravens had left us, being the first we had eaten in that 48 hours.

28th November, Friday.—Marched at nine

the territory. Thomas Freeman journeyed through the far Southwest region still owned by the Spanish, but was forced to turn back by hostile soldiers. Between 1805 and 1807, Lieutenant Zebulon Pike explored the upper Mississippi Valley and the area of present-day Colorado. In the latter region he discovered, but failed to scale, the peak named after him. Eventually he made his way down into Spanish-held New Mexico, where he was arrested. Although he did not keep accurate records of his observations, he was eventually able to draw a map of the far Southwest and bring back the first detailed reports of the Rockies and the Great Plains.

By 1812 there were seventy-five thousand people in the territory of Louisiana adjacent to the mouth of the Mississippi River, and Louisiana entered the Union that year as the eighteenth state. Although John Jacob Astor and a few other fur traders pushed into the northern regions, it remained virtually unsettled for many years to come.

THE ESSEX JUNTO

From the point of view of the Federalist party, the Louisiana Purchase meant certain political disaster. With the exception of New England and Delaware most of the country had already gone over to Jefferson's side, and Federalist leaders were sure that settlers in the new territory would also be Democratic Republicans. This bleak outlook led some of the most extreme Federalists to consider a plan to secede from the Union. Proposed by a political group centered in Massachusetts known as the Essex Junto, the new country was to include Newfoundland, New England, Pennsylvania, and New York. The Junto was headed by Senator Timothy Pickering, who declared, "The people of the East cannot reconcile their habits, views, and interests with those of the South and West."

The secessionist plan, however, found little support, even among Federalists. Hamilton refused to take part in the plot, so Pickering turned to Hamilton's archenemy, Aaron Burr. Burr had become discontented with his position as vice-president. Jefferson openly disliked and distrusted him, excluding him from any important decision-making. Hungry for power, Burr decided to run for governor of New York in 1804. Pickering approached Burr during the campaign, promising Federalist support if Burr would then bring New York into the "Northern Confederacy." Burr's answer was somewhat encouraging, and the Federalists backed him against the Jeffersonian candidate, Morgan Lewis. Hamilton, despising Burr, campaigned for Lewis.

Burr lost the election overwhelmingly, a result which had several important consequences. First, the Essex Junto collapsed along with Burr's campaign. Second, Hamilton's low opinion of Burr got into public print. And third, Burr demanded a retraction and challenged Hamilton to a duel. Hamilton tried to evade the challenge since his own son had died in a duel and he wished to shun the custom. Yet he felt his honor was at stake and so he reluctantly accepted. The two met with pistols on July 11, 1804, at Weehawken, New Jersey. According to some observers, Hamilton aimed his gun to miss. Burr's bullet found its mark, though. Thirty hours later, Alexander Hamilton, the great financial wizard of the first years of the republic, was dead.

OPPOSITION TO JEFFERSON

Jefferson won the presidential election of 1804 by a landslide. He received 162 electoral votes, while his opponent, C. C. Pinckney, carried only Connecticut and Delaware. Jefferson triumphed because he had shown that a limited and frugal federal government was possible without creating economic and political disorder. There had been no lawlessness during his first term and internal taxes had been abolished with no harm to the nation. "What farmer, what mechanic, what laborer ever sees a tax-gatherer in the United States?" asked Jefferson in 1805.

Within the Jeffersonian coalition, however, there were some dissidents. One group, led by John Randolph of Roanoke, advocated an extreme states' rights position. Originally a supporter of Jefferson, by 1804 Randolph began to fear that the federal government was becoming too powerful. For example, he opposed Jefferson's attempts to buy West Florida from Spain as unconstitutional. Randolph's defiant attitudes won him some sympathy, but he also suffered from periodic bouts of insanity and was never a serious force within the Democratic Republican party.

Jefferson's other great opponent was Aaron Burr. Burr's unsuccessful campaign in New York and his duel with Hamilton had left him politically isolated, but he was still a dangerous schemer. A short, bald dandy, Burr was a descendant of the famous Puritan clergyman Jonathan Edwards. Although he started his career full of promise, his excessive ambition and unstable mind proved his ruin in the long run. John Quincy Adams described Burr in these words: "Ambition of military fame, ambition of conquest over female virtue was the duplicate passion of his life." Many women succumbed to his personal magnetism, but his military adventures were less successful.

While still vice-president, Burr asked the British minister, Anthony Merry, to make a deal with him. If England would supply him with one-half million dollars, Burr would lead the Western part of the United States in an insurrection to create a separate confederacy. Merry was interested enough to relay news of the proposal back to London, little knowing that Burr was conniving with the French and Spanish for support as well. Without waiting for a response, Burr traveled west to join forces with another expert at intrigue, General James Wilkinson, Jefferson's military commandant of the Louisiana Territory. Burr organized a small band of soldiers on Blennerhassett Island in the Ohio River and on December 10, 1806, began to lead them south to join Wilkinson at New Orleans.

Aaron Burr disguised as a priest.

No one knows exactly what Burr intended to do; he himself might not have been quite certain. He may have been planning to take New Orleans and use it as a base for his efforts to lead the Western states in revolt. Or he may have meant to capture Mexico as a beginning for his personal empire. In any event, Wilkinson suddenly changed his mind and denounced Burr. He revealed the entire plot to Jefferson, and Burr was soon captured while trying to escape to Florida.

Burr's trial on the charge of treason began in Richmond, Virginia on August 3, 1807. Chief Justice Marshall, who conducted the proceedings, and President Jefferson were both thoroughly partisan in their approach to the trial. Jefferson was determined to see his political enemy convicted, and perhaps was guilty of misusing his presidential powers to that end. He went so far as to instruct the government attorneys on how to organize the case, and took personal charge of assembling the evidence.

Marshall, in his hostility toward Jefferson, was clearly sympathetic to the defendant. The chief justice tried to subpoena Jefferson himself, but the president refused to appear on constitutional grounds. Then Marshall defined the crime so narrowly that the jury was virtually forced to acquit Burr.

The final outcome rested on what actually constituted treason. Burr's defense was based on the fact that he was not actually on Blennerhassett Island when the force left, and thus was not party to an overt act of treason. The government claimed that Burr was guilty anyway, because he had instigated the plot. Marshall agreed with the defense position. According to his interpretation, the meaning of "treason" under the Constitution was such that only *acts*, not words, could be considered treasonable. This narrow definition not only led to Burr's acquittal, but also set an important precedent for the future of civil liberties in the United States.

Unfortunately for Burr, he was still wanted for murder in six states, so he was forced to flee to Europe. He immediately asked for an audience with Napoleon, somehow hoping to persuade France to make peace and form an alliance with England. According to the new scheme, Burr would then be appointed commander of a combined army that would conquer Mexico and eventually the United States. The plan never got off the ground, but Burr did manage to return to America and spend most of the rest of his life practicing law in New York City.

International Problems

While Jefferson's first term was peaceful in the area of foreign affairs, his second was difficult and full of controversy. Once he had finally gained the support of most Americans for his approach to domestic issues, a new set of international problems began to emerge. His solutions to these problems were the cause of much discontent, resulting in the loss of much of his prestige. His second term was so trying that Jefferson wrote a friend: "Never did a prisoner, released from his chains, feel such relief as I shall on shaking off the shackles of power."

The one major foreign crisis of Jefferson's first term occurred in 1801, when Tripoli declared war on the United States. For many years America, along with the European powers, had paid tribute to the rulers of Morocco, Algiers, Tunis, and Tripoli in order to protect commercial shipping from pirate raids along the northern coast of Africa. American shipping was particularly vulnerable because the United States had no effective regular navy and its merchant vessels could not depend on British protection after the Revolution. Consequently, the United States was forced to pay approximately $100 thousand per year to avoid the Barbary pirates, a practice which infuriated Jefferson. "When this idea comes across my mind, my faculties are absolutely suspended between indignation and impatience," he claimed.

Jefferson finally reached the limit of his tolerance when the Dey of Algiers publicly humiliated an American naval officer at the same time the Pasha of Tripoli tried to squeeze still more money out of the United States. With these provocations, Jefferson firmly refused to pay any more. The Pasha responded by having the flagpole in front of the American consulate chopped down as a declaration of hostilities. The ensuing conflict lasted until 1805 and was fought mainly by American naval forces off the North African coast. Unfortunately, the president's earlier budget-cutting activities had greatly weakened the navy. It was not strong

The burning of the frigate Philadelphia *in the harbor of Tripoli in 1804.*

enough to overwhelm the pirates, but it did manage to establish a blockade in 1805. Some form of tribute was still paid for another ten years, but America was now in a position to demand a lower price for the "protection." The Pasha settled with Jefferson for a mere $60 thousand, to be paid to the Pasha personally. In addition to this price reduction, the war with the Barbary pirates provided the inexperienced American navy with excellent practice. The officers, including Stephen Decatur, learned much about warfare at sea, knowledge they later put to good use in the War of 1812.

THE FRENCH AND BRITISH CONFLICT

Two weeks after Napoleon arranged for the sale of Louisiana, he renewed hostilities with England. This new conflict, which ravaged all of Europe, lasted on and off for the next twelve years. At first America was able to stay out of it, and make immense profits from her neutral position. Between 1803 and 1812 the United States became the world's most important neutral carrier and the leading wholesaler of tropical produce. In fact, American trade flourished to such an extent in this period that it was not equalled again in real value until the late 1940s. Shipbuilding boomed and American tonnage increased prodigiously.

Between 1803 and 1805 neither Britain nor France interfered with American commerce. American ships were free to deal openly with the two competing powers. England and the United States were on fairly good terms, and the French Navy was not strong enough to patrol the Atlantic. France never had as many ships as England, and those she did have were demolished by the British fleet in 1805 during the Battle of Trafalgar.

The war was a strange stalemate though, for British triumphs at sea were matched by French victories on land. In November 1805 Napoleon defeated the combined armies of Russia and

Austria at Austerlitz in central Europe. Thus while England ruled the seas, Napoleon reigned supreme over most of the Continent.

Because Britain and France could not strike directly at each other they turned to commercial warfare. In April 1806, Britain issued an Order in Council, closing the northern coast of Europe to all trade. In November Napoleon answered with the Berlin Decree, declaring a blockade of the British Isles. In 1807 Britain issued further Orders, forbidding all coastal trade between European ports under French control and requiring all neutral vessels to obtain a British license before entering a European port. Napoleon then took the final step in this economic battle. In December 1807 he issued the Milan Decree, making all ships with a British license subject to immediate seizure.

The United States was now caught in a vise. If American vessels sailed between French ports without a British license, they could be taken by the British. But if they entered a French port with a British license, they would be seized by the French. Jefferson and other Americans regarded these Anglo-French regulations as insulting. But they were effective. British merchants were soon satisfied to see their government undermining America's expanding trade, which had become a threat to British commercial supremacy. In 1805 the *Essex*, an American vessel carrying cargo from Spain to Cuba by way of Salem, Massachusetts, was seized by an English frigate. This was the beginning of a campaign during which scores of American merchant vessels were captured, on the grounds that they were trading illegally between enemy ports in the Caribbean normally closed to foreign trade. British men-of-war hovered off the coast of the United States to capture the reshipment of these goods to European ports. The result was a virtual blockade of the key ports on the Atlantic seaboard and in the Gulf of Mexico.

In addition to interfering with shipping, the British infuriated many Americans by their practice of impressment. For more than four

The British navy impressing American seamen.

hundred years the British navy had been raiding English villages and carrying off able-bodied men to serve aboard its ships. Since the pay was poor and the discipline was severe, it was difficult to find "recruits" any other way.

When war resumed in 1803 the British navy was once again in desperate need of recruits. Under British law the navy was permitted to stop any neutral vessel, capture all English subjects, and impress them into service. With this official sanction, many American ships were stopped at sea and searched for potential recruits. In truth, many British sailors were working in the American merchant marine. Attracted by the comparatively high wages and good working conditions, Englishmen regularly deserted their own vessels to join American crews. In 1804, for example, twelve British men-of-war were detained in the port of Norfolk, Virginia because their crews had all jumped ship.

British officers were not particularly scrupulous, however, when searching for Englishmen among the American crews. Swedes, Danes, and Portuguese sailors were often hauled away, and between 1793 and 1811 the British impressed about ten thousand native-born Americans.

AN AMERICAN EMBARGO

By 1807 the British had seized more than five hundred American ships and the French had captured another two hundred. This interference, plus the practice of impressment, caused much bitterness; but Jefferson still continued to believe that prosperity was more important than glory and national honor. "We have principles from which we shall never depart," he insisted, "We do not want war, and all this is very embarrassing."

In 1807, though, another incident occurred which struck such a blow to American pride that war seemed almost inevitable. In February a British crew deserted an English man-of-war and four of the sailors enlisted on an American warship, the *Chesapeake.* Under international practice at the time, neutral merchant ships could be stopped at sea, but not naval vessels such as the *Chesapeake.* However, a British admiral stationed in Nova Scotia was so outraged at the desertion that he ordered the capture of the fugitive sailors. Carrying out this order, the British frigate *Leopard* stopped the *Chesapeake* ten miles off Norfolk, Virginia, and demanded the right to board ship. When the American captain refused, the *Leopard* opened fire. Three men were killed, eigtheen were wounded, and the *Chesapeake* was forced to surrender.

The American people rose up in righteous indignation at the surprise attack. Jefferson wrote of the nation's mood: "Never since the battle of Lexington have I seen this country in such a state of exasperation as at present, and even that did not produce such unanimity." While the public clamored for war, Jefferson realized that America's tiny navy was no match for British seapower. Knowing that he had to strike back in some way, he turned to a strategy of economic coercion. In December 1807, his congressional supporters passed the Embargo Act, prohibiting all exports by land or by sea from the United States. Under the act only coastal trade between American ports was permitted. It was expected that the embargo would be an effective tactic since many nations were heavily dependent on America for food and other commodities.

Some segments of the British economy were adversely affected by the embargo. Textile factories which needed American cotton were forced to shut down and thousands of factory workers were suddenly unemployed. On the other hand, 1808 was a good year for English crops, greatly offsetting the effects of the embargo. Moreover, the embargo helped many English merchants get some of their markets back.

As it turned out, the embargo created the greatest hardships in America itself. Exports fell

The Leopard *takes the* Chesapeake.

from $108 million in 1807 to $22 million in 1808. Commercial wharves had no business, and the prices of manufactured goods and farm products suffered a sharp decline. New England Federalists now became the strongest proponents of states' rights, and New England merchants once again spoke of seceding from the Union. Even though some Yankee skippers were able to evade the embargo by smuggling goods into Canada, the country faced a serious depression. One New Englander said that Jefferson had resorted to "cutting one's throat to cure the nosebleed." Jefferson himself later wrote: "I felt the foundation of the government shaken under my feet by the New England townships."

Nevertheless, the president refused to give up his unpopular law. Rather than trying to enforce American rights by building a bigger navy, he obtained from Congress the Force Act of 1809 which gave federal collectors almost arbitrary power over American trade. He was willing to accept this increase in centralized power because he felt that war would mean an even more dangerous centralization. Even so, the law still proved unworkable since the New England states were defiant. On March 1, 1809, three days before Jefferson was scheduled to leave office, Congress revoked the Embargo Act and replaced it with the Nonintercourse Act. Under this less stringent law, trade was prohibited only with Britain and France.

Ironically, the Embargo Act may have had at least one beneficial side effect. Cut off from international trade, many Northern merchants were forced to invest their capital in manufacturing enterprises. Jefferson, who was opposed to the development of factories in the United States, had unintentionally laid the foundations for the industrialization of America.

Madison As President

By the end of his second term, Jefferson was ready to leave active political life. He had always disliked the speech-making, the bickering, and the direct confrontations involved in politics. He also believed, as had Washington, that no president should serve more than two terms. This conviction, plus his growing weariness with America's international problems, led to his decision to step down. In one of his final political acts, he personally intervened in the legislative caucus to win the next presidential nomination for his close friend James Madison.

Madison won the election of 1808 by 122 electoral votes to 47 over the Federalist candidate C. C. Pinckney of South Carolina. Unfortunately, the new president did not have the political skills of his brilliant predecessor. A scholarly, even bookish man, Madison was a serious student of political philosophy. But despite his training and intellectual accomplishments, Madison was subject to fits of indecision and poor judgment. He was no match for stronger, more aggressive politicians and was the first president to have cabinet choices forced upon him by the Congress. Although Madison wanted former Treasury Secretary Albert Gallatin to be his secretary of state, the Senate forced him to accept a nonentity named Robert Smith for the post and to keep Gallatin in the treasury position. In 1813 Madison succumbed to similar pressures from his party. He appointed a greedy, untalented New Yorker as secretary of war, causing Gallatin to resign in disgust. After Gallatin's departure, Madison was said to have appeared brokenhearted.

THE FAILURE OF PEACEABLE COERCION

The great problem facing Madison when he took office was to avoid war with Britain. The

Embargo Act had failed, but the Nonintercourse Act passed early in 1809 was beginning to have some effect on the English economy. Napoleon had already sealed off most of continental Europe from trade with Britain, so America was the only important remaining consumer of British industrial goods. Since they needed the American market, British industrialists began to put great pressure on Foreign Minister George Canning to repeal the Orders in Council. They argued that as long as the Orders continued to operate, the Americans would not be able to trade openly with England. Canning responded only half-heartedly to these pressures. He was willing to admit that Britain had no right to search American warships, but he would make no apology for the attack on the *Chesapeake.*

Canning also went so far as to open some European ports to American trade and to instruct the British minister in Washington, David M. Erskine, to attempt to negotiate a settlement. Erskine was married to an American woman and was quite fond of the United States. Soon he was able to reach an agreement which provided that Britain would withdraw the Orders in Council and ask for no concessions in return. Madison was obviously delighted, but unfortunately Erskine's terms were far more lenient than Canning had intended. Nevertheless, Madison lifted the embargo on June 10, 1809, without waiting for the agreement to be approved in London.

Canning was furious when he received news of the generous settlement. He immediately repudiated it, summoned Erskine back to London, and replaced him with a disagreeable man who abhorred Americans. The new minister, Francis James Jackson, found Madison a "plain, rather mean-looking man," and his wife Dolley, "fat and forty, but not fair." His presence obviously put a further strain on Anglo-American relations.

Embarrassed by the haste with which he had lifted the embargo, Madison was forced to restore nonintercourse. In the interim, however, hundreds of American vessels had already unloaded tons of produce in England, bringing relief after the long period of hardship the embargo had caused. Now that its warehouses were stocked with food and cotton, England was in a much better position to drive a hard bargain with the United States.

On May 1, 1810, the United States instituted yet another economic policy, embodied in a measure called Macon's Bill Number 2. This action restored trade with Britain and France, but offered each of the belligerents an opportunity to be the favored nation. If France would agree to respect America's neutral rights, the United States would suspend trade with Britain. If Britain would repeal its Orders in Council, America would reward her by suspending trade with France.

Napoleon immediately saw a chance to manipulate the new law to his advantage. In the famous Cadore Letter he professed his love for America and promised that France would repeal its commercial restrictions. But he went on to hedge the promise with a number of qualifying clauses that made the pledge virtually meaningless. Madison swallowed the bait, though. He asked England for a similar concession and when she refused, Congress again moved to prohibit trade with the British. Meanwhile, Napoleon was not fulfilling his pledge at all. On the very day he made his offer, France raised the tariffs on American goods and seized all American ships in French ports. Outmaneuvered by the Europeans, Madison's new strategy had accomplished nothing.

At this point, Britain finally made a few vague attempts to win American friendship. Two of the three Americans who had been captured aboard the *Chesapeake* were returned to American soil (the third had died in captivity). An editorial on the subject printed in a Baltimore newspaper was typical of the American reaction: "Presented at such a time," it said, "the reparation was like restoring a hair after fracturing the skull." Ironically, on June 6, 1812, Britain finally decided to suspend the hated Orders. But it was too late. On June 1

Madison had asked Congress for a declaration of war. On June 4 the House complied by a vote of seventy-nine to forty-nine. Fourteen days later the Senate made it final, voting nineteen to thirteen in favor of war with Britain.

WAR HAWKS

When Congress met on November 11, 1811, its membership had changed considerably. Most of the representatives who had opposed war with Britain had been voted out of office and replaced by a new group of congressmen. Sensitive to American honor, these incoming representatives became even more anti-British as they learned of her wartime activities.

The leaders of the war faction were a small band of youthful Democratic Republicans from the Southern and Western states popularly known as the "War Hawks." They were dominated by the new Speaker of the House, Henry Clay of Kentucky, and they clamored for revenge on England. These angry young men—who included Richard M. Johnson of Kentucky, Felix Grundy of Tennessee, and John C. Calhoun of South Carolina—had little interest in the old question of states' rights and were quite willing to delegate more power to the federal government, particularly in wartime. They tended to be intensely nationalistic, eager for territorial expansion, and furious at Britain's lack of respect for America.

By the middle of 1812, even the president and Secretary of State James Monroe were becoming more warlike and receptive to the aggressive demands of the War Hawks in their own party. In the end, it was not only the Westerners and Southerners who favored war; forty-six of the sixty-five Jeffersonians in Congress eventually voted in support of the conflict. Thus there was ultimately no split within the Democratic Republican party between War Hawks and peace doves. When it came to voting for war, party regularity more than public opinion or section-

War Hawks in Congress

"An honorable peace is attainable only by an efficient war. My plan would be to call out the ample resources of the country, give them a judicious direction, prosecute the war with the utmost vigor, strike wherever we can reach the enemy, at sea or on land, and negotiate the terms of a peace at Quebec or Halifax. We are told that England is a proud and lofty nation that disdaining to wait for danger, meets it half-way. Haughty as she is, we once triumphed over her, and if we do not listen to the councils of timidity and despair we shall again prevail. . . ."

Henry Clay,
Annals of Congress, January 1813

New England Doves

"The war cannot be carried on by the Militia. A regular army will be enlisted with the utmost difficulty; besides money cannot be raised by Loans; and if Taxes be collected, the popularity of the Party according to Mr. Jefferson's former opinion, must be destroyed. I infer that the war will drag on heavily; that it will become very, and extensively, unpopular; that the dread of French connexion will greatly increase the mass of discontent; that the Congressional Elections will show the perilous unanimity of the Northern States agt. the war, and if England have a wise ministry, we must soon return to Peace."

**Rufus King,
Letter to C. Gore**

alism actually produced the conflict. Although they were definitely in the minority, the Federalists were even more cohesive on the issue than the Jeffersonians. Fearing the wartime assumption of power by the federal government, not a single Federalist broke ranks to vote for war with Britain.

Those who supported the war were driven by a strong desire to vindicate the nation's honor after years of British impressment of American sailors and seizure of American merchant vessels. They argued that France had seemed to change her ways recently and was no longer interfering with American commerce. Clay put it this way: "As to France we have no complaint . . . but of the past. Of England we have to complain in all tenses." In addition, the attacks on American shipping had resulted in a downturn in the economy of the West and South. A serious depression had settled over the United States since 1808, and prices for hemp, cotton, and tobacco had fallen steadily. Farmers blamed these conditions on English commercial restrictions. In urging war Henry Clay said, "We are asserting our right . . . to export cotton, tobacco and other domestic produce to market."

New Englanders had a similar need for a free flow of trade with Europe, but people in this region had a lingering emotional attachment to Britain which influenced their view on the war issue. New England was still the stronghold of Federalism. Politically and culturally its conservative citizenry sympathized strongly with England in her great struggle with the French. They believed that a war with England would be a blow against the tradition of parliamentary government and a triumph for Napoleon, who now held all of Europe in his autocratic grip. Such ideological considerations did not impress the fiery "backwoodsmen" of America.

WESTWARD EXPANSION

Maritime problems were not the entire reason for the War of 1812. In part, the conflict arose out of sentiment to expand American territory and remove the Indians who occupied land within America's boundaries. Many westerners living on frontier settlements were certain that England was behind the continuing series of Indian raids. Even though the British had advised the Indians to make peace, frontier people still believed that British officials in Canada were supplying the Indians with weapons and paying a bounty of six dollars apiece for American scalps.

Actually, the Indian attacks were mainly prompted by American plundering of the Indians' fields and hunting lands. General William Henry Harrison, the Governor of the Indiana Territory, considered Indians "wretched savages" and mere obstructions to American "civilization." Through deceptive treaty arrangements he was able to deprive several tribes of their lands. When Shawnee chief Tecumseh and his half-brother Tenskwatawa (known as "the Prophet") tried to reverse this trend, General Harrison began to prepare for an all-out battle. By 1806 Tecumseh had organized all the tribes east of the Mississippi into a confederacy. Traveling from the Great Lakes to the Gulf of Mexico, he had forged a vast number of Indians into a solid union. Tecumseh preached that the Indians should live separately from the white people, safe from their power, corrupting laws, and liquor. So great was the influence of this movement that even Harrison was obliged to say of Tecumseh: "He is one of those uncommon geniuses which spring up occasionally to produce revolutions and overturn the established order of things."

When Harrison came in November 1811 to wipe out Tecumseh's camp, the inevitable clash occurred. Trying to keep the Americans away, Tenskwatawa attacked Harrison's troops. Harrison was able to repel the Indians and destroy their camp on Tippecanoe Creek near the Wabash River in Indiana. Although the battle was indecisive, it was enough to throw Tecumseh's confederacy into disarray and to alarm the American people. They were convinced that the British had been backing Tecumseh and believed

General William Henry Harrison and Tecumseh.

this to be yet another reason for going to war. They saw it as an opportunity not only to drive the Indians farther west, but also to strike at the British bases which supposedly supplied them.

Some War Hawks even hoped to annex Canada and the Floridas (still held by Spain, which was now England's ally). Once Canada was part of America, the continent would be free of the Union Jack forever. Since Canada was populated by many Tories who had fled during the Revolution, a number of Americans believed that the huge territory should be annexed. Congressman Harper of New Hampshire saw it as the work of Divine Providence: "To me, sir, it appears that the Author of Nature has marked our limits in the south by the Gulf of Mexico, and on the north by the regions of eternal frost." This idea was expressed in more concrete terms by Felix Grundy of Tennessee: "We shall drive the British from our continent. . . . They will no longer have an opportunity of intriguing with our Indian neighbors. . . . That nation will lose her Canadian trade, and, having no resting place in this country, her means of annoying us will be diminished."

The War of 1812

The United States was so poorly prepared and deeply divided that the War of 1812 was almost a national disaster. The country was unprepared financially. Early in 1811 the Bank of the United States had been allowed to expire and now there was no central agency that could handle the complex job of issuing war bonds. Moreover, when the bank died, so did many investors' confidence in the government's ability to redeem the bonds once they were finally issued. As a consequence, only one-half of the $11 million in bonds offered for sale were bought. Congress had equal difficulty raising money from other sources. It finally doubled tariffs and introduced new excise taxes, but these were widely evaded.

The inadequacy of the army and navy was an even more serious problem. In their anxiety to reduce the national debt, Jefferson and Gallatin had trimmed America's armed forces down to a bare minimum. As late as 1811 Madison was still pursuing this policy. The new president made no recommendation for naval expansion in his annual messages to Congress, and the legislature voted overwhelmingly against adding ten new ships early in 1812. It was not until several months after the war had started that Congress finally authorized the construction of new frigates. And none of them was ready to sail until after the war was over. In short, the United States was taking on the world's most powerful navy, which had hundreds of men-of-war, while she herself owned only a tiny fleet of sixteen vessels.

But the War Hawks were not particularly concerned about the size of the American navy. They were planning to defeat Britain on land by capturing Canada, an easily obtainable goal in their opinion. Jefferson, now retired to Monticello, was confident that taking Canada "will be merely a matter of marching." Little resistance was expected from the Canadians themselves, and Americans felt certain that the British could not withdraw any troops from their struggle against Napoleon to protect the northern territory.

Unfortunately for these plans the American army was a poorly commanded force of only thirty-five thousand soldiers. As one young officer commented: "The old officers had very generally slunk into either sloth, ignorance, or habits of intemperate drinking." Most of the new ones were either "coarse and ignorant," or "swaggerers, dependents, decayed gentlemen and others unfit for anything else." The strongest land forces in America were the state militias, which together included over one-half million men. But many of the enlistees refused to serve outside of their state boundaries, and the strongest units were in New England—a region strongly opposed to participating in the war at all.

THE CANADIAN CAMPAIGN

To the disappointment of the expansionists, Canada did not want to be part of the United States. Her five thousand professional soldiers were well trained, and all three of America's invasions turned into fiascoes. In the first attempt, Revolutionary War hero William Hull was surrounded near Detroit by a small British force backed by Tecumseh and several hundred Indians. Tecumseh disliked the British, but he hated the Americans. Paralyzed by fear and indecision, Hull surrendered without even firing a shot. The American public was outraged and Hull was sentenced to death for his cowardice. Madison pardoned him, however, because of his record in the Revolutionary War.

A second invasion force which attempted to cross the Niagara River ended in an American defeat when the New York militia refused to cross its state boundary. The New Yorkers watched from safety as their countrymen were mowed down by the Canadians. General Henry

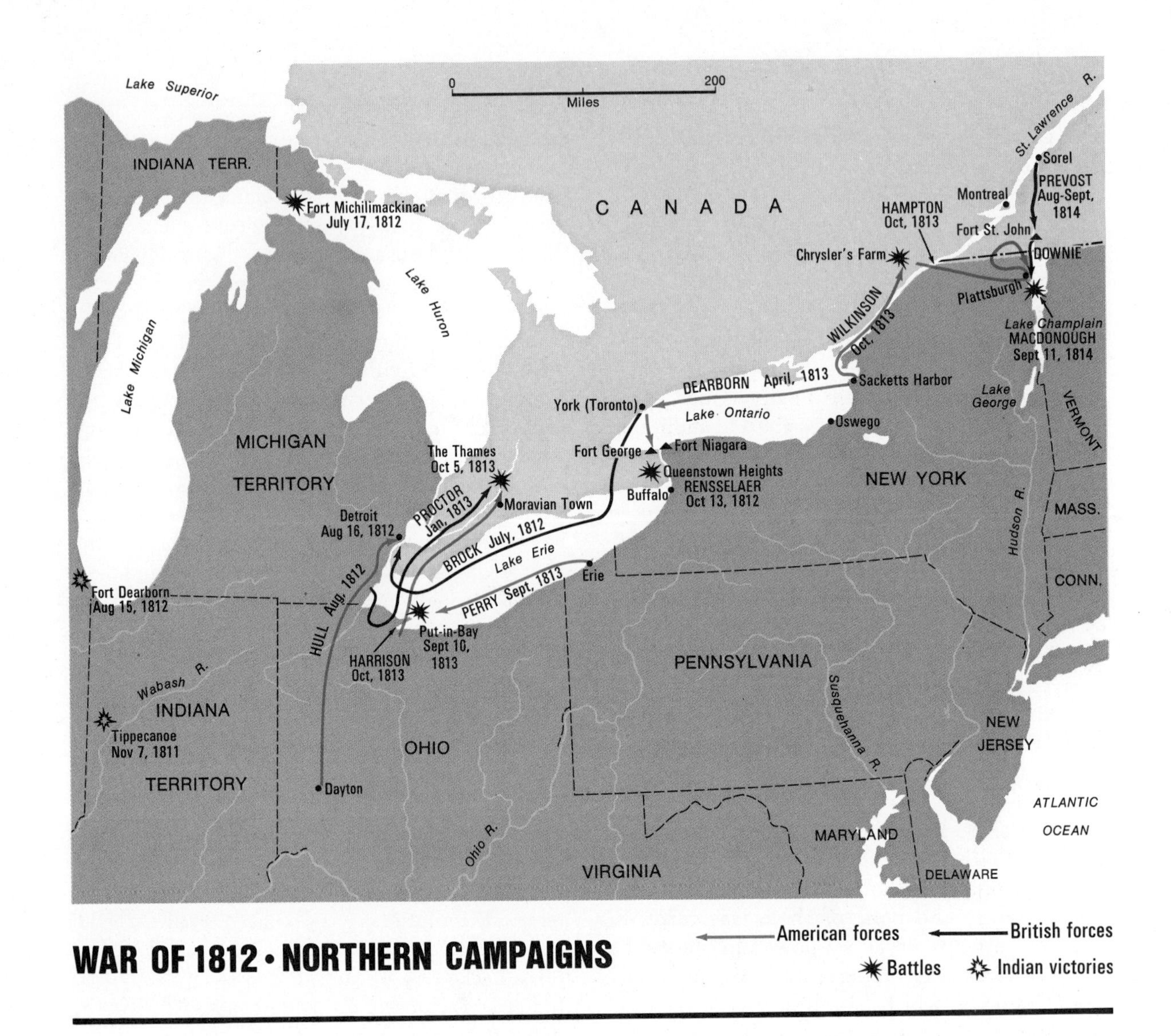

WAR OF 1812 • NORTHERN CAMPAIGNS

Dearborn led the final campaign into Canada, along Lake Champlain toward Montreal. Dearborn's militiamen also balked at the boundary line, and the general was soon forced to march back to Plattsburgh, New York without accomplishing anything. Thus ended the American offensive of 1812. Jefferson's "mere matter of marching" had fallen far short of defeating the British.

In 1813 America's poor war record was partially vindicated by Captain Oliver Hazard Perry's brilliant victory on Lake Erie. In ships he had designed and built himself Perry defeated

"Queen Charlotte and Johnny Bull Got their dose of Perry," a cartoon celebrating Perry's naval victory on Lake Erie. ▶

a British squadron on the lake in September 1813. This triumph secured American control over the Great Lakes, and Perry reported it in the now famous phrase, "We have met the enemy and they are ours." After receiving the good news, General Harrison gained a second American victory in October at the Battle of the Thames in northern Ohio. With a troop of Kentucky militiamen, Harrison routed a British force and their Indian allies under Tecumseh. Tecumseh died mysteriously in the battle; his body was never found. With his death the last remnant of the Indian confederacy was demolished. Despite these triumphs, however, the goal of conquering Canada remained out of reach.

THE NAVAL WAR

Although it was described by the *London Evening Star* as a "few fir-built frigates, manned by a handful of bastards and outlaws," the small American fleet scored a series of dazzling triumphs in the first few months of the war. Part of the reason for the successes was that the American frigates were larger and better armed than their British counterparts. Two months after the war began Captain Isaac Hull of the U.S.S. *Constitution* gunned the English *Guerrière* into submission in the middle of the Atlantic. In October 1812 Stephen Decatur, who had already demonstrated his skill in the war against the Barbary pirates, pitted the *United*

An anti-British cartoon from the War of 1812: "John Bull making a new Batch of Ships to send to the Lakes."

States against the H.M.S. *Macedonian*. Decatur's ship emerged victorious, hauling the battered enemy vessel into New London, Connecticut as a prize. Soon the *Constitution* (nicknamed "Old Ironsides") was in action again. This time it engaged the British frigate *Java* off the coast of Brazil, shot the *Java*'s mast and reduced her to rubble.

Nevertheless, the American navy was simply too small. By 1813 most of the American men-of-war were bottled up in their home ports by the Royal Navy, and British squadrons roamed up and down America's coast at will. American privateers were able to harass British commerce, but the English blockade in turn almost destroyed American shipping. Since the United States had few roads and most shipments were still made along coastal waterways, interstate trade suffered as much as international commerce. Looking back, one New Englander described the blockade in this way: "Our harbors were blockaded; communications coastwise between our ports were cut off; our ships were rotting in every creek and cove where they could find a place of security; our immense annual products were mouldering in our warehouses; the sources of profitable labor were dried up."

This sort of economic disaster was exactly what the New England Federalists had feared and predicted. In the peak year of 1807 American imports and exports had totaled one-quarter billion dollars. By 1814 they had declined to one-tenth of that figure. Federalists regarded President Madison as a greater enemy than George III, and the governors of Massachusetts and Connecticut refused to send their state militias to the aid of the national government. Daniel Webster, a young Federalist congressman from New Hampshire, asked, "Where is it written in the Constitution that you may take children from their parents, and parents from the children, and compel them to fight the battles of any war in which the folly or the wickedness of government may engage it?" The Jeffersonians temporarily lost ground throughout New England, and this richest section of the country subscribed to only a tiny fraction of the government's war bonds.

THE BRITISH ATTACK

When Napoleon's abdication in April 1814 finally ended the war in Europe, the British were able to devote their attention to chastising their troublesome former colonies. Some of England's best troops, many of whom had served under Wellington at Waterloo, were shipped to American or Canadian shores. With these new forces, the British soon inflicted one of the worst psychological blows ever experienced by Americans during wartime. In August 1814 the redcoats invaded Washington and burned the Capitol, the White House, and other public buildings. The rout was so complete that Madison himself was forced to flee the city.

The nation's capital was captured and burned by the British in August 1814, shortly after President Madison had fled.

The sacking of Washington, though, was not even the main British thrust. The most serious British attacks took place at three strategic points: Niagara, Lake Champlain, and New Orleans. The first offensive was launched at Niagara in July 1814. But General Jacob Brown and his subordinate Winfield Scott quickly turned it back by taking Fort Erie and outfighting the British at Lundy's Lane. Two months later Sir George Prevost attempted to capture Lake Champlain. The British were successful in this effort, which threatened to cut off New England and restore the region to the British Empire. In September, however, the American fleet under Captain Thomas Macdonough won a decisive victory at Plattsburgh, New York, forcing Prevost to retreat into Canada. This was the last battle fought before a treaty brought the war to a close.

Because transatlantic and transcontinental communications were so slow, the most spectacular American victory of the entire war actually occurred after the peace treaty was signed. General Andrew Jackson of Tennessee had already defeated the Creek Indians on March 27, 1814 at the Battle of Horseshoe Bend. Jackson then went on to capture and destroy Pensacola in Spanish Florida to prevent the British from using it as a base. Next, the general marched his men through Mobile to New Orleans.

In a countermove the British set sail from Jamaica and approached New Orleans from the Gulf of Mexico. On January 8, 1815, between six and eight thousand British troops under Sir Edward Pakenham met Jackson's army. The American force of about forty-five hundred was composed of local pirates, government soldiers, and French-speaking militia. Pakenham ordered an assault on Jackson's defenses and the Americans opened fire. Jackson was outnumbered but he used brilliant tactics in the placement of his artillery. As a result, in less than one-half hour the Americans sustained less than twenty-five casualties while the British suffered some twenty-six *hundred*. Badly crippled, the British army was forced to retreat in haste.

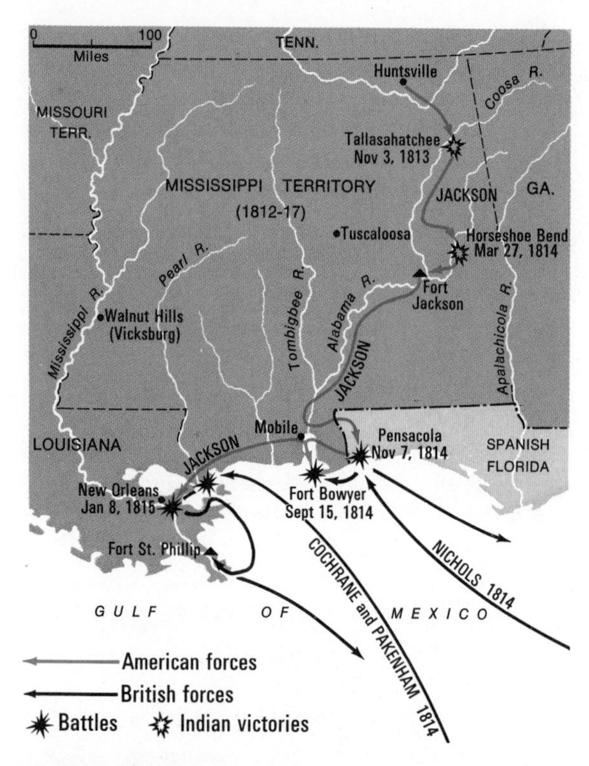

**WAR OF 1812
SOUTHERN CAMPAIGNS**

The great victory in the Battle of New Orleans made Andrew Jackson the most popular American hero since George Washington. Of Jackson's campaign in the South, the historian Marshall Smelser has written: "Had not the United States crushed the Creeks, defended Mobile, seized Pensacola, and held New Orleans, all of the Louisiana Purchase could have been lost and part, perhaps, given to Spain. . . ."

THE HARTFORD CONVENTION

Despite British interference with American shipping, New Englanders actually made a great deal of money during the War of 1812. Massachusetts and Rhode Island were not blockaded throughout most of the conflict, and merchants in the region continued to carry on their lucrative trade with the British whenever possible. As late as 1813 New England was sending one million bushels of grain per year to British armies.

Prosperity, however, did not diminish political opposition to the war. In December 1814 the Massachusetts legislature called for a convention in Hartford, Connecticut which attracted twenty-six delegates. Some of the members planned to propose a number of constitutional amendments, while others hoped to sign a separate peace with England or even secede from the Union. Following three weeks of debate the convention adopted the more moderate stand.

All of the suggested amendments were designed to restore the dominance of New England and its commercial interests. Specifically, the convention proposed to repeal the Three-fifths Compromise concerning the enumeration of slaves and to apportion representatives according to the number of free people in each state. The delegates also proposed to reduce the power of the federal government by limiting embargoes to sixty days, and by requiring a two-thirds majority in Congress to declare war, restrict foreign trade, or admit new states. Finally, the representatives sought to bar all naturalized citizens from holding federal office and to restrict any president to one term in office.

Unfortunately for the conventioneers, their demands were poorly-timed. By the time their delegation arrived in Washington, the war was over, Jackson had scored his great triumph at New Orleans, and a peace treaty had just been signed. Madison paid no attention to the gloomy New Englanders, and the authors of the ultimatum were regarded by the public with ridicule and a suspicion of traitorous intent.

Peace and Postwar Diplomacy

The War of 1812 was generally viewed as a second war for independence, finally securing favorable international recognition for the United States. Unlike most wars, however, peace negotiations began soon after the outbreak of hostilities. The first unsuccessful attempt took place in June 1812, only one week after the war began. A second effort was made the following fall, when the Czar of Russia offered to mediate between America and Britain. Madison was optimistic at that point, but the English distrusted Russian motives and the diplomatic moves never really materialized.

By August 1814 Britain and the United States had settled down to direct negotiations in Ghent, Belgium. The British representatives were men of little stature, controlled by the British foreign minister, Lord Castlereagh. The American delegation, however, was made up of some of the most respected politicians in the country, including John Quincy Adams, Albert Gallatin, and Henry Clay.

Signed on December 24, 1814, the Treaty of Ghent did little more than return to prewar conditions. Such issues as neutral rights, impressment, national boundaries, fisheries, and compensation for shipping losses were not even mentioned in the treaty. "Nothing was adjusted, nothing was settled," said Adams, "nothing in substance but an indefinite suspension of hostilities." The only real losers in the war were the Indians. After suffering heavy casualities, they no longer had any promise of British firearms or supplies. In effect, the Indians were left to the mercy of the land-hungry American people.

Although British industrialists were pleased with the outcome, the treaty was unpopular in England with shippers, the landed gentry, and the press. In America, on the other hand, peace was greeted with total jubilation. Suddenly the

This 1815 cartoon depicts tough Yankee resistance to John Bull (Britain). The swamp John Bull refers to is Jackson's defeat of the British at New Orleans.

ineptness, the lack of public support, and the nasty infighting were forgotten. Holidays were proclaimed and cheering patriots embraced each other in a mood of happy celebration. Many Americans had feared that after defeating Napoleon, the British would turn vengefully on the United States. But instead, "Not one inch of territory ceded or lost" was the slogan of the hour. Madison promptly submitted the treaty to the Senate, which ratified it unanimously the next day. As the historian Thomas A. Bailey has written, "The Treaty of Ghent certainly was the most popular peace pact with a major power ever concluded by the United States."

EFFECTS OF THE WAR

As soon as the War of 1812 ended, most Americans turned their backs on Europe and returned to domestic concerns. Tecumseh's Indian confederacy was crushed, opening the area east of the Mississippi to settlement by frontier farmers. American manufacturing had been forced to develop, so the country was now more self-sufficient. The most widely felt effect of the war was probably the rebirth of pride in the United States. Since the war in Europe had ended almost simultaneously, the country was no longer divided in its foreign sympathies. Gallatin wrote: "The war has renewed and reinstated the national feelings and character which the Revolution had given. . . . The people now have more general objects of attachment. . . . They are more Americans; they feel and act more as a nation." They forgot the humiliating moments of the war and made heroes of Andrew Jackson

Detail of a handkerchief commemorating American naval victories of the War of 1812. ▶

and Oliver Hazard Perry. The country had not suffered financially very much, except for the heavy losses incurred by the shipping industry. Most important, they felt they had "licked the British twice."

Even though a great deal of ill feeling prevailed between England and the United States, further settlements were reached by statesmen of the two countries on several important issues in the years immediately following the war. By the Rush-Bagot Agreement of 1817, each nation promised to demilitarize its side of the Great Lakes. In 1818 a convention successfully established the northern boundary of the Louisiana Territory at the forty-ninth parallel, provided a ten-year joint occupation of the Oregon Territory, extended an earlier agreement banning discriminatory duties on each other's goods, and reopened the Newfoundland fisheries to Americans.

These agreements signaled a new era of rationality on both sides. The arrangements concerning the Canadian border were especially beneficial since money would no longer have to be spent on building up large fleets on the Great Lakes or Lake Champlain. Eventually, the entire border between America and Canada was demilitarized, an unparalleled achievement.

THE FLORIDAS AND THE LATIN AMERICAN REPUBLICS

Jefferson had thought that the Louisiana Purchase included West Florida, and he also claimed East Florida as compensation for Spanish interference with American commerce. In 1805 and

1806 he tried to talk Napoleon into forcing Spain to sell the Floridas to the United States. Congress even appropriated $2 million in secret funds to start the negotiations. But Napoleon had meanwhile decided against the deal.

Americans had had their eyes on East and West Florida ever since. In part this was because they were hungry for new lands to settle, but there were other reasons, too. The territories could be used as a base from which to attack the United States—and many Americans feared that Britain might buy them from Spain for this purpose. In addition, the Floridas would have the advantage of linking the Atlantic coast to New Orleans and providing new river transportation to the Gulf of Mexico.

American desire for the Floridas had been partially satisfied by the end of the War of 1812. In 1810 a group of American settlers in West Florida tore down the Spanish flag, declared the Republic of West Florida, and petitioned to join the United States. One month later Madison granted the request. Although this illegal land grab embarrassed the president, he faked the needed documents for posterity's sake. John Quincy Adams was also embarrassed when he tried to explain the incident to the czar of Russia. But the czar replied diplomatically, "Everyone always grows a little in this world."

Now Americans began to eye East Florida greedily. Spanish forces were so busy putting down revolutions in South America, that Florida was left unguarded. Certain elements in America had already rushed into this vacuum: white renegades, escaped American slaves, and hostile Indians who used Florida as a base from which to raid Georgia outposts.

In March 1812 General George Matthews, a former governor of Georgia acting as Madison's special agent, led a revolution of American settlers in East Florida. He was supported in this effort by United States Navy gunboats. Matthews occupied East Florida and claimed it for the United States. Madison disavowed his actions, but the United States retained East Florida until the end of the war.

The new president, James Monroe, also had ambitions for the area. He took steps quickly and peacefully to secure the rest of Florida and to establish the western boundaries of the Louisiana Purchase. Monroe was especially anxious to settle American territorial problems with Spain so that the United States could be the first country to recognize the independence of Spain's Latin American colonies. He believed that the only impediment to these plans was the Holy Alliance: a coalition of Russia, Prussia, and Austria which pledged to crush revolution wherever it appeared. It was possible that these powers would try to put down the revolutions in Spanish America.

To set the president's plans in motion Secretary of State John Quincy Adams began negotiating the territorial and boundary issues with the Spanish Minister Luis de Onís in December 1817.

In the midst of the negotiations Monroe unintentionally created an incident which provoked the Spanish. He authorized Andrew Jackson to cross the American border into East Florida, if necessary, to chastise marauding Indians. General Jackson interpreted his orders quite liberally. Never one to hesitate, Jackson seized a Spanish military outpost and replaced Spain's flag with that of the United States. He then executed two British subjects he suspected of inciting the Indians to attack American settlers. Within a few weeks Jackson had captured every Spanish fort in East Florida except St. Augustine. He had also deposed the Spanish governor, replaced him with an American, and declared that henceforth the revenue laws of the United States would be in force in Florida. He later said that he should have hanged the Spanish governor as well.

When news of the execution of the two Englishmen reached London the people were outraged. "We can hardly believe," one London journal wrote, "that anything so offensive to public decorum could be admitted, *even in America!*" But the British government did not protest the incident.

Meanwhile, Jackson's enemies in Congress initiated an investigation of his conduct. But every resolution to condemn the popular general was defeated and the American public erupted in long victory celebrations when Jackson was finally cleared. New Yorkers celebrated for five days and Jackson received the keys to the city.

The situation temporarily embarrassed Adams' negotiations. Spain demanded an apology, but the secretary of state took the offensive. He pointed out that the Spanish, by their own admission, were powerless to govern Florida. He asserted that if Spain could not restrain the Indians, she should immediately cede the territory to the United States. Adams also demanded a westward line stretching to the Pacific for the Louisiana Purchase. After months of hard bargaining, Spain finally agreed to all American demands, except for the territory of Texas. She ceded East and West Florida, accepted the Rocky Mountains as the western boundary of Louisiana, and the forty-second parallel as the northern boundary of her North American claims west of the Rockies. This last provision excluded her from any further claim to the Oregon Territory.

The Adams-Onís, or Florida, Treaty gave the United States undisputed control of the territory to the Rocky Mountains and a window on the Pacific by virtue of her joint control of the Oregon Territory with Great Britain. These remarkable gains cost the United States a mere $5 million worth of American claims against the Spanish government.

Following the successful negotiations President Monroe recognized the independence of Latin American colonies in 1822. The Holy Alliance had taken no steps to suppress the revolutions there.

THE MONROE DOCTRINE

Even though the United States had taken its stand on Spain's Latin American colonies, she still had to face the possibility that the Holy Alliance might decide to help Spain recover these provinces. The question became of immediate concern when the Monroe administration received a dispatch from its minister to Great Britain in the fall of 1823. The dispatch indicated that England was interested in issuing a joint statement with the United States denouncing the transference of the Spanish colonies to any other power. Britain also hoped that the United States would deny any interest in controlling the territories and leave open the question of their independence or negotiated return to Spanish control. By October the British Foreign Office had lost interest in a joint statement, but the president and his cabinet had begun to consider the project seriously. In fact, Britain was busy securing France's promise not to intervene on the side of Spain in Latin America. The United States gradually abandoned the idea of a joint declaration with England and decided to issue a statement of its own.

The president enunciated the Monroe Doctrine in a message to Congress delivered on December 2, 1823. It was a general statement which committed the nation to no specific action and has been interpreted in many different ways ever since.

The basic points of the doctrine were that the Western Hemisphere was no longer open to colonization or military intervention by the European powers and that the United States would not intervene in the affairs of Europe. It recognized the existence of spheres of influence in the world, and implicitly claimed the Western Hemisphere as the area of American dominance. In addition, it represented America's belief in the superiority of her own political system and her determination to prevent the "decadent" powers of Europe from interfering with her national destiny or with that of any other country in the hemisphere. Following the tradition of isolation begun during the early years of the republic, the doctrine was directed against no nation in particular but against all those not in the Western Hemisphere.

UNITED STATES • 1822

Although the United States could not enforce the Monroe Doctrine herself, she knew that she had nothing to fear. European intervention in Latin America would restrict British trade there, and the British navy would no doubt prevent such interference.

The cabinet debate over the original English proposal of a joint statement indicates clearly that John Quincy Adams was the real inspiration behind the Monroe Doctrine. It was Adams who favored rejecting the British offer in favor of an independent statement. It was Adams who saw that Russian attempts to settle the Alaskan panhandle might renew European efforts to colonize North America and limit American expansion and political dominance on the continent. Finally, it was Adams who was astute enough to see that, because of the power of the British fleet, America was safe in making an independent statement.

The Monroe Doctrine drew little international attention when it was first uttered. The Russian czar had retracted his threat against the Americans entering Alaskan coastal waters even before Monroe spoke. France had also abandoned her rather vague plans to help Spain in Latin America nearly two months before Monroe made his now-famous statement because England had disapproved of the project.

The new Latin American republics regarded the Monroe Doctrine with indifference once they realized that the United States had no intention of making specific commitments to Latin America. At the time America was too small and too weak to back her foreign policy statements with action. Nevertheless, the Monroe Doctrine did clearly establish the principle of America for the Americans. And it was only a few decades before the United States had the resources to back her words with military power.

Readings

GENERAL WORKS

Adams, Henry, *History of the United States During the Administration of Jefferson and Madison.* Englewood Cliffs, N.J.: Prentice-Hall, 1963.

Borden, Morton, *Parties and Politics in the Early Republic, 1789–1815.* New York: Crowell, 1967.

Channing, Edward, *The Jeffersonian System.* New York: Harper and Brothers, 1906.

Cunningham, Noble E., Jr., *The Jeffersonian Republicans in Power.* Chapel Hill, N.C.: University of North Carolina Press, 1963.

Fischer, David H., *The Revolution of American Conservatism.* New York: Harper & Row, 1965.

Horsman, Reginald, *The Frontier in the Formative Years, 1783–1815.* Albuquerque: University of New Mexico Press, 1973. (Paper)

Peterson, Merrill D., *The Jefferson Image in the American Mind.* New York: Oxford University Press, 1960.

Smelser, Marshall, *The Democratic Republic, 1800–1815.* New York: Harper & Row, 1968.

Wiltse, Charles M., *The Jeffersonian Tradition in American Democracy.* Chapel Hill, N.C.: University of North Carolina Press, 1935.

Wiltse, Charles M., *The New Nation: 1800–1845.* New York: Hill and Wang, 1961.

SPECIAL STUDIES

Abernethy, Thomas P., *The Burr Conspiracy.* New York: Oxford University Press, 1954.

Banner, James M., Jr., *To the Hartford Convention.* New York: Alfred A. Knopf, 1970.

Bemis, Samuel F., *John Quincy Adams and the Foundations of American Foreign Policy.* New York: Knopf, 1949.

Brown, Roger H., *The Republic in Peril: 1812.* New York: Columbia University Press, 1964.

Burt, A. L., *The United States, Great Britain and British North America.* New Haven, Conn.: Yale University Press, 1940.

Coles, Harry L., *The War of 1812.* Chicago: University of Chicago, 1965.

Commager, Henry S., *Thomas Jefferson, Nationalism and the Enlightenment.* New York: George Braziller, 1974.

Ellis, Richard E., *Jeffersonian Crisis: Courts & Politics in the Young Republic.* New York: Oxford University Press, 1971.

Horsman, Reginald, *The Causes of the War of 1812.* New York: Octagon, 1970.

Levy, Leonard W., *Jefferson & Civil Liberties: The Darker Side.* New York: Quadrangle, 1973. (Paper)

Perkins, Bradford, *Castlereagh and Adams.* Berkeley, Calif.: University of California Press, 1964.

Perkins, Bradford, *Prologue to War*. Berkeley, Calif.: University of California Press, 1963.

Perkins, Dexter, *A History of the Monroe Doctrine*. Boston: Little, Brown, 1963.

Pratt, Julius W., *Expansionists of 1812*. Gloucester, Mass.: Peter Smith, 1957.

Whitaker, Arthur P., *The United States and the Independence of Latin America, 1800–1830*. New York: W. W. Norton, 1964.

PRIMARY SOURCES

DeVoto, Bernard (Ed.), *The Journals of Lewis and Clark*. Boston: Houghton Mifflin, 1953.

Koch, Adrienne, and William Peden (Eds.), *The Life and Selected Writings of Thomas Jefferson*. New York: Random House, 1944.

Padover, Saul (Ed.), *The Complete Madison*. New York: Harper and Brothers, 1953.

BIOGRAPHIES

Bedini, Silvio, *The Life of Benjamin Banneker*. New York: Charles Scribner & Sons, 1973. (Paper)

Brant, Irving, *James Madison: Commander-In-Chief*. Indianapolis, Ind.: Bobbs-Merrill, 1961.

Brant, Irving, *James Madison: The President*. Indianapolis, Ind.: Bobbs-Merrill, 1956.

Dangerfield, George, *Chancellor Robert R. Livingston of New York, 1746–1813*. New York: Harcourt, Brace & World, 1960.

Hecht, Marie B., *John Quincy Adams: A Personal History of an Independent Man*. New York: Macmillan Publishing Co., 1972.

James, Marquis, *Andrew Jackson: Border Captain*. New York: Grosset & Dunlap, 1933.

Malone, Dumas, *Jefferson the President: First Term, 1801–1805*. Boston: Little, Brown, 1970.

Malone, Dumas, *Jefferson the President: Second Term, 1805–1809*. Boston: Little, Brown, 1974.

Tucker, Glenn, *Tecumseh: Vision of Glory*. Indianapolis, Ind.: Bobbs-Merrill, 1956.

Schachner, Nathan, *Aaron Burr: A Biography*. Cranbury, N.J.: A. S. Barnes, 1961.

HISTORICAL NOVELS

Roberts, Kenneth L., *Captain Caution*. New York: Fawcett World, 1970. (Paper)

Vidal, Gore, *Burr*. New York: Bantam Books, 1974. New York: Random House, 1973. (Paper)

Locks on the Erie Canal. ▶

8

Social and Economic Patterns of the Young Republic

Mr. Chairman, our confederacy comprehends within its vast limits great diversity of interests —agricultural, planting, farming, commercial, navigating, fishing, manufacturing. No one of these interests is felt in the same degree, and cherished with the same solicitude, throughout all parts of the Union. Some of them are peculiar to particular sections of our common country. But all these great interests are confided to the protection of one government—to the fate of one ship; and a most gallant ship it is, with a noble crew. If we prosper, and are happy, protection must be extended to all: it is due to all.

Henry Clay

After the War of 1812 the United States began to mature as an independent nation. New technologies gradually brought the country into effective competition with European markets. Leading politicians sought to use the federal government to strengthen national unity.

In New England new industries reaped handsome profits, and the Northeast began shifting from commerce to manufacturing. In the South cotton replaced tobacco and rice as the region's leading export. In 1816 and 1817 poor harvests in Europe led to an increased demand for American grain. The West had welcomed 2.2 million settlers by 1820, and now outranked New England in population. During the next decade new transportation systems (steamboats, roads, and canals) connected the West to the seaboard, and Western agricultural produce found new markets in the Atlantic coastal states and in Europe.

The Postwar Culture

AMERICANS ON THE MOVE

New England had the largest and most stable population in the country. Most of New England had been settled by 1800. From 1790 to 1820 the population of Connecticut increased by only ten percent, and the population of Rhode Island and Massachusetts grew just as slowly.

The Middle Atlantic states and the West, on the other hand, experienced sharp increases in population. Between 1815 and 1820 about 100 thousand foreigners emigrated to the United States, most of them settling in the Middle Atlantic states and the West. In the nineteenth century a restrictive land policy which had discouraged immigration was generally abandoned. The Iroquois, who had dominated western New York, were expelled by the turn of the century, and this territory was opened to white settlers. By 1820 New York, which had been the fifth

The Frederick Road, west of Baltimore, was a stagecoach line, a cattle run, and an artery to the West.

Brooklyn, New York, in 1816.

most populous state in 1790, had the largest population in the country.

Almost all the cities of the Northeast grew dramatically with the advent of industrialization. By 1810 New York City and Philadelphia had become the two largest cities, with populations of more than 90 thousand each; by 1830 they had more than 150 thousand inhabitants each. Only Boston, which lacked a navigable river connecting it to the West, remained relatively stable. During the 1820s the number of American towns with more than 8000 inhabitants rose from eleven to forty-four. Most of these towns were in the Northeast.

In the South the growth of an economy based on the export of cotton affected the growth and power of the states. South Carolina and Georgia, the new centers of cotton agriculture, doubled in population between 1790 and 1820.

"Old America seems to be breaking up and moving westward," observed an Englishman in 1817. In 1810 only one-seventh of the American people lived west of the Appalachians; thirty years later more than one-third of the country's population had crossed the mountains. From 1810 to 1820 the population of Ohio doubled and by 1840 it had climbed from 230,760 to 1,519,467. Other Western states experienced similar influxes of settlers.

DECLINE IN THE CITIES

In contrast to the growth of new rural settlements, a process of deterioration had already begun in the cities. Eighteenth-century American cities had reflected the comfortable economic circumstances of the merchants and craftsmen who lived there, but in the first decades of the nineteenth century large slum areas began to appear. New York City may have boasted of its literary groups and its centers of intellectual life, but it also had slums worse than those in London. Members of wealthy old Dutch families lived in stately yellow brick houses, but pigs were allowed to forage in the garbage that littered every public avenue. The city had the wealth of more than a mile of warehouses along the East River but it also swarmed with thousands of penniless immigrants.

American cities were a study in contrast. Philadelphia was probably the most progressive American city of the day, with its well-planned, well-lit, well-paved streets, a good water supply, and handsome houses and public buildings. Boston offered its citizens similar improvements. On the other hand, no city had an adequate sewerage system. Lacking proper treatment facilities, cities allowed wastes to run into nearby rivers, often the same rivers from which they drew their water. Philadelphia, for example, used the already polluted Delaware River to meet its water needs. No wonder the city suffered two separate plagues of yellow fever in the 1790s. The first claimed 4000 lives (more than ten percent of the city's population) and the second took an additional toll of 3500. Yellow fever also hit New Haven, Baltimore, New York, and Boston in the 1790s.

Disease, poverty, and overcrowding caused a severe drain on public services such as fire and police protection. American cities had almost no police protection and people out walking at night had to carry pistols. Large cities had an average of one fire a night, and there were only volunteer fire companies, or firemen hired by insurance firms, to battle the flames.

The resulting increase in crime and disorder led many to argue that cities were immoral, unnatural institutions. In 1800 Thomas Jefferson condemned the growth of large cities in America:

> When great evils happen, I am in the habit of looking out for what good may arise from them as consolations to us, and Providence has in fact so established the order of things, as that most evils are the means of producing some good. The yellow fever will discourage the growth of great cities in our nation, and I view great cities as pestilential to the morals, the health, and the liberties of man. True, they nourish some of the elegant arts, but the useful ones can thrive elsewhere, and less perfection in the others, with more health, virtue, and freedom would be my choice.

MANNERS AND ATTITUDES

For all their problems cities remained centers of culture and social style. Urban life and the intense nationalism of the postwar years created a new kind of social behavior. Americans began moving away from self-conscious imitation of European manners. Old World etiquette, concerned with the proper ways to curtsy and talk to the rich and famous, was now rejected as un-American. Contemporary writers advised Americans to "get rid of imported superfluities of etiquette," and to develop "a distinctively American school of good manners." As a result many Americans discarded European pretensions and insisted on social equality.

American manners and attitudes were analyzed by a number of European visitors after 1816. While many were quite critical of the young nation, some tried to give a balanced view of the American outlook and way of life. Foreign visitors tended to direct their criticism to certain areas. Many attacked the Americans' materialistic outlook, their use of wealth to measure an individual's success. They also pointed to the hypocrisy of putting so much emphasis on the idea of equality while the institution of slavery existed in their midst. Most annoying to foreigners was the lack of refinement in American life: they observed much rough speech, a lack of cultural accomplishment, heavy drinking, bragging, and tobacco chewing.

On the other hand, many postwar visitors were impressed by American energy, ingenuity, and physical well-being. They also looked favorably on the general lack of class distinctions, and on the economic opportunities available in the United States. Finally, they were happy to find most Americans, if not cultured, at least generous and kind.

READING HABITS

Nineteenth-century Americans strove for a lifestyle that was simple and natural but not lacking in culture. The Northeast took pride in being the intellectual and artistic center of America. The West had no highly developed culture to speak of, although most towns had subscription libraries, and Cincinnati had an important book publishing firm. The South presented certain contradictions. Charleston had a public library before Boston. The wealthier citizens of Richmond, Norfolk, and New Orleans regularly imported the latest books from England, as well as paintings and sculpture from various parts of Europe. Many Southern towns had Shakespeare libraries and clubs. Yet the rate of illiteracy for whites was higher in the South than in any other section of the United States.

Smith Attacks American Culture

"In the four quarters of the globe, who reads an American book? or goes to an American play? or looks at an American picture or statue? What does the world yet owe to American physicians or surgeons? What new substances have their chemists discovered? or what old ones have they analyzed? What new constellations have been discovered by the telescopes of Americans?—what have they done in the mathematics? Who drinks out of American glasses? or eats from American plates? or wears American coats or gowns? or sleeps in American blankets?—Finally, under which of the old tyrannical governments of Europe is every sixth man a Slave, whom his fellow-creatures may buy and sell and torture?"

Sydney Smith,
Edinburgh Review, 1820

Ingersoll Defends Cultural Advances

"The American mind has been called more to political, scientific, and mechanical, than to literary exertion. . . . In the literature of imagination, our standard is considerably below that of England, France, Germany and perhaps Italy. . . . In the literature of fact, of education, of politics, and of perhaps even science, European pre-eminence is by no means so decided. The American schools, the church, the state, the bar, the medical profession, are, all but the last, largely, and all of them adequately, supplied by their own literature. Respectable histories are extant by American authors. . . . In biography, without equal means, have we not done as much since we began as our English masters? In the literature as well as the learning of the sciences, botany, mineralogy, metallurgy, entomology, ornithology, astronomy, and navigation, there is no reason be be ashamed of our proficiency. . . ."

**Charles Jared Ingersoll,
A Discourse Concerning the Influence of America on the Mind, 1823**

Most of the country's population was literate, however, and the reading public was served by a growing number of libraries. More and more books were being produced at lower cost as materials became cheaper and publishing was mechanized.

Americans expected creative talent to thrive in an atmosphere of intellectual freedom. In the late 1700s playwrights such as Royall Tyler and William Dunlop paid homage to the superior morals and manners of the new republic. The poetry of Philip Freneau and William Cullen Bryant drew inspiration from distinctly American scenes and experiences. Phillis Wheatley, brought from Africa as a slave and educated by her Boston owners, celebrated the events of the Revolution in her couplets. The Hartford Wits, a coterie of Yale graduates, vied with each other to create an American epic to equal Vergil's *Aeneid*, but their attempts "merely imitated the rhapsodic effusions of debased eighteenth century European epic poetry." As one critic observed, "Despite all these efforts to create a truly distinctive literature, it was apparent . . . that Americans had not gotten off their literary knees to Europe."

This drawing from Washington Irving's Sketchbook *illustrates the fictitious figure of Ichabod Crane from the famous "Legend of Sleepy Hollow."*

The books Americans bought were, for the most part, written by foreign authors. American intellectuals called for a native literature but the reading public continued to stock their bookshelves with English fiction.

Before 1830 only two American writers were as popular in the United States as their foreign rivals: James Fenimore Cooper and Washington Irving. The prejudice against American novelists was so strong that Cooper pretended his first novel, *The Spy* (1821), was written by a "prominent Englishman." Cooper's best-selling novels depicted highly romanticized confrontations between Indians and settlers. Irving's *Sketchbook* (1819), which included the famous tale "Rip Van Winkle," brought him recognition as an author of literary merit with a uniquely American flair.

EDUCATION

During the early years of the republic there was an increased concern for public education. People of ambition had always thrived in America but chances for advancement now became linked to education, especially for certain kinds of work in urban centers. The Northeast, for example, was no longer a land of pioneers; a young person could not hope to carve a fortune out of a wilderness that no longer existed. But, equipped with a background in mathematics and technology, an enterprising individual could become an engineer, an architect, or a bridge or road builder.

Unfortunately, state school systems in the Northeast were slow to respond to the demand for public education. Teachers were terribly underpaid. Writer–reformer Bronson Alcott, for example, earned only $120 for teaching eighty students for four months in 1820. And even though teaching was one of the first professions open to women, it was largely because they were a source of cheap labor for expanding the educational system.

The Land Ordinance of 1785 contained a provision for reserving a section of every township in the Northwest Territory for public education. But little public education resulted there either.

Public primary and secondary education was almost nonexistent in the South in the early nineteenth century. Jefferson had proposed a system of free education in Virginia, but the state rejected his plan. He blamed the inefficient, aristocratically selfish, and often corrupt local governments for his failure. Indeed, political domination by the planter class militated against good public education in the South. Wealthy plantation owners preferred to educate their sons privately, often in the North or in England, and they remained indifferent and unresponsive to the needs of the rest of the population.

American colleges were also poorly financed. The faculty of Amherst had to go without salary for several weeks when money ran low. Princeton reduced its deficit in 1821 by cutting the salaries of two professors. College presidents conducted fund-raising drives every year, but tuition continued to be the primary source of income of every college. Thus, to attract more students, many schools lowered admission standards and relaxed academic requirements. As a result, the quality of American higher education suffered.

The curricula of most American colleges had changed little since colonial times. They generally focused on the Greek and Latin classics, and added a small measure of philosophy, mathematics, and theology.

A college education was for the most part a luxury limited to the sons of the affluent.

NEW RELIGIOUS ENTHUSIASM

Religious expression found its most fervent voice in a new revivalist movement called the Second Great Awakening. The movement began in New England and spread through revivals which took place between 1791 and 1801 in towns from Connecticut to New Hampshire. Traditional Calvinists continued to preach predestination and salvation through grace, and they frowned on revivalistic excesses. But religious emotionalism spread rapidly to the rest of the country and lasted almost until the Civil War. Its appeal was especially strong in the South and the West, where it had a major impact on the social life of frontier settlers.

The Second Great Awakening virtually swept the West, with wandering preachers attracting thousands of new believers. The itinerant ministers were usually Congregationalists, Baptists, or Methodists. Revival meetings were scenes of emotional preaching and mass conversions. A typical gathering usually began on a Thursday and lasted until the following Tuesday. Members of the congregation brought their own bedding and food. Western revivals began in the 1780s and culminated in a huge meeting at Cane Ridge, Kentucky, in 1801. Forty ministers

Methodist camp meeting.

preached for a week to fifteen thousand "sinners." At one point, more than one hundred members of the congregation had passed out from exhaustion following outbursts of evangelical frenzy.

Revivalism became a major force in the growth or decline of certain denominations. Presbyterian leaders, for example, were repelled by emotional frenzy, opposed revivalism, and lost membership as a result. In contrast, the methodists and Baptists made wide use of revival meetings and lay preachers. The Methodists, who emphasized universal salvation, grew from three thousand worshipers in 1800 to more than one million members by the middle of the century.

Perhaps the most important contribution the Second Great Awakening made to the settling of the West was its effect on the social life of frontier towns. When evangelists moved on they usually left established churches behind. These churches became the cultural centers of the Western towns. They served as information clearing centers and meetinghouses for social visits. As one contemporary put it, people went to church "almost as much to meet each other as to attend upon the means of grace." After the service, boys courted girls, farmers exchanged bits of farming wisdom, wives shared recipes, and everyone mulled over the latest bits of local gossip and current events.

Churches also encouraged moral standards of behavior often lacking in rough pioneer conditions. Church elders continuously waged battle against such evils as drinking, gambling, swearing, and fighting. Sometimes recalcitrant reprobates, moved by the evangelical spirit of a camp meeting, would change their ways, much to the satisfaction of their preachers. The Reverend David Rice reported, "drunkards, profane swearers, liars, quarrelsome persons, etc. are remarkably reformed. . . . Some neighborhoods, noted for their vicious and profligate manners are now as much noted for their piety and good order."

The Second Great Awakening also nurtured the growth of religious colleges, particularly in the West. The Baptist Convention of 1820 adopted as its slogan, "Every state its own Baptist college." Methodists opened Wesleyan universities in Ohio, Illinois, Dakota, Iowa, and Nebraska. The primary purpose of such schools was expressed in the charter of Western Reserve: to train "an able, learned and pious ministry for the infant churches. . . ." These institutions, organized and supported in their early years by the churches, set a valuable precedent for the development of higher education in nineteenth century America.

The Changing Economy

THE AMERICAN SYSTEM

By the end of the War of 1812 the United States was experiencing a political transition. The original Jeffersonian principles were being exchanged for the principles of Neo-Federalism. At a time when the Federalist party existed in only a few areas, its principles were being adopted by large numbers of the opposition. Whereas the Jeffersonians had originally championed states' rights, a strict construction of the Constitution, and the agrarian way of life, Madison now pointed his party toward new goals: broadening the federal government's authority and taking up industry's cause. This change in attitude extended to the nation's military strength and finances, and to manufacturing, trade, and transportation.

Before the War of 1812 the Jeffersonian Republicans had been opposed to keeping a large army and navy. They doubted that the country could support such organizations and feared that a national military was dangerous to the liberties of the people. The War of 1812, however, had demonstrated the need to build national defenses. In his 1815 Annual Message to Congress Madison therefore urged expansion of the navy, reorganization of the militia, and development of the military academy at West Point (established in 1802).

Both Jefferson and Madison had raised constitutional objections to the chartering of the first Bank of the United States in 1791. Renewal of the bank's charter was defeated in 1811 by a combination of agrarian and new business interests which found the bank's policies too restrictive. But the management of the country's finances had been so chaotic during the war that Madison now proposed the creation of a new national bank.

Jefferson and his early supporters had envisioned America as an agrarian paradise and had feared the effects of industry on the American people. The war had exposed America's weakness as a nation with little industry. Before 1812 the United States had basically traded its raw materials for European manufactured goods, but during the war the country had been cut off from these markets and had been compelled to develop its own industries. Even Jefferson had modified his views on the value of industry, admitting that "manufacturers are as necessary to our independence as to our comforts." Madison proposed the institution of a federal tariff to protect native industries.

The Jeffersonians had always feared that the federal government might overstep its powers and encroach on areas best left to the states. Madison continued to agree with this position in principle, but now he advocated federal planning in the matter of transportation. The war had demonstrated how vital it was for the nation to have a good system of inland transportation after the British blockade of the Atlantic coast brought nearly all interstate commerce to a halt. Madison proposed an amendment to the Constitution that would give the federal government the right to establish "throughout our country the roads and canals which can best be executed under national authority."

The American public was receptive to these trends. An important aspect of America's growing national pride was a policy based on an integrated economy at home and expansion of trade abroad. Madison supported internal improvements, domestic production, and an independent American commercial policy. It was during his administration that Henry Clay of Kentucky, the brilliant Speaker of the House, developed the nationalistic program known as the American System. The American System aimed at binding all sections of the country together through economic interdependence. The most clearly articulated aspects of the American System dealt with protective tariffs, the second national bank, and the federal involvement in internal improvements.

Madison's 1815 Address pointed the way to a broader role for the federal government in shaping the American economy. It was Henry Clay who developed these ideas into the American System.

Protective tariffs

Higher tariffs to protect American manufacturing was one of Clay's main objectives. When the war ended British manufacturers began flooding American markets with the surpluses they had been accumulating since 1812. Cheaply produced goods easily outsold American commodities and threatened to destroy America's infant industries. Manufacturers, particularly in New England, felt the need for tariff protection. Other parts of the country also had something to gain from protectionist measures. In the Carolinas and New England new cotton mills were suffering from English competition. In western Pennsylvania iron smelters had to compete with Scottish and Swedish iron. In Kentucky manufacturers of hemp bags were outdistanced by Russian hemp merchants and the Scottish bagging industry. In New York grain farmers, no longer permitted to sell to England, demanded sole rights to the American market. In Vermont and Ohio wool growers sought measures to protect them from English wool merchants.

In response to these needs Congress passed the rather mild Tariff of 1816, which maintained the wartime rates of about twenty to twenty-five percent on imported goods. The vote in the House of Representatives revealed the diversity of economic interests in the country. New England, which had the most to gain, voted for the tariff, but only by seventeen votes to ten. The dissenting votes represented New England's shipping interests who feared that higher duties would diminish foreign trade and thus reduce profits. The South, with almost no industry, voted thirty-four to twenty-three against the bill. Southern representatives who supported the measure did so as a patriotic gesture. Some Southerners, like John C. Calhoun, believed that if there were another war with England, the American army and navy would need American industries to manufacture goods. Moreover, many Southerners expected their region to experience its own industrial boom in the near future. Only the Middle Atlantic and Western states gave their wholehearted support to the measure.

Revival of the national bank

Five years after the first Bank of the United States had expired, some 250 state and private banks had been chartered. Since there was no national currency these banks issued about $100 million of their own paper money. Few state-chartered banks had adequate reserves of gold and silver, and only New England banks were able to back up their paper dollars with specie (gold and silver). The paper money offered by individual banks was frequently not negotiable in neighboring areas. Worse still, the various paper currencies were seldom able to command their face value. As in the days of the Continental Congress, the country was plagued by a host of different currencies, most of them devalued.

The absence of a national bank caused other problems, too. The federal government no longer had a place to deposit its funds or a reliable system for transferring money from one place to another. Neither did it have a financial institution through which to sell government bonds for needed revenue. The inconvenience and fiscal chaos created by the lack of a national currency were described by Albert Gallatin in December 1815. "Public credit, heretofore supported simply by common honesty, declines at home and abroad; private capital placed on a still more uncertain basis; the value of property and the nature of every person's engagements equally uncertain; a baseless currency varying every fifty miles and fluctuating everywhere."

To solve these problems the Second Bank of the United States was chartered by Congress in 1816. The new national bank's structure was similar to its predecessor's, except for an increase in its capitalization from $10 million to $35 million. As before, the federal government provided one-fifth of its capital; however, this time five of the twenty-five directors were appointed by the president and approved by the Senate.

A national program for improvements

Clay's system included a land bill which would raise revenue from the sale of Western lands. The revenue would then be distributed to the states for financing internal improvements.

The nation had a pressing need for improvements in interstate transportation. American commerce moved in a clumsy pattern. Western goods going east traveled on barges down the Mississippi and then on ships around Florida and up the Atlantic coast. Eastern goods traveled west in wagons across poorly built roads, many of which were only dirt paths. Leading politicians in Washington had long recognized the need for such internal improvements as a national highway and canal system, if only for military transport. In 1817 John C. Calhoun had addressed a congressional committee, saying:

> Let it not be forgotten, let it be forever kept in mind, that the extent of the republic exposes us to the greatest of calamities—*disunion.* We are great, and rapidly—I was about to say fearfully—growing. This is our pride and danger, our weakness and our strength.

> . . . We are under the most imperious obligations to counteract every tendency to disunion. . . . Whatever impedes the intercourse of the extremes with this, the centre of the republic, weakens the union. . . . Let us, then, bind the republic together with a perfect system of roads and canals. Let us conquer space.

Yet much resistance had to be overcome before Calhoun's ideas could be implemented. New England was opposed to a national system of roads; the region already had good roads, and merchants feared that an improved interstate system might divert trade to Philadelphia, Baltimore, or New York. The South felt it had little to gain from what was essentially the establishment of communications and trade routes between the Northeast and the West. Neverthless, after much debate, a transportation bill passed both houses of Congress. Surprisingly, President Madison vetoed it. Although he agreed with the need for national roads, he felt that the Constitution should first be amended to permit Congress to intervene in this area.

When another transportation bill was introduced in the 1820s President Monroe also opposed it on constitutional grounds. By this time sectional rivalries had become even more pronounced. People who lived in the West favored a national system of roads but those in New England and the old South still opposed the project. After listening to objections on constitutional grounds, Henry Clay, a champion of federally sponsored highways, exclaimed in irritation: "A new world has come into being since the Constitution was adopted. Are the narrow, limited necessities of the old thirteen states, of indeed, parts only of the old thirteen states, as they existed at the formation of the present Constitution forever to remain the rule of interpretations?"

The protests of Clay and members of Congress who agreed with him had little effect on the reluctant federal government. The government would occasionally subscribe to stock in private companies engaged in roadbuilding, but a real, long-range federal highway program was not begun until the twentieth century. Federally sponsored internal improvements, an important part of Clay's American System, were never put into effect in his time.

EARLY INDUSTRIALIZATION

The War of 1812 underscored America's need for greater economic independence. It also brought the country closer to this goal. The United States had been all but completely cut off from foreign commerce during the embargo and the war, and a number of small Northeastern manufacturing establishments had arisen to fill the gap. Shipping and commercial interests, which would not regain their prewar international strength until the 1840s and 1850s, began to focus more intently on internal trade.

Alexander Hamilton had once noted that there existed "in the genius of the people of this country, a peculiar aptitude for mechanical improvements." Hamilton's observation was soon borne out; a number of minor inventions and mechanical improvements led to major changes in American industry after 1815.

Improved waterwheels, leather transmission belts, and metal gears made machines more durable and more efficient. The rolling mill eliminated the need to hammer out sheet metal by hand. A new process for refining pig iron facilitated a switch from coal to the cheaper charcoal. The perfection of the cylinder process for making paper led to the mechanization of that industry. A new method of canning food in airtight containers conserved perishable foods for transportation from the country to the city.

Eli Whitney, best known for inventing the cotton gin in 1793, was an important inventor of the early republic. In 1800 he devised a way of manufacturing rifles using machinery with interchangeable parts—a highly significant advance toward the assembly line method of production. American manufacturers were particularly interested in mechanized production because of the high cost of labor. American workers earned as much as fifty percent more than their British counterparts.

The development of the factory

Despite advances toward industrialization in the years following the War of 1812, most workers continued to labor in their houses or in small shops. The typical American was still a farmer living isolated from the city. Only 700,000 out of a national population of 9.6 million lived in urban centers of more than 2,500 persons. Indeed most Americans were hardly aware of the beginnings of industrialization.

The Napoleonic Wars had stimulated not only American industry but domestic manufacturing as well. By 1823 most of the country's one-half million urban laborers were still engaged in household manufacturing while at the same time producing most of their own food. These craftsmen made everything from pianos and cigars to pencils and barrels.

Even small remote towns had their own ironworks, brickyards, flour mills, and lumberyards. In 1810, for example, the tiny town of Lebanon, Ohio (population 300) had three tanners, four shoemakers, two blacksmith shops, a hatter, a nail maker, and two saddle shops. Few worked full-time at these occupations, however; most domestic manufacturing was a sideline conducted in basements or spare rooms by farmers, shopkeepers, lawyers, and doctors. Such shops

Home industry.

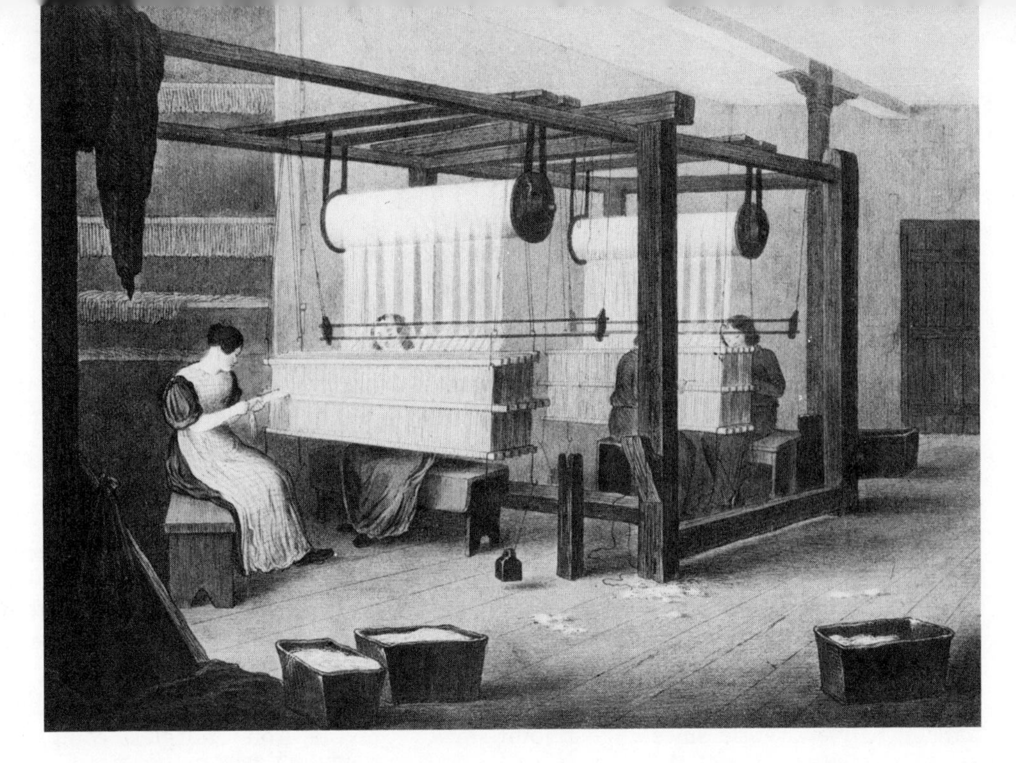

A cotton loom in a New England factory.

usually turned out only small quantities of goods and sold only to the immediate neighborhood. Occasionally, however, domestic manufacturers would sell to a national market. For example, merchants in the Northeast bought shoe leather in wholesale quantities and distributed it to cobblers who worked in their homes. The finished shoes were then collected, inspected for quality, and packaged in a central warehouse, from which they were shipped all over the country.

It soon became clear that production would be cheaper and more efficient if labor and resources were consolidated in a factory setting. An Englishman, Richard Arkwright, had devised a rudimentary assembly line for producing cotton fabric. Arkwright used newly invented machines such as the flying shuttle, spinning jenny, and water frame to manufacture machine-spun cotton that was less expensive and more durable than hand-spun cotton. As a result English factories had had a monopoly on the cotton-spinning trade since the 1770s.

Americans were eager to copy Arkwright's factory system, but British inventions were closely guarded. No one was allowed to take the plans for these machines out of England and skilled textile workers were not permitted to travel abroad or to emigrate. Nonetheless, a young Englishman named Samuel Slater slipped out of Britain, came to America, and reconstructed the machines from memory for the Pawtucket, Rhode Island, firm of Almy & Brown. This company—which had the first effective factory in America—began manufacturing cotton thread early in 1791. Nine children, most of them from poor farming families, tended its seventy-two spindles and each earned less than a dollar a week. The only product was thread; no cloth was made.

During the Napoleonic Wars many more cotton mills opened in America. By 1815 there were 213 factories, although most were forced out of business by tough British competition before the Tariff of 1816 could come to their rescue. One factory, however, opened its doors in 1816, survived, and prospered. The Boston Associates, led by the wealthy merchant Francis Cabot Lowell, built a cotton mill at Waltham, Massachusetts.

◀ *A carpenter's clothier shop in which Samuel Slater's spinning machines were installed. (Smithsonian Institution)*

Under one roof, raw cotton was unbaled, corded, and spun by efficient power looms; the finished cloth was then dyed and printed. This factory was the first wholly integrated cotton manufacturing plant in the world, a testament to American ingenuity and efficiency.

The rise of the corporation

As the factory system gradually replaced individual crafts new legal entities came into prominence. The corporation is perhaps the most important. By the 1820s the corporation—which made it possible to finance large factories—was the nation's principal economic institution.

The corporation had not played a significant part in the New World since English joint-stock companies had financed the early settlements. But its advantages were becoming increasingly obvious to manufacturers and merchants of nineteenth-century America. The corporate form was attractive to business because issuing stock to many investors simplified the matter of acquiring capital. It was attractive to investors because they were not legally responsible for the corporation's debts; individual stockholders risked only the depreciation or loss of the original investment. The corporate form made is possible to raise large sums of money by allowing many people to pool their resources for the needed amounts. In addition, stocks could be bought and sold without disturbing the financial structure of the business and without requiring a lot of paperwork or stockholders' meetings.

Although corporations were relieved of certain kinds of internal red tape, they were governed by external regulations. Throughout the early 1800s incorporation required obtaining a special charter from the state legislature. There were so many rules governing the establishment of new corporations that most businesses remained unincorporated until the second half of the century. Many people felt that special incorporation through legislative charter was creating monopolies. Some argued that general incorporation laws—laws that would extend the right of incorporation to all—would restore and preserve free enterprise. Others argued that incorporation was monopolistic by nature, but reluctantly accepted general incorporation as an alternative preferable to special incorporation.

The first general incorporation laws vastly simplified and improved the procedure of incorporation. Charters could be issued to corporations without specific legislative action in every case. The individual states began passing general incorporation laws by the late 1830s.

Tax benefits were also introduced to aid new businesses. New York, for example, passed a law in 1817 that exempted textile mills from taxation; Ohio extended tax benefits in 1823 to textile, iron, and glass companies.

The United States Patent Law further helped business not only by encouraging the invention of new industrial products and processes but also by protecting manufacturers who bought the exclusive rights to these inventions.

America's first successful use of the corporation took place in the cotton textile industry, notably in plants under the management of the Boston Associates. In the first year of operation the Boston Associates' Waltham factory paid a dividend of twelve percent. By 1822 the original stockholders were reaping handsome yearly dividends. The incorporated Boston Associates was so successful that it opened nine new companies in Massachusetts and New Hampshire between 1821 and 1825. Each specialized in the large-scale production of a single commodity. The factory at Lowell, Massachusetts, soon became the center of the Boston Associates' activity and Lowell became the leading industrial city of the time.

Like the great industries that dominate American manufacturing today, these early corporations were geared not to the individual craftsman but to the machine; they were financed not by one great capitalist but by many investors; and they were managed not by the owners but by hired professional managers.

THE DOMINANCE OF COTTON

The technological innovations that fostered the rise of manufacturing also changed the nation's agriculture. In particular, the application of new machinery to cotton production in the South had far-reaching economic and political effects in pre-Civil War America.

Eli Whitney's invention of the cotton gin made cotton the leading cash crop in the South and in the nation. Before the cotton gin only long-staple cotton could be grown profitably because its black seeds could easily be removed by hand at a reasonable cost. This variety, however, would grow only in warm, humid lands free of even the lightest frost. The hardier short-staple variety could grow in greater varieties of soil and weather, provided the growing season was sufficiently long. Its green seeds, however, were extremely hard to remove; a person who worked all day could clean only about one pound.

Eli Whitney's original, hand-cranked model of the cotton gin. (Smithsonian Institution)

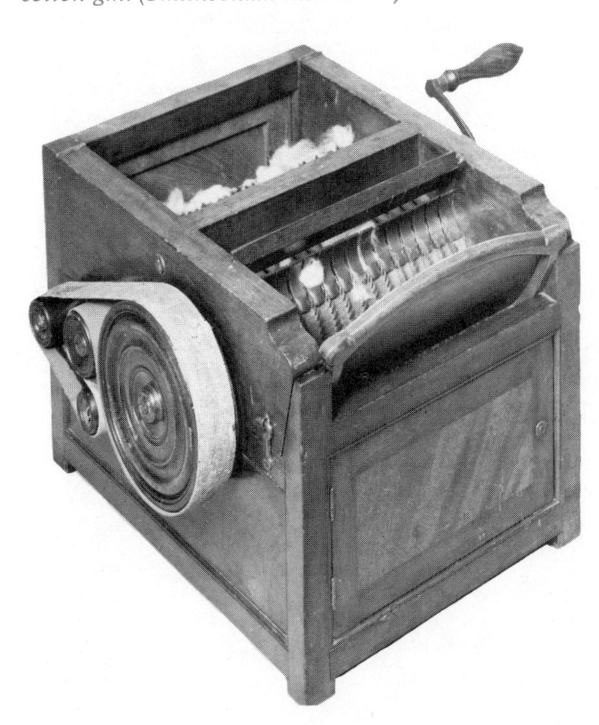

With Whitney's gin it became quick, efficient, and easy to clean both varieties of cotton. The design was so simple that Whitney was never able to enforce his patent; anyone who saw the invention could easily copy it. At least fifty pounds of cotton could be cleaned in a day with this machine, and soon huge, horse-driven gins were cleaning thousands of pounds a week. By the 1820s the South was producing three-quarters of the world's supply of cotton.

The opening up of fresh new lands was as significant as the gin to the growth of the cotton industry. The profitable raising of cotton required rich black topsoil, and the soil of the Southeastern states had been exhausted from nearly two hundred years of planting tobacco. When Jackson defeated the hostile Indian occupants of the Southwest during the War of 1812, the way was cleared for white settlement of the Black Belt (so named for its rich black soil). As a result cotton production rose from 80 million pounds per year in 1810 to nearly 500 million pounds per year in the 1830s.

Cotton had a major impact on the economy of the period. Most American cotton was exported to the textile factories of England and the Continent in exchange for imported manufactured goods. Northern merchants became rich by arranging the sale and transportation of Southern cotton crops. The crop was so profitable that Southerners used every inch of land to grow it and, as a result, came to depend heavily on the Western states for foodstuffs and work animals.

WATERWAYS AND OVERLAND TRANSPORTATION

When Western farmers were finally able to grow surplus produce they had difficulty finding markets for it. Farm products could be floated down the Mississippi on rafts and flatboats, but with spring floods and summer droughts, this was a risky business. Even under ideal conditions the trip from Pittsburgh to New Orleans took at least a month. And once a farmer reached the Gulf of Mexico, there was no easy way to travel upriver again. So although the Mississippi River network made it possible for the West to sell some of its produce to the East, there was no equivalent system enabling the East to sell to the West. Eastern products had to come overland and roads were needed.

Roads and bridges

In the days before explosives and modern road-building machinery, building a road through a mountain range or leveling uneven ground was a slow, laborious, and expensive operation. The Lancaster Turnpike, an excellent road complete with drainage ditches, firm foundations, and a gravel surface was built as early as 1794 to connect Lancaster, Pennsylvania, with Philadelphia. By 1825 private companies in the Northeast and Middle Atlantic states had built about ten thousand miles of turnpike roads. Wooden and stone bridges, spanning creeks and lakes, had been built as early as the 1790s.

Most of these bridges and turnpikes were found in the East. A few highways served the

COMMERCIAL

MAIL STAGE,

IN THIRTY-NINE HOURS,

From Boston to New York,

CARRYING ONLY SIX PASSENGERS.

Runs by the way of Worcester, Stafford Springs,
Hartford, Middletown, New-Haven to New-York....Leaves Boston every day at 1 o'clock, P. M.---arrives at Hartford at 7 o'clock, A M.---arrives at New-Haven 3 o'clock P. M.---arrives at New-York, 6 o'clock, A. M.

Returning*......Leaves *New-York* for *Boston
every day at half past seven o'clock, A. M.---leaves New-Haven at 10 o'clock, P. M.---leaves Hartford half past 5 o'clock, A. M.---arrives at Boston half past 11 o'clock, P. M.---making *Thirty-nine hours*, it being seven hours sooner than ever performed before.

The Proprietors solicit the Patronage of the Public, and pledge themselves that every exertion shall be made for their accommodation.

Fare to be paid in Boston, New Haven and New York.

For Seats apply at the Stage Office, Exchange Coffee-House, entrance in Congress-Street—Boston.—Col. Reuben Sikes, Worcester.—Bennett's Coffee-House, Hartford,—Butler's Hotel, New-Haven,—Courtland-Street, No. 1, New-York.

For Seats in the *Accommodation Stages*, apply as above.

BOSTON, *February*, 1815.

(Courtesy, American Antiquarian Society) ▲

A toll gate on the Baltimore-Reisterstown Road. (The Metropolitan Museum of Art, Gift of Mrs. John Sylvester, 1936)

West: the National Road, which connected Maryland with Illinois by the 1840s; the Wilderness Road, which crossed on a diagonal down from the northern boundary of Virginia through the Cumberland Gap into Kentucky; and the Natchez Trace, which lay between Nashville, Tennessee, and Natchez, Mississippi.

Financed by private companies (frequently with the aid of state or federal money), these projects were terribly expensive. An average road cost between $5,000 and $10,000 per mile. The sixty-two-mile Lancaster Turnpike, for example, cost $465,000. Because of the expense of building roads, turnpike owners were forced to charge high tolls. The National Road and the Wilderness Road provided feasible routes for settlers migrating to the Western lands, but were too expensive for transporting goods. The cost of long-distance transportation pushed the price of common foodstuffs much higher than the cost of the same items grown nearby. The cost of transporting a ton of oats from Buffalo to New York, for example, was twelve times greater than the value of the cargo. This discouraged traffic to such an extent that by the 1830s thousands of miles of turnpike had to be abandoned or handed over to the states.

Steamboats

The expense of hauling goods overland and the lack of a federally financed road system focused increasing attention on water transportation. Two developments made inland water transportation so successful that the entire nation was soon bound together in economic interdependence: the steamboat and the Erie Canal.

During the 1790s John Fitch and some other engineers had been experimenting with the steam engine in water transportation. But it remained for Robert Fulton, a young American artist and engineer, to make steam navigation commercially successful. Fulton devised a workable means of combining all the essential elements: the engine, the paddlewheels, and the steam boiler.

Fulton entered into partnership with Robert R. Livingston, whom he had met in Paris in 1802. Livingston and his wealthy brother-in-law John Stevens (who had designed an improved steam boiler), had obtained from New York state a monopoly for steam navigation on state waters. When Fulton returned to the United States he was commissioned to build a steamboat. In 1807 he made his famous voyage up the

▼ *Steam travel at the mouth of the Ohio River.*

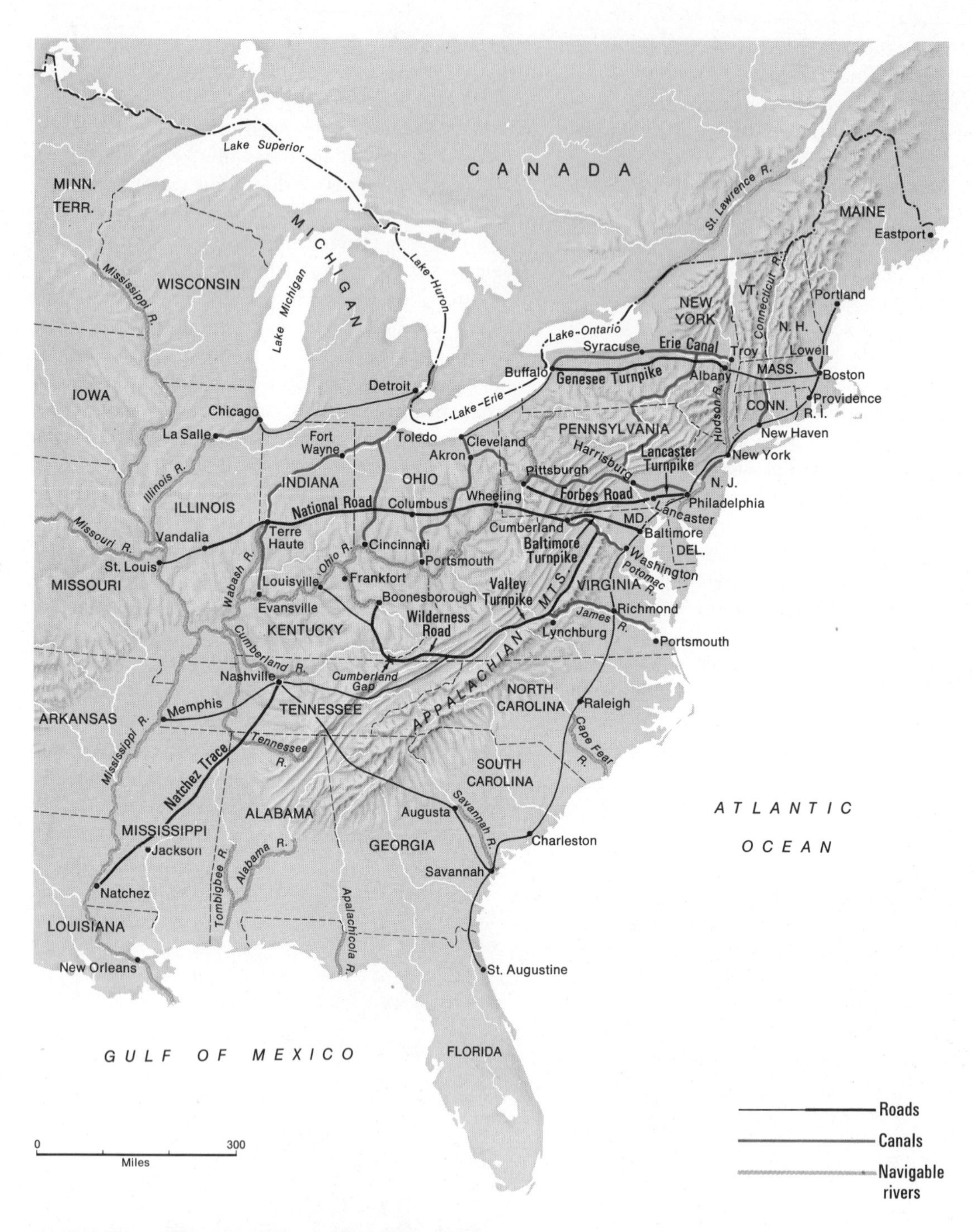

CANALS AND ROADS • 1820 TO 1850

Hudson River in the *Clermont*. The ship, 142 feet long, drew only 7 feet of water; the shallow draft made the boat ideal for most river traffic. Four years later another Fulton steamboat, the *New Orleans*, sailed down the Mississippi from Pittsburgh to its namesake city.

By 1830 some 200 steam-powered shallow-draft vessels were sailing freely through the waterways of the West. Since the steamboat could travel upstream it turned the major waterways into two-way highways. Frequent steamboat travel along the Mississippi reduced transportation costs and established regular trading routes between the West and the East.

It was in the West that the steamboat made its greatest contribution to the development of the American economy. Steamboats could move much faster than flatboats. Previous shipping on light keelboats poled along by strong men was slow and the rates were high—as much as $5.00 for every one hundred pounds. By 1820 steamboats had lowered this rate to $2.00. By 1842 competition had lowered the rate even further, to 25 cents per one hundred pounds. Steamboats also offered an attractive alternative to bumpy coaches careening over dusty roads. Luxury passenger vessels, with comfortable cabins decorated with carpets and mirrors, offering entertainment and good food, soon turned long-distance travel from an agony into a reasonably enjoyable experience.

The steamboat, however, could not conquer all the problems of travel on the Mississippi. The river's floods, droughts, and other hazards such as shallows and overhanging branches, made it and its tributaries difficult to use. And even steamboats took a long time transporting manufactured goods from Boston to Cincinnati, since they had to go by way of New Orleans.

The Erie Canal

The Erie Canal finally created a direct route between the Northeast and the West. As the Great Lakes were all connected with each other much of the West could be reached directly by waterways. At the other end of the canal vessels could sail down the Hudson River from Albany to New York City, and from there ships could sail to all of the Eastern seaboard and Europe. The Erie Canal turned New York City into a great trade center for Western livestock and grain by redirecting much of the trade that used to flow through New Orleans to the harbor of New York City.

The Erie Canal was built at the urging of the former mayor of New York City, DeWitt Clinton. In 1816 Clinton convinced the New York legislature of the wisdom of building a canal between Albany and Buffalo. Clinton quite correctly predicted that with the canal "the whole island of Manhattan, covered with habitations and replenished with a dense population, will constitute one great city." The legislature appropriated $7 million for the enterprise. The money was raised from such sources as land sales, taxes on salt, lotteries, and special appropriations.

The canal, 363 miles long and equipped with 83 locks, was completed in 1825. Although the engineers in charge had had little experience constructing canals, they learned by trial and error and by studying British canals. The chief engineer, Benjamin Wright, was an excellent organizer and promoter of new talent. One of his protégés, Canvass White, was sent to Britain to study the design of locks. Another of Wright's associates, John B. Jervis, later became the most famous American civil engineer of his generation. The builders devised a new kind of plow to cut the matted roots of trees and learned how to turn limestone into waterproof cement.

The Erie Canal proved to be a sound financial venture. Tolls paid off the original investment in the first nine years of operation and were soon bringing $3 million a year into the state treasury. Freight rates from Buffalo to Albany were reduced from $100 to $15 a ton, and the trip was shortened from twenty to eight days. As Clinton had predicted New York City experienced rapid new growth and soon became the country's leading city. In 1818 a regularly scheduled passenger and freight service opened be-

Building the Erie Canal, 1825.

tween New York and the English port of Liverpool. Most of the goods sent from Europe to the West now passed through New York rather than through New Orleans.

A canal boom

Canals were not designed for the steamboat but for barges pulled by horses walking along towpaths on the banks. This method of transportation was vastly cheaper than moving goods over roads. But even though transportation was cheaper, construction was considerably more expensive. Canals cost some $20,000 per mile to construct, and even a short canal took as many as ten years to build. In 1816 there were only three canals in the country that were as long as two miles and only one hundred miles of canal altogether.

Even so, the success of the Erie Canal inspired many other canalbuilding projects. New York State opened a second canal, between Lake Champlain and the Hudson River, in 1823. New England promoters sponsored the digging of a series of short canals connecting Worcester and Northampton, Massachusetts to the coast. In 1828 a canal running from northeastern Pennsylvania, across New Jersey and New York, to the Hudson River was completed. It was used to carry Pennsylvania coal in barges to the Eastern seaboard. Pennsylvania built a route that was part canal and part railroad across the Allegheny Mountains from Philadelphia to Pittsburgh. However this system, with its 177 locks and stretches of railroad in between, proved too cumbersome and slow to be a great success. In addition, construction costs were so high that Pennsylvania ended by defaulting on its debts to European investors during the Panic of 1837. This unique case is a good illustration of the canal mania of the times: building a canal across the Alleghenies was obviously unfeasible, but the success of the Erie Canal had created virtually limitless and, in this instance, extremely shortsighted enthusiasm.

West of the mountains canalbuilding also met with great popular support. By 1837 Ohio had 750 miles of canals. The most important, the Ohio and Erie, connected Portsmouth on the Ohio River to Cleveland on Lake Erie. Another canal linked Toledo to Cincinnati. Indiana constructed the 450-mile Wabash and Erie Canal. By 1840 there were some 3300 miles of canals in the United States, most of them in the Northeast and the West. The cost was high for those days, about $125 million, but well worth it to the national economy. Only the Southern states, with their excellent natural river system, had not felt the urgency to invest heavily in public roads and canals.

The Supreme Court under John Marshall

New technologies were not the only significant factor in the expansion of the nation's economy. The economy also had an ally in the judicial system: Chief Justice John Marshall, whose decisions were consistently sympathetic to the protection of business. Political and economic developments would later modify public opinion toward increased states' rights, but right after the war the Court was in tune with the nationalistic mood in the country. During the first half of the nineteenth century the Supreme Court's decisions were a direct result of John Marshall's influence.

Appointed by President John Adams, Marshall served as chief justice of the Supreme Court from 1801 to 1835. Marshall was a Federalist and a thoroughgoing supporter of a strong central government. He was also an ardent defender of private property who regarded the business community as the federal government's ally in resisting the power of state governments.

A former Virginia lawyer and congressman, Marshall had been John Adams' secretary of state for a brief time, but his lasting fame came from his years on the Supreme Court. He was often not an impartial judge, frequently deciding the case before hearing the arguments. He so completely dominated the Court that in over thirty-four years he was part of the minority opinion in only eight cases. Although Marshall was an unpretentious man with simple tastes, he entertained a lifelong suspicion of putting too much power in the hands of the masses. Most of his decisions reflected his defense of a strong central government and vested property rights.

When Marshall retired he was eighty years old. He had shepherded the Supreme Court through five administrations. He had seen the country progress from a loosely knit collection of states into a unified new nation. And he had played a significant part in this process by handing down a number of decisions that set Congress and the Supreme Court above state legislatures and state courts.

Marshall had established the right of judicial review in the 1803 case of *Marbury* v. *Madison* (Chapter 7). Marshall's decision in this case asserted the Supreme Court's right to decide whether a law passed by Congress and signed by the president was constitutional. The Constitution itself did not grant the Court this privilege, but most of the Founding Fathers probably

Federal Supremacy

"That the United States form, for many, and for most important purposes, a single nation, has not yet been denied. In war, we are one people. In making peace, we are one people. In all commercial regulations, we are one and the same people. In many other respects, the American people are one; and the government which is alone capable of controling and managing their interests in all these respects, is the government of the Union. . . . For all these purposes, her government is complete; to all these objects, it is competent. The people have declared, that in the exercise of all powers given for these objects, it is supreme. It can, then, in effecting these objects, legitimately control all individuals or governments within the American territory. The constitution and laws of a State, so far as they are repugnant to the constitution and laws of the United States, are absolutely void. These States are constituent parts of the United States. They are members of one great empire—for some purposes sovereign, for some purposes subordinate."

John Marshall,
Cohens v. Virginia, 1821

Federal Supremacy

"The great question, whether a federal or a national system of government will best secure the liberty and happiness of the people, remains to be more fully considered. . . .

The geography of our country and the character of our people, unite to demonstrate that the ignorance and partiality of a concentrated form of government, can only be enforced by armies; and the peculiar ability of the states to resist, promises that resistance would be violent; so that a national government must either be precarious or despotick. By dividing power between the federal and state governments, local partialities and oppressions, the common causes of revolution, are obliterated from our system."

**John Taylor,
New Views of the Constitution
of the United States, 1823**

expected the Court to review legislation. Because Marshall was a nationalist, however, he wanted to enhance the prestige of Congress, not undermine it. During the rest of his tenure he never again declared a federal law unconstitutional.

The Marshall Court handed down major decisions in cases involving monopolies in interstate commerce, state taxation of a federal bank, and contractual obligations under state laws. The decisions in each of these instances set precedents which remain today.

INTERSTATE COMMERCE

The Marshall Court declared state laws unconstitutional on thirteen occasions. In one of these cases, *Gibbons* v. *Ogden* (1824), Marshall ruled that Congress had virtually absolute power to regulate interstate commerce.

New York had granted Robert Fulton and Robert R. Livingston a monopoly over all steam navigation within the state. In 1815 Aaron Ogden purchased from Fulton and Livingston the right to operate a ferry between New York

City and Elizabeth Point, New Jersey. Later, Thomas Gibbons, who held a federal license to operate a vessel along the Atlantic coast, set up a rival ferry line. Ogden sued Gibbons, arguing that Gibbons had no right to enter waters on the New York side of the state line.

When the case was appealed to the Supreme Court Marshall decided in favor of Gibbons. Unlike many of Marshall's decisions this one was quite popular. Soon dozens of ferries were crossing New York waters. The New York monopoly had been destroyed. Even more important, *Gibbon* v. *Ogden* disallowed *all* interstate monopolies. From now on steamboats could go wherever they pleased with only a federal coasting license.

In *Gibbons* v. *Ogden* Marshall ruled that a state could regulate commerce and navigation within its own boundaries, but that these same activities carried across state lines were subject to regulation by Congress. The decision had two important legal consequences. First, Marshall firmly stated that "an act of Congress is supreme: and the law of the state . . . must yield to it." Second, Marshall interpreted the Constitution's reference to *commerce* so that it included navigation. This broad interpretation of the word *commerce* enabled later Supreme Court justices to grant Congress the right to regulate electric power companies, radio and television transmission, and even factory conditions.

DEFENDING THE NATIONAL BANK

Marshall's earlier decision in *McCulloch* v. *Maryland* (1819) also strengthened both business and the federal government's authority.

The state of Maryland had sought to tax the Baltimore branch of the Bank of the United States, in fact, to tax it out of existence. The Constitution does not specifically grant Congress the right to charter a bank. However Marshall, following in Hamilton's footsteps, held that such authority was implied in the Constitution. Marshall claimed that states did not have the power to "retard, impede, burden, or in any manner control" the operations of constitutional laws passed by Congress. "Let the end be legitimate," Marshall wrote, "let it be within the scope of the Constitution, and all means which are appropriate, which are plainly adapted to that end, which are not prohibited, but consistent with the letter and spirit of the Constitution, are constitutional." This broad interpretation of the powers of Congress extended its authority into finance. By defending the Bank of the United States against state regulation Marshall again aided the business community: the bank could now give businessmen loans, provide them with a safe place for investment, and help maintain a reliable national currency.

In *McCulloch* v. *Maryland* Marshall again placed federal authority over the authority of the states.

THE SANCTITY OF CONTRACTS

Marshall made two other significant decisions in 1819 that aided the business community by establishing the inviolability of contracts.

The first case involved Dartmouth College. Dartmouth had received a royal charter in 1769 from King George III. This charter was later acknowledged by the New Hampshire legislature, but it was subsequently ignored when the legislature, without Dartmouth's agreement, sought to turn the private college into a public institution. Dartmouth sued the state in *Dartmouth College* v. *Woodward*. The chief justice ruled in favor of the college, stating that such a charter could not be changed unilaterally. This decision defined charters as contracts that could be altered only with the consent of both parties. It also determined that licensed corporations could not be regulated by states except under restrictions written into the original charter. The second case, *Sturges* v. *Crowninshield*, declared unconstitutional a New York law that relieved debtors of their obligations. In rendering this decision Marshall cited a constitutional provision that forbade all legislation which impaired contractual obligations.

REACTION TO MARSHALL'S DECISIONS

The long-range effects of Marshall's rulings were to: (1) establish the right of judicial review, an important factor in balancing power among the three branches of the federal government; (2) extend congressional authority over interstate commerce; (3) set the Supreme Court and Congress above state legislatures and state courts; (4) affirm the sanctity of contracts; and (5) ally the Court with a broad and flexible interpretation of the Constitution.

People such as Jefferson, suspicious of concentrating power in the federal government to the diminishment of states' rights, were alarmed by Marshall's decisions. Jefferson declared: "The Constitution is a mere thing of wax in the hands of the judiciary, which they may twist and shape into any form they please." However, the use of the Constitution which Marshall had envisioned—as a buttress and protection for the business community—was not fully realized until after the Civil War. And Marshall's emphasis on a strong central government regulating the economy on behalf of the national welfare did not become an acceptable development to the majority of Americans until the twentieth century.

Readings

GENERAL WORKS

Billington, Ray A., *Westward Expansion.* New York: Macmillan, 1967.

Burlingame, Roger, *The March of the Iron Men.* New York: Grosset & Dunlap, 1960.

Cochran, Thomas C., and William Miller, *The Age of Enterprise.* New York: Macmillan, 1943.

Dorfman, Joseph, *The Economic Mind in American Civilization,* Vols. I–V. New York: Viking, 1946–1959.

Nagel, Paul C., *One Nation Indivisible: The Union in American Thought, 1776–1861.* New York: Oxford University Press, 1964.

North, Douglass C., *The Economic Growth of the United States, 1790–1860.* Englewood Cliffs, N.J.: Prentice-Hall, 1961.

Taylor, George R., *The Transportation Revolution.* New York: Harper & Row, 1968.

SPECIAL STUDIES

Commons, John R., et al., *History of Labor in the United States,* Vols. I–IV. New York: Macmillan, 1918–1935.

Curti, Merle, *The Roots of American Loyalty.* New York: Columbia University Press, 1946.

Goodrich, Carter, *Government Promotion of Canals and Railroads, 1800–1890.* New York: Columbia University Press, 1960.

Gray, Lewis C., *History of Agriculture in the Southern United States to 1860,* Vols. I–II. New York: Kelley, 1969.

Havighurst, Walter, *Voices on the River: The Story of the Mississippi Water Ways.* New York: Macmillan, 1964.

Miller, Nathan, *The Enterprise of a Free People.* Ithaca, N.Y.: Cornell University Press, 1962.

Mohl, Raymond A., *Poverty in New York, 1783–1825.* New York: Oxford University Press, 1971.

Shaw, Ronald E., *Erie Water West: A History of the Erie Canal, 1792–1854.* Lexington, Ky.: University Press of Kentucky, 1966.

Wade, Richard C., *The Urban Frontier.* Chicago: University of Chicago Press, 1959.

Warren, Charles, *The Supreme Court in United States History,* Vols. I–III. Boston: Little, Brown, 1923.

BIOGRAPHIES

Ammon, Harry, *James Monroe: The Quest for National Identity.* New York: McGraw-Hill Book Co., 1971.

Baker, Leonard, *John Marshall: A Life in Law.* New York: Macmillan Publishing Co., 1974.

Beveridge, Albert J., *The Life of John Marshall,* Vols. I–IV. Boston: Houghton Mifflin, 1916–1919.

Green, Constance M. L., *Eli Whitney and the Birth of American Technology.* Boston: Little, Brown, 1956.

Nevins, Allan and Jeannette Mirsky, *The World of Eli Whitney.* New York: Macmillan, 1962.

Porter, Kenneth W., *John Jacob Aster,* Vols. I–II. New York: Russell & Russell, 1966.

Early American Industry, Invention, and Science

At the age of eighty-one, Benjamin Franklin wrote, "I have sometimes wished that it had been my destiny to be born two or three centuries hence." When Franklin wrote these words, he was looking forward to the outburst of industrial growth which characterized American life in the nineteenth and twentieth centuries. But he was also looking back on the previous 20 years which had fashioned a country of international import out of dense woods, rich deposits of minerals, and a variety of crops which could be grown in the fertile soil.

It is hard to imagine how the first settlers could have survived without the native Americans since the technology of the New World was quite different from that of the Old World. The Indians shared their knowledge of how to grow the unfamiliar crop, corn, how to clear the thick forests, and how to use dead fish to fertilize the soil. Without these basic skills, it would have been pointless for the Europeans to consider settling permanently in a land 3000 miles across the ocean from their nearest center of commerce.

The fundamental knowledge of how to farm the soil became the economic backbone of colonial development. At the close of the eighteenth century the first census reported that nine out of ten people were engaged primarily in food production. In addition to corn, colonial farmers grew great quantities of wheat, rice, and tobacco. Eventually food products began to be transported from one place to another. Philadelphia alone had shipped five million tons of flour by 1770.

Industry began to develop early in colonial America and shipbuilding was one of the first. Perhaps the psychological security of being able to go back to their homeland motivated the early colonists to develop this commercial interest. The first six shipwrights on record settled in Salem, Massachusetts in 1629; on July 4, 1631, they launched their first ship, the *Blessing of the Bay*.

Within thirty years, 200 ships, including the shallow water ketch, had been designed and built in the colonies. By the turn of the century 1000 ships bearing the mark of colonial manufacture had been built. It was not long before the schooner, the early version of the nineteenth-century American clipper, had been designed. Needless to say, English shipbuilders were not unaware of the burgeoning colonial industry, and in 1720 the master shipwrights of London filed a formal protest against the competition.

It was a futile gesture. Britain's attempts to stop a process already in motion were soon replaced with orders for more

Early ketch typical of those used in the colonial trade about 1670. ▶

ships. When Britain went to war against the colonies, one-third of her merchant marine sailed in colonial ships. The maturity of the shipbuilding industry also enabled the colonial forces to raise a navy rather rapidly in the 1770s, a necessity since the British had one of the most powerful fleets in the world.

The process which made it possible for colonial industries to eventually take over where English industries had previously prevailed was, in fact, funded by the British. Beginning around 1640, land grants, cash subsidies, and the rights of monopoly were being awarded to encourage the growth of industry in the colonies. The principle of exclusive rights to manufacture created economic forms which depended upon controlling the market. It was in this environment that the iron industry began in 1643.

In that year, the Crown granted a Massachusetts ironworks group a twelve-year exclusive franchise. Within 100 years, the colonial iron industry had grown to be more of a threat to England's economic stability than the shipbuilding industry ever could have been.

Massachusetts, Maryland, Virginia, and particularly Pennsylvania were found to be rich in iron ore. When this discovery was made in the 1600s, English capitalists were anxious to invest their money in New World ventures. This, together with the British government's policy of subsidizing colonial enterprises, helped the fledgling industry grow rapidly.

In 1720 the first iron was exported to England from Maryland and Virginia. From 1730 to 1760, the number of foundries and forges in New England grew from twenty-five to fifty-five. By 1750 Maryland, Virginia, and Pennsylvania were providing 3000 tons of iron ore per year to England, an amount equal to one-sixth of England's total iron output.

Again British industry filed a protest. This time the government responded with the Iron Act of 1750 which provided that no new forges could be built in the colonies. But the British order was irrelevant since the world's need for iron was growing and since the ore was too abundant to be left untapped. Within another quarter century, 200 iron forges were operating in the colonies, together producing one-seventh of the world's iron. Only Russia and Sweden produced more.

It was during the same crucial years in which the iron industry was emerging (1630–50) that the seeds were planted for a number of different American industries, many of them in Massachusetts. Five weavers settled in Rowley, Massachusetts, and wove the colonies' first piece of cloth, measured to be 83½ yards long. Monopoly rights were granted for a corn mill in Newbury, Massachu-

◀ *Iron casting furnace, 1787.*

In the House of [R]epresentatives, *February* 16, 1776.

W*HEREAS this Colony* c[an]not *be ſupplied with a ſufficient Quantity of* Paper *for its own Conſ[um]ption, without the particular Care of its Inhabitants in ſaving RAGS for the Paper-Mills* : Therefore,

Resolved, That the Committees of Correſpondence, Inſpection, and Safety in the ſeveral Towns in this Colony be, and they hereby are required *immediately* to appoint ſome ſuitable Perſon in their reſpective Towns (where it is not already done) to receive Rags for the Paper-Mills : And the Inhabitants of this Colony are hereby deſired to be very careful in ſaving even the ſmalleſt Quantity of Rags proper for making Paper, which will be a further Evidence of their Diſpoſition to promote the Public Good.

Sent up for Concurrence. William Cooper, Speak. Pro. Tem.

In Council, Feb. 16, 1776. Read and Concurred,
Perez Morton, Dep'y. Sec'y.

Conſented to, by the Major Part of the Council.

A true Copy, Atteſt. Perez Morton, Dep'y. Sec'y.

PAPER-MILLS,

At the SLITTING-MILL, in Milton.

In Compliance with the foregoing Resolve,

and to *Encourage* the

PAPER-MANUFACTURE,

WE now propoſe to give *Three Coppers* per Pound for all white *Linnen*, and *Cotton* and *Linnen RAGS*, ſuitable for making Writing-Paper ; which is Three Pence O. T. per Pound more than has been given :---- Alſo, One Copper and an Half per Pound is now given for Check and courſe Rags, and Two Coppers for Canvaſs, that is either made of Hemp or Flax ; and Half a Copper a Pound for old Ropes and Junk.---Ropes and Junk that are too bad for Oakum will make good Paper.

☞ It is therefore hoped, that more Attention will be paid to this Affair in future, both from a Principle of *Patriotiſm* and *Frugality*. The preſent alarming Situation of the *Colonies*, renders it entirely needleſs to point out the Utility of eſtabliſhing this, and every Kind of *Manufacture* among us ; and if each Family will but lend their Aid, to encourage this Buſineſs, by ſaving their *Rags*, there may be a Sufficiency of Paper made here, and entirely prevent the Importation of that Article into this Country.

⁂ Any Gentlemen, Traders, or others throughout this Country, that will ſo far promote the Intereſt of America, by receiving *Rags* for the aforeſaid Purpoſe, ſhall be paid Ten per Cent. Commiſſions, and neceſſary Charges of Tranſportation, either by Land or Water to ſaid Mills : And the ſmalleſt Favors gratefully acknowledged by their very Humble Servants,

HUGH McLEAN and Co.

TO BE SOLD at ſaid Mill, all Sorts of Printing

PAPER,

Writing ditto, *London* Brown, Whitiſh Brown, Bonnet Paper : Likewiſe Preſs Paper for Clothiers, for glazing and goodneſs ſuperior to any made in *America*, and not inferior to the beſt made in *England*.

CASH given for RAGS by

[S]*ALEM* : Printed by E. Russell, Upper End of Main-ſtreet : Who gives Cash for all K[inds] of Cotton and Linnen and Check Rags. for the Uſe of the above Paper-Mills.

setts. A land subsidy was granted for a glass-making plant in Salem, Massachusetts. And the first diversified conglomerate was started by one Joseph Jenks who, after securing a patent and a fourteen-year franchise for his furnace, went on to receive the first patent for a scythe in Massachusetts, then set up the first wire-making plant, and finally cast the die for the first piece of money minted in the colonies.

The wood industry also developed early. The first sawmill was built in Massachusetts in 1635. The sawmill implied not only the ability to make wooden boards from logs, but also the ability to make paper. In 1690, the paper industry itself was put on firm footing when William Rittenhouse built the first paper mill in Germantown, Pennsylvania, near Philadelphia. By 1700, sawmills were common in New England and the Middle colonies. At the time of the Revolution, some seventeen paper mills were operating, fifteen of them in the Philadelphia area. Without the ability to communicate on paper, the American revolutionary movement might have taken a lot longer to develop.

When Benjamin Franklin was born, in 1706, the population of the twelve colonies numbered more than 250,000 and was doubling every twenty years. The amenities of life to which people were accustomed in the Old World had begun to be more common in the New World.

A year after Franklin was born, the colonial postal service was officially declared a branch of the British postal service. In Boston, the postmaster was publishing a successful newspaper, the *Boston Newsletter*. Even public transportation was beginning to be available in the first, not-so-comfortable, wagons. In the meantime, the vehicle which would one day come to symbolize conquering the frontier was being built in a valley in Pennsylvania—the Conestoga wagon.

By the time Franklin was in his thirties, Harvard College had been graduating students for nearly a hundred years. An educated elite had been produced, and it was with these American-born colonials that Franklin formed the nucleus of the Junto, the predecessor of the American Philosophical Society. Comprehensive in its goals, the original plan was for the organization to be intercolonial and, later, international. The Philadelphia chapter consisted of a representative from each of seven branches of "science": medicine, botany, mathematics, geography, chemistry, mechanics, and natural philosophy.

In 1743 Franklin wrote that the colonies' material needs were primarily satisfied, and that it was time to turn to the life of the mind. He took his own advice and within the next thirty years made a great number of contributions to American society. Beginning with the highly efficient Pennsylvania fireplace, now known as the Franklin stove, "Poor Richard" went on to develop the lightning rod which led to his famous experiments with electricity. It was Franklin who contributed the concepts of *plus* and *minus* and *negative* and *positive* to the field of electricity.

As an urban planner, he drew up plans for paving streets, designed drainage systems, and established the first library, the first fire company, and the first insurance company. A thoroughly practical inventor, he also designed bifocal lenses which he himself wore. When he took charge of the post office in 1753, moving the mail became an around-the-clock operation. As a result of this, the time for a letter to go from Boston to Philadelphia and back was reduced from three weeks to six days.

Within 150 years the colonies had evolved from being consumers of a few British goods to being one of England's major suppliers. In 1772 England's trade with the colonies was equal to her trade with the entire world just sixty-eight years earlier.

Having lived through this most rapid period in colonial expansion, it is not surprising that Franklin wrote, just two years before his death, of what the twentieth and twenty-first centuries might look like: "... invention and improvement are prolific, and beget more of their kind. The present progress is rapid. Many of great importance, now unthought of, will, before that period, be produced."

Suggested Reading

Bridenbaugh, Carl, *The Colonial Craftsman* (New York: New York University Press, 1950). A detailed description of how each craft developed in the colonies, including woodworking, candlemaking, glassblowing, etc.

Oliver, John W., *History of American Technology* (New York: Ronald Press, 1956). This exhaustive work traces the development of each important American technology from the time the first settlers arrived to 1950.

Roe, Joseph Wickham, *English and American Tool Builders* (New Haven: Yale University Press, 1916). Tools have their own fascinating history, carefully followed in this book.

Sloane, Eric, *A Museum of Early American Tools* (New York: Ballantine Books, 1964). A pictorial representation of the many different kinds of tools which the early settlers invented.

Thompson, Holland, *The Age of Invention* (New Haven: Yale University Press, 1921). Beginning with the life of Benjamin Franklin, this book documents in biographical style the nineteenth-century developments which came to be known as "the age of invention."

Philadelphia's Second Street with Christ Church in the background.

9

The Emergence of Sectional Strains

I have found the backwoodsmen to be . . . a hardy, adventurous, hospitable, rough, but sincere and upright race of people . . . If we were to try them by the standard of New England customs and opinions, that is to say, the customs of a people under entirely different circumstances, there would be many things in the picture, that would strike us offensively. They care little about ministers, and think less about paying them. They are averse to all, even the most necessary restraints. They are destitute of the forms and observances of society and religion; but they are sincere and kind without professions, and have a coarse, but substantial morality.

Timothy Flint
Recollections of the Last Ten Years

From 1816 to 1819 the United States enjoyed a period of political harmony known as the Era of Good Feelings. Pride in the quality of American accomplishments and faith in the superiority of the American way of life characterized this era. Americans believed that their political institutions were superior to all others, and that their country offered unbounded economic opportunity. However, until this time, most Americans had associated these achievements with a federal government of limited power. In fact, early American nationalism had been based on the idea that the government should not interfere with political and economic freedom. But after the War of 1812 many of the country's leaders began to support a political program based on a stronger central government. In its similarity to Hamilton's ideas, this program became a form of neo-Federalism. For a few years neo-Federalist policies had wide, if not universal, support.

The Era of Good Feelings was destined to be short-lived. Economic difficulties, culminating in the Panic of 1819, and political differences focusing around the issue of slavery, led to a return of the Jeffersonian ideals of self-determination by the states and a growing awareness of sectional differences and conflicting needs.

Good Times and Bad

JAMES MONROE AS PRESIDENT

James Monroe, who had served as Madison's secretary of war, succeeded Madison as president. In 1816, at Madison's insistence, the Jeffersonians nominated Monroe as their official presidential candidate. He won easily over his Federalist opponent, Rufus King. King, a New Yorker, had been nominated in an effort to downplay the New England character of the Federalist party. The strategy failed and King was the last Federalist candidate ever nominated for the presidency. He carried only Massachusetts, Connecticut, and Delaware.

Monroe had served the public for many years. He was Madison's secretary of state from 1811 on and was secretary of war as well during 1814. His vigorous handling of the end of the war won him considerable popular support. The third Virginian in a row to become president, he was also third in ability. He had neither Jefferson's remarkable idealism and encyclopedic interests, nor Madison's fine, theoretical mind. However, he did have an admirable record of service to the nation. In addition to his two cabinet posts, Monroe had fought under Washington during the Revolution, served twice as governor of Virginia, and was later elected to the Senate. A stately, dignified man with rather old-fashioned manners and dress, Monroe earned his greatest distinction as a diplomat to Paris, Madrid, and London.

Monroe's appearance was reminiscent of the heroic days of the Revolution. Historian George Dangerfield has described him in the following manner.

> On certain special occasions, his tall, raw-boned, venerable figure would appear in the faded uniform of a Revolutionary officer; otherwise he wore the plain dark coat, the knee-length pantaloons, the white-topped boots of an earlier day; his hair was powdered and tied in a cue at the back; his manners were mild, but constrained, awkward, formal and old-fashioned.

Monroe had more than his record and stately appearance to aid him; he also had the best cabinet since the administration of George Washington. John Quincy Adams, Monroe's secretary of state, was well-prepared for the office he held. Adams had served as America's ambassador to Russia, Prussia, The Netherlands, and England. William H. Crawford, originally appointed by Madison, continued as Monroe's secretary of the treasury. William Wirt, one of the leading lawyers of the day, was named attorney general. John C. Calhoun was appointed secretary of war. These were all gifted men who possessed sound administrative abilities.

Monroe has been described as "one of those men of persistent mediocrity from whom useful and attractive Presidents have been made." The Monroe Doctrine, a landmark in foreign policy, was formulated chiefly by John Quincy Adams. Adams also negotiated the acquisition of Florida and the settlement of the boundary between Canada and the United States. Most of the Monroe administration's domestic policies had been designed under Madison. Monroe's first term was so peaceful that when he was elected for a second term in 1820, only one electoral vote was cast against him. Even this seeming triumph, however, probably reflects the fact that the opposition Federalist party had died.

THE ERA OF GOOD FEELINGS

The country, proud of its technological accomplishments and confident of the superiority of its government, moved forward, for a time, together.

Symbolic of the new harmony was the renewal of friendship between Thomas Jefferson, the nation's most famous Democratic Republican, and John Adams, the most famous living Federalist. In 1801 Adams had skulked angrily out of Washington without attending Jefferson's inauguration. The two men had not corresponded for years. Now, however, they were again exchanging voluminous letters and addressing each other as "My dear friend."

Monroe rode this wave of good feeling which he had not created and could not maintain. He began his first term with a goodwill tour of New England, formerly the center of Federalist opposition. The president's visit had even been scheduled by a Federalist newspaper, the *North American Review.* Monroe was greeted everywhere by cheering crowds. He enjoyed six days in Boston, the Federalist stronghold, and when he addressed the Massachusetts legislature, he embraced political opponents with these words: "I indulge a strong hope that our principal dangers and difficulties have passed, and that the character of our deliberations and the course of the government itself, will become more harmonious and happy than it has heretofore been." Another Federalist newspaper, the *Columbian Centinel,* delighted with the political harmony engendered by the president, published an article about the new administration entitled, "Era of Good Feelings." The slogan caught on; it seemed an apt expression of the domestic harmony and prosperity of the postwar period.

RECONCILIATION OF THE PARTIES

One of Monroe's concerns was the rivalry between the political parties. Moderates in both parties wished to reconcile Federalists and Jeffersonians. And this desire was compatible with Monroe's desire to end partisan politics, which he considered contrary to republican principles.

In November 1816 General Andrew Jackson had written to the president-elect urging him to forget party feeling in forming his administration and to draw on the ablest men of both parties. Monroe's reply was very carefully worded. He stated that he wanted, not to absorb the Federalists, but to eliminate all parties. He cited the Jeffersonian belief that the Federalists were the party of monarchy, and noted that appointing Federalists to high posts might revive the fading party. He also expressed concern that too rapid an elevation of Federalists would arouse opposition within his own party.

Nevertheless, Monroe was careful to avoid making any public references which could be viewed as politically insulting to the Federalists

A city election at the State House in Philadelphia.

as a group. He also cultivated personal friendships with individual Federalists. The next logical step would have been to appoint some former Federalists to high office, but increasing criticism, within his own party, of the mild pro-Federalist attitude Monroe had already shown made it impossible to take that step.

Monroe failed to eliminate party division. He underestimated the intensity of sectional differences, and mistakenly viewed the divisiveness they caused as a practical problem capable of solution through compromise.

The Era of Good Feelings lasted only a few short years—from 1816 to 1819. The large Jeffersonian coalition split into factions; the Panic of 1819 generated sentiment against the national bank; sectional animosities were heightened by the Missouri crisis; squabbles arose over the disposition of Western lands, federally sponsored internal improvements, the tariff, and suffrage; and there was infighting in Monroe's cabinet, notably between Calhoun and Crawford.

SECTIONAL STRAINS ON NATIONAL UNITY

By 1820 the outburst of nationalism that had united Americans after the War of 1812 subsided and the sectional differences that had prevailed since colonial times resurfaced. Different economies, manners, and even accents had always distinguished the various regions of the United States. Southerners and Northerners had long been suspicious of each other; pioneers on the frontier had a well-defined distrust of their fellow citizens in the East.

During the War of 1812 these differences had been more or less submerged as Americans united to fight their common enemy. However the war itself set in motion certain processes which would exaggerate the differences between the various regions. The development of manufacturing in the Northeast ultimately brought New England's factories into competition with Britain's, and the United States began to consider the advantages of a self-sufficient economy with high tariffs to restrict foreign imports.

The South, however, did not industrialize. It remained a specialized agricultural economy in the colonial tradition, exporting its crops to Europe in exchange for manufactured commodities. Southerners knew that they could not rely on Northern mills to consume all the cotton they produced. The region's major customers were, and would continue to be, the English textile factories of Lancashire. The economic interests of the North and the South were therefore in opposition. While the North had everything to gain from restricting imports, the South had nothing to gain. As far as the South was concerned, tariffs meant only that the Southern customer would pay higher prices for imported goods.

The West was also a significant factor in the American economic equation. Before 1812 most settlers west of the Appalachian Mountains were Southerners. Most had migrated from Virginia and North Carolina to Kentucky and Tennessee. Thus the early West was basically an extension of the old South. After the war, however, many Northerners joined small farmers from the South to settle the Illinois and Indiana territories of the Northwest. This section of the country soon held one-quarter of the nation's population and had a strong influence on national politics.

Conflicts of interest, particularly over the issue of slavery, divided the Northwest and the Southwest, much as the Northeast and Southeast were divided on such issues as the tariff. Yet the West still displayed a political cohesiveness on specifically Western issues such as internal improvements, Indian affairs, and government land policy. Regardless of their origins or views on slavery, all Westerners wanted better roads linking them to the East, protection against the Indians, and cheap farmland.

THE PANIC OF 1819

Early trends had pointed to a unity born of economic interdependence: as the nation slowly started to shift from an agrarian to an industrial economy in the early 1800s, the various self-sufficient regions gradually evolved into a mutually-profitable system of mass markets. The shift was caused by industrialization in the Northeast, the advent of cotton as a major cash crop in the South, and the linking of the West to the East through improved transportation systems. The Marshall Court's protection of the manufacturing and business interests also helped accomplish the changeover.

The great economic expansion between 1816 and 1819 had not been regulated by government policy, nor by the national bank's sound fiscal control. Europeans, starved by the Napoleonic Wars and suffering from two bad harvests, bought unprecedented quantities of American corn, beef, pork, flour, cotton, and tobacco. Britain's textile manufacturers purchased American cotton at extremely high prices to provide clothing, which had been scarce during the war years.

But by 1818 Europe was recovering. Good harvests replenished European wheat. Cheap cotton from India began replacing America's expensive cotton in Britain's textile factories. While these developments were healthy for Europe, they had an adverse effect on the American economy. The prosperity of the postwar years was followed by the country's first nationwide depression, the Panic of 1819.

Overproduction of cotton in the United States caused a great drop in cotton prices. The amount of precious metals on the world market declined when mining in Mexico and Peru was disrupted during the Latin American revolts against Spain. World prices declined severely after 1815. And Americans were unprepared for this turn of events.

Unaware of international economic conditions, Americans had responded to the boom in the United States by speculating wildly in Western lands. By 1819 Americans owed the government some $22 million for lands purchased on credit. Moreover, Western farmers, eager to buy farm equipment and additional land, had become heavily indebted to the Bank of the United States. The bank, particularly its Western branches, had pursued a foolishly generous policy in making loans on mortgages, renewing notes repeatedly, and issuing new loans without making certain that they could be repaid. When Europe's demand for American cotton and wheat declined, farmers made less money and became less able to pay for agricultural equipment and to meet their mortgage payments.

To make matters worse the Bank of the United States was terribly mismanaged. It issued great quantities of inflationary paper money without having adequate supplies of gold and silver on hand to back it up. The president of the Baltimore branch and several of his subordinates absconded with bank funds. By July 1818 the bank had liabilities of $22 million and only $2 million worth of gold and silver reserves.

The bank's collapse appeared imminent. Jefferson, writing to John Adams, blamed the panic on the issuance of too much paper money. "The paper bubble is then burst. That is what you and I, and every reasoning man, seduced by no obliquity of mind or interest, have long foreseen." The president of the bank, William Jones, and his successor, Langdon Cheves, attempted to curtail the inflated economy by recalling loans and pressuring state banks to redeem their notes in specie. After making the mistake of lending too much money too easily, the bank blundered further by taking too stern an attitude at a time when money was scarce.

In the depression that ensued the Bank of the United States became known as "the Monster." One after another, state banks closed their doors. Prices fell drastically. Cotton dropped to ten cents a pound. Almost one-third of the population of Pittsburgh abandoned the city; its textile, glass, and iron manufacturers closed shop. The aggregate value of property in New York declined from $315 million to $256 million in one year. In Kentucky two political parties clashed over controversial laws designed to aid debtors. In Cincinnati the national bank suddenly became the unwilling owner of hotels, stables, and stores when debtors defaulted on their loan payments.

The federal government took limited action to alleviate the crisis. Many Jeffersonians still believed that the federal government had no responsibility for the country's economic problems. Also, sectional tensions and disagreements over economic policy prevented wide support for any specific government measures.

As a result, Congress passed only the following few measures: in 1820 a new land act allowing a settler to buy an eighty-acre homestead for $100; in 1821 a relief act to assist people with shaky credit; and in 1824, when the country was already on the way out of its economic doldrums, a new tariff.

Land policy

The people's attitudes toward government land policy reflected the diversity of sectional interests in the country. The federal government owned millions of acres in the West. Westerners wanted to be able to buy this land as cheaply as possible, whereas Northerners and Southerners regarded it as a public asset which should be sold for large sums to ease the nation's tax burdens. Northern industrialists also feared that if land were cheap, many factory workers would abandon their jobs and head West, while those who stayed behind would be able to command steep wages as factory owners competed for their services. The cotton planters of South Car-

Settlement of immigrants in Missouri. ▶

olina and Georgia also feared—quite correctly—that cheap land in the Southwest would create a rival cotton-growing area.

Despite these pressures the government's land policy had grown increasingly liberal. The Land Act of 1800 specified that land could be sold in lots of no less than 320 acres at no less than $2.00 per acre. In 1804 the minimum lot size was reduced to 160 acres, and the price was reduced to $1.64 per acre. Now, moreover, buyers could pay for the land over a five-year period. This attractive policy promoted huge land sales. The government sold one million acres in 1815 and five million in 1819. Then the panic struck. The land that farmers had purchased through bank loans was repossessed.

To relieve the distress of Western farmers, and despite protests from the North and the South, the government passed the Land Act of 1820. The minimum lot size was again reduced, this time to eighty acres, and the minimum price was also reduced, to $1.25 per acre. However, the government now had to be paid immediately, and in cash. The installment plan, which had led to so many foreclosures during the panic, was abolished. Land was offered at a government land auction and went to the highest bidder. Much of the land, especially the more fertile areas, went for a great deal more than the minimum price. In some areas of Alabama and Mississippi, for example, it sold for as much as $100 per acre.

The tariff question

Immediately after the War of 1812 the concept of a protective tariff had been popular throughout the country. The North was strongly in favor of the tariff as a means of shielding its infant industries against competition from cheap European imports (although New England shipowners resisted the tariff, fearing it would inhibit international commerce and thus diminish their business). Many in the South viewed the tariff as a way to develop industry below the Mason–Dixon Line. The West was convinced that the tariff would create markets in the North and South for its produce and livestock. Efforts to set duties higher than those in the Tariff of 1816, and the Panic of 1819, however, soon destroyed this consensus.

The Tariff of 1816 had itemized certain imported goods and taxed them at about twenty-five percent of their value. Northeastern manufacturers wanted to increase these duties. At the same time, the panic was hurting Southern cotton growers as much as it was Northern manufacturers. The price of cotton had dropped in a few months from thirty-three to ten cents per pound. Furthermore, the South was not developing the anticipated industries. Now the South had no reason to support a higher tariff; in fact it had every reason to defeat one. Southern votes in Congress defeated both a proposed tariff in 1820 and a bill to provide money for the National Road in 1822. The South's stand on these two issues alienated Northern manufacturers and Western farmers. These two groups believed that the depression would end only if there were tariffs to protect American industry and federally sponsored transportation systems to connect the West to the East.

In 1824 a new attempt to raise the tariff had the support of the Ohio Valley and the Middle Atlantic states, and was finally successful. The new tariff was designed to place such a high

A large version of Eli Whitney's cotton gin.

duty on the itemized imports that they could no longer compete with American products.

Commercial interests opposing the bill could not defeat it, even with the aid of the South and the Southwest. The bill barely scraped through the Congress, however. Competing interests in the country had pressured Congress with opposing demands. American wool growers, for example, wanted a high duty on imported wool, but woolen manufacturers proposed an increased duty only on imported woolen fabrics. Iron manufacturers called for a duty on pig iron from Scotland, but manufacturers who used Scottish pig iron for casting small mechanical parts opposed this part of the tariff. Southerners had fought the duty on hemp, since they preferred Russian hemp baggings (used to bag raw cotton) to Kentucky hemp. In general, the grain, wool, and manufacturing interests supported the Tariff of 1824; the planting, commercial, and fishing interests opposed it. The net effect of the tariff was to boost duties to between thirty to thirty-six percent of the value of certain imported goods. The cost of pig iron from Scotland rose from fifty to fifty-six cents per one hundred pounds; the price of hemp jumped from $15 to $35 per ton; the duty on cotton fabrics increased eight percent.

By the middle of the 1820s prosperity returned to the United States. But the panic had left deep scars, especially with regard to the Bank of the United States. Large numbers of Americans found they distrusted banking in general and paper money in particular. Many held paper money responsible for the inflationary cycle that had culminated in panic and depression. Lingering resentment against the Bank of the United States was strengthened when the Congress investigated certain financial irregularities and then took no action to chastise or control the national bank.

Western settlers viewed the bank as the darling of Eastern financiers, which added to their distrust of Eastern business interests. Yet, a new economic interdependence was growing between the Northeastern states and such Northwestern states as Ohio, Indiana, and Illinois. For a time the new West continued to support positions taken by Southern politicians. Ultimately, however, economic ties with the Northeast destroyed this alliance. The nation's three geographical regions merged into two: the North and the South.

The Slavery Issue

Nowhere did sectional differences become more bitter than over the issue of slavery. Never economically important to the North, slavery had been abolished in all states north of Maryland by 1804. Slavery had also been legally excluded from the Northwest Territory. In the South, however, the institution became an even more important part of the economy after the introduction of the cotton gin and after the settlement of new lands made cotton a profitable crop.

A number of Southerners had long opposed slavery and believed in extending to slaves the principles of liberty embodied in American Revolutionary thought. Of the 130 antislavery societies established in America before 1827, more than 100 were in the upper South. Twice, Virginia almost abolished slavery. But states in the upper South insisted that freed slaves leave the state, and early in the century states in the deep South had made it illegal for private individuals to free their slaves. The growth of the new cotton economy reversed the antislavery trend throughout the South.

Slave labor was perfectly suited to cotton farming. Tobacco required careful planting and delicate pruning, but cotton could be managed

BY
HEWLETT & BRIGHT.

SALE OF
VALUABLE
SLAVES,

(On account of departure)

The Owner of the following named and valuable Slaves, being on the eve of departure for Europe, will cause the same to be offered for sale, at the NEW EXCHANGE, corner of St. Louis and Chartres streets, on *Saturday*, May 16, at Twelve o'Clock, *viz.*

1. **SARAH, a mulatress, aged 45 years, a good cook and accustomed to** house work in general, is an excellent and faithful nurse for sick persons, and in every respect a first rate character.

2. **DENNIS, her son, a mulatto, aged 24 years, a first rate cook and steward** for a vessel, having been in that capacity for many years on board one of the Mobile packets; is strictly honest, temperate, and a first rate subject.

3. **CHOLE, a mulatress, aged 36 years, she is, without exception, one of** the most competent servants in the country, a first rate washer and ironer, does up lace, a good cook, and for a bachelor who wishes a house-keeper she would be invaluable; she is also a good ladies' maid, having travelled to the North in that capacity.

4. **FANNY, her daughter, a mulatress, aged 16 years, speaks French and** English, is a superior hair-dresser, (pupil of Guilliac,) a good seamstress and ladies' maid, is smart, intelligent, and a first rate character.

5. **DANDRIDGE, a mulatoo, aged 26 years, a first rate dining-room servant**, a good painter and rough carpenter, and has but few equals for honesty and sobriety.

6. **NANCY, his wife, aged about 24 years, a confidential house servant,** good seamstress, mantuamaker and tailoress, a good cook, washer and ironer, etc.

7. **MARY ANN, her child, a creole, aged 7 years, speaks French and** English, is smart, active and intelligent.

8. **FANNY or FRANCES, a mulatress, aged 22 years, is a first rate** washer and ironer, good cook and house servant, and has an excellent character.

9. **EMMA, an orphan, aged 10 or 11 years, speaks French and English,** has been in the country 7 years, has been accustomed to waiting on table, sewing etc.; is intelligent and active.

10. **FRANK, a mulatto, aged about 32 years speaks French and English,** is a first rate hostler and coachman, understands perfectly well the management of horses, and is, in every respect, a first rate character, with the exception that he will occasionally drink, though not an habitual drunkard.

☞ All the above named Slaves are acclimated and excellent subjects; they were purchased by their present vendor many years ago, and will, therefore, be severally warranted against all vices and maladies prescribed by law, save and except FRANK, who is fully guaranteed in every other respect but the one above mentioned.

TERMS:—One-half Cash, and the other half in notes at Six months, drawn and endorsed to the satisfaction of the Vendor, with special mortgage on the Slaves until final payment. The Acts of Sale to be passed before WILLIAM BOSWELL, *Notary Public*, at the expense of the Purchaser.

New-Orleans, May **13, 1835.**

PRINTED BY BENJAMIN LEVY.

by unskilled workers of any age. The plant, which could be cultivated year-round, grew only waist high. A single overseer could keep track of many slaves at once. Slave labor became particularly profitable on large plantations which had a need for constant labor.

As provided in the Constitution, the federal government outlawed the foreign slave trade in January 1808. But ships continued to smuggle as many as five thousand Africans into America almost every year to meet the demand for more laborers.

The sale of slaves also became a major source of profit in the upper South. States with surplus slaves—such as Virginia, Maryland, and Kentucky, whose diminishing cotton production did not require extensive slave labor—became the slave producers for the cotton kingdom. Licensed traders bought slaves at auctions in these states and sent them to the states of the deep South—Alabama, Mississippi, Tennessee, Arkansas, and Florida. Slaves bought in eastern Virginia or Maryland were shipped to the Florida towns along the Gulf of Mexico. Those purchased in Kentucky and western Virginia were forced to march to the Mississippi River, where they were loaded on flatboats and shipped off to New Orleans. New Orleans was the slave emporium of the cotton kingdom: its streets were lined with slave showrooms, depots, and auction marts. In the forty years before the Civil War 742,000 blacks were transported from the upper South to the cotton-growing states.

For almost 150 years slaves had been legally defined as property. They were sold at auctions along with paintings, furniture, land, and other valuables. A slave represented a significant capital investment, some selling for as much as $1800. Separation of families was common; when families were advertised for sale, usually only the mother and her youngest children were included.

THE MISSOURI COMPROMISE

Since the debates over ratification of the Constitution, slavery and its expansion had not been an issue in national politics. Slavery was tolerated as the "peculiar institution" of the South. If Northerners discussed the issue at all, they deplored its existence, although not always with an easy conscience (Illinois and New Jersey, for example, had their own forms of black servitude). Northerners occasionally grumbled at the constitutional provision which allowed the Southern states to count three-fifths of their slaves in determining their share of congressional representatives. And Southern slaveowners protested the federal law which closed the African slave trade, but since smugglers constantly broke the law their complaints had little substance.

When Louisiana became a state in 1812 the rest of the Louisiana Purchase was organized into the Missouri Territory. By 1820 this territory had a population of 66,000, of which

10,000 were slaves. When Alabama entered the Union in 1819 an exact balance of power was achieved in the Senate: there were eleven free states and eleven slaveholding states. That part of the Missouri Territory west of Illinois between the Mississippi and Missouri rivers had petitioned Congress for admission to the Union as early as 1817. Admitting a new state to the Union had always been a routine matter, but Missouri's application created a furor that occupied Congress from 1819 to 1821. The request greatly aggravated the nation's increasingly sectionalist attitude toward slavery.

Northerners opposed the petition for several reasons. First, they disliked the practice of apportioning representatives on the basis of three-fifths of the slave population, and they did not want this practice extended west of the Mississippi River. Second, the creation of a new slave state would give the South an advantage in the Senate. Third, abolitionist societies such as the Manumission Society of New York and

Attacking the Expansion of Slavery

"Sir, extend your view across the Mississippi, over your newly acquired territory; . . . Look down the long vista of futurity. . . . Behold this extended empire, inhabited by the hardy sons of American freemen—knowing their rights, and inheriting the will to protect them—owners of the soil on which they live, and interested in the institutions which they labor to defend— . . . . Compared to yours, the Governments of Europe dwindle into insignificance, and the whole world is without a parallel. But, sir, reverse this scene; people this fair dominion with the slaves of your planters; extend slavery—this bane of man, this abomination of heaven—over your extended empire, and you prepare its dissolution. . . . The envious contrast between your happiness and their misery, between your liberty and their slavery, must constantly prompt them to accomplish your destruction. Your enemies will learn the source and the cause of your weakness. . . . With this defect, your Government must crumble to pieces, and your people become the scoff of the world. . . ."

James Tallmadge,
United States Congress,
Debates and Proceedings,
February 15, 1819

Defending the Expansion of Slavery

"The real question is, what disposition shall we make of those slaves who are already in the country? Shall they be perpetually confined on this side of the Mississippi, or shall we spread them over a much larger surface by permitting them to be carried beyond that river? . . . Now, sir, in relation to the physical force of the country, if ever the time shall come when we shall be engaged in war, and they should be excited to insurrection, it is obvious that there must be an immense subduction from the efficiency of the slave-holding section of our country; its actual efficiency would consist only, or nearly so, in the excess of the white beyond the black population; by spreading them over a more extended surface, you secure these advantages; first, by diminishing the proportion which the slaves bear in point of numbers to the whites, you diminish their motives to insurrection. Secondly, that if that event ever should occur, it would obviously be much more easily and certainly suppressed, because. . . . they would have a much smaller relative proportion of physical force."

**Philip P. Barbour,
United States Congress,
Debates and Proceedings,
February 16, 1819**

Quaker organizations in Pennsylvania had moral objections to the admission of another slave state. In February 1819 James Tallmadge, Jr., a New York representative, proposed to bar further introduction of slavery into Missouri after it became a state.

The Northwest Ordinance of 1787, written by Thomas Jefferson, had barred slavery from the first territory created by the United States—the Northwest Territory (today's Midwest). This set a precedent against extending slavery into territories outside the South, and the precedent stood until Missouri requested entry into the Union as a slave-holding state. Missouri's request led Southerners to work aggressively to extend slavery beyond the area of containment that had been tacitly, and in part legally (according to the precedent of the Northwest Ordinance), agreed upon since the Revolution.

The Tallmadge Amendment was the first serious challenge to the extension of slavery in the United States. It provided,

> That the further introduction of slavery or involuntary servitude be prohibited except for the punishment of crimes whereof the party shall have been duly convicted: and that all children born within the said State after the admission thereof into the Union shall be free, but may be held to service until the age of twenty-five years.

The amendment passed the House of Representatives by a small majority, but was defeated in the Senate. A few Northern senators had voted against it because they felt that the government did not have the constitutional right to meddle in the internal affairs of a state.

When the next Congress met in December

◀ *"Senate Chamber U.S.A. Conclusion of Clay's speech in defense of slavery."*

1819 statehood for Missouri was again proposed. Now, however, the issue was complicated by the fact that the District of Maine, having separated itself from Massachusetts, was also applying for statehood. Henry Clay, the Speaker of the House, used this opportunity to effect a compromise. "Equality is equality," he said, "and if it is just to make the restriction of slavery the condition of the admission of Missouri, it is equally just to make the admission of Missouri the condition of that of Maine."

In 1820 Clay worked out a compromise which earned him the nickname, "the Great Pacificator." According to the terms of the compromise Missouri entered the Union as a slave state and Maine as a free state. To prevent similar conflicts in the future another provision was added: slavery was to be "forever prohibited" in all other parts of the Louisiana Purchase north of the 36° 30′ line. This left Arkansas and Oklahoma as the only two territorial areas open to the expansion of slavery. The rest of the Louisiana Purchase—a vast and as yet unsettled area—was north of the demarcation line, and was thus closed to slavery. This territory included the future states of Kansas, Nebraska, Iowa, Minnesota, the Dakotas, Montana, and Colorado. The 36° 30′ demarcation line lasted until 1854, when it was repealed by Congress in response to pressure from advocates of slavery expansion.

In 1820 Maine was duly admitted as a state but Missouri was only authorized to write a constitution. When it was presented for congressional approval, Missouri's constitution contained a clause forbidding free blacks or mulattoes from other states from entering Missouri "under any pretext whatever." This clause clearly violated the federal Constitution's provision that "the Citizens of each State shall be entitled to all Privileges and Immunities of Citizens in the several States." Under the Missouri clause a black citizen of Massachusetts, for example, would not be allowed to enter Missouri—a flagrant violation of national authority. Missouri's constitution was accepted, however, with the proviso that no law passed in Missouri should ever violate the United States Constitution. Missouri's constitution was already in clear violation of the federal Constitution, but Missouri was admitted as a state in 1821.

IMPACT OF THE COMPROMISE

The Missouri Compromise made slavery a national issue and polarized the country even further. The Northwest, despite the large number of settlers from the South, generally voted with the Northeast; similarly, the Southwest was aligned with the Southeast. Thus the issue of slavery had much to do with the development of a political North and a political South.

Defensive as a result of the Missouri debates, Southerners no longer argued for slavery as a necessary evil but began defending it as a positive good. Charles Pinckney of South Carolina insisted: "Every slave has a comfortable house, is well fed, clothed, and taken care of; he has his family about him, and in sickness has the same medical aid as his master, and has a sure and comfortable retreat from old age. . . . During his whole life he is free from care, that canker of the human heart."

Two years after the Missouri debates a freedman, Denmark Vesey, taking his authority from the Bible and the Declaration of Independence, planned a massive uprising in Charleston. The plot was unsuccessful, but it made Southern whites fearful of future uprisings. They restricted life even more for slaves and free blacks.

In the North the rights of free blacks were also restricted. The Missouri Compromise called attention to black people at a time when the country was not willing to accept true racial equality. For instance, the Supreme Court of New Jersey—a state which had legally abolished slavery in 1804—proclaimed in 1821 that "black men are *prima facie* slaves." This ruling severely retarded the elimination of slavery in that state; it required that, in court cases where slaveholders claimed fugitive slaves as their property, the burden of proof was upon the blacks to bring evidence that they were free. Other states limited or denied free blacks equal opportunities for education, economic advancement, and the right to vote.

The question of slavery, conveniently buried for three decades, was now being debated again—at a time when the South was more than ever fiercely dedicated to preserving the institution. Jefferson wrote John Adams that the dispute, "like a fire bell in the night, awakened and filled me with terror." Adams responded: "I take it for granted that the present question is a mere preamble—the title page to a great tragic volume."

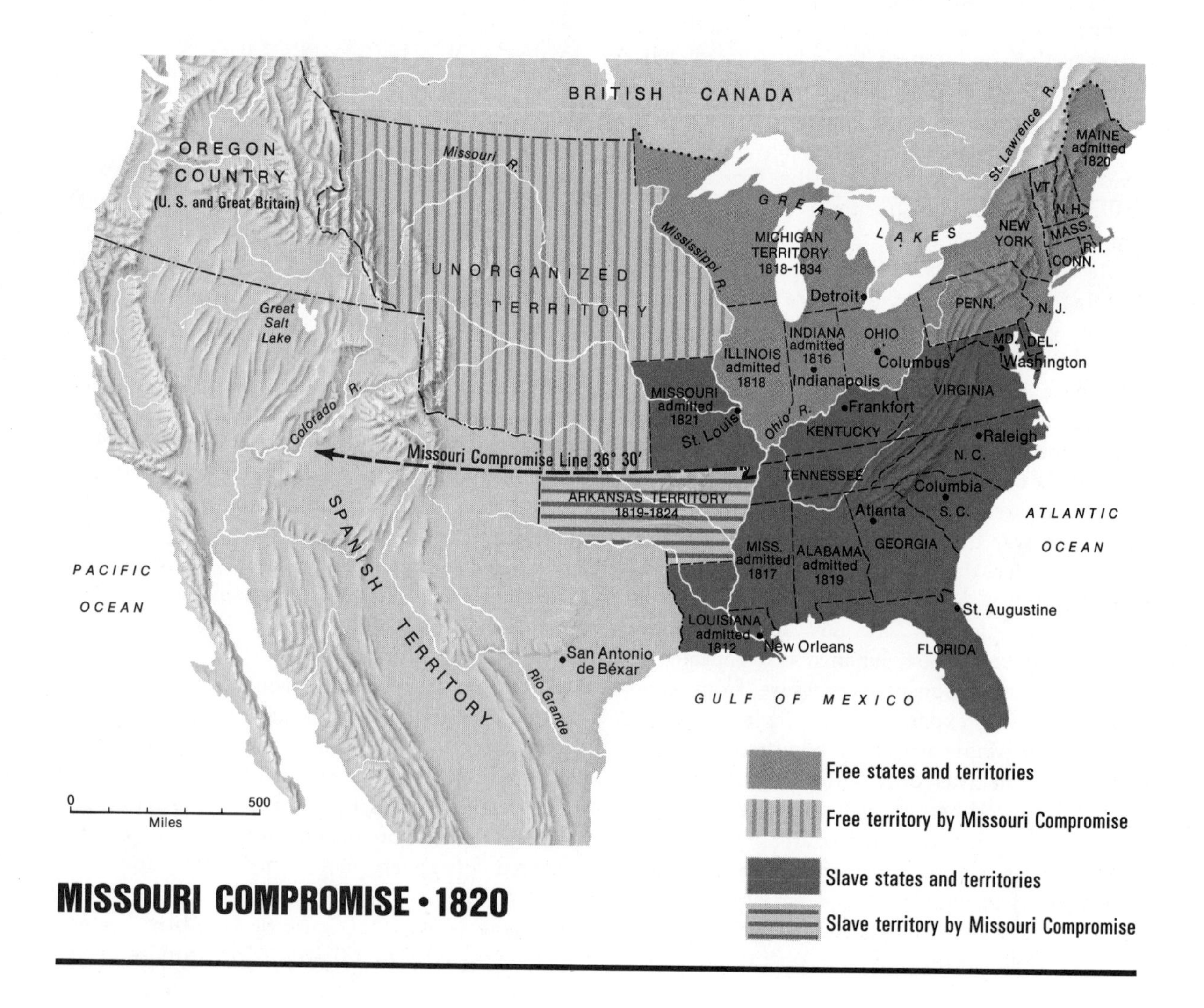

MISSOURI COMPROMISE • 1820

Sectional Politics

By 1820 sectional economic and political interests were putting strains on American leaders quite unlike those experienced by the nation's Founding Fathers. The great leaders of the Revolutionary era—Washington, Hamilton, Franklin, Jefferson, John Adams, and Madison—had had strong ties to their native states, but were usually able to "think continentally," as Hamilton had put it. Now these giants were gone. A new era of sectional politics was emerging which hampered the effectiveness of such nationalists as Henry Clay of Kentucky and John Quincy Adams of Massachusetts. Others, such as John C. Calhoun of South Carolina, Daniel Webster of Massachusetts, and Martin Van Buren of New York, while they defended the Union, were equally devoted to the advancement of their own regions.

NORTHERN POLITICAL LEADERS

John Quincy Adams

The best-known Northern political figure was John Quincy Adams, son of the second president and soon himself to become the chief executive. The younger Adams, an able diplomat, had held various posts in Europe. He served on the commission that forged the Treaty of Ghent, and tenaciously negotiated the brilliant Adams-Onís Treaty of 1819 with Spain.

Adams' strict Puritan upbringing left him with the lifelong habit of microscopically examining his own character flaws as well as everyone else's. He entered the presidency a bald, stout man with a tense and compulsive attitude toward work. His highly developed moral sense often made him harsh and dogmatic. Intelligent and courageous, he was also suspicious and fearful of the future. His enemies accused him of being a monarchist, but he had the manner of a republican. An Englishman who saw Adams at the Russian court reported that the American sat "with cotton in his leathern ears . . . like a bulldog among spaniels." Introspective and vain, he regarded his voluminous diary as, "next to the Holy Scriptures, the most precious book every written by human hands."

Adams was as ardent a nationalist as the great leaders of his father's generation. He subscribed enthusiastically to the strong financial role played by the federal government under Henry Clay's American System. Economic nationalists like Adams and Clay sought to serve the nation's interests by controlled expansion and rational planning on the federal level. While they believed in a democratic suffrage, they also believed that the federal government and its policies could best be managed by an intellectual elite. Moreover, they believed the Federalist notion that the most reliable supporters of nationalism were the nation's merchant and manufacturing interests.

Daniel Webster

Another great exponent of economic nationalism was Daniel Webster, a famous orator and lawyer of imposing appearance. Although Webster was an intelligent man, he did not have an independent mind. He has been called "a perfect barometer of opinion among men of wealth," and a political reflection of the changing economic interests of New England. Like the New England merchants he so much admired, Webster opposed the War of 1812; on the strength of this opposition, he was elected to Congress.

Webster fought both a cheap land policy and federally sponsored internal improvements, which he felt would benefit only the West. At first he also opposed a protective tariff and the creation of a second national bank. By the 1820s, however, Webster's views began to change to reflect the growing influence of the manufacturing interests on the New England economy. He became an ardent supporter of high tariffs and of the second Bank of the United States. While he was a member of the United States Senate, Webster also served simultaneously as a director of the national bank and as its leading attorney. He was also in debt to the bank for thousands of dollars, conduct which today would be regarded as a conflict of interest.

Always a staunch defender of the Union, by the 1830s Webster was brilliantly defending the supremacy of the national government against the sectional interests of the South. Although he yearned for the presidency, he never earned wide enough political appeal to become a serious contender.

Ralph Waldo Emerson once described Webster as follows:

> He obeys his powerful animal nature;—and his finely developed understanding only works truly . . . when it stands for animal good; that is, for property. He believes, in so many words, that government exists for the protection of property. He looks at the Union as an estate, a large farm, and is excellent in the completeness of his defense of it. . . . Happily he was born late,—after independence had been declared, the Union agreed to, and the Constitution settled. What he finds already written, he will defend. Luckily that so much had got well-written when he came.

Martin Van Buren

Another bright young lawyer of the period, Martin Van Buren was described by one of his contemporaries, a bit unfairly, as "a first-rate second-rate man." He was a member of the New York State Legislature by the time he was thirty, and in 1820, he won a seat in the United States Senate.

In his early career he was a fence-straddler on the major issues of the day. No one knew what he thought about slavery, although years later he became its outspoken opponent. His attitude toward the Bank of the United States was unclear, and he was equally vague about the protective tariff. Once he avoided casting a vote on a controversial matter simply by not showing up in the Senate; he later casually explained that he had promised to walk with a friend through the congressional cemetery. His speaking style was so complex that, although he always sounded intelligent, it was frequently difficult to be sure which side of an issue he was defending. The shrewd John Randolph of Roanoke said maliciously of Van Buren that he "rowed to his objective with muffled oars."

Van Buren was very much opposed to the economic nationalism represented by the American System. Not only did he believe this political philosophy to be contrary in certain of its aspects to the interests of his state of New York, but he also felt that it was incompatible with the old Jeffersonian concept of a central government with limited powers and a laissez-faire economic system. As a result, Van Buren began to work assiduously for a revival of pure Jeffersonian republicanism. As a master of the art of politics, he greatly aided the creation of a new national two-party system.

SOUTHERN POLITICAL LEADERS

William H. Crawford

William H. Crawford was perhaps the most prominent Southern politician. Elected senator from Georgia in 1807, Crawford became Monroe's secretary of the treasury in 1816.

The modern picture of Crawford is rather blurred, since his private papers have been lost, leaving documents generally written by his enemies. We do know that he was a crude, boisterous, but good-natured man with an immense physique. Despite his rough manners he was quite popular in Washington society. He was a smart politician, and one of the first leaders to try to build a national machine. But there was little consistency in his political views. As a

Jeffersonian Republican, he favored the states' rights position; as a conservative, he defended the interests of Georgia's rich planters against its poor white farmers. Despite his conservatism and sectionalism, however, he also favored federal control of internal improvements and a mild protective tariff. As secretary of the treasury, he also supported the second Bank of the United States. Dismissed by many of his enemies as a cunning opportunist, Crawford nonetheless proved to be an excellent and even a progressive administrator of the treasury.

John C. Calhoun

John C. Calhoun was more brilliant, if less popular, than Crawford. Born in South Carolina in 1782, he graduated from Yale in 1804 and was further educated at Tapping Reeve's law school in Litchfield, Connecticut. Calhoun displayed a logical and precise mind, one that was always dazzling in argument, but not always adapted to practical politics. A Calvinist who had converted to Unitarianism, he combined the rigor and gloom of his first religion with the rationality of his second. To one observer he seemed a "cast-iron man who looks as if he had never been born."

His political career, like Daniel Webster's, reflected the changing temper of his native state. Elected to Congress in 1811, Calhoun had persuaded South Carolina to adopt the postwar nationalism of the Era of Good Feelings. South Carolina, the dominant state of the Southern cotton kingdom, went so far as to support a moderately protective tariff, sacrificing its own interests to strengthen the nation's economy. In 1817 Calhoun became secretary of war under Monroe. Endorsing the American System, Calhoun felt that America needed to become stronger and more unified in the event of a future war. Accordingly, he called for a well-trained army, a large navy, and a federally supported, unified system of roads and canals. All of these measures would have a defensive value. Calhoun's support of a moderate tariff and of the national bank were also based on the idea of making the United States more self-sufficient. "Our true system is to look to the country," stated Calhoun, "and to support such measures and such men, without regard to sections, as are best calculated to advance the general interest."

His disinterested nationalism did not last long. The Panic of 1819 brought a strong reaction from South Carolina. The panic had severely depressed the South's economy. In the previous decade, when South Carolina had led all other states in cotton production, it had been able to endure generously the inconvenience of a protective tariff. Now the state was less prosperous and the newly settled states of the lower South were becoming dangerously competitive. The tariff became an obvious scapegoat for all of South Carolina's woes. By 1826 Calhoun, reflecting his state's attitude, had become an eloquent champion of free trade. By 1829 he had become so firm a defender of state's rights that he declared the protective tariff unconstitutional as well as objectionable.

WESTERN POLITICAL LEADERS

Henry Clay

The most intelligent and flamboyant Western leader of the 1820s was Henry Clay of Kentucky. Gray-eyed, lean, and handsome, Clay was almost as persuasive and hypnotic an orator as Daniel Webster. Little of his magic in debate can be gleaned from the written records of his speeches, for they do not show "the strange posturings and glidings, the punctuating pinches of snuff, the pointed finger, the unforgettable smile, and all the music of that wonderful voice."

Clay was born in Virginia, but at twenty he moved to Kentucky, where he practiced law. Like Calhoun, he was one of the War Hawks, earning the epithet, "Glorious Harry of the West." Elected congressman from Kentucky in

1810, Clay served as speaker of the house from 1811 to 1820, and again from 1823 to 1825.

Clay is celebrated for his American System, which he formulated during the early 1820s. As already noted, the system—which involved government support for higher traiffs, internal improvements, and a national banking system—was intended to benefit all parts of the country. Roads and canals would improve transportation between East and West. Tariffs would protect manufacturers in the East. A government bank would regulate national and inter-regional concerns. Northeastern industries would consume Southern cotton, Southern cotton growers and Northern city dwellers would consume Western farm produce. Western farmers would purchase Northern manufactured goods, and the national bank would make all these economic exchanges run smoothly. Everybody would profit. Unfortunately, for Clay, both in theory and in practice, the appeal of his plan was short-lived.

Andrew Jackson

Andrew Jackson entered the political scene at the turn of the centruy. A member of the convention which drafted the Tennessee Constitution, Jackson was elected to the House of Representatives in 1796 as the first congressman from the new state. Following a term in Congress, Jackson returned to Tennessee to serve as the judge of its supreme court from 1798 to 1804. As a general in the Tennessee militia and as a brilliant general in the War of 1812, Jackson's aggressiveness against both the Indians and the British won him widespread popularity, particularly in the West. Forceful and somewhat dictatorial as a leader, he was courteous and gentlemanly as an individual. He was independent in his behavior and determined in his ideas. Gradually becoming associated wtih the movement toward increased popular involvement in government, Jackson became the symbol of what was later referred to as "Jacksonian democracy."

Thomas Hart Benton

Thomas Hart Benton of Missouri was another important Western politician of the 1820s. Benton was a man of great vanity who could also be gracious and urbane. He was considered by some to be a man of learning and the best constitutional lawyer in the country. Benton's voting record was basically Jeffersonian and devoted to Western interests, although he supported parts of the American System. He endorsed free homesteads for small farmers and opposed all banks, all paper money, and easy credit. He disliked Clay's proposed tariffs, but voted for them in order to obtain protection for Missouri's lead and furs. He also advocated an extensive federal transportation network.

Benton served in Congress for thirty years, making speeches in a booming voice and colorful style. He was fond of affirming that he and the people were one: "Benton and democracy are one and the same, sir; synonymous terms, sir; synonymous terms, sir."

The Adams Administration

The election of 1824 showed clearly how political alliances were being drawn along sectional lines. Jefferson had chosen Madison to succeed him in the presidency and Madison had passed the mantle on to Monroe. Monroe selected his secretary of the treasury, William H. Crawford, who was then nominated by a congressional caucus as the official presidential candidate of the Jeffersonian party. The party, however, was in a shambles as a result of sectional strife. Three other men decided to throw their hats into the ring, all of them as Jeffersonians: these

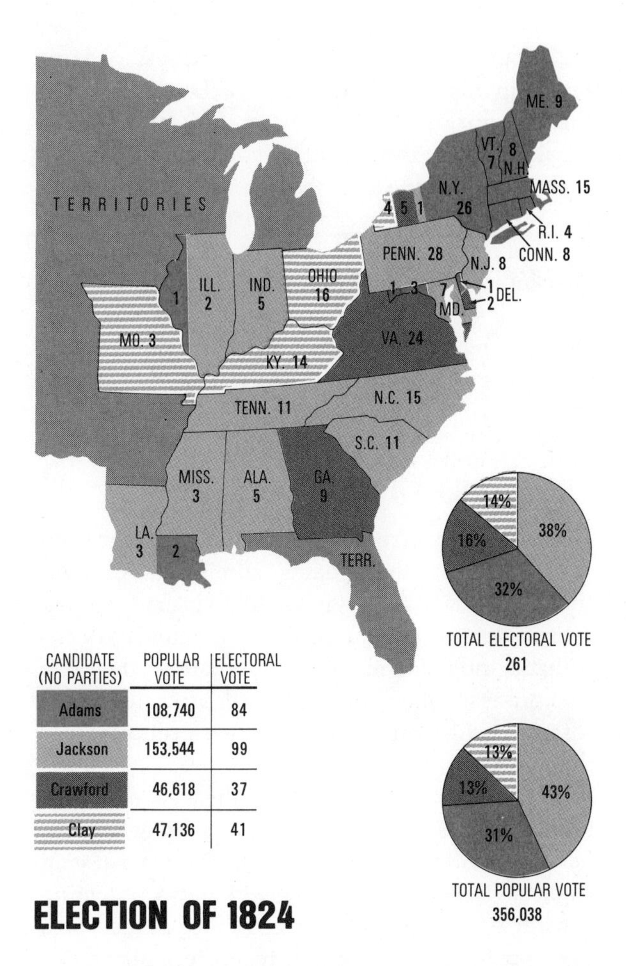

CANDIDATE (NO PARTIES)	POPULAR VOTE	ELECTORAL VOTE
Adams	108,740	84
Jackson	153,544	99
Crawford	46,618	37
Clay	47,136	41

ELECTION OF 1824

were John Quincy Adams, Henry Clay, and Andrew Jackson. The party, already weakened by the Panic of 1819 and the Missouri controversy, never recovered from this disastrous splintering among candidates.

A political novice, Andrew Jackson emerged quite unexpectedly as a serious presidential contender, and succeeded in building a national following where his rivals had failed. In part, he appealed to the nation's patriotic memories of his heroism at the Battle of New Orleans. But he also appealed to a rapidly-growing electorate that was disgusted with the caucus system, the closed political mechanism whereby officeholders determined who would be nominated for office. Jackson was regarded as pure and unspoiled because he was not part of the political establishment.

Jackson had the highest popular vote and also led in the electoral college with ninety-nine electoral votes; Adams received eighty-four votes; Crawford forty-one, and Clay thirty-seven. Jackson had received a plurality but not a majority. According to the Constitution the decision had to go to the House of Representatives. Under law the House could choose from only the three leading candidates, and so Clay was automatically eliminated. Crawford, who had become quite ill, was no longer regarded as a serious contender.

The choice was between Jackson and Adams. Clay was not on warm terms with Adams personally, but he did recognize that Adams was much more likely to support the American System than was Jackson, whose political views had never been clearly stated. Therefore Clay, ignoring the fact that his own state of Kentucky had instructed him to vote for Jackson, met secretly with Adams. Then, after announcing his support for Adams, Clay persuaded several other representatives to follow his example. When the votes were counted, Adams received thirteen, Jackson seven, and Crawford four.

One of President Adams' first acts was to appoint Clay secretary of state. Jackson, furious, accused Clay and Adams of having made a corrupt bargain, complaining: "So you see the Judas of the West has closed the contract and will receive the thirty pieces of silver. His end will be the same." Clay's decision to support Adams was justified in terms of national policy, but his acceptance of an appointment in the new administration was a serious political blunder. Jackson's supporters used it at every opportunity for their own advantage.

The dissolution of the Jeffersonian Republican party, the persistent name-calling by the Jacksonians, and the failure of his later foreign negotiations damaged Adams' prestige as president.

In his first Annual Address to Congress, Adams was greeted with scorn, even though most of his proposals were remarkably farsighted. Unfortunately, he always remained out of step with popular sentiment in the country. After the congressional election of 1826, a new Jacksonian coalition of Adams' enemies, renamed the Democratic Republicans, gained control of both houses of the Congress. Thereafter every move the President made was blocked by a hostile legislature.

ADAMS AND THE AMERICAN SYSTEM

Adams was determined to extend the American System. In fact, his desire for federally sponsored improvements went beyond even Clay's earlier proposals, to the dismay of his cabinet. Adams, however, ignored their warnings and proceeded with his "perilous experiment" of bold recommendations to Congress. He suggested that Congress pay for expeditions to explore the Far West, establish a uniform standard of weights and measures, found a national university, and erect an astronomical observatory. He urged general laws "promoting the improvement of agriculture, commerce, and manufactures, the cultivation and encouragement of the mechanic and of the elegant arts, the advancement of literature, and the progress of the sciences, ornamental and profound. . . ."

These recommendations seemed farfetched and absurd to a nation internally divided and basically devoted to the concept of a federal government with limited power. Adams also made the error of comparing American progress in the sciences unfavorably with that of the Europeans. And when he told congressmen not to be "palsied by the will of our constituents," his enemies claimed that he held American democracy in contempt.

The president was ridiculed and most of his proposals were sidetracked. His reference to observatories as "lighthouses of the skies" became a national joke. Only fragments of his grand design were ever realized. Two and one-half million dollars were appropriated for the maintenance of the National road and an additional sum of roughly $2 million was allocated to support private canal companies. Adams failed in his efforts to create a Department of the Interior, and his massive federal program for internal improvements was defeated.

Twelve years later Adams reflected: "With this system in ten years from this day the surface of the whole Union would have been checkered over with railroads and canals. It may still be done half a century later and with the limping gait of State legislature and private adventure. I would have done it in the administration of the affairs of the nation."

THE TARIFF OF ABOMINATIONS

The most controversial piece of legislation passed during the Adams administration was the Tariff of 1828. Adams and Clay had wanted a tariff that would help America achieve a centralized, independent economy. Instead, the tariff was an assortment of piecemeal provisions representing different special interest groups rather than a truly rational system.

Manufacturers in the Northeast demanded higher duties on foreign factory-made goods. Senator Benton clamored for duties on fur and lead. Levi Woodbury of New Hampshire, acting contrary to his belief in free trade, asked for a duty on manufactured silk to protect his state's silk mills. Similarly, the hemp raisers in Kentucky, the wool growers of New York, and other regional groups each called for their own protective tariffs. The tariff was passed, supported by a majority of Western and Northern votes. New England merchants, who formerly advocated free trade, retrenched and instructed Webster, who was directing administration forces in the Senate, to vote for the bill. Van Buren and other supporters of Andrew Jackson apparently voted for the tariff in the belief that it would add Western and Northern voters to the Democratic Republican party. The bill, called by its enemies the "Tariff of Abominations," finally passed with the Northwest and Middle Atlantic states for it, the South and Southwest against it, and the Northeast divided. This alignment of votes echoed the regional reaction to the Tariff of 1824. The ever-rising tariff was now as high as sixty percent on some items. The South, increasingly opposed to a high tariff, was again frustrated. Within a few years this frustration would have ominous results.

INTERNATIONAL PROBLEMS

In the area of diplomacy, Adams had shown great skill as Monroe's secretary of state. But as president, he suffered defeat and humiliation. In 1825 Simon Bolivar, the liberator of much of South America, called for a Pan-American Congress in Panama. Clay, eager to foster Pan-American harmony, obtained an invitation to the conference on behalf of the United States and persuaded Adams to send two delegates. Adams, unnecessarily, asked Congress for approval and received a conflicting and hostile response. Many isolationist congressmen were opposed to participating in any international gathering. Southerners, in particular, disapproved of the convention in Panama because they feared that Latin Americans might raise the question of slavery in the United States. Some resisted participating in a conference that might involve recognition of the black republic of Haiti. On the other hand, Northern commercial interests thought contacts with South American countries would be economically beneficial. After four months of debate, Congress gave its reluctant approval. It came too late and the conference was held, ironically, without United States' participation: one of the delegates died on his way to the conference and the other delayed his departure and missed the conference completely.

Adams also bungled negotiations with Britain over American access to West Indian trade. In 1825 Parliament, which had kept this lucrative trade closed to the United States, offered to lift some of its restrictions on trade. Adams considered the British offer inadequate. After a year's delay he instructed his minister in London to demand better terms. Galled by the president's stubbornness, the British once again blocked American trade with the West Indies. The American public blamed Adams for mishandling the entire affair.

Simon Bolivar.

THE JACKSONIANS AWAIT THEIR TURN

The puritanical, soul-searching Adams had been a failure as president. His aloof manner attracted little sympathy to his causes. His custodial approach to government—his attitude that an educated elite should shape the destiny of the nation for the benefit of the ordinary citizen—repelled the fiercely individualistic farmers of the West. His high-minded ideals hampered his relationship with his supporters and made him all the more vulnerable to the Jacksonian Democrats. Jackson's supporters relentlessly criticized Adams for four years, making the American people receptive to "Old Hickory" as their next national leader.

Readings

GENERAL WORKS

Abernethy, Thomas P., *The South in the New Nation.* Baton Rouge, La.: Louisiana State University Press, 1961.

Brooks, Van Wyck, *The World of Washington Irving.* New York: Dutton, 1944.

Dangerfield, George, *The Awakening of American Nationalism, 1815–1828.* New York: Harper & Row, 1965.

Dangerfield, George, *The Era of Good Feelings.* New York: Harcourt, Brace & World, 1962.

Eaton, Clement, *The Growth of Southern Civilization.* New York: Harper & Row, 1961.

Eaton, Clement, *The Mind of the Old South.* Baton Rouge, La.: Louisiana State University Press, 1964.

Hammond, Bray, *Banks and Politics in America from the Revolution to the Civil War.* Princeton, N.J.: Princeton University Press, 1957.

Larkin, Oliver W., *Art and Life in America.* Rev. ed. New York: Holt, Rinehart and Winston, 1960.

Nye, Russel B., *The Cultural Life of the New Nation.* New York: Harper, 1960.

Wish, Harvey, *Society and Thought in Early America.* Vols. I–II. 2nd ed. New York: David McKay, 1962.

Wright, Louis B., *Culture on the Moving Frontier.* Bloomington, Ind.: Indiana University Press, 1955.

SPECIAL STUDIES

Haines, Charles G., *The Role of the Supreme Court in American Government and Politics, 1789–1835.* Berkeley: University of California Press, 1944.

Livermore, Jr., Shaw, *The Twilight of Federalism.* Princeton, N.J.: Princeton University Press, 1962.

Moore, Glover, *The Missouri Controversy.* Lexington: University of Kentucky Press, 1953.

Rothband, Murray N., *The Panic of 1819.* New York: Columbia University Press, 1962.

Turner, Frederick J., *Rise of the New West.* New York: Collier, 1962.

Weisberger, Bernard A., *They Gathered at the River.* Little, Brown, 1958.

PRIMARY SOURCES

Benton, Thomas H., *Thirty Years View,* Vols. I–II. New York: Greenwood Press, 1968.

Nevins, Allan (Ed.), *The Diary of John Quincy Adams.* New York: Ungar, 1929.

Van Buren, Martin, *Autobiography.* J. C. Fitzpatrick, ed. New York: Kelley, 1969.

BIOGRAPHIES

Bemis, Samuel F., *John Quincy Adams.* New York: Knopf, 1956.

Chambers, William N., *Old Bullion Benton.* Boston: Little, Brown, 1956.

Current, Richard N., *Daniel Webster and the Rise of National Conservatism.* Boston: Little, Brown, 1955.

Current, Richard N., *John C. Calhoun.* New York: Washington Square Press, 1963.

Dalzell, Robert F., *Daniel Webster & the Trial of American Nationalism, 1843–1852.* Boston: Houghton Mifflin Co., 1973.

Eaton, Clement, *Henry Clay and the Art of American Politics.* Boston: Little, Brown, 1957.

Remini, Robert V., *Martin Van Buren and the Making of the Democratic Party.* New York: Columbia University Press, 1959.

Wiltse, Charles M., *John C. Calhoun: Nationalist.* Indianapolis: Bobbs-Merrill, 1944.

FICTION

Melville, Herman, *Moby Dick.* New York: Modern Library, 1950.

Twain, Mark, *Life on the Mississippi.* New York: Signet New American Library, 1961.

Opposite: "General Jackson, President-Elect, on his Way to Washington," drawn by Howard Pile. ▶

10

The Jacksonian Era

But the experience of the world goes to prove that there is a tendency to monopoly wherever power is reposed in the hands of a minority. Nothing is more likely to be true than that twenty wise men will unite in opinions in opposition to a hundred fools; but nothing is more certain than that, if placed in situations to control all the interests of their less gifted neighbors . . . , fifteen or sixteen of them would pervert their philosophy to selfishness. This was at least our political creed, and we therefore admitted a vast majority of the community to a right of voting. Since the hour of the Revolution, the habits, opinions, laws, and I may say principles of the Americans are getting daily to be more democratic.

James Fenimore Cooper,
Notions of the Americans

Jackson Takes Command

By the time Andrew Jackson became president Americans believed not only that all men were created equal but that all men were entitled to the same opportunities. The emphasis on political equality was an important difference between Jeffersonian and Jacksonian democracy. Jefferson had stood for the right of the "common man" to choose leaders from among those qualified to lead. Jackson enabled the ordinary man to consider himself worthy of political office. Jacksonian democracy made Americans distrustful of social rank and proud to be one of the great mass of average citizens.

Jackson himself was the prime example of this outlook. The first American president born in a log cabin, he had tremendous popular support as the hero of the common people. Since he entered the presidency with a limited understanding of the complexities of government, he and his followers insisted that social status and education were unnecessary for political leadership. Careers in politics were theoretically open to all men of talent, no matter how simple their origins.

Yet the Jacksonian era did not advance political democracy quite so much as many historians have claimed. Political power came not so much to the common man as to the shrewd, ambitious, and nouveaux-riches politicians who knew how to flatter the common man.

THE DEMOCRATIZATION OF POLITICS

It had been relatively easy to remove property qualifications for voting, state by state, in the decades following the Revolution. And the new Western states never placed any property restrictions on the franchise. By the 1850s all adult white men in the country could vote. However, there was no state in which women were allowed to vote, and only New England (with the exception of Connecticut) allowed free black men to vote. Free black men had once voted legally in certain other states as well, but only because of omissions in the voting laws. During the 1820s and 1830s these laws were deliberately changed to exclude blacks.

While the vote was being extended to larger numbers of white men, the social and economic structure of the country did not change significantly. Although men of talent and ambition could rise from poverty to positions of power, the luxurious homes of the very rich still contrasted sharply with the humble dwellings of the working classes. Pauperism was on the rise. Most city-dwellers were unable to climb out of the artisan and mechanic class; they continued to face long hours, frequent unemployment, and payment in depreciated money. Although they were better off than their European counterparts, most small farmers were still trapped in a life of frugality, hard work, monotony, and little leisure.

In fact political reformers did not claim that any social and economic changes would result from giving more people access to the political process. Mass suffrage, they reassured those in power, would have no effect on the class structure of society. "Will not our laws continue the same?" they asked. "Will not the administration of justice continue the same?"

Although a liberalized suffrage did not extend the vote to women and blacks, nor radically alter the class structure, it did create demands for certain political changes. Many state offices became elective, and voters began to participate more directly in the selection of the president. By 1832 presidential electors were chosen directly by the voters, in all states except South Carolina. Party nominating conventions replaced the secret congressional caucus which had named presidential candidates since Jefferson's time.

The vote came to be seen, for the first time, as a tool for influencing government policies. Such interest groups as small businessmen, unskilled workers, and large-scale farmers dis-

County election day was a festive affair. There is little evidence of piety at the polls in George Caleb Bingham's painting. (Boatmen's National Bank of St. Louis)

covered that tariffs, banking laws, and internal improvement legislation could all be changed by using their vote.

The mass of American voters began to take a personal interest in public policies. By the early 1800s their dislike for special privilege had led to the complete separation of church and state and to laws against monopolies in most states. The people were also becoming interested in educating themselves: the free school movement had begun, more people were acquiring secondary education, and there was a glimmer of enthusiasm for adult education. The number of newspapers grew, their prices declined, and political affairs received more publicity than ever before.

Office-seekers responded to the increasing political awareness of the American voters by openly and actively wooing them. The political parties had to appeal to broader sections of the public than they had when only men of property could vote. Mass enthusiasm for certain candidates was stimulated by increasingly theatrical campaigns. Political candidates staged parades and rallies, held barbecues, and gave away lavish amounts of hard cider. Their speeches often played on popular fears and prejudices.

Politicians of this era tended to be well-to-do (for such public appeals were expensive), but seldom were they aristocrats. Men of old wealth had been turned away by the increasing vulgarity of politics. Ambitious, opportunistic, and frequently hypocritical, the new breed of politician often cared more for success than for principle.

While the new political leaders of the 1820s debated such issues as the tariff, the national bank, and the sale of public lands, they all had the same attitude toward the proper order of society. They believed in the sanctity of property and accepted class structure and growing economic inequalities without question. Most of them accepted the institution of slavery, and most were unconcerned with the problems of working people. Reform movements to aid the enslaved, the poor, and the weak were largely led by people outside the mainstream of American politics.

JACKSON: THE PEOPLE'S CANDIDATE

Andrew Jackson was no exception. His background was perfectly suited to the demands of the new democratic politics. Born in the backwoods of South Carolina, he had lost his family and fought in the Revolutionary War by the time he was fourteen. After a few years spent carousing and brawling, he became a self-taught lawyer and moved into the Tennessee Territory. There he practiced law, married, and made friendships with influential people. He became a well-to-do planter and land speculator with a large plantation near Nashville which was worked by slave labor.

Jackson held various political jobs in the new state of Tennessee and eventually became general of the Tennessee militia. After his victory against the Creek Indians at the Battle of Horseshoe Bend in the War of 1812, he was made a general in the United States Army. His tremendous success in the Battle of New Orleans made him a great popular hero.

Jackson began to be mentioned by friends and politicians around the country as a presidential possibility in the 1824 election. His campaign appeal would be based on his record as a military hero, an Indian fighter, and as a symbol of the democratic forces of the West. His understanding of national issues, however, was hazy. While he was a man of intelligence, he had received little formal education, and his spelling and grammar were poor. His enemies thought of him as brutal and vulgar.

There was little, however, that was common or vulgar about Jackson himself. "Old Hickory" was a natural gentleman with easy manners and an independent mind. His judgment, though based on instinct, was usually sound. Over six feet tall, with proud military bearing and an impressive shock of white hair, the hot-tempered general was once characterized as "not taking kindly to culture but able to achieve wonderful things without it." He had an iron will and an iron constitution, as witnessed by his ability to withstand a persistent siege of illnesses that plagued him throughout his years in the White House.

Jackson's rise from humble origins to the nation's highest office made him a symbol of what could be achieved under a democratic system of government. The key to his success in politics was the same as it had been in war: he was a natural leader, a man whom people instinctively followed. He was supported and admired by people in every section of the country and in every social class. Since his convictions on public issues were virtually unknown when he ran for president, he was elected on the basis of personality alone.

THE ELECTION OF 1828

Picking up the pieces after the election of 1824, Senator Martin Van Buren recognized that the formless coalition of politicians calling themselves Jeffersonian Republicans was finished. He therefore conceived a plan to create in its place a new political coalition based on pure Jeffersonian principles—a coalition which would survive the country's growing sectionalism. He particularly wanted to purge the Jeffersonian party of neo-Federalist politicians like Clay, Webster, and Adams.

Van Buren was motivated in part by personal ambition, but he was also dedicated to the principle that government should be as limited and decentralized as possible in order to protect the people's liberty. His hopes rested on the people of the South and on the small farmers of the North because he believed that the Jeffersonian principles of equalitarianism and states' rights were most strongly held by these elements. The South was also most important in winning an election. It was Van Buren's hope to unite these elements behind the candidacy of the popular General Jackson.

By 1827 Van Buren's tireless behind-the-scenes efforts had produced a regrouping of political forces in the country. Now there were the Democratic-Republicans (called Democrats by the early 1830s) led by Jackson and the National Republicans (later called the Whigs) led by Adams and Clay. Along with Van Buren himself, those who backed Jackson's candidacy were all masters of the new party politics: Thomas Hart Benton of Missouri, John H. Eaton of Tennessee, and John C. Calhoun of South Carolina (who became Jackson's running mate in 1828).

In 1826 Adams lost his majority in Congress to Jackson's followers, and he knew then he had little chance of reelection. Adam's critics included those who disapproved of the American System, as well as those who disapproved of the president's handling of both public affairs and public relations. The antiadministration majority in Congress spent the full preelection year trying to undermine Adams' position by attacking his conduct of the presidency and his personal life.

In the meantime, Jackson, who believed he had been robbed of the election in 1824, spent the following four years trying to arouse popular support for his candidacy in 1828. Although his previous career had hardly shown him to be a devoted champion of democracy, he almost instinctively associated himself with that position after 1824. He had taken a firm stand against paper money and inflationary banking policy during the Panic of 1819, and this endeared him to many who saw banks as undemocratic institutions.

The campaign of 1828 degenerated into a hostile personal clash; there was almost no discussion of national issues. It was the first really expensive campaign in American history (it cost the Jacksonians $1 million). Mud-slinging, misrepresentation, and name-calling escalated on both sides. Jackson was accused of being a "drunk," a "tyrant," and a "gambler." His ailing wife Rachel was attacked by the opposition as a "convicted adulteress" (her divorce from a previous husband was discovered not to have been legally final when she married Jackson). Adams, on the other hand, was accused of paying for private possessions with public money, of supplying the Russian Czar with a young American mistress, and of pandering to private interests in the administration of public lands. The accusations from both sides descended to the most degrading depths the country had yet seen in a political campaign.

Unaided by party platforms or debates on the issues, the voters followed their emotions. Most backed the candidate they thought would

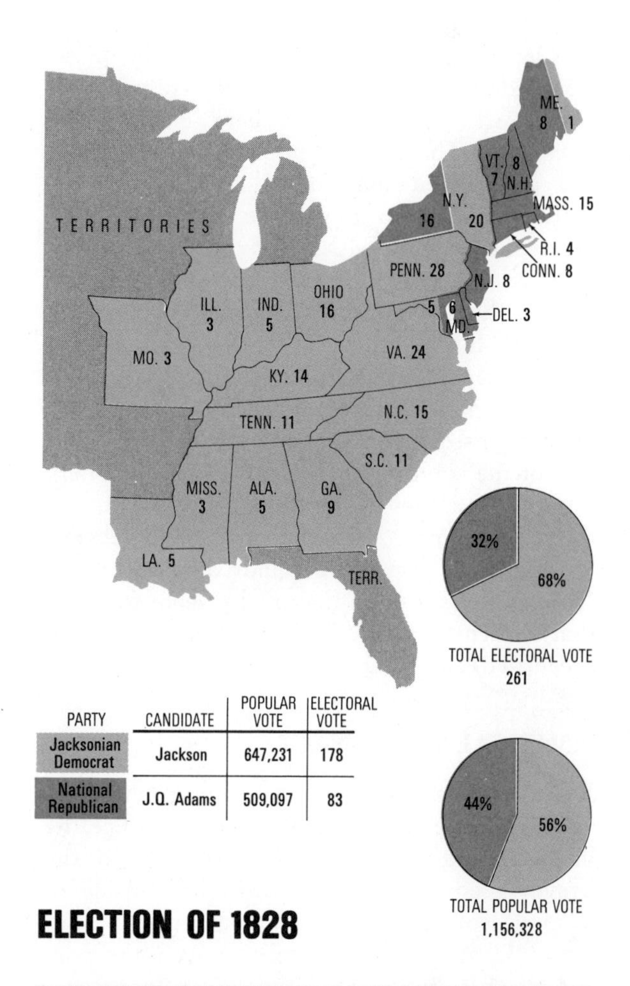

PARTY	CANDIDATE	POPULAR VOTE	ELECTORAL VOTE
Jacksonian Democrat	Jackson	647,231	178
National Republican	J.Q. Adams	509,097	83

ELECTION OF 1828

protect the interests of the people against special privilege. Jackson received fifty-six percent of the popular vote, taking all nine states west of the Appalachians and a substantial portion of the urban labor vote in the East. In the electoral college he won with 178 votes to Adams' 83. The Jacksonians also controlled both houses of Congress.

Jacksonian Politics

On March 4, 1829, the day of Jackson's inauguration, ten thousand visitors jammed into Washington, whose population was only eighteen thousand. When Jackson emerged on the Capitol portico, the crowd cheered wildly. After taking the Oath of Office, he pushed through the mobs, mounted his horse, and rode to the White House. The crowd followed on horseback, on foot, and in wagons. They surged into the White House and interrupted the official reception. Well-wishers climbed up on delicate chairs, swarmed over valuable rugs with muddy boots, shouted, overturned furniture, broke glassware, and even pressed the new president helplessly against the wall—all to express their approval. Their hero had to escape through a rear window.

The unplanned celebration evoked a variety of reactions. Some political observers expressed fear of the coming rule by "King Mob." Others saw the festivities as symbolic of the victory of the common man. According to Daniel Webster, "People have come five hundred miles to see General Jackson, and they really seem to think that the country has been rescued from some dreadful danger."

POLITICAL PATRONAGE

Jackson immediately set out to bring new faces into the government. Long terms in office, he claimed, had corrupted many officials in the previous administration. "Office is considered a species of property," he complained to Congress. Conveniently, "reform" paved the way for a redistribution of this political "property" to Jacksonians.

Party workers who had proven their loyalty were frequently rewarded with public offices. Ideally, such appointees would be most able to carry out the party's principles and the voters' desires. This, however, was not always the case. Many political appointees began to view their jobs as a lucrative livelihood, rather than as a responsibility. The term for this practice, the "spoils system," carried an apt connotation of plunder.

There was nothing new about firing opposition officeholders to give jobs to deserving partisans. It had long been the policy in New York and other Northern states. Previous presidents had removed men from office without creating much attention. But there had not been a real political shift in the national government for many years; there had been virtual one-party rule since Thomas Jefferson's presidency. Jackson's actions thus seemed revolutionary.

In practice, President Jackson used the spoils system with moderation. He wisely did not fire experts in the departments of the army and navy. Nor did he dismiss judges or high-ranking diplomats. In fact, he replaced only about 252 presidential appointees out of 612, and only about 900 of the more than 10,000 officeholders on the government payroll.

The concept of reward was not the only key to understanding Jackson's use of the spoils system. Jackson believed that appointive offices should be democratically rotated among different people, both to prevent corruption and to increase opportunities for wider participation in government. Jackson tended to play down the importance of training and experience in politi-

"Office Hunters for the Year 1834" is an anonymous cartoon. In it Jackson is depicted as a winged demon dangling offices, bags of money, and other "spoils" within tantalizing reach of the crowds below.

cal office. He felt that the duties connected with such offices were essentially simple, and that any man of intelligence could readily assume them. Holding the same office for a long time bred indifference, he felt, and this was far worse than any of the problems that might arise from periodic rotation in office.

As it turned out, some of Jackson's appointees were more corrupt and inefficient than their predecessors. Samuel Swartwout was a flagrant example; he was given the collectorship of the Port of New York for his diligence in the 1828 campaign. In less than ten years Swartwout managed to steal over one million dollars from the government.

A STRONG PRESIDENCY

During the presidential campaign Jackson's opponents had portrayed him as a simple soldier being manipulated by greedy politicians. His behavior in office, however, left little doubt that he was clearly his own master. Although Jackson had his speeches written for him and sought advice from his personal friends and campaign backers in his unofficial "Kitchen Cabinet" (which included Martin Van Buren, whom he had appointed secretary of state), he ultimately made his own decisions.

Whereas earlier presidents had accepted the idea of an equal balance among the three branches of government, Jackson felt that the executive branch was supreme. The president alone, he maintained, was elected by the whole country. The people were always right, and as president he was their spokesman.

To exercise this supreme power given him by the people, Jackson did not hesitate to use his power to veto congressional legislation. Together, all of his predecessors had vetoed only

◀ *Jackson's adversaries attacked his position on the veto, the spoils system, and internal improvements. Here they caricature him as King Andrew I, a power-hungry monarch grinding the Constitution underfoot during his "reign."*

nine bills, in every case on the grounds that the bill in question was unconstitutional. Jackson alone vetoed twelve bills. In some cases he acted on the basis of personal disapproval; in other cases he thought the bills would have granted powers to the federal government which had already been delegated to the states. Jackson was also the first president to use the "pocket veto"—leaving a bill unsigned until Congress adjourned, automatically preventing it from becoming law.

By his dramatic use of the office of president, Jackson made policy rather than merely carrying out the law. He announced policies, vetoed bills, and appointed and dismissed subordinates, all in the name of the people. This innovative concept of presidential power enabled the chief executive to put pressure on Congress, the Supreme Court, and foreign governments. Jackson's determination to play a powerful role in the government ended an era of strong congressional leadership and contributed directly to the modern concept of the presidency.

FOREIGN AFFAIRS UNDER JACKSON

In foreign affairs Andrew Jackson was stubborn and extravagantly patriotic. These qualities often caused him to take unnecessary risks for petty victories, but they also helped him straighten out several longstanding diplomatic tangles. In addition, his strongly nationalistic foreign policy helped Jackson strengthen loyalty and cohesion within the Democratic party.

Ever since the Revolution the United States had been trying to persuade the British to reopen West Indian trade to American shipping. It was Jackson, negotiating with patience and tact, who finally succeeded. Though he privately threatened to respond "with the promptness and energy due our national character" if Britain continued to delay a settlement, he made a concession to which the British finally responded. In what was called the "Reciprocity of 1830," Jackson granted British ships the same access to American ports that ships of all other countries enjoyed, repealing retaliatory duties. The British government then opened its West Indian islands to direct trade with the United States, but subject to such duties as it might decide to impose.

Using a tougher approach, the president also succeeded in forcing foreign countries to settle damage claims from the Napoleonic Wars. France, for example, had agreed in 1831 to pay

American claims against ships and cargoes damaged or destroyed in the wars. In 1833 the United States presented France a $1 million bill for the first payment and the French Chamber of Deputies refused to provide the funds. Jackson was furious, especially since the government now owed the Bank of the United States $170,000 for preparing the bill. When the French continued to delay, he sent a message to Congress calling for "a law authorizing reprisals upon French property." Congress refused to act on his request, believing it might lead to war. Jackson countered by breaking off diplomatic relations with France and ordering the navy readied. Insulted, the French sent a fleet of their own to the West Indies.

In 1835 France changed course and voted the money to pay the claims. However she refused to turn over the funds until given "satisfactory explanations" of the language used by Jackson. "We will not permit France or any, or all European governments to dictate to the President what language he shall use," thundered Jackson, and the crisis mounted.

War was averted, however, when Jackson's advisers convinced him to modify the tone of his comments and disclaim any intention of insulting France. The quarrel was resolved and in 1836 the French payments began to flow regularly into the American treasury.

INDIAN REMOVAL

Jackson's Indian policy was as forceful as his diplomacy. It repelled only a few humanitarian critics in the Northeast, most of whom were already anti-Jacksonian National Republicans anyway.

Southerners, Westerners, and land speculators everywhere were delighted when the president introduced a plan to remove all Indian tribes to reservations west of the Mississippi. Removal had been started by Jefferson, but it had not been carried out with dispatch and had slowed down considerably under Adams' even-handed approach.

Jackson vigorously revived the removal policy soon after he took office. He based his actions on his professed belief that Indians were unhappy living among white people, and also on the grounds that removal was the only way to protect the tribes from extermination by white settlers. Jackson was a Westerner, an expansionist, and an old Indian fighter. He had refused to enforce the Act of 1802 in which the federal government promised to oust intruders on Indian lands. He claimed to believe the act unconstitutional. He also claimed that it was lawful for the president to use military force to remove intruders only when force was absolutely necessary. Even if it had wanted to, the federal government could not have provided a standing army large enough to protect the Indians' ancestral lands from encroachment by white settlers. "Doubtless it will be painful to leave the graves of their fathers," Jackson acknowledged, but it was only necessary to "open the eyes of those children of the forest to their true condition" to make them recognize the "humanity and justice" of their removal.

The plan was insensitive to the claims and traditions of the Indians and its execution was brutal. Tribes were given "evacuation treaties" and token payment for their lands, and then they were made to move west. Federal agents often tricked, coerced, or bribed tribal chiefs into signing away their lands. If these methods did not work, the chiefs were plied with liquor. Grasping white settlers often drove Indians off their property before preparations to migrate could be completed. The land the Indians were forced to settle was rarely as fertile as that from which they were driven.

The migrations themselves were poorly planned and caused great suffering. Indians from the South, for instance, thinly dressed and without moccasins, were forced to move North in December. They crossed the Mississippi in zero degree weather. During the journeys, measles took hundreds of lives. A cholera epidemic in 1832 further thinned out the tribes.

Alexis de Tocqueville, author of *Democracy*

Robert Lindneux represented the Indians' suffering on the Trail of Tears in this painting. (Woolaroc Museum, Bartlesville, Oklahoma)

in America, watched as a group of Choctaw Indians began crossing the Mississippi River at Memphis. "Never will that solemn spectacle fade from my remembrance," he wrote. "No cry, no sob, was heard among the assembled crowd; all was silent. Their calamities were of ancient date, and they knew them to be irremediable." Later historians have called this western trek of the Indians a "trail of tears." Ralph Waldo Emerson protested that "such a dereliction of all faith and virtue, such a denial of justice, and such deafness to screams for mercy were never heard of in time of peace . . . since the earth was made."

The forced migration of Indians went on for more than ten years. Only a few tribes resisted the policy and these were treated severely. In 1832 Chief Black Hawk led about one thousand Sac and Fox Indians back across the Mississippi River to Illinois, hoping to find a hospitable prairie in which to plant a crop of corn for his starving people. Their attempted return, referred to as the Black Hawk War, was quickly ended by militia and regular army troops.

In the vastness of the Florida Everglades, however, the Seminoles were able to wage a more effective, though equally futile fight. Led by Chief Osceola and supported by a great number of runaway slaves, the Seminoles managed to hold off the United States Army from 1835 to 1842. Their rebellion cost the United States about $40 million and two thousand lives. Most of the Seminoles were wiped out, and the army only managed to capture Osceola himself by treacherously seizing him during a peace conference.

The Cherokees of Georgia fought for their cultivated lands with legal action. They had adopted many of the white people's ways, becoming farmers and cattle raisers, building roads, houses, churches, and schools. Convinced that literacy was the key to their survival, they developed a written language, printed Bibles, and published a weekly newspaper. In 1827 they drafted a constitution and formed a Cherokee state within the state of Georgia. The United States formally recognized the Cherokee nation, but Georgia did not. In 1828 Georgia passed a law nullifying all Cherokee laws and claiming Cherokee lands.

Friends of the Cherokees appealed to the Supreme Court to restrain Georgia from enforcing its laws over the Indians and from seizing their lands. In *Cherokee Nation* v. *Georgia* (1831) the Court ruled that an Indian tribe was not a state nor a foreign nation. Therefore it could not maintain an action in the federal courts. However, Indians were "domestic dependent nations" under United States sovereignty and they had a right to the land they occupied until title to it had been transferred to the federal government. The following year, in *Worcester* v. *Georgia* Chief Justice Marshall held further that the Cherokee nation was a distinct political community where Georgia law

"A Bivouack in Safety, or Florida Troops Preventing a Surprise" shows the cartoonist's (and the public's). skepticism about the army's role in the Seminole War in Florida. ▼

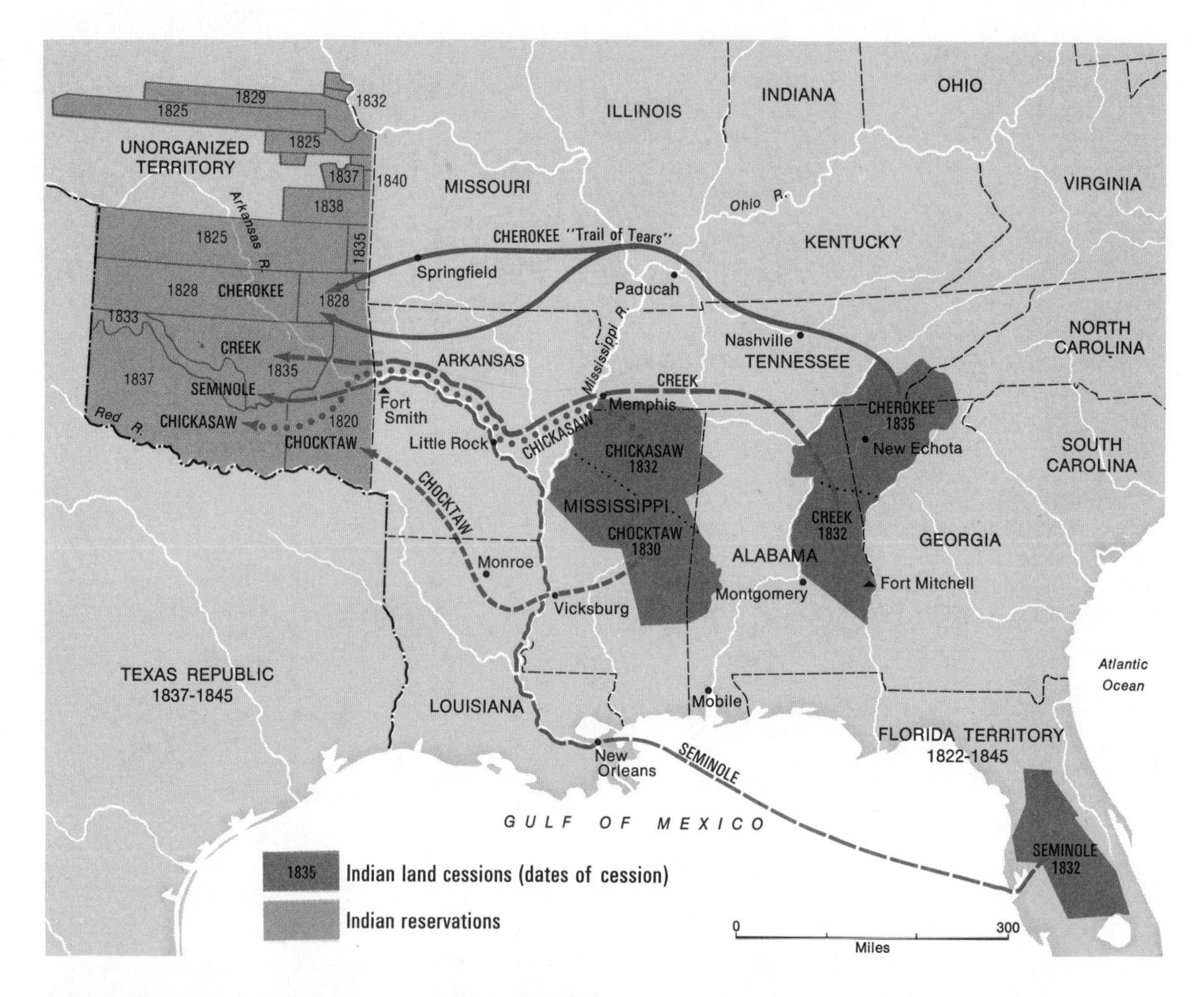

INDIAN LAND CESSIONS AND MIGRATIONS • 1820 TO 1840

had no force and Georgia citizens could not enter without consent.

Without legal support, but with the tacit approval of the White House, Georgia defied the Supreme Court rulings and forced the evacuation of the Cherokee nation to Oklahoma. The Cherokee removal began without notice in the middle of winter. Whites took the Indians' livestock, farm tools, and household belongings. On the trek west, about one hundred Cherokees died each day from cold, hunger, or disease.

The only Western statesman to denounce the treatment of the Cherokees was Henry Clay. Although the Indians had no vote, and although his constituents in Kentucky had no interest in the matter, Clay made a fervent speech in the Senate in 1835. He accused Georgia of violating the most elementary principles of justice and decency, and severely criticized Jackson. But Jackson refused to oppose Georgia. He was a Westerner, forever unsympathetic to the Indians, and convinced that their removal was desirable and endorsed by the majority of Americans. Opposition to Indian removal would also have cost him the votes of several Southern states.

Jackson's Indian policy was typical of his party's pro-Western, agrarian, states' rights outlook, and of its inconsistent interpretation of the Constitution. Although the Democrats claimed that using federal troops to protect the Indians from white expansion would be unconstitutional, they apparently had no constitutional compunctions about using federal military might to enforce the removal of Indians from their lands. Despite the Democrats' pious statements about protecting the Indians, they betrayed their expansionist bias when they set up the Bureau of Indian Affairs as an agency within the War Department. They cited states' rights in their refusal to interfere with Georgia's internal affairs. Strict construction was the basis for their claim that recognizing the Cherokee nation would violate the constitutional provision that no state could be established within another state without the approval of the state legislature as well as Congress. By tacitly supporting Georgia's defiance of Supreme Court decisions, Jackson's administration also betrayed some sympathy for the notion that states could nullify federal laws or court decisions they considered unconstitutional.

Sectional Controversy

From the very beginning of his presidency Jackson faced the problem of holding together the separate factions that had elected him. The Democratic party was a loose coalition of different and often conflicting sectional interests. Northern Democrats wanted to maintain a high tariff; Southern Democrats to reduce it. Westerners wanted to lower the price of federal lands; New Englanders wanted to leave it as it was.

The Democrats had a majority in Congress but they seldom voted as a unit. Some Democratic representatives even changed parties when they found themselves disagreeing with the president. Other representatives who originally opposed Jackson came into the Democratic party when they discovered that they agreed with him on a crucial issue.

INTERNAL IMPROVEMENTS

One of the early issues that caused shifts in party affiliations concerned internal improvements. Democrats in the West firmly supported federal financial backing for roads and canals. Democrats in the South, New York, and Pennsylvania were adamantly opposed to this part of the American System. New York and Pennsylvania had financed their own internal improvements and were not enthusiastic about Western competition. No matter what position he took the president was sure to antagonize some elements of his party.

Jackson announced his position on internal improvements in 1830, when he vetoed a bill authorizing federal funding for a sixty-mile road from Maysville to Lexington, Kentucky. The road was to be a part of a projected interstate system. Jackson said that he opposed as unconstitutional the use of federal monies for internal impovements within a state; he was not opposed if the projects were national in scope. At Van Buren's suggestion, he even hinted that all public programs at federal expense might be unconstitutional.

The Maysville Road veto was a shrewd political move aimed at pleasing the majority of voters, which it did. Most people agreed with

Jackson that federal funds should be saved to pay off the public debt. His veto did not affect many votes, and it showed the administration's regard for economy and their determination to show that they were strict constructionists. The veto had also enabled Jackson to strike a blow at Clay, who had fervently backed the Maysville Road for his home state. After the veto, Clay took up the issue with even greater passion. He exploited it particularly in the West, where the construction of improved transportation was often the only national issue of interest to voters.

The Maysville Road veto did not completely stop the use of federal funds for internal improvements. Jackson himself actually endorsed an average of $1.3 million per year in internal improvement bills, including some that gave federal funds for local projects. But he had made his point: his party stood for limiting the use of federal power.

PUBLIC LANDS

Jackson agreed with Westerners that the government should encourage the settlement of public lands by selling it cheaply. The alternative, Adams' policy, had been to keep land prices high in order to bring as much money as possible into the federal treasury.

Senator Thomas Hart Benton of Missouri suggested that the government gradually lower the price of poor public land from one dollar and a quarter per acre to fifty cents an acre, and finally give away free to settlers whatever remained unsold. This scheme was called graduation. Under another plan, squatters already settled illegally on 160 acre quarter-plots of public land would be given an option to buy as soon as the government offered the land for sale. This scheme was called preemption.

These two plans, which Jackson liked, placed more importance on opening up the country to settlement than on financial gain for the treasury. Jackson believed that settlers should be able to buy land in small tracts for little more than it cost to survey and clear away Indian titles. He also felt that each new state should be given the public lands that lay within its borders. In 1832 he told Congress that "the public lands shall cease as soon as practicable to be a source of revenue."

Moderate though these plans were, they greatly displeased Easterners, who viewed western migration as a severe drain on their sources of labor. They feared that those who stayed behind would demand higher wages for their scarce services. Completely opposed to graduation and preemption, Easterners proposed legislation to halt altogether the survey and sale of new lands in the West.

To resolve this conflict, Clay suggested a compromise. Instead of giving public lands to individual Western states, the land should be sold; ten percent of the proceeds could go to the Western states and the remaining revenue could be distributed among all the states. Congress passed Clay's distribution scheme in 1833, but Jackson, still siding with the West, vetoed it. Jackson never did settle the land question during his time in office.

NULLIFICATION

The most divisive sectional controversy of Jackson's administration arose over Southern opposition to protective tariffs passed after 1816. Because the tariff raised the price of everything they bought but protected nothing they sold, Southerners felt that they were paying too large a share of federal taxes. To make matters worse, much of the income from the tariff was going for internal improvements outside of the South.

As the tariff increased, many Southerners began to feel more and more discriminated against. The loudest outcries came from South Carolina. The state was in economic and social trouble, and it saw the spirit of nationalism in the country and the tariff as the cause of its ills.

South Carolina's plantation aristocracy was already uneasy over race relations and feared that a powerful federal government might tamper with the institution of slavery. The state's slave population already outnumbered its white citizens. The white population had also been badly shaken by Denmark Vesey's unsuccessful slave conspiracy of 1822. South Carolina was the first Southern state to develop an acute nervousness on the subject of slavery. This uneasiness made South Carolinians particularly sensitive to the need to protect their state's right to define her own institutions and way of life without federal interference.

Uneasiness over slavery was a chronic condition, but South Carolina's acute economic difficulties in the 1820s increased the state's paranoia. The days when the state had flourished and planters had made huge fortunes cultivating rice and cotton had ended with the Panic of 1819. Cotton prices had dropped in the ensuing depression and had fallen even lower as the new states of Alabama and Mississippi increased the world's supply of cotton. South Carolina's profits fell disastrously as its worn-out fields produced smaller yields at higher production costs. The state's population stagnated as ambitious farmers emigrated west looking for better land. Unwilling to blame their misery on soil exhaustion and competition from newer states, South Carolinians blamed the tariff and other federal encroachments as the real culprits.

By the 1820s people all over the South were swarming to public meetings to protest the tariff. When Jackson first took office he had pleased protectionists by endorsing import duties on "all products that may be found essential to our national independence." As Southern objections increased, however, he saw that the tariff was a divisive issue. So he shifted his position by asking Congress for a revenue tariff that would give only "temporary and, generally, incidental protection," a position more in line with traditional Jeffersonian economic theory. The president's reversal, while antagonizing the protectionists, encouraged the South Carolina legislature to assume (incorrectly) that he would tolerate direct state action against the high import duties.

Calhoun's doctrine

Southern opposition to protective tariffs also posed a dilemma for Vice-President Calhoun, South Carolina's leading politician. For several years after 1816 he had been both a nationalist and a protectionist. But by the 1820s he had to modify his views to satisfy his constituency, without at the same time offending Northern and Southern friends whose support he needed to further his ambition for the presidency.

In 1828 Calhoun published an unsigned essay attacking that year's Tariff of Abominations. It was apparent from the document that Calhoun had become a strong supporter of states' rights. He proposed the doctrine of nullification as a means for a numerical minority, such as the South, to protect itself from offensive laws passed by the majority. Nullification would give a state legislature the right to decide whether or not a federal law was constitutional and if it was not, to vote to prevent its intrastate enforcement.

Calhoun's nullification doctrine borrowed a line of reasoning from the Virginia and Kentucky Resolutions of 1798. Like them, he argued that the states had been completely sovereign before 1787 and that they had not surrendered their sovereignty when they ratified the Constitution. They had merely formed a "compact" creating a federal government to serve as their "agent" for executing the powers provided in the compact. The agent had limited powers and these were determined, not by the Supreme Court, but by the sovereign states. Since the protective tariff resulted in one-third of the country paying two-thirds of the federal government's expenses, the federal government had obviously exceeded its powers.

Unlike Jefferson in the Kentucky Resolutions, Calhoun did not propose that a majority of the states would be needed to nullify a federal law. Each state had the right to judge when its "agent" had overstepped its authority. Delegates to a popularly elected state convention could vote to declare a law null and void within their state. Congress could only prevent them from doing so by getting three-quarters of the states to ratify a new amendment which would establish the constitutionality of the controversial law. If the federal government tried to coerce a state into accepting legislation, the state had the right to secede from the Union. Calhoun believed this scheme would protect the minority South and encourage Congress to pass only those bills that would benefit the entire country.

In 1830 Calhoun's doctrine had a full-scale review in the Senate when a debate over public land policy expanded to an examination of the nature of the federal union. Calhoun, vice-president and presiding officer of the Senate, listened as his spokesman, Robert Hayne of South Carolina, brilliantly explained and defended the concept of nullification, recited the South's grievances, and appealed to the West to adopt the doctrine as a means of preventing enforcement of policies that would limit the sale of public lands.

Daniel Webster responded to Hayne in the most eloquent speech of his career. Webster held the attention of the Senate galleries for two days while he argued that the sovereignty of the states was limited by the Constitution. He denied that the federal government was an agent of the states. "It is," he said, "the people's constitution, the people's government, made for the people, made by the people, and answerable to the people." If a state felt that it had not been justly treated, it could seek action in the courts, at the polls, or in the amending process. Otherwise, any disturbance of federal sovereignty by a state would be considered treasonable and could lead to civil war. Webster closed his speech with the phrase, "Liberty and Union, now and forever, one and inseparable!"

Jackson splits with Calhoun

Although the Democrats tended to favor states' rights and a low tariff, Jackson would not tolerate an attack on the legitimate use of federal power which had been specifically provided in the Constiution. He made his position quite clear at a Democratic party banquet celebrating Jefferson's birthday shortly after the Webster–Hayne debate. Calhoun and his followers tried to use the occasion to gather support for their cause. They proposed toast after toast, each subtly implying a connection between nullification and Democratic party principles. Jackson sat patiently and silently through twenty-three toasts. Then he rose, raised his glass, and said "Our Federal Union—It must be preserved."

Calhoun, his political career already in jeopardy, brought his relations with the president to the breaking point with his immediate and defiant countertoast: "The Union—next to our liberty, the most dear! May we all remember that it can only be preserved by respecting the rights of the states and distributing equally the benefits and burdens of the Union."

The rift between the president and vice-president was encouraged by Secretary of State Van Buren, who hoped to take Calhoun's place as Jackson's presidential heir. Van Buren had two episodes, other than the banquet encounter, going for him. The first was a social clash created by administration wives when Secretary of War John Eaton married Peggy O'Neale, the attractive but morally suspect daughter of a tavernkeeper. Mrs. Calhoun's refusal to receive the "hussy" was quickly imitated by the wives of other cabinet members, senators, and representatives. Always gallant about ladies and still passionately haunted by the memory of slander against his own wife before her death, Jackson was outraged by the incident. He promptly pronounced Peggy Eaton "as chaste as a virgin." Van Buren, also a widower, went out of his way to pay Mrs. Eaton marked attention.

The second episode working in Van Buren's favor was built on the division caused by the Eaton gossip. William H. Crawford, an old political enemy of Calhoun's, let it be known that in 1818, when he was secretary of war, Calhoun had criticized Jackson's invasion of Florida. Calhoun defended himself with a long, explanatory letter, but Jackson immediately rejected it as "full evidence of the duplicity and insincerity of the man."

In 1831 Jackson reorganized his cabinet at Van Buren's urging, and forced Calhoun's friends out of the administration. Shunted aside as a national leader, Calhoun was now in the position of being chief defender of the South.

The South Carolina showdown

While Jackson and Calhoun were drifting apart the nullification controversy simmered for a few years and South Carolina waited for Congress to reduce the Tariff of Abominations. But when Congress passed a new tariff in 1832 the controversy flared up again. Although the new legislation reduced tariffs to their 1824 levels, the duties were still considered intolerably high by the South.

The South Carolina legislature called for a convention to draw up an Ordinance of Nullification. The delegates declared the tariffs of both 1828 and 1832 null and void, and forbade the collection of federal duties within the state. Furthermore, the state legislature voted funds to raise a volunteer army to defend the state from "invasion."

Interpreting South Carolina's actions as open defiance, Jackson quickly reinforced the federal army and navy; he hoped that a show of force would result in a peaceful political solution. Jackson did not want war, and he rightly calculated that South Carolina felt the same way. He issued an official proclamation on December 10, declaring nullification "incompatible with the existence of the Union, contradicted expressly by the letter of the Constitution, unauthorized by its spirit, inconsistent with every principle on which it is founded, and destructive of the great object for which it was formed." Nullification was treasonous; nullifiers were traitors to be punished by force. Jackson concluded, "The laws of the United States must be executed. I have no discretionary power on the subject; my duty is emphatically pronounced in the Constitution."

Jackson asked Congress to pass a force bill giving him the authority to use the army and navy, if necessary, to collect customs duties. But at the same time, he called for a new tariff bill that would significantly lower duties.

Meanwhile, South Carolina was weakened. Not only was it divided within its own ranks, but the support it had counted on from the other Southern states had not materialized. Virginia said that nullification was a caricature of her Resolutions of 1798, Georgia "abhorred the doctrine," and Alabama denounced it as "unsound in theory and dangerous in practice." South Carolina stood alone.

It was all too obvious that a military showdown would be virtually suicidal for South Carolina. But conceding defeat would incur a loss of prestige and the ruination of its political leaders. The state and Calhoun were saved by the intervention of the "Great Pacificator," Henry Clay. He devised a compromise that would gradually lower tariff rates over a ten-year period to no higher than twenty percent. Calhoun endorsed the plan as a means of compromise.

The tariff bill was passed, ironically, on the same day as the force bill. Daniel Webster objected to making any concessions to the nullifiers, but Jackson signed both measures, confident that national harmony would now be restored. Although he had not effected a permanent solution, he nevertheless managed to relax national tensions on a crucial issue and avoid a military confrontation.

The South Carolina convention reassembled and repealed its Ordinance of Nullification. But to save face it also nullified the force bill, even though it had already been withdrawn. Since the crisis had actually resulted in the lowering of the tariff, Calhoun and his followers claimed a victory. They continued to work for nullification by building Southern solidarity until that day when a united Southern front might effectively resist federal political and military power. Calhoun's group also worked more closely with Clay for the next few years in an effort to embarrass Jackson whenever possible.

The Bank War

As the election of 1832 approached, Jackson's stand against the Bank of the United States became an extremely popular, if not prudent, issue in his campaign. Jackson had opposed the bank before he became president and had criticized it steadily during his first term. The bank became the primary issue of his reelection campaign, and his second term was dominated by his obsession to destroy the "monster." The old general's combative position was based on instinct rather than a sound understanding of economics.

Jackson was supported in his passion to destroy the bank by a coalition of agrarian-minded Southerners, ambitious Westerners, and Eastern intellectuals and workers. Some of these people resented any central bank with the power to control state banks. Others distrusted all banks and regarded the Bank of the United States as a prime offender and natural target for reform. All feared the power and monopolistic privilege of the national bank, with its enormous sums controlled by a few rich and powerful people with little regulation from the Congress or the chief executive.

The Bank of the United States had been a stabilizing factor in the nation's economy. Its power needed to be checked, not crushed. As the American economy entered a dangerous inflationary cycle in the 1830s, the destruction of the national bank removed the only remaining brake on credit expansion. The nation plunged into frenzied speculation that culminated in panic and a major depression.

THE "MONSTER" INSTITUTION

In 1823 a sophisticated and brilliant banker, Nicholas Biddle, had become the president of the second national bank. Under his direction it became a conservative and responsibly administered business enterprise. Biddle was an astute economist who recognized that the bank and its twenty-nine branches had the potential to regulate the growing American economy. Under his careful direction, the bank bought and sold government bonds, advanced loans to the business community, and issued bank notes that gave the country a sound and uniform paper currency. It also restrained state banks from reckless lending policies by forcing them to back their own notes with gold and silver and to repay loans from the national bank on demand. This control over the flow and exchange of money gave the national bank tremendous influence. And since Biddle knew much more about banking than did his board of directors, the power of the bank lay entirely in his hands.

Biddle's careful regulation protected the state banks and the nation's economy as well as the bank itself, but the institution still met with considerable opposition. A distrust of paper money and bankers still lingered from the days of Adams and Jefferson. Jackson was among those who wanted all transactions to be made in hard money, gold and silver. Many workers whose wages were paid in fluctuating paper agreed. Resentment of the great power of the institution was increased by the fact that it ultimately acquired much of the coin that had been in the other banks.

The business community was divided in its opinions of the bank. The more stable and traditional business elements, such as the old merchant firms, wanted sound money and supported the institution. But the newer, less-established elements wanted more inflated paper money rather than less.

Because the national bank controlled the amount of money available to state banks, local businesses found it more difficult to borrow. They resented the Bank of the United States because they considered its credit policies too tight. They wanted the bank to allow more paper to circulate. Some business and government officials also condemned the bank as a monopoly that held federal funds without being subject to federal controls. States' rights and working-class groups opposed the bank because it was not provided for in the Constitution. Their antagonism was certainly not lessened by the fact that Biddle was wealthy, charming, and cultured. New Yorkers were particularly hostile to the bank, for it diverted the financial plum of customs revenues from the port of New York to the bank's head office in Philadelphia.

Jacksonians suspected the bank of supporting their political rivals. Biddle's bank had, in fact, been relatively circumspect before 1832. But that changed when Biddle found himself in a life-or-death struggle with the president. Biddle was frequently accused of corrupting politicians and editors with generous loans. Daniel Webster not only borrowed heavily but was on the bank's payroll, supposedly as a legal counselor. "I believe my retainer has not been renewed or *refreshed as usual,*" he wrote Biddle on one occasion. "If it be wished that my relation to the bank should be continued, it may be well to send me the usual retainer."

Wary of all this opposition, the bank's supporters tried to outmaneuver Jackson. Biddle visited the president and assured him of the bank's sound financial position. He appointed Democrats as directors of branches and told the president he would accept some restrictions on the bank's power. But Biddle was sure that Jackson remained hostile. He therefore worked with Clay and Webster to get the bank rechartered before the election of 1832, even though the charter would not expire until 1836.

Clay assured Biddle that the bank would be rechartered. This put the president in an embarrassing position. Since Clay believed that the bank was popular in the country, he thought Jackson would not dare veto the bank bill. But if the president signed the bill, the nation would believe him to be a hypocrite. If he vetoed it, he would provide the National Republicans with a winning issue for the 1832 campaign.

As Clay had predicted, the bank bill did pass both houses (with restrictions on its powers) by July 1832. It then went to the White House for the president's signature.

"Race over Uncle Sam's Course" satirizes the battle over the Bank of the United States. Henry Clay (right) supported the bank and is shown winning the race. Andrew Jackson (with Van Buren on the back of a jackass) is shown losing the race. Jackson did eventually win his battle.

Attacking the Constitutionality of the National Bank

"It is maintained by the advocates of the bank that its constitutionality in all its features ought to be considered as settled by precedent and by the decision of the Supreme Court. To this conclusion I can not assent. Mere precedent is a dangerous source of authority, and should not be regarded as deciding questions of constitutional power except where the acquiescence of the people and the States can be considered as well settled . . . .

If the opinion of the Supreme Court covered the whole ground of this act, it ought not to control the coordinate authorities of this Government. . . . The opinion of the judges has no more authority over Congress than the opinion of Congress has over the judges, and on that point the President is independent of both. The authority of the Supreme Court must not, therefore, be permitted to control the Congress or the Executive when acting in their legislative capacities, but to have only such influence as the force of their reasoning may deserve."

Andrew Jackson,
July 10, 1832

Defending the Constitutionality of the National Bank

"I now proceed, Sir, to a few remarks upon the President's constitutional objections to the Bank; and I cannot forbear to say, in regard to them, that he appears to me to have assumed very extraordinary grounds of reasoning.

Hitherto it has been thought that the final decision of constitutional questions belonged to the supreme judicial tribunal. The very nature of free government, it has been supposed, enjoins this; and our Constitution, moreover, has been understood so to provide, clearly and expressly . . . .

The President is as much bound by the law as any private citizen, and can no more contest its validity than any private citizen. He may refuse to obey the law, and so may a private citizen; but both do it at their own peril, and neither of them can settle the question of its validity. The President may *say* a law is unconstitutional, but he is not the judge. The judiciary alone possess this unquestionable and hitherto unquestioned right. . . ."

**Daniel Webster,
July 11, 1832**

THE BANK VETO

Jackson promptly vetoed the bill, with the following statement:

> There are no necessary evils in the government. Its evils exist only in its abuses. If it would confine itself to equal protection, and, as Heaven does its rains, shower its favors alike on the high and low, the rich and the poor, it would be an unqualified blessing. In the act before me [for rechartering the Bank of the United States] there seems to be a wide and unnecessary departure from these just principles . . . .

Jackson's veto message is the first instance in American history of a president taking his appeal directly to the people. His opponents, more comfortable with the old style of politics which left decision-making to the statesmen, were offended and alarmed by this new democratic tactic. They accused Jackson of stirring up the poor against the rich, and predicted the onset of class conflict if this style of political behavior were to succeed.

Jackson's veto message, intended for the general public, largely ignored the complex economic questions involved in the bank issue and concentrated its arguments on those points most likely to arouse emotion. Jackson—like others before him—attacked the bank as a monopoly with a stranglehold over the nation's economic development. Much of its stock was not even in American hands but had been bought by foreigners. He charged that since the Constitution had not specifically provided for a national bank, the bank was unconstitutional. Finally, he claimed that the bank was an invasion of the states' rights and favored the economic development of the East at the expense of the West.

The president's message was a masterpiece of political propaganda. He clearly saw the bank's political weaknesses and exploited them for party advantage. While his definition of the bank as a monopoly was technically incorrect (it made only twenty percent of the country's bank loans and issued only twenty percent of the paper money), it was in fact a powerful institution. Jackson's stand on behalf of economic equality and against special privilege strengthened his reputation as the champion of the common people.

Even though the Supreme Court had ruled that the bank was constitutional in *McCulloch v. Maryland* (1819), many people, including the president, did not accept the validity of that decision. Jackson's message was a dramatic appeal to American patriotism and to states' rights.

Clay and Webster made the counterattack in the Senate. But their reasoned economic arguments, directed to a handful of national leaders, were no match for the president's popular appeal. It was not until the Whigs abandoned their aristocratic style and adopted the democratic tactics of the Jacksonians that the party found the secret of political success in the democratically inclined country.

Despite Jackson's veto of the bank bill, the institution was not dead yet. Its charter had four more years to run.

THE ELECTION OF 1832

Because of his stand on the bank issue, Clay was the National Republican's overwhelming choice as their presidential candidate in the election of 1832. Jackson, with Van Buren as his running mate, carried the banner for the Democratic-Republicans. The campaign of 1832 also included, for the first time, a third party: the Anti-Masons, led by William Wirt, a well-known Baltimore lawyer.

The new party had begun to take shape in 1826 around the disappearance of a New York bricklayer named William Morgan. Morgan had planned to publish a book that supposedly revealed the secrets of his Masonic Lodge. Rumors began circulating that Morgan had been murdered by the Masons, reviving old prejudices against secret societies. Because a large number of political leaders and judges were Masons, many people began to suspect that Masonic secrecy might be covering up a widespread aristocratic conspiracy against democratic principles.

The impression spread despite the fact that the popular Andrew Jackson was himself a Mason.

The movement against the Masons grew large enough to destroy Freemasonry in much of New England and the Northwest. Rising young politicians such as William H. Seward and Thaddeus Stevens skillfully forged the movement into an anti-Jackson party, more extreme in its attitudes than the National Republicans. In September 1831 the Anti-Masonic party held a national nominating convention in Baltimore, the first national political convention of its kind. It set the precedent, followed to this day, for nominating presidential and vice-presidential candidates.

Although the Anti-Masonic party was anti-Jackson, its entrance into the campaign as a third party actually bolstered the president's chances for reelection. Wirt had accepted the party's nomination because he believed his candidacy would be endorsed by the National Republicans, who were also strongly against Jackson.

But the National Republicans nominated Clay instead. They also adopted the country's first party platform, which attacked Jackson for misuse of patronage and the veto and which demanded the recharter of the national bank. The Democrats, as the Jacksonians were now called, nominated Jackson as a matter of course and a platform seemed unnecessary.

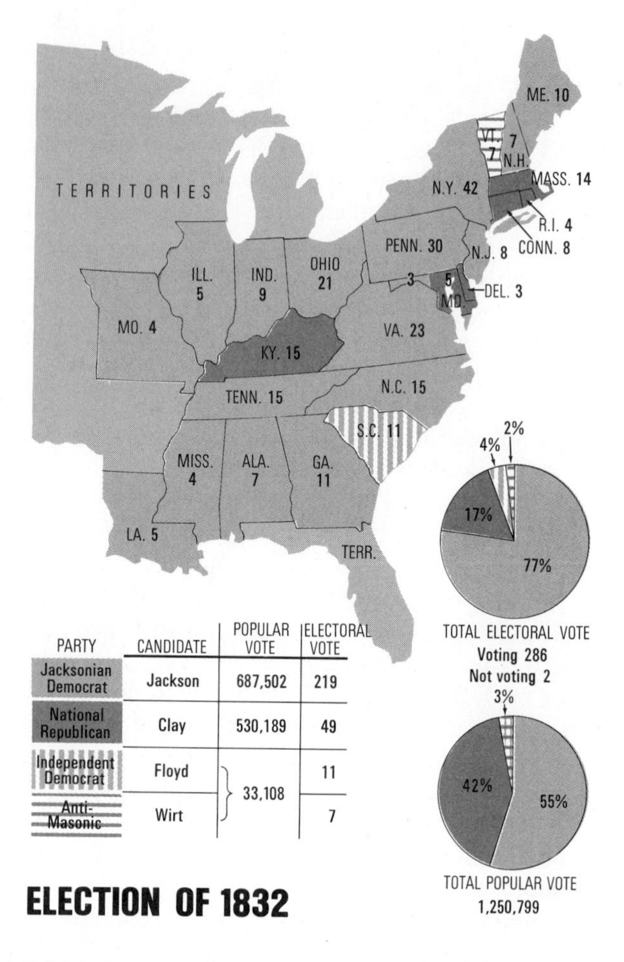

PARTY	CANDIDATE	POPULAR VOTE	ELECTORAL VOTE
Jacksonian Democrat	Jackson	687,502	219
National Republican	Clay	530,189	49
Independent Democrat	Floyd	33,108	11
Anti-Masonic	Wirt		7

ELECTION OF 1832

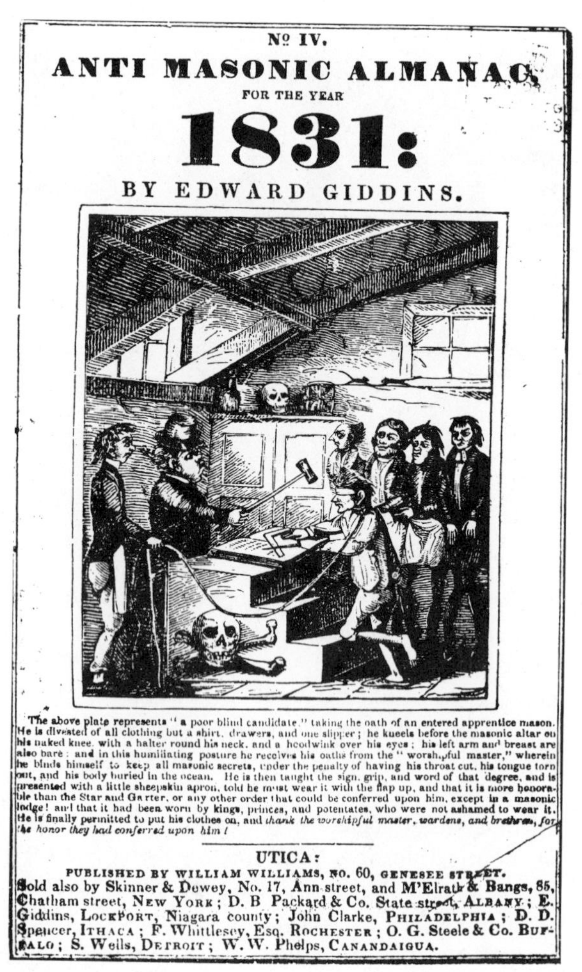

Nº IV.

ANTI MASONIC ALMANAC,

FOR THE YEAR

1831:

BY EDWARD GIDDINS.

The above plate represents "a poor blind candidate," taking the oath of an entered apprentice mason. He is divested of all clothing but a shirt, drawers, and one slipper; he kneels before the masonic altar on his naked knee, with a halter round his neck, and a hoodwink over his eyes; his left arm and breast are also bare: and in this humiliating posture he receives his oaths from the "worshipful master," wherein he binds himself to keep all masonic secrets, under the penalty of having his throat cut, his tongue torn out, and his body buried in the ocean. He is then taught the sign, grip, and word of that degree, and is presented with a little sheepskin apron, told he must wear it with the flap up, and that it is more honorable than the Star and Garter, or any other order that could be conferred upon him, except in a masonic lodge! and that it had been worn by kings, princes, and potentates, who were not ashamed to wear it. He is finally permitted to put his clothes on, and *thank the worshipful master, wardens, and brethren, for the honor they had conferred upon him!*

UTICA:

PUBLISHED BY WILLIAM WILLIAMS, NO. 60, GENESEE STREET.

Sold also by Skinner & Dewey, No. 17, Ann-street, and M'Elrath & Bangs, 85, Chatham street, NEW YORK; D. B Packard & Co. State street, ALBANY; E. Giddins, LOCKPORT, Niagara county; John Clarke, PHILADELPHIA; D. D. Spencer, ITHACA; F. Whittlesey, Esq. ROCHESTER; O. G. Steele & Co. BUFFALO; S. Wells, DETROIT; W. W. Phelps, CANANDAIGUA.

◀ *Anti-Masonic Almanac for the year 1831.*

The 1832 contest was a bitter campaign in which the parties denounced each other in cartoons, pamphlets, and speeches. Jackson was at the peak of his popularity, while the opposition was weakened by being split into two parties. Votes that went to Wirt merely drained support away from Clay.

Jackson won by the comfortable majority of 219 to 49 in the electoral college. His party also picked up more seats in Congress. To the reelected president, his clear-cut victory could mean only one thing: the people had given him a mandate to fight and destroy the Bank of the United States.

DEATH OF THE BANK

Since the bank's charter had four years to run, Jackson could not immediately kill the institution. Moreover, he feared that Clay and Biddle were spreading money and influence among the members of Congress in an effort to overturn his veto. Convinced that he must "cripple the bank" in order to "deprive the conspirators of the aid which they expect from its money and power," Jackson and his advisers hit upon a plan that would render the bank virtually impotent. Much of the bank's power came from its favored position as fiscal agent for the government. The administration could withdraw that power by removing the federal deposits from the bank.

Such a policy could legally only be carried out by the secretary of the treasury. When the incumbent secretary refused to give the order, the president replaced him. And when his replacement also delayed, Jackson removed him and appointed a third secretary, Roger B. Taney, a close friend who had encouraged him to veto the bank bill.

Taney began the systematic removal process immediately. The government opened accounts with a group of state banks, made no new deposits in the Bank of the United States, and drew on its existing deposits to pay government bills. The federal reserves in the Bank of the United States dwindled rapidly, while those in the state or "pet" banks, chosen for their political affiliations, rose.

The Senate, already angry at Jackson's use of executive authority, now opened a harsh attack on him. Many Senators believed the president needed the Senate's approval to remove an officeholder who had been appointed with the

"The Political Barbecue, Going the Whole Hog" shows Jackson as a "pig" being roasted by his enemies.

"Set to between Old Hickory and Bully Nick" shows Jackson squaring off against Nicholas Biddle, president of the Bank of the United States.

Senate's consent. In December 1833 Clay pushed through resolutions censuring Jackson for removing a second secretary of the treasury and the bank deposits without asking the Senate's agreement. Taney's appointment was also rejected. Jackson fought back by declaring that as chief executive he inherently had the power to dismiss officeholders who would not carry out his policies, a position later upheld by the Supreme Court. In 1837 the censure resolutions were stricken from the official records by Jackson's supporters.

Biddle, meanwhile, was not about to witness the bank's destruction without a fight. As the federal withdrawals from the bank began to run into the millions, Biddle decided to call in loans made to the state banks and to raise considerably the interest rates for borrowing money. By thus creating a credit shortage, he hoped to produce a business panic so widespread that the resulting depression would turn public sentiment against Jackson. Biddle believed this would force the president to return the deposits to the Bank of the United States and to call for its recharter. "Nothing but the evidence of suffering . . . will produce any effect," he asserted.

The suffering which Biddle relied on did indeed come about. During the winter of 1833 to 1834, interest rates almost tripled, businesses collapsed, and unemployment rose rapidly. The administration denied any responsibility. Biddle relentlessly kept up the pressure on the economy. Soon even business leaders who sympathized with Biddle were urging him to give in. He did finally reverse himself and began to grant credit at reasonable rates. The panic subsided, but it had failed to help the bank and had shown, in fact, how dangerously powerful the institution had become. Its charter expired in 1836 and with it, the restraining influence on state banks.

If Jackson had been less determined in his convictions against banks in general, he might more wisely have chosen only to reduce the bank's power. A central bank that could control credit to other banks in the country was indeed too important and powerful to be left unchecked in the hands of a small group, even though some members were appointed by the government. The bank recharter bill in 1832 had provided for some needed restrictions on its operations, but the president and his advisers found these restrictions insufficient. For his part, Biddle ruined any hope of recharter when he placed the country's economy in jeopardy to retaliate against Jackson, an indication that he would place personal power before the country's welfare.

Jackson had won the war on the bank, but the desirability of such a victory was questionable. The bank had been an extremely useful institution for controlling credit and preventing wild speculation.

FINANCIAL CHAOS

With the national bank's restraining influence removed, the many state banks began to lend vast sums regardless of their gold and silver reserves. In January 1835 there were $83 million in bank notes in circulation; by December 1836, the amount had leaped to $120 million. Prices rose, and with them the nation's economic optimism. Expansion soon began to get out of hand. The most serious aspect was a speculative land boom. Buying land to sell in the future at even higher prices became the national mania. Chicago, for example, was only a village of some two or three thousand people, but speculators sold and resold small lots for twenty-five miles around, confident that the area would expand. Throughout the West, land speculation became a feverish activity because the government put the vast public lands on the market at the same time that lending loosened up and interest rates declined. Many Western farmers mortgaged their own property to buy more government lands and then mortgaged these to buy still more.

The government itself contributed to the spiral by depositing money from land sales in pet banks that eagerly lent it out again. The land boom produced a demand for internal improvements and much of the borrowed money went to reckless canal, turnpike, and railroad projects, financed both privately and by the states.

Political leaders were divided in their reaction to the speculation and growing inflation. Many of them, in fact, had become speculators themselves. Senator Benton made the ominous prediction that this "bloat in the paper system" would only bring on another depression.

Foreseeing the truth of Benton's warning, Jackson issued a Specie Circular in 1836, ordering all federal land offices to accept only gold and silver in payment for public lands. The administration was signaling its determination to bring the dangerous inflationary spiral under control. The demand for payment in specie did sharply curtail Western land sales, but in the end had no effect in curbing inflation. Demand was simply diverted from land to other goods. In addition, the Specie Circular with its implication that boom times were coming to an end, may have reduced public confidence. But the real crisis of confidence came, not from administration policy, nor from within the country, but from the international market. In 1837 Americans were suddenly hit with a sharp contraction of credit from abroad, together with a rapid fall in the price of cotton on the world market. The precarious American economy simply could not withstand the strain, and plunged into panic and depression.

In the resulting Panic of 1837, prices plunged. Speculators who could not sell their lands abandoned them to the banks that held their mortgages. But the foreclosed property could not make up for the banks' losses on loans. By the time Jackson left office in the spring of 1837, many banks had been forced to close their doors. Booming prosperity based on widespread borrowing disappeared, and the United States sank into a depression from which it would not recover for seven turbulent years.

The New Two-Party System

By Jackson's second term in office a new two-party system had developed. It had grown out of the breakdown of the massive Jeffersonian coalition that had controlled political life for a decade after the War of 1812. The Democratic-Republicans led by Andrew Jackson, were simply called the Democrats. The National Republicans under Clay called themselves Whigs, a label they borrowed from English history in symbolic protest against the "reign" of "King Andrew."

Although by 1840 the two-party system was active in every state except South Carolina, the Democratic and Whig parties were only in part split along ideological lines. Both parties attracted equal numbers of former Federalists. The competition between the two parties, almost evenly balanced in most areas, produced a massive voter turnout in that year's election. Yet their differences were to some extent a matter of tone. The Whigs tended to be uncomfortable with demagogic appeals to the people and preferred to aim their campaigns at a small circle of business and political leaders. At the same time, leaders of both parties spent most of their efforts organizing their followers and competing for office. For the first time, party loyalty was elevated to a virtue.

In addition to building strong local organizations to get out the vote, the Democrats geared their policies to the new mass electorate. They professed a concern for the welfare of the average citizen and a distrust of business and commercial interests and special privilege. Dominated by Jackson's personality, the Democratic party reflected his beliefs: in free economic opportunity with neither government nor private interference, in states' rights (with the federal government asserting only those powers specifically granted to it by the Constitution), in universal white male suffrage, in the ability of ordinary people to conduct the affairs of government, and in a strong presidency acting in the name of the people.

As the election of 1836 approached the Democrats were still a diverse group. Jackson's forceful personality held together a coalition of small farmers from the North and South, urban workers (particularly Irish immigrants), middle-class business people and state bankers, and moderately well-to-do slaveholders. Ultraconservative planters and extreme states' rights advocates had, however, left the party. The urban members of Jackson's party found it had to stomach his idealization of an agrarian society (he felt that agricultural interests were "superior in importance" to any others and that farmers were the "best part" of the population). But they followed the president out of a sense of personal loyalty and a conviction that his popularity had opened to them many political opportunities.

Jackson had been an extremely popular president. He had the great politician's feel for what the average citizen thought. Much of his appeal came from his uncanny talent for reducing the most complex issues to a simple clash between good and evil. His defense of the Union in the nullification crisis, his attack on the national bank, his vetoes, and his support of the nominating convention as opposed to the undemocratic congressional caucus made him a national hero.

The Jacksonian movement represented some of the deep dilemmas of American democracy. With the new concept of the common citizen as a fit candidate for political office came the demand for more political jobs often leading to the abuses and corruption of the spoils system. Jackson had destroyed the Bank of the United States, an institution most Americans saw as a monopolistic monster. But in so doing he had set the stage for a seven-year depression. The Jacksonian movement championed political and economic equality in theory. But since the party was dominated by Southern planters and Western farming interests, their rhetoric applied only to white men, not to blacks, Indians, or women. There were few Jacksonian Democrats in such humanitarian activities as the antislavery and women's rights movements.

The Whig party, which had emerged by 1834, encompassed a variety of groups who rarely agreed except in their opposition to Jackson. The Whigs generally included former National Republicans such as wealthy Southern planters, well-to-do Northern farmers, some business, commercial, and banking interests, and native workers whose jobs were protected by the tariff. There were also Anti-Masons (whose party was absorbed by the Whigs by 1834), a scattering of Northern abolitionists, blacks who could vote, and Democrats who had become disillusioned with Jackson. Although both parties attracted equal support from the middle classes, the socially conservative, commercially active communities with cosmopolitan contacts tended to vote Whig, while isolated, sparsely populated communities tended to vote Democratic.

Because of its extremely diverse nature, there were many conflicts over policy within the Whig party. But, alarmed by Jackson's financial policies, they generally supported Clay's American System. National in their outlook, they wanted federally sponsored internal improvements, high protective tariffs, a national bank, and a strong Congress. Led by Clay, they also demanded respect for the rights of Indians and free blacks. In sum, the Whigs sought the prosperity of the people as a whole. Through a constructive national government policy they were ready to build roads, canals, schools, and promote the welfare of the poor.

The Whigs' political style differed in different parts of the country. In New England and the new West the reformers in the party frequently gave their campaigns a moralistic, evangelical tone. They were the party of temperance, strict laws against immorality, and respect for the Sabbath. In the South, on the other hand, the party was so hungry for office that it concentrated on building an effective organization and sidestepped the difficult issues.

Interpreting Jacksonianism

Historians have seen the Jacksonian era and Jackson himself in varying ways. Throughout the nineteenth century most important historians admired the outlook of the Whigs. Authors such as James Parton and William G. Sumner criticized Jackson as spiteful, coarse, illiterate, and despotic. They pointed out that the Jacksonians had used the spoils sytem to allow the vulgar and uneducated to hold important government positions while people of worth were excluded from public office. Late nineteenth-century historians saw the debasement of political life in their own times as a direct result of Jacksonian politics.

But in 1890 Frederick Jackson Turner began a new school of interpretation that admired the American frontier and its democratic legacy. And, at the turn of the century a revival of faith in democratic reform created a new respect for the Jacksonians' emphasis on popular control of government. This idea dominated the interpretation of the Jacksonian period for several decades. It was evident in Claude Bowers' *Party Battles of the Jacksonian Period* (1922), in Marquis James' popular biography of Jackson (1933–1937), and in Arthur Schlesinger, Jr.'s *Age of Jackson* (1945). At the same time there were other critics who continued the older, more critical view of the Jacksonians as wily politicians mainly concerned with obtaining the spoils of office. This view was evident in T. P. Abernethy's *From Frontier to Plantation in Tennessee* (1932) and in Charles M. Wiltse's biography of Calhoun (1944–1951).

Arthur Schlesinger Jr.'s *Age of Jackson* also shifted the debate on Jacksonianism away from Turner's frontier thesis. While Schlesinger, like Turner, stressed the importance of the growth of democracy in American life, he questioned that its roots were in the West among frontier farmers. Schlesinger claimed that Jacksonian democracy was "a problem not of sections but of classes." He pointed out that Eastern workers, disillusioned by the hard times following the Panic of 1819, had formed an important element in the Jacksonian coalition. According to Schlesinger, Jacksonianism reflected above all the wish of urban workers as well as farmers "to restrain the power of the business community."

Richard Hofstadter's *American Political Tradition* (1948) and Bray Hammond's work on early American banking (1950s) have challenged Schlesinger's emphasis on class conflict and have denied that Jackson's party opposed business interests. According to Hofstadter and Hammond, many rising entrepreneurs were drawn to the Jacksonian movement because it attacked the monopolistic power held by a few wealthy men. Far from restraining business, they argue, Jackson's party aimed at and achieved the liberation of business enterprise.

Hofstadter's and Hammond's work, while disagreeing with Schlesinger's, continued the trend of deemphasizing the role of the frontier and agrarian forces played in shaping American democracy. Their new emphasis on urban factors in part reflects the influence of the urban environment on the outlook of twentieth-century historians.

More recently Michael Lebowitz, like Bray Hammond, has pointed out that a central problem in anlyzing the Jacksonian is the fact that they were a coalition of credit-hungry, expectant capitalists and hard-money people who were injured by economic change and opposed to all banks. On the bank issue they united behind Jackson in opposition to the existing bank system, even though the system they wanted to put in its place differed from Jackson's.

In the later 1950s historians such as Marvin Meyers and John Ward turned their attention to the intellectual and psychological aspects of the Jacksonian movement. In so doing they have in part returned to Turner's theme of the frontier influence on Jacksonian democracy. Meyers has described the movement as an effort to preserve the virtues of the simple, agrarian republic the Jeffersonians bequeathed to the Jacksonians. Uneasy with the rapid industrialization of the country, the Jacksonians struck out at the national bank as the symbol of the corporate money power. Yet their destruction of the bank hastened the development of an unregulated capitalist economy.

In the early 1960s historian Lee Benson questioned whether the label "Jacksonian democracy" is appropriate. Benson does not believe that there was a well-organized political reform group centered around Jackson. The Jacksonians' emphasis on states' rights, strong executive leadership, and limited government power was not necessarily the same thing as a commitment to expand democracy. The struggle between the parties of this period was over means, not ends, with both coalitions mainly interested in obtaining jobs, not in debating issues. Benson has suggested that the term "Jacksonian democracy" should be replaced by the "Age of Egalitarianism."

In the last few years historians have tended to reinforce Benson's emphasis on the political opportunism of the Jacksonian movement. Richard P. McCormick's *Second American Party System* (1966) underlines the fact that Jacksonian politics was characterized by demagoguery and a cult of personality rather than by principles. He also shows that poor voters were not especially drawn to the Jacksonians.

Other revisionist interpretations can be seen in other new books on the period. Jean A. Wilburn's *Biddle's Bank: The Crucial Years* (1967) clearly demonstrates that the second bank was popular in the country and even with many state bankers. Robert V. Rimini's *Election of Andrew Jackson* (1963) describes the sordid realism of the men who organized Jackson's election victory. Finally, Glyndon Van Deusen in his biographies of Clay and other important Whigs, as well as *The Jacksonian Era, 1828–1848* (1963) has done much to show the importance of Whig thought as a forerunner of the trend toward government planning in the twentieth century.

THE ELECTION OF 1836

By 1836 lack of unity among the Whigs was matched by factionalism among the Democrats. Clay and Webster, the Whig party's leaders, managed the 1836 campaign. They adopted the tactic of "favorite son" candidacies, recognizing that the Whig party itself had no leader who could successfully oppose the Democrats. They chose to have popular Whig candidates run in each section of the country, with no national nominating convention and no party platform. The favorite son, it was hoped, would draw local votes away from Jackson's hand-picked successor, Van Buren, and thereby prevent him from winning a majority in the electoral college. The election would thus be forced into the House of Representatives. Daniel Webster ran for the Whigs in New England, Hugh Lawson White ran in the South and Southwest, and General William Henry Harrison ran in the Northwest.

The strategy failed. Martin Van Buren, the choice of Andrew Jackson, was elected with 170 electoral votes to 124 for his combined opponents. However, Van Buren had only a slight popular majority since he was not well liked in the South. The House was dominated by a combination of Whigs and Southern Democrats opposed to the new president.

VAN BUREN'S TROUBLED PRESIDENCY

Van Buren's presidency coincided with the great Panic of 1837. British demand for American cotton fell, and construction projects came to a halt throughout the United States as British capitalists began calling in their loans. With

"The Times" depicts the Panic of 1837. ▼

construction down and factories closing, thousands of workers were left without any prospect of employment. Many Americans faced starvation as crop shortages turned the winter of 1837 to 1838 into an unforgettably grim experience. State banks folded and the United States entered seven years of depression.

Van Buren had little responsibility for the depression and, because of his economic philosophy, he took little responsibility for trying to end it. "The less government interferes with private pursuits the better for the general prosperity," he said. A true laissez-faire Jacksonian, he felt that the government should not intervene in the economy despite his sympathy for individuals ruined by the depression. Van Buren's chief interest was to keep the federal treasury from going into the red. This, he thought, would maintain confidence in the economy and therefore encourage business to revive.

Though Van Buren favored the reform of banking procedures he was adamant in his belief that the government should remain entirely out of banking. He therefore proposed an independent treasury system. Under this plan, all connections between the federal government and any other banks were to be cut. Vaults were to be constructed in various cities to take in and pay out government funds strictly in gold and silver. The country's banking business would be carried on by state-regulated private banks.

The new president's scheme naturally aroused the opposition of the Whigs. Clay and Webster charged that it would sabotage the country's existing banking structure. It would, they admitted, protect the government from loss, but it would also keep gold and silver out of banks that needed it desperately to back their loans, thus curtailing credit.

Those who had lost their lifetime savings in a state bank favored Van Buren's proposal, for it reinforced their own suspicion of banks. Congress, however, did not immediately yield to public clamor. It did not pass the Independent Treasury Act until 1840, when Van Buren's term in the White House was virtually at an end.

THE "HARD-CIDER" ELECTION OF 1840

Van Buren, though tainted by the economic panic, was renominated for the presidency by the Democrats in 1840. The Whigs referred to him as "Martin Van Ruin," and for the Democrats not to have him run again would only have been to admit that the Whigs were right.

Given the country's woeful circumstances, the Whigs scented victory. Drawing upon the lessons learned in Jackson's campaign, they prevailed upon Clay not to seek the nomination. Instead, they deliberately nominated a military hero, General William Henry Harrison of Ohio, who had achieved some notoriety in the battles of Tippecanoe and the Thames during the War of 1812. The Whigs used Harrison's robust military image as a direct contrast to that of Van Buren, a man who drank not hard cider but expensive French wines. For vice-president the Whigs ran John Tyler of Virginia, a states' righter who was meant to balance the ticket.

The issues of the day were the depression and the independent treasury, but the campaign was based mostly on personalities and ballyhoo. Harrison had lived in a log cabin and was pictured as a fit candidate, in the Jacksonian tradition, to truly represent the people. Van Buren had no such background and was described by the Whigs as dining off imported gold plates. The fact that Harrison was not really low-born, or poverty-stricken, or raised in a log cabin did not seem to matter. His shrewd political backers knew what was needed to offset and ultimately defeat Van Buren's aristocratic image. They managed to create absurd misimpressions in the public mind. On the one hand, there was the educated Harrison, whose father had been one of the signers of the Declaration of Independence, made out to be a rough-hewn frontiersman. On the other hand, there was the politically wily Van Buren, the son of a tavernkeeper, now denounced as an aristocrat who wore corsets and ate French food.

The Whigs jeered that the party of Jackson was saddled with a highfalutin dandy from the

This cartoon characterizes the presidential campaigns of Harrison and Van Buren. Harrison was elected on his log cabin and hard cider platform.

East. Having learned all about successful politicking from the Democrats, the Whigs now chanted or shouted such slogans as "Two Dollars a Day and Roast Beef," and "With Tip and Tyler We'll Bust Van's Biler!" And of course there was the well-known:

> Tippecanoe, and Tyler too.
> And with them we'll beat little
> Van, Van, Van,
> Oh! Van is a used-up man.

Almost 2.5 million voters turned out to vote in 1840. This was seventy-eight percent of the electorate, compared with a fifty-six percent turnout in 1828. Probably voting mostly against hard times, they swept Harrison into office. The electoral college vote was a resounding 234 to 60. The Democrats had been beaten by their own methods.

Though conducted on trivial and demagogic issues the election of 1840 was of major significance in the history of American democracy. The Whigs had made a major change in their political style by recognizing that an aristocratic manner could no longer succeed in American politics. From then on, all political parties in America would use democratic strategies in their appeal to votors.

TYLER BECOMES PRESIDENT

When Harrison entered office in the winter of 1841 the leaders of his own party felt that he would be a puppet president. But it was not sure exactly whose puppet he would be: Henry Clay's or Daniel Webster's. The question had not been settled before the election, and after the election Clay, who remained in the Senate, and Webster, who was now secretary of state, became rivals for influence in the White House. And, while they squabbled for control Harrison was besieged by Whig officeseekers looking for the same patronage they had condemned under the Democrats.

The pressure was too much for Harrison and he became gravely ill with pneumonia. He died on April 4, 1842, one month after inauguration. John Tyler became president, the first vice-president to reach the office because of the death of his predecessor.

A states' righter receiving most of his support from the South, Tyler ran almost immediately into a clash over policy with Clay and the Whig majority in Congress. Twice he vetoed their bills to raise the tariff. But he finally accepted its upward revision, reneging on the promise made to the South in the Tariff of 1833 to reduce tariffs to twenty percent in ten years.

On the issue of federal banking arrangements, Tyler went along with Clay on the repeal of the independent treasury. But in an effort to wrest control of the Whigs from Clay, Tyler vetoed a bill that would have established a third national bank in its place. When he vetoed a second bank measure pushed through by Clay, his entire cabinet, with the execption of Webster, resigned in protest. Clay called the Whig representatives into caucus. They drew up a statement denouncing the president and reading him out of the Whig party.

Spurned by the Northern and Western factions of the Whigs and receiving only lukewarm support from the Southern Democrats, Tyler became, in effect, a president without a party. Though honest and conscientious, Tyler was virtually powerless without the backing of the cabinet and Congress. He had none of Jackson's combative strength or national popularity.

Tyler had little choice but to court the Southerners. He gave Calhoun the opportunity to regain Southern leadership by appointing him secretary of state. With renewed prestige, Calhoun devoted his efforts to making himself a national figure and making the South a unified political force.

THE SUPREME COURT UNDER TANEY

Although the Whigs now controlled Congress and were in nominal control of the White House, the Jacksonians still controlled the Supreme Court. Jackson had named seven of the nine justices, including Chief Justice Roger B. Taney, appointed when Chief Justice Marshall died in 1835. The nomination of Taney, a states' rights agrarian, had been bitterly contested in the Senate. Webster and other nationalists feared the possibility of a too-strict interpretation of the Constitution and reversals of the Court's earlier decisions.

In fact, however, the main body of the Marshall Court decisions survived almost intact. The Taney Court tended to be less nationalistic and to give the states more power to regulate corporations. For example, in the 1837 case of *Charles River Bridge* v. *Warren Bridge*, The Charles River Bridge Company challenged the Warren Bridge Company's right to build a bridge. The state had chartered the company to build and run a toll bridge over the Charles River and then chartered a second company to build another, toll-free bridge over the same river. But although the second bridge would compete directly with the first, the Taney Court upheld the state's action. Sharing Jackson's distrust of special corporate charters, the Court asserted that the rights of corporations are less important than those of the community, and that "the happiness and well-being of every citizen depends on their faithful preservation."

As chief justice Taney did not let his sympathy for states' rights undermine Marshall's precedents. But he did make definite distinctions between those areas of government under federal law and those under state law. A true Jacksonian, Taney said in one opinion:

> The object and end of all government is to promote the happiness and prosperity of the community by which it is established, and it can never be assumed that the government intended to diminish its power of accomplishing the end for which it was created.

Here was a lesson in Jacksonian democracy.

Readings

GENERAL WORKS

Benson, Lee, *The Concept of Jacksonian Democracy.* Princeton, N.J.: Princeton University Press, 1961.

Hammond, Bray, *Banks and Politics in America.* Princeton, N.J.: Princeton University Press, 1957.

McCormick, Richard P., *The Second American Party System: Its Formation in the Jacksonian Era.* Chapel Hill, N.C.: University of North Carolina Press, 1966.

Pessen, Edward, *Jacksonian America: Society, Personality, & Politics.* Homewood, Ill.: Dorsey Press, 1969. (Paper)

Schlesinger, Arthur M., Jr., *The Age of Jackson.* Boston: Little, Brown, 1945.

Syrett, Harold C., *Andrew Jackson: His Contribution to the American Tradition.* Indianapolis, Ind.: Bobbs-Merrill, 1953.

Temin, Peter, *The Jacksonian Economy.* New York: W. W. Norton & Co. (Paper)

Van Duesen, Glyndon G., *The Jacksonian Era.* New York: Harper & Row, 1963.

White, Leonard D., *The Jacksonians.* New York: Macmillan, 1954.

Williamson, Chilton, *American Suffrage: From Property to Democracy.* Princeton, N.J.: Princeton University Press, 1960.

SPECIAL STUDIES

Foreman, Grant, *Indian Removal: The Emigration of the Five Civilized Tribes.* Norman, Okla.: University of Oklahoma Press, 1969.

Freehling, William W., *Prelude to Civil War.* New York: Harper & Row, 1966.

Hugins, Walter, *Jacksonian Democracy and the Working Class.* Stanford, Calif.: Stanford University Press, 1960.

Meyers, Marvin, *The Jacksonian Persuasion.* Stanford, Calif.: Stanford University Press, 1957.

Miller, Douglas T., *Jacksonian Aristocracy: Class and Democracy in New York, 1830–1860.* New York: Oxford University Press, 1967.

Remini, Robert V., *Andrew Jackson and the Bank War.* New York: W. W. Norton & Co., 1967. (Paper)

Remini, Robert V., *Martin Van Buren and the Making of the Democratic Party.* New York: Columbia University Press, 1959.

Rogin, Michael Paul, *Fathers and Children: Andrew Jackson and the Subjugation of the American Indian.* New York: Knopf, 1975.

Ward, John W., *Andrew Jackson: Symbol for an Age.* New York: Oxford University Press, 1962.

PRIMARY SOURCES

Benton, Thomas H., *Thirty Years' View,* Vols. I–II. New York: Greenwood, 1968.

Chevalier, Michael, *Society, Manners, & Politics in The United States.* (Reproduction of 1839 edition.) Clifton, N.J.: Kelley Publishers.

Cooper, James F., *The American Democrat.* Baltimore: Penguin Books, 1962.

Grund, Francis J., *Aristocracy in America.* New York: Harper Torchbooks, 1959.

Martineau, Harriet, *Retrospect of Western Travel.* New York: Johnson, 1970.

Nevins, Allan (Ed.), *America Through British Eyes.* New York: Oxford University Press, 1948.

Tocqueville, Alexis de, *Democracy in America,* Philip Bradley, ed. New York: Vintage Books, 1945.

Trollope, Frances, *Domestic Manners of the Americans,* Donald Smalley (Ed.). New York: Vintage Books, 1960.

Van Buren, M., and John C. Fitzpatrick (Eds.), *The Autobiography of Martin Van Buren,* New York: Plenum, 1969.

BIOGRAPHIES

Chambers, William N., *Old Bullion Benton: Senator from the New West.* Boston: Little, Brown, Atlantic Monthly Press, 1956.

Coit, Margaret L., *John C. Calhoun: American Portrait.* Boston, Houghton Mifflin, 1950.

Current, Richard N., *Daniel Webster and the Rise of National Conservatism.* Boston: Little, Brown, 1955.

Goven, Thomas P., *Nicholas Biddle: Nationalist and Public Banker.* Chicago: University of Chicago Press, 1959.

James, Marquis, *Andrew Jackson: Portrait of a President.* Indianapolis: Bobbs-Merrill, 1937.

Swisher, Carl B., *Roger B. Taney.* New York: Macmillan, 1935.

Wiltse, Charles M., *John C. Calhoun: Nullifier,* Vol. II. Indianapolis: Bobbs-Merrill, 1949.

FICTION

Adams, Samuel H., *The Gorgeous Hussy.* Boston: Houghton Mifflin, 1934.

Gerson, Noel B., *Old Hickory.* New York: Doubleday & Co., 1964.

11

Conditions of Life in the Mid-nineteenth Century

"The Progress of the Century," a lithograph by Currier and Ives.

What indomitable enterprise marks the character of our people! What immense forests have disappeared, and given place to cultivated towns, thriving villages, and wealthy cities! Agriculture, and manufactures, and commerce, and schools, and public buildings, and houses of public worship; all these testify to our matchless enterprise. The rapidity of our progress throws all Eastern countries into the shade. We build steamboats for the Sultan of Turkey, and railroads for the Autocrat of Russia; and our enterprises extend to the icebergs of the poles—to India, China, and Japan.

Orin Fowler

From 1820 to 1865 the United States experienced rapid geographical, agricultural, and industrial growth. But at the same time many Americans experienced a deterioration in the quality of their lives.

In the decades before the Civil War Americans rushed to settle the new Western lands acquired by their government. The frontier seemed to hold the possibility of realizing the American dream of individual fulfillment and equal opportunity. But those who made the move often found frontier life grim and the burden of financial indebtedness for their land oppressive. Their attempts to suppress the native Americans who occupied the land they wanted also reveal the limited application of their ideals.

Many farmers switched from bare self-sufficiency to commercial farming during this period, and the country's agricultural output soared. But although cash crops provided them with a new source of income, the necessary investments in land and machinery left them heavily indebted.

In the North the burgeoning industrial economy seemed to offer many people the opportunity of raising their standard of living. Yet the life of industrial workers was dreary and their wages were poor. Immigrants especially suffered from poverty, contrary to their hopes of bettering their lives in the New World.

In the South the expansion of the cotton kingdom profited some, but many people were unable to climb the social and economic ladder based on land and slave ownership. The expansion of slave labor during the antebellum period was a major blot on the American dream of freedom and equality for all expressed in the Declaration of Independence.

The Growth of the West

THE NATIVE AMERICANS

White settlement of the West paralleled the declining power of the Indians. After 1815 many tribes were rendered helpless by military action and the advancing frontier settlers.

Since white settlers came to occupy and exploit the Western lands and had no interest in preserving the native Americans' way of life, their main contact with the Indians, other than trade, involved open conflict over possession of the land. Most frontier settlers saw the Indian as an adversary in war, and a very brutal one at that.

As already noted, there were great cultural differences between the two races. The Indians had their own civilizations. Their social structures were based on the limited authority of tribal leaders and communal use of land; their religious practices differed from the Judeo-Christian tradition, and they were unfamiliar with European political, economic, and social structures. Because the native Americans had a lifestyle that was different from their own, the European-Americans judged them to be inferior.

Some early writers saw the Indians as innocent, childlike persons who spent their time in the pursuit of pleasure—a romantic picture of the naturally free individual. But frontier conflicts with neighboring tribes soon led most settlers to view the Indians as bloodthirsty savages. According to one Oregon settler, native Americans "came to be thought of as game to be shot or vermin to be destroyed." Only those settlers who lived far from the frontier came to desire justice for the Southern and Western tribes.

According to federal treaties assigning the native Americans to reservations on land the white settlers considered undesirable, the Indians were to receive payments for the lands they relinquished and annual government support. No white person was to enter Indian country without a license. But despite the good intentions of some government officials, the pressures of the westward movement undermined all efforts to protect the tribes. Many traders insisted that the Indians pay their debts before receiving compensation for lands taken. As a result, many tribes received next to nothing for the massive territories they had been forced to relinquish. Moreover, after 1854 the Government Land Office began selling Indian lands in spite of the law.

In addition to geographical confinement west of the Mississippi River, many Indians suffered other disasters. Whites relentlessly slaughtered the buffalo, chief food of many Western tribes, and introduced smallpox, tuberculosis, venereal disease, and whiskey. More Indians died from these disasters than from warfare. Missionaries tried to convert some tribes to Christianity and teach them new skills, undermining the native institutions and often creating bitter internal factionalism that weakened the tribes. By the outbreak of the Civil War, only the Plains Indians still withstood the westward march of the white settler.

MIGRATION PATTERNS

In 1810 only one-seventh of the European-American people lived west of the Appalachians. By 1870 over one-half of the country's population had crossed the mountains.

Those who moved west during the antebellum period were part of an irregular flow of settlers which had begun to cross the continent back in 1607, with the founding of Jamestown. During the seventeenth century fur traders and trappers had extended the frontier to the Fall Line, the western origin of the rivers flowing into the Atlantic Ocean. These first American frontiersmen had given guns to the Indians, unintentionally handing them the means to resist the further advance of settlers. In the eighteenth century Indian resistance and the Allegheny Mountains formed a new frontier barrier. But the native Americans were subsequently weakened by military defeats and government removal programs, foreign governments' claims were set aside, and steamboats and canals were developed. The settlers took advantage of these situations and pushed the farming frontier to the Mississippi River by 1800 and all the way to the West Coast by the 1840s.

In the great pre-Civil War migration, some areas were settled faster than others. After 1816 tobacco farmers moved westward in their search for virgin land. Cotton-growers seeking to profit from the increased international demand for cotton were attracted to the rich soils of the Black Belt states (Georgia, Alabama, and Mississippi). Hordes of farmers also made their way to Texas and California by the 1830s and 1840s. According to an 1853 account, "Marvelous reports had gone forth of the fertility of the virgin lands; and the productions of the soil were commanding a price remunerating to slave labor as it had never been remunerated before."

Most frontier settlers avoided settling the open prairies at first. Thinking that land on which trees did not grow was infertile, they skirted the productive grasslands of Indiana and Illinois. The region which was to become Oklahoma and Kansas also appeared so unsuitable for cultivation that it was relegated to the Indians. Pioneers from the South had to hurdle the huge reservation, as well as the Great American Desert, in their westward movement. Only after a rise in world grain prices in the 1840s and the development of railroad links with the East did pioneers begin trying to plow the dense prairie sod. Many Southerners too poor to own slaves now moved into Indiana and Illinois, where slavery was forbidden.

WAVES OF SETTLEMENT

The frontier was settled in stages. Often the first white people to reach an area were the fur traders, miners, and loggers. The pioneers' crude camps drew farmers who hoped to cultivate lands already cleared by loggers and to sell their

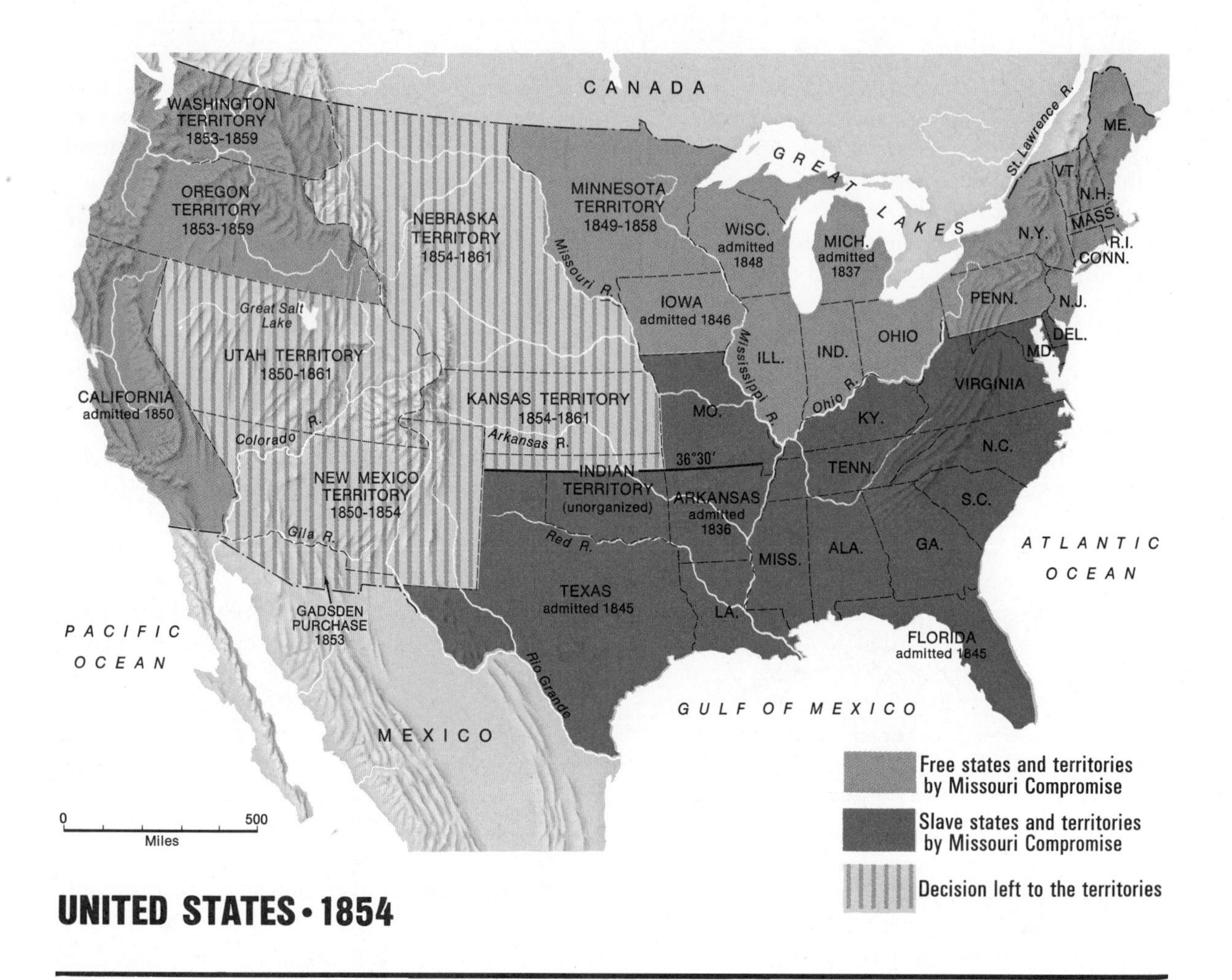

UNITED STATES • 1854

produce at high prices to the original nonfarming population. Despite conflicts between loggers and farmers over land use, lumber camps often became the core for larger agricultural settlements, such as St. Paul, Minnesota.

In his 1837 manual, *A New Guide for Emigrants to the West*, J. M. Peck offered this description of the waves of immigration into lands already explored by adventurers.

> Generally, in all the western settlements, three classes, like the waves of the ocean, have rolled on after the other. First comes the pioneer, who depends for the subsistence of his family chiefly upon the natural growth of vegetation, called the "range," and the proceeds of hunting. His implements of agriculture are rude, chiefly of his own make, and his efforts directed mainly to a crop of corn, and a "truck patch." The last is a rude garden for growing cabbage, beans, corn for roasting ears, cucumbers and potatoes; a log cabin, and, occasionally, a stable and corncrib, and a field of a dozen acres, the timber girdled or "deadened" and fenced, are enough for his occupancy. It is quite immaterial whether he ever becomes the owner of the soil.

The next class of emigrants purchase the lands, add field to field, clear out the roads, throw rough bridges over the streams, put up hewn log houses, with glass windows, and brick or stone chimneys, occasionally plant orchards, build mills, school houses, court houses, etc., and exhibit the picture and forms of plain, frugal, civilized life.

Another wave rolls on. The men of enterprise and capital come. The "settler" is ready to sell out and take advantage of the rise of property—push farther into the interior, and become, himself, a man of capital and enterprise in turn. The small villages rise to spacious towns or cities; substantial edifices of brick, extensive fields, orchards, gardens, colleges and churches are seen. Broadcloths, silks, leghorns, crapes, and all the refinements, luxuries, elegancies, frivolities and fashions are in vogue. Thus wave after wave is rolling westward. . . .

An ad from Harper's Weekly *in 1863 offers land for sale in Illinois.*

LAND SPECULATION

Accounts like Peck's tended to gloss over the harsher realities of Western settlement. Rampant land speculation profited many, but made life more difficult for others. In 1853 Joseph Glover Baldwin cynically described the period as "the era of the second great experiment in independence; the era, namely, of credit without capital, and enterprise without honesty."

Inflated land prices were directly linked to laissez-faire government policies which enabled the state banks to extend credit lavishly, and which lowered the price of land to the point that by 1820 an eighty acre farm could be purchased for a mere $100. With land so cheap and credit so readily available, Americans of all types became land speculators. A group of New York bankers with ties to the Jackson administration bought up one-third of a million acres spread across eight states and territories. Less wealthy speculators also sought to buy land at government auctions and then resell pieces of it at higher prices and usurious interest rates. Their customers often overextended themselves and could not afford to cultivate their lands or pay their real estate taxes. Even the very poor speculated. They squatted on good pieces of land and then, rather than exercise their right to buy it, sold it to someone else.

Even Jackson's 1836 Specie Circular, which required that all land be paid for in gold or silver, did not stop the spiraling speculation and inflation of land prices. Since Eastern banks were the only ones able to provide the gold and silver specie, they began to dole it out at interest rates of up to thirty percent per year. Many small farmers who accepted such heavy financial burdens were forced to foreclose, saddling banks and larger landowners with unmarketable land. In order to keep such properties income-producing, creditors convinced the indebted small landowners to stay on as tenant farmers. Tenancy thus became a common feature of Western frontier settlement.

Land speculators, especially absentee owners, had a generally negative influence on frontier life. By not improving their lands, they bore less of the local tax burden than settlers who had made improvements. Absentee speculators were often slow to pay taxes for community services,

In the mid-nineteenth century some Easterners, concerned about losing their workforce, produced propaganda to discourage Midwestern settlement. "Major Walter Wilkey's unhappy return to New England from a twelve months' miserable half-starved residence" in Illinois (see photo above) was invented in 1839 for this very purpose. In 1841 a farmer in New England complained about the many young New Englanders being lured away from their native soil to attractive-sounding lands in the Midwest: "A great portion of our young men, on arriving at the age of manhood, push their fortunes in the West . . . leaving the agricultural portions of New England, with help scarcely sufficient to cultivate their lands in the ordinary way." Midwestern land interests were busily pushing their interests in the old world (opposite) as well as in the already settled areas of their own country. Below, a successful farm in the Midwest.

Für westliche Einwanderer!

Iowa Land

im Thale des

Des Moines Flusses.

Eine Million Acker

Zu verkaufen gegen Credit von der

Des Moines Navigation Compagnie.

angering the farmers and inhibiting development. On the other hand, speculators actively fought to have internal improvements situated near their land in order to increase its value. As a result, many railroads, county seats, state capitols, and public institutions were built in unsuitable places.

Speculators also considered Indian lands fair game. Using their influence with high-placed friends in the Bureau of Indian Affairs, speculators soon took over nine million acres of Indian lands in Kansas alone.

LIFE ON THE FRONTIER

In spite of the financial burdens of frontier life introduced by loan sharks and land speculators, vast numbers of Americans were still willing to uproot themselves from more developed society and cart their families, worldly goods, and livestock great distances to begin a more primitive life. They were caught up in the national urge for personal economic and social growth.

That half of the population which thus uprooted itself seemed to feel the West offered vast untapped resources and opportunities. They believed it to be a place where a free person could, almost without restrictions, stake out a claim and create a home, and perhaps eventually a prosperous farm or a thriving business. According to historian Frederick Jackson Turner, the West was "the richest free gift that was ever spread out before civilized man."

But frontier life was never easy. The land speculators' propaganda seductively glossed over the drudgery and loneliness of life in an isolated wilderness and the poor quality of some of the land. As frontier settlers struggled to clear and cultivate land on which to grow their own food, they had little time for house-building. Their first homes were usually primitive shacks or dirt-floored cabins. Their animals often had to fend for themselves. Hogs were so scrawny that they were often called "wind-splitters."

As pioneers moved into the prairie their log cabins gave way to houses made of sod that were smoky, damp, and vermin-ridden. Water often had to be hauled for miles in a barrel. Without forests, settlers had to burn dried buffalo dung in primitive stoves for fuel.

The veneer of civilization was extremely thin in frontier areas. Aggressive actions were restrained by some social codes but little formal law. People had to defend their own reputation and property. The law would supposedly step in to impose capital punishment on those guilty of cattle rustling, horse-stealing or "dry-gulching" (shooting an enemy in the back). But officers of the law frequently resembled "Old Necessity," a justice of the peace on the Texas plains in the 1880s. He literally knew no law, but kept a mail-order catalogue bound in sheepskin on his bench, so that it would look like an impressive law book. Once, when a man pleaded guilty, "Old Necessity" opened his book at random and said, "I fine you $4.98." The man jumped up in protest, but his attorney hissed, "Sit down. Be thankful he opened it at trousers instead of at pianos!"

OCCUPATIONAL AND SOCIAL MOBILITY

The West was famed as the "land of opportunity" where people of European background could break with the tradition that a man inherited the occupation and social status of his father. On the frontier people could rise as high on the economic and social ladder as their ambitions and talents would take them. Or so it seemed.

The myth of Western mobility has been disputed by recent studies of settlement patterns. According to Ross M. Robertson, the Southern frontier displayed none of the looseness and fluidity that was thought to characterize Western society. When the new Southern lands were settled by both small yeoman farmers looking to better themselves and planters with their slaves, the planters monopolized the best lands. The small farmers were forced to take

Turner on the Frontier and Democracy

"The most important effect of the frontier has been in the promotion of democracy here and in Europe. As has been indicated, the frontier is productive of individualism. Complex society is precipitated by the wilderness into a kind of primitive organization based on the family. The tendency is anti-social. It produces antipathy to control, and particularly to any direct control. The taxgatherer is viewed as a representative of oppression. . . . The frontier individualism has from the beginning promoted democracy.

The frontier States that came into the Union in the first quarter of a century of its existence came in with democratic suffrage provisions, and had reactive effects of the highest importance upon the older States whose peoples were being attracted there. An extension of the franchise became essential."

Frederick Jackson Turner,
The Frontier in American History, 1893

Wright on the West as Imitative

"In their choice of political institutions the men of this section were imitative, not creative. They were not interested in making experiments. Their constitutional, like their domestic, architecture was patterned after that of the communities from which they had moved westward. . . . To be sure they ordinarily, although not invariably, adopted the more democratic practices where there was variation in the East, but even in this respect they never varied from some well-established seaboard model, unless it was in the case of the proportion of elected officials. And even in this instance . . . one can trace precedents and some tendencies in this direction in the older states. In short, the result of the developments in the newer section seems to have been somewhat to accelerate the rate of growth of the democratic movement, not to change its direction."

**Benjamin F. Wright,
Sources of Culture in the Middle West, published 1961**

marginal lands or to move even farther west, and the class lines were immediately rigidified in the image of the old South.

In the northern frontier regions small farmers and poor families looking for opportunities had to face competition from land speculators and estate-builders. Many were forced into tenancy by inflation and speculation.

But despite these difficulties many frontier settlers apparently did manage to improve their standard of living. Lots of Western farmers switched from self-sufficient farming to commercial agriculture. Improved transportation facilities—roads, canals, steamboats, and eventually railroads—made it profitable for them to grow money crops for sale in the distant markets of the Eastern seaboard and Europe. And although frontier life was difficult at first, it became less harsh as more neighbors moved in, as schools and churches were built, as transportation improved, and as manufactured goods shipped from the East became cheaper.

Western expansion created important urban centers west of the Appalachians which consumed the industrial products of the East as well as the produce of an expanding agricultural base. The speed of urban growth in mid-America between 1830 and 1860 was phenomenal. It helped decrease America's economic dependence on Europe and promoted a spirit of nationalism.

RAILROADS

The isolation of the West was considerably eased by the advent of the railroad. Before the railroad, canal building had allowed phenomenal growth of some regions, such as the Great Lakes area. Chicago, an insignificant village in the 1820s, had grown to a city of over 100,000 by 1860. But the national craze for canalbuilding was halted by the Panic of 1837 and the resulting collapse of the country's already shaky monetary structure. Some states, particularly those in the West, had overbuilt. Eight Western and Southern states defaulted on payments to canal investors. As a result, public sentiment against state ownership of transportation facilities ran high. People were more receptive to the construction of railroads, which were to be built and run by private enterprise.

After a thriteen-mile segment of the Baltimore and Ohio opened in 1830, many Eastern regions pushed the building of local railroads in an effort to compete with New York for trade with the interior. In the thirty years before the Civil War railroad building boomed. As the earliest small, independent lines were consolidated, they joined previously unconnected parts of the country. Lines were eventually laid east from Chicago to meet the Eastern trunk lines and westward into Iowa and Missouri. By 1860 over thirty thousand miles of track linked most of the great cities east of the Mississippi and north of the Ohio.

These early railroads were for the most part built by state-chartered private companies which were granted the power of eminent domain, monopoly rights, and freedom from taxation. These companies received financial assistance from state, county, and municipal governments in the form of heavy investment in stock, and from the federal government in the form of land grants. By 1860 twenty-eight million acres of land from the public domain had been turned over to private companies for the construction of railroads.

State and local financial support of railroad-building placed heavy burdens on taxpayers, and the advantages of railroads were not immediately apparent to their passengers. At first—with primitive locomotives and tracks—schedules were most irregular, breakdowns were commonplace, and passengers in open cars were showered with sparks from the wood-burning locomotives. Soon, however, safety and efficiency were increased by the use of solid roadbeds and iron "T" rails, and by the substitution of coal for wood as fuel. The design of the locomotives and cars was improved, sleeping cars were added to passenger trains, and the invention of the telegraph made it easier to supervise railroad operations, by quickly relaying messages. As more refinements were introduced the railroads became the ideal solution to the large country's transportation needs. Trains were fast, they could be built through rough terrain to service the most remote markets, and they were dependable in winter when water in the canals often froze.

In addition to helping draw the West and the East together, the railroads promoted the development of remote areas, stimulated agricultural production in the West by providing improved transportation to Eastern markets, and boosted mining and smelting industries by their use of iron. Even on the edge of the frontier, the cheaper transportation raised the Westerner's income and standard of living, and helped to erase the isolation of earlier days.

The South, meanwhile, had not been active in building railroads. Southerners relied on the Mississippi and other rivers to carry their traffic.

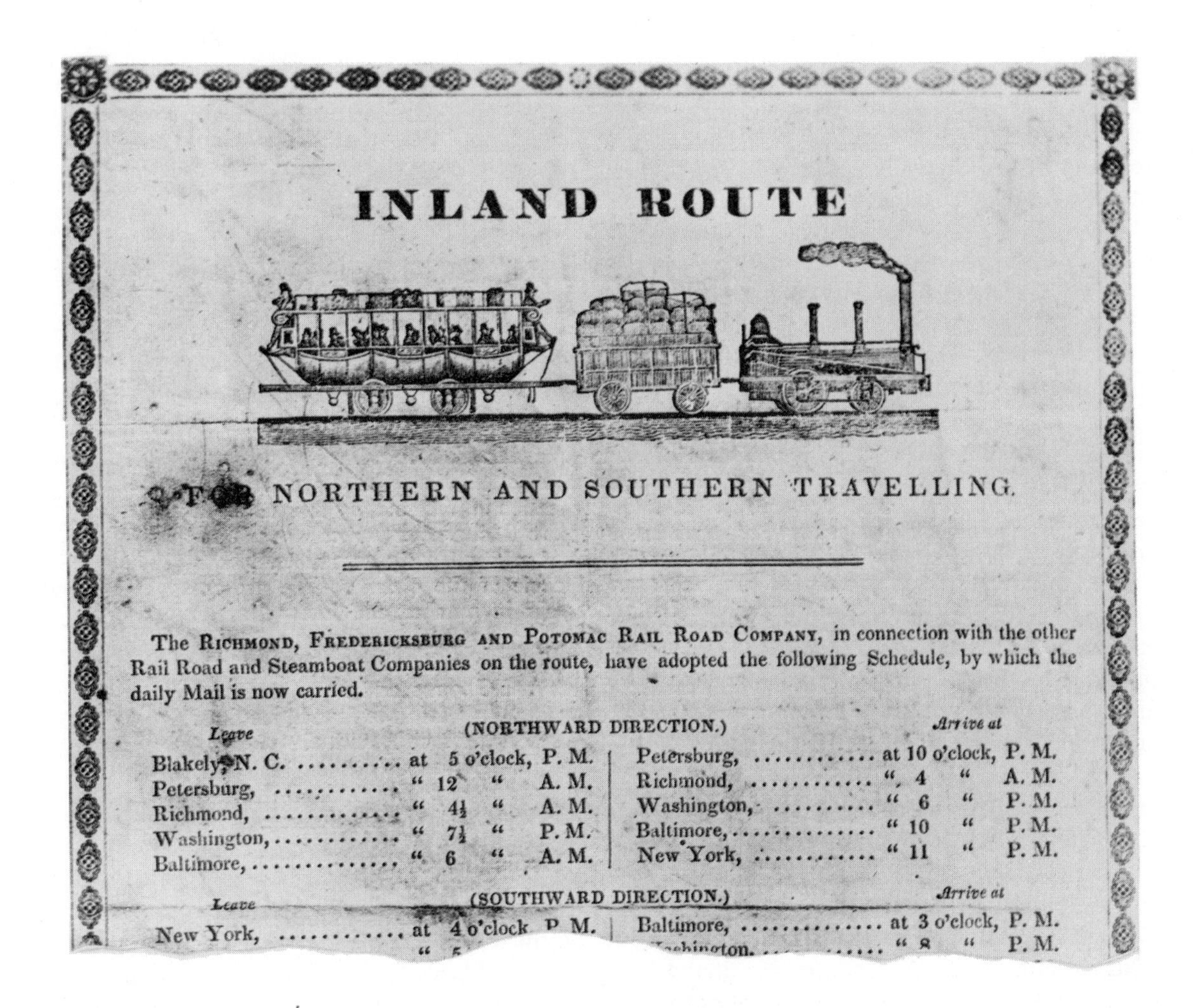

INLAND ROUTE

FOR NORTHERN AND SOUTHERN TRAVELLING.

The Richmond, Fredericksburg and Potomac Rail Road Company, in connection with the other Rail Road and Steamboat Companies on the route, have adopted the following Schedule, by which the daily Mail is now carried.

(NORTHWARD DIRECTION.)

Leave		Arrive at	
Blakely, N. C.	at 5 o'clock, P. M.	Petersburg,	at 10 o'clock, P. M.
Petersburg,	" 12 " A. M.	Richmond,	" 4 " A. M.
Richmond,	" 4½ " A. M.	Washington,	" 6 " P. M.
Washington,	" 7½ " P. M.	Baltimore,	" 10 " P. M.
Baltimore,	" 6 " A. M.	New York,	" 11 " P. M.

(SOUTHWARD DIRECTION.)

Leave		Arrive at	
New York,	at 4 o'clock P. M.	Baltimore,	at 3 o'clock, P. M.
	" 5		" 8 " P. M.

As a result, their share of the nation's trade declined sharply at the time that the industrial Northeast and agricultural Northwest were becoming more interdependent. With increased economic ties came greater social and cultural connections. These links helped forge a feeling of nationalism in the North which would be important in preserving the Union.

Commercial Expansion

In the decades before the Civil War Americans greatly increased their trading activities, both among themselves and with foreign nations. The new trade contacts were made possible by transportation improvements and also by the invention of the telegraph. In 1832 Samuel F.B. Morse, a New England painter, developed the idea of an electromagnetic telegraph. He had to wait eleven years, however, before he received a $30,000 appropriation from Congress to build an experimental telegraph line from Washington, D.C., to Baltimore. Finally, on May 1, 1844, the first message was sent over the line. The invention was such a triumph that by 1850 thousands of miles of line had been installed across the United States east of the Mississippi. In 1858 a transatlantic cable was buried under the ocean. The United States was at last only seconds away from Europe. No longer would week-long lags in communication separate the New World from the Old.

FOREIGN TRADE

American shipowners, merchants, and manufacturers were hurt by the Panic of 1837 and the depression that followed. Within ten years, however, internal economic recovery and a series of favorable foreign developments gave a tremendous boost to overseas trade. In 1846 Britain repealed the Corn Laws which had protected its domestic agriculture, thereby opening up a large market for American wheat. That same year America passed lower tariff rates, attracting more European manufactured goods to the United States. As a result, the combined value of American exports and imports increased from $222 million in 1840, to $318 million in 1850, and $687 million in 1860.

During this period the country continued to import manufactured goods and a supply of raw materials to foreign buyers, and imports still led exports. Textiles and iron products were the chief imports, while cotton was still the major export, bringing in $191 million in 1860. American whalers sailed the world's oceans, making the country the leading exporter of whalebone and whale oil. Gold, too, gained immediate importance as an export after its discovery in California in 1848.

Throughout the antebellum period Great Britain was not only America's leading foreign supplier but her best customer as well. At the same time that trade with England grew, commercial activity between the United States and the West Indies declined. The islands, once major consumers of American goods, accounted for only twenty percent of the country's exports in the 1820s. Purchases fell sharply to a mere seven percent in the years before the Civil War.

Trade with the Orient

Most American commerce was with Europe, but trade inroads were being made in other parts of the world. Early nineteenth-century American merchant ships stopped in the Philippines, India, and Java. And by the 1840s the country had signed a trade agreement with Siam.

In 1844 the Treaty of Wanghia opened five Chinese ports to American trade, a privilege the British had received two years before. The treaty also established specific customs duties and granted the United States control over her own nationals in the trading ports. But China resented these concessions which she had been forced to make. In 1858 when China attempted to evade the treaty commitments, British and French gunboats were sent to enforce them, with America's tacit support.

While America had hitchhiked on the imperialist policies of Britain and France in China, it took a more direct approach in Japan, a nation isolated for two centuries from the rest of the world. In an effort to pry the islands open, the United States government sent Commodore Matthew C. Perry and his fleet of steam warships to Japan in 1853. Though Perry had the strength of his warships to back up any claims or entreaties, his initial dealings with the Japanese government were exploratory and peaceful. He presented the Japanese emperor with letters from President Pierce and a gift consisting of an array of Western gadgetry. In 1854 he returned and found the Japanese officials, who in the meantime had apparently considered the alternative to a peaceful agreement, were eager to come to terms.

After Perry secured the opening of two small ports to American trade, the United States Department of State sent diplomat Townsend Harris to Japan as its first American consul. Harris' charm and diplomatic abilities were even more persuasive than Perry's warships. He

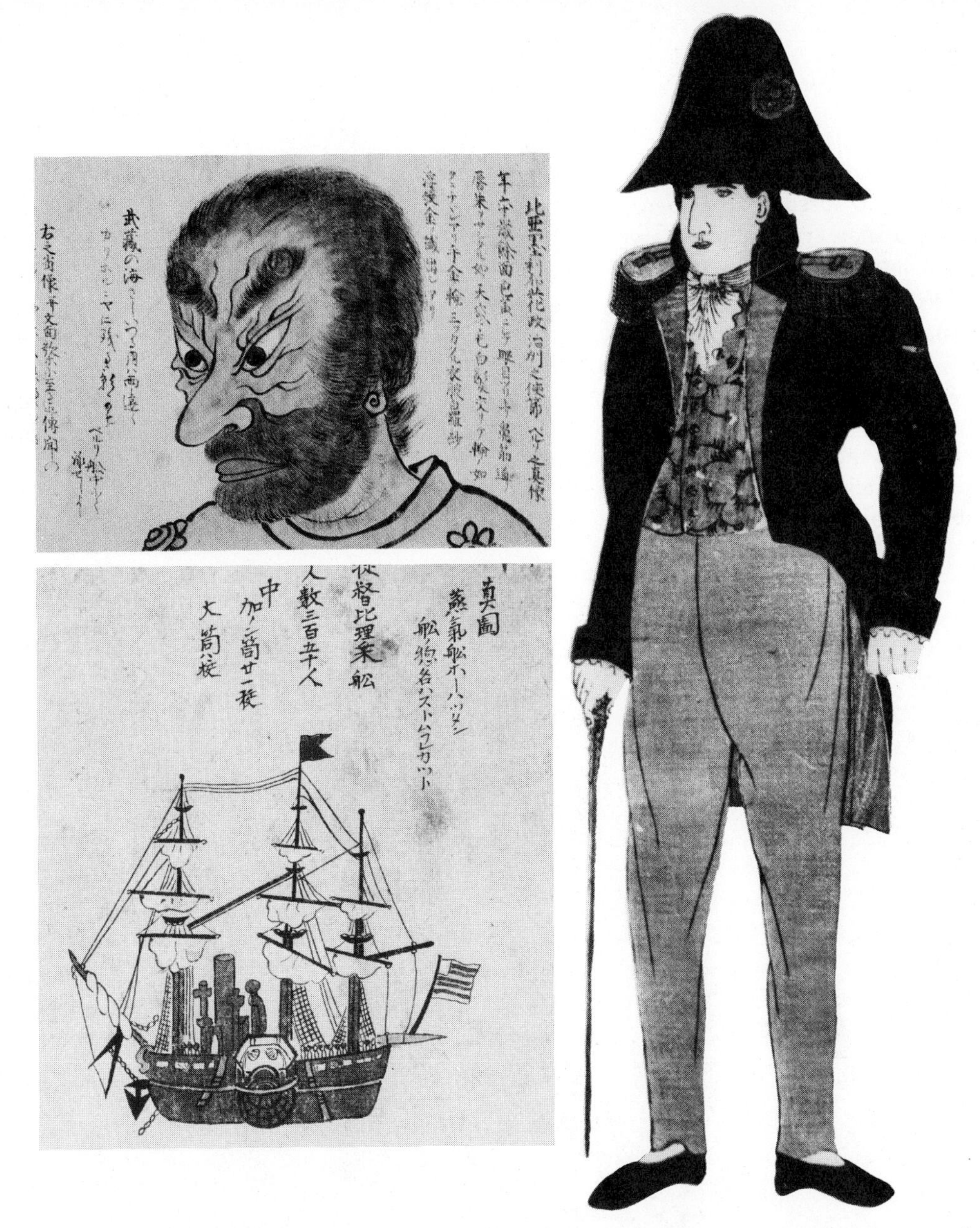

Two Japanese renditions of Commodore Perry, and a Japanese drawing of Commodore Perry's steam warship, the Powhatan.

managed to convince the Japanese that the United States had no territorial ambitions in the Pacific, and obtained further commercial concessions in an 1858 agreement. In 1860 relations were firmly established by a visit of the first Japanese mission to the United States.

Clipper ships

Though America's diplomatic contacts were sometimes carried on by gunboats, her commercial cargoes were carried by a new kind of sailing vessel, still unmatched in its beauty.

With the 1845 launching of the *Rainbow*, a radical improvement over the old three-masted packet ships, the era of the famed clipper ships was ushered in. The *Rainbow's* hull was long and sleek, her stern rounded, and her bow concave. Her tall, raking masts held an enormous spread of canvas that moved her 750 tons with ease through the water. Clipper ships later set records for speed that helped give the United States a more prominent share of the international carrying trade than it had ever had before.

Even though they were mostly used in trade with Europe and the Far East, the clipper ships reached a peak of performance in the 1850s as a vital link between the Atlantic and Pacific coasts. On a voyage from New York to San Francisco, the *Flying Cloud* averaged an incredible 433 miles a day; the clippers took three months to make the trip around Cape Horn in South America, whereas the older boats took over five months.

The clippers carried the fast freight and passenger traffic of the world until about 1875, but years earlier their supremacy began to be threatened by the Panama Railroad, which deprived them of much of the California trade, and by the appearance of the British iron steamships.

Some American steamships were successfully used for ocean travel, but they were no competition for their British rivals which had the advantage of being ironclad and driven by a

The USS Constitution*, an American frigate.*

huge screw propeller. America's carrying trade position declined, and not until World War I did she regain the mastery of the sea that she had achieved in the days of the clippers.

DOMESTIC TRADE

While American foreign trade grew to five times its previous level from 1843 to 1860, domestic trade expanded at twice that rate. The vitality of the international trade helped spur domestic commerce, for imports and exports were deposited at port cities, creating a great deal of business for home carriers.

The expansion of internal trade was also strongly aided by population increases and by regional specialization. As the various areas began to specialize in distinct commodities, they experienced a growing need to exchange goods. These exchanges were further served by the mining of gold in California, which produced a stable monetary basis for transactions. The invention of the telegraph made speedier transactions possible. As the amount of money in circulation increased, the pace of domestic economic activity quickened further.

The country's railroad network and excellent system of waterways were a great asset to growing domestic traffic. Coastal vessels carried Southern cotton to the cities of New York and New England. Steamboats plied the Mississippi River, hauling both freight and passengers, and controlling the flow of goods from farm to market until the elaborate network of canals began diverting much of the business to the Great Lakes.

Agricultural Expansion

As increased survival rates, continuing high birth rates, and enormous waves of immigration added to the nation's population during the 1840s and 1850s, and as improved transportation facilities were built, farmers could grow more crops for more consumers. But although the production of cash crops increased greatly during the antebellum period, many involved in farming became less free.

Droves of farmers left the rocky soil of New England and the wornout farms of the old South to begin farming the rich soils of the West. At the same time an effort was made to modify the American practice of overusing and then abandoning land. Because of the growing importance of agriculture to the nation's economy, agricultural reformers developed and promoted new methods for utilizing and preserving the land. Jesse Buel of New York developed soil conservation techniques. Buel advocated crop rotation and the use of fertilizers, promising that "by draining, manuring, ploughing, harrowing, hoeing . . . we may preserve, unimpaired, the natural fertility of our soils."

Marl, an earth rich in calcium, was introduced into Virginia to counteract the acidity of fields that had been depleted by the planting of tobacco. As its use spread to other areas, marl eventually multiplied corn and wheat harvests.

Production in the Corn Belt (which reached from Pennsylvania to Iowa) rose to a record 838 million bushels in 1860, a forty percent increase in less than ten years. Corn was the predominant crop in the North as well as an important crop in the South. People all over the country ate lots of fresh corn, corn bread, and corn-fed pork.

Wheat production for domestic and international consumption also soared before the Civil War. Less bulky than corn, wheat was cheaper to transport and therefore more profitable.

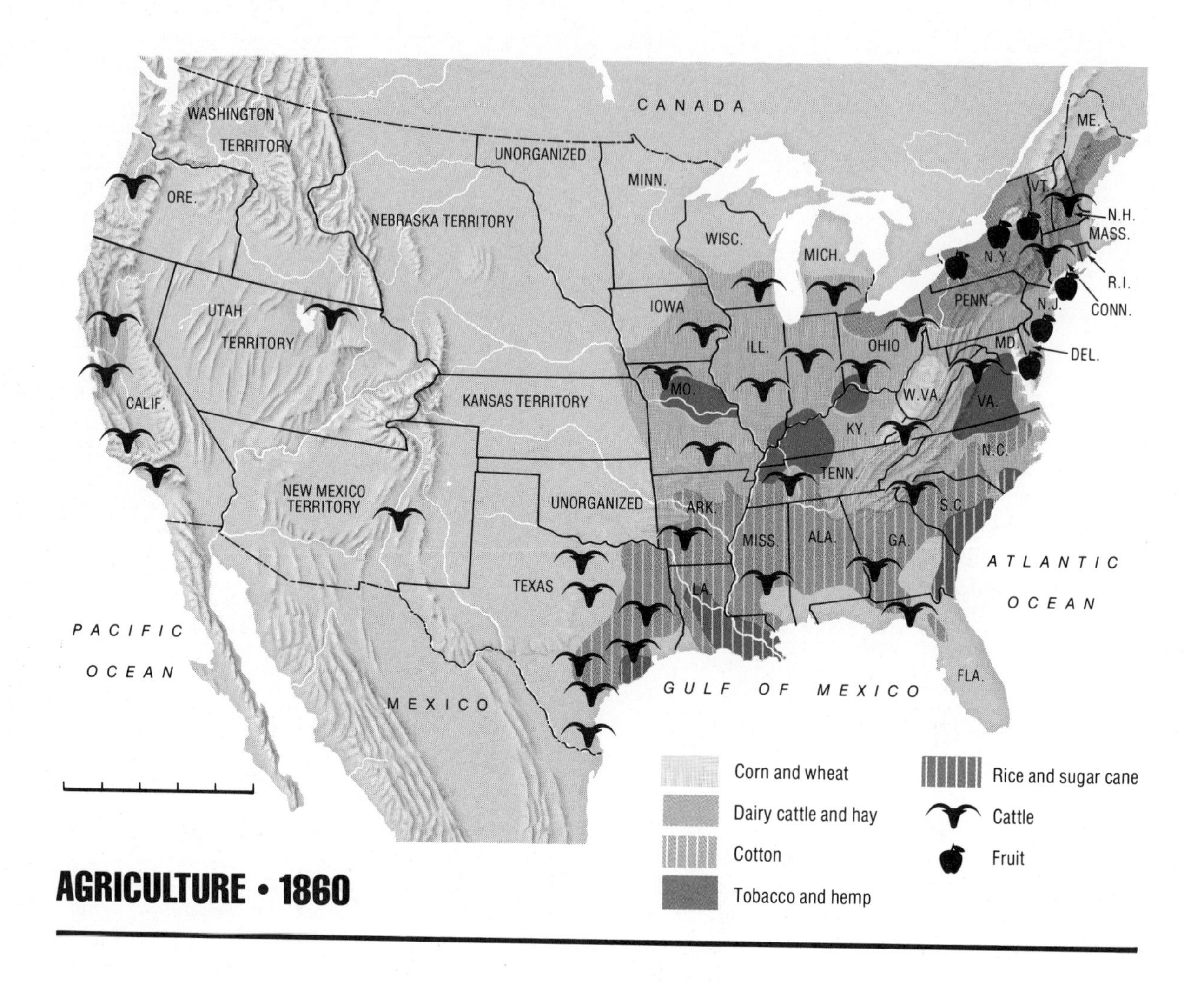

AGRICULTURE • 1860

MECHANIZATION

In addition to boosting their production through fertilization, farmers also cultivated more acreage with better machinery.

At the beginning of the nineteenth century Americans were still farming new land the same way it had been cultivated for centuries. After setting aside a patch of earth for a vegetable garden, which usually became the wife's responsibility, the farmer fenced in his main field at a cost of $1.25 an acre. Because the ground was hard, the initial plowing was often done by a hired team of professional "breakers." Steering huge plows drawn by a dozen oxen, these breakers would cut the first furrows in the land. Then the farmer would dig deeper holes into the furrows with an ax, and in these holes plant Indian corn, pumpkins, and beans. After the ground had been sufficiently broken during the first season, the family would do all the plowing and planting themselves.

In 1800 farmers had only wooden plows and harrows, pulled by oxen and horses, and a few hand tools. The most a farm family could cultivate was a little over one acre a day, and most of what they grew, they ate.

" 'Westward the Course of Empire Takes Its Way' with McCormick Reapers in the Van." (Chicago Historical Society)

Though farmers tended to resist change, they recognized that mechanization was essential if agriculture was to grow into a commercial enterprise. Many were interested when John Deere, an Illinois blacksmith, invented a steel plow in 1830. Deere's plow was light enough for a single person to guide while driving a team, and capable of cutting clean, deep furrows. Deere continued to make improvements in his original design, and by 1858 he was turning out thirteen thousand steel plows a year.

Cyrus McCormick of Virginia and Obed Hussey of Ohio built reapers which greatly reduced the labor of harvesting. With one of their steel-toothed, horse-drawn machines, a single person could do as much work as five people with scythes. But the reapers did not achieve widespread use until McCormick moved his plant to Chicago in 1848 and sent salesmen with demonstration models to the frontier areas. Ten years later, McCormick was manufacturing five hundred reapers a month and still could not keep up with the demand.

Further mechanization occurred in the 1850s with the invention of mechanical threshers, cultivators, hayrakes, and mowers which reduced the need for field hands in the chronically labor-short country.

But mechanization, while reducing the human labor necessary for farming, also increased the costs of farming. Whereas in 1800 the average farmer rarely spent more than $20 on tools, by 1857 farmers with one hundred acres of land needed some $600 worth of machinery. The heavy cost of mechanization diminished opportunities for farm laborers and tenant farmers to climb the occupational ladder. It also made farmers more dependent on credit agencies and banks.

COMMERCIALIZATION AND SPECIALIZATION

Investments in machinery forced farmers to grow larger crops on more land in order to pay for the machinery and to specialize in a few crops in order to minimize the number of machines they needed. By the 1850s large-scale, specialized agriculture geared to the market was firmly established as far west as Illinois and Wisconsin.

The South, including the newly settled lands of the rich Black Belt, specialized in growing cotton. But there were other regional specialties, too: tobacco, widely grown for export in Virginia, Kentucky, Tennessee, and Missouri; rice, in the Carolinas and Georgia; sugarcane in Louisiana; and hemp in Kentucky. Most other Southern crops were raised for home consumption, with the large planters concentrating their efforts on producing a cash crop for the commercial market.

As transportation links improved the West quickly assumed dominance in the growing of staple food crops and livestock. In 1840, for instance, New York, Pennsylvania, and New England were the principal cattle-raising areas. Within ten years they had been replaced by Illinois, Indiana, Iowa, and Texas. The development of the refrigerator car made it easy to ship slaughtered hogs, cattle, and sheep from the Mississippi Valley to the Eastern seaboard. Western urban centers such as Cincinnati and Chicago began to specialize in meat-packing as well as flour milling.

The farmers of the Northeast, working poor or exhausted soil, found that they could not compete with the West in the production of wheat, corn, hogs, and sheep and so stopped trying. Many moved west themselves; others gave up farming and worked in the mills. Those who persisted switched to dairying and to growing fruits and vegetables for nearby markets. In New York City, Boston, and Philadelphia, they at first had a distinct price advantage over distant competitors. Also, fruit and vegetable sales were boosted when an Englishman invented the tin can, a handy device for packaging and preserving fresh produce.

THE GROWTH OF SLAVERY

As cotton, rice, and sugar production mushroomed in the South, demand for slave labor also soared. Since the African slave trade had been outlawed in 1808 the lower South bought its slaves from the upper South. This created a dramatic shift in the distribution of the slave population. Most slaves lived in the deep South. For example, they were 57 percent of the population in South Carolina but only 1.5 percent in Delaware. The slave population of Alabama was eight times larger in 1850 than it had been thirty years before, when the new cotton-growing state entered the Union.

Despite the ban on the African slave trade, the total number of slaves in the country grew from 857 thousand at the turn of the century to almost 4 million by the beginning of the Civil War. This increase was accomplished partly by smuggling slaves from Africa illegally, but mostly by natural reproduction within the slave population.

"Group of Slaves on Parade, Fort Augusta" from the Illustrated London News *of 1857.*

Slave ownership and class structure

While most Southern farmers wanted to own slaves, only about one-fourth of the population actually did own any. By 1860, of a free population of 1,500,000 families, only 385,000 owned slaves. Of these, only 12 percent qualified as planters by owning 20 slaves or more. A mere 3000 families had over 100 slaves and lived on large plantations. Plantation owners were few because the investments required in land and slaves were so high.

There were economic drawbacks to depending on slave labor. The labor force could not be adjusted to meet business fluctuations. And it cost more to keep slaves than to hire free labor. Slave labor limited the Southern economy to a few crops and prevented the rapid diversification which was taking place in the North. The slave system also impeded the introduction of new machinery and required constant control. But the rewards were often well worth the expense. Cotton planter Stephen Duncan of Natchez, Mississippi, for example, owned 1000 slaves and had an annual income of $170,000.

The slave system also created a self-conscious aristocracy. Despite its small size compared to the total population, the planter class dominated the economic, social, and political life of the South. Planters lived and entertained lavishly. They also set the tone for the unwritten social code which tended to supersede written laws in the South. The Southern code based on personal honor was the best instrument for self-government, according to apologists, since it left areas like master-servant relations to the master's conscience. That conscience, more fixed than any legal code, was supposedly characterized by generosity, warmth, and charity, distinguishing it from the Northern conscience which, according to the Southern view, based human relationships on their money value.

Southern class structure was clearly based on how many slaves one owned. Below the planter class was the gentry, people who owned five to twenty slaves and who dreamed of joining the exclusive group above them. The next rung on the social ladder was occupied by those who owned five slaves or less and who usually worked in the fields with them. This group comprised the bulk of slave-owning whites. The rest of the small farmers in the South—three-quarters of the white population—owned no slaves at all. In this category, the lowlands whites who worked as mechanics, lesser tradespeople and small cotton farmers strongly supported slavery as an institution. It gave them a sense of racial superiority and their desire to own a slave or two made them identify with the planter class. Many small farmers, on the other hand, despised the planter class with their slaves. Scattered through the valleys of the Appalachians, these yeoman farmers were to form a strong contingent of pro-Unionism in the South during the Civil War.

At the bottom of the social and economic ladder were the poor whites, despised by those above them as "hillbillies," "crackers," or "clay-eaters." And below all whites were the approximately 240,000 free blacks. These people, though legally free, lived severely restricted lives because so many Southerners feared they would encourage the slaves to rebel.

Laws enforced the low status of the free blacks. They were not allowed to migrate freely to other Southern states and, if caught without their freedom certificates, they could be claimed as slaves. They could not vote, testify against whites, or serve on juries. They were subject to curfews and largely prevented from assembling without the presence of a white person. Toward the end of the antebellum period they were not even allowed to attend meetings of charitable organizations. Although blacks made up a sizable part of the population of Southern cities, some municipalities barred free blacks as well as slaves from the skilled trades.

Migrating out of the slave states was of little help for their treatment in the North was not much better than it was in the South. There they faced the race prejudice of whites and competition for jobs from immigrants. Public transportation, schools, prisons, hospitals, and even cemeteries were segregated. White mobs in Northern cities sometimes killed blacks and destroyed their property. In Illinois and Indiana laws were passed regulating the behavior of free blacks and, by the end of the antebellum period, Illinois, Indiana, and Oregon had forbidden free blacks from entering their states. Between 1807 and 1837 five of the Northern states which had allowed blacks to vote disenfranchised them. Finally, the federal government excluded blacks from the army and from most of its jobs.

Despite job discrimination free blacks in the North found work as fruit and produce vendors, barbers, stevedores, brick masons, wood sawyers, cooks, house servants, and managers of small stores with black customers. But in even the most menial jobs, such as bootblacking, they were often replaced by white immigrants. A few free blacks were visibly successful. Among them were Benjamin Banneker, a city surveyor who helped draw up plans for Washington, D.C., and John Russworm an editor in New York who established America's first black newspaper, *Freedom's Journal*, in 1827. But such instances were rare.

The organization of slave labor

On Southern farms most slaves were used as field hands under either the gang system or the task system. The cultivation of cotton, a sturdy crop not easily damaged by unskilled labor, easily lent itself to the gang system, in which a single overseer supervised as many as forty slaves. Their labor was highly organized and intensive. At planting time five waves of hands moved through the fields like an assembly line. First came plowers of the soil, followed by harrowers of dirt lumps, drillers of holes for the seeds, droppers of seeds, and finally rakers to cover the holes. At harvest time gangs were forced to compete. Each slave was assigned a weight of cotton he or she would be expected to pick. Under some masters, a slave who failed might be whipped and a slave who succeeded might receive an increased assignment. Some planters, however, offered positive rewards to encourage greater effort.

Picking cotton off the low-growing plants was back-breaking work but it required no mental effort and could be handled by slaves of most ages and both sexes (an estimated eighty percent of all female slaves were used as field hands). Under the gang system slaves usu-

Planting sweet potatoes on a South Carolina plantation in 1862.

ally worked from dawn to dusk with a short rest at midday. They received a weekly food allowance, generally salt pork or bacon and corn, and often slept on a narrow plank in a dark cabin with a stick of wood for a pillow and perhaps some burlap for a blanket.

The cultivation of other crops was somewhat less rigorous, if only because of the nature of the plants. Under the task system, used in the cultivation of tobacco, rice, and sugar, slaves were carefully taught how to care for and harvest the plants. Each slave was assigned a specific amount of work. This was an incentive for intensive labor, because once the daily task was completed the slave had the rest of the day off.

In the slack periods between planting and harvesting, field slaves were used for making land improvements, construction, home manufacturing, rearing livestock, and cultivating corn and other crops.

About twelve percent of the adult male slaves on the farms and twenty-five percent in the cities were skilled workers and crafts people: trained carpenters and blacksmiths, shoemakers, chair makers, and harness makers. Since these artisans brought higher prices than field hands on the domestic slave market, they received better treatment from their owners.

The slaves who fared best in the agricultural regions of the South were the domestics—butlers, gardeners, cooks, housemaids, personal maids, and coachmen. Their work was lighter and their food, clothing, and housing considerably better than that of field hands. Some were even taught to read and write (although for a master to allow this was against the Southern slave codes), and some traveled extensively with their owners as maids and valets.

The foreman or "driver" commanded the highest price of all plantation slaves. The foreman was the plantation superintendent's right-hand man. He called the hands to work, laid out their specific chores, and checked individual quotas at the end of the day. The driver's food rations and his clothing were better than those of the other field hands, and he was occasionally awarded a bottle of rum.

Some slaves were allowed to hire themselves out to other masters or were rented out by owners or commercial agencies. Such rentals, five times more common than sales, were commonly used for temporary harvest help or such jobs as railroad construction. In return for their services, hired slaves generally received better food and clothing than the plantation field hands and sometimes a weekly allowance. Their owners received a percentage of their wages.

The extent of exploitation

The inhumanity of slavery in a society which preached the ideal of individual opportunity has been debated since before the Civil War. In 1838 Calhoun told congress: "We see it [slavery] now in its true light, and regard it as the most safe and stable basis for free institutions in the world." Calhoun's statement was strongly contradicted by New England historian Richard Hildreth, whose visit to the South left him convinced that slavery, "is a far more deadly and disastrous thing, more fatal to all the hopes, the sentiments, the rights of humanity, than almost any other system of servitude which has existed in any other community."

Belying the common notion that most slaves were contended, slaves themselves told of the dehumanizing nature of the system. Frederick Douglass, who fled from slavery in Maryland in 1838, described it as a life of, "perpetual toil; no marriage; no husband, no wife, ignorance, brutality, licentiousness; whips, scourges, chains, auctions, jails and separations; an embodiment of all the woes the imagination can conceive."

Robert W. Fogel and Stanley L. Engerman have recently argued, in *Time on the Cross,* that despite the undeniable hardships of slavery, slaves did not suffer from deprivation. Fogel and Engerman, using new mathematical techniques, concluded that the energy value of the slaves' diet exceeded that of free men. Rations of corn and pork were adequate, they claim, and were supplemented by sweet potatoes and other vitamin-rich products grown on the plantation. Fogel and Engerman also challenged the idea that the slaves' family life was limited. Slaves lived in single-family households, and the construction of their housing compared well with that of free workers of the period. Only occasionally were there slave "dormatories," and these were for unmarried men and women. However, since slaves could not make contracts, their marriages were not legally binding under state law.

While the slave's life expectancy was twelve percent below that of white Americans, Fogel and Engerman maintain that it was greater than that of urban industrial workers and "well within the range experienced by free men during the nineteenth century."

Historians generally agree that while fear of physical brutality was used to force slaves to work harder, most masters were not sadistic, if only for economic reasons. Fogel and Engerman stress that brutal whippings would have injured a slave's value. There were also those slaveowners who offered positive incentives to work hard: these included holidays, extra food, cash or land for the slave's exclusive use. Some slaves could grow marketable crops on their land and were allowed to keep the earnings.

On the other side of the debate, Kenneth Stampp in *The Peculiar Institution* has shown that cruelty was endemic in all slaveholding communities, especially in the newly settled regions close to the frontier. And in *The Slave Community* John Blassingame concludes that one-third of all slave families were broken up and that whippings were common on plantations.

The historical debate over the extent to which slaves were exploited has increased our knowledge of the slave's daily life but has tended to prevent a real appreciation of the distinctiveness of Afro-American culture. The historian, Eugene Genovese, has recently studied black personality, religion, language, music, and society in the environment of slavery. He has shown that within severe limits slave society provided a variety of experiences. There was an interdependent relationship between the slave and master based on rights and obligations on both sides. It was not a relationship of equals, but both sides understood its terms. Genovese maintains that a black culture based on a combination of the African heritage and the conditions of slave life existed and grew despite the slave system.

The desire for freedom

The black response to slave life varied. Some slaves found that Christianity offered a retreat from the harsh realities of the system. Others may have accommodated themselves to their life by playing a docile and helpless role. Many competed with each other for recognition by their master, while the slave elite—house servants, foremen, and skilled artisans—often identified themselves with the master class. At the same time many engaged in sabotage, stealing, and running away. And the records indicate that a high proportion of runaways were the more privileged slaves—which suggests that the childlike role may have been consciously

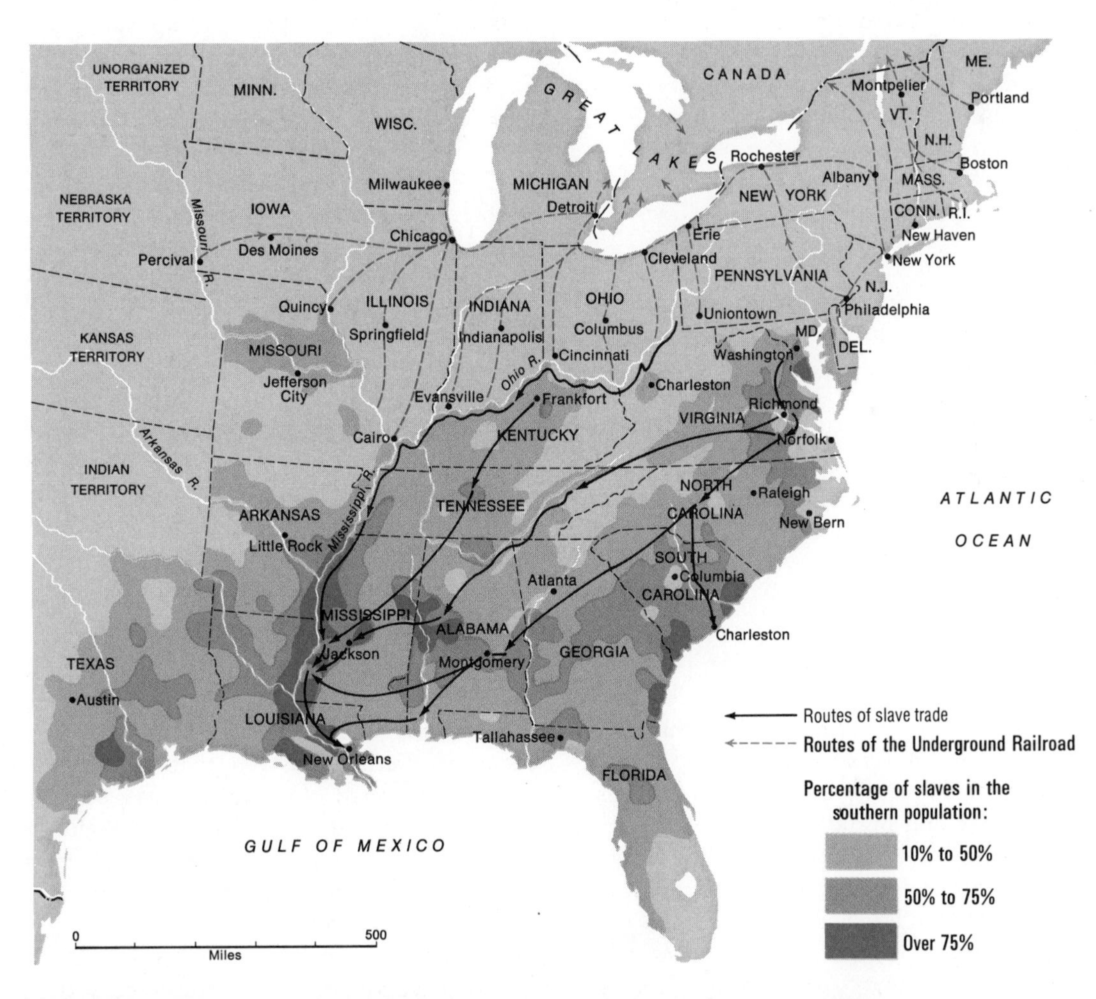

SLAVERY AND THE UNDERGROUND RAILROAD • 1840 TO 1860

Nat Turner's Plans for Rebellion

"On the 12th of May, 1828, I heard a loud noise in the heavens, and the Spirit instantly appeared to me and said the Serpent was loosened, and Christ had laid down the yoke he had borne for the sins of men, and that I should take it on and fight against the Serpent, for the time was fast approaching when the first should be last and the last should be first. . . . And by signs in the heavens that it would make known to me when I should commence the great work—and until the first sign appeared, I should conceal it from the knowledge of men—And on the appearance of the sign, (the eclipse of the sun last February) I should arise and prepare myself, and slay my enemies with their own weapons."

The Confessions of Nat Turner, 1831

Thomas R. Gray Comments on Nat Turner

"He is a complete fanatic, or plays his part most admirably. On other subjects he possesses an uncommon share of intelligence with a mind capable of attaining any thing; but warped and perverted by the influence of early impressions. . . . I shall not attempt to describe the effect of his narrative, as told and commented on by himself, in the condemned hole of the prison. The calm, deliberate composure with which he spoke of his late deeds and intentions, the expression of his fiend-like face when excited by enthusiasm, still bearing the stains of the blood of helpless innocence about him; clothed with rags and covered with chains; yet daring to raise his manacled hands to heaven, with a spirit soaring above the attributes of man; I looked on him my blood curdled in my veins."

The Confessions of Nat Turner, 1831

adopted and was cast off lightly when it became possible.

Many slaves tried, to little avail, to buy their freedom. Those who ran away were tracked down with bloodhounds and, if caught, were beaten severely and branded as troublemakers.

Perhaps the most successful method of escape from slavery was the Underground Railroad to the North. Three thousand of the railroad's "conductors" (those who helped escaped slaves in their journey to the North) were escaped slaves or blacks who had been born free in the North.

Nat Turner led the most sensational of all the slave revolts, and the one that had the greatest repercussions. A Virginia slave and Baptist preacher, Turner believed that his plans were divinely inspired. On an August evening in 1831, Turner and a small band of eight slaves killed Nat's master and his family. Then they pushed through the countryside gathering additional recruits along the way until they numbered seventy. In forty-eight hours Turner's renegade band seized and murdered sixty people. The terrified local white population mobilized volunteer reprisal forces and called out the state militia. Turner was caught, briefly imprisoned, and hanged, together with about twenty other blacks.

The South was terror-struck after Turner's Rebellion. One Northerner wrote:

> They lie down to sleep with fear. They hardly venture out on nights. A lady told me, that for weeks after the tragedy, she had quivered at every blast of wind, and every blow of the shutter. Bolts and bars were tried, but the horrid fear haunted the whole population day and night.

Insurrection panics occurred many times between 1831 and 1860, but Turner's was the last of the organized slave revolts. Remembering the bloody slave rebellions in the West Indies and South America, Southerners imposed such strict controls over slave behavior that open revolts had little chance of success. Slaves were forbidden to own firearms, and they could not visit or be visited by whites or free blacks. A slave could only preach to the slaves belonging to his or her own master, and only on the master's land with whites present. Night patrols were on constant alert throughout the South, supported by money which poured into town and county police departments from fearful whites. The movements of free blacks were restricted and emancipation was almost impossible.

Industrial Growth

During the pre-Civil War period the foundation was laid for the country's rising industrial economy. By 1850 the value of American manufacturing output topped one billion dollars, surpassing agricultural products by several million dollars.

The nation had enormous industrial potential which began to be realized through the technological developments of the antebellum period. There were massive deposits of coal, salt, oil, copper, lead, zinc, sulfur, limestone, and iron ore. Lumber and water for power were plentiful.

In the first half of the nineteenth century new techniques were devised for extracting and processing those natural resources into usable forms. In 1844, for example, Charles Goodyear patented a method for "vulcanizing" rubber, making it strong, elastic, and nonsticky even under extreme temperatures. This development triggered the rapid growth of the rubber-goods industry. Also before the Civil War a process was devised for turning the country's plentiful iron ore into steel, a durable, malleable, and inexpensive structural metal.

Increased demand for improved transportation and mechanization fanned the growth of American industry. Between 1840 and 1860 the production of pig iron tripled to meet the needs of railroad builders and farm machinery producers. The oil industry made huge profits selling to new markets created by the internal combustion engine and the kerosene lamp.

Mass production methods introduced during this period increased manufacturing capability. Assembly lines, standardized procedures for labor, and the use of machines with interchangeable parts enabled factories to make more efficient use of people and materials. Improvements in one area triggered expansion in another. When Isaac Singer began mass producing his sewing machine in 1851, he stimulated the growth of the garment industry.

Industrial expansion was also bolstered by a generous flow of capital into the new enterprises, and by the emergence of business initiative and leadership. The industrial entrepreneur and the corporate form were becoming established features of American economic life. Wealthy and

Type foundry around 1840. ▲

"Domestic Felicity with a Sewing Machine." ▼

sometimes unscrupulous individuals used the corporation as a means for setting up and operating huge businesses. A powerful business community became the moving force in the development of the country's natural resources, as business interests gained control of the railroad, oil refining, banking, meat packing, and farm machinery industries.

By 1857 one billion dollars in private capital had been invested in the railroads and another one billion had been channeled into various manufacturing enterprises. Much of this money had come from speculative overinvestment in corporate stocks and bonds which were frequently purchased with minimal down payments and high-interest loans from New York banks. Such overspeculation was a very important factor in the crash of 1837. After the crash speculation was still considered attractive, but some industrialists had learned financial discipline.

Government on all levels recognized the needs of big business and directly or indirectly encouraged private enterprise on a grand scale. After the fall of the Bank of the United States, the individual states established stable banking systems, benefiting business in general, and the federal and state governments made impressive land grants to the railroads. Liberal government land policies allowed timber and mineral interests to create monopolies over these natural resources. And reasonably high government tariffs protected American industry from foreign competition.

While government assisted the developing industries, it also adopted a laissez-faire attitude toward regulating them. Government on all levels failed to pass legislation regulating business practices or preventing the trend toward monopoly. At the same time the states prevented labor from hampering the growth of business. They used troops and court injunctions to quell boycotts and strikes.

SECTIONAL ASPECTS

America's industrial development was concentrated in the East. Industries in New England and the Middle Atlantic states hired over seventy percent of all Americans involved in manufacturing. Eastern industries were led by the manufacture of cotton cloth in New England. The important iron and steel industries were likewise centered in the East, along the rivers which supplied water power for the first large-scale factories.

Only about fifteen percent of the manufactured goods the United States produced came from the South. Although some Southern planters invested a portion of their capital in Northern manufacturing, they saw to it that their own society remained essentially agrarian. Southern cotton planters flourished, but their economy relied on Northern textile mills, Northern transportation, and Northern brokers and bankers.

Some attempts were made at manufacturing in the South. William Gregg of South Carolina established a textile mill in 1846. Gregg successfully employed over three hundred workers in 1850, but his operation was insignificant compared to the extensive Northern textile industry. Lowell, Massachusetts, alone had more spindles revolving in 1860 than did the entire South.

In the West the availability of natural agricultural resources also allowed the development of related industries. Factories sprang up to make wood products from the extensive virgin forests. By 1860 lumber production in the country was equal in value to cotton textile production. Western cattle provided the raw material for the meat packing and leather tanning industries. Grain was turned into flour and meal, liquor and beer, by a growing number of Western mills and distilleries.

THE AMERICAN WORKER

Americans believed that industrial progress would fulfill part of the nation's destiny: the expansion of economic well-being. But while the gross national product was rising and some people enjoyed a higher standard of living, many others felt the quality of their life deteriorating. The entrepreneur and the factory system may have contributed a great deal to the country's economic development but almost from the outset they also revealed a distinct tendency toward human exploitation.

America had always faced a scarcity of labor. In 1800 ninety percent of Americans still lived and worked on farms. Those who worked in the cities were skilled artisans, not factory hands. However, in response to the increasing demands of new industries, a sizable class of wage earners took form. Its members came from the farms of the East and later from Europe. Many wage earners were women and children.

The accelerating economy used new machinery that required fewer specialized skills and less physical strength. By the early 1820s half the workers in the cotton textile factories were children under sixteen. Many argued that such employment was a blessing for children and young women. Factory work, they said, gave young girls an opportunity to escape the doldrums of the farm, to save for a trousseau, to meet new people, or to help educate a younger brother. By midcentury, twice as many females as males worked in the cotton mills. They were preferred by employers because, as one manufacturer put it, "Women are much more ready to follow good regulations, are not captious, and do not clan as men do against the overseers."

Some companies transported whole families from the farm to the mill. Parents and children as young as four or five years worked side by side tending looms in the textile factories. Under the "Family System," they lived in factory towns provided by their employers and had little contact with the outside world. Although later generations frowned on child labor, antebellum apologists argued that it helped maintain family solidarity and provided a reasonable standard of living for the people involved.

On the other hand, the Boston Associates enlisted unmarried women in their late teens and early twenties to work in their Lowell, Massachusetts, mills. Since those hired under this "Lowell System" returned after a few years to the farms, they did not form a permanent working class.

WORKING CONDITIONS

The girls at the Lowell factory were treated relatively well. Charles Dickens observed approvingly:

> They were all well dressed. They were healthy in appearance, many of them remarkably so, and had the manners and deportment of young women. . . . The rooms in which they worked were as well ordered as themselves.

The Lowell girls enjoyed better wages and working conditions than their English counterparts. They lived in relatively pleasant boarding houses, attended lectures regularly, organized sewing circles, and edited their own literary periodicals.

On the whole, however, American workers labored long hours for low pay. Unskilled workers made only one dollar a day, and skilled workers from one to two dollars. Mill hands worked twelve to fifteen hours a day, but most of them came from farming families and were used to working hard for less money than they earned in the mills.

Even the more favorable working conditions in the Lowell textile mills began to deteriorate rapidly, as management of the Boston Associates' mills was turned over to hired professionals. In their eagerness to increase profits, these new managers lowered wages and turned the factories into places of drudgery. They forced the Lowell girls to wake up at 4:30 A.M., start work precisely at 5:00, and allowed them only two thirty-minute breaks for meals, at 7:00 and 12:00.

Industrialization gradually changed the behavior of American workers so that it fit the regulated demands of machine-oriented processes. Americans had always taken time off from work for celebrations, hunting, and harvesting. Such habits were vigorously suppressed. In Philadelphia tardy and absent workers were fined. To prevent their attention from straying from their assigned tasks, Philadelphia workers were forbidden to "carry into the factory nuts, fruits, etc., books or paper."

Historian Paul Faler examined the Lynn, Massachusetts shoe factories and found that from 1826 to 1860 the entrepreneurs gradually imposed a new morality on their workers. They especially tried to end drinking on the job. Lynn's shoemakers had long expected a daily ration of liquor as part of their wages, and treated each other to drinks twice a day. Influenced by the temperance movement, employers began refusing to employ workers who drank.

By 1840 exploitation of factory workers had worsened as employers shifted from daily wages to piece rate payments in order to increase production. Skilled craftspeople witnessed the degeneration of their trades as the crafting of a product, such as a shoe, by a single person, gave way to the division of tasks among several people.

THE LABOR MOVEMENT

Deteriorating working and living conditions blighted Eastern factory towns. The workers were legally free, but the drudgery of their lives was a form of bondage. Those who came from the farms to raise their standard of living by taking factory work found that their new lives were bleak, that the routine was oppressive, and that living was expensive in the company boardinghouses. Even worse off than the mill hands were the unskilled laborers who worked in

"The shoemakers' strike in Lynn, Massachusetts." Eight hundred women operatives struck in March 1860.

construction gangs on railroads, turnpikes, and canals. They were unable to earn enough to support a family.

Eventually laborers began to organize to improve their lot. They formed rudimentary unions, but strikes were prohibited by law and repressed by their employers.

In 1834 one thousand Lowell girls went on strike to protest a fifteen percent wage cut. According to a Boston newspaper, one of the leaders of the protest made a "flaming" speech from a stump about "the rights of women and the inequities of the 'monied aristocracy' which produced a powerful effect on her auditors, and they determined to 'have their way, if they died for it.' " But they got nowhere. Striking was regarded as a crime, and the poorly organized workers had no precedents for such protests. The leaders of the strike were fired; the rest of the young women went back to work at the reduced wages.

Other workers during this period also tried to use the strike to force employers to meet their demands. There were 114 strikes between

1831 and 1840 in Pennsylvania alone. Although the workers involved were threatened with criminal prosecution and the use of state troops, they believed there was no other way to press for higher wages and improved working conditions.

Instead of striking over poor working conditions, many factory workers and craftspeople moved west to look for new opportunities. An estimated one-third of the Midwestern farmers of the antebellum period had earned the money for their land as craftspeople or laborers in the East. Even though new workers moved in to replace them, employers could not degrade labor to European standards as long as there was land available on the continent.

Guild-style craft unions existed very early in the nation's history. They were composed of independent, skilled artisans who employed journeymen and apprentices. By the beginning of the nineteenth century these artisans had expanded their businesses and become "merchant capitalists." As competition among them grew, they were forced to cut their employees' wages. Their workers, in turn, formed the country's first unions when their income dwindled and their status was threatened by mass production.

These early efforts to organize labor unions were opposed at first by both management and government. Labor combinations were regarded as illegal conspiracies to inspire revolt and violence. Their very existence was considered a menace to both employers and nonunion workers.

Labor was further discouraged from organizing by the traditional emphasis on individual effort to overcome obstacles, the use of children for unskilled jobs, and the instability introduced into American society by the lure of the frontier and by the influx of destitute immigrants.

In 1842 the Massachusetts Supreme Court ruled that labor unions were not illegal combinations unless they were planning a conspiracy. Now unions finally had some official sanction to exist. Lasting organizations for the protection of American workers did not develop until after the Civil War, but during the boom years 1834 to 1837, trade union membership rose from 26,000 to 300,000. Most of these unions were nonpolitical organizations, but Philadelphia unions organized into the American Working Men's Party in order to more effectively seek a ten-hour day, an end to licensed monopolies, equal property taxes, and free education for their children.

The Panic of 1837 dealt a staggering blow to the trade union movement. Some craft unions, such as the printers, managed to weather the worst years, but most of the crafts were unable to compete with the rising mass production techniques. These crafts, together with their unions, gradually disappeared. By the 1840s labor organizations in other trades began to revive along with the economy. By the mid-1850s almost all skilled workers were organized. In addition to increased wages, labor's greatest cry was for reducing the working day to ten hours. By 1855 seven states had passed laws ensuring laborers' a ten-hour working day.

IMMIGRANTS AS WORKERS

The European immigrants who flooded the country before the Civil War could rightfully claim to have been exploited. One-half million of them entered the United States in the 1830s, 1.5 million in the 1840s, and over 2.5 million in the 1850s. They came from northern and western Europe, especially Germany and Ireland, driven by unemployement, religious persecution, and famine in their native countries. Steamships that carried American cotton and lumber to Europe converted unoccupied space on their return trips into rough passenger quarters. An immigrant could travel in steerage on these cargo vessels from Liverpool to New York for under $15. But the food was bad and quarters were crowded, stuffy, and unsanitary. Outbreaks of epidemics were common. On one crossing of the steamship *Lark,* for example, 158 out of 440 steerage passengers died of typhus.

Germans and some Scandinavians pushed into the Western regions of America. The poorer immigrants, however, had no money to purchase farmland. Most of them remained in the Eastern seaports. They were usually destitute, often unskilled, and eager for work of any kind. They were swiftly absorbed into the factories of the Northeast.

Because the immigrants demanded less comfort and stayed on over the years mill owners gradually replaced their farm girls with Irish immigrants. Desperation forced them to accept lower wages than the American workers and to shun unionization so as not to displease their employers. By 1860 Irish immigrants accounted for over half of the labor force in the New England mills.

The influx of immigrants was a major factor in the rapid growth of the American economy in the antebellum period. Welsh and some English workers labored in the coal mines of Pennsylvania and in the lead mines of Missouri and Wisconsin. German and English workers increased the country's supply of skilled craftspeople. Irish workers toiled in New England's factories, built the nation's railroads, and dug her canals. Chinese immigrants provided an important source of labor for the Western mines and railroads.

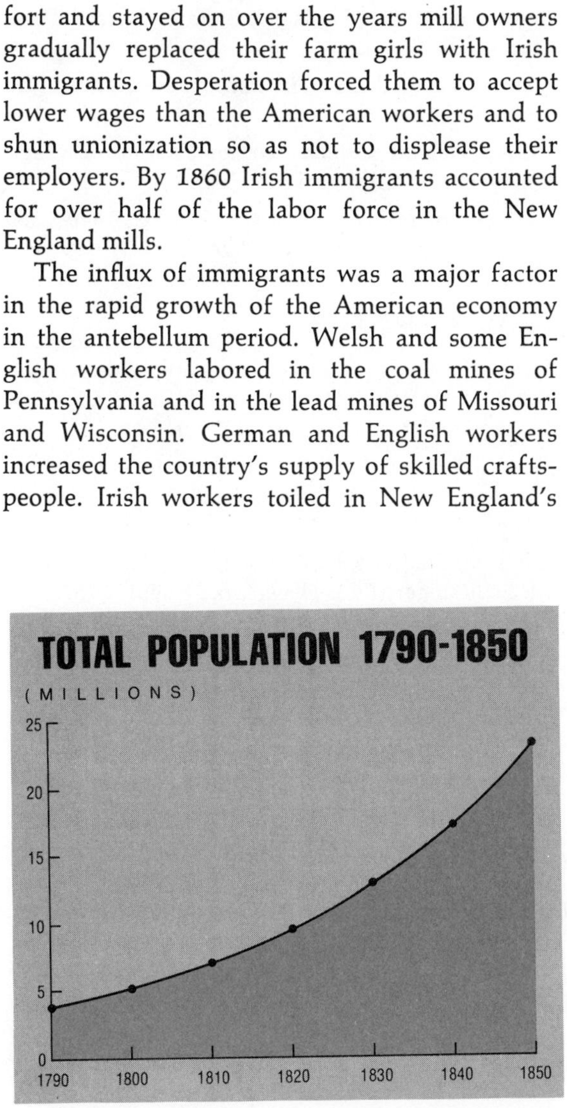

But despite their hopes, their hard work, and their contribution to American growth, the immigrants were often exploited and unhappy. Like the Americans they replaced, they had to face the new industrial work ethic and be bent to industrialized patterns. Their depressed wages were hardly sufficient to live on. New arrivals were easy prey for swindlers who overcharged them for food, lodging, and transportation. Because they could afford only the cheapest housing, most lived in dire poverty in the slums of the larger Eastern cities. They were ideal prospects for greedy realtors who crowded their tenements with as many families as possible. A typical New York tenement housed as many as 4000 people, most with nowhere else to go. Sanitary conditions in these buildings were deplorable, life expectancy was low, and the mortality rate high.

In some cities Irish Roman Catholics faced the strong prejudices of American Protestants. The newcomers were blamed for their own poverty and wretched living conditions, for urban crime, and for spreading disease. A leading New York citizen blamed the 1832 cholera epidemic on immigrants, "the lower classes of intemperate, dissolute and filthy people huddled together like swine in their polluted habitations."

Though they were not as readily exploited as the other immigrants, the Scandinavians, Germans, Dutch, Czechs, and Finns who moved into the interior of the country also found hardships. Their new life was considerably different from the one they had left behind. They were unfamiliar with the soil crops in America, and American frontier life differed radically from European village life. American farmers lived in houses that were widely separated from their neighbors. The loneliness and isolation the Europeans experienced in their new country told heavily upon their families.

TOTAL POPULATION 1790-1850
(MILLIONS)

Readings

GENERAL WORKS

Billington, Ray A., *America's Frontier Heritage.* New York: Holt, Rinehart & Winston, 1966.

Billington, Ray A., *Westward Expansion.* New York: Macmillan, 1967.

Clark, Thomas D., *Frontier America.* New York: Scribner's, 1969.

Davis, David B., *The Problem of Slavery in Western Culture.* New York: Cornell University Press, 1966. (Paper)

Eaton, Clement, *The Growth of Southern Civilization.* New York: Harper & Row, 1961.

Eaton, Clement, *A History of the Old South.* New York: Macmillan, 1966.

Gates, Paul W., *The Farmer's Age: Agriculture, 1815–1860.* New York: Holt, Rinehart & Winston, 1960.

Genovese, Eugene, *The Political Economy of Slavery.* New York: Pantheon, 1965. (Paper: Random).

Pessen, Edward, *Riches, Class, and Power before the Civil War.* New York: Heath, 1973.

Riegel, Robert E., and Robert G. Athearn, *America Moves West.* New York: Holt, Rinehart & Winston, 1970.

SPECIAL STUDIES

Blassingame, John W., *The Slave Community: Plantation Life in the Antebellum South.* New York: Oxford University Press, 1972.

Degler, Carl N., *Neither Black nor White: Slavery & Race Relations in Brazil & the U.S.* New York: Macmillan, 1971. (Paper)

Dick, Everett, *The Dixie Frontier.* New York: Knopf, 1948.

Elkins, Stanley M., *Slavery.* Chicago: University of Chicago Press, 1968.

Fogel, Robert W., and Engerman, Stanley, *Time on the Cross.* Boston: Little, Brown, 1974.

Genovese, Eugene, *Roll, Jordan, Roll: The World the Slaves Made.* New York: Pantheon, 1974.

Genovese, Eugene, *World the Slaveholders Made.* New York: Pantheon, 1969.

Gutman, Herbert G., *Slavery and the Numbers Game: A Critique of Time on the Cross.* Urbana, Ill.: University of Illinois Press, 1975.

Jones, Maldwyn A., *American Immigration.* Chicago: University of Chicago Press, 1960.

Owsley, Frank L., *Plain Folk of the Old South.* Baton Rouge, La.: Louisiana State University Press, 1949.

Stampp, Kenneth M., *The Peculiar Institution.* New York: Knopf, 1956.

Wade, Richard C., *The Urban Frontier.* Chicago: University of Chicago Press, 1959.

Ware, Norman J. *The Industrial Worker, 1840–1860.* Boston: Houghton Mifflin, 1924.

PRIMARY SOURCES

Fishel, Leslie H., Jr., and Benjamin Quarles, *The Black American: A Documentary History.* Glenview, Ill.: Scott, Foresman, 1970. (Paper)

Goodrich, Carter (Ed.), *The Government and the Economy, 1783–1861.* Indianapolis: Bobbs-Merrill, 1966.

Olmsted, Frederick L., *The Cotton Kingdom.* Arthur M. Schlesinger (Ed.). New York: Knopf, 1953.

Wish, Harvey (Ed.), *Slavery in the South.* New York: Farrar, Straus & Giroux, 1964.

BIOGRAPHIES

Green, Constance M., *Eli Whitney and the Birth of American Technology.* Boston: Little, Brown, 1956.

Lane, Wheaton J., *Commodore Vanderbilt.* New York: Knopf, 1942.

Ortiz, Victoria, *Sojourner Truth.* Philadelphia, Pa.: Lippincott, 1974.

FICTION

Bontemps, Arna, *Black Thunder.* Boston: Beacon Press, 1968. (Paper)

What hath God Wrought?

The American Telegraph System 1844–1866

For thousands of years the ability to communicate between distant points was limited by the speed of the horse and the sailing ship. For almost two centuries the properties of electricity were studied and the idea of communicating by wire slowly developed.

Suddenly, in the 1840s, the American telegraph system was born. In just two decades the system expanded into a profusion of different companies and routes, then contracted to become the nation's first great industrial monopoly.

The telegraph was the first of the wire technologies, the first continental communications system, and the first modern application of electricity.

In the spring of 1844 Samuel Finley Breese Morse successfully demonstrated the practicality of telegraphic transmission along a route from Baltimore to Washington, D.C. Within a decade thousands of miles of wire had been strung between the cities east of the Mississippi.

The telegraph was carried to the Pacific coast just when the Civil War was beginning, eight years before the railroad crossed the American continent. A year after the war's end, the transatlantic cable was successfully completed and Western Union had established the first national communications system as a private monopoly.

Centuries before Morse began his work, the ancient Greeks had discovered electricity as the mysterious sparks which appeared as a consequence of rubbing together pieces of amber. During the eighteenth century numerous scientists and amateur experimenters had explored the nature of static electricity.

By 1800 a number of discoveries crucial to the development of the telegraph had been made. Volta had developed a primitive battery which provided a way of storing electricity; Georg Ohm had published the first laws of the "galvanic circuit" which explained the principles of using a battery to send a current (signal) through a resistance medium (wire); and Hans C. Oersted had established the connection between electricity and magnetism which provided control over the detection of signals sent along a wire.

Thus, by the time Morse entered the process, much of the developmental work had already

Morse's original message.

been done. Morse was a painter who knew nothing about electricity. He turned his talents to invention at a desperate point in his life when painting had failed to provide him with a living.

With the help of an important American scientist, Joseph Henry, Morse was able to develop a simple machine for sending and detecting signals sent over a wire. By 1837 he had a working model.

At the same time he invented a code which consisted of a basic alphabet of two beats, one long *da* or dash (–), and one short *dit* or dot (·). Used in combination, these two signals formed letters and a series of letters formed words. The most frequently used letters had the simplest code. The letter *e,* for example, is simply a dot (·). Less commonly used letters, like *b,* have longer codes, such as dash dot dot dot (–···). One of the most commonly known Morse-invented words is the distress signal, SOS (··· –––···).

Improved form of telegraph key.

Morse code caught on because it was simple, just like the telegraph machine which Morse had built to send the code. Elaborate printing instruments were soon developed to decode the telegraphic messages, but eventually it was found that a person could decode the telegraphic messages faster than any machine if the signal was in the form of a sound. When the signal decoder triggered a machine which made a clicking sound, SOS became three long clicks, three short clicks, and three long clicks. The sound of the clicks became the familiar noise of the telegraph office, and good telegraphers, such as Andrew Carnegie, were among the first of the modern communications professionals.

Yet the path was not so easy for Morse himself. He tried for many years to interest the American and European governments in funding the development of his invention. Finally, he received a subsidy of $30,000 from Congress to construct a telegraph line along the railway between Baltimore and the capitol. Coincidentally, the two national political parties were holding their conventions in Baltimore, thus providing an audience for testing the new system. From the Supreme Court chambers on May 24, 1844, Morse clicked out his famous first words by telegraph: "What hath God wrought?"

No one really knew, and few could have foreseen, what a great resource had been tapped by a machine which clicked. In his report to Congress on the experimental telegraph line, Morse pointed out the great potential for good or evil

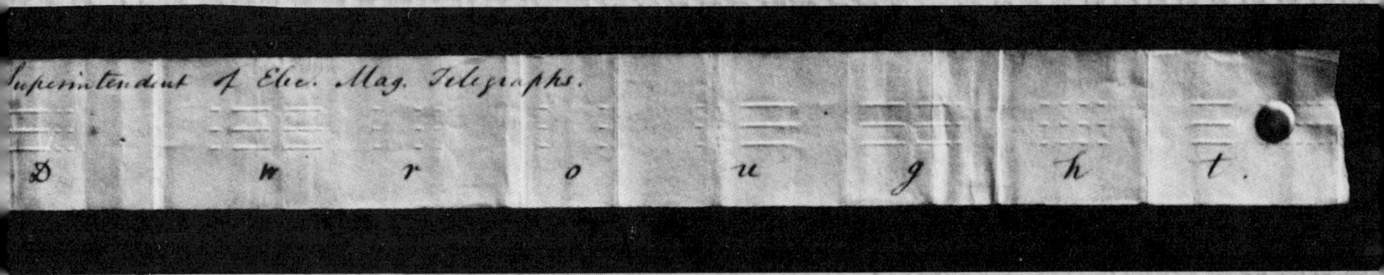

which the new invention represented. He suggested that the government acquire his patent rights and take responsibility for constructing the telegraph system throughout the nation. However, he received no response from Washington and finally turned to private interests to raise the necessary capital to continue building.

The telegraph was an idea whose time had come. By the fall of 1845, just a little more than a year after the first experiment, construction of telegraph lines was proceeding between all the major eastern cities. By the end of 1846, telegraphy was firmly established as a reasonable commercial venture. From this point on, Morse faded into the background and the development of telegraphy was dominated by the organizational and financial structure of the companies building the telegraph systems.

It took little time for newspapers to find a use for the new communications system. News about the Mexican War was the first big story to "come across the lightning wire." The ability to communicate from city to city was also a boon to the financial community, providing the early beginnings of the ticker tape which has come to symbolize Wall Street.

But even though telegraphy filled many needs, it took years for it to become a stable business enterprise. From the beginning, there was a tension between the people who wanted to build one large national telegraph system and those who wanted to develop a number of small local systems. The financiers who bought an interest in the Morse patent favored the former plan. They envisioned an initial system of national trunk lines interconnecting the major cities. Local distribution lines within cities would be built at a later time, they believed. This vision foreshadowed the eventual structure of the telegraph industry but the immediate future was one of explosive growth. The initial years of expansion were characterized by the Morse interests splitting into factions, competitive devices entering the market, and rival telegraph lines being constructed everywhere.

Demands for expansion quickly fractured the Morse patent "family" which consisted of two major personalities: Amos Kendall, a former Postmaster General in Andrew Jackson's cabinet, who was the agent for the patent rights of the majority of the Morse interests, and F. O. J. "Fog" Smith, a former Congressman from Maine, who had been chairman of the House Commerce Committee in 1838 when Morse first came to Washington seeking government support. As part-owner of the patent, Smith proved to be a major element of disruption and discord throughout most of the developmental period of the telegraph.

A third person, a man by the name of Henry O'Rielly, also occupied an important role in early telegraph history. Just two weeks after hearing about telegraphy for the first time, he signed a contract with Kendall to construct telegraph lines from the eastern seaboard to the Mississippi and Great Lakes. O'Rielly proved to be the pop-

"Landing the Atlantic Cable in Heart's Content Bay, Newfoundland."

ulist of the telegraph movement. He looked forward to a great democratic association of local companies with representatives from each town along the route. His hopes for telegraphy stood in opposition to the plans of the Morse interests.

One might think that the telegraph system was carefully thought out and financed ahead of time. Instead, the telegraph industry was built on a shoestring and capital was raised as the wire progressed from community to community.

Despite these problems, seven years after the first 40 miles of wire had been laid between Baltimore and Washington, over 23,000 miles of wire connected most of the important commercial centers east of the Mississippi.

However, the structure of the infant industry was far from settled. In 1851 and 1852, a small company called the New York and Mississippi Valley Printing Telegraphy Company competed with Morse lines for the Buffalo–New York City business. This Rochester, New York company was organized by Hiram Sibley with the explicit aim of acquiring *all* telegraph interests west of Buffalo and making them into one system under one management.

At one crucial organizational meeting held to raise capital, Sibley openly admitted that he thought telegraphy to date had been a failure. Yet the company which Sibley was founding did flourish under the strategy of one system/one management, and in little more than a decade a number of individual failures had been consolidated into one giant success which was the first national monopoly.

In the spring of 1856, Sibley reorganized his company as the Western Union Telegraph company. Simultaneously, Cyrus Field appeared with his twin dream of a unified telegraph system on the Atlantic seaboard and a link to Europe. Although Field's obsession with the Atlantic project would not be satisfied for ten years, the company he helped form in 1855—the American Telegraph Company—was to succeed in its effort to unify the East Coast and proved to be Western Union's final competition for total monopoly.

As Field and the American Telegraph Company, which eventually absorbed the original Morse interests, looked to the Atlantic cable and future business with Europe, Sibley and Western Union, which eventually absorbed all non-Morse interests, looked west to California. When gold was discovered in 1848, the overland stage took sixty days to reach the Pacific coast while clipper ships took ninety days. Beginning in 1853, telegraph systems were expanding throughout California, and were so important that in 1859, the state legislature voted to subsidize the first system that connected with a line from the East. In 1860 the United States Congress passed the Pacific Telegraph Act which authorized the subsidization of the transcontinental link.

The Civil War was already underway as the Pacific line was being built. For the most part, the fortunes of war favored Western Union which was well-suited with its east–west lines to take advantage of the greatly increased volume of business brought on by the war. American Telegraph, with its north–south system, was severely crippled.

Within a year Western Union's geographic advantages were to prevail, and by June 1866, American Telegraph had been absorbed. A month later, Cyrus Field landed the transatlantic cable at Heart's Content, Newfoundland, establishing the connection with Europe. Thus, within twenty years, Morse's Baltimore-to-Washington experimental link had grown into a national telegraphic monopoly and the basis for the first global communications system.

Suggested Reading

Clarke, Arthur C., *Voice Across the Sea* (New York: Harper & Brothers, 1958). This talented science fiction writer turns his attention to the history of the transoceanic cable from the 1850s to the 1950s.

Field, Henry, *The Story of the Atlantic Telegraph* (New York: Charles Scribner's Sons, 1893). A personal chronicle of the twelve-year story of the laying of the first transatlantic cable as told by Cyrus Field's son.

George, Lloyd and Gilman, James, *Modern Mercuries* (New York: Robert McBride & Co., 1932). An easy-to-read, illustrated history of communications from the development of speech to air mail.

Still, Alfred, *Communication Through the Ages* (New York: Murray Hill Books, 1946). The subtitle of this book, "From Sign Language to Television" describes the span of time the book covers.

Thompson, Robert Luther, *Wiring A Continent* (Princeton: Princeton University Press, 1947). An exhaustive study of the history of the telegraph industry in the United States from 1832–1866.

Lyceum lectures became a popular form of adult education in the 1840s. This lecturer is explaining the science of meteorology to an adult audience in New York City.

12

Religion, Romanticism, and Reform

The old and moth-eaten systems of Europe have had their day, and that evening of their existence which is nigh at hand will be the token of a glorious dawn for the down-trodden people. Here we have planted the standard of freedom, and here we will test the capacities of men for self-government. We will see whether the law of happiness and preservation upon each individual, acting directly upon himself, be not a safer dependence than musty charters and time-worn prerogatives of tyrants. Doctrines that even now are scarcely breathed, innovations which the most fearless hardly dare propose openly, systems of policy that men would speak of at the present day in the low tones of fear . . . will, in course of time, see the light here and meet the sanction of popular favor and go into practical play. Nor let us fear that this may result in harm. All that we enjoy of freedom was in the beginning but an experiment.

Walt Whitman, *Brooklyn Daily Eagle*

The great political and economic changes which characterized American life in the forty years preceding the Civil War were accompanied by tremendous social and intellectual ferment. Alexis de Tocqueville, a young Frenchman who visited the United States from 1831 to 1832, witnessed many of the trends himself and wrote about them with an accuracy and insight which has never been surpassed. His enduring work, *Democracy in America,* is based upon his personal observations and still serves as a valuable introduction to a study of the American character.

Tocqueville believed that the emphasis on equality had become *the* dominant influence in America by the 1830s. While he recognized that individual liberty had always been an important American ideal, he argued that the desire for equality, or "the sovereignty of the people" as he called it, was the most vital force in shaping the American way of life: "In America, the principle of the sovereignty of the people is not either barren or concealed, as it is with some other nations; it is recognized by the customs and proclaimed by the laws; it spreads freely, and arrives without impediment at its most remote consequences. If there be a country in the world where the doctrine of the sovereignty of the people can be fairly appreciated, where it can be studied in its application to the affairs of society, and where its dangers and advantages may be judged, that country is assuredly America."

Tocqueville was careful to point out the potential danger of the American love of equality. He saw that an excessive emphasis on equalitarianism could lead to a "tyranny of the majority," showing itself in conformity of thought and a decline of individual freedom. As he put it, "... every citizen, being assimilated to all the rest, is *lost in the crowd,* and nothing stands conspicuous but the great and imposing image of the people at large." In other words, while the desire for equality seemed to be linked with freedom, it could eventually lead to an enslavement of individuals to the opinions of the majority. Thus Tocqueville believed that the future greatness of America depended on its ability to strike the proper balance between freedom and equality. The sovereignty of the people would have to be matched by the development and survival of personal liberty.

In addition to warning of the dangers of equalitarianism, Tocqueville observed many ways in which the ideal was influencing American life. For instance, he saw that equality of opportunity had helped make the American people very pragmatic, and given them an intense love of wealth and material comfort. "They will habitually prefer the useful to the beautiful, and they will require that the beautiful should be useful," he wrote. He also noted a growing preference for commerce and industry over agriculture, and realized that the abundance of natural wealth had made the United States into a middle-class country. He saw American economic and social life as a unique phenomenon, characterized more by fluidity than by rigid stratification: "The Americans are a very old and enlightened people, who have fallen upon a new and unbounded country, where they may extend themselves at pleasure, and which they may fertilize without difficulty. This state of things is without a parallel in the history of the world."

Tocqueville noticed two other American qualities which came together in the first half of the nineteenth century to produce a powerful spirit of reform: the tendency to create organizations for civic improvement and the belief in human perfectibility. He wrote that, "... as castes disappear and the classes of society approximate, ... as ancient opinions are dissipated, and others take their place—the image of an ideal but always fugitive perfection presents itself to the human mind. Continual changes are then every instant occurring under the observation of every man..." In *Democracy in America,* Tocqueville did not comment directly on the reform movements which were beginning to take shape, but he did describe the two most important factors which characterized those efforts. He understood the theoretical ideals which motivated American reformists, and he observed the strong tendency in America for individuals to join groups in order to further their goals.

Tocqueville also perceived that a democratic and pragmatic people could still appreciate fine art and literature. "As soon as the multitude begin to take an interest in the labors of the mind, it finds out that to excel in some of them is a powerful means of acquiring fame, power, or wealth. The restless ambition which equality begets instantly takes this direction, as it does all others. The number of those who cultivate science, letters, and the arts, becomes immense." As we will see, the tremendous volume of American literary and artistic production during this period testifies to the accuracy of Tocqueville's observation.

Finally, in the area of religion, Tocqueville believed that a democratic country would emphasize the substance of beliefs more than external observances. Again, the intellectual and religious developments of the pre-Civil War era tend to bear out this basic assumption.

The Religious and Philosophical Background

Like the period of the Great Awakening in the early eighteenth century, the pre-Civil War era was a time of tremendous religious change in America. Some of the changes were disruptive—such orthodox doctrines as Puritanism and the Enlightenment emphasis on rationalism were rejected by many people. On the other hand, the same religious currents which undermined some established churches often led to the creation of brand-new sects. The belief in perfectibility and the value of personal experience, and in the Second Coming of Christ formed the basis for new types of religious expression. Instead of demanding obedience to a given body of doctrine, the religious movements of the early nineteenth century stressed the importance of a personal, emotional response.

ORGANIZED RELIGION

Most of the established churches with European ties, such as the Anglican, Lutheran, and Roman Catholic churches, found it necessary to reorganize and take on a more American look. The Anglican Church became the Episcopal Church shortly after the Revolution. Its new American hierarchy severed all direct connections with English church officialdom. Although the church was out of favor for a time after the Revolutionary War, the reorganization gradually enabled it to reclaim some of its former adherents. Virginians, particularly members of the upper class, were predominantly Episcopalian. As one wealthy Virginian put it: "No gentleman would choose any road to heaven but the episcopal." The new cotton aristocrats of Mississippi and South Carolina sometimes followed the religious example of the Virginia planters, but more often they favored the emotionally oriented denominations that were having a great revival throughout the South and West.

The Lutherans also broke their European ties and began using English rather than German in their services. Small in number until the 1840s, Lutheran churches began to increase rapidly with the great influx of German immigrants during that decade.

Another church that expanded in the early nineteenth century was the Roman Catholic. By 1846 there were twenty Roman Catholic bishoprics in the United States. Ethnic differences between the newly arrived Irish immigrants and the German and French church hierarchy was a threat to church unity, but the pressure of dealing with this problem helped the Catholic Church develop into an institution that was basically American. Eventually, the Church was able to assist immigrants in adapting to life in the United States as well as attract some American Protestants who were dissatisfied with their religions.

In the Boston area many Congregationalists began to desert their church for Unitarianism. Part of the reason for the shift was that Unitarianism, breaking with Calvinist outlooks, stressed the basic goodness of human beings and interpreted God as a merciful, benign being. Deeply influenced by the philosophy of the Enlightenment, Unitarians preached toleration of other faiths, urged individuals to come to their own interpretations of the Scriptures, and rejected the doctrine of the Trinity. In fact, the name Unitarian comes from the belief that God is a single being, not three beings in one God. Whereas Unitarianism tended to appeal to a small, well-educated group (such as the Harvard faculty), a watered-down version of the movement called Universalism attracted other segments of the New England population. Based on the belief that it was God's purpose to save every human being from sin, it gradually spread throughout the North in the pre-Civil War period. Thus the pessimistic world view of Puritanism, which had held many Americans in its grip for so long, was first weakened by the Enlightenment and then seriously undermined by Unitarianism and Universalism.

Scene at an 1858 camp meeting.

EVANGELICALISM

While Unitarianism was winning many converts in New England, by the 1820s the South and West were in the throes of yet another outburst of revivalism. Like the Puritans, evangelical groups such as the Baptists and Methodists believed in a literal heaven and hell and emphasized the Bible as an infallible record of divine revelation. Unlike the Puritans, however, most of the new evangelical religions taught that redemption could be earned by performing good works. Instead of believing in a preordained salvation, they preached that people could be reborn by freely confessing their sins and opening their hearts to God.

The belief in individual and social perfectibility was one of the doctrinal sources for the revivalism of the 1820s and 1830s. Perfectionism spurred the growth of the Methodist Church and was a basic element in the preaching of the country's greatest revivalist ministers such as

Charles G. Finney and Phoebe Palmer. According to Finney, "All sin consists in selfishness; and all holiness or virtue, in disinterested benevolence." Luther and Calvin, the two founders of Protestantism, had both doubted the effectiveness of good works. But American revivalists, led by Finney, combined an interest in saving souls with a conviction that Christians must help make society better. Thus the new evangelicalism reintroduced a belief in the saving grace earned by moral, benevolent behavior, especially if it led to social reform. "And what is to reform mankind but the truth?" asked Finney. "And who shall present the truth if not the church and the ministry? Away with the idea that Christians can remain neutral and keep still, and yet enjoy the approbation and blessings of God."

Thus the religious revivalism of the 1820s and 1830s was also significant as a social phenomenon. Because of its new emphasis on the moral and spiritual importance of reform, evangelicalism had its greatest impact on those socioeconomic groups that stood to gain the most from changing society.

In addition to strengthening the Methodists, the Baptists, and the social reformers, the strong tide of religious ferment led to the creation of several new religious movements, many of them short-lived. One sect which survived was a denomination founded in 1832 called the Disciples of Christ, now known as the Christian Church. Organized as an attempt to restore Christian unity and return all believers to a simple faith in the Gospels, the Disciples of Christ claimed one hundred thousand converts by 1850.

The Seventh Day Adventists, founded upon a belief of Christ's Second Coming, were another one of the new sects. The group began in the 1830s when a Baptist minister from Vermont named William Miller predicted the exact day in 1844 on which the Second Coming, or Advent, would occur. As the judgment day approached, Miller's disciples sold their belongings, dressed in white, and assembled on hilltops to await the coming of the Lord. When the prophecy failed to materialize many of the faithful gave up the idea entirely and the group nearly dissolved. However, a hard-core of believers justified the "Great Disappointment" and in 1846 organized a formal denomination under the leadership of Ellen G. Harmon. The new church was known as the Seventh Day Adventist Church because its members contended that Saturday, rather than Sunday, had been the Lord's day of rest and hence should be the sabbath.

Of all the unconventional religious currents circulating during this period, Swedenborgianism probably had the most intellectual impact. Swedenborg was an eighteenth-century Swedish philosopher who taught that the Second Coming of Christ would not be an actual event, but a spiritual one. As such, it could occur for anyone who studied the Bible and truly understood the relationship between human beings and the natural, spiritual, and celestial worlds. The cosmic ideology of Swendenborgianism had a profound impact on another important movement of the period, transcendentalism.

TRANSCENDENTALISM

Transcendentalism was the American counterpart of European romanticism. The movement had started in Germany in the last quarter of the eighteenth century. It steadily gained momentum until it came to dominate the artistic and philosophical output of all Europe. Romanticism was not a precise philosophy, but a vague term that described a cluster of loosely related attitudes. Basic to the romantic spirit was a rejection of the Enlightenment position that reason could solve all human problems. Romanticists believed that instinct, or intuition, was the true guide to ultimate wisdom. Where the Enlightenment had cultivated the normal, the rational, the ordered, and the familiar, romanticism searched out the bizarre, the instinctual, and exotic areas of experience. The Enlightenment had stressed the universality of human characteristics, while romanticism emphasized the uniqueness and genius of each individual and nationality. Romantics also loved untamed nature and the natural person. Less intellectual and closer to the instincts, the natural person was considered more in touch with essentials than the city dweller or the overrefined aristocrat. This democratic aspect of romantic thought appealed to Americans.

The transcendentalists were not so much a religious sect as a loosely knit group of individuals with similar philosophical attitudes. Emphasizing intuition and the importance of nature, they were closely connected with the first flowering of American literary genius and with the important reform movements of the early nineteenth century. Most people associated with this school of thought came from New England, and a surprising number of them had attended Harvard University and served as Unitarian ministers. Starting as an informal discussion club in 1836, the group met and exchanged ideas in and around Concord, Massachusetts for several years.

Transcendentalism was based on a rejection of the rational theology of Unitarianism. The transcendentalists dismissed the Unitarian faith as "corpse-cold," uninspiring, too impressed with human reason, and too neglectful of the human spirit. They wanted a living religion, and it had to be one which did not depend on a rigid theological creed. The transcendentalists also argued against some of the Enlightenment theories of John Locke. Locke had claimed that ideas do not arise spontaneously in the mind, but that they come about through sense impressions received from the external world. The transcendentalists, on the other hand, contended that ordinary experience could never be a guide to understanding ultimate reality. They believed that real knowledge could only be gained by intuition, the process of looking within oneself.

The transcendentalists stressed that in order to find reality one had to rise above, or transcend, the level of knowledge obtained through reason. They urged people to trust their intuition, not their reason. For the transcendentalists, an almost mystical perception of God, or the "Over-Soul," was the most important goal in life. This led them to celebrate nature which they believed to be divine, a direct expression of God. The leading transcendentalist, Ralph Waldo Emerson, wrote that, "Standing on the bare ground . . . all mean egotism vanishes. I become a transparent eyeball; I am nothing; I see all; the currents of the Universal Being circulate through me; I am part and parcel of God."

Like the revivalists, the transcendentalists wanted an emotional acceptance of God's power. But unlike most revivalists, they were intensely intellectual and had a great respect for formal learning. Since they stressed progress through the process of individual inspiration, most transcendentalists shared Tocqueville's fear of a stifling conformity to which the egalitarian spirit of America could eventually lead. They also disliked the trends in American life toward industrialism and granting paramount importance to material comfort. Many transcendentalists were prominent social activists, supporting and often working in the various reform groups of this period.

Literature

A phenomenal burst of literary activity took place in the decades before the Civil War. So great was the artistic achievement during this period that one author, Herman Melville, referred to the inherent potential of American writers by saying, "Believe me, men not very much inferior to Shakespeare are this day being born on the banks of the Ohio." With the works of such geniuses as Emerson, Thoreau, Poe, Hawthorne, Melville, and Whitman, the pre-

Civil War era represented a golden age in American literature. Between 1850 and 1855 the following masterpieces were published: Nathaniel Hawthorne's *The Scarlet Letter* and *The House of Seven Gables,* Herman Melville's *Moby Dick,* Henry David Thoreau's *Walden,* and Walt Whitman's *Leaves of Grass.* As the modern critic F. O. Matthiessen has written: "You may search all the rest of American literature without being able to collect a group of books equal to these in imaginative quality."

Romanticism was beginning to influence the American imagination, and many American authors turned to Europe as a symbol of romance. Literary pioneers such as Washington Irving and Henry Wadsworth Longfellow traveled to Europe in order to stimulate their creative powers and to escape certain aspects of democratic life in America. At the same time, the use of themes drawn from a romanticized feudal past betrayed a nostalgia for the simpler American past. The United States was being drastically changed during this period by immigration and urbanization, and many Americans were bewildered by what was happening. Romantic literature could calm some of the anxieties without really challenging American principles. A good example of this type of writing is Washington Irving's "Rip Van Winkle," a romantic story about a man who falls asleep for twenty years, then wakes up to find everything changed. Another important literary theme was the contrast between American and European life. Although the European past was often portrayed positively, many plays and books used the contemporary high culture of the Continent as an object of derision. By contrast, the simple virtues of the American yeoman could then be emphasized favorably.

RALPH WALDO EMERSON

Emerson (1803–1882) was the leading transcendentalist and the most famous American writer and thinker of his day. Descended from a long line of New England preachers, he graduated from Harvard in 1821 and soon became a Unitarian minister. After several years in the ministry he found that he disliked many of the mundane duties of his profession, and that the rational theology of Unitarianism was no longer satisfying to him. Because of his need to be free of the confinements of organized religion, he resigned as pastor of the Second Church of Boston in 1831. In his resignation address he claimed that the Church was a decaying institution, responsible for filling people with a "wasting unbelief." He also rejected the personality of God and the idea of miracles, speaking instead of "divine laws" and a beautiful, sentimental approach to the human soul.

Next Emerson set out on the first of his three trips to Europe, where he met many of the leading intellectuals of the Continent, including the English poet William Wordsworth and the Scottish philosopher Thomas Carlyle. When he returned to America Emerson settled in Concord, Massachusetts, and began to earn his living as an essayist and lecturer. He traveled far and wide speaking on philosophical subjects, receiving as much as fifty dollars a talk. On the platform, his manner was grave. But his speaking voice was so beautiful that one small-town observer said, "Our choir was a pretty good one, but its best was coarse and discordant after Emerson's voice."

His first book, *Nature,* was published in 1836. Calling for a new, independent American philosophy, this work marked the beginning of the transcendental movement. "There are new lands, new men, new thoughts," he wrote. "Let us demand our own works and laws and worship." Next he criticized the establishment culture of New England in his American Scholar Address at Harvard in 1837, and broke further with orthodox Calvinism with the Divinity School Address in 1838. By this time the Transcendental Club had been meeting on an informal basis for several years. In 1840, led by Emerson and the literary critic Margaret Fuller, the members started to issue a publication called *The Dial* through which they hoped to inspire many writers with the idea of an American national literature.

Ralph Waldo Emerson.

Emerson's frequent lectures served as the basis for several books of essays. Never systematic, his work consisted of brilliant flashes of insight, attempts at showing the value of previously unnoticed parts of the American experience. Believing in human perfectibility Emerson considered organized religion superfluous to the accomplishment of anything worthwhile. To him, the pursuit of virtue was the single most important human activity. He believed in accomplishing his goals by relying on inner strength, not organized religion. Knowing oneself was crucial to Emerson. Like so many Americans, he was a rugged individualist; one of his most famous essays is entitled "Self-

Individual Reform

"Whoso would be a man, must be a nonconformist. He who would gather immortal palms must not be hindered by the name of goodness, but must explore if it be goodness. Nothing is at last sacred but the integrity of your own mind. . . . No law can be sacred to me but that of my nature. Good and bad are but names very readily transferable to that of this; the only right is what is after my constitution; the only wrong what is against it. . . . I am ashamed to think how easily we capitulate to badges and names, to large societies and dead institutions. Every decent and well-spoken individual affects and sways me more than is right. I ought to go upright and vital, and speak the rude truth in all ways. . . . I do not wish to expiate, but to live. My life is for itself and not for a spectacle. . . ."

Ralph Waldo Emerson
"Self-Reliance," 1841

Communal Reform

"The most prevailing fear about Association is on the score of that undefined thing, Individuality. The very vagueness of the term, as used, however, is proof that it covers more than is understood. . . . We are prepared to take the ground that there is not and never can be Individuality, so long as there is not Association. Without true union no part can be true. The members were made for the body; if the whole body be incoherent, every member of it will be developed falsely, will become shrunken or overgrown, distorted and weakened, since it will have either more or less than its share, both of duty and of sustenance. Variety itself is dull, if it lack unity; for unity is the beginning and end of variety. . . ."

John S. Dwight,
"Lecture on Association," 1844

Reliance." In it he wrote, "Nothing is at last sacred but the integrity of your own mind."

Another American attitude which Emerson embodied was the belief in equality. Though he was not an admirer of General Jackson, Emerson was nevertheless quite in tune with the concept of Jacksonian democracy. In fact much of his work was really an intellectual form of democratic theory. On the theme of equality, he stated: "I believe it is the conviction of the purest men that the net amount of man and man does not much vary." Finally, he believed that all people were not only equal, but that they were also part of one great spiritual mind, the Over-Soul: "There is one mind common to all individual men. Every man is an inlet to the same and to all of the same. . . . Who hath access to this universal mind is a party to all that is or can be done, for this is the only and sovereign agent."

HENRY DAVID THOREAU

Born in Concord, Massachusetts, Thoreau (1817–1862) was a close friend and former student of Emerson. In 1837 he graduated from Harvard where he had been an outstanding student in the field of literature. In delivering the class commencement address, he first began to express a somewhat unconventional view of the world: "This curious world which we inhabit is more wonderful than it is convenient; more beautiful than it is useful; it is more to be admired and enjoyed than used."

After graduation Thoreau tried in vain to carry on his family's pencil-making business. He also taught school for a while in Concord, but resigned when the directors insisted that he dispense corporal punishment. Next Thoreau and his brother opened their own school and ran it from 1839 to 1841. In September 1839 he and his brother took a two-week river journey which became the subject of his first book, *A Week on the Concord and Merrimack Rivers.* It was published in 1849 at his own expense and sold only three hundred copies during his lifetime.

In 1849 Thoreau went to stay with the Emerson family and served them as a handyman for two years. He also associated with the Transcendental Club, which was active in Concord during this period. In March 1845 he built a small cabin at Walden Pond on the Emersons' property, a mile and a half from the center of Concord. For two years he used the area for his retreat from civilization. He spent his time writing, hiking, and gardening, or as he put it, "making the earth say beans instead of grass." He also spent one night in jail in 1845 for refusing to pay a poll tax in protest against slavery and the Mexican War. He justified this protest in an essay called "On Civil Disobedience," which has become one of the most famous works ever written on the subject of nonviolent resistance.

Thoreau's masterpiece, *Walden,* appeared in 1854. The book is a condensation of most of the journals he kept throughout his life, summing up his individualistic philosophy and his love of nature. As a modern critic has written: "The lesson he had taught himself, and which he tried to teach others, was summed up in the one word 'simplify.' That meant simplify the outward circumstances of your life, simplify your needs and your ambitions; learn to delight in the simple pleasures which the world of Nature affords. It meant also, scorn public opinion, refuse to accept the common definitions of success, refuse to be moved by the judgment of others." In *Walden* Thoreau also wrote of his objections to certain changes in the American way of life. He was especially opposed to the encroachment of the new industrial and urban forms of civilization. After *Walden* Thoreau devoted himself to lecturing in support of the antislavery movement and to continuing his explorations into natural history.

Thoreau's life was indeed as simple as the virtues which he preached. As Emerson said in his moving portrait of his younger friend: "He was bred to no profession; he never married; he lived alone; he never went to church; he never voted; he refused to pay a tax to the state; he ate no flesh, he drank no wine, he never knew the use of tobacco; and though a naturalist, he used neither trap nor gun. He chose, wisely no doubt for himself, to be the bachelor of thought and Nature."

Thoreau has become famous in the twentieth century for his defense of individual nonconformity. He stated clearly and poetically his belief that it is more important to obey one's conscience than to obey the laws of the land. In his love of nature and his ability to see the natural world as an expression of God Thoreau was a romanticist. When Thoreau was on his deathbed a friend asked him if he had made peace with God. Thoreau responded, "I am not aware that we ever quarreled."

Walt Whitman.

WALT WHITMAN

In 1842 Emerson had called for a great national poet: "We have yet had no genius in America . . . which knew the value of our incomparable materials, and saw, in the barbarism and materialism of the times, another carnival of the same gods whose picture he so admires in Homer."

The nation finally received exactly the poetic genius Emerson had requested in the person of Walt Whitman (1819–1892). Born in Long Island, Whitman left school when he was thirteen. In 1832 he began his long association with the newspaper business, starting as a printer's devil for the *Long Island Patriot.* By the 1840s he had worked his way up to the writing staff of the paper, and from 1846 to 1848 he served as editor of the Brooklyn *Eagle.* His journalistic efforts on behalf of various social reform movements eventually led to his dismissal from the *Eagle.*

Whitman's life changed dramatically in 1848, when he began to work on *Leaves of Grass.* The first edition appeared in 1855, transforming him from a traveling journalist to a major poet. This early version contained twelve poems, including the famous pieces later titled "Song of Myself." In the preface to the original edition he set forth his artistic ideals, asserting that a poet must be in harmony with the common people of the time. This belief in the artistic value of everyday life made the subject matter of his poems quite unique, even shocking. Whitman's themes were based on "common idioms, manners, the earth, the rude visage of animals and trees, and what is vulgar," as he himself remarked. The style of his poetry was also unconventional. Instead of the normal repetitious rhythms which people expected, Whitman's verse was plain and unornamented. He employed broad cadences, more typical of biblical prose than ordinary verse.

By 1860 *Leaves of Grass* had grown to 456 pages, with 122 new poems. For the rest of his life Whitman continued to add to the volume. It went through nine editions altogether, the last one appearing in 1892, the year of Whitman's death.

Nathaniel Hawthorne.

NATHANIEL HAWTHORNE

In a sense, Emerson, Whitman, and Thoreau were all optimists. Each of them was critical of certain aspects of American culture—its conformity, its inequalities, and its materialism. But because of their belief in the essential goodness of all human beings they all felt that American life could be progressively improved. Writing at the same time, however, were three figures of equal literary importance who did not hold such a hopeful view of life. Nathaniel Hawthorne, Herman Melville, and Edgar Allan Poe were romantic writers in that they ardently studied nature, valued instinct more than the intellect, and were fond of exotic places and faraway times. On the other hand, they were also part of the older Puritan tradition. They each saw evil as an active, inescapable force in human affairs, and as artists they were basically haunted by the notions of sin, vice, and pride.

Hawthorne (1804–1864) was born in Salem, Massachusetts, the son of a local shipmaster. After four years at Bowdoin College, Hawthorne retired to Salem where he lived a lonely, secluded existence. His only amusements were long walks along the Salem seashore, reading, and daydreaming. As the years went by his daydreams became more and more morose. During this period he wrote his old Bowdoin classmate, the poet Longfellow, saying: "Since we last met . . . I have secluded myself from society; and yet I never meant any such thing, nor dreamed what sort of life I was going to lead. I have made a captive of myself and put me into a dungeon, and now I cannot find the key to let myself out—and if the door were open, I should be almost afraid to come out."

Like his Puritan ancestors Hawthorne was obsessed with sinfulness, which in his opinion was a matter of individual selfishness. Although he did not attend church he spent much of his time brooding over religious concepts and filling his notebooks with short stories of evil impulses and the mysteries of sin. After his marriage in 1842 he started to become truly productive, writing four major novels and many short stories over the next twenty years. The books were moderately successful, but the income was not sufficient to support the Hawthornes. So he also held a variety of government posts, from weigher and gauger at the Boston Customs House to United States consul in Liverpool, England.

Many critics recognized Hawthorne's mastery of prose, but the skepticism and sense of hopelessness in his work went against the popular outlook. For instance, his masterpiece, *The Scarlet Letter,* is the story of a Puritan woman who commits adultery with a minister. After giving birth to an illegitimate child, the adulteress is forced by the members of the community to wear a scarlet letter *A* sewn to her dress. At the end of his life the minister finally confesses his part in the sinful situation by opening his shirt to reveal an identical letter *A* branded into his flesh by God. Hawthorne's preoccupation with this kind of tragic subject offended many Americans caught up in the prevailing optimism of the mid-nineteenth century.

Hawthorne was also drawn to the problem of the exceptional individual, the artist, within a democratic, mass society. Like Tocqueville, he was extremely concerned by the level of mediocrity which equalitarianism seemed to impose. But he also saw that an artist had to be able to establish close, human relationships with others. Even though some amount of solitude was required in order to be an artist, he considered withdrawal as an aristocratic, European attitude. This was the paradox he faced in seeking to reject solitude and affirm American values. To Hawthorne, human fulfillment meant resolving the contradiction, and his explorations of the issue took on a deeply religious tone.

Herman Melville.

HERMAN MELVILLE

One of Hawthorne's few close friends was the novelist and poet Herman Melville (1819–1891). After working as a bank clerk and a schoolteacher in Albany, New York, Melville shipped out to sea as a cabin boy in 1837. Shortly after his return he went off again on a series of South Sea voyages, including an eighteen-month trip on the Whaler *Acushnet*. In 1842 he jumped ship in the Marquesas Islands, spending an idyllic month with friendly natives before sailing to Tahiti on an Australian ship. He finally returned to Albany after serving in the United States Navy.

Melville now began writing, using his voyages as material for his first two books, *Typee* and *Omoo*, published in 1846 and 1847. *Mardi*, *Redburn*, and *White-Jacket* were further stories of adventure at sea, but Melville did not reach his full artistic stature until the publication of *Moby Dick* in 1851.

Considered by many as one of the finest novels ever written, *Moby Dick* has been interpreted in many ways. On one level it is a superb adventure story with a wealth of detailed information about whaling. Moreover, it is a penetrating psychological study of human obsession, and a serious exploration of the human need to find meaning in the universe. The book's plot concerns a Yankee skipper, Ahab, who lost one leg in a struggle with the great white whale, Moby Dick. Driven by a desire for revenge, Ahab forces his crew to pursue Moby Dick from one end of the Pacific to the other. In the end the ship is attacked by the whale, and Ahab and all but one of the crew members are killed.

According to some modern critics the story represents Melville's belief that the world is as morally colorless as the white whale. Melville seems to be saying that human beings cannot tolerate such meaninglessness, however, and Ahab is both heroic and insane in attempting to conquer Moby Dick as the embodiment of evil.

EDGAR ALLAN POE

Poe (1809–1849) was born in Boston. He was orphaned at the age of three and raised by a wealthy tobacco merchant. In 1826 he enrolled at the University of Virginia. While in college he drank and gambled so much that his adopted father disowned him. Although his literary brilliance was soon apparent in "Tamerlane and Other Poems" (1827) gambling debts and alcoholism were already shaping the pattern of his life. Despite his great talent Poe was never able to earn more than $300 a year as a journalist, critic, editor, and writer.

In 1836 he married his cousin and they moved to New York in search of broader literary horizons. Still troubled by gambling and drinking, he went from one position to another, writing prolifically in order to support himself. In 1845 his wife died of tuberculosis and Poe's private life became even more chaotic. As he described it to a friend, "I became insane, with long intervals of horrible sanity. During these fits of absolute unconsciousness, I drank—God only knows how often or how much. As a matter of course, my enemies referred the insanity to the drink, rather than the drink to the insanity."

In spite of his personal tragedies Poe managed to turn out a truly impressive body of work. His literary criticism was highly original and insightful, and his fine short stories included some of the first detective stories ever written. As a poet his bizarre symbolism and his experiments in pure sound had a great influence on the French symbolist movement. Like Hawthorne and Melville, Poe never reflected the prevailing American belief that human nature was perfectible. He wrote in one letter: "I have no faith in human perfectibility. I think that human exertion will have no appreciable effect upon humanity. Man is now only more active—not more happy, nor more wise—than he was 6,000 years ago."

The Visual Arts

While American literature scaled new heights, the visual arts were not far behind. Americans of the mid-nineteenth century began to take an active interest in their own society, and this new inward turn was reflected in painting, sculpture, and architecture, as well as in literature.

In the 1820s neoclassicism, an outgrowth of the Enlightenment, was the ruling style in American art. According to its standards artists were to ignore the unusual and emotional aspects of a scene and were to stress instead the rational and the ideal. The artist's job was to eliminate all the "accidents" of nature and simplify every scene until the underlying perfect form was revealed. Thus, rather than showing real people, neoclassical painting showed idealized human beings, freed of all their individuality. The style was mostly used to praise such American virtues as the opportunity for upward mobility. Portraits of the merchant elite, for example, used classical backdrops and poses drawn from Greek art to give dignity to the subjects.

By the mid-1840s, however, a new mood had set in. Just as religion and literature reacted against the Enlightenment's emphasis on rationality, the visual arts now turned away from neoclassical values. "Picturesqueness" became the most desired quality in painting, straightforward depictions of simple, natural scenes. Themes were drawn from natural landscapes and the American frontier, reflecting the prevailing mood of romantic nationalism.

The American clergy's attitude toward art also underwent a tremendous change at this time. Instead of seeing art as a frivolity, they decided to use it as an ally in their effort to reform society. As Edward Everett Hale stated, "We believe that God wants to educate the whole man—body, mind, and soul—that to God's eye, therefore, the hours of rest are worth as much as the hours of labor." Since people would always seek amusement it would be better to guide their tastes than to allow them free rein. In order to uplift the tastes of the lower classes and the nouveaux riches, ministers urged an identification of art with religion. Landscape art made one aware of nature, and many ministers felt that nature was the "interpreter of God." Thus, insofar as art developed an awareness of nature, it was good.

This trend was reinforced by the fact that many American artists of this period were inspired by the British Pre-Raphaelites. According to Pre-Raphaelite theory, the artist had a duty to uplift the masses. The Pre-Raphaelite school had a romantic view of the visual arts; its purpose was to democratize art. In the words of one artist, its goals were, "to make Art popular, not by making it low, but by opening its principles to the comprehension of all kinds in the proportion of their intelligence and moral development. . . ." In order to obtain truthfulness, the artist had to paint directly from nature.

THE HUDSON RIVER SCHOOL

Thomas Cole (1801–1848), founder of the Hudson River School of landscape painting, emigrated to America from England at the age of seventeen. He worked for awhile as an engraver at his father's wallpaper factory in Ohio, eventually moving east to make his living by painting portraits. After studying at the Pennsylvania Academy in 1825, he turned to painting landscapes, attempting to capture a sense of the vast American wilderness. By the time he established his own studio in New York in 1827, he was the acknowledged leader of a group of American romantic painters who drew their inspiration from the countryside along the Hudson River.

In Kindred Spirits *Asher Brown Durand painted William Cullen Bryant and Thomas Cole on a walk through the Catskill Mountains. Cole was considered to be America's greatest landscape painter, a position Durand inherited when Cole died.* ▶

Cole was infected with a love of nature typical of romanticism. On his long rambles through the Catskills and along the Hudson he continually made sketches which he would later work into full oil paintings. His works are distinguished by their wonderfully luminous quality, capturing the quality of light and air at a specific moment of time. Nevertheless, Cole had mixed feelings about the natural world. Sometimes he felt that whatever was natural was good, and that contemplation of a landscape could lead a person to a religious experience. But sometimes he assumed the old Puritan view, the feeling that nature was frightening, sinful, diseased, and unbearably lonely. As he put it: "There was an awfulness in the utter solitude that was almost painful. Man may seek such scenes and find pleasure in the discovery, but there is a mysterious fear that comes over him and hurries him away. The sublime features of nature are too severe for a lone man to look upon and be happy."

When Cole died Asher Durand (1796–1886) took his place as America's greatest living painter. Durand had none of Cole's ambivalence about the absolute goodness of nature. Convinced that God was in every mountain stream, he regarded landscape as the perfect form of moral art. Durand promoted a purely Emerso-

nian view of the natural world, marked by optimism over what could be learned from artistic images drawn directly from nature.

Overall there were about a dozen painters who were considered to be part of the Hudson River School. Most of them did paint scenes of the Hudson River Valley and many of them also lived in the Catskill Mountain area of southern New York State. Although the members of the group differed widely in style, training, and even subject matter, they had in common a strong view of the importance of people's relationship to the natural world. In many ways the Hudson River School expressed in painting what the Transcendentalists were saying with words —that nature is full of meaning and that Americans should develop more respect for the vast wilderness of their own country.

PAINTINGS OF AMERICANA

The new interest which painters were showing in American subjects was not confined to landscapes or to the natural beauty of the country. During this period there were several important painters who drew their inspiration from scenes out of the everyday life of the people of America. One of the most famous was William Sidney Mount (1807–1868), a self-taught artist who began work as a sign painter. Seeking to be entirely original, Mount declared: "I launched forth on my sea of adventure with the firm determination to avoid the style of any artist and to create a school of my own." His most popular canvases were of black people at their daily activities on Mount's native Long Island. Unlike the neoclassicists who had wanted to remove all topical or accidental details from their "pure" subjects, Mount tried to catch "the unstudied circumstance of the moment." Traveling around in a horse-drawn studio, Mount attempted to make his paintings seem like actual scenes from life. He had a great respect for all human beings and presented their actions with simplicity and directness. His paintings were popular in his own country as well as in Europe where many people were curious about American life.

Another well-known genre artist of the pre-Civil War period was George Caleb Bingham (1811–1879), who also started out as a sign painter. After a brief period of formal study Bingham worked successfully as a portrait painter in Washington, D.C. He eventually returned to his home in Columbia, Missouri, where he became interested in depicting the everyday activities he saw around him. Concentrating on styles of life along the Mississippi River, Bingham began to produce works with titles like *The Jolly Flatboatman in Port.* His paintings show men playing cards, making

The Jolly Flatboatman in Port *by George Caleb Bingham.* ▼

George Catlin's respect for the native Americans' way of life is evident in his portrait of the Chief of the Blackfeet. *(Smithsonian Institution)*

music, dancing, or fishing off boats or docks. He also created many canvases which capture moments in the political life of Missouri, such as stump speakers or election-day scenes.

Another group of mid-nineteenth century painters turned to the West for subjects. One of these artists was George Catlin (1796–1872) who had been fascinated with Indians ever since he had encountered them during his boyhood in Wyoming County, Pennsylvania. As an adult Catlin maintained his interest in native American life, traveling across the Great Plains to paint hundreds of portraits of the Indians he met and lived with. Driven by the romantic belief that "a state of primitive wilderness and rudeness" was a sure guide to ideal beauty, Catlin trekked through the wilds carrying oil pigments and canvases on his back. He worked at such great speed that in 1832, for example, he managed to cover 1500 miles and paint 135 canvases in just 86 days. In addition to portraits, he painted scenes of warriors enduring ritual tortures or hunting buffalo, and of medicine men dancing in splendid plumage.

Catlin referred to the Indians as a "truly lofty and noble race," and he genuinely lamented the white people's destruction of the native American way of life. Acting on his convictions, he attempted to raise money and gain sympathy for the Indians by touring Europe with his paintings and a troupe of braves who performed war dances for the awed spectators.

Reform Movements

"It may be said, without much exaggeration, that everything is done now by Societies," wrote the Unitarian minister William Ellery Channing. "You can scarcely name an object for which some institution has not been formed." From the 1820s until the outbreak of the Civil War a host of humanitarian reform movements flourished in the North, particularly in the Northeast. For those who sought to correct the evils of society the main issues of concern included: schools, prisons, mental hospitals, factory conditions, alcoholism, war, the status of women, and—above all else—slavery.

The sources of this reformist activity were as varied as the goals. One important factor already described was the decline of Puritan theology and its gloomy assessment of human nature. As Puritanism steadily lost its grip a new spirit swept through the Protestant denominations. The adherents of Unitarianism and Universalism strove to reform society by calling on people to exercise the power of reason. Supporting the view that human progress was possible, these religions preached human perfectibility through rational effort.

The revivalist movement was also committed to reforming society, although from a different set of motives than Unitarianism. The central figure in the reform movement of the evangelical churches was Charles G. Finney, who maintained that "the church must take right ground on the subject of Temperance, and Moral Reform, and all the subjects of practical morality which come up for decision from time to time." According to Finney, certain practices such as gambling, intemperance, and infidelity were sinful and had to be eliminated from society. Many Presbyterians, Baptists, and Congregationalists responded enthusiastically to this call to support the reform of society.

The wide-ranging spirit of reform in the 1830s and 1840s was a social response to the same intellectual currents that were shaping religion and the arts during the period—evangelicalism, Unitarianism, transcendentalism. The revival movement intensified the mood of self-examination and purification leading to a general desire to root out the ills of society. Unitarianism fit perfectly with the optimism of the Jacksonian era, enabling men and women to believe that the possibilities were limitless for those with a righteous cause. Finally, transcendentalism provided a basis for linking religion and an ethical life. Considered as a whole, the reform movements of the pre-Civil War period were essentially moral crusades aimed at bringing human experience into harmony with God's will. Participants usually stressed the ideals of individual self-fulfillment, equal rights for all, and service to humanity.

MODEL COMMUNITIES

Industrialization was having a noticeably detrimental effect on the living conditions of most American working people. In an effort to upgrade the style of life which many workers experienced, some reformers wanted to totally reorganize society into self-sufficient communal units. The formation of model communities was fostered by the same outlooks that motivated many of the new religious sects. It was a reaction against the disruptive effects industrialization and urbanization were having on the established order. By setting up model communities the reformers hoped to have a gradual and deeply curative effect on the country as a whole.

The most famous of the nonreligious experimental communities was New Harmony, Indiana. Organized in the 1820s by Robert Owen, a successful Scottish industrialist and social philosopher, New Harmony was planned to function as a socialist venture. Owen believed that the social environment was the most decisive factor in personal development. He thought that people had to be happy in order to work well. He had already tested some of these theories in a model industrial community, called New Lanark, which he had established in Scotland. In 1826 his American experiment was launched. As in New Lanark, property was cooperatively owned by all members of the village, and the community was governed by a democratically elected assembly. Work was limited to an eight-hour day and a variety of extra activities were provided to interest the inhabitants. Most of the people who came to live there, however, were too individualistic to adjust to communal living. Moreover, Owen wanted to run the community himself, based upon his own radical ideas. He was firmly opposed to organized religion, marriage, and the holding of private property. As a result, the project soon broke down and was abandoned after a few years.

Another utopian experiment involved a group of forty communities which were set up in the 1840s on principles established by the French socialist Charles Fourier. Unlike Owen, Fourier proposed that each community (called a phalanx) should be organized as a business unit. Profits from all the enterprises were to be divided. One-third would be paid out as dividends to the stockholders, and the remainder would be fed back into the community in the form of salaries and cash rewards for the members. All participants would live together and work on community projects. Each member would also be allowed to choose his or her occupation; and for the sake of variety, people were to change jobs *eight* times a day. As with Owen's project, each community in the phalanx movement was to be a self-sufficient unit, operating outside of the rest of society.

Brook Farm was founded in 1841 to provide a center for the application of transcendentalist views. At one time or another many of New England's leading intellectuals lived at Brook Farm, which was located only ten miles outside of Boston. The goal of its chief sponsor, George Ripley, was to combine the life of the thinker and worker, to develop the complete individual. Activities at Brook Farm included manual labor, manufacturing, several progressive schools, and stimulating conversation in the evenings. In 1845, however, it was converted into a Fourierist phalanx, and a year later a disastrous fire completely destroyed the farm building. The community was forced to disband as an economic failure.

One after another the other Fourierist phalanxes failed, although not always for economic reasons. Exactly why they did disband is a matter of conjecture, for many of them were actually not in debt at all. One reason was probably that many of the farmers on these communities were city-bred intellectuals, not really cut out for rural life.

On the other hand, several experimental communities based upon religious principles were able to survive and flourish during this period. One example was the Amana Society in Iowa. Unlike the Fourierist experiments, the Amana Society was composed of people who shared a religious and cultural identity and were used to simple village life. Another religious community, the Perfectionist settlement of John Humphrey Noyes at Oneida, New York, lasted until the 1880s. Noyes, who had been expelled from the ministry, formed the Perfectionist sect in 1846. Its members believed in complete release from sin through faith in God, faith healing, and a complex system of marriage in which all men and women in the community were each other's husbands and wives. Attempting to create the Kingdom of Heaven on earth through communal living, the members devoted themselves to logging, farming, and the manufacture of fur traps. Yet in spite of internal success, popular antagonism to the community's marital practices ultimately forced its abandonment.

Of all the religious communities, the largest and most successful were founded by the Shakers, also known as the United Society of Believers in Christ's Second Coming. Founded by Mother Ann Lee, the Shakers established over a dozen economically self-supporting communities, some of which lasted well into the twentieth century. These Shaker villages grew because they offered a fulfilling life to people who had undergone the emotional transformation of revivalism and yet had no other way to express their profound change in feelings. More than any other group, it was the Shakers who demonstrated that utopian communities were both socially and economically viable.

EDUCATIONAL REFORM

The progressive spirit of the pre-Civil War years had a gradual effect on American educational philosophy. Before the 1820s most Americans

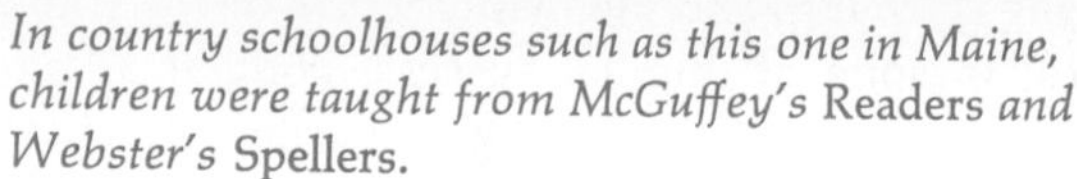

In country schoolhouses such as this one in Maine, children were taught from McGuffey's Readers *and Webster's* Spellers.

The title page of McGuffey's Second Eclectic Reader. *The first* Readers *contained stories and poems that stressed honesty and morality; the more advanced* Readers *contained masterpieces of literature and famous speeches.* ▶

had not considered free public education a duty of the state, and even in the following decades many traditionalists continued to insist that people should not be able to receive an education at public expense. As one North Carolina legislator shouted during a debate over tax-supported schools, "I hope you do not conceive it at all necessary that *everybody* should be able to read, write, and cipher." During the 1830s, however, large segments of the population did begin to demand state-supported primary education as a prerequisite for a truly democratic society.

As in so many other struggles, Massachusetts led the way. America's first public high school was built in Boston in 1821, and in 1837 the Commonwealth of Massachusetts established the first board of education. Horace Mann, the first secretary of the board, was an enthusiastic supporter of public education who believed that the democratic system of government could work only if all citizens were educated: "If we do not prepare children to become good citizens, if we do not enrich their minds with knowledge . . . then our republic must go down to destruction, as others have gone before it."

The goal of the educational reformers was to make the United States a land of greater equality. Mann and most other reformers had a positive belief in the ability of people to reshape themselves. But they were also aware of the growing tendency for one class in society to possess all the wealth and education, while the rest remained in poverty and ignorance. So Mann took the lead with such specific measures as lengthening the school term in Massachusetts, organizing a state association of teachers, and increasing teachers' salaries. Later he also helped create the first teacher-training college in America.

By the 1850s most states had agreed with Mann's position that education should be tax-supported. Several states passed laws requiring local communities to open public primary schools, and tax-supported public high schools also began to be built across the country. In addition, the system of state universities was gaining some ground. Funded by government land grants, seven state universities had been opened by 1860. Despite this proliferation of public schools, however, nowhere in the United States was education compulsory.

Young people were not the only beneficiaries of this upsurge of interest in education. Publishing was a thriving industry well before the Civil War so that many books, newspapers and periodicals were available to the general public. Many of the books sold in America appealed directly to the strong instinct for self-improvement: readers could buy how-to-do-it manuals on every subject from raising chickens to carving tombstones. Moreover, newspapers, once relatively expensive, were now being sold for only a penny a copy. This enabled the ever-growing number of readers to keep informed on such subjects as domestic politics and innovations in the arts and sciences.

Adult education was furthered in a somewhat more formal manner by the lyceum movement which started in Massachusetts in 1826 under the influence of Joseph Holbrook. A nationally organized system of public lectures on important topics of the period, the lyceum movement brought famous thinkers and writers to large audiences in hundreds of small communities across the country. Leaders of the various reform movements, such as abolitionists or temperance workers, were also frequent lyceum speakers. By 1860 about three thousand lyceums had been established, most of them in New York, New England, and the Northwest. In addition to the lectures, many local lyceums formed their own discussion groups to contemplate subjects as widely different as "wealth" and "electromagnetism."

PRISONS AND MENTAL HOSPITALS

Many pre-Civil War humanitarians turned their attention to improving the American prison system. In essence this was a struggle to change the emphasis from punishing the guilty to reforming the weak. Immediately after the Revolutionary War many Americans believed that the cause of crime lay in the uncertainty of punishment. That is, the punishments laid out in the colonial criminal codes were so severe and cruel that juries were often reluctant to convict anyone. The mandatory punishments were simply out of proportion to the crimes in most cases. Thus, before the early decades of the nineteenth century, most states had amended their criminal codes in an attempt to create more humane laws. By the 1840s nine states had abolished imprisonment for debt, some states had provided for the separation of young offenders from hardened criminals in prisons, and a number of reform schools had been established. A few states even did away with capital punishment altogether. Once the mandatory sentences were made reasonable it was expected that the certainty of punishment would restrain most people from crime.

In the 1820s penologists began shifting their interest away from the legal system toward a study of the criminal and the penitentiary environment. The failure of the more humane laws to stop crime was part of the reason, but a deeper cause was a new concern over the breakdown of a stable, ordered society. Many Americans realized that their society was changing rapidly, and that the roots of criminal behavior often lay in the breakdown of traditional family life and discipline. People also came to see the penitentiary as a place where the criminal could be removed from social disorder, kept in a controlled environment, and hopefully be rehabilitated. The prison reform movement, then, was based on the idea that the source of corruption was usually external rather than inherent in the human mind. In this way prison reformers shared some of the values of the leaders of the communal movements. Both emphasized the importance of the external environment in creating the mental outlook of its inhabitants.

Some of the prison reforms of this period would seem very harsh to us today. In 1821 advanced penologists introduced a new system into a New York prison, consisting of solitary confinement by night, and absolute silence during meals and work by day. Reformers believed that this procedure would lead convicts to reflect at length on their wrongdoings. Pennsylvania went so far as to subject its prisoners to total isolation around the clock. Strangely enough, many visiting European penologists hailed this system as the most enlightened approach they had ever seen.

The construction of publically supported institutions for the insane came out of the same impulse as prison reform. Between 1830 and 1860 many asylums were built on the theory that mentally-deficient behavior was caused by the environment, and that rehabilitation could be achieved by removing disturbed people from a disordered atmosphere. A Boston schoolmistress named Dorothea Dix was the leading crusader for improved conditions for the mentally ill. For almost fifty years she toured the country speaking on behalf of better treatment for the insane, helping to convince most states to open public asylums.

While the new special institutions for criminals and the insane created an improved environment for rehabilitation, they were highly restrictive. They completely isolated the inmates from society, without really attempting to prepare them for an eventual return to real-world conditions. Visits and correspondence were discouraged. Work, punctuality, and regimentation were the central aspects of both types of institution.

THE TEMPERANCE MOVEMENT

The temperance movement paralleled the rise of industrialism and probably commanded more attention than any cause other than the abolition of slavery. Heavy consumption of liquor was an old English custom imported to America. But whereas the English generally consumed nothing more potent than ale or wine, Americans took to much stronger drink, such as distilled whiskey or hard cider. Drinking was almost universal among both sexes, and drunkenness was usually treated more as an occasion for jokes than for condemnation or pity. Some ministers were permitted to sell liquor to their congregations. And even the Puritans drank large quantities of alcohol.

Revivalists of the early nineteenth century, however, began to denounce drunkenness. Excessive drinking was condemned as contributing to poverty, crime, and mental illness. Led by Dr. Justin Edwards, the issue developed into a movement in its own right after 1825. Soon many local temperance societies were formed, and in 1833 the United States Temperance Union became a national organization. Requiring a pledge of total abstinence from liquor, the Union had more than one million members within a year.

To publicize their cause, temperance workers distributed many tracts which illustrated the harmful effects of alcohol. In an age which saw the rapid growth of the factory system in America, temperance advocates were particularly concerned about the detrimental influence of alcohol on workers' productivity. Temperance workers also sang songs outside of bars, songs that were

"The Drunkard's Progress," an 1846 lithograph.

highly reminiscent of the revivalist hymns they had been brought up on.

Before 1860 legislatures in some Northern states made attempts to control the sale of liquor, but most of the laws were repealed during the Civil War. Undaunted, the temperance crusade continued until it reached its ultimate goal in the twentieth century, a national prohibition law.

THE PEACE MOVEMENT

Although it did not have as wide an appeal as the crusade against liquor, the peace movement also attracted many reformers. One American denomination, the Quakers, had long held that wars were evil and that conscientious people should not participate in them. After the War of 1812 many Americans were ready to agree with the Quaker point of view.

Moreover, many of the revivalist sects of the early nineteenth century began to argue that killing was absolutely inconsistent with the teachings of Christ. By 1819 more than a dozen local peace societies had been created, and in 1828 a Maine merchant named William Ladd established the American Peace Society to coordinate activities by the local chapters. Ladd also proposed a version of world organization like the later United Nations, which he hoped would be able to interpret and administer international law. Unfortunately, the Civil War and its aftermath sidetracked most pacifist efforts, and the early peace movement all but evaporated.

WOMEN'S RIGHTS

America's four leading crusaders for women's rights—Lucretia Mott, Susan B. Anthony, Elizabeth Cady Stanton, and Frances Wright—each gained firsthand organizational experience through their participation in other reform movements. However, when Lucretia Mott and Elizabeth Cady Stanton traveled to London in 1840 to attend the World Anti-Slavery Convention, they were excluded from the proceedings because they were women. The irony of being treated as inferiors by a radical organization dedicated to the liberation of all human beings, dramatized the plight of women in society.

At that time women could not vote or hold public office. As late as 1850 many states permitted husbands to beat their wives "with a reasonable instrument." Every cent a wife earned was legally her husband's. Women were denied custody of their children and, in divorce cases, husbands were far more likely to be given the children. Women could not manage their own property, nor could married women hold property in their own names. Women could not sign papers or be called as witnesses in trials. They could not sue or be sued. Except that they could legally hold property, single women enjoyed as few civil rights as married women. Legally, women were the equivalents of children, the insane, or the mentally retarded.

Aside from such legal discrimination, women suffered from many social taboos. They were not allowed to speak before mixed audiences, deliver sermons, or enter any of the professions. Women were barred from higher education on the theory that they were physically unable to take the strain of studying certain subjects.

According to Kate Millett, author of *Sexual Politics,* it was in the abolitionist movement that women first began to evolve a philosophy of their basic rights and place in society. As Millett has written, "It was the Abolitionist Movement which gave American women their first opportunity for political action and organization. In the United States, where the Women's Move-

"The Age of Iron, or Man as He Expects to Be" is a satirical comment on the women's rights movement.

ment began and from whence it spread to other Western countries and beyond the Western world, it was the cause of eradicating slavery which provided the impetus for the emancipation of women." Two of the pioneer female activists during the abolitionist movement were Sarah and Angelina Grimké who were the first to win the right to speak on the evils of slavery at mixed public gatherings. In response to various attacks on their participation, they answered that if a great moral reformation of American society was to occur, women had to take a part in it on an equal footing with men. In the words of Angelina Grimké, "What can *woman* do for the slave when she herself is under the feet of man and shamed into silence?"

The revival movement of this period also encouraged women to participate in social action by working in voluntary evangelical associations. Women were permitted to speak out at most revival meetings, rather than maintain St. Paul's directive to remain silent in church. It was also a religious institution of higher education, Oberlin, which first offered a college education to women. The religious spirit which led to reform in education opened up other opportunities as well. In 1837 the first women's college, Mount Holyoke, was established. By the 1850s Antioch College and the University of Iowa were accepting young women as students. In 1850 the Women's Medical College of Pennsylvania was founded, creating not only an educational but also a professional breakthrough since women had formerly been excluded from practicing medicine.

Before the Civil War some changes were also achieved in the legal status of women. As a result of the first Women's Rights Convention at Seneca Falls, New York in 1848, women activists adopted the goal of equality with men and stressed their demand for the right to vote. Although this "inalienable right to elective franchise" was not gained until 1920, there were

◀ *"The May Session of the Woman's Rights Convention: The Orator of the Day Denouncing the Lords of Creation." From* Harper's, *1859.*

several significant victories in the period before the Civil War. Massive petition campaigns, for instance, forced most states to pass some kind of legislation recognizing the right of married women to hold property. In addition, the new profession of teaching in elementary schools was opened everywhere to women. A few women were licensed to preach, and many more gradually began to address audiences in formal lectures, usually on the subject of abolition or women's rights. Several women did attain noteworthy stature despite various legal limitations imposed upon them: Dr. Elizabeth Blackwell became famous as a doctor; Dorothea Dix was famous as a champion of reform in mental hospitals; Emma Willard and Catherine Beecher made important contributions to progressive education; and Margaret Fuller, a transcendentalist, became the brilliant literary critic of the New York *Tribune*, coeditor of the transcendentalist magazine *The Dial*, and author of a controversial best-seller, *Women in the Nineteenth Century*.

THE ABOLITIONIST MOVEMENT

The use of slave labor was perhaps the most explosive issue of the day. By 1804 all Northern states had arranged for an immediate or gradual abolition of slavery. By 1808 Congress had banned all importation of slaves into the United States. At the end of the 1700s optimists in the North and the South had imagined that slavery would soon die out. However, as the world cotton market expanded, slavery grew in importance instead of diminishing. And as the use of slave labor became more economically significant in the South, it became more repellent to Northern reform leaders.

The abolitionist movement which emerged in the 1830s was based on the idea that slavery was a sin on the part of the slaveowner. Furthermore, abolitionists believed that it was their mission to make slaveowners aware of the immorality of slavery and bring them to seek redemption. Because of the moralistic thrust of abolitionism, it had much in common with revivalism. It used many of the techniques developed by revivalists, techniques such as highly emotional lectures, mass printing of tracts and petitions, and a constant series of meetings to publicize the cause. The abolitionist movement was also similar to revivalism in that it began by urging moral, not political reform.

Religious impulses such as perfectionism and revivalism provided the intellectual foundation for much of this antislavery movement. Established Protestant churches formed auxiliary organizations which became centers for concern and agitation. Religion also motivated some of the major antislavery tracts, including *Uncle Tom's Cabin*, which Harriet Beecher Stowe declared had been written by God. On the other hand, Southerners also used religion in defending slavery. Southern theologians were able to cite biblical texts on black inferiority, Moses' acceptance of servitude, and St. Paul's advice to be obedient toward one's master. Placed in this religious context, the controversy over slavery helped tear churches apart.

Abolitionist efforts in the North

Free blacks in the South could do little to protest their conditions. Free blacks in the North, however, could and did protest vigorously, but without much success. One reaction was to establish strong organizations in the free black communities of Northern cities. Blacks formed benevolent societies, mutual aid associations, and secret fraternal orders in their effort to assist other members of their community. Separate churches were also created in the Methodist and Baptist denominations because of discrimination in the white-dominated churches. The African Methodist church, for example, was founded after a black preacher and black members of the congregation were told to sit in the rear of a Philadelphia Methodist church.

Free Northern blacks and former slaves were also primarily responsible for the Underground Railroad. Harriet Tubman risked her life by

◀ *Frederick Douglass.*

venturing into the South on countless occasions to help over three hundred slaves to freedom. After making his own escape from slavery in 1838, Frederick Douglass became an active participant in the Railroad in Rochester, New York. In addition, "personal liberty" laws passed by Northern states in the 1840s barred local officials from assisting in the capture of fugitive slaves which greatly aided the Underground Railroad. Black-run Vigilance Committees were organized in the 1830s to help clothe, feed, and shelter fugitives from the South.

"Practical Illustration of the Fugitive Slave Law," 1851 lithograph. ▼

Many black fugitives eventually became active in the abolitionist movement: Frederick Douglass, Henry Bibb, William Wells Brown, and others spoke to audiences all over the North. Their speeches provided the most compelling evidence against slavery.

The abolitionist movement truly got underway in the North when William Lloyd Garrison began to publish his newspaper, *The Liberator*, in 1831. In the first issue of this controversial publication Garrison gave firm notice of his fierce determination, "I am in earnest—I will not equivocate—I will not excuse—I will not retreat a single inch—and I WILL BE HEARD."

Born in Massachusetts, the son of a poor sailor and a deeply religious mother, Garrison began work at the age of thirteen as an apprentice printer before becoming involved in the temperance and peace movements. During the 1820s he worked with a New Jersey Quaker named Benjamin Lundy who published an emancipation newspaper called the *Genius of Universal Emancipation*. Believing Lundy to be too moderate, Garrison eventually left for Boston where he soon founded *The Liberator*.

In *The Liberator* Garrison called for total and immediate freedom for all blacks. He opposed the idea of gradual emancipation, as well as a much-discussed plan for the state governments to compensate slaveowners for freeing their slaves. Although he did not really believe that slavery could end immediately, he argued that moral people should talk and act as though they thought it could. Since he was also a pacifist, Garrison did not recommend armed coercion against the South. His only weapon was moral persuasion, through which he hoped to show Southerners the error of their ways and lead them to reform. To this end he founded the New England Anti-Slavery Society in 1832, and helped organize the American Anti-Slavery Society a year later.

Garrison was one of the most radical of the abolitionist leaders. Because the Constitution specifically recognized the legality of slavery, he considered the entire federal government to be as immoral as any slaveowner. He called the Constitution "a covenant with death and an agreement with hell," and publicly burned a copy of it. As the abolitionist movement grew, Garrison's extremism and his inability to compromise diminished the influence he could exert outside of New England.

With the organization of the American Anti-Slavery Society, several other leaders began to emerge. The most prominent abolitionist in the West was Theodore Dwight Weld. Weld began his career as an evangelist, preaching in favor of temperance and eventually abolition. He had been converted by the famous evangelist Charles G. Finney, and soon began using revivalist techniques himself in the crusade against slavery. Weld was a powerful speaker, able to hold audiences spellbound for days at antislavery meetings. As one witness reported, he "held increasing audiences at fever pitch, with his flashing eye, his clarion tones and marvelous eloquence, without manuscript or note, for sixteen successive evenings." Within the American Anti-Slavery Society Weld also brought together some seventy apostles and sent them out to preach abolitionism. Weld's eloquence and organizational abilities helped carry the abolitionist movement to the small town and farming population of the Midwest.

The period following the establishment of the Anti-Slavery Society saw several incidents of violence against abolitionist speakers. Garrison was repeatedly threatened by mobs, but the high point of antiabolitionist resentment was the shooting of Reverend Elijah P. Lovejoy in 1837. Lovejoy, the editor of an antislavery newspaper, had moved from St. Louis, Missouri to Alton, Illinois because of the hatred inspired by his publication. In Alton, though, the violence continued. When, despite constant intimidation, he refused to stop publishing, Lovejoy was finally shot and killed by a rioting mob. Abolitionists mourned him as a martyr to the cause of human dignity and freedom of the press.

The Argument against Slavery

"As anti-slavery Christians, our duties in regard to this horrible and sinful system extend beyond the jurisdiction of the Federal Government, and reach even to the slave-holders themselves. True Christianity is an aggressive religion. 'Go ye into all the world,' was the command of its divine founder. Can it be our duty to send missionaries into China and Hindostan, to rebuke the sins of their inhabitants, and to prostrate in the dust their altars and their gods, and yet to observe the silence of the grave in regard to a sin which, in our own country, reduces millions to ignorance, degradation, and wretchedness, and, by denying them the lamp of life, keeps them in virtual heathenism? Convinced that slavery is a sin, we have not only the right, but are bound by the obligations of Christianity, to oppose it, and to use all lawful means for its abolition, whether in our own or other countries. If slavery be not sinful, then we know not what degree of cruelty and injustice amounts to a violation of the law of God."

William Jay,
"An address to the Anti-Slavery Christians of the United States," 1852

The Argument for Slavery

"I think, then, I may safely conclude, and I firmly believe, that American Slavery is not only not a sin, but especially commanded by God through Moses, and approved by Christ through his apostles. And here I might close its defense; for what God ordains, and Christ sanctifies, should surely command the respect and toleration of man. But I fear there has grown up in our time a transcendental religion, which is throwing even transcendental philosophy into the shade—a religion too pure and elevated for the Bible; which seeks to erect among men a higher standard of morals than the Almighty has revealed, or our Saviour preached; and which is probably destined to do more to impede the extension of God's kingdom on earth than all the infidels who have ever lived. . . . When the abolitionists proclaim 'man-stealing' to be a sin, and show me that it is so written down by God, I admit them to be right, and shudder at the idea of such a crime. But when I show them that to hold 'bondmen forever' is ordained by God, *they deny the Bible, and set up in its place a law of their own making.* I must then cease to reason with them on this branch of the question. Our religion differs as widely as our manners. The great judge in our day of final account must decide between us."

**James H. Hammond,
"Letters on Slavery," 1852**

The abolitionist appeal to the small town and farming populations of the Northern states gradually widened after the middle of the 1830s. Slavery was thereafter not only associated with immorality, but also with the denial of civil rights. Southern Congressmen were so outraged by a flood of petitions to end the slave trade in the District of Columbia that they persuaded Congress to pass the Gag Rule in 1836, providing that none of the petitions should be read to the members. John Quincy Adams, not an abolitionist but a strong defender of free speech, fought the rule until it was repealed in 1844. In the minds of many Northerners, the antislavery crusade was now related to the protection of civil rights.

From the very beginning of the movement, the abolitionists were seriously divided among themselves. Subgroups with different views or alternative approaches were constantly splitting off to form their own factions. One cause of dissension was the participation of women and blacks in the movement. Radicals such as Garrison supported the women's demands for equal rights and the opportunity to speak in public for the movement. A few other leaders were willing to recommend certain blacks as antislavery lecturers. Most abolitionists, however, believed that women speakers would ruin any chance for a widespread public appeal. Many also felt that black lecturers would precipitate feelings of racial prejudice and possibly even mob violence.

The issue of working through the political process to gradually undermine the institution of slavery ultimately led to a major split in the abolitionist movement. Garrison and the radicals opposed involvement in politics, since it would require many compromises. Garrison's differences with more moderate abolitionists reached a breaking point at the annual meeting of the Anti-Slavery Society in 1840, when most of the moderates left the organization. Some of them went on to form their own American and Foreign Anti-Slavery Society and to create a political party dedicated to the abolition of slavery. Out of their efforts came the Liberty party, which polled 7000 votes in the presidential election of 1840. Garrison's supporters ridiculed these meager results, claiming that the moderates had sold their moral purity in vain. Four years later, however, Liberty party candidate James G. Birney was able to increase the total to 62,000 votes.

Soon, abolitionism was to gain even wider appeal as it became associated with the question of westward expansion. Many Northerners who had not originally been sympathetic to the cause of antislavery began to fear for the future of the Western territories. If slavery was allowed to expand into them, free workers would be forced to compete with slave labor. No longer an abstract moral question, slavery was starting to become a tangible economic problem for many Northerners. These concerns were reflected in the slogan of the Free Soil party, political successor of the Liberty party: "Free Soil, Free Speech, Free Labor, and Free Men." In 1848 the party gave its nomination to ex-president Martin Van Buren, who received almost 300,000 votes. Moreover, there was now a small but formidable group of political abolitionists sitting in Congress who constantly attacked the expansion of slavery into the Western territories. This group included such senators as Charles Sumner of Massachusetts, Salmon P. Chase of Ohio, William H. Seward of New York, and congressmen Joshua R. Giddings of Ohio and George P. Julian of Indiana.

The Southern defense of slavery

Before the rise of abolitionism there was an attempt, fostered mainly by Southern whites, to find a solution to racial tensions by transporting free blacks to Africa. In 1816 the Virginia legislature suggested that a territory be found in Africa, or elsewhere if necessary, for colonization by American blacks. In the following year the American Colonization Society was formed, and under its auspices the black republic of Liberia was established in West Africa. The Society was supported by private donations, federal aid, and appropriations from the Virginia and Maryland legislatures.

The movement, however, proved to be unsuccessful. Northerners began to suspect that the Society, composed mainly of Southerners, was simply looking for a way to rid the United States of free blacks, who represented a threat to slavery. Most blacks themselves refused to leave the country, feeling that America was now their home and that they should receive their full rights as citizens. Between 1821 and 1867 fewer than 15,000 blacks left the United States to settle in Liberia.

By the late 1830s, however, many Southerners began to take the offensive in support of slavery. With John C. Calhoun as their leading spokesman, they now described the institution as a "positive good." In a famous statement in 1837, Calhoun said:

> I hold that in the present state of civilization, where two races of different origin, and distinguished by color, and other physical differences, as well as intellectual, are brought together, the relation now existing in the slave-holding States between the two is, instead of an evil, a good—a positive good. . . . I hold then, that there never has yet existed a wealthy and civilized society in which one portion of the community did not, in point of fact, live on the labor of the other. . . . I may say with truth that in few countries is so much left to the share of the laborer, and so little exacted from him, or where there is more kind attention paid to him in sickness or infirmities of age.

Many of the most commonly advanced proslavery arguments are expressed in Calhoun's statement. In essence, the champions of slavery contended that every advanced society needed slaves, whether called by that name or not. They also claimed that Southern slaves enjoyed much more security and comfort than Northern industrial workers, the "wage slaves" of the factory system. Another argument was that slaves were a form of private property, and no outsider had a right to interfere with someone else's belongings. Finally, many believed that slavery was justified by references in the Bible and in the works of ancient Greek and Roman philosophers. Some people even claimed that blacks were destined to servitude on the grounds that they were anthropologically inferior to whites.

Slavery's apologists liked to picture the condition of the blacks in the rosiest tints. George Fitzhugh, a Virginia lawyer, wrote in 1854:

> A Southern farm is the beau ideal of Communism: it is a joint concern, in which the slave consumes more than the master, of the coarse products, and is far happier, because . . . he is always sure of a support.

So moved was one poet by this image of black contentment that he wrote:

> Secure they toil, uncursed their
>   peaceful life,
> With labor's hungry broils and
>   wasteful strife,
> No want to goad, no faction to deplore,
> The slave escapes the perils of the
>   poor.

One Virginian gentleman insisted, "A merrier being does not exist on the face of the globe, than the Negro slave of the United States."

Proslavery spokesmen also argued that all civilizations depended on the use of slave labor. According to James H. Hammond, governor of South Carolina: "In all social systems there must be a class to do the menial duties, to perform the drudgery of life. . . . Such a class you must have or you would not have that other class which leads progress, civilization, and refinement. It constitutes the very mud-sill of society and of political government." This "mud-sill" theory was widely accepted among Southern intellectuals, causing many of them to renounce the principle of equality as advanced in the Declaration of Independence. As Professor Thomas Cooper of South Carolina wrote: "We talk a great deal of nonsense about the rights of man. We say that man is born free and equal to every other man. Nothing can be more untrue: no human being ever was, nor is or ever will be born free."

In truth, slave life became increasingly intolerable as the Southern masters became more and more anxious about revolts and abolitionism. Slaves were forbidden by law to read or write in most Southern states. Punishments became harsher, living and working conditions more deplorable, controls tighter as slaveowners feared for the future of the institution of slavery.

Ironically, as the debate on the morality of slavery intensified, the civil liberties of whites in the South became more tightly restricted. Most states made it illegal for postmasters to accept abolitionist literature. Southern education was carefully planned to exclude all mention of abolitionist ideas. Books were banned or censored, liberal teachers were fired, and reform for any cause whatsoever was grounds for suspicion. As the South fought to save slavery, it became the bastion of reaction.

Readings

GENERAL WORKS

Boorstin, Daniel, *The Americans: The National Experience.* New York: Random, 1965.

Eaton, Clement, *The Mind of the Old South.* Baton Rouge: Louisiana State University Press, 1964.

Griffin, Clyde S., *The Ferment of Reform, 1830–1860.* New York: Thomas Y. Crowell, 1968. (Paper)

Jones, Howard M., *Revolution and Romanticism.* Cambridge, Ma: Harvard University Press, 1974.

Larkin, Oliver W., *Art and Life in America.* New York: Holt, Rinehart & Winston, 1960.

Levin, David, *History as Romantic Art.* Stanford, Calif.: Stanford University Press, 1959.

Marty, Martin E., *Righteous Empire: The Protestant Experience in America.* New York: Dial, 1970. (Paper)

Matthiessen, F. O., *American Renaissance.* London: Oxford University Press, 1941.

Parrington, Vernon L., *Main Currents in American Thought,* Vols. I–III. New York: Harcourt, Brace, 1927–1930.

Tyler, Alice F., *Freedom's Ferment: Phases of American Social History from the Revolution to the Outbreak of the Civil War.* New York: Harper & Row. (Paper)

Wright, Louis B., *Culture on the Moving Frontier.* Bloomington, Ind.: Indiana University Press, 1955.

SPECIAL STUDIES

Bartlett, Irving H., *The American Mind in the Mid-Nineteenth Century.* New York: Crowell, 1967.

Bestor, Arthur J., Jr., *Backwoods Utopias.* Philadelphia: University of Pennsylvania Press, 1950.

Brooks, Van Wyck, *The Flowering of New England.* Cleveland: World, 1936.

Cash, W. J., *The Mind of the South.* New York: Knopf, 1941.

Donald, David, *Lincoln Reconsidered.* New York: Knopf, 1956.

Duberman, Martin (Ed.), *The Antislavery Vanguard.* Princeton, N.J.: Princeton University Press, 1965.

Dumond, Dwight L., *Antislavery.* Ann Arbor, Mich.: University of Michigan Press, 1961.

Filler, Louis, *The Crusade Against Slavery.* New York: Harper, 1960.

Flexner, Eleanor, *Century of Struggle: The Women's Rights Movement in the United States.* Cambridge, Ma: Harvard University Press, 1959.

Fredrickson, George M., *Black Image in the White Mind: The Debate on Afro-American Character and Destiny, 1817–1914.* New York: Harper & Row, 1972. (Paper)

Jenkins, Williams, *Pro-Slavery Thought in the Old South.* Chapel Hill, N.C.: University of North Carolina Press, 1935.

Kraditor, Aileen, *Means and Ends in American Abolitionism: Garrison and His Critics on Strategy and Tactics, 1834–1850.* New York: Pantheon, 1969.

Quarles, Benjamin, *Black Abolitionists.* New York: Oxford University Press, 1969. (Paper)

Rothman, David, *The Discovery of the Asylum: Social Order and Disorder in the New Republic.* Boston: Little, Brown, 1971. (Paper)

Smith, Timothy L., *Revivalism and Social Reform in Mid-Nineteenth Century America.* New York: Abingdon Press, 1957.

Tyler, Alice F., *Freedom's Ferment.* Minneapolis: University of Minnesota Press, 1944.

PRIMARY SOURCES

Commager, Henry S., *The Age of Reform 1830–1860.* Princeton, N.J.: Van Nostrand, 1960.

McKitrick, Eric L. (Ed.), *Slavery Defended.* Englewood Cliffs, N.J.: Prentice-Hall, 1963.

Miller, Perry (Ed.), *Margaret Fuller: American Romantic.* Garden City, N.Y.: Doubleday Anchor, 1963.

Miller, Perry (Ed.), *The Transcendentalists.* Cambridge, Ma.: Harvard University Press, 1950.

Thomas, John L., *Slavery Attacked.* Englewood Cliffs, N.J.: Prentice-Hall, 1965.

Tocqueville, Alexis de, *Democracy in America,* Vols. I–II. Phillip Bradley (Ed.). New York: Viking, 1945.

BIOGRAPHIES

Arvin, Newton, *Herman Melville.* New York: William Sloane, 1950.

Krutch, Joseph W., *Henry David Thoreau.* New York: William Sloane, 1948.

Marshall H. E., *Dorothea Dix: Forgotten Samaritan.* Chapel Hill, N.C.: University of North Carolina Press, 1937.

Nye, Russel B., *William Lloyd Garrison and the Humanitarian Reformers.* Boston: Little, Brown, 1955.

Oates, Stephen B., *To Purge This Land With Blood: A Biography of John Brown.* New York: Harper & Row, 1970.

Rusk, Ralph L., *The Life of Ralph Waldo Emerson.* New York: Scribner's, 1949.

Thomas, John L., *The Liberator: William Lloyd Garrison.* Boston: Little, Brown, 1963.

13

Mid-nineteenth Century Expansion: Manifest Destiny

Why, were other reasoning wanting, in favor of now elevating this question of the reception of Texas into the Union, out of the lower region of our past party dissensions, up to its proper level of a high and broad nationality, it surely is to be found, found abundantly, in the manner in which other nations have undertaken to intrude themselves into it, between us and the proper parties to the case, in a spirit of hostile interference against us, for the avowed object of thwarting our policy and hampering our power, limiting our greatness and checking the fulfilment of our manifest destiny to overspread the continent allotted by Providence for the free development of our yearly multiplying millions. . . .

John L. O'Sullivan

"The Independent Gold Hunter on His Way to California" is equipped with pick and shovel, a pan for mining, and a scale for weighing, and other necessities for the adventure.

From the beginning of the colonial period Americans had been constantly moving westward, even when forbidden to do so by the British government. Both Thomas Jefferson and John Quincy Adams believed the United States would ultimately control the whole North American continent. The Louisiana Purchase, the War of 1812, and the Adams-Onís Treaty of 1819 were other manifestations of the country's expansionist tendencies. Even the Monroe Doctrine can be seen as an attempt to prevent European interference in what was considered an area designed to be controlled by the United States. For thirty years after the Monroe Doctrine was announced in 1823, American foreign policy was concerned almost exclusively with the Western Hemisphere. In particular, the United States was vitally interested in acquiring all the land between the Louisiana Purchase and the Pacific Ocean.

The movement to push the country's boundaries to the Pacific reached its peak during the 1840s. In a period of ten years, the United States did the following.

1. Acquired seven thousand miles of territory on the border between Maine and Canada;
2. Annexed the Republic of Texas;
3. Settled the Oregon boundary dispute with England; and
4. Fought a war with Mexico which resulted in the acquisition of the territories of New Mexico and California.

This aggressive wave of expansion was dignified by the term "manifest destiny." The phrase was coined in the middle of the decade to describe the widely held belief that the people of the United States were destined to possess all of North America to the Pacific Ocean. The term first appeared in an article by John L. O'Sullivan, editor of the *Democratic Review* in New York. It is "our manifest destiny," wrote O'Sullivan in July 1845, "to overspread the continent allotted by Providence for . . . our yearly multiplying millions." Because it gave to America's expansion a sense of lofty inevitability, the phrase "manifest destiny" caught on quickly and became part of the American vocabulary.

Origins of the Expansionist Movement

One reason westward expansion was able to become an American preoccupation was that it satisfied such a diverse set of needs. It was vital to Southerners since it created the possibility of more slave states. Already outnumbered in the House of Representatives, the South needed to maintain the balance between free and slave states in order to protect what it considered its vital interests. An equal number of slave and free states would mean equality in the Senate, and no bill could become law without the approval of both houses of Congress. Similarly, the Northern states wanted to add new territories out of which to carve free states. By increasing free-state influence in the Congress, Southern opposition to the demands of Northern business interests could be overcome.

Westward expansion, though, was more than a race between North and South to gain political leverage. There was a sense in which the mood of manifest destiny was part of the spirit of adventure so characteristic of nineteenth-century America. Many Americans went west out of the same pioneering instinct which originally drove people to leave Europe and come to the New World. Henry David Thoreau spoke for his entire generation when he said, "I am leaving the city more and more and withdrawing into the wilderness . . . I must walk toward Oregon and not toward Europe."

Much of this movement was touched off by the phenomenal growth of the American population. Immigrants were moving into the older regions of the country in great numbers between

1830 and 1860, and many small farmers and cotton planters sought the border lands of Texas, California, and Oregon almost as much to get away from the "crowded" areas as to fulfill a desire for new lands. As Americans began to settle new parts of the continent, the promise of new and increased commerce further reinforced the trend. The spread of cotton culture aroused the avarice of planters, textile manufacturers, and merchants who dreamed of an ever-expanding market for cotton products. In addition to Thomas Hart Benton's dream of developing America's inland waterways, there were also the superb natural harbors at Puget Sound, San Diego, and San Francisco to tempt shippers. According to an American captain in the 1820s, San Diego Bay was "as fine a bay for vessels under three hundred tons as ever was formed by Nature in her most friendly mood to mariners." With such harbors as terminals for a planned transcontinental railroad, merchants dreamed of the American Pacific Coast as the jumping-off place for extensive trade with the Orient.

In addition to political and commercial motives and the pressures of population growth, the fear of Europe was an important impetus for expansion. Americans believed that if European countries acquired a foothold on the continent, they would threaten the American democratic mission. In addition to competing with the United States commercially, countries such as England might even try to establish colonies on the West Coast of North America. These misgivings made Americans want to ensure their safety by expanding the country's borders. But in so doing, a vicious circle was created: the European countries, fearing America's political and economic ambitions, tended to be more interested than ever in North America.

The American ambition for expansion can be seen in many ways. On the one hand, it represented blatant aggression against the Indian tribes occupying the western parts of the continent as well as against Mexico. But on the other hand, it was also part of the same nationalistic spirit expressed by many Western countries in the nineteenth century. Americans thought that their system of government was superior to all others, and that they had the right, perhaps even the responsibility, to spread their institutions across the continent. Most Americans felt that Divine Providence had ordained the country's expansion to the Pacific Ocean. In their optimism, many people actually believed that by taking lands away from England, Spain, Mexico, and the Indians, they were providing a haven for the oppressed masses of Europe. As one orator explained, "It is not good taste in individuals to indulge in boasting; but a nation is allowed to assume an elevated tone." Such comments reflected the self-confidence of Americans who maintained that by providing adequate space for its own political and economic development, the United States would undermine tyranny all over the world.

THE MAINE BOUNDARY DISPUTE

The explosive decade of expansionism began modestly in 1842 with a treaty settlement between the United States and England over the Maine–Canada border. Known as the Webster-Ashburton treaty, it was intended only to adjust contested areas, but it helped set the tone of manifest destiny because it put the American flag in a part of the continent that another country claimed. Five years before the treaty was signed, such an amicable agreement had not seemed likely. In addition to a strong sense of mutual mistrust between Britain and the United States, several incidents along the Canadian-American border appeared to make open war between the two countries a very distinct possibility.

In 1837 a group of Americans had supported a minor Canadian insurrection, hoping it would lead to American annexation of Canada. The British were able to suppress the revolt easily, but Americans living near the border continued to help the rebels slip back into Canada on regular raiding parties. One night Canadian officials crossed the Niagara River, killed an American, and set fire to an American boat, the

"The American Steam Packet Caroline, *Descending the Great Falls of Niagara, after being set on fire by the British, Dec. 29th, 1837."*

Caroline, which had been carrying supplies for the rebels.

The burning of the *Caroline* created an instant uproar along the border from Vermont to Michigan. Thousands of American backwoodsmen banded together in a secret society of "Hunters and Chasers of the Eastern Frontier," a well-armed organization whose members swore to destroy British power in North America. But the excitement did not extend to London or Washington. Both President Van Buren and British Foreign Secretary Lord Palmerston recognized that the incident did not justify a war, and Van Buren sent General Winfield Scott to the border to curb the "Hunters" during negotiations over the Maine boundary. A New York jury also acquitted the Canadian accused of killing an American at the time the *Caroline* was burned. The *Caroline* incident was settled by a mutual admission of fault. The British expressed regret for the raid and the Americans did not demand indemnity for the ship.

A second near-clash occurred over the right to control the Aroostook River Valley, an area claimed by the Canadian province of New Brunswick and by the state of Maine. The British felt the area was of strategic importance and planned to build a railroad through the region. The Maine militia refused to permit such a "foreign intrusion," and war fever began to rise in Congress. However, through a representative, President Van Buren interceded once again and persuaded the governor of Maine to withdraw the militia. For their part, the Canadians agreed to stay out of the area until the dispute was settled by a boundary commission. The Aroostook War of 1838 to 1839 had ended before it began.

The Aroostook War had resulted from the imprecise wording of the Treaty of Paris, the agreement which had ended the Revolutionary War. The description of the Canadian-American boundary from the Atlantic Ocean to the St. Lawrence River was left so vague that the exact line could not be determined. In negotiating to settle the dispute Secretary of State Daniel Webster had to achieve a compromise with Britain and at the same time satisfy the people of Maine and Massachusetts. These states were initially unwilling to surrender any territory whatsoever, but were finally somewhat placated by receiving cash indemnities. The friendly attitude of Lord Ashburton, the British negotiator, was also instrumental in producing an amicable settlement.

In the end, the United States conceded five thousand square miles of territory between Quebec and New Brunswick and kept seven thousand square miles as part of Maine. Since this settlement gave the British a right of way for the strategic railroad from New Brunswick to Quebec and Montreal, the British were willing to give up important claims elsewhere. For instance, the boundary drawn in the northern Minnesota area gave the United States possession of iron ore deposits discovered in the region years later. Although the American gains were substantial, they did not satisfy everyone. Manifest destiny was already on the rise, and Webster was criticized by many Americans for not obtaining every bit of the disputed territory.

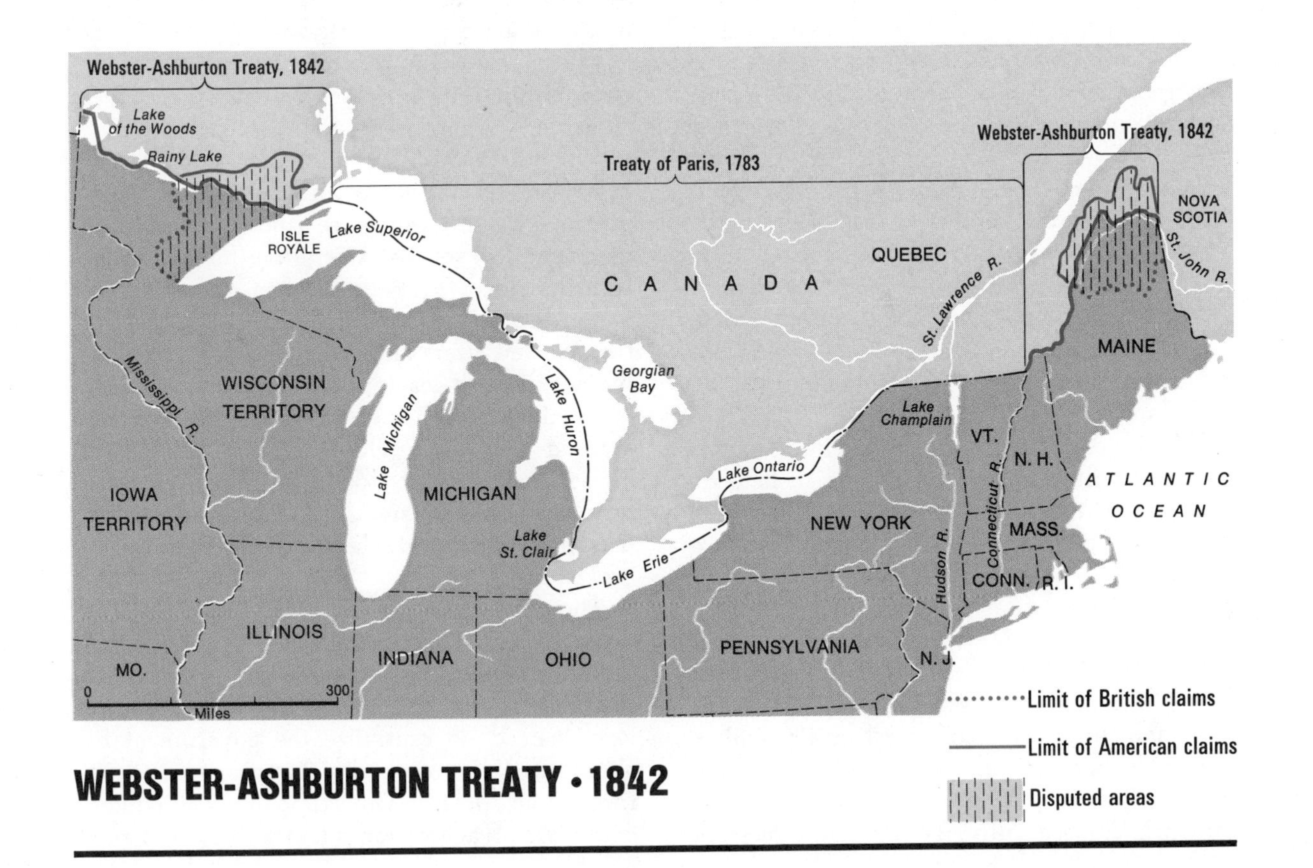

WEBSTER-ASHBURTON TREATY • 1842

Annexation of Texas

The first area beyond the borders of the United States to arouse the spirit of manifest destiny was the warm, rich land of Texas. Larger than France and blessed with a good climate and a large variety of natural resources, Texas was a likely but difficult prospect for annexation. It was desirable territory because it offered a vast new area for Southern cotton planters, but expansion of the Southern economy also presented major problems. Cotton meant a slave economy, and abolitionists forcefully objected to the spread of slavery. Since feelings were strong on both sides, presidents Jackson and Van Buren had refused to take up the issue. By 1843, however, the national urge for more territory could no longer be resisted, and President Tyler began negotiations with Texas.

Americans had begun to settle the Mexican province of Texas in 1823, two years after Mexico became independent of Spain. To encourage immigration, the Mexican government offered low-priced land grants to American promoters such as Stephen Austin who would bring in groups of families to colonize the area. Mexico had several reasons for wanting to attract the foreigners: development of natural resources, increased tax revenues, and the establishment of a buffer against Indian raids and American land hunger were among the most important.

Thousands of Americans flocked into Texas in the 1820s, attracted by reports of rich land for farming. Southerners often brought their slaves with them, avoiding Mexican laws against slavery by freeing them, then making them bonded servants. Almost from the start, the newcomers clashed with their Mexican neighbors and the Mexican government. The underlying friction was cultural, but there were also specific troubles over land titles, taxes and, most of all, politics. Although there were many Americans in Texas, the area was only a tiny part of a much larger province. Consequently, Texans had almost no support or representation in the provincial legislature, seven hundred miles away. Resentment was strong on both sides. The Mexican government felt threatened by American belligerence and by pressure from the American government to sell Texas. The settlers, on the other hand, resented Mexican attacks on slavery, as well as the government's failure to provide adequate marketing facilities for agricultural produce.

In 1830 Mexico sought to limit the problem by banning further immigration from the United States. The new law did not stop immigrants from coming, however. Colonists fought with Mexican troops, immigrants settled illegally, and the Americans began to demand that they be granted some privileges of self-government. In 1832 a particularly determined American arrived in Texas and soon actively participated in the fight that freed the territory from Mexico and later brought it into the United States: Sam Houston.

When he was still a young man Houston had enjoyed a spectacular political career as a congressman from Tennessee and a favorite of President Jackson. At thirty-five his promising future suddenly collapsed when damaging rumors about his private life became public. For the next few years he lived among the Cherokee Indians, finally leaving for Texas after being inspired by a feeling that a great new destiny awaited him there. Houston soon established himself in the stormy political life of the territory as a shrewd and skillful leader, just the person Texas needed when open rebellion finally broke out.

The insurrection became inevitable in 1835 when General Antonio Santa Anna became dictator of Mexico. In 1832 he had promised to grant Texas self-rule, but his first act as dictator was, instead, to centralize the government by abolishing all powers at the provincial level throughout Mexico. The Texans took this move as an act of aggression against them and pro-

Against Texas Annexation

"I observe, that the cause of Liberty, of free institutions, a cause more sacred than union, forbids the annexation of Texas. It is plain from the whole preceding discussion, that this measure will exert a disastrous influence on the moral sentiments and principles of this country, by sanctioning plunder, by inflaming cupidity, by encouraging lawless speculation, by bringing into the confederacy a community whose whole history and circumstances are adverse to moral order and wholesome restraint, by violating national faith, by proposing immoral and inhuman ends, by placing us as a people in opposition to the efforts of philanthropy, and the advancing movements of the civilized world. . . ."

William Ellery Channing,
1837

For Annexation of Texas

"The addition of new and adjacent regions to our dominion, instead of weakening, greatly strengthens the bonds of our Union. It augments the power against which the spirit of disunion must contend whenever it awakens. It multiplies counteracting interests, and lessens the danger of its influence. . . . Sir, you cannot, if you would, set bounds to the indomitable energy of our noble race. Where has the Creator raised mountains so high that we cannot scale them—ay, and subdue and cultivate them? or spread an ocean so broad and so deep that we cannot swim it, and whiten its bosom with our commerce? No, sir. To arrest our peaceful and onward march would be treason to the cause of human liberty. . . ."

**Rep. Chesselden Ellis,
1844**

claimed the independent Republic of Texas. In November 1835 a group of representatives met to set up the new government. They immediately sent Stephen Austin to obtain support from the United States and placed Sam Houston at the head of their insurgent army.

THE WAR FOR INDEPENDENCE

The War for Independence lasted six months and consisted of one Texan defeat and one Texan victory. The first of the two conflicts took place shortly after several companies of Texas volunteers captured the small town of San Antonio. Leaving only 145 men to guard the town under the command of Colonel W. B. Travis, the Texans then departed. Soon General Santa Anna crossed the Rio Grande and marched on San Antonio, where Travis herded his men into an old walled mission called the Alamo. There, for ten days, the Texans held off four thousand Mexican troops. On March 6, 1836, however, Santa Anna's all-out assault could not be stopped. In the slaughter that followed, every defender was killed, including the famed Davy Crockett and Jim Bowie. Although the defense of the Alamo was a foolhardy military tactic, it created one of the most dramatic legends of bravery in American history.

After the Alamo Sam Houston led the Texan army in a skillful retreat, avoiding the advancing Mexicans whose forces outnumbered his two to

▲
"The Fall of the Alamo" from Davy Crockett's Almanack, *first published in 1835.*

one. On April 21, 1836, Houston finally decided that his army was ready for battle, and he chose a place along the San Jacinto River (near present-day Houston) to make the stand. While Santa Anna's forces were taking their customary midday siesta, Houston and his men rushed the camp shouting, "Remember the Alamo!" In eighteen minutes of furious hand-to-hand fighting, 630 Mexicans were killed and 700 more, including Santa Anna, taken prisoner. Texan casualties totalled only 9 dead and 34 wounded. Santa Anna soon agreed to sign a treaty recognizing the Republic of Texas. Mexico refused to acknowledge the treaty, but the new republic immediately sent an envoy to Washington asking for annexation to the United States or recognition of independence.

SENTIMENT FOR AND AGAINST ANNEXATION

With typical boastfulness, Americans cheered the triumph over the "bloodthirsty barbarians of Mexico." Believing that the rebels had fought a war for democracy, hundreds of adventurers journeyed to Texas to settle and join its army. Although President Jackson did nothing to stop American citizens from offering support, the American government remained officially neutral. Jackson did not want to invite a war with Mexico by American complicity in the revolt. Sensitive to the delicacy of the situation, Jackson would not commit himself beyond formally recognizing the Lone Star Republic, and this he waited to do until his very last day in office.

If Jackson was cautious on "the Texas question" it was primarily because annexation raised the thorny question of the expansion of slavery. Southerners saw in the huge area a chance to shift the balance of American political power in their favor. Southern leaders were uneasily aware that the recent admissions of Arkansas and Michigan had given the Union thirteen free and thirteen slave states. However, Florida was the only slave territory left, while the free territories of Wisconsin, Iowa, and Minnesota would soon be demanding statehood. The annexation of Texas could help counterbalance this Northern advantage, putting additional Southern votes in the Senate and the Electoral College.

Among many Northerners the annexation of Texas began to look like a Southern plot to extend slavery. In 1836 the Quaker abolitionist Benjamin Lundy published a pamphlet entitled "The War in Texas: A Crusade Against the Government Set on Foot by Slaveholders." In his pamphlet Lundy claimed that the Texas revolution was nothing more than a Southern proslavery conspiracy. Abolitionism was also gaining political influence by this time, as some Northern members of Congress openly denounced slavery and the possibility of extending it. In 1837 the Vermont legislature also "solemnly protested" admitting any state "whose constitution tolerates domestic slavery."

In an attempt to influence Northern attitudes, Sam Houston predicted that Texas would become an enormous market for manufactured goods. This did not work so Houston turned to the strategy that had worked so well at San Jacinto: "concentrate, retreat, and conquer." If the United States did not want to annex Texas, Texas would simply find "some other friend" to protect it. With this in mind, Houston approached the English with the idea of creating an enormous southwestern country that would stretch to the Pacific and rival the United States in size and strength. The British were very interested since they would obtain a buffer against American expansion and possibly even break the American cotton monopoly. Moreover, British abolitionists hoped they could convince Texas to end slavery and show that free labor could also produce cotton profitably. As Houston had hoped, his diplomatic maneuvering soon developed an irresistible desire for Texas on the part of both Northerners and Southerners.

THE ELECTION OF 1844

By 1844 the country was dominated by the aggressive spirit of manifest destiny. Fever to annex Texas ran high, but the expected Whig nominee, Henry Clay, and the Democratic favorite, Martin Van Buren, both tried to avoid the subject as a campaign issue. Because the Texas question might intensify the sectional battle over slavery as well as provoke a war with Mexico, they decided it was better to keep it out of the campaign. In separate public statements they both said they opposed annexation of Texas without the consent of Mexico. This cautious action cost Van Buren the nomination.

More in touch with the mood of the country, expansionist delegates at the Democratic convention blocked Van Buren's nomination and instead named James K. Polk. A dedicated expansionist and former governor of Tennessee, Polk was the first presidential "dark horse." The Democrats based their campaign strategy on their desire to avoid charges of sectional favoritism while at the same time exploiting the issue of expansionism. To accomplish these goals they produced a party platform linking the annexation of a slave holding Texas to a demand for the free territory of Oregon. "The re-occupation of Oregon and the re-annexation of Texas," said the platform, "at the earliest practicable period are great American measures, which this convention recommends to the cordial support of the Democracy of the Union." By using the words *re-occupation* and *re-annexation,* the Democrats attempted to make the proposed acquisitions seem legal, even without the consent of Mexico or England.

The campaign itself was one of slogans and personalities instead of rational debate of the issues facing the country. Clay was willing to

"The Returns of the Election," an 1844 cartoon. A caption underneath the cartoon explains: "This Plate is intended to represent the returns of the Presidential Election as they will be received in Philadelphia; the different States are represented by Balloons."

support annexation only if it could be accomplished without bringing on a war with Mexico. He also suggested that the Oregon border, which the United States shared with England, might one day be settled at the forty-ninth parallel. In answer, Western Democrats called for "all of Oregon or none." Their slogan was "Fifty-four forty or fight!" which meant that they wanted to obtain the entire Oregon Territory all the way north to 54 degrees 40 minutes north.

It was a close contest. Although Polk won the vote in the Electoral College by 170 votes to 105, his margin in the popular vote was only 38,181. Clay's loss of New York, where he had to compete not only with Polk but with the abolitionist Liberty party as well, cost him the election.

TEXAS JOINS THE UNION

President Tyler had tried to acquire Texas through a treaty of annexation earlier in 1844. But Calhoun, now secretary of state, undermined the project by publicly asserting that the United States should annex Texas to protect the institution of slavery. Antislavery senators killed the treaty in June. After the election Tyler was still determined to acquire Texas before Polk took office in March 1845. He decided that if the required two-thirds majority of the Senate would not approve a treaty, Texas could be invited to join the Union by a joint resolution, which needed only a simple majority in both houses of Congress. Thus Tyler offered a resolution which gave Texas control over its public lands, allowed the territory to be divided into no more than five states, and protected slavery by including Texas in the provisions of the Missouri Compromise. The measure was passed in the House of Representatives by a comfortable margin, but squeaked through the Senate by only two votes. On February 28, 1845, Tyler signed the resolution, and by the end of the year Texas accepted the invitation to become the twenty-eighth state in the Union.

Polk's Administration

Few presidents had ever entered the White House with so clearly defined a program as James K. Polk. His main concern was westward expansion, in an era when Americans were moving into Texas, Oregon, and California. Polk helped spread American influence all over the globe, but most of his effort was spent acquiring a landed empire in North America. Although a Southern Democrat, Polk was very impressed by the desire of the commercial interests for control of the Pacific Coast, hence his emphasis on settling the Oregon boundary dispute and acquiring California from Mexico.

In the area of domestic policy the Polk administration clearly reflected the growing power of the South in the Democratic party. Polk was a Tennessee planter and slaveowner. He did not want to extend slavery, but otherwise his opinions on the subject supported the Southern viewpoint. If slavery was abolished, he felt, "the dissolution of the Union . . . must speedily follow."

On the question of protective tariffs Polk also had Southern ideas. One of his achievements was the Walker Tariff of 1846, which reduced the tariff Congress had raised in 1842. By lowering the tariff wall so that duties averaged about twenty-five percent, Polk put the United States in line with the prevailing European tendency of facilitating world commerce by limiting trade restrictions. Also, the cheaper iron that could now be imported aided in the construction of American railroads.

This was generally a period of growth and expansion for America's foreign trade. In the late 1840s large American surpluses of cotton and wheat were sold abroad for good profits. Yankee skippers carried goods from California to Asian ports and even as far as Zanzibar and the Persian Gulf. Trade treaties were established with Latin American countries as well as with England and France. Trade relations were being established with Japan, and America offered to pay Spain $100 million dollars for Cuba to prevent its sale to another power.

Finally, Polk stayed in the tradition of the Democratic party by vetoing internal improvement bills, which annoyed many Westerners. On the other hand, Westerners and Southerners were both pleased by the reinstitution of Van Buren's independent treasury, which the Whigs had killed in their efforts to set up a new national banking system during Tyler's administration.

All of these internal measures, plus the settlement of the Oregon dispute, and the acquisition of a vast new territory west of Texas, were accomplished in four years. Polk's failing health limited his presidency to one term, and three months after leaving office, he died.

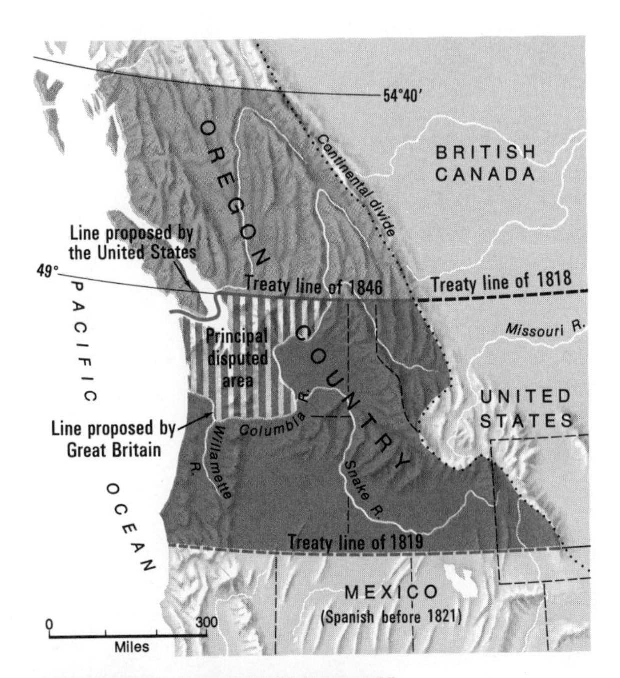

OREGON CONTROVERSY 1818 TO 1846

THE OREGON CONTROVERSY

When Polk took office Tyler had already accomplished half of the Democratic party's 1844 expansionist platform by annexing Texas. Thus the new president immediately set out to fulfill the second half: the annexation of Oregon. The problem was how to live up to the campaign promise, "Fifty-four forty or fight," for the United States had never previously claimed the entire Oregon Territory. The question had previously been whether to extend the northern boundary of the Louisiana territory, the forty-ninth parallel, through Oregon to the Pacific Ocean, essentially cutting the territory in half, or to accept the British demand for all the territory north of the Columbia River. Polk realized that to demand all of Oregon now would probably mean war with England. Nevertheless, in his Inaugural Address he spoke of the "right of the United States to that portion of our territory which lies beyond the Rocky Mountains," also claiming: "Our title to the country of Oregon is clear and unquestionable, and already are our people preparing to perfect that title by occupying it with their wives and children."

SETTLEMENT OF OREGON

Until the 1840s England and the United States had occupied Oregon jointly. England's explorations of the area started with the discovery of the Oregon coast by Sir Francis Drake in 1579. The American claim was based on treaties, voyages, and explorations dating back to Captain Robert Gray's voyage to the mouth of the Columbia River in 1792. Through the years the two countries had never been able to agree on a dividing line which would give each of them a portion of the territory. As noted, the United States suggested the forty-ninth parallel, a direct westward extension of America's northern border. The British, however, wanted to maintain control of the fur trade in northwest Oregon and the natural harbor of Puget Sound. Thus England was willing to agree on the forty-ninth parallel only as far west as the Columbia River. Since neither side would yield, in 1818 they decided to postpone the decision by means of an agreement to leave Oregon open to both countries all the way north to 54° 40′ for a period of ten years. Nine years later the agreement was extended to run indefinitely, or until

"Uncle Sam's Taylorifics" shows a bull-headed John Bull (Britain) trying to use Uncle Sam's preoccupation with Mexico to catch more of the Oregon Territory.

one country gave the other a year's notice that the agreement was to be cancelled.

Until the 1840s the United States had shown little interest in the isolated Oregon wilderness beyond the Rockies. England, though, had built the area around Vancouver into a profitable fur-trading center, operated by the great Hudson's Bay Company. In the 1830s a few American adventurers began to find their way to Oregon, but the Hudson's Bay Company, although not wanting them, hardly felt threatened by their presence.

Gradually, more and more Americans were infected with "Oregon fever." Methodist, Presbyterian, and Catholic missionaries were among the earliest settlers there, having flocked to Oregon in the 1830s. Their letters and reports praised the area's rich soil and fine climate, and the Eastern newspapers picked up the word. Soon Americans were convinced that Oregon's Willamette Valley was a virtual Garden of Eden. In search of new lands in the West, thousands of people began setting off on the difficult two-thousand-mile journey along the famed Oregon Trail. The trail began in Independence, Missouri and followed the Platte River through the Nebraska Territory into Wyoming. It then went through the tortuous Rocky Mountain passes, and finally along the Snake River into Oregon.

THE OREGON TREATY

Although Polk was publicly committed to "Fifty-four forty or fight!" privately he was more than ready to compromise on the boundary. In addition, few Americans were really willing to fight in order to acquire all of the Oregon Territory. Merchants wanted a port on the Pacific Coast for American ships, but the Puget Sound area at the forty-ninth parallel was sufficient. Once Texas had joined the Union, many Southerners lost interest in the whole of Oregon and also sided with the compromise position. Finally, the annexation of Texas meant that California might soon follow. This possibility convinced many who desired a Pacific harbor that America's manifest destiny lay further south, in California. Therefore, in July 1845, Polk informed the British minister in Washington that the United States would accept the forty-ninth parallel as the dividing line in Oregon.

The British, however, were not willing to compromise at first. Without consulting his government, the British envoy turned the American offer down. Now Polk was forced to take the offensive. As a first step, he urged Congress to give the one-year notice of the end of joint occupation. A crisis was now in the making, but England, like the United States, did not want to go to war over Oregon. Great Britain did not consider the distant territory vital to her interests. Already most of Oregon's settlers were Americans, and the fur trade had declined so that it was no longer of major importance. Also, in the mid-nineteenth century, England had become more interested in free trade than in territorial acquisitions. Thus the British ultimately suggested that Oregon be divided at the forty-ninth parallel, turning Polk's proposal into their own. Polk blustered that the offer should be rejected, but he allowed his cabinet to send it to the Senate for advice. With the decision in the hands of Congress, Polk was confident that he could have the compromise agreement he wanted, yet appear politically uncompromised.

By the time the Senate was able to vote on the final Oregon treaty, in June 1846, the Mexican War had already begun. Then Senate advised acceptance of the compromise by forty-one votes to fourteen. This wide margin of votes reflected annoyance with the extremist views of American expansionist policy. Under the terms of the treaty the Louisiana boundary line was extended westward to the coast, giving the United States control of the Columbia River Valley and the Puget Sound area. Vancouver Island was left to the British. The compromise settled a long-standing dispute in a manner that was agreeable to both countries.

Sacramento, California (above) was a thriving river port in 1848, while St. Helen's on the Columbia River in the Oregon Territory (left) was still a small frontier settlement in 1852. Below, a scene from the end of the Oregon Trail, travel down the Columbia River.

The Oregon Trail began at Independence, Missouri (right). Fort Laramie (below), in present-day Wyoming, was one of a series of forts along the trail that served as meeting places for pioneer emigrants, hunters, traders, and Indians. Located in the heart of Sioux country, it was a strategic point along the trail for some thirty years.

Life on the 2000-mile-long trail (left) was full of hardship: it took some seven months to reach Oregon from Independence, the travelers were subject to Indian attack, and life in the evening campsites demanded constant work and vigilance.

Further Westward Expansion

While the main focus of American expansionist interest as late as 1844 was Texas and Oregon, most Americans wanted to acquire all of the trans-Mississippi region to the Pacific Ocean. Not only did this idea fit with the motives behind manifest destiny, but Americans could also point to the growing number of settlers in territory supposedly under Mexican control: New Mexico, Utah, and California.

SANTA FE TRADE

At the same time the question of Texas held the attention of most of the country, a group of enterprising small businessmen sought to include the New Mexico territory in the Union as well. In 1821 a Missouri trader named William Becknell had marked out the eight-hundred mile trail from Independence, Missouri, through Kansas, to Santa Fe, the capital and only town in New Mexico. Thereafter, every spring for almost twenty-five years an armed caravan of American merchants had driven to the outpost with wagon-loads of hardware and cotton cloth to trade for silver bullion, furs and mules. It was a dangerous but profitable undertaking, averaging $130,000 in annual revenues.

In 1844, out of anger over the proposed annexation of Texas, the Mexican General Santa Anna banned Americans from trading in Santa Fe. The move came too late, however, for the route had been opened and American appetites whetted. Though few of the traders had actually settled in the region, New Mexico was on the way to becoming a territory which Americans considered their own.

THE MORMONS

Although many Americans went west to "perfect" American rights to the continent, one group made the journey in order to escape the United States. That group was the Mormons, who settled in the Utah territory in 1848.

The Mormon religion, or Church of Jesus Christ of Latter-Day Saints, was founded by Joseph Smith in western New York state. Deeply influenced by the early-nineteenth century revival movement which had centered in this area, Smith claimed in 1827 that angels had led him to a place where "there was a book deposited written upon gold plates." Smith translated these tablets with the aid of Divine Providence and published them as the *Book of Mormon*. Written in the style of the Old Testament, the book is a mystical interpretation of the origins of the American Indians and the role to be played by the spiritual descendants of the "good" tribes. In 1830 Smith organized his church as a theocracy, with himself in complete charge as God's "prophet." An elaborate hierarchy below him gave opportunity for leadership to the talented among the church members.

As the movement grew, the Mormons' attempts to establish themselves through a communal economic and social life aroused the opposition of surrounding communities. The anger of the "gentiles" (the Mormon name for other Christians), forced the sect to move first to Ohio, then to Missouri, and then, in 1839, to Illinois, where they established the town of Nauvoo and prospered. In the early 1840s Smith claimed to have received a revelation approving the practice of polygamy. As many other Mormons began to follow the example of their leader and take several wives, the anger of their neighbors increased. A wave of violence against the settlement reached its crest when the Mormons destroyed the opposition newspaper in the town. Smith was arrested and then murdered before he could be brought to trial.

Brigham Young, a brilliant and strong-willed follower of Joseph Smith, became the Mormons' new "Lion of the Lord." Hoping to find a safe new homeland, Young decided to take his people into "the midst of the Rocky Mountains . . . where we can . . . build a city in a day and have a government of our own." Soon, in one of the most remarkable westward migrations in American history, Brigham Young organized several thousand Mormons and journeyed with them into the Utah territory. In July 1847 they arrived at the Great Salt Lake basin. About them stretched the most inhospitable of lands: "a broad and barren plain . . . a seemingly interminable waste of sagebrush . . . the paradise of the lizard, the cricket, and the rattlesnake." Although they never asked the Mexican government for permission to settle that part of Mex-

TRAILS TO THE FAR WEST

"Persecution and Expulsion of the Mormons from the City of Nauvoo, Ill. September 1846."

ican territory, within a year five thousand Mormons were living there. Within ten years they had transformed the grim landscape into a prosperous farming area.

Unlike many Western pioneers, the Mormons did not work as individuals in competition with each other. Under the forceful control of Brigham Young and the church organization, they functioned as a vast cooperative community. Governing through a complicated church hierarchy, Young regulated both the religious and the civil affairs of the Mormon people. With shrewdness and a firm system of justice, he created the most successful communitarian project America has ever known.

However, the Mormons were unable to remain apart from the rest of the United States. The war with Mexico pulled them into American territory when, in 1850, their remote region came under Union jurisdiction. The authorities in Washington appointed Young to serve as the territorial governor, and the Mormons gave up little of their independence. They drove out any federal judges who ruled against Young's decisions, and when a new territorial governor was named in the late 1850s, the federal government had to send troops in to support him. Many Americans were hostile to the Mormons because of their customs and their tightly knit system. They were frequently accused of being undemocratic and were sometimes regarded as a conspiracy to destroy the United States. Despite the feelings against them, however, the Mormon's polygamous theocracy survived intact until well after the Civil War.

CALIFORNIA

The first American contacts with California were made when New England whaling and trading ships stopped at various Pacific ports to purchase supplies or sell their products. In the 1830s the first American settlers arrived to trade with the Indians and the Mexicans. They found a small and scattered population dominated by a few large ranchers who controlled the local Indians and forced them to do manual labor. The Mexican government's control of the territory was weak, and many American merchants believed that the United States could easily take over the territory.

These merchants began promoting immigration to the area and by the 1840s many caravans of covered wagons began turning south off the Oregon Trail near the Snake River to head for the Sacramento River Valley. By 1845 California was home to at least seven hundred Americans, few of whom planned to give up their American citizenship or to stay for long under Mexican jurisdiction.

Once in the Sacramento Valley, most of the emigrant carvans made their way to Sutter's Fort—a vast private domain controlled by John Augustus Sutter, a Swiss-born merchant who had become a Mexican citizen. Sutter was able to operate independently of the Mexican government, however, to the point of issuing his own passports to people wishing to travel further into the region.

When the first American immigrants arrived, Sutter was well on his way to expanding the

The Spanish had established Franciscan missions in California in the late sixteenth century. By the middle of the seventeenth century the missionaries claimed one hundred thousand native American converts.

California miners digging for gold on John Sutter's property.

fort into an independent state, with himself as absolute overlord. The dream ended in 1848, when gold was discovered on his property. Sutter tried to keep the news secret, but rumors passed from one traveler to another and soon the word was out. In the gold rush that followed, miners overran Sutter's land and Sutter himself died penniless in Washington trying vainly to reclaim his property.

Americans were so intent on having California that the town of Monterey was temporarily captured in 1842, four years before the territory was officially taken. After picking up a rumor that British warships were sailing toward California, Commodore Stockton of the United States Navy became convinced that hostilities had broken out. He promptly sailed into Monterey Bay, forced the astonished Mexican commander to surrender, and announced that the United States had annexed California. The State Department was forced to apologize for the awkward mistake, but the incident made Mexicans more certain than ever that North Americans were untrustworthy, aggressive people.

The Mexican War

Although California was not a major campaign issue in the 1844 presidential election, the public soon began coupling it with the annexation of Oregon. By the following summer there was widespread talk about a great nation extending from the Atlantic to the Pacific, talk matched by the expansionist ambitions of the new president. California was being extravagantly praised as "the richest, the most beautiful and the healthiest country in the world." In addition, American commercial interests were quite aware that California could provide several ports on the Pacific, as well as a logical terminus for the projected transcontinental railroad. Polk almost desperately wanted to get California's actual and potential riches into United States' hands before they fell to England or France.

Given the American desire for California, war with Mexico was a distinct possibility. Many Americans believed that Britain and France were encouraging Mexico to resist further expansion by the United States, and there were rumors that the two European powers were willing to recognize an independent California, if it would promise not to let itself be annexed. Although there was no foundation to the rumors, Polk acted as if there were. An agent was sent to California to persuade the citizens of the territory to place themselves under American protection. Soon a fleet of warships was dispatched with orders to take San Francisco if war broke out with Mexico.

Next, in his first Annual Message to Congress, Polk declared that the United States would not permit European countries to establish colonies in North America, nor to keep an independent territory from coming into the Union. "The people of *this continent* alone have the right to determine their own destiny," Polk said. The message was actually a restatement in specific terms of the Monroe Doctrine which had been almost forgotten since 1823. It soon came to be known as the Polk Corollary to the Monroe Doctrine.

Despite the agitation over California, hostilities between Mexico and the United States actually began over the boundary of Texas. Many Texans claimed the border was the Rio Grande, while Mexico insisted it was the Nueces, a river 150 miles further north. Early in 1845, when Texas was invited into the Union, Mexico broke off diplomatic relations with the United States and moved troops into the area of the Rio Grande.

For a time Polk seemed to believe that he could use frontier pressure to badger Mexico into accepting the Rio Grande as the southern boundary of Texas and into giving up California. To this end, he tried to get Texas to seize the disputed territory between the Rio Grande and the Nueces rivers. But the government of Texas would not act, and in the fall of 1845 Polk was forced to send American troops under Zachary Taylor into Texas to protect the border. Taylor crossed the Nueces into the disputed territory and stationed his army at Corpus Christi.

In December of the same year the president sent John Slidell, a diplomat and former representative from Louisiana, to negotiate directly with the Mexican government. Slidell was to demand the Rio Grande as the southern boundary of Texas; he was also instructed to offer as much as $25 million for all of New Mexico and California. Viewing Americans as deceitful, the Mexican government, on hearing rumors of the American proposals to carve up their country, refused to even see Slidell. Returning after three frustrating months, Slidell asserted that "nothing is to be done with these people until they have been chastised."

When Polk heard of Slidell's treatment, he ordered Taylor to advance to the Rio Grande. By March 1846 Taylor was at Matamoras and was ready to send his army into action when a Mexican force crossed the river and attacked one of his mounted patrols. All of the Americans were killed or captured. American blood had been shed "on American soil," Polk announced to Congress. A state of war existed "notwithstanding all our efforts to avoid it," he said. Actually, Polk had been preparing a war message before the attack. Now he simply revised the address to blame Mexico directly for the hostilities. Both houses quickly voted for war and the president issued a declaration on May 13, 1846.

Polk's war plan had two major components. First, he wanted to take possession of California and New Mexico. Second, by clearing the Mexicans out of Texas and by taking Mexico City, he hoped to compel the Mexican government to make peace on American terms. However, the idea of war was not universally popular in

"The American Flag going up over the Old Custom House at Monterey, California, on July 7, 1846."

America. Many Northern Whigs and abolitionists refused to support the conflict, viewing it as a conspiracy of Southern slaveowners. They were only willing to repel a Mexican invasion of Texas and were not thinking of an aggressive war to seize California, or of the deep thrust into Mexico that ensued.

California and New Mexico were easily taken by American forces. In June 1846 an expedition led by Colonel Stephen W. Kearny set out from Fort Leavenworth, Kansas to march to the Pacific. The progress of this "Army of the West" had an almost epic quality, as it traveled along the Santa Fe Trail past blazing fields of flowers and great herds of buffalo. After marching for two months Kearny and his men entered Santa Fe and captured it without firing a shot. Kearny announced that New Mexico was now annexed by the United States, and the force moved right on to California.

Most of the work there had already been done by American settlers who, under the leadership of John C. Frémont, had taken most of the region without difficulty. All that was left for Kearny was to put down scattered resistance near Los Angeles and San Diego in southern California. Thus by January 1847 New Mexico and California were American possessions, and the first of Polk's goals had been achieved.

THE MEXICAN CAMPAIGN

The most difficult part of Polk's plan was the campaign against Mexico itself. It meant that Americans would have to march south through hundreds of miles of rough country dotted with virtually impregnable defense points before they would even reach the capital city. Moreover, the invasion was complicated by Polk's desire to find a good general who was also a loyal Democrat to take charge of the war. General Taylor, who had been involved in the beginning of the war at the Rio Grande, was a Whig. He was also an outspoken soldier who was becoming dangerously popular as a military hero in the mold of Andrew Jackson. Nicknamed "Old Rough and Ready," Taylor began to be mentioned as a prominent candidate for the White House shortly after the war began.

In the words of Democratic Senator Thomas Hart Benton, Polk wanted a "small war, just large enough to require a treaty of peace, and not large enough to make military reputations dangerous for the presidency." In order to bypass Taylor, then, the president eventually turned to General Winfield Scott. Scott too was a Whig, but his personality did not attract political popularity.

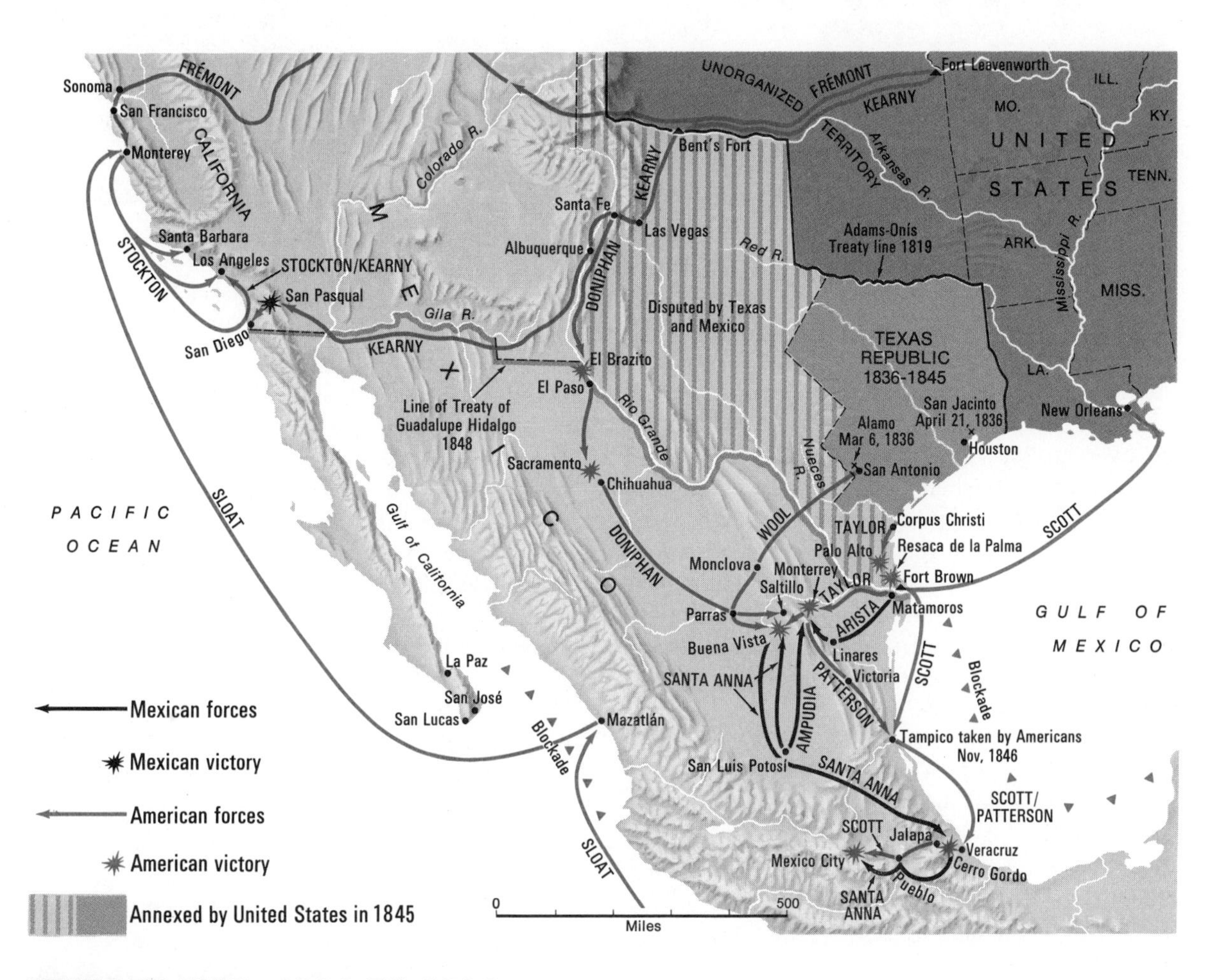

MEXICAN WAR • 1846 TO 1848

"The Battle of Veracruz—Night Scene," 1847.

Although Polk's attitude was partisan, it was also realistic. Taylor, though competent and very popular with his troops, was not a brilliant soldier. He had definite limitations when it came to campaign tactics, and was inclined to be overcautious. This became quite evident in September 1846 when he led his forces against the city of Monterrey in northern Mexico. After a three-day battle in the city streets, Taylor was able to defeat the Mexican defenders. His popularity rose to new heights in the United States, but he let the Mexicans withdraw instead of making them surrender. In addition, he agreed not to continue the offensive against them for eight weeks.

In February 1847 Taylor fought another important battle, this one at Buena Vista, south of Monterrey. His army was under government orders to stay on the defensive and keep out of Mexican territory. Convinced that the orders were part of a plot to downgrade him politically, Taylor decided to march south anyway. Soon Santa Anna marched north to meet him, with troops outnumbering the Americans four to one. At first the armies clashed inconclusively, with neither side winning any permanent ground. On the second day, however, it became clear that the American line would not break. Santa Anna, his troops demoralized, was forced to retreat in virtual defeat.

Polk's judgment was correct when he chose General Winfield Scott to lead the major campaign of the war, the assault on Mexico City. According to one of his young officers, Lieutenant Ulysses S. Grant, Scott was "the finest specimen of manhood my eyes ever beheld." In Washington, Scott had made a permanent contribution to the American army by modernizing military administration and strengthening the professional training of officers. His greatest achievement, however, was the brilliant strategy he planned and carried out for the entire Mexican campaign.

Scott decided to invade Mexico by sea, at the Gulf Coast, and march from there straight to the capital. The first step was to land his army near Veracruz, where the Americans established their beachhead. Soon they laid siege to the city of Veracruz and, with a loss of only a handful of men, captured it in less than three weeks. From Veracruz Scott marched inland to complete the invasion, one of the most daring and best managed in American military annals. Since Mexico's government and economy had been gravely weakened by the conflict, Scott and a small army were able to advance 260 miles through enemy territory without losing a battle.

At the edge of Mexico City, Santa Anna fought back desperately, but Scott hammered him into defeat in two hard battles. On September 14, six months after landing at Veracruz, Scott and the American army overwhelmed the Mexican defenders, and entered and occupied the enemy capital. Santa Anna's government collapsed, but it was four months before a new government recognized defeat and negotiated a treaty.

NEGOTIATIONS

Nicholas Trist, the chief clerk of the State Department, had accompanied Scott's army from Veracruz; he had instructions from Polk to "take advantage of circumstances as they might arise to negotiate a peace." He was to offer terms similar to those Slidell had carried to Mexico earlier. Because of the confusion that

War with Mexico: Right or Wrong?

"But now, after reiterated menaces, Mexico has passed the boundary of the United States, has invaded our territory, and shed American blood upon the American soil. She has proclaimed that hostilities have commenced, and that the two nations are now at war.

As war exists, and, notwithstanding all our efforts to avoid it, exists by the act of Mexico herself, we are called upon by every consideration of duty and patriotism to vindicate with decision the honor, the rights, and the interests of our country."

President James K. Polk,
May 1846

War with Mexico: Right or Wrong?

"It is a singular fact that if any one should declare the President sent the army into the midst of a settlement of Mexican people who had never submitted, by consent or by force, to the authority of Texas or of the United States, and that there and thereby the first blood of the war was shed, there is not one word in all the President has said which would either admit or deny the declaration. This strange omission it does seem to me could not have occurred but by design. . . . I have sometimes seen a good lawyer, struggling for his client's neck in a desperate case, employing every artifice to work round, befog, and cover up with many words some point arising in the case which he dared not admit and yet could not deny. Party bias may help to make it appear so, but with all the allowance I can make for such bias, it still does appear to me that just such, and from just such necessity, is the President's struggle in this case. . . ."

**Abraham Lincoln,
January 1848**

followed the fall of Mexico City, however, Trist could not start peace talks until January 1848. By that time, Polk wanted to demand more concessions from Mexico than originally planned, and he ordered Trist home for further instructions just as negotiations were about to begin.

Trist, on the other hand, believed that Mexico would not be willing to grant more than the huge territorial concessions already being asked. Moreover, he feared that any further demands could lead to a guerrilla war, which would be to America's disadvantage. Thus he decided to ignore the summons from Polk. On February 2, 1848 he signed the Treaty of Guadalupe Hidalgo, under whose terms the United States received California, the New Mexico territory, and the Rio Grande as the southern border of Texas—all for just $15 million. Although Trist had done well and had actually spent $5 million less than initially authorized, Polk was furious when he heard that his emissary had acted against orders. Polk called his peace commissioner an "impudent and unqualified scoundrel," and fired him from the State Department as soon as he returned home.

Trist's action was insubordinate, but courageous. It came at a time when opinion in the country was very much divided on the merits and possible continuance of the war. On one side, a number of expansionists were calling for all of Mexico. Such sentiment was strongest in the East where commercial interests were already savoring the great profits to be generated from a complete takeover. The belief that slavery would not flourish in Mexico also brought some Westerners, who were against the expansion of slavery, to the cause. Furthermore, many Americans had become convinced that the United States was obligated to absorb the whole country and rule it—for the benefit of Americans, for the well-being of Mexicans, and for the advancement of world civilization.

Arguing against further expansion were many Whigs and Northern Democrats who had always opposed the invasion of Mexico. They disliked the expense of the conflict, and still feared the expansion of slavery. At the same time many Southern Democrats were also against continuing the war because they did not believe that Mexico would be useful for agriculture. Since Whigs were in control of the House of Representatives after 1846, Polk knew that he would not be able to get enough funds to carry on with the war as he wished. So despite his disappointment, he decided to submit the treaty which Trist had negotiated to the Senate for approval. It passed easily by thirty-eight to fourteen.

What were the results of the Mexican War? The United States gained over five-hundred thousand square miles of territory, outlets for trade on the Pacific Coast, and the soon-to-be-discovered gold mines in California. Compared to future wars, the losses in money and lives were small. However, the acquisition of this new territory intensified the growing sectional conflict over the expansion of slavery, a conflict which ultimately split the Union. The war was also a manifestation of the tendency to rationalize aggressive deeds by cloaking them in idealistic statements. Finally, the war embittered Mexican-American relations for many years to come.

Actually, the problem of the further expansion of slavery had arisen even before the end of the Mexican War. In 1847 David Wilmot, a Democrat from Pennsylvania, attached an amendment called the Wilmot Proviso to an appropriation bill. Under Wilmot's scheme, the funds authorized by the bill would be denied unless "neither slavery nor involuntary servitude shall ever exist" in territory acquired from Mexico. The House voted for the amendment, but the Senate turned it down. Nevertheless, Wilmot persistently added his stipulation to other bills in Congress, and the idea was vigorously debated throughout the country. Northerners were indignant that the "land of the free" should consider introducing slavery where it did not already exist, while Southerners felt that such a formal amendment was discriminatory against their way of life. In essence, the Wilmot Proviso helped polarize opinion on the question of extending slavery in the years before the Civil War.

The Election of 1848

By 1848 the issue of expansion of slavery into new territories was agitating the whole country and dividing the leadership of the two major parties. Early in the year Congress voted to bar slavery from Oregon, but this was hardly a test of the nation's acceptance of antislavery laws since there was no demand for slavery in an area where cotton was not grown. The election campaign of 1848 could have provided a forum for discussing the issue, but the political leaders refused to debate it.

DEMOCRATS, WHIGS, AND FREE-SOILERS

The Democratic candidate, Senator Lewis Cass of Michigan, was an expansionist who tried to placate the South with the new doctrine of popular sovereignty. An early opponent of the Wilmot Proviso, Cass believed that the people in each territory should decide for themselves whether or not to have slavery. Unfortunately, certain issues were left unclear in Cass' position. For example, he never stated whether a territory should decide the slavery question before or after slaves were brought into a territory which had been first occupied by settlers without slaves. Cass' failure to answer such questions made him a lackluster candidate. As for the Democratic platform, it failed to mention slavery altogether.

The Whigs also hoped to ignore slavery. To direct attention away from it and other issues, they nominated the popular military hero, General Zachary Taylor. Taylor was completely lacking in political sophistication and refused to give his opinion on any current subject, except to say that if elected he would govern without catering to the politicians. One of his campaign comments was: "I am a Whig, *but not an ultra Whig.*" In accordance with the style of "Old Rough and Ready," the Whigs offered no party platform at all.

The creed of the party regulars was "party harmony." However, both Democrats and Whigs overlooked the rabid antislavery factions in their parties which were determined to make the expansion of slavery an issue one way or another. Leading the antislavery struggle within the Democratic party was a group known as the "Barnburners," who called for a "burning of the barn" of the Democratic party in order to get rid of the proslavery "rats." In the Whig party the Northern "conscience" Whigs refused to compromise with the "Cotton" Whigs. Eventually, antislavery elements in both parties bolted and combined to form their own party. Known as the Free-Soil party, its platform was expressed in the slogan: "Free Soil, Free Speech, Free Labor, and Free Men." Martin Van Buren, now an antislavery Democrat, was nominated as their presidential candidate.

The electorate responded with very little enthusiasm to the election campaign. Neither of the major candidates appealed to party workers, and Van Buren was limited by the lack of a national party machine to support his efforts. Influential national leaders found themselves backing one candidate or the other mostly for negative reasons. For example, Horace Greeley supported Van Buren only because he thought

"The Modern Colossus, or Eighth Wonder of the World." This 1848 lithograph depicts Van Buren, ex-president and Free-Soil party candidate, trying to bridge the gap between the Whig's antiabolition platform and the Democrat's platform in the 1848 election.

that Lewis Cass was a "pot-bellied, mutton-headed cucumber."

Although Taylor won the election, the Free-Soilers turned out to be a very important factor in the final outcome. They polled ten percent of the vote nationally, and split the Democrats in New York sharply enough to give the state to Taylor. In Ohio and Indiana they divided the Whig vote, giving those states to Cass. In the House of Representatives, the small band of Free Soilers held the balance of power. Thus they had shown the disruptive effect of a party based on a single strong issue. The Free-Soilers had also shown that the subject of the expansion of slavery could not be shunted aside. Their emergence set the stage for a realignment of the political parties in the next decade.

Sectionalism and the New Territories

Slavery and all other sectional issues relaxed for awhile in 1848, when news spread that gold had been discovered in California. Americans were joined by gold-miners from all over the world in a mad rush to get at the riches in California. Some made the perilous voyage around Cape Horn or through the Isthmus of Panama to get there. Others made the journey overland, stopping at Salt Lake City where the Mormons grew rich supplying miners at exorbitant prices.

Within a year California had a population of one-hundred thousand. San Francisco alone grew from a squalid village to a city of twenty thousand inhabitants within a matter of months.

As a result of this rapid growth the government of California began to demand entrance into the Union without first going through the territorial process. President Taylor's major problem became the issue of California's statehood and the organization of the rest of the territory acquired from Mexico. Northerners generally wanted the territories organized without slavery, or through popular sovereignty by letting the people in each area decide what they wanted. Most Southerners wanted to be able to take their slaves anywhere, since they considered them to be property protected under the Constitution. Finally, some people in all parts of the country wanted the issue to be decided by extending the Missouri Compromise line to the Pacific Coast.

Taylor's decision was that California should be admitted as a state without going through the intermediate step of becoming a territory. This would relieve Congress of making the slavery decision because, as a state, California could decide for itself. He also thought that New Mexico could follow a similar course.

Southerners were horrified by this prospect, for a free California would destroy the balance in the Senate between free and slave states. Furthermore, if all the new lands were permitted to enter the Union as free states, the South would end up surrounded by hostile states capable of destroying her way of life. Thus Taylor's move played directly into the hands of Southern extremists who began to declare themselves in favor of secession as early as 1850.

CLAY'S RESOLUTIONS

Of all the leaders who understood the mounting crisis, the most perceptive was the aging Henry Clay. Clay felt that the Union was close to dissolution, and that if California was admitted as a free state, the South was entitled to some concessions. After consulting with his old Whig rival, Daniel Webster, Clay offered the Senate a number of proposals designed to satisfy North and South. The principle measures were:

1. that California would be admitted as a free state;
2. that territorial governments to be set up in Utah and New Mexico should decide for themselves whether slavery should be permitted.
3. that the western boundary of Texas would be adjusted to exclude the eastern part of New Mexico;
4. that in return for this concession by Texas, the United States would assume the portion of the public debt contracted by Texas prior to annexation;
5. that the slave trade, but not slavery, would be outlawed in the District of Columbia;
6. that a stricter fugitive slave law would be adopted; and
7. that Congress could not interfere with the interstate slave trade.

Clay's compromise proposals initiated a magnificent Senate debate, which covered a period of seven months. Clay and Webster made their last great speeches in defense of the Union, and Calhoun bitterly denounced the North for its attacks on slavery. In closing, he raised the specter of the breakup of the Union. After many lengthy speeches and numerous changes in the wording of specific measures, a majority of the Senate came to support some form of compromise. President Taylor, however, stubbornly refused to consider any proposal that conflicted with his own plan to take California and New Mexico into the Union unconditionally and without congressional direction. But on July 9, 1850, Taylor died suddenly of a stomach disorder, and Vice-President Millard Fillmore succeeded him. A political moderate, Fillmore favored the compromise and the deadlock between Congress and the White House was broken.

THE COMPROMISE OF 1850

Each section of the proposed compromise had to be voted on separately. Great numbers of congressmen were absent when the time came to vote on aspects of the settlement that were unpopular in their home districts. Many Southerners, for instance, stayed away for the vote on California's admission, while strongly supporting the fugitive slave sections. Some Northern antislavery politicians, on the other hand, missed the votes on a new fugitive slave law and the organization of the New Mexico Territory, and came to approve California's admission and the abolition of the slave trade in the District of Columbia.

Under the compromise finally passed, California entered the Union as a free state in 1850, and its eastern boundary was fixed at the 120th meridian. Texas received $10 million in return for giving up all claims to the New Mexico Territory. Utah and New Mexico were formed as new territories, with the slavery question left open for their own voters to decide. The slave trade was outlawed in the nation's capital, but slavery itself was allowed to continue there. A

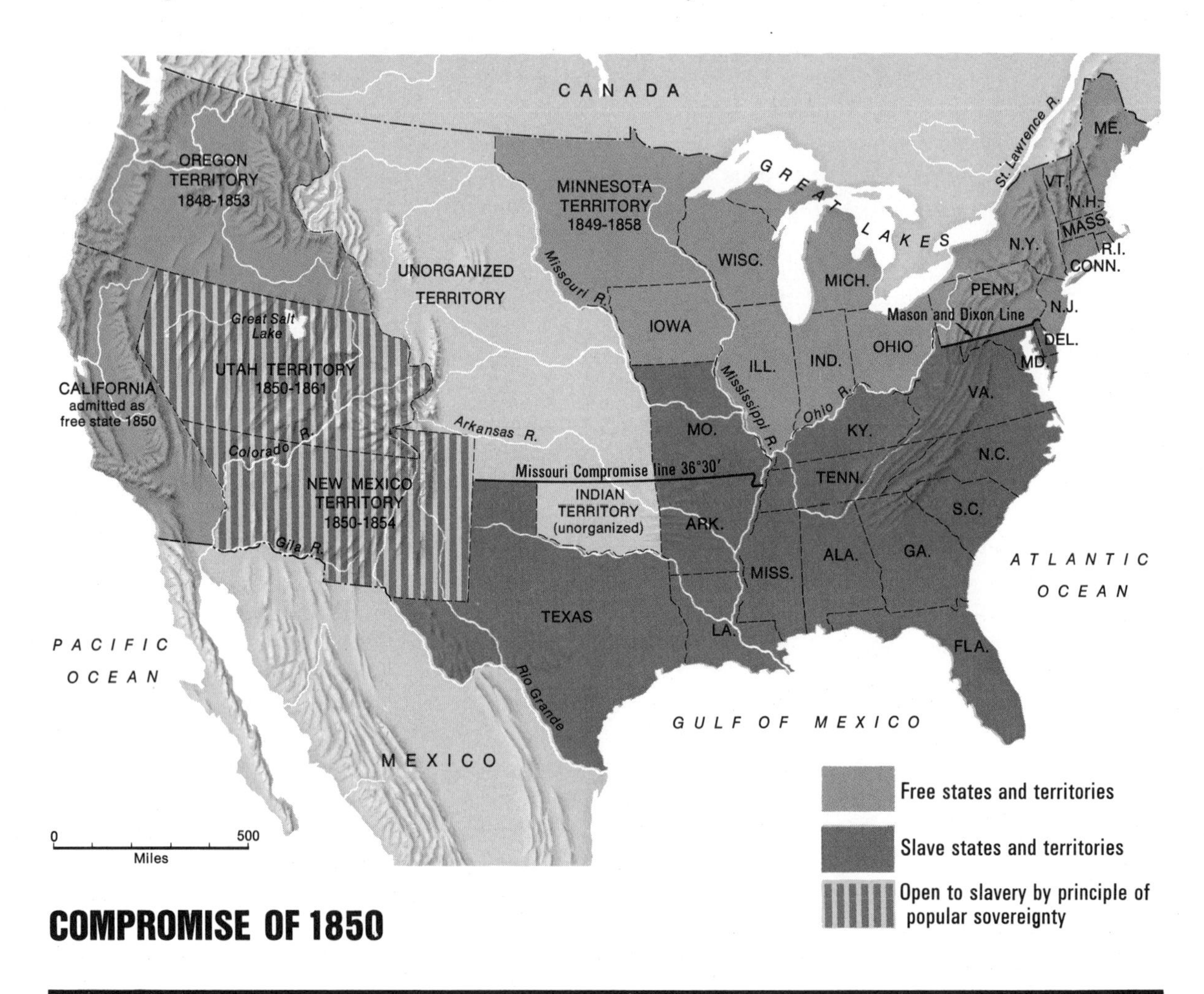

COMPROMISE OF 1850

most fateful measure was the Fugitive Slave Law, which promised strong federal action to end the abolitionist practice of aiding runaway slaves.

Thus despite the turmoil that arose from America's drive to the Pacific, through the Compromise of 1850, the Union remained intact. However, sectional differences had been clearly identified and the compromise did not end the hostility felt by both sides. Some time had been bought, but the crucial issues had not been resolved. Manifest destiny had embodied the nation's most enduring political and economic ideals—the expansion of individual liberty, free government, and equality of opportunity—but it had also shown that there were great differences of opinion among Americans as to what those ideals really meant. One split was over the means of acquiring new lands. A small band of pacifists was opposed to westward expansion if it was accomplished by force. A more far-reaching division of opinion existed over how to organize the territories once they were acquired. Those who wanted slavery introduced into the new territories believed the country's ideals applied only to the white population. But the conscience of the antislavery reformers was gradually having an effect on a large portion of Northern public opinion. The moral aversion to slavery was becoming a great force in American life, along with the economic and political opposition to the expansion of slavery.

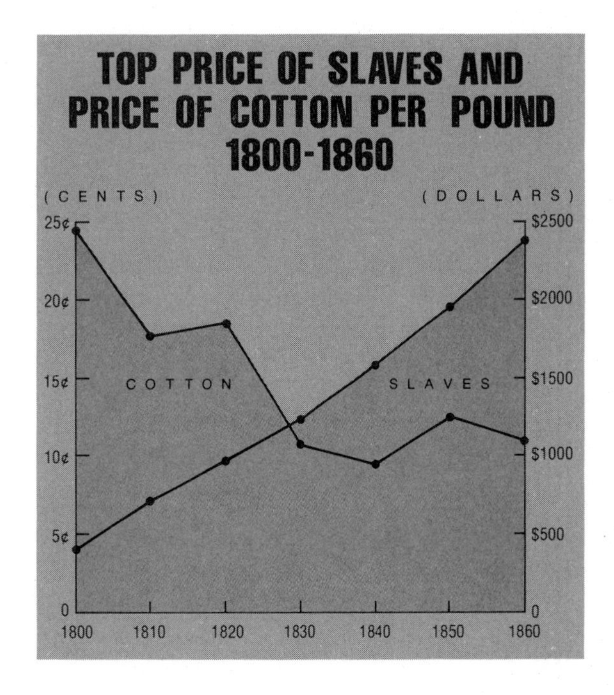

Readings

GENERAL WORKS

Billington, Ray A., *The Far Western Frontier.* New York: Harper, 1965.

Graebner, Norman A., *Empire on the Pacific.* New York: Ronald Press, 1955.

Lavender, David S., *Westward Vision: The Story of the Oregon Trail.* New York: McGraw-Hill, 1963.

Merk, Frederick, *Manifest Destiny and Mission in American History.* New York: Knopf, 1963.

Parkman, Francis, *The Oregon Trail.* New York: Holt, Rinehart & Winston, 1931.

Weinberg, Albert K., *Manifest Destiny.* Baltimore, Md.: The Johns Hopkins University Press, 1935.

SPECIAL STUDIES

Allen, Harry C., *Great Britain and the United States.* London: Odhams Press, 1954.

Cleland, Robert G., *This Reckless Breed of Men.* New York: Knopf, 1950.

DeVoto, Bernard, *The Year of Decision: 1846.* Boston: Little, Brown, 1943.

Gunderson, Robert G., *The Log-Cabin Campaign.* Lexington, Ky.: University of Kentucky Press, 1957.

Merk, Frederick, *The Monroe Doctrine and American Expansionism, 1843–1849.* New York: Knopf, 1966.

Morgan, Robert J., *A Whig Embattled.* Lincoln: University of Nebraska Press, 1954.

Pletcher, David M., *The Diplomacy of Annexation: Texas, Oregon and the Mexican War.* Columbia, Mo.: University of Missouri Press, 1973.

Ruiz, Ramón E. (Ed.), *Mexican War: Was it Manifest Destiny?* New York: Holt, Rinehart & Winston, 1963.

Seager, Robert, *And Tyler Too!* New York: McGraw-Hill, 1963.

Siegel, Stanley, *A Political History of the Texas Republic.* Austin: University of Texas Press, 1956.

Singletary, Otis A., *The Mexican War.* Chicago: University of Chicago Press, 1960.

Stegner, Wallace, *The Gathering of Zion: The Story of the Mormon Trail.* New York: McGraw-Hill, 1964.

Weems, John E., *To Conquer a Peace: The War Between the United States and Mexico.* New York: Doubleday, 1974.

PRIMARY SOURCE

Nevins, Allan (ed.), *Polk: The Diary of a President.* London: Longmans, Green, 1929.

BIOGRAPHIES

Brodie, Fawn, *No Man Knows My History.* New York: Knopf, 1945.

Hamilton, Holman, *Zachary Taylor,* Vols. I–II. Indianapolis: Bobbs-Merrill, 1941–1957.

James, Marquis, *The Raven.* Indianapolis: Bobbs-Merrill, 1929.

Morgan, Dale L., *Jedediah Smith and the Opening of the West.* Indianapolis: Bobbs-Merrill, 1953.

Nevins, Allan, *Frêmont: Pathmarker of the West,* Vols. I–II. New York: Frederick Unger, 1955.

Nibley, Preston, *Brigham Young, the Man and His Work.* Salt Lake City, Utah: Deseret Books, 1936.

Sellers, Charles, *James K. Polk,* Vols. I–II. Princeton, N.J.: Princeton University Press, 1957–1966.

14

The 1850s: The Gathering Storm

CHARLESTON

MERCURY

EXTRA:

Passed unanimously at 1.15 o'clock, P. M. December 20th, 1860.

AN ORDINANCE

To dissolve the Union between the State of South Carolina and other States united with her under the compact entitled "The Constitution of the United States of America."

We, the People of the State of South Carolina, in Convention assembled, do declare and ordain, and it is hereby declared and ordained,

That the Ordinance adopted by us in Convention, on the twenty-third day of May, in the year of our Lord one thousand seven hundred and eighty-eight, whereby the Constitution of the United States of America was ratified, and also, all Acts and parts of Acts of the General Assembly of this State, ratifying amendments of the said Constitution, are hereby repealed; and that the union now subsisting between South Carolina and other States, under the name of "The United States of America," is hereby dissolved.

THE

UNION

IS

DISSOLVED!

I believe this government cannot endure, permanently half slave and half free. I do not expect the Union to be dissolved—I do not expect the house to fall—but I do expect it will cease to be divided. It will become all one thing, or all the other. Either the opponents of slavery will arrest the further spread of it, and place it where the public mind shall rest in the belief that it is in the course of ultimate extinction; or its advocates will push it forward, till it shall become alike lawful in all the States, old as well as new—North as well as South.

Abraham Lincoln, 1858

An 1860 poster hailing the secession of South Carolina from the Union.

Poster advertising Uncle Tom's Cabin.

The Compromise of 1850 was the second attempt to create national unity on the settlement of new territories despite growing economic and social differences between the North and the South. The country's leaders hoped the compromise would endure. However, beneath a calm surface old attitudes and problems persisted. No section of the country was wholly satisfied with the compromise. Southerners objected to California's admission as a free state, and many Northerners violently attacked the Fugitive Slave Law.

In the North population was increasing and industry expanding. The entire coastal trade was in Northern hands. And the railroad was daily creating closer political and economic ties between the Northeast and Northwest. The South had become a virtual financial colony of the North, and Southerners saw no end to Northern demands for higher tariffs, federal support of internal improvements, and free public lands for yeoman farmers.

In addition to the economic and political tensions between the North and the South, events in the early 1850s heightened the controversy over slavery. Extreme abolitionists sought to keep their crusade alive by preventing enforcement of the Fugitive Slave Law. Some even spirited fugitives over the border into Canada, beyond the reach of American Laws. In 1850 Vermont was the first of several Northern states to enact a "personal liberty law" in opposition to the Fugitive Slave Law. Fugitives began receiving legal support and jury trials in the Northeast. The black leader Frederick Douglass advocated a new militancy: "Every slavehunter who meets a bloody death in this infernal business, is an argument in favor of the manhood of our race."

The 1852 publication of Harriet Beecher Stowe's *Uncle Tom's Cabin* added to the emotional furor surrounding the issue of slavery. The daughter of a New England clergyman, Mrs. Stowe had never traveled in the South. She was careful to attack the institution of slavery rather than the Southerners who perpetuated it. In fact, Simon Legree, the novel's sadistically cruel overseer, was a Northerner. The novel sold three hundred thousand copies within a year. The melodramatic appeal of the book, particularly as dramatized on stages across the country, turned thousands against slavery.

Pierce Becomes President

Even as slavery divided the country on moral grounds, it also undermined the institutions that held the country together. The effect was most clearly seen in the splits within the political parties.

The Free-Soilers were seriously weakened because they were the only party to oppose the Compromise of 1850. Moderate Northerners in the Free-Soil party returned to the Democrats.

The Democrats embraced several factions in an uneasy alliance: the small farmers of the West who were against the expansion of slavery into the territories; many planters and most small farmers in the South who defended the expansion of slavery; Eastern merchants whose business was mainly in the South; and many skilled and unskilled workers in Northern towns who were not abolitionists but who were against slavery. The Democrats had pledged their unreserved devotion to the compromise and had promised to oppose attempts of "any shape or color" to open the question of slavery to debate again.

Despite their unanimous support of the compromise, the Democrats had a hard time selecting a presidential candidate for the election of 1852. Forty-nine ballots were cast before they chose Franklin Pierce, the governor of New Hampshire.

The Northern Whigs hated the Fugitive Slave Law and saw to it that President Fillmore was not nominated. But the Whig platform agreed to "acquiesce in" the Compromise of 1850. Pierce triumphed over their final choice, General Winfield Scott, largely because he endorsed the compromise more energetically than the Whigs. Pierce won twenty-seven states, while Scott carried only four. In the Electoral College Pierce's victory was a stunning 254 votes to 42. The Free-Soil party suffered a major setback: its candidate, John P. Hale, attracted only half as many votes as the party had received in 1848.

The election took a fatal toll of the Whigs. Never again would a Whig candidate campaign for the presidency. Southerners were abandoning the party, fearing that a strong central government in the control of Northern antislavery politicians would destroy slavery and with it the whole Southern way of life. The great Unionists in the Whig party, Webster and Clay, had held the rival factions together in an alliance to preserve the nation, but they both died in 1852. Within a few years the party, its Northern and Southern factions hopelessly divided, would be extinct.

Campaign poster from the election of 1852 displays Pierce and his running mate.

Franklin Pierce had received the nomination for president because he was considered unobjectionable to the South. Pierce was one of the handsomest chief executives ever to hold that office, and at forty-nine, the youngest thus far. But his congenial personality and sturdy military appearance belied a weak, irresolute nature. As president, Pierce was dominated by the strong men in his cabinet, men such as Secretary of War Jefferson Davis from Mississippi and Secretary of State William L. Marcy of New York. When circumstances forced him to take a stand, Pierce tended to allow his Southern friends to dictate his action.

THE KANSAS-NEBRASKA ACT

The Pierce administration was soon embroiled in a domestic controversy that shattered the superficial calm created by the Compromise of 1850. In 1830 the area west of Missouri and Iowa (known as the Nebraska Country) had been set aside as a permanent Indian reserve. By the 1850s, however, land hunger, fed by plans to run the projected transcontinental railroad through the area, prompted the government to revise its policy on the land originally deeded in perpetuity to the Indians.

In 1854 Stephen A. Douglas, a Democrat from Illinois, submitted a bill to the Senate proposing to break the government's treaties with the Indians and to organize the land west of Missouri and Iowa into territories and eventually into states. Few congressmen objected to breaking the treaties, but Douglas' bill raised once again the troublesome issue of the expansion of slavery into new territories. The Missouri Compromise of 1820 forbade slavery forever "in all territory ceded by France to the United States . . . which lies North of 36° 36'." Thus, the entire Nebraska Country area was by law closed to slavery. However Douglas, advocating popular sovereignty, suggested that the people of Nebraska should be allowed to decide for themselves whether they wanted slavery or not. A similar plan had recently been worked out for the territories of New Mexico and Utah. Douglas believed that since most of Nebraska was too far north for cotton agriculture, it was unlikely to become a slaveholding area; but he suggested self-determination for the territory in the hopes of ensuring Southern support for his proposal.

Before formal debate began, Southern congressmen brought pressure on Douglas to make three changes in the bill. The measure originally allowed Congress to reject a proslavery constitution, even if the people of the territory voted to legalize slavery under their state constitution. The revised bill removed that power from Congress and left it solely with the people of Nebraska. Second, Douglas' bill contradicted but did not repudiate the Missouri Compromise. The revised bill explicitly stated that the compromise was henceforth "inoperative and void," an important psychological victory for the South. Third, the revised bill specifically divided the Nebraska Country into two territories: the larger Nebraska to the North, and Kansas to the South. This provision made it much more likely that Kansas, which lay immediately to the west of the slave state of Missouri, would itself become a slave state.

Douglas made these changes in his bill simply to speed its passage through Congress. Though he viewed slavery as an outdated, inefficient institution, he had no deep feelings about the slavery question. In fact he was fond of saying, "I don't care whether slavery is voted up or down." He expected the bill to generate some controversy, but thought it would please most people: his constituents in Chicago, because they would be at the western terminus of the proposed transcontinental railroad to be built through the territory; Westerners, because they would now have free access to lands formerly reserved for the Indians; Southerners, because the principle of popular sovereignty could extend slavery to parts of the Louisiana Purchase formerly closed to it under the Missouri Compromise; the nation as a whole, because a new sectional controversy would have cleverly been avoided and the Union preserved. In fact, Douglas hoped to be elected president because of his success with the Kansas-Nebraska bill. Unfortunately, he failed to gauge the depth of the North's opposition to slavery expansion.

As it turned out, the bill destroyed Douglas' dominant position in the Democratic party and seriously split the party. The Senate passed the bill by 37 votes to 14, but the more sharply divided House passed it by only 113 to 100. Despite its passage, the Act had reopened old wounds temporarily patched by the Compromise of 1850. Only seven of the forty-two Northern Democrats who voted for the Kansas-Nebraska Act were reelected to office. Douglas was mobbed by abolitionists in his own state of Illinois, and ruefully claimed he could have traveled from Chicago to Boston by the light of his burning effigies.

THE SETTLEMENT OF KANSAS

With the passage of the Kansas-Nebraska Act, the new territory of Kansas immediately became a battleground. Northern abolitionists, determined to make the territory a free state, financed the migration of antislavery Yankees to Kansas. In New England, emigrant aid societies spon-

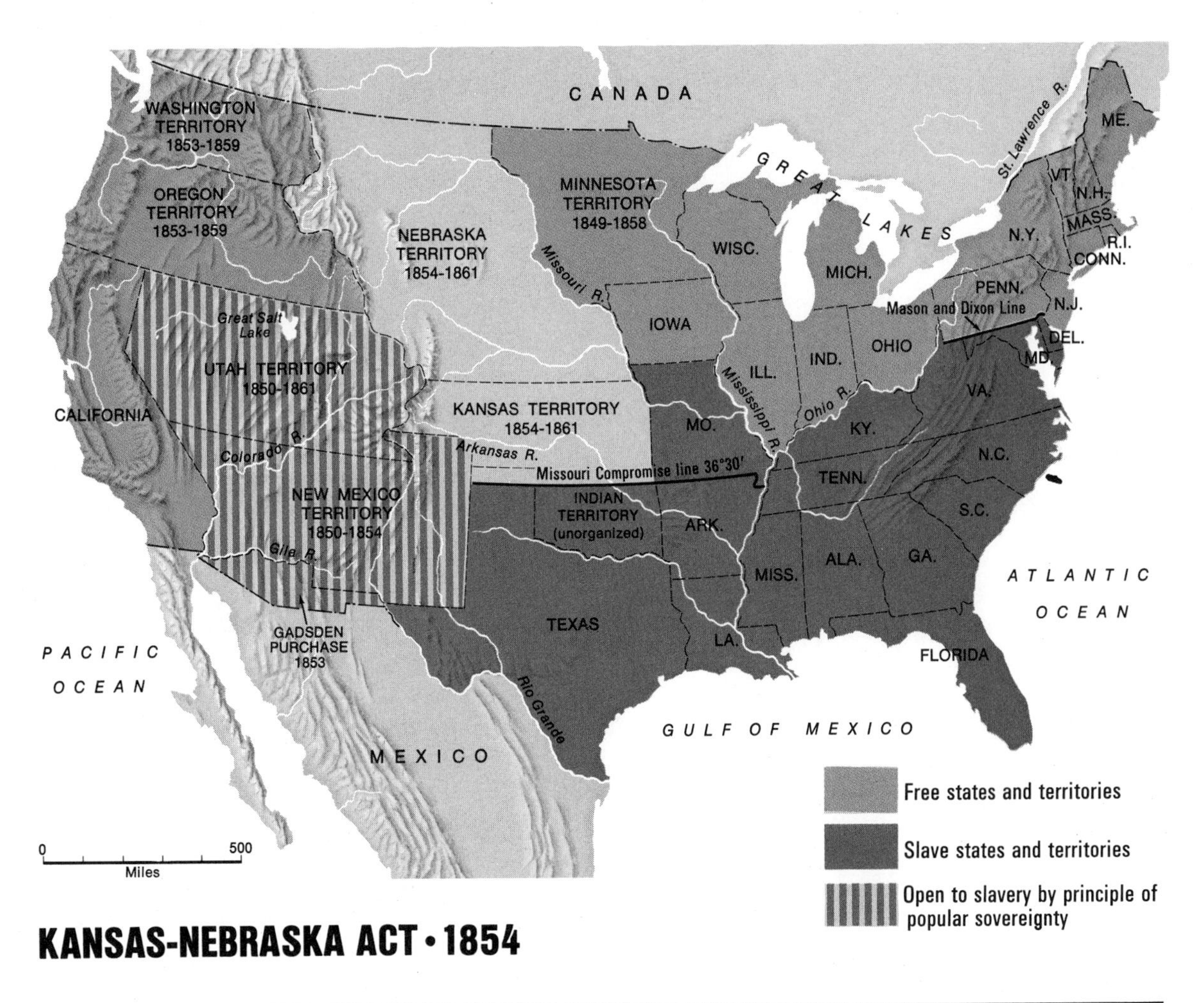

KANSAS-NEBRASKA ACT • 1854

This 1856 cartoon shows Buchanan and Breckinridge, discussing "these dam'd poor whites with their Free notions," overlooking slaves trying to enter Kansas and dead poor white farmers across the border.

sored two thousand new settlers to the area. At the same time, proponents of slavery from Missouri, Alabama, Georgia, and South Carolina also moved into the region.

When Kansas held its first territorial election in 1855, there were only about three thousand registered voters, most of them from the North. Some three thousand proslavery Missourians crossed the border and cast ballots illegally. Andrew H. Reeder, appointed governor of Kansas by President Pierce, tried to disqualify eight of the thirty-one members of the territorial legislature on the grounds that they had been elected irregularly. Southern congressmen put pressure on Pierce to veto this move since the disqualified legislators were all proslavery men. Pierce acceded to their demands and refused to support Reeder. The illegally elected Kansas legislators remained in office. The legislature then asked the president to remove Reeder from office. Pierce complied, naming William Shannon of Ohio as the new governor.

The proslavery Kansas legislature now passed a series of stringent laws designed to drive antislavery people out of Kansas. Anyone caught harboring a fugitive, or even speaking out against slavery, was subject to a fine and a prison term. However, those Kansans who were against the expansion of slavery into the territories were not intimidated by these measures. These "freesoilers" called a convention of their own, framed a state constitution that made slavery illegal in Kansas, held their own election, and announced that Charles Robinson would be their governor. They also sent Andrew H. Reeder, the ousted former governor of Kansas, as their territorial delegate to Washington.

Kansas now had two governors and two legislatures, representing two sharply antagonistic factions. Pierce might have been able to pacify both sides if he had called for a new, carefully monitored election, but he hesitated, and the territory was plunged into violence.

In May 1856, fighting erupted in Kansas, ultimately claiming two-hundred lives. The chief free-soil towns were Lawrence and Topeka, while proslavery settlers were clustered in Atchinson and Leavenworth. A drunken United

States marshal and impromptu proslavery posse raided the town of Lawrence and arrested several free-soil leaders. John Brown, a fanatical abolitionist who would earn notoriety and martyrdom three years later, led a counterattack. Seeing himself as an avenging angel sent by the Lord to chastise slaveowners, Brown led a band of six followers into enemy territory and murdered five proslavery settlers.

In the meantime, Pierce had appointed yet another governor, John W. Geary. In an effort to control the explosive Kansas territory, Geary dispatched federal troops. Gradually the conflict subsided. Although no more blood was shed, tension over the slavery question in "Bleeding Kansas" intensified.

Few of the Kansas free-soilers were true abolitionists. Most opposed slavery not because they considered it a sin but because they feared that cheap slave labor would threaten their own livelihoods. When Kansas finally became a state in 1861, its constitution forbade slavery but also excluded free blacks. Abolitionists in faraway New York and New England, however, were not concerned with the economic side of the issue in 1856. They thought of Kansas as a battleground where divinely inspired abolitionists were fighting to crush the satanic forces of slavery.

BROOKS AND SUMNER

Violence over the slavery question surfaced even in Congress. Legislators carried knives and pistols with them into the chambers. On May 19, 1856, Charles Sumner of Massachusetts delivered an impassioned speech denouncing slavery and arguing for a free Kansas. In the course of his oration, Sumner railed against the proslavery Missourians who had participated illegally in the Kansas election. Sumner directed particularly harsh criticism at Senator Andrew P. Butler of South Carolina, and others he viewed as proslavery spokesmen, calling them "hirelings picked from the drunken spew and vomit of an uneasy civilization." Butler's enraged nephew, Congressman Preston Brooks, anxious to defend his uncle's honor, attacked Senator Sumner in the Senate, crying: "Mr. Sumner, I have read your speech against South Carolina, and have read it carefully, deliberately and dispassionately, in which you have libelled my State and slandered my white haired old relative, Senator Butler, who is absent, and I have come to punish you for it." Brooks struck Sumner a dozen times with his cane, making the senator an invalid for more than three years. News of the attack sped over telegraph lines to all parts of the country. One cartoon in a North-

A Northern cartoon of Brooks' attack on Sumner in the Senate chambers. In the background Southern senators look on in amusement.

ern newspaper depicted a noble Sumner, quill in hand, falling before the merciless onslaught of "Bully" Brooks, while crude-looking Southern congressmen stand aside snickering in the background. Brooks resigned from the House of Representatives, but was reelected by his North Carolina constituents. Sumner's seat in the House was held for him until he was able to serve again some three years later.

THE REPUBLICAN PARTY

An important result of the Kansas-Nebraska Act was the alignment of antislavery and free-soil factions from all parties into a new political organization, the Republican party. Almost immediately, it became the country's second major political party. Its initial platform opposed the Kansas-Nebraska Act and denounced the spread of slavery. By the end of the summer of 1854, the Republicans had united members of several political factions: Northern Whigs (Lincoln joined in 1856), many Northern Democrats, former Free-Soilers, abolitionists, and temperance advocates. Despite a variety of opinions on other issues, all were solidly united against the Kansas-Nebraska Act. Republican candidates did not appear on the ballots in most states of the South, where it was considered "a stinking, putrid, abolition party." In the past, parties had been national organizations, cutting across sectional lines. Now a party was emerging that was purely regional.

The Republican party grew rapidly, scoring impressive political gains. In the congressional elections of 1854 it scored a stunning victory in the House of Representatives: Republicans won 108 seats, Democrats only 83, and another new party, the Know-Nothings, took the remaining 43.

The American, or Know-Nothing party, formed in 1852, appealed to the prejudices of native-born Americans who wanted to keep new immigrants out of the country. As much a secret society as it was a political party, it derived its name from the fact that candidates were instructed to keep their inflammatory prejudices secret and to answer when questioned that they "knew nothing" about the matter. Paradoxically, many antislavery people were opposed to the influx of new immigrants. So for a few years a number of politicians were both Republicans and Know-Nothings. The party also attracted nativists from the Whig and Democratic parties: native-born working people who feared competition from cheap foreign labor, and Southerners who feared the population advantage increased immigration gave the North.

The Decline of Manifest Destiny

Undaunted by sectional hostility over the slavery issue, Pierce planned to continue the expansionist foreign policy of his Democratic predecessor, James K. Polk. Pierce's Inaugural Address had urged America to view territorial growth without "any timid forebodings of evil." Yet for most Northerners, foreign expansion under a president they considered the pawn of Southern proslavery forces inevitably raised "forebodings of evil" regarding slavery expansion. In the past, the majority of Americans heartily endorsed the acquisition of new territory, but now the ever-present issue of slavery affected almost every consideration of foreign as well as domestic policy.

CUBA

Outside the United States, Cuba and Brazil were the last strongholds of slavery in the Western world. Pierce's interest in acquiring Cuba confirmed the worst suspicions of Northerners opposed to slavery. If Cuba became a United States possession, it would ultimately join the Union as a slave state.

Despite such objections, the acquisition of Cuba would have provided strategic advantage for the United States. Ownership of the island, which commands the entrance to the Caribbean, would have ensured the safety both of American commerce in the Gulf of Mexico and of a proposed interoceanic canal through Central America. By contrast, as long as Cuba remained in foreign hands the island could be used as a base for attacking the United States. As early as 1848 President Polk had offered Spain $100 million for Cuba, but the Spanish foreign minister had replied that he would rather see the island sunk than sold.

Many Southerners could not easily dismiss their dream of acquiring Cuba. Some supported a Venezuelan adventurer named General Narciso López in his efforts to take Cuba by force. After making three unsuccessful attempts between 1849 and 1851, López was captured and executed by the Spanish. Disappointed Southern expansionists retaliated by destroying the Spanish consulate in New Orleans.

President Pierce made the acquisition of Cuba one of his prime objectives. He appointed an ardent but indiscreet senator from Louisiana, Pierre Soulé, as his minister to Spain and informed him that the acquisition of Cuba was the goal of his mission. Soon after arriving in Spain, Soulé made several gross blunders. Among them was challenging the French ambassador to a duel in which he injured him for life.

Then, early in 1854, an American ship, the *Black Warrior,* was seized in Havana for violating Spanish customs laws. Pierce sought to use this incident as an excuse to declare war. Soulé was instructed to obtain an indemnity of $300,000 and an apology from the Spanish government. Soulé decided to present this demand with a forty-eight-hour ultimatum. When Spain refused to comply, Soulé threatened war. Recognizing that the envoy had exceeded his instructions, the Spanish foreign minister ignored Soulé's ultimatum and settled the matter directly with the ship's owners and with Pierce's secretary of state, William L. Marcy. As the New York *Herald* commented about Soulé: "We wanted an Ambassador there, we have sent a matador."

Despite these setbacks, Pierce did not relinquish the idea of buying Cuba. Secretary of State Marcy now instructed Soulé to confer on the subject with James Buchanan, the American minister in London, and John Y. Mason, the American minister in Paris. Marcy wanted to know how the European powers would respond if America should invade the island. But the ministers misunderstood their instructions. Instead of sounding out European opinion, they sent Marcy a confidential dispatch from Ostend, Belgium, recommending that the United States offer Spain $120 million for Cuba. If the offer were rejected, the United States, "by every law, human and divine, shall be justified in wresting" Cuba from Spain "if we possess the power."

When this recommendation, known as the Ostend Manifesto, was made public in the United States, Southerners greeted it with enthusiasm while Northern free-soilers branded it as a plot to add another slave state to the Union. The New York *Tribune* called it a "Manifesto of Brigands," and Northern indignation forced President Pierce to repudiate its recommendations. Marcy sent a sharp rebuke to Soulé who resigned in anger and humiliation. Cuba's fate remained unsettled.

CENTRAL AMERICA

With the acquisition of California, the United States seriously contemplated digging a canal through Central America to shorten the sea voyage from coast to coast. Several American diplomats viewed the tiny republic of Nicaragua as the best site. Great Britain, however, resisted United States control of such a vital link between the oceans. To block American plans, Britain declared herself protector of the Mosquito Indians living on the eastern coast of Nicaragua at the proposed site of the canal. For

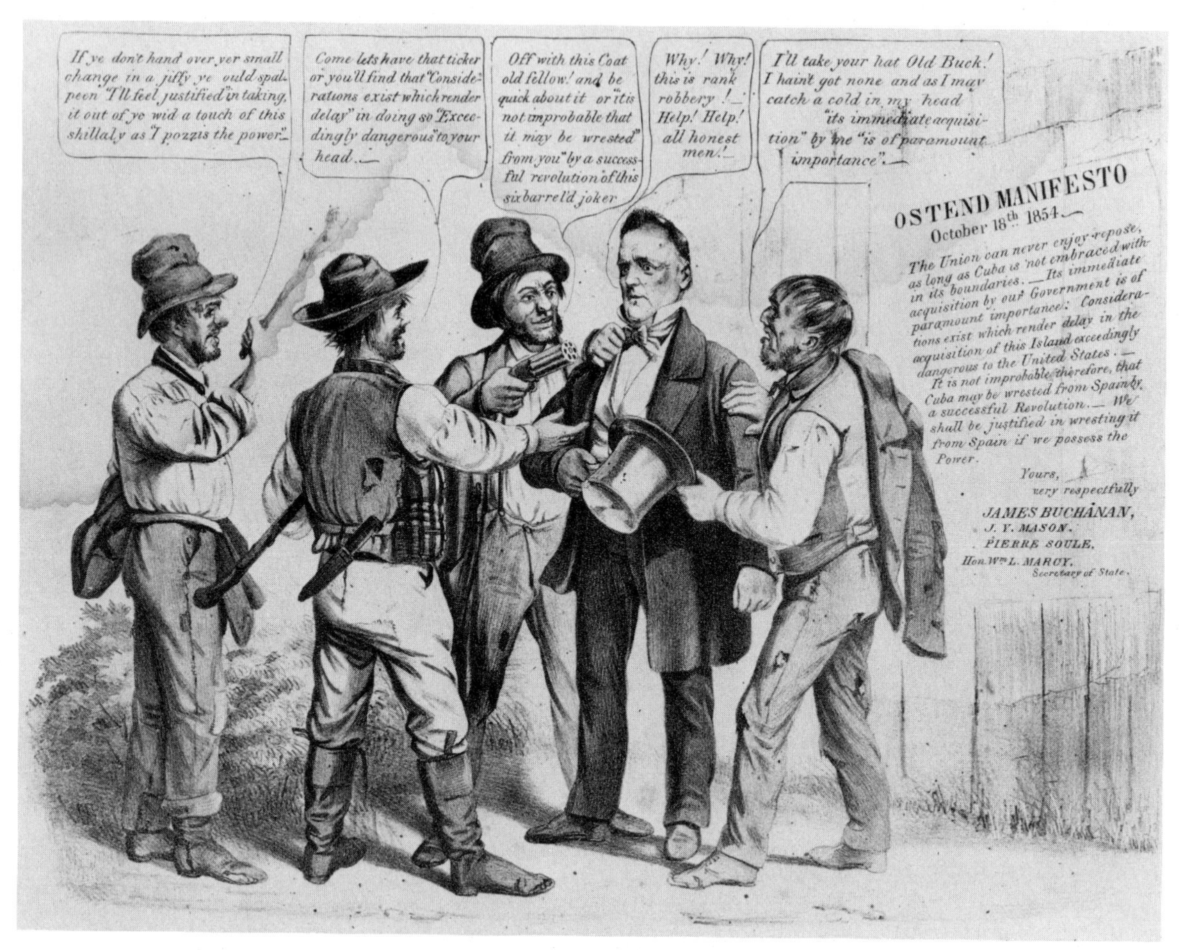

"The 'Ostend Doctrine,' or Practical Democrats carrying out the principle." In this 1854 cartoon James Buchanan, United States minister to Great Britain, is being robbed by a group of ruffians who are justifying their actions by quoting the "Ostend Manifesto."

its part, the United States opposed Great Britain's attempt to gain control of the area. The dispute was finally settled by the Clayton-Bulwer Treaty of 1850 which provided that any canal built by either country would be open to ships of all nations and would remain unfortified even in time of war. Furthermore, the United States and Britain promised not to attempt to gain political control of Central America. American expansionists regarded the treaty as a diplomatic defeat, but it did prevent a showdown with a powerful adversary and established the principle of a neutral, unfortified canal.

Ignoring their government's pledge, some American entrepreneurs persisted in interfering with the region's economic and political affairs. A group of businessmen formed the Panama Railway Company and began to operate a railroad line across Panama in 1855. At the same time, railroad promoter Commodore Cornelius Vanderbilt subsidized a scheme to seize control of Nicaragua. In 1855 an adventurer named

William Walker proclaimed himself president, apparently planning to make himself dictator of all of Central America and to open the area to slavery. The Democrats obligingly expressed approval of Walker's government in their 1856 platform. Involved in a controversy with Vanderbilt, however, Walker lost his supplies, and was ousted by the neighboring republics. When Walker attempted to return to power in 1860, British naval officials arrested him and turned him over to authorities in Honduras who executed him.

Northern fears about adding Central America to the Union as a slave state increased when another adventurer, George W. L. Bickey, tried to organize an expedition to conquer Mexico and divide it into twenty-five slave states. Only one important Southern leader, the governor of Mississippi, offered assistance.

THE GADSDEN PURCHASE

Despite Pierce's expansionist ambitions, the United States acquired only one small territory during his administration. In 1853 the War Department surveyed possible routes for an intercontinental railroad. The shortest southern route would cross Mexican territory south of the Gila River. Pierce's secretary of war, Jefferson Davis, sought to forestall Northern objections to a Southern railroad through foreign territory by proposing the annexation of part of Mexico. Davis persuaded the president to send James Gadsden, a Southern railroad promoter, to negotiate a treaty with Mexico. Gadsden, claiming that American absorption of Mexico was inevitable, used threats of force to urge Mexican president Santa Anna to cede a large part of northern Mexico and Baja, California. Mexico, however, sold only enough land for the proposed railroad. In 1853 Gadsden purchased forty thousand square miles of desert for $10 million.

In approving the sale, the United States Senate annulled the provision in the Treaty of Guadalupe Hidalgo which made the United States responsible for controlling Indian raids into Mexico. Furthermore, the amended treaty opened the Isthmus of Tehuantepec in Southern Mexico to American traffic. The Gadsden Purchase was so unpopular in Mexico that Santa Anna was removed from office the following year.

Buchanan Becomes President

The continuing controversy over the slavery issue, the violence in Kansas, and the controversies over Pierce's expansionist, pro-Southern foreign policy dominated the election campaign of 1856.

The Democrats cautiously endorsed the Kansas-Nebraska Act and supported the use of popular sovereignty to determine the status of slavery in a new territory. However, they realized that their two best-known defenders of popular sovereignty, Pierce and Douglas, were political liabilities. Therefore, the Democrats ignored them both and settled on the uncontroversial James Buchanan, a stalwart party man who had spent the last few troubled years as the American minister to Great Britain.

Four years earlier the Democrats had selected Pierce because he was a "dark horse" unlikely to arouse strong antipathies. Now they adopted the same strategy by nominating the politically neutral Buchanan. At a time when strong leadership was needed, political expediency resulted in chosing a man who would be either an indecisive president or would cater to the interests of the influential Southern leadership of the party.

The new Republican party nominated John C. Frémont, a glamorous explorer whose primary

In this cartoon from the 1856 presidential election, John C. Frémont, the Republican candidate, is approached by six would-be supporters. Left to right they are: a prohibitionist-vegetarian, a feminist, a socialist, a free-love advocate, a Catholic priest, and a free black. Frémont promises, "You shall all have what you desire."

distinction was his military leadership during the war with Mexico and his role in the annexation of California in 1846. Frémont's views on key issues were as much a mystery as Buchanan's. But like his opponent, Frémont had avoided any association with the Kansas dispute. In the tradition of Andrew Jackson, William Henry Harrison, and Zachary Taylor, Frémont was drawn into politics as a war hero more respected for his victories than for his political views.

The Republican party itself, however, stood firmly in opposition to the Kansas-Nebraska Act. It also supported a federally financed program of internal improvements which were opposed by Southerners. These two positions established still more clearly the fact that the Republicans were a Northern-based party whose appeal was only to that section.

In its platform for 1856, the American, or Know-Nothing party, with a stated policy against foreign immigration, urged "a change in the laws of naturalization, making a continued residence of twenty-one years . . . an indispensable requisite for citizenship." Like the Whigs and the Democrats, however, the Know-Nothings were split on the issue of slavery. The free-soilers had been absorbed into the Republican party. Proslavery Southern Know-Nothings nominated former president Millard Fillmore who was also endorsed by the few surviving Whigs.

Buchanan scored impressive majorities in the election of 1856, winning the presidency with 174 electoral votes. Frémont polled 114 electoral votes and Fillmore received only Maryland's 8. Buchanan carried five Northern states and every Southern state except Maryland. The Republicans did not win a single Southern electoral vote. Indeed, some Southern politicians threatened secession if "black Republicans" were elected.

Obviously, even though the Democratic party was a national organization, it owed its victory to the South. Just as clearly, the Republicans were an exclusively Northern party. If they had won a few more popular votes in two more large Northern states, such as Pennsylvania and Illinois, Frémont would have been president. Considering that this party was a recent phenomenon, it had made a remarkably good showing in the election.

James Buchanan had been in government service for forty-three years, and his long public career had been favorably regarded. A lawyer, he was experienced in constitutional law, which he revered both as an early Federalist and later as a conservative mainstay of the Democratic party. His most important appointments were as minister to Russia under Jackson, as minister to England under Pierce, and as secretary of state under Polk. Buchanan was sixty-six, the first bachelor and only Pennsylvanian to serve as president. His career in public service had been so long and varied that many people expected him to steer the ship of state expertly out of troubled waters.

Unfortunately, Buchanan was inclined to vacillate and to accept the views of his Southern advisers. Furthermore, in trying to maintain the "sacred balance" between proslavery and antislavery factions, he alienated both. Although he believed slavery to be morally wrong, he felt that it had to be protected under the Constitution in states where it was already established. He also angered Northerners with his expansionist policies.

THE DRED SCOTT DECISION

Two days after Buchanan's inauguration the Supreme Court announced its controversial decision in the case of Dred Scott, a black man seeking freedom from slavery. Dred Scott's owner, Dr. John Emerson of St. Louis, Missouri, was an army surgeon who had been stationed at Rock Island, Illinois and later, at Fort Snelling in the Wisconsin Territory. Through all these changes of residence, Emerson had been accompanied by Dred Scott. After Emerson died, abolitionists persuaded Scott to sue for his freedom in the courts of Missouri on the grounds that his residence in Illinois and in the Wisconsin Territory, where slavery was prohibited, had made him free. Scott lost his case in the Missouri Supreme Court.

In the meantime, however, Scott had become the property of J. F. A. Sanford of New York. Because Sanford lived in another state, Scott's appeal could now go to the federal courts which had jurisdiction over all interstate matters. The case was important to abolitionists as a test of the laws. Buchanan urged Supreme Court justice Robert C. Grier of Pennsylvania to make the Court's decision as broad as possible to determine congressional power to outlaw slavery in the territories. Buchanan was informed of the Court's proslavery judgment before his inauguration. He approved it and, in his Inaugural Address, asked the American people to abide by the Supreme Court's up-coming decision.

The Supreme Court handed down a six-to-three decision against Scott. The decision was based on the grounds that Dr. Emerson's temporary residence in Illinois and the Wisconsin Territory had not waived the jurisdiction of Missouri slave laws governing Scott. Chief Justice Taney's opinion declared further that

Dred Scott *v.* Sanford

"The question then arises, whether the provisions of the Constitution, in relation to the personal rights and privileges to which the citizen of a State should be entitled, embraced the negro African race, at that time in this country, or who might afterwards be imported, who had then or should afterwards be made free in any State; and to put it in the power of a single State to make him a citizen of the United States, and endue him with the full rights of citizenship in every other State without their consent. Does the Constitution of the United States act upon him whenever he shall be made free under the laws of a State, and raised there to the rank of a citizen in every other State and in its own courts?

The court think the affirmative of these propositions cannot be maintained. . . ."

Chief Justice Taney,
1857

Dred Scott *v.* Sanford

"I can find nothing in the Constitution which. . . . deprives of their citizenship any class of persons who were citizens of the United States at the time of its adoption, or who should be native-born citizens of any State after its adoption; nor any power enabling Congress to disfranchise persons born on the soil of any State, and entitled to citizenship of such State by its constitution and laws. And my opinion, is, that, under the Constitution of the United States, every free person born on the soil of a State, who is a citizen of that State by force of its constitution or laws, is also a citizen of the United States. . . .

I dissent, therefore, from that part of the opinion of the majority of the court, in which it is held that a person of African descent cannot be a citizen of the United States. . . ."

**Justice Curtis,
1857**

blacks were not citizens of the United States, that they were not entitled to the rights of citizens, and that the Supreme Court thus had no jurisdiction in the case.

Having denied its jurisdiction, the Court had no reason to rule on any other constitutional points in the case. But it nonetheless proceeded to lay down broad principles that created violent controversy across the nation. The majority of the justices declared that the Missouri Compromise was unconstitutional. They argued that neither Congress nor the territorial legislatures had the right to outlaw slavery. The Fifth Amendment expressly guaranteed the protection of personal property, and a slave was considered property. In a complicated, 240-page decision, the Court flatly contradicted Douglas' doctrine of popular sovereignty. Whereas Douglas had assured the people of Kansas that they could ban slavery from their territory if they chose to do so, the Court now ruled that only a state, and not a territory, could make such a decision.

Two justices expressed dissenting opinions, with Benjamin F. Curtis, a free-soil sympathizer, filing a sixty-nine-page decision. He argued that free blacks were indeed citizens of the United States and that Congress was constitutionally empowered to exclude slavery from the territories, since the constitutional right to create territories obviously included the right to govern them.

Southerners rejoiced over the Court's decision. The highest tribunal of the land had forbidden Congress to interfere with what henceforth had to be regarded as a purely local issue. Northern free-soilers denounced the decision, claiming that slavery could now be extended into the Minnesota Territory and even Oregon. The Republicans promised that when they were in power they would pack the Court with their own justices who would reverse the Dred Scott decision. Abolitionists jeered at the irony of the Court's defense of slavery in the name of the Bill of Rights. Typical of the Northern response was an editorial in the Chicago *Tribune:*

> That bench full of Southern lawyers which gentlemen of a political temperament call "august tribunal" is that last entrenchment behind which despotism is sheltered, and until a national convention amends the Constitution so as to defend it against the usurpations of that body, or until the Court itself is reconstructed by the dropping off of a few of its members and the appointment of better men in their places, we have little to hope for by congressional action in the way of restricting slavery.

BUCHANAN AND KANSAS

Before the Dred Scott decision Buchanan had secretly encouraged the Court to deprive Congress and the territorial legislatures of the power to ban slavery. After the decision, in an effort to further appease the Southern wing of the party, he tried to bring Kansas into the Union as a slave state, although most Kansans were free-soilers.

The president appointed Robert J. Walker as territorial governor of Kansas. Walker, an able administrator, quickly recognized that most Kansans wanted to bar slavery from their state. Accordingly, although he was from the slave state of Mississippi, Walker worked to help the citizens of Kansas to turn their preference into law. By 1857 Kansas had enough settlers to apply for statehood on a popular sovereignty basis. The proslavery faction, however, had already convened a constitutional convention of its own in the town of Lecompton and drafted a proslavery state constitution. The Lecompton Constitution guaranteed the protection of slavery and was presented to the voters in such a way that they did not have the chance to vote on the issue at all. The antislavery faction, infuriated by the trick, refused to vote, and the constitution was ratified by the proslavery faction.

Walker went to Washington to urge the president to reject the Lecompton Constitution and to convene a new, more representative convention in Kansas. Buchanan, however, was now completely under the influence of his Southern-dominated cabinet. Fearing Southern threats of secession if the constitution was not accepted, Buchanan refused Walker's request and stated that the Lecompton constitution was valid.

Douglas felt the election had been a fraud and opposed the Lecompton Constitution on the grounds that it betrayed popular sovereignty. However, Buchanan would not listen to him and submitted the document to Congress for approval. It passed in the Senate, but in the House, Republicans and "Douglas Democrats" forced the president to withdraw it. Now Buchanan shifted his support to the English bill which provided that if a new referendum in Kansas accepted the Lecompton Constitution, Kansas would immediately be admitted to the Union and receive a federal grant of about four million acres of land. If rejected, statehood and the land grant would be delayed for two years or until the territory had ninety thousand inhabitants. The English bill passed both houses, even though Douglas himself and many Republicans opposed it.

In the meantime, a fairly elected Kansas legislature took office for the first time and called a referendum on the Lecompton Constitution. The document was voted down on January 4, 1858, by a vote of 10,226 to 162. Despite its overwhelming rejection, Buchanan stubbornly persisted in regarding the Lecompton Constitution as a legitimate document. The United States Congress called for another referendum under the terms of the English bill and Kansans again rejected the Lecompton Constitution, this time by a vote of 11,812 to 1,926. When Kansas finally entered the Union in 1861, it did so as a free state.

Buchanan's stubborness had not only alienated the North but had also further split the Democratic party. Stephen A. Douglas was the most powerful Democrat in the country after the president. Buchanan's rejection of Douglas' cherished theory of popular sovereignty permanently estranged Douglas and his followers. Now the party was divided into Southern Democrats, who backed the president, and "Douglas Democrats," who supported the senator from Illinois.

THE PANIC OF 1857

In 1857 sectional strains were intensified by a downturn in the economy which mainly affected the North. When the panic came, more than five thousand businesses failed within a year. Unemployment was widespread.

Because of the country's preoccupation with slavery and territorial expansion people had neglected other economic and political factors which were leading to the depression. Frenzied speculation in railroads and land had undermined the economy. New railroad lines had been built at a breakneck pace. Since many of them extended into thinly settled areas in the Northwest where there was as yet little demand for railroad service, the value of railroad stock soon tumbled. Farmers were being hurt by an event halfway around the world. The Crimean War had created a temporary demand for surplus American grain and meat, but when the conflict ended in 1856, the European market was glutted and food prices fell drastically. State banks had overextended credit to farmers in the Midwest and Northwest, and the farmers began defaulting on their mortgages. Financial distress in agriculture gave new vigor to the demand for free land. In 1860 a homestead act was passed only to be vetoed by Buchanan, who feared that if free land were more available, the territories would be filled with free-soilers. Finally, the discovery of gold had inflated the currency, creating an unstable economy.

The South was relatively unaffected by the depression since world demand for cotton remained high. Exultant Southerners, smarting under Northern attacks on their way of life, pointed to their economic invulnerability as proof of the superiority of their slave-based cotton economy. Northerners, failing to understand the true causes of the panic, blamed it on the low Tariff of 1857, which had been pushed through Congress by the South. So the Republican party, incurring further wrath, demanded a higher protective tariff for Northern industry.

The Congressional Elections of 1858

Increasing sectional tensions, heightened by the economic dislocations in the North, caused the Democrats to fear a hard battle in the upcoming congressional elections. The question of slavery expansion was still the key issue. The most dramatic debate on the subject was conducted in Illinois, where Stephen A. Douglas, the colorful Democratic leader, sought reelection as senator. The choice of Illinois' next senator lay with the state legislature rather than the people, since senators were not popularly elected at this time. But a popular election was generally held so that the people of Illinois could indicate their preference.

The Republicans nominated Abraham Lincoln to oppose Douglas.

One of the Lincoln-Douglas debates.

ABRAHAM LINCOLN

Abraham Lincoln, the son of an uneducated frontier farmer, was born in Kentucky in 1809. When he was seven the family moved to Indiana, and they finally settled in southern Illinois in 1830. Lincoln received almost no formal schooling. He educated himself by reading widely. At twenty-three he won his first political post as a Whig member of the Illinois state legislature. He studied law and was admitted to the Illinois bar in 1836. Lincoln became the leading Whig in Illinois, and in 1846 he was elected to the House of Representatives. After the Kansas-Nebraska Act was passed Lincoln joined the new Republican party. As a lawyer his name was well known in Illinois, and he was the strongest candidate the Republicans could have nominated. His national reputation, however, was not made until his debates with Douglas in 1858.

Lincoln once described himself thus: "It may be said I am, in height, six feet four inches, nearly; lean in flesh, weighing an average one hundred and eighty pounds; dark complexion, with coarse black hair and gray eyes. No other marks or brands recollected." Lincoln's image as a homely, rough-hewn figure was in large part the creation of Lincoln himself. He was keenly aware of his role as an example of the self-made man. The virtues attributed to him—his simplicity, meekness, and honesty—were real, but Lincoln was complex enough to know their value. In his first political speech he struck a humble pose: "I was born and have ever remained in the most humble walk of life. I have no popular relations or friends to recommend me." Thereafter, he constantly sounded this theme.

Lincoln always believed that frugality, industriousness, and ability were the building blocks of success. He once declared in a public address, "Twenty-five years ago, I was a common laborer. The hired laborer of yesterday labors on his own account today, and will hire others tomorrow. Advancement—improvement in condition—is the order of things in a society of equals." This belief was the key to his career.

Lincoln challenged Douglas to seven debates. The continuing contest between these two men soon attracted national interest, and their views were reported in newspapers across the land.

The debates covered many topics, but each focused on the expansion of slavery into the territories. Douglas tried to depict Lincoln as an abolitionist in order to frighten moderates away from the Republican camp. Although Douglas personally was opposed to slavery, he insisted upon the right of people in each territory to decide whether they wanted slavery or not, according to the theory of popular sovereignty.

Lincoln pointed out that he was not an abolitionist. Neither he nor the Republican party wanted to prohibit slavery in the Southern states where it already existed, at least not by force. Courting the southern Illinois vote, Lincoln stated that he did not favor the destruction of all social distinctions between the two races: "I am not, nor ever have been, in favor of bringing about in any way the social and political equality of the white and black races." This position, in part, reflected the atmosphere of his youth in Indiana and Illinois, states which had been hostile to blacks, free or slave.

Nevertheless, Lincoln staunchly condemned slavery as "a moral, social and political wrong," something Douglas carefully avoided doing. The expansion of slavery had to be stopped, Lincoln said, lest it become so divisive an issue as to create a civil war. In a speech in Peoria Lincoln explained why slavery should be kept out of the territories: "We want them for homes of free white people. This they cannot be, to any considerable extent, if slavery is planted within them." The territories were "places for poor people to go to, and better their condition." If slavery was permitted, poor people would have to compete with slave labor or even become slaves themselves. Moreover, if so patent an evil as slavery could be restricted, Lincoln felt, it might even die a "natural death" in the South someday without bloodshed. These arguments appealed to the large mass of whites who feared blacks, as well as to the abolitionists.

The crucial moment in the debates came in Freeport, Illinois, when Lincoln asked Douglas to reconcile his doctrine of popular sovereignty with the Supreme Court's recent Dred Scott decision. Lincoln knew that no matter what Douglas said, he would offend some supporters. If he rejected popular sovereignty, the free-soilers in Illinois would denounce him. If he rejected the Dred Scott decision, he would lose Southern support. With strong presidential ambitions, Douglas certainly did not wish to offend proslavery sentiment or alienate the Southern politicians who were in control of the Democratic party. Douglas tried to solve the dilemma with his "Freeport Doctrine." He modified the Supreme Court decision, claiming that the people of a territory had the lawful means to introduce slavery "or exclude it as they please, for the reason that slavery cannot exist a day or an hour anywhere, unless it is supported by local police regulations. Those police regulations can only be established by the local legislature; and if the people are opposed to slavery, they will elect representatives to that body who will by unfriendly legislation effectually prevent the introduction of it into their midst."

The Freeport Doctrine displeased many Northerners because it glossed over the moral question of slavery. It horrified Southerners because it suggested a loophole whereby a territory could exclude slavery. Douglas had already lost much Southern support by opposing Buchanan's endorsement of the Lecompton Constitution. Now the rift between Northern Douglas Democrats and Southern proslavery Democrats widened.

THE ELECTION

Lincoln received a few more popular votes than Douglas in the congressional election of 1858. But the Democrats had won control of the Illinois legislature, and it voted to return Douglas to his seat in Congress. Lincoln had driven an effective wedge between Douglas and the Southern Democrats, however, hastening the breakup of the Democratic party. In addition, Lincoln had won prominence throughout the North as a sane, articulate, and moderate spokesman of Republican ideals.

In the elections, Democrats lost ground in almost every state, including President Buchanan's own state of Pennsylvania. They regained control of the Senate, but the Republicans won a plurality in the House. Despite their gains, however, the Republicans were unable to get their bills through Congress or past the White House. Southern congressmen and presidential vetoes blocked such Republican measures as a higher protective tariff, a homestead bill, a transcontinental railroad, and federal land grants for the endowment of agricultural colleges.

The Election of 1860

As the presidential elections of 1860 drew closer, the hostility between North and South increased. John Brown's raid on the federal arsenal at Harpers Ferry, Virginia, exemplified the tension that would soon lead to civil war.

Brown, the "avenging angel" who had killed five supporters of slavery in Kansas in 1856, now shifted his abolitionist activities to the upper South. Brown planned to capture the arsenal, arm his followers, and establish a black state in the mountains of Virginia. He was convinced his new black state would attract a spontaneous army of rebellious slaves who would ultimately force the white South to its knees.

Financed by Northern abolitionists, Brown and a small band of followers attacked Harpers Ferry on October 16, 1859, and recruited a few slaves. A hastily assembled local militia soon counterattacked. Dangerfield Newby, a fugitive slave fighting to liberate his wife and seven children, was the first of Brown's men to die. Buchanan ordered Colonel Robert E. Lee and Lieutenant J. E. B. Stuart to lead a detachment of marines to Harpers Ferry to stop the raid. The next day Stuart regained the arsenal, capturing Brown and five of his men. Ten of Brown's men had died in the exchange of fire.

Brown, tried for treason at Charlestown, was convicted and sentenced to be hanged. Governor Wise of Virginia ignored the pleas of Brown's relatives and friends to place him in an insane asylum. Wise, like thousands of other Southerners, resented the fact that Northern abolitionists had backed Brown, and feared that Brown's raid could spark a general slave insurrection throughout the South.

The majority of Northern moderates condemned Brown's violent tactics. His behavior during the trial, however, was so dignified and eloquent that he became a martyr for freedom. Before he died, Brown stated:

> Now, if it is deemed necessary that I should forfeit my life for the furtherance of the ends of justice, and mingle my blood further with the blood of my children and with the blood of millions in this slave country whose rights are disregarded by wicked, cruel, and unjust enactments, I say, let it be done.

John Brown (left) at his trial in Virginia.

In this cartoon of the 1860 presidential election, Dred Scott fiddles while the candidates dance. Abraham Lincoln (upper right) won. The other candidates were John C. Breckinridge of Kentucky (upper left), Stephen A. Douglas (lower left), and John Bell of Tennessee (lower right).

After his execution, John Brown, according to Thoreau, became "more alive than ever." At the same time, Southern antipathy toward the North hardened further. One North Carolinian wrote: "I have always been a fervid Union man [but now] I am willing to take the chances of every probable evil that may arise from disunion, sooner than submit to Northern insolence and Northern outrage."

The nation approached the presidential election of 1860 with grave apprehension. The North feared that the South had become more rigid than ever in its defense of slavery; the conflict over the fate of Kansas, the Dred Scott decision, and John Brown's raid had done much to fire Southern pride and anger. The South feared that the North had gained a pronounced political advantage with the admission of the free states of California, Minnesota, and Oregon.

The great issue of the election, once again, was the fate of slavery in the territories. The Republicans were clearly against the expansion of slavery. The Democrats were split: the Southern wing advocated federal protection of slavery in all territories, and the Northern wing, led by Stephen Douglas, wanted the question of slavery to be solved by popular sovereignty.

THE DEMOCRATIC CONVENTION

In April 1860 the Democrats met in Charleston, South Carolina, to nominate their presidential candidate. Southern extremists were unhappy over Douglas' Freeport Doctrine attempting to reconcile the Dred Scott decision with the theory of popular sovereignty. They demanded a plank in the party platform explicitly stating that it was the duty of the national government to protect the rights and property of persons in the territories.

Douglas could not accept a plank which refuted the doctrine of popular sovereignty. As one of his spokesmen said, "We cannot recede from this doctrine without personal dishonor, and so help us God, we will never abandon this principle." Douglas was backed by a majority of the delegates at the convention, and a popular sovereignty platform was adopted. Delegates from eight Southern states walked out in protest. Douglas needed the support of two-thirds of the delegates in order to receive the nomination; and this he did not have. A new convention met in Baltimore on June 18. Again the Southern delegates withdrew, but this time they were replaced by new Southern delegates who were favorable to Douglas. The official convention nominated Douglas on a popular sovereignty platform while the Southerners who had walked out met independently and nominated John C. Breckinridge of Kentucky. Breckinridge, Buchanan's vice-president, was a moderate, but his wing of the Democratic party adopted a platform calling for a federal code to protect and expand slavery in the territories, and for the annexation of Cuba.

THE REPUBLICAN CONVENTION

On May 16 the Republicans held a convention in Chicago that attracted more spectators than had any previous political gathering in American history. More than ten thousand people attended every day. The leading contender for the presidential nomination was William H. Seward of New York who had been the dominant figure in the party from its inception. But there was strong opposition to his candidacy. For one thing, he was considered a "political abolitionist (he had incautiously spoken of a coming "irrepressible conflict" between the North and South, distressing the moderate faction of former Whigs in the party who feared a civil war). For another, Seward had aroused antipathy by his association with Thurlow Weed, the wily political boss of New York State, and was opposed by Know-Nothings for his friendly attitude toward the new immigrants.

Only Lincoln, among all the contenders for the nomination, was without important political enemies.

On the third ballot the convention unanimously nominated Abraham Lincoln. A compromise candidate, Lincoln was an ardent enough opponent of slavery on moral grounds to satisfy abolitionists in the Northeast and yet a moderate enough spokesman for the peaceful, legal containment of slavery to win the confidence of former Whigs and other delegates from the Midwest.

The Republican platform took the position that slavery had already been outlawed in the territories: "We deny the authority of Congress, or a territorial legislature, or of any individuals, to give legal existence to slavery in any territory of the United States." This was a direct refutation of the Dred Scott decision based on the Republicans' interpretation of the clause of the Fifth Amendment of the Constitution which guarantees personal liberty.

The Republicans also broadened their appeal by promoting several measures which had failed in Congress during the preceding session. These measures were the immediate entrance of Kansas into the Union (to appeal to free-soilers); a protective tariff (to appeal to Eastern manufacturers and factory workers); a homestead law that would provide free land for settlers (to attract the votes of Western farmers); internal improvements and a transcontinental railroad (to win the allegiance of Californians and the business community); and a plank attacking any abridgment of the right of citizenship (to win votes from recent immigrant arrivals).

The Republican ticket was also well balanced. Lincoln himself was certain to draw support from voters in the Midwest while his running mate, Hannibal Hamlin of Maine, a former Democrat, would presumably win votes from disaffected Democrats and from people in the Northeast.

THE CONSTITUTIONAL UNION PARTY

The race for the presidency was complicated by the entrance of a new party, the Constitutional Union party. Composed of old-line Whigs, Know-Nothings, and dissident Democrats, the new party nominated John Bell of Tennessee. Characterized as the "Old Gentlemen's party," it campaigned on one simple slogan: "It is both the part of patriotism and of duty to recognize

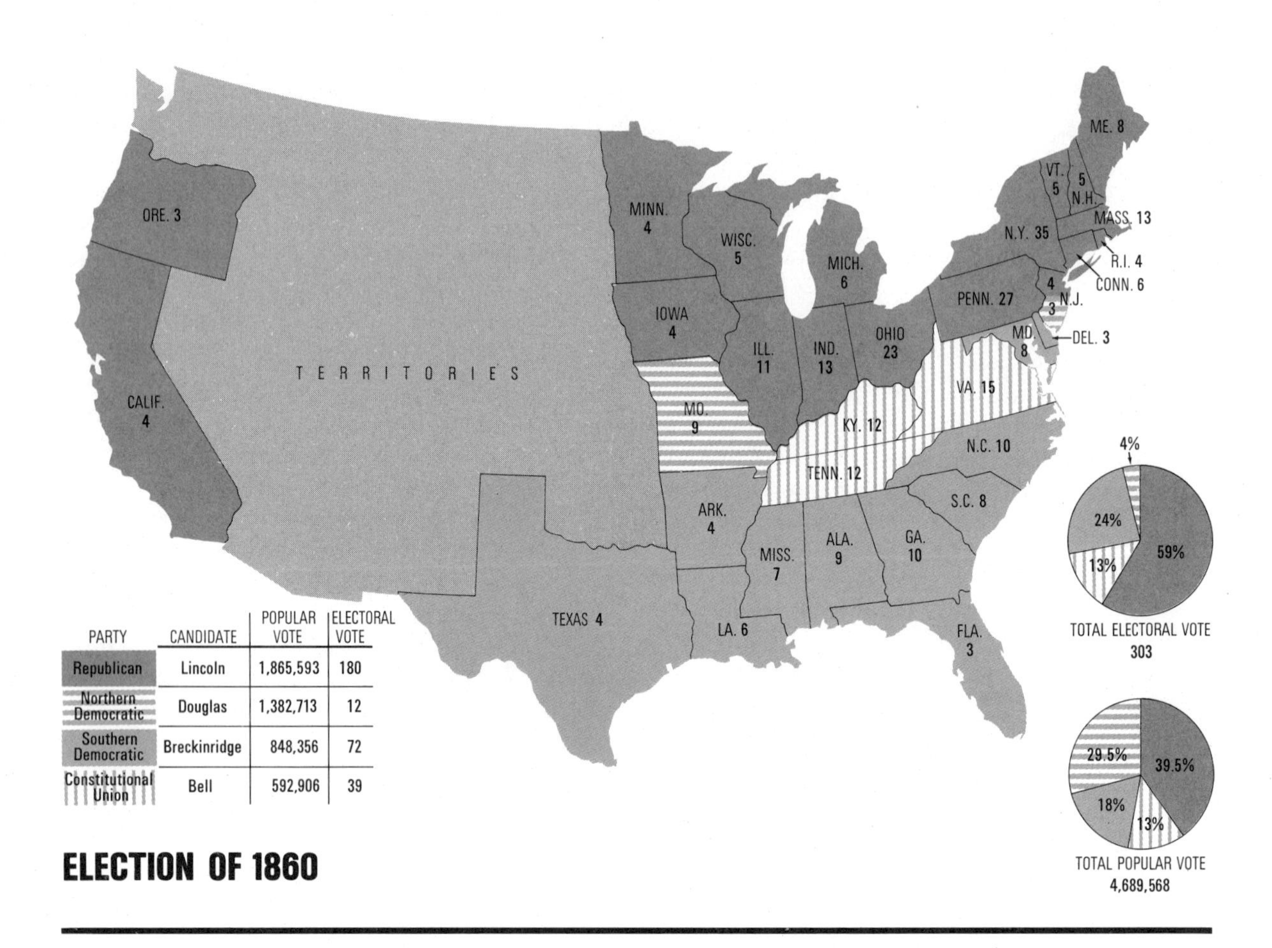

PARTY	CANDIDATE	POPULAR VOTE	ELECTORAL VOTE
Republican	Lincoln	1,865,593	180
Northern Democratic	Douglas	1,382,713	12
Southern Democratic	Breckinridge	848,356	72
Constitutional Union	Bell	592,906	39

ELECTION OF 1860

no political principle other than the Constitution of the country, the union of the states, and the enforcement of the laws." On the crucial question of the expansion of slavery into the territories, the Constitutional Union party took no stand at all. Its appeal was limited, and it won votes primarily in the border states along the Mason-Dixon Line which had the most to lose in the event of a civil war.

THE CAMPAIGN

The campaign was spirited. Lincoln made no speeches so others could not twist his opinions. But Republican orators led by Seward and Salmon P. Chase of Ohio toured the country on behalf of the Republican ticket. By election time some fifty thousand speeches, generally moderate in tone, had been made. The tremendous enthusiasm of the party, displayed in rallies and parades, distracted its supporters from thinking seriously about Southern threats of secession should Lincoln win. Lincoln himself thought the threats were a bluff.

The contest was a peculiar one; in reality, it was two contests. In the South Bell and Breckinridge competed against each other; in the North Lincoln and Douglas fought it out.

Breckinridge defeated Bell by some 250,000 votes. Lincoln won a mere 1,926 votes in the South; in many states his name did not even appear on the ballot.

There were many parades for Douglas, and he spoke widely throughout the North. Douglas also broke with precedent by delivering many campaign speeches in the South. He had decided to campaign actively there, primarily to prevent the South from seceding following a Republican victory, a prospect which he regarded as inevitable. As he said, "Mr. Lincoln is the next President. We must try to save the Union. I will go South." Unfortunately, Douglas made almost no impression south of the Mason-Dixon Line.

The race in the North was extremely close in some states. For example, Lincoln carried California by only 643 of that state's 119,000 votes, and Oregon by only 264 out of a total of 13,000 votes.

Lincoln won the election by a decisive margin in the electoral college. He received 180 electoral votes, while all of his rivals combined received only 123. However, he received only thirty-nine percent of the popular vote. Almost one million more votes were cast for his opponents than for Lincoln. Douglas alone received well over one million votes. Yet Lincoln carried every free state but New Jersey and his popular vote was distributed in such a way that it paid off in electoral votes.

Although Lincoln did not win by a clear majority, he had a strong free-soil mandate. By casting ballots for Douglas and Lincoln, more than two-thirds of the country's voters had expressed their determination in some way to stop the expansion of slavery. Lincoln and Douglas together had received sixty-nine percent of the total vote.

Secession

Southern reaction to the Republican victory was summarized by an editorial in the New Orleans *Daily Crescent* on November 13, 1860:

> They have robbed us of our property . . . they have set at naught the decrees of the Supreme Court, they have invaded our States and killed our citizens, they have declared their unalterable determination to exclude us altogether from the Territories, they have nullified the laws of Congress, and finally they have capped the mighty pyramid of unfraternal enormities by electing Abraham Lincoln . . . on a platform and by a system which indicates nothing but the subjugation of the South and the complete ruin of her social, political, and industrial institutions.

In moving toward secession white Southerners believed they were preserving a way of life that provided them with individual freedom and economic opportunity. Many of them deeply feared that the restriction of slavery would destroy the economic and cultural foundations of their society.

Throughout the fifteen slave states people were angry and anxious over the election of Lincoln. For years Southerners had threatened secession. The South considered the Union a voluntary association of sovereign states, and believed that states could separate from the rest of the nation whenever they chose to do so.

Although many Southerners continued to be Unionists after Lincoln's election, the secessionists were better organized. South Carolina, with its unified economic and social outlook, had long been the center of Southern separatism. Even before the 1860 election the governor of South Carolina warned that a Republican victory would "inevitably destroy our equality in the Union, and ultimately reduce the Southern states to mere provinces of a consolidated despotism, to be governed by a fixed majority in Congress hostile to our institutions and fatally bent upon our ruin." The South Carolina legislature had

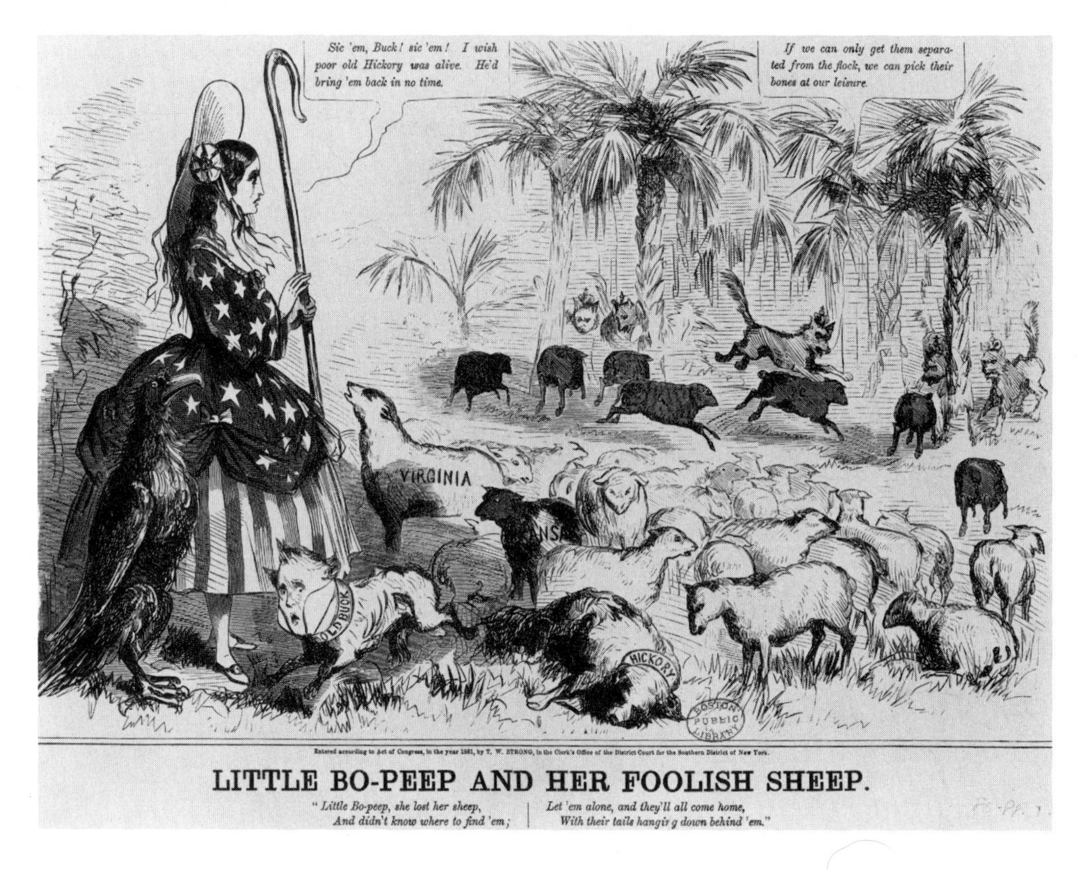

In this 1861 cartoon Little Bo-Peep, dressed in stars and stripes, laments the ineffectuality of her sheepdog "Old Buck" (President Buchanan) while her black sheep, two of which are named Georgia and South Carolina, stampede toward the woods where the European wolves await.

remained in session during the campaign. As soon as the returns were counted, it called for a convention to provide for the state's secession from the Union. While that convention was meeting, President Buchanan gave a speech denying the right of states to secede from the Union. He admitted, however, that he could find no constitutional authority for coercing states to remain in the Union. Furthermore, Buchanan hesitated to take action with a tiny standing army of fifteen thousand men, many of whom were stationed in the West to control the Indians. With public opinion in the North divided on the use of force, the president wanted to avoid confrontation.

On December 20, 1860, the South Carolina convention voted unanimously to withdraw from the United States.

SECESSION SPREADS

Six more states of the deep South soon followed South Carolina's lead. Mississippi chose to withdraw on January 9, 1861. By January 26 Florida, Alabama, Georgia, and Louisiana had also left the Union.

The last of the states in the deep South to secede was Texas, which withdrew on Febuary 1. Governor Sam Houston, a strong Unionist, had refused to call the legislature into session, hoping to forestall a vote on secession. As Houston warned, "You may after the sacrifice of countless thousands of treasure and hundreds of thousands of precious lives, as a bare possibility, win Southern independence, if God is not against you; but I doubt it." Despite Houston's stand, the secessionists forced a public vote on the issue and the people, later backed by their legislature, voted overwhelmingly to withdraw from the Union.

When Lincoln assumed office he inherited the first stages of dissolution of the Union. Seven states had already broken away and had formed a new government in Montgomery, Alabama. That new nation, the Confederate States of America, chose Jefferson Davis of Mississippi as its provisional president. A new Southern Congress began to draft a constitution, and a new flag, the Stars and Bars was designed.

Secessionists viewed the new nation with confidence. The insults of Northerners would be silenced. Tension created by conflicts over the fate of slavery in the territories would be broken. And Southerners would no longer have to pay high tariffs on manufactured goods. Secession would allow the South to break its dependency on Northern manufacturing and to develop its own balanced, self-sufficient economy. The world market for cotton remained profitable and sound. Adventurers backed by the Confederacy would soon bring Cuba, Mexico, and Central America into the Southern confederation. Most Southerners were also convinced that the North would not fight a war over secession.

Secession had not yet swept the upper South and border states. From Virginia to Missouri, eight slave states remained in the Union. Even in the seceding states the separatist urge was not nearly as unanimous as the voting statistics might indicate. A group of moderates, called "cooperators," at first worked to preserve the Union. They pointed out that Lincoln had promised not to advocate abolition where slavery already existed. They also underlined the fact that Southern Democrats could still control the Senate and the Supreme Court. The small farmers in northern Georgia and Alabama who did not own slaves tried to persuade rich plantation owners from the southern parts of their states to wait until a slave-state convention had presented its demands to the North. But the cooperators eventually saw that their cause was hopeless, and decided to cast their lot with the secessionists.

THE CRITTENDEN COMPROMISE

Meanwhile, in an effort to halt the spread of secession, Buchanan had asked Congress to frame compromise measures to reduce Southern fears. The House drafted an amendment that would forever deny Congress the power to abolish slavery in states where it already existed. Southern spokesmen rejected the proposal because it said nothing about slavery in the territories.

A Senate committee, headed by John J. Crittenden of Kentucky, then recommended a series of amendments that would guarantee the permanence of slavery in the District of Columbia and in the states where it already existed, strengthen the Fugitive Slave Law, prevent interference with the interstate slave trade, and, most important, reestablish the Missouri Compromise line of 36° 30′ (slavery would be allowed South of the line and prohibited north of the line).

Despite support throughout the country for the Crittenden Compromise, few Northern and Southern leaders endorsed it. Moreover, when Lincoln was approached for his approval, he rejected the plan. He pledged never to compromise in his determination to keep slavery from expanding into new territories. He also feared that the compromise would encourage the South to embark on expansionist attacks south of the Rio Grande. Lincoln suspected that Southerners had visions of turning parts of Mexico and Central America and all of Cuba into slave states.

The legislature of Virginia tried to act as a mediator by inviting the other states to a peace conference in Washington, D.C. Delegates from twenty-one states attended, but the reconciliation plan they devised merely followed the broad outlines of Crittenden's scheme. Furthermore, their proposal, made public in February 1861, came after seven states had already seceded.

FAILURE TO COMPROMISE

Why did the spirit of compromise, which had always prevailed in past national controversies, fail this time? In the country as a whole, among the people of the border states, the Douglas Democrats, and the conservative business interests, there was still a widely held hope for compromise. But gone were the great statesmen who had initiated past successful efforts to save the Union. Men like Clay, Webster, and Calhoun had now been replaced by new leaders in both sections who were less willing to compromise, men like Seward, Chase, Sumner, Jefferson Davis, Alexander H. Stephens of Georgia, William B. Yancy of Alabama, and Robert Barnwell Rhett of South Carolina. Also, enmity between the sections had increased almost beyond hope of reconciliation. Lincoln's position was crucial. He insisted that any compromise had to exclude the expansion of slavery, and yet there was no chance the South would accept any such compromise plan. Even as compromises were being proposed, sectional economic and political interests were undercutting their prospects for adoption. Finally, events had progressed so rapidly that by the time compromises were proposed, the precedent for secession had been set seven times.

BUCHANAN'S POLICY

Now Buchanan stiffened his opposition to the separatist movement. He replaced secessionists in his cabinet with reliable Unionists. In his last message to Congress he also emphasized his duty as president to collect federal revenues and protect properties in the South: "The Union must and shall be preserved by all constitutional means. . . . The present is no time for palliations. Action, prompt action, is required."

South Carolina flouted Buchanan's authority by demanding that the president relinquish federal property in the South, such as Fort Sumter

This cartoon attacks President Buchanan's handling of the presidency.

in the harbor of Charleston. Buchanan refused, and sent supplies to strengthen the fort defended by a small garrison under Major Robert Anderson. To avoid antagonizing South Carolina Buchanan dispatched an unarmed merchant ship, the *Star of the West*, instead of an armed naval vessel. But when the ship entered Charleston harbor, fire from shore batteries forced it to return to New York.

The South had fired on the Stars and Stripes, but Northerners, bewildered by the event, did not react by demanding war. Everyone waited to see what course Lincoln would pursue.

Lincoln Takes Command

On March 4, 1861, when Lincoln gave his long-awaited Inaugural Address, states in the upper South—Virginia, Maryland, North Carolina, and Delaware—were still debating whether to stay in the Union. The slave states farther west—Tennessee, Kentucky, Arkansas, and Missouri—were also discussing secession.

Lincoln took a firm but cautious stance. He entreated the states of the Confederacy to return to the Union. He reassured the South that he had no intention of trying to abolish slavery where it already existed and promised to support the Fugitive Slave Law. He emphatically denied the right of any state to secede from the Union: "I hold that, in contemplation of universal law and of the Constitution, the Union of these States is perpetual. . . . No State, upon its own mere motion, can lawfully get out of the Union." He pledged to protect federal property, collect federal revenues, and maintain federal services.

"My countrymen, one and all," Lincoln said, "think calmly and well upon this whole subject. Nothing valuable can be lost by taking time. If there be an object to hurry any of you in hot haste to a step which you would never take deliberately, that object will be frustrated by taking time; but no good object can be frustrated by it." The new president insisted that hostili-

Abraham Lincoln.

ties would not be initiated by him:

> In your hands, my dissatisfied fellow-countrymen, and not in mine, is the momentous issue of civil war. The government will not assail you. You can have no conflict without being yourselves the aggressors. You have no oath registered in Heaven to destroy the Government, while I shall have the most solemn one to "preserve, protect and defend it."

In a final eloquent passage Lincoln appealed to the patriotic memories of Southerners:

> I am loath to close. We are not enemies, but friends. We must not be enemies. Though passion may have strained, it must not break, our bonds of affection. The mystic chords of memory, stretching from every battlefield and patriot grave to every living heart and hearthstone all over this broad land, will yet swell the chorus of the Union, when again touched, as surely they will be, by the better angels of our nature.

FORT SUMTER: THE WAR BEGINS

The day after his inauguration Lincoln received a letter from Major Anderson warning that Fort Sumter could be held only if the president dispatched twenty thousand additional men, a large naval force, and ample provisions.

For six weeks the president hesitated. He was determined to keep Fort Sumter, but he still believed there was enough Union sentiment in the South to settle the matter without the use of force. As weeks passed, however, the press and then the people of the North began to express impatience. By the time Lincoln decided on a policy of action, Northern public opinion was ready to support strong moves to save the Union.

Lincoln realized that the Confederacy would consider an armed naval expedition to Fort Sumter as an act of war. On the other hand, if Fort Sumter were allowed to fall into Confederate hands, Lincoln would seem to be recognizing the independence of the seceding states. Most of the members of his cabinet advised him not to send food to Fort Sumter. Only Secretary of the Treasury Salmon P. Chase and Postmaster General Mongomery Blair favored aiding Anderson. Assuming that a major conflict with a foreign enemy would bring the seven states of the Confederacy back into the Union, Secretary of State William H. Seward proposed a scheme to provoke war with France or Spain over Mexico or Santo Domingo.

Lincoln decided to send relief to Fort Sumter, but he chose to send only food in unarmed ships. "If such attempt be not resisted," Lincoln wrote the governor of South Carolina, "no effort to throw in men, arms or ammunition will be made without further notice, or in case of an attack upon the Fort." Thus Lincoln, sensing that a conflict could not be averted, forced the Confederacy to take the next step. If the South shelled a peaceful expedition bringing food to a beleaguered fort, then the Confederacy would be responsible for firing the first shot of a civil conflict. The president was determined to save the Union even if it meant war.

The governor of South Carolina, Francis W. Pickens, forwarded Lincoln's message to Jefferson Davis in Montgomery. The president of the Confederacy immediately ordered General Pierre G. T. Beauregard to request that Major Anderson evacuate Fort Sumter by 4:00 A.M. on April 12, 1861. When Anderson refused, Beauregard opened fire. The shelling began at 4:30 A.M. and continued for the next thirty-four hours, when Anderson lowered the Stars and Stripes in defeat. Lincoln's unarmed flotilla then approached the fort and, with Confederate permission, carried away Anderson's troops. Not a single soldier had died on either side, but the war had begun.

Many Americans still doubted that a real war would follow. Some radical abolitionists such as William Lloyd Garrison and the Quaker poet John Greenleaf Whittier recommended that Lin-

THE UNITED STATES ON THE EVE OF THE CIVIL WAR

coln permit the Confederate states to depart from the Union in peace. Many businessmen in the North also wished for peace. They were fearful that a war would interrupt commerce, reduce the value of government securities, and interfere with the collection of debts owed by Southerners. Many Southerners also expected peace to follow. They were convinced that Northerners were too obsessed with making money to allow their economy to be disrupted by war.

Yet despite initial Northern hesitation to fight, the desire to keep the nation together was a strong force. The North was divided on the question of fighting over the slavery issue, but not on fighting to preserve the Union. Continued use of the Mississippi River and unhampered access to the Southern markets for Northern agricultural and manufactured goods played a part in the decision. But there were other powerful ideas shaping pro-Union sentiment in the North. Some abolitionists saw the war as a means of destroying slavery. Most important, Northerners generally believed that the United States had a special mission to establish an enduring democratic society.

Interpreting the Causes of the Civil War

Was the Civil War inevitable? If so, what forces brought it about? Was slavery the decisive issue? Which section was guilty of causing the conflict: the North or the South? How important were the roles of opposing economic interests? Could war have been avoided if hotheads had not stirred up animosities and if the nation's leaders had been wiser during the 1850s?

Immediately after the war Northern historians, many of whom had participated in the struggle or had lost relatives on the battlefield, argued that the South had plotted the destruction of the Union in order to preserve the evil institution of slavery. Henry Wilson, in his three-volume *History of the Rise and Fall of the Slave Power in America* (1872–1877), embodied the viewpoint that the North had fought a crusade against an absolute moral wrong. Postwar Southern historians, however denied the importance of slavery as a cause of the war and blamed Lincoln and the Republican party's overbearing and unconstitutional actions in 1860 and 1861. Others, such as former president Buchanan, felt that extremists in both the North and South were at fault. Had Northern abolitionists and Southern advocates of slavery been more temperate, war might have been avoided.

By the 1890s the first generation that could look at the Civil War from some distance viewed the conflict in the context of intense economic nationalism. Historians such as James Ford Rhodes regarded the Civil War as a blessing in disguise. Sectionalism and slavery had hampered American growth. The war had abolished both evils and permitted the United States to become a unified nation and a first-rate industrial power. Slavery and the South had been at fault, Rhodes wrote, but individual slaveowners were merely victims of impersonal economic forces. Southerners, not personally to blame, deserved sympathy more than censure. The Civil War had been an "irrepressible conflict" between two economic systems: the industrial wage system of the North and the agricultural slave system of the South.

Rhodes had an obvious Northern bias, but contemporary Southern historians agreed that the war had been waged between two different ways of life and two economies. Buoyed by a return to prosperity in the South, they also regarded the Civil War favorably. Southern historians of the period viewed slavery and secession, not as moral wrongs, but as hindrances to economic progress in the South. Woodrow Wilson, for example, believed that the Civil War was an unfortunate but inevitable event that had a fortunate outcome.

The complacency and optimism of the nationalist school was sharply challenged in the early twentieth century by the historians of the progressive era. Perhaps the greatest work of this new movement was Charles and Mary Beard's *The Rise of American Civilization*, published in two volumes in 1927. Like the nationalist historians, the Beards believed that economic forces had caused the Civil War, but unlike the nationalists, they did not see the results as an unmixed blessing. Rather, they viewed the war as a "social cataclysm in which the capitalists, laborers, and farmers of the North and West drove from power in the national government the planting aristocracy of the South." Furthermore, in the postwar era, a small band of Northern capitalists had ruthlessly exploited the great mass of American workers. The Beards and other Progressives were eager to curb the power of big business in their own day. Thus they saw the post-Civil War period as the beginning of the development of great social and economic inequities in American life.

Although the Progressives were influenced by the economic writings of Karl Marx, they were not orthodox Marxists. They did not want a revolution, but rather, democratic reform. In the 1930s a small group of American Marxist historians presented their perspective on the Civil War. Unlike the Beards, they did not deplore the outcome of the conflict. In classical Marxist terms, every economy must progress from feudalism to capitalism and then to socialism. Since the Civil War had brought an end to a slave economy, regarded as a form of feudalism, and strengthened American capitalism, the conflict was regarded as an important step toward a socialist economy in the United States. As one Marxist, James Allen, put it: "The destruction of the slave power was the basis for real national unity and the further development of capitalism, which would produce conditions most favorable for the growth of the labor movement."

During the Depression, two other schools of interpretation arose. One was a movement of Southern nationalists who blamed the conflict on the North. Typical of these was Frank L. Owsley, a professor at the University of Alabama. Not surprisingly, he attacked pre-Civil War Northerners for their rudeness:

> . . . an impatient generation who had no . . . understanding of the essence of national unity. The result was that urbanity, self-restraint, and courtesy—the ordinary amenities of civilized intercourse—were cast aside; and in their gracious place were substituted the crude, discourteous, and insulting language and conduct in intersectional relations. . . . It was the Missouri debates in which intersectional comity was first violated; and it was the political leaders of the East, particularly the New Englanders and those of New England origin, who did it when they denounced in unmeasured terms slavery, the slaveholder, and southern society in general.

Owsley refused to see slavery as a moral issue. Slavery had been merely a system of discipline necessary for social control.

The third and probably most important school of thought to arise in the 1930s was the revisionist movement. Profoundly disillusioned over the outcome of World War I, the revisionists regarded all wars as pointless and unavailing. Whereas the nationalists, the progressives, and the Marxists had all considered the Civil War an inevitable outburst of violence, the revisionists thought that it might easily have been averted if the country's leaders had been more skillful during the 1850s. Historians such as Avery Craven and James G. Randall insisted that the war had been "a repressible conflict" caused by the "Blundering Generation." Whereas earlier historians had been influenced somewhat by Marx, the revisionists reflected the ideas of Sigmund Freud. As Randall wrote on the eve of World War II:

> War-making is too much dignified if it is told in terms of broad national urges, of great German motives, or of compelling Russian ambitions. When nations stumble into war, or when peoples rub their eyes and find they have been dragged into war, there is at some point a psychopathic case. Omit the element of abnormality, or of bogus leadership, or inordinate ambition for conquest, and diagnosis fails. . . . The writer doubts seriously whether a consensus of scholars who have competently studied the Civil War would accept either the cultural motive or the economic basis as the effective cause.

Craven also emphasized the irrationality of leaders as a cause of the war and charged that Americans had

> . . . permitted their shortsighted politicians, their overzealous editors, and their pious reformers to emotionalize real and potential

> differences and to conjure up distorted impressions of those who dwelt in other parts of the nation. . . . In time a people came to believe that social security, constitutional government and the freedom of all men were at stake in their sectional differences; that the issues were between right and wrong; good and evil. Opponents became devils in human form. Good men had no choice but to kill and be killed.

The revisionist position was in essence a more sophisticated restatement of Buchanan's thesis that the war had been caused by extremists on both sides.

After World War II, historians such as Allan Nevins and Arthur M. Schlesinger, Jr., returned to the theory that the Civil War was fought over the moral issue of slavery and that the North was justified in prosecuting a war against the institution. Schlesinger also rejected what he characterized as the easy optimism of the revisionists concerning the basic rationality of human nature. Having just endured a war against the Nazis, Schlesinger wrote:

> . . . the experience of the twentieth century has made it clear that we gravely overrated man's capacity to solve the problems of existence within the terms of history. . . . Man generally is entangled in insoluble problems; history is consequently a tragedy in which we are all involved, whose keynote is anxiety and frustration, not progress and fulfillment.

The revisionists had contended that slavery would have eventually disappeared without the Civil War since it was an "outmoded" institution. Given the emotional attachment of the South to slavery, Schlesinger gravely doubted the validity of their arguments.

The civil rights movement of the 1950s and 1960s caused historians to reexamine the position of blacks in American society and to set the institution of slavery and the Civil War within this context. Allan Nevins in *The Emergence of Lincoln* (1950) hypothesized that a "major root of the conflict was the problem of slavery with its complementary problem of race-adjustment.

Readings

GENERAL WORKS

Craven, Avery O., *Civil War in the Making*. Baton Rouge: Louisiana State University Press, 1959.

Craven, Avery O., *The Growth of Southern Nationalism, 1848–1861*. Baton Rouge: Louisiana State University Press, 1953.

Dumond, Dwight L., *Anti-Slavery Origins of the Civil War*. Ann Arbor: University of Michigan Press, 1959.

Nevins, Allan, *The Emergence of Lincoln*, Vols. I–II. New York: Scribner's, 1950.

Nevins, Allan, *Ordeal of the Union*, Vol. II. New York: Scribner's, 1947.

Nichols, Roy F., *The Disruption of American Democracy*. New York: Macmillan, 1948.

Potter, David, *South and the Sectional Conflict*. Baton Rouge: Louisiana State University Press, 1968. (Paper)

. . . It was a war over slavery and the future position of the Negro." However, this did not mean that the North was fighting for the equality of the races; there was too much evidence that Northerners as well as Southerners considered the blacks to be inferior.

Other historians have also placed the Civil War within the history of race relations in the United States. They have shown that while the war brought emancipation, it made little impact on racism. David Brion Davis' *The Problem of Slavery in Western Culture* (1967) shows the depth of the roots of belief in slavery, and Winthrop Jordan's massive study, *White Over Black: American Attitudes Toward the Negro, 1550–1812* (1968) noted the long duration and the pervasiveness of the rejection of blacks by white Americans. Leon Litwack's *North of Slavery: The Negro in the Free States, 1790–1860* (1964) concluded that complete segregation, formalized discrimination, and belief in black inferiority prevailed throughout the states that fought for the Union in the Civil War.

Thus most historians tend to agree that the North did not hate slavery enough to go to war because of it and certainly was not fighting for racial equality. The use of slave labor in a form of agrarian capitalism also makes it impossible to claim that the conflict between an industrial society and an agrarian society in itself caused the war. The definitive explanation of the conflict still eludes students of American history.

Yet slavery played an important part in every aspect of the sectional conflict. According to historian David M. Potter:

> Economically, it was an immensely powerful property interest, somewhat inimical to the interests of free farming, because the independent farmer could not compete with the slave. Socially, it was the keystone of a static society of social hierarchy which challenged the dynamic, mobile, and equalitarian modes of life and labor that prevailed in the free states. Ideologically, it was a negation of the basic American principles of freedom and equality.

SPECIAL STUDIES

Crandall, Andrew W., *The Early History of the Republican Party, 1854–1856.* Boston: Badger, 1930.

Current, Richard N., *Lincoln and the First Shot.* Philadelphia: Lippincott, 1964.

Fehrenbacher, Don E., *Prelude to Greatness, Lincoln in the 1850s.* Stanford, Calif.: Stanford University Press, 1962.

Foner, Eric, *Free Soil, Free Labor, Free Men.* New York: Oxford University Press, 1970.

Formisano, Ronald P., *Birth of Mass Political Parties in Michigan, 1827–1861.* Princeton, N.J.: Princeton University Press, 1971.

Hopkins, Vincent, *Dred Scott's Case.* New York: Atheneum, 1967.

Jaffa, Harry V., *Crisis of the House Divided.* Garden City, N.Y.: Doubleday, 1959.

Luthin, Reinhold H., *The First Lincoln Campaign.* Cambridge, Mass.: Harvard University Press, 1944.

Malin, James C., *John Brown and the Legend of Fifty-Six.* New York: Haskell, 1970.

Malin, James C., *The Nebraska Question, 1852–1854.* Gloucester, Mass.: Peter Smith, 1968.

Phillips, Ulrich B., *The Course of the South to Secession.* New York: Hill & Wang, 1964.

Potter, David M., *Lincoln and His Party in the Secession Crisis.* New Haven, Conn.: Yale University Press, 1942.

Stampp, Kenneth M., *And the War Came: The North and the Secession Crisis, 1860–1861.* Baton Rouge: Louisiana State University Press, 1960.

PRIMARY SOURCES

Angle, Paul M. (Ed.), *Created Equal.* Chicago: University of Chicago Press, 1958.

Johannsen, Robert W. (Ed.), *The Letters of Stephen A. Douglas.* Urbana, Ill.: University of Illinois Press, 1961.

Scarborough, William K. (Ed.), *The Diary of Edmund Ruffin, Vol. I: Toward Independence: October 1856–April 1861.* Baton Rouge: Louisiana State University Press, 1972.

BIOGRAPHIES

Capers, Gerald M., *Stephen A. Douglas, Defender of the Union.* Boston: Little, Brown, 1959.

Donald, David, *Charles Sumner and the Coming of the Civil War.* New York: Knopf, 1960.

Johannsen, Robert W., *Stephen A. Douglas.* New York: Oxford University Press, 1973.

Klein, Philip S., *President James Buchanan.* University Park: Pennsylvania State University Press, 1962.

Swisher, Carl B., *Roger B. Taney.* New York: Macmillan, 1935.

Thomas, Benjamin P., *Abraham Lincoln.* New York: Knopf, 1952.

FICTION

Allis, Marguerite, *The Rising Storm.* New York: Putnam's, 1955.

Nelson, Truman, *The Sin of the Prophet.* Boston: Little, Brown, 1952.

Seifert, Shirley, *Senator's Lady.* Philadelphia: Lippincott, 1967.

Stowe, Harriet Beecher, *Uncle Tom's Cabin.* New York: Macmillan, 1962.

LET MY PEOPLE GO

The Life of Harriet Tubman

Dere's two *things I've got a* right *to, and dese are, Death or Liberty—one or tother I mean to have.*

The events which wove the extraordinary fabric of Harriet Tubman's life are almost unbelievable. Born a slave, she escaped to the North as a young woman, only to return nineteen times on the dangerous mission of freeing her family and hundreds of other enslaved blacks. Over the course of her long life she was a laborer, domestic, "conductor" on the Underground Railroad, abolitionist organizer, farmer, soldier, nurse, baker, psychic, visionary, religionist, reconstructionist, advocate of women's rights, speaker, fund-raiser, peddler of produce, and founder of a home for indigent and aged black people.

Harriet Tubman was born in Maryland around 1820—as nearly as she could remember. Her days of hard labor, whippings, and beatings began at the age of five. Harriet's duties included working as a field hand, doing housework, cleaning wheat, husking corn, cutting wood, hauling logs, driving oxen, plowing, and carrying heavy burdens. She preferred hard labor over housework, for at least she could breathe freely outdoors. Her feats of strength were famous and her master exhibited her as a spectacle of muscular power. She worked from dawn until dusk and often into the night as well, receiving no wages whatsoever for her labors.

Harriet Tubman.

Twenty-eight fugitives escaping from the Eastern Shore of Maryland.

When she was about fifteen, Harriet Tubman received a shock which affected her for the rest of her life. One evening one of the slaves with whom Harriet was laboring suddenly put down his work and headed for town. The overseer noticed that he was missing and angrily marched off to find him. Fearing trouble, Harriet followed the overseer, who found the slave in a store and demanded that he submit to a whipping. When the slave would not cooperate, the overseer ordered Harriet to grab him. She refused, and the slave made a break for the door. The overseer seized a two-pound counterweight and hurled it after the fleeing slave. The weight hit Harriet, bashing in her skull. She fell to the floor, unconscious.

For many months, Harriet Tubman lay on a bed of straw in her mother's simple cabin, wavering dangerously between life and death. She had been a rebel before this incident, but during her long illness, her bitter opposition to slavery grew. She also became deeply religious and spent much of her time in prayer. "Pears like I prayed all de time," she said. At long last, and very slowly, she recovered, but she remained the victim of a strange affliction for the rest of her life. A number of times each day, no matter what she was doing, Harriet Tubman would, suddenly and without warning, fall into a deep sleep. Her slumber would last for several minutes and it was impossible to awaken her. This malady was with her for the rest of her life.

Harriet's master died when she was a young woman. One day soon after his passing, she received a warning that she would be taken that night to be sold into a chain gang in the deep South, a fate all slaves dreaded. So Harriet knew that she had to escape that evening or suffer a fate which was worse to her than death. She did not dare tell her mother or anyone else, for she knew that if she did, a commotion would be raised and escape would be impossible. But she had to say good-by somehow, so she strolled through the slave quarters singing this song:

When dat ar ole chariot comes,
I'm gwine to lebe you;
I'm boun' for de promised land,
I'm gwine to lebe you.

Harriet Tubman did not know where she was going when she set out alone that night in 1849, but she was determined to follow the North Star until it led her to freedom. She traveled by night, on foot, through fields and forests and across streams and marshes. She slept during the daytime, usually in the open but sometimes aided to shelter by sympathetic blacks and Quakers. At last she reached Pennsylvania and freedom.

Her initial reaction was one of ecstasy. "There was such a glory ober eberyting; de sun came like gold through the trees, and ober the fields, and I felt like I was in Heaben." Later, however, she felt like she was arriving home after 25 years in prison, with no house, family, or friends to welcome her. "I was a stranger in a strange land," she said. It was then that she decided to bring her family to the North and make a home for them there.

Harriet moved to Philadelphia, where she worked as a domestic in hotels and clubhouses. But even with her new freedom, she never forgot those she left behind in slavery. "I have heard their groans and sighs, and seen their tears," she said, "and I would give every drop of blood in my veins to free them." She saved all her money and, whenever she had enough, she made the dangerous journey back to her home to free members of her family and other slaves.

In her work freeing slaves, Harriet Tubman became known as a "conductor" on the Underground Railroad. The Underground Railroad was a secret and unlawful system for the freeing of slaves, a series of land and sea routes to the North which were linked together by "stations" where fugitives could find aid from sympathizers. Hundreds of blacks risked their lives as conductors during the 1850s, the period when Harriet was active. In all, some 75,000 slaves reached the North via the Underground Railroad.

After the Fugitive Slave Law was passed in 1850, it became necessary to conduct slaves all the way to Canada. For Harriet, this meant a journey of some 500 miles across Maryland, Delaware, Pennsylvania, New Jersey, and New York to Ontario Province in Canada. The dangers increased. Runaways were causing a decrease in the market value of slaves, so proslavery uniformed police, government authorities, and citizen vigilantes doubled their efforts to hunt down Harriet Tubman and her groups of fugitive slaves. Forty thousand dollars was offered for her capture, and there were dark threats of the long, slow process by which she would be tortured to death if found.

In addition to the danger, there was the hardship of the long journey, which was conducted mostly at night, on foot and in all kinds of weather. Also, there were "perils among false brethren." In spite of all this, Harriet Tubman never lost a "passenger." None of the fugitives she conducted to the North was ever lost, killed, or captured. She succeeded in bringing out her parents and all but one of her ten brothers and sisters, in addition to the hundreds of other slaves she led to freedom and the thousands of fugitives she inspired. Harriet became known as the "Moses" of her people. The old spiritual took on a new meaning:

> Go down, Moses
>   Way down in Egypt's land
> Tell ole Pharaoh
>   To let my people go!

Harriet said that her strange sleeping spells played an important role in her work. During these spells she felt her soul leave her body and travel to lands and people which she would later experience in her journeys. She received messages from God, who, she said, guided her every movement. As she put it, "t'wasn't me, 'twas *de Lord!* I always *tole* him, 'I trust to you. I don't know where to go or what to do, but I expect you to lead me,' an' he always did." During one of her slumbers, Harriet received a message that she must go at once to free three of her brothers. She arrived in Maryland on Christmas Eve, and learned that her brothers were to be sold into slave gangs on Christmas Day. She rescued

Satire of the Underground Railroad.

them just in time. On another occasion, she received a similar message about her parents. She arrived a few days before her father was to be tried for aiding in the escape of a fugitive. Harriet "removed his trial to a higher court," as she humorously put it, and rushed him and her mother to Canada. Another of Harriet's psychic experiences is particularly noteworthy. On October 16, 1859, Harriet announced to her friends that she felt that some tragedy had suddenly befallen her friend and ally, John Brown. It turned out that the attack on Harper's Ferry occurred that day. It was only because of a flare-up of her head injury that Harriet herself was not with Brown for that historic event.

There are numerous similar stories about Harriet's powers as a psychic and visionary, most of which have been verified by other witnesses. However, the bulk of such stories have been lost. Harriet's contemporary and biographer, Sarah H. Bradford, decided not to record most of the stories of Harriet's psychic abilities, for fear that such stories would discredit her and her work in the eyes of the unbelieving.

When the Civil War broke out, Harriet joined the Union forces. She was a spy, scout, commando, and guerilla warrior. She was also an extraordinary nurse. With her knowledge of herbal medicine, she cured black and white soldiers of dysentery, fevers, and various other diseases.

Rather than draw army rations, Harriet returned to her small cabin late every night after a long, hard day and made fifty pies, a large amount of gingerbread, and two casks of root beer. These she sold to support herself and her aged parents in the North.

On the Combahee River in South Carolina Harriet Tubman accomplished one of the great exploits of the Civil War. This effort resulted in freedom for nearly 800 slaves, and may be the only time in American history that a woman planned and led a military campaign.

After four years of war service, Harriet returned to the North to join her parents in their home on a modest farm which Harriet had purchased for them in Auburn, New York. On the train home, Harriet was brutally thrown into a baggage car by a conductor and three assistants, all white, who refused to recognize her army pass. To them, it was inconceivable that a woman, a black woman, could legally hold such a pass. Harriet's arm was nearly torn off and she was physically and spiritually wounded for life by this incident.

Harriet spent the rest of her busy days in poverty. She took care of her parents, fed and housed the needy and sick, worked as a domestic, supported two schools for blacks in the South, raised funds, made speeches, peddled produce, worked with the women's suffrage movement, was active in the development of the African Methodist Episcopal Church, established a home for the black indigent and aged, and did temperance work.

Harriet fought for years to obtain a pension for her involvement in the Civil War, but it was not until she was nearly eighty years old, that the government finally awarded her a pension of twenty dollars a month for her Civil War effort.

In 1913, at the age of ninety-three, Harriet Tubman died with the same spirit, energy, and strength which had characterized her life. Who else but Harriet would conduct her own farewell services? In her last moments, she led the friends and ministers gathered at her bedside in the singing of her favorite spirituals.

Suggested Reading

Bradford, Sarah H., *Scenes in the Life of Harriet Tubman* (Auburn, New York: W. J. Moses, Printer, 1869). The first biography, based on interviews with Harriet Tubman.

Conrad, Earl, *Harriet Tubman* (Washington, D.C.: The Associated Publishers, Inc., 1943). Comprehensive biography.

Conrad, Earl, *Harriet Tubman, Negro Soldier and Abolitionist* (New York: International Publishers, 1973). Short biography, in paperback.

Sickels, Eleanor, *In Calico and Crinoline, True Stories of American Women 1608–1865* (New York: Viking Press, 1935). Short biographies of a number of women who played important parts in American history.

Opposite:
"Yankee Volunteers Marching into Dixie," 1862.

15

The Civil War

After passing General Lee and his staff, I rode on through the woods in the direction in which I had left Longstreet. I soon began to meet many wounded men returning from the front; many of them asked in piteous tones the way to a doctor or an ambulance. The farther I got, the greater became the number of the wounded. At last I came to a perfect stream of them flocking through the woods in numbers as great as the crowd in Oxford Street in the middle of the day. Some were walking alone on crutches composed of two rifles, others supported by men less badly wounded than themselves, and others were carried on stretchers by the ambulance corps. . . .

Arthur J. L. Fremantle

The Civil War revealed the gap between America's professed ideals and her actual practices. The warring parties had once fought together for the right of self-determination—one of the rights they had proclaimed was theirs in the Declaration of Independence. Now the South was fighting to preserve a system that oppressed the black people in its midst, a system that contradicted the ideals expressed in the Declaration, and the North was fighting to preserve the Union, not to abolish the institution of slavery and extend the Declaration's principles to the oppressed minority. Furthermore, President Lincoln, usually remembered for his great humanity, bypassed federal laws and suppressed many people's civil liberties in his effort to preserve the Union.

For Lincoln as for most Northerners preservation of the Union, rather than the abolition of slavery, was the central issue of the Civil War. In a letter to Horace Greeley on August 22, 1862, the president wrote:

> I would save the Union. I would save it the shortest way under the Constitution. . . . If there be those who would not save the Union, unless they could at the same time save Slavery, I do not agree with them. My paramount object in this struggle is to save the Union, and is not either to save or destroy Slavery.

Hoping for a swift end to the conflict with the South, Lincoln issued a call to arms immediately after the attack on Fort Sumter. It was the equivalent of a declaration of war in an internal conflict and it was prompted by what was considered an illegal attempt at secession from an unbreakable Union. The president issued a call for seventy-five thousand state militia to serve for ninety days to "put down" the rebellion. The call was answered quickly because of the intense concern Northerners felt at first for preserving the Union. The initial Confederate call for one hundred thousand volunteers was met equally enthusiastically.

Contrary to Lincoln's hopes, America's internal disagreement was not to be resolved easily. Many of the men who answered the calls and their replacements were to become casualties in one of the bloodiest of all wars. By 1865, 620,000 of them would be dead.

The Two Sides Take Shape

Americans were forced to take sides against each other. Many made their choices for philosophical, rather than geographical or even family reasons. Several of the Confederate president's in-laws chose to fight for the Union; three of the Union president's brothers-in-law would die fighting for the South.

FORMATION OF THE CONFEDERATE GOVERNMENT

The Southern states, which had seceded separately from the Union, did not intend to try to exist separately. Ardent in their determination to win their independence from the United States government, they nonetheless acknowledged their dependence on each other. In February 1861, before the attack on Fort Sumter, delegates to the first convention of the seceding states met in Montgomery, Alabama, to draft a form of government for a new Southern republic.

The document the convention devised did not differ greatly from the United States Constitution, except on a few crucial points. The Confederate Constitution declared that it was established by the "people of the Confederate states, each state acting in its sovereign and independent character." The secessionist states were a confederation of sovereign states, not a federation of united ones. The central government was given no authority to impose tariffs, finance internal improvements, interfere with the governing of the states, or control slavery. It could acquire new territories, but was forbidden to interfere with slavery there either. This states' rights philosophy would greatly handicap the South's mobilization effort and hamper its success in the war.

Although the Confederate Constitution made provisions to protect the states' sovereignty, it said nothing about their right to secede. Ironically, the new government of states fighting for their right to secede from the United States was itself described as "permanent."

Under the Confederate Constitution, the structure of government was to be very similar to that of the United States, with the exception that the president was to serve only one term of six years. This provision tended to undermine the little political leverage the first and only Confederate president was to have with the Congress.

The Montgomery Constitutional Convention named Jefferson Davis of Mississippi provisional president and Alexander H. Stephens of Georgia provisional vice-president. Though neither man sought nor really wanted the job, Confederate voters confirmed the convention's choices in their first election. While Lincoln's task was to preserve a nation, Davis' was to make one.

A native of Kentucky, Jefferson Davis grew up in Mississippi, graduated from West Point, and served as Franklin Pierce's secretary of war. Then as a senator he made a reputation as the spokesman for Southern interests in the Senate. Honest, energetic, and devoted to duty, he could also be unyielding and petty.

Davis' slight executive experience and lack of forcefulness made him inadequate for the task of drawing the Confederacy together. He was unable to foster loyalty even among those who worked closest to him and he could not bind them into a smoothly functioning government organization. He meddled constantly in other

Jefferson Davis, president of the Confederacy.

officials' responsibilities, played favorites, and often switched personnel out of whim or impatience. His military judgment was highly erratic, but he rigidly refused to accept counteradvice from his brilliant commanders. His energies were spent largely in quarrels with the Confederate Congress over wartime legislation and with his staff, including Vice-President Stephens.

Stephens was a thorn in Davis' side, even though he remained at home in Georgia throughout most of the war. He was a scholar who yearned for the solitude of study. Stephens was fanatical about states' rights, but he opposed the draft and other wartime measures necessary for achieving a Confederate victory. Most important, he detested President Davis. Whenever Davis exercised presidential power,

Stephens complained that he was becoming a despot. Stephens was never convinced that the Confederacy could succeed and his pessimism increased during the course of the war.

The Confederate president's official advisers were no more help to him than was his vice-president. Throughout the war, Davis' cabinet continued to squabble and shift its position on issues with irritating regularity. Most of its members displayed only an average ability, largely because Davis had initially distributed the cabinet posts on a geographical basis. As a result, men were named for one post even though they might have been better qualified for another. For example, the first Confederate secretary of state, Robert Toombs, did not have the temperament for diplomacy; he did, however, have great financial expertise, and might have been an excellent secretary of the treasury.

Perhaps the ablest of all Davis' cabinet members was Judah P. Benjamin, a lawyer from New Orleans who served first as attorney general, then as secretary of war, and finally as secretary of state. Intelligent and farsighted, he tried in vain to make the Confederacy face its financial, economic, and diplomatic shortcomings. However, his informed opinions and earnest concern ran counter to popular opinion and only earned him ceaseless criticism from Southern newspapers and legislators.

DISUNITY IN THE NORTH

The times called for a president who would not crumble under pressure but be a bold and decisive head of state as well as a military strategist. Because he largely met these qualifications, Lincoln proved to be infinitely superior to Davis as a war leader, even though Davis was a professional soldier. Both men decided military policy. Lincoln did so for much of the war because he could find no generals capable of formulating overall strategy. He also understood the relationship between economic strength and the mobilization of military power. Davis, on the other hand, had extraordinarily capable officers but refused to delegate overall planning to them. Unlike Davis, Lincoln was tolerant, flexible, and politically shrewd. He was willing to suffer much criticism and also false flattery to achieve the results he wanted. It was said of him, "He had a genius for giving men enough rope to hang themselves."

Convinced of the righteousness of the cause, Lincoln acted boldly to preserve the Union. But his extensive use of executive power to bring the war to a satisfactory conclusion aroused considerable controversy in the North.

Once Lincoln had acknowledged that the rift between the North and the South could only be mended by war, he lost no time implementing his decision. Congress was not in session from April through July 1861, so Lincoln acted on his own as commander-in-chief, stretching executive power further than any president before him and leading many on his own side to call him a "despot," "tyrant," and "dictator."

On April 19 Lincoln proclaimed a maritime blockade of the South. Then on May 3, without any precedent, he issued a call for forty regiments of three-year United States volunteers to supplement the state militia he had called out in April. He further usurped congressional power by expanding the navy. He ordered $2 million for military expenditures, although the Constitution states: "No money shall be drawn from the Treasury, but in consequence of appropriations made by law." Ultimately, however, Congress sanctioned these actions.

More widely opposed than these military and financial decisions was Lincoln's seeming disregard throughout the war for the constitutionally protected personal rights of citizens. With his approval, the federal government examined private mail and telegrams and detained anyone whose passport was questionable in any respect. As early as April 27, 1861, Lincoln gave his military commanders the power to make summary arrests without warrants and to suspend habeas corpus in cases of "extreme necessity," as he put it. Although Lincoln was known for his clemency, in September 1862 he issued a presidential proclamation announcing that anyone who discouraged enlistments, resisted the draft, or committed other disloyal acts would be tried by a military court-martial. At least fifteen thousand Americans were imprisoned under this order. Many remained in jail until the end of the war without ever knowing who their accusers were or what the charges were against them.

When the Sixth Massachusetts Infantry Division passed through Baltimore on its way to Washington, it opened fire on mobs of anti-Union demonstrators who were blocking their way. Both soldiers and civilians were killed in the fighting which ensued. Lincoln sanctioned the act by sending a garrison of federal troops to occupy the city and arrest all suspects. Many were subsequently tried by military courts.

Most Northern Democrats were loyal to the Union and supported the war, but they strongly objected to the autocratic authority with which the Republican president had denied habeas corpus in Maryland and tried civilians under military law. Although the Democrats' chief spokesman, Stephen A. Douglas, had died in 1861, they strove under the leadership of Horatio Seymour to keep their party organization strong and active in the hope of regaining power in the next election.

There was a small faction in the Northern Democratic party, however, whose sympathies lay with the South. The "Peace Democrats," or "Copperheads," wanted a negotiated peace with the South and opposed all war measures, especially if they were linked to proposals to abolish slavery. They also feared that the popularity of the Republican prosecution of the war would undermine the Democratic party.

When a Copperhead spokesman, former Ohio congressman C. L. Vallandigham, publicly demanded an end to the "wicked and cruel" war, he was arrested, tried in a military court, and deported behind Confederate lines. Vallandigham fled to Canada and eventually returned unmolested to Ohio, where he led peace demonstrations before the 1864 elections.

As the Confederacy's chances for victory clearly grew dimmer, the Copperheads became even more insistent in their demands for a compromise, ignoring the fact that the South was not interested in making concessions. They encouraged Northerners to fight for the South and actively tried to retard Union enlistments. But the overwhelming majority of Democrats, while they opposed Lincoln's methods, favored the preservation of the Union.

In addition to the peace demands of the Copperheads, the president faced just the opposite criticism from an extreme faction within his own party. Although Lincoln's emphasis on the preservation of the Union as the central issue of the war initially won the support of most Republicans, the "Radicals," or abolitionist wing, worked to make the end of slavery the main aim of the conflict. They attacked anyone who wanted to restore the Union to its prewar status. As they saw it, the South had to be not only conquered but remade.

The most influential and vindictive of the Radicals was Pennsylvania representative Thaddeus Stevens, chairman of the powerful Ways and Means Committee. Early in his career he denounced slavery as "a curse, a sham, and a crime." Moreover, he demanded that blacks be enfranchised and admitted to the armed forces. The Radicals had considerable strength in both houses of Congress, and Stevens applied continual pressure on the president, who needed the Radicals' vote for reelection.

The Radicals wanted to take control of military policy and to formulate a plan for the emancipation of the slaves. To this end they created the Congressional Committee on the Conduct of the War, in December 1861. Its representatives went so far as to crossexamine military commanders about their battle strategies and to challenge Lincoln's choice of military commanders. General McClellan, a Democrat, was the chief target of their charge that the war was not being prosecuted vigorously enough. The Radicals also pushed through Congress the Confiscation Act of 1862, providing for presidential seizure of all property (including slaves) used in furthering the insurrection. The Act had little effect and the Radicals hated to term slaves "property," but its passage showed that Northern feeling against slavery was hardening.

Although the Radicals were harsh and abusive in their manner, their committee's reports did succeed in uncovering scandals and inefficiency in the military, and their idealism had a powerful effect on Northern public opinion.

THE UNDECIDED BORDER STATES

One of the most pressing problems Lincoln faced after the episode at Fort Sumter was how to keep the border states within the Union. His official statement that the North was fighting to preserve the Union, rather than to free the slaves, was partly intended to prevent the border states from seceding. But some of them decided that they could not fight against the South.

Shortly after Lincoln called for troops in April, Virginia, North Carolina, Tennessee, and Arkansas joined the Confederacy. Of all the slave states, only Delaware was openly loyal to the Union cause. Kentucky, Maryland, Missouri, and the western part of Virginia remained undecided; their populace was divided, and they initially refused to furnish troops for the Union Army. Together with Delaware, their white population was more than half the size of the Confederacy.

Kentucky at first tried to proclaim her neutrality but decided to stay in the Union after Lincoln authorized pro-Union people in Kentucky to create armed resistance to secession. Maryland also decided to stay in the Union after Lincoln sent a force to arrest secessionist leaders there. Maryland's pro-Union governor even sent troops to the Union army, although they were to be used only for the defense of Washington and not for fighting in the South.

In Virginia many mountain whites in the western part of the state strongly resented the plantation interests in the eastern part. Lincoln capitalized on their anti-Confederate feelings. In June he ordered thirty thousand troops into western Virginia. The presence of these soldiers encouraged the separatist tendencies of the people. In November 1861 the western counties split away and formed the new state of West Virginia, admitted into the Union in 1863.

Missouri did not give in so easily. When her pro-South governor tried to use the state militia to seize a federal arsenal near St. Louis, Lincoln authorized a Missouri congressman to gather a "home guard" pledged to federal service. The home guard attacked the governor's militia and forced its surrender. As the federal troops marched away, they clashed in a riot with St. Louis civilians, killing many of them. Guerrilla warfare followed in Missouri, and lasted until federal troops achieved a firm victory. The governor and his supporters then proclaimed an independent Missouri government which seceded and operated as a government-in-exile in Texas. Ultimately about thirty thousand Missourians fought for the South, but more than three times that number served in the Union army.

Factors in the War Effort

SOUTHERN CONFIDENCE

The South fully expected to win its independence. It believed it was fighting for its liberty. Yet its confidence was based on three miscalculations. First, Southerners believed war was simply a test of bravery in combat and overlooked the crucial factors of firepower, transport, food supplies, and logistics. The Civil War was the first industrialized war. Second, Southern leaders believed that cotton was so important to the English and French textile manufacturers that they would force their governments to grant the South diplomatic recognition. Eventually, the Confederates thought, European powers would enter the war on the South's side and break the Northern blockade because Confederate independence would be economically profitable to them. Third, Southern leaders decided to pursue a defensive strategy, forcing the Union army to conduct an offensive war against the South which would be difficult militarily, especially if it did not have strong popular backing in the North. To defeat the South, the North would need more men and equipment, as well as longer lines of communication, all of which needed defending. The North must seem to be the aggressor, a factor which Confederate leaders hoped would elicit support from Northern sympathizers.

"Line Officer of Artillery, full dress, and Railroad battery, 1862."

RAILROADS

This was the first war in which railroads were used extensively to transport men and supplies, and the North's superior railroad network gave it a distinct advantage. The Union claimed nearly twenty-two thousand miles of track, over two times more than the Confederacy could claim. In addition, the Confederate tracks were not connected. The Southern railroads were only short lines, with major gaps between vital points. Supplies had to be detoured for long distances or transported between railroads by wagons. Also, the track gauge was less uniform in the South than in the North, preventing the interchange of railroad cars on different lines. Most of the through lines that did exist in the South connected with the Atlantic or Gulf Coast and were easy targets for enemy bombardment. And when equipment broke down in the South it could not be replaced, since train manufacturers were in the North. As the war dragged on, Southern troops suffered severely from the Confederacy's inability to transport supplies, clothing, and ammunition to them.

COMPARATIVE RESOURCES

The fact that the Civil War stretched over years instead of months magnified another of the South's liabilities, its agrarian-based economy. The South's industrial growth had been stunted by its attachment to an agricultural economy based mainly on the export of cotton. At the beginning of the war the North had nearly 110,000 manufacturing concerns that were turning out products valued in excess of $1.5 billion annually and employing 1.3 million workers. The South, on the other hand, had only about 20,000 manufacturing concerns that were producing about $155 million worth of goods annually and employing 110,000 workers. The North produced seventeen times as much cotton and woolen goods, twenty times as much pig iron, and thirty-two times as many firearms as the South.

While the South was at an economic disadvantage, 3.5 million of its population were slaves. Although many fled to Northern lines when they could, there were no slave revolts and they were available to perform the labor

needed to carry on the war. This allowed a large number of Southern whites to serve in the Confederate Army.

The South was unable to exchange its cotton for foreign manufactured goods, at first because of a cotton embargo it imposed in hopes of forcing countries dependent on a supply of raw cotton to enter the war on its side. Then the Confederate lifeline to Europe was cut by a Union blockade of Southern ports. The Union, meanwhile, began importing even more firearms from abroad than it manufactured at home.

Whatever resources the South had at the beginning of the conflict were gradually consumed by the war machine. The North could replace equipment faster than it wore out, but there was no way for the Confederacy to acquire vitally needed new supplies. Throughout the war Southern troops lacked food, uniforms, rails, locomotives, textiles, and ammunition. In reduced circumstances, the South was compelled to turn most of its possessions into war material. Church bells were cast into cannons, carpets were made into clothes, and newspapers were printed on the back of wallpaper. Its defensive military strategy also exposed its railroads and crops to all the destructiveness of war.

On the Northern homefront the war actually acted as a stimulus to production. Although the rate of industrialization may not have increased during the war years, industries that produced iron and steel, woolens, boots and shoes, arms and ammunition, railroad equipment, petroleum, prepared foods, coal, and lumber all met the demands put on them. With increased production came the remodeling of old factories and the building of new ones, all spurred by the war effort. Wages increased forty-three percent but prices rose more, reducing real wages to two-thirds of their 1861 level.

At the same time, however, the new boom brought out profiteering contractors and suppliers who overcharged the government and delivered inferior goods. The ethical conduct of business and commercial leaders was more questionable during the Civil War than during any previous period in the nation's history.

FINANCES

While Washington was being assailed by critics of its too-wealthy suppliers, the South was having grave difficulties paying for its war needs. It had no treasury and only a small supply of capital. Contrary to its expectations, it was un-

◀ *"That Feed Won't Do," a cartoon of 1861, illustrates the Confederacy's financial troubles.*

able to obtain needed loans from Europe. Since its banking facilities were inadequate and its population hostile to taxation, the Confederacy was forced to issue paper currency to help pay the cost of the war. All told, it issued $1.5 billion in paper, more than three times the amount of federal greenbacks in circulation. But because of inadequate gold backing, Confederate currency dropped in value more dramatically than did Union greenbacks.

When the war began the Union government was operating with an empty treasury. Eventually, however, the administration was able to finance the war by raising tariffs to an all-time high of forty-seven percent; raising excise taxes and levying the country's first income tax (five to ten percent); printing $400 million worth of paper money, which was legal tender and at the end of the war was still worth about sixty cents on the dollar; and selling over $2 billion worth of war bonds to patriotic citizens. The war cost the Union over $2 million a day.

The Union government also enacted a new National Bank Act in 1863, creating the National Banking System. The system enabled the administration to market its bonds more economically and to aid the financing of the war by issuing a new national currency.

EUROPEAN INVOLVEMENT

The European powers looked favorably on the South's attempt to gain its independence for several reasons. They would have been delighted to see a democracy fail and would have welcomed the break-up of the fast-growing United States which they began to view as a threat to their own dominance. Especially in England, the aristocracy cherished fellow feelings for the highly class-conscious Southern society. British merchants and industrialists looked forward to having access to the South's cotton without having to pay tariff duties.

But Southern hopes of active support from the European powers were doomed to disappointment. Confederate leaders made the mistake of thinking that Southern cotton was more important to the European economy than it actually was. Britain had stockpiled large surpluses of Southern cotton in 1859 and 1860, so that the Southern embargo on cotton shipments and then cutbacks in its cotton crop failed to bring England and France into the war on the Confederate side. In 1862, when Britain's cotton supply began to run so low that workers were laid off, she turned to India and Egypt for replenishment.

Since English merchants did a brisk business with the North, buying wheat and selling arms, they had strong economic reasons for not wanting to officially interfere in America's Civil War. And many in Britain and France were morally opposed to the use of slave labor.

At first Europeans were confident that the South could win its independence on its own anyway. And by 1863 Northern victories ended the likelihood of European intervention on behalf of the South.

In 1861, however, there was an incident that brought England to the verge of war with the Union. Jefferson Davis had sent two commissioners to plead the Confederate cause in England and France. His representatives, James Mason and John Slidell, were heading for Europe aboard the British steamer *Trent* when it was detained and boarded by a Union officer, Captain Charles Wilkes, commander of a warship which was part of the Union's blockade of Southern ports.

Wilkes took Mason and Slidell off the British ship and transported them to the United States, where they were imprisoned. Although Wilkes' act was very popular with the Northern public, he was denounced in London. The British foreign secretary sent a caustic note to the United States demanding the release of the prisoners and a public apology.

Lincoln did not want a war with England, but neither did he wish to back down before British threats. To save face, Secretary of State Seward provided for Mason's and Slidell's release on technical grounds without ever admitting that the United States had been wrong to seize them.

Though Britain did not intervene directly in the war, she was a constant irritant to the North in her willingness to allow English shipyards to build sea raiders for the Confederacy. British law permitted the building of ships in England for belligerents, but it forbade these vessels from being "equipped, fitted out, or armed for fighting purposes." British shipbuilders got around these legal restrictions by allowing unarmed ships to leave England for an island port such as Nassau, where they were provided with British guns and ammunition. Several of the so-equipped "brigands of the sea" plied the Atlantic and preyed on Northern shipping. The most famous and successful of the raiders were the *Alabama* and the *Florida*, built for the Confederacy in Liverpool in 1862.

Lincoln protested strongly against this practice through Charles Francis Adams, the American minister to London and by threatening to unleash a "flood of privateers" against British sea trade. The *Florida* was eventually captured and the *Alabama* sunk by the Union navy, but not before they had destroyed over $15 million in Northern commerce.

In 1863 the British government finally interceded to stop the building of ships with the obvious purpose of destructive attacks on a friendly power. Two heavy ironclad ships destined to be equipped with deadly battering rams for the South were seized, unfinished, by the British government after the United States threatened to attack neutral shipping if the ironclad ships broke the Northern blockade. Perhaps even more important, the British recognized by this time that the South was being defeated and did not want to be associated with the losing side.

TWO ARMIES

At the outbreak of the war the Union's twenty-three states had a population of approximately twenty-two million. The eleven Confederate states had only a little over nine million people, more than one-third of them slaves. But this great disparity was not at first reflected in the relative size of the armies of the two sides.

Large segments of the North did not supply troops for the Union effort. The one-half million people scattered from Dakota to California made no substantial contribution to the war effort. Furthermore, even during the Civil War some Union regiments had to serve in the West to counter attacks from Indian tribes fighting with the Confederacy or to keep loyal Indians in the Union fold. Some in the border states favored allowing the South to secede and would not fight in the Union Army. Massachusetts, Vermont, Michigan, and Wisconsin even furnished some men for the Southern cause.

As a result, in order to raise an adequate army, the Union had to resort to enticements and, eventually, conscription. In 1861 the United States government offered $100 to each volunteer. This amount was later increased to $302 for new recruits and $402 for veterans. States, cities, and counties sometimes paid additional bonuses, too. In time, Illinois soldiers were offered combined bonuses totally $1056 per volunteer. This system had its drawbacks, since some men would enlist, pick up their bonuses, and desert. Some would even reenlist under assumed names to collect more money.

In March 1863 the Union had to resort to conscription to enlarge its regular army and navy, the latter for a blockade of the Confederate coast. About 300 thousand men out of a total call-up of 1.9 million were eventually drafted despite much draft evasion, substitute-buying, and resistance, including some bloody draft riots. The unpopular draft laws were particularly disliked because they discriminated in favor of the well-to-do. The rich were either

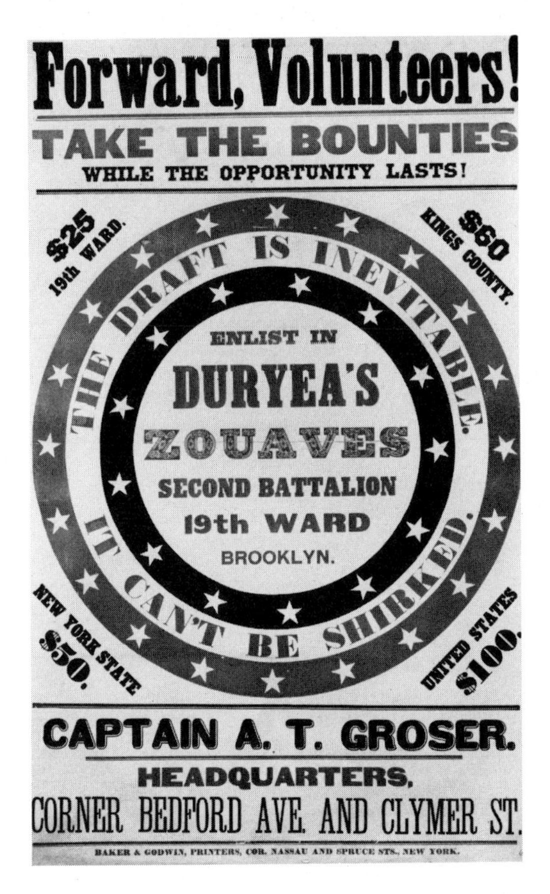

(Courtesy New York Historical Society, N.Y.C.)

exempted or were able to pay someone to serve in their place.

On the other hand the North was considerably aided by heavy immigration during the war years. Over eight hundred thousand newcomers arrived between 1861 and 1865, more than the total casualties of the North. So many immigrants joined up that the Union forces were eventually one-fifth foreign-born in composition. In one division commands were given in four different languages.

In the South Jefferson Davis at first called for one hundred thousand volunteers. The Confederate Congress later authorized a volunteer army of four hundred thousand troops for three years. The number that enlisted, however, did not reach this figure, even though the initial response was enthusiastic. Although the South had far more volunteers than the North, more than were needed immediately, most joined for only twelve months.

By April 1862 the South, too, had to institute a draft. Its First Conscription Act declared that all able-bodied white males between eighteen and thirty-five years of age were liable to three years of military service. Like the draft act in the North, however, the South's Conscription Act exempted certain professional and wealthy people which alienated many of the less privileged and aroused resistance to volunteering. The average young Southern male began to view the effort as "a rich man's war and a poor man's fight." Moreover, states' rights sentiment was so strong among some state leaders that they refused to allow their troops to become part of the Confederate Army.

With resistance to volunteering and evasion of conscription on both sides, it was difficult at times to maintain military discipline. There are no reliable figures as to exactly how many men served on either side. Estimates suggest that some two million men probably wore the Union blue and less than half that number wore the Confederate gray. Terms of enlistment varied from two weeks to the duration of the war.

In a short war the North's numerical superiority would have meant relatively little, given the South's original military superiority. As the conflict ground on, the North built its armies to twice the size of those of the South. Its advantage in numbers became an important psychological, as well as physical weapon. Gradually the Confederate Army's strength was sapped and its reinforcements almost ceased. Southern losses weakened the will to continue the conflict. Meanwhile the Northern armies, despite heavy casualties, seemed to grow more powerful with every battle.

COMMANDERS

The South had an initial advantage over the North in the brilliance of its field commanders. For twenty years before the war a coterie of

◀ *Confederate generals (from left to right): "Stonewall" Jackson, Albert Sidney Johnston, and Robert E. Lee.*

Southern officers had dominated the United States Army under the leadership of General Winfield Scott of Virginia. Many Northern West Pointers found little opportunity for advancement under Scott, so they left the army. Southerners, on the other hand, moved up the ladder of command and became well-trained, superior officers. When the war broke out they embraced the Confederate cause.

Robert E. Lee, Joseph E. Johnston, and Albert Sidney Johnston, the finest of the West Point alumni, were relied upon to give the South the fighting edge in a war they expected to be brief and defensive. But despite the superiority of its generals, the South had no centralized military authority—except for Jefferson Davis who insisted on determining strategy himself. Until the Confederate Congress created the post of commander in chief in the closing months of the war, the most important Southern military post seemed to be that of Commander of the Army of Virginia, where much of the fighting took place. In June 1862 this position was given to Robert E. Lee.

The son of General "Light-Horse Harry" Lee of Revolutionary War fame, Lee was the supreme military genius of the South. He graduated from West Point with an outstanding record and served as Scott's right-hand man during the Mexican War. Although he was dismayed by the disruption of the Union, after secession Lee dutifully heeded the call of his native state of Virginia. Duty, in fact, was the ultimate motivating force in Lee's life. He himself said it was "all the pleasure, all the comfort, all the glory we can enjoy in this world."

When the war began Lee was fifty-four years old. His jet-black hair had turned completely white and he had a statuesque military bearing. Lee became a legend in his own time, both because of his personal qualities and because of his military intelligence and courage. Although usually outnumbered and undersupplied in battle, he had the capacity for building his army while he fought, and he was bold in forming and carrying out plans.

Lee received his strongest assistance from the tactical genius of General Thomas Jonathan Jackson, nicknamed "Stonewall" for his unyielding stand at the Battle of Bull Run. Jackson was a grave and simple man imbued with evangelical piety and a profound belief in the holiness of the cause for which he fought. His extraordinary skill in military maneuvers caused the Union army some surprising setbacks.

At first the Union had no officers who could match the revered Confederate generals. Such was the state of the Northern army at the beginning of the war that its commander, General Winfield Scott, was one of only two officers in the entire Union service who had ever commanded troops large enough to be called an army. The other was John E. Wool who was seventy-seven years old, two years older than Scott himself.

As the war progressed Lincoln repeatedly shifted his generals about in an effort to find strong leadership. When Scott retired as general in chief in the fall of 1861, Lincoln replaced him with General George B. McClellan. Although he was a good army man, McClellan was not aggressive, and he formulated strategy only for the defense of Washington and attacks on nearby Richmond, Virginia, the Confederate capital.

In an effort to centralize the command of Union armies in all theaters of the war, Lincoln demoted McClellan to Commander of the Army of the Potomac in the spring of 1862. After directing action on all fronts for a short time himself, the president placed General Henry Wager Halleck in supreme command. But Halleck, too, proved unable to direct the movements of the scattered Union contingents. It was not until March 1864 that Lincoln found the general in chief he had been looking for in Ulysses S. Grant.

Unlike his Confederate counterparts, Grant did not come to his command from a long and distinguished military career. Born in 1822, the son of an Ohio tanner, he had been a poor student at West Point. Though he had served capably under Scott and Taylor in the Mexican War, he was a Northerner and thus not advanced by Scott.

In addition to resenting his failure to be promoted, Grant was bored by the inactivity of the peacetime army. When he took to drink and was demoted in rank, he simply resigned. At the outset of the war he was working in his family's leather store in Illinois. In June 1861 he entered the Illinois militia as a colonel. Several months later he was raised to the rank of brigadier general.

Grant was short, bearded, squarely built, and often slovenly in appearance. He was shy, with sluggish movements, and a somewhat forlorn look. One observer said of him, "He habitually wears an expression as if he had determined to drive his head through a brick wall."

Ulysses S. Grant.

Grant may not have looked like an officer, but there was no mistaking his courage and his eagerness to take responsibility. Though modest, he was self-confident and systematic in his understanding of military situations. He would plunge into battle fearlessly and demand the same of his men. He was so zealous that he was sometimes accused of having a callous disregard for human life. But his enormous determination and aggressiveness helped fire the Union armies and eventually led them to victory after a series of defeats. He struck the South ferociously with all the military power available to him. Careful maneuvering for position, a strategy which aided the South in the early phases of the war, gave way before Grant's use of the North's superior weapons, numbers, and transportation facilities.

Grant's chief of staff, John A. Rawlins, was not a West Point graduate but an Illinois lawyer. He was intelligent and supplied the ambition and political polish that Grant lacked. He was Grant's closest associate. As one commentator put it: "If you hit Rawlins on the head, you knock out Grant's brains."

The greatest of all Grant's generals was William Tecumseh Sherman of Ohio. Sherman was tall and gaunt, with an impressive military bearing, tousled red hair, and piercing eyes. He had a reputation for eccentricity, but actually he was cool and quick-thinking, and a tough fighter. Yet Sherman never displayed great ambition for leadership. He had little interest in army political intrigues, and when he was asked to run for president in 1884 he replied, "I will not accept if nominated and will not serve if elected."

1861–1862 Campaigns

Although the North won the Civil War by years of wearing the South down, most Northerners wanted to take the offensive and move fast to put down the rebellion. At the beginning of the war, General Winfield Scott offered Lincoln a plan to blockade the South along its sea and land frontiers. Then, with the enemy under pressure, the Union would send in the powerful armies it had built up. This tactic of gradually squeezing the South to death, called the Anaconda Plan, resembled what finally happened, but at first it appeared too slow to meet the popular demand for a quick and decisive end to the war.

The war began without any definitive strategy on either side. The South pursued a largely defensive policy of trying to hold as much territory as it could rather than striking a blow on Northern soil when it had the military advantage. By the time Lee tried the alternate strategy of invading Pennsylvania in the fall of 1862 and the summer of 1863, the North was better organized. Both times, first at the Battle of Antietam and then at the Battle of Gettysburg, the Union managed to prevent the South from getting a strategic foothold in the North, but at a terrible cost to both sides.

The pattern of the fighting was largely shaped by the Union's determination to take the Confederate capital of Richmond and by the geography of the South. Although the Northern armies repeatedly battled their way toward the Southern capital, it did not fall until the end of the war. There was often unrelated fighting in several places at once, since geographical barriers prevented unified campaigns in the South. The Eastern theater, from the Appalachian Mountains to the Atlantic coast, was dominated by the fighting for Richmond; and the Western theater, from Tennessee to Mississippi, was dominated by the Union's effort to wrench control of the Mississippi Valley away from the South.

MAJOR BATTLES OF THE CIVIL WAR • 1861 TO 1865

An overall Union strategy following Scott's earlier plan began to succeed as the fighting ground on. The Union blockade of the Atlantic and Gulf coasts isolated the South from trade with Europe. When Northern naval and land forces managed to take control of the Mississippi River by the summer of 1863, they cut the Trans-Mississippi states of Louisiana, Arkansas, and Texas off from the rest of the Confederacy. The next Union objective in the Western theater was to gain control of the Tennessee River, an excellent route to the center of the South. Using the river as a springboard, Union troops could dissect the Confederacy even further. This they did, with General Sherman's devastating march across Georgia. Sherman so weakened the Confederacy that it could no longer hold its only remaining territory in the Eastern theater.

BULL RUN

The first major battle of the Civil War occurred as inexperienced Union troops fought inexperienced Confederate troops for control of Richmond. Urged on by the popular cry, "Forward to Richmond!" thirty-five thousand Union troops under Brigadier General Irvin McDowell began an overland advance toward the Confederate capital. On July 21, 1861, they met twenty-five thousand Confederate troops commanded by Brigadier General P. G. T. Beauregard, later joined by a contingent under General Joseph E. Johnston. Only thirty miles from Washington, raw recruits under confusing orders attacked each other at Bull Run (the stream for which the North named the battle; the South referred to battles according to the nearest settlement, in this case, Manassas Junction).

Neither side was successful. As McDowell pulled his men back, his army began to fall apart in a wild retreat to Washington. The Confederate troops were unable to pursue McDowell because they, too, had become disorganized.

Bull Run was a terrible shock to Northern leaders. It helped convince them that this war was not going to be won by calling out the militia for ninety days. The short-term regiments were sent home. McClellan now replaced McDowell as the commander of the new Army of the Potomac. Until the spring of 1862, McClellan patiently worked to create a real fighting force out of "a mere collection of regiments . . . [some] perfectly raw, others dispirited by the recent defeat." When Scott retired in the fall of 1861, McClellan was made general in chief of all the Union armies.

THE SEA BLOCKADE

In the fall of 1861, while McClellan was trying to train a professional army, the Union launched a land and sea expedition to seal off the Confederate coastline. These forces took five Confederate forts during the winter, giving them a secure base for their blockading operations, and forcing the Confederate government to divert some of its Richmond troops to guard against invasion from the sea.

With ships deployed along the Atlantic and Gulf coasts, the North managed to choke off about eighty percent of the South's exports and imports soon after the war began, creating serious supply problems for the Confederacy and depressing its morale. The British could easily have broken the blockade at this point if they had wanted to. They could have legally continued to trade with the South because under international law, a blockade had to be effective in order to be binding on third parties. In other words, there had to be enough ships stationed outside the blockaded port to make its use clearly dangerous. This was not the case, but Britain chose to recognize the blockade anyway since it served her long-term interests. She might in the future (as she had in the past) want the United States to recognize the principle of a loose but legal blockade.

The North also extended the legal principles of the blockade by seizing neutral ships on the high seas. Many ships thus seized belonged to

British shippers, but England did not protest since she had done the same thing herself and foresaw using the tactics again someday.

THE BATTLE FOR THE MISSISSIPPI VALLEY

In 1862, while the Union was continuing to seal the Confederacy in along the seacoast, it tried to pave the way for opening a path through the Confederacy in the West by gaining control of the Mississippi Valley.

By the autumn of 1861 the Union army had built a base at Cairo, Illinois with Brigadier General Grant in charge. The Confederates occupied Columbus, Kentucky, and Grant countered by taking Paducah. The Union troops now occupied northern Kentucky, while the Confederates held the southern part of the state. Jefferson Davis sent General Albert Sidney Johnston to take command of the Confederate forces in the Mississippi area, but neglected to give him enough soldiers and Johnston was outnumbered two to one.

Forts Henry and Donelson

Early in February fifteen thousand Union troops moved up the Tennessee River with a flotilla of gunboats under the command of Grant and captured Fort Henry, the Confederate bastion on the Kentucky-Tennessee border. This wiped out Johnston's access to transportation on the Tennessee River, and he was forced to retreat to nearby Fort Donelson, Tennessee, on the Cumberland River. Now General Henry Wager Halleck brought his troops to meet Grant's. Their combined forces seized Fort Donelson on February 16, capturing twelve thousand Confederate prisoners.

Halleck convinced the Lincoln Administration that he was responsible for the Union successes at Forts Henry and Donelson and he was rewarded with the combined command of the West, over Grant and General Don Carlos Buell.

The Union occupation of the forts was a decisive step in the war. The seizures had destroyed Johnston's entire defensive line against invasion from the north. He was left no choice but to abandon his stronghold at Columbus and regroup his army farther south, in northern Mississippi.

Shiloh Church

The Confederates had been thrown off balance, and Lincoln was extremely anxious to capitalize on that advantage. He sought to move Union troops into eastern Tennessee as soon as possible. With McClellan's backing, the president urged Buell to occupy Knoxville, but Buell protested that the terrain was too poor to keep his army sufficiently supplied. Halleck sided with Buell. Their hesitancy cost the Union precious time which the Confederate generals Johnston and Beauregard used to revitalize their forces at Corinth, Mississippi.

When Halleck finally did send Grant up the Tennessee River, the Confederates were prepared. Grant, with forty thousand men, established himself at Pittsburg Landing on the Tennessee. While Grant waited for the reluctant Buell to join him there with twenty-five thousand more men, Johnston advanced with forty-five thousand Confederate troops. On April 6 and 7, in the woodlands and pastures near a country meetinghouse known as Shiloh Church, Johnston and Grant fought the most extensive battle to take place on the North American continent up to that time.

On the first day Grant was nearly driven into the river because Buell's forces did not arrive in time to counter the first Confederate attack. Twenty-four hours later Grant finally received reinforcements, and only then was he able to challenge the Confederate forces. The armies battled on for another full day—the South now without the leadership of the courageous Johnston, who had died of a leg injury. Finally overwhelmed by Union numbers, the battered

Farragut captures the ram Tennessee.

Confederate Army under Beauregard was forced to retreat back to Corinth.

In a tactical sense, the Northern victory at Shiloh Church was an extremely narrow one. Both sides suffered severely. There were more than ten thousand Confederate and over thirteen thousand Union casualties. Many of these died from untreated wounds. The battle began in the rain on Sunday and ended on Monday. By Tuesday it was still raining, and nine-tenths of the wounded still lay where they had fallen. Many had died from shock and exhaustion; some had drowned in areas filled in by the heavy rains.

Strategically, the North had gained a decisive advantage. Its forces were now in possession of much of Tennessee and Kentucky. The South had failed to prevent a concentration of federal troops within its territory, and its own forces were left in a vulnerable defensive position in the Mississippi Valley.

Farragut takes New Orleans

After the battle of Shiloh Church, a powerful Union fleet under Flag Officer David Glasgow Farragut entered the Mississippi River from the Gulf of Mexico. Under heavy firing from forts which had been built to protect the approach to New Orleans, the brilliant and determined Farragut, who had almost fifty years experience in the American Navy, managed to "run the forts." On April 25, 1862, Farragut took possession of New Orleans, the largest city in the Confederacy and its principal seaport.

Confederate troops were forced to withdraw and the city was placed under the control of General Benjamin F. Butler, whose army had accompanied Farragut. Butler's occupation of New Orleans was harsh and controversial. He even issued an order stating that any female caught insulting a Union soldier would "be regarded and held liable to be treated as a woman of the town plying her trade." This was considered an unforgivable insult by Southerners, and the act inflamed the entire South.

Union overconfidence

By the spring of 1862 the Confederacy appeared to be near defeat. Most of the South's Atlantic coastline had been sealed off by the Union blockade, and Halleck was in northern Mississippi. Following the taking of New Orleans, Butler moved up the river and seized Baton Rouge. In June federal gunboats wiped out a Confederate fleet at Memphis and the Union was able to take that city and open the entire Mississippi to Union control. Halleck joined his forces with those of Grant, Buell, and General John Pope, and finally drove Beauregard out of Corinth, Mississippi. In the Eastern theater, McClellan was preparing to advance against Richmond. The Lincoln administration was so confident that the war was about to end that it halted all further troop recruitments.

This confidence proved premature, however. Federal progress was impeded by a critical lack of leadership at the top of the military command, and actions in the different theaters of the war were not being coordinated. Lincoln, distrusting McClellan's inertia, removed him as general in chief of the Union armies, but left him as commander of the Army of the Potomac. As McClellan began his drive on Richmond, there was no comparable offensive in the West. Just when a Union offensive in the West might have been decisive, that theater of the war became inactive.

McCLELLAN'S PENINSULAR CAMPAIGN

In the East McClellan was carefully preparing to lay siege to Richmond by an approach from the sea. In mid-March of 1862 he had floated a large number of troops guarding Washington down Chesapeake Bay in steamboats to the tip of the Virginia peninsula; there he took a position at Fort Monroe. Gradually and methodically he moved up heavy artillery for bombarding the Confederate capital. By the end of May his forces were less than ten miles from Richmond.

McClellan's buildup on the peninsula was threatened by the startling introduction into the naval engagements of an ironclad warship by the Confederacy. The steam frigate *Merrimack*, scuttled in 1861 by the Union, had been recovered and rebuilt in the Confederate naval yard at Norfolk, Virginia. They added several innovations to the original ship, including an iron-plated citadel amidship, powerful guns behind it, and an enormous iron ram at the bow.

The vessel was slow and clumsy, but its iron plating made it invulnerable to gunfire. When it first engaged Union warships on March 8, 1862, it caused a near panic in the North. It sank a Union frigate, brought another wooden ship to surrender, grounded a steamer, and loomed as a threat of destruction to the entire Union fleet around McClellan's bastion of Fort Monroe on the Virginia coast.

The Union, however, immediately countered with an ironclad vessel of its own, the *Monitor*. Construction began when reports reached Washington that the South was building a ship which would make wooden battleships useless, and it was completed in time to be sent down to Hampton Roads, Virginia, to challenge the *Merrimack* in a wearying battle the next day. Neither ship sank, but the *Monitor* won a distinct advantage for the Union by ending the fear that the *Merrimack* would be able to take control of Chesapeake Bay.

THE SOUTHERN OFFENSIVE IN THE EAST

Meanwhile, McClellan waited with over one hundred thousand men in northern Virginia for several thousand more troops from the Washington area to join him in his long-planned attack on Richmond. His caution gave the South time to place fifteen thousand soldiers in the Shenandoah Valley northwest of Richmond under the wily military genius "Stonewall" Jackson.

With comparatively few troops but shrewd military tactics, Jackson began a series of brilliant offensive maneuvers in the Shenandoah Valley. His feints managed to convince the Union army and the Lincoln administration that he had a much larger force than he actually had, and he let it be known that with this force he intended no less than the capture of Washington.

Alarmed, the president sent a great number of the men McClellan was depending upon to the valley to drive out Jackson.

The Union forces numbered forty-five thousand, three times those under the Confederate general's command. But in a series of dazzling military tactics, Jackson eluded his pursuers, defeated them in several engagements, and rejoined Lee in the defense of Richmond. The Union army was left totally confused regarding Jackson's strength, location, and plans.

Meanwhile, Confederate General Joseph E. Johnston, who held a defensive position at Yorktown, waited until McClellan was practically at the gates of the Confederate capital to attack him on May 31 at Seven Pines. It was a bloody and indecisive battle for both sides. Johnston was critically wounded and President Davis now appointed Robert E. Lee to command the Army of Virginia.

McClellan settled down next to the Chickahominy River to await reinforcements and make preparations in his methodical fashion for a siege from the north, a change in plans resulting from confusion over Jackson's movements.

The Seven Days' Battle

Meanwhile, Lee brought Jackson and his men down from the Shenandoah Valley. By the last week in June, Lee had gathered an army of eighty thousand men. In a series of savage assaults they forced McClellan to retreat. As McClellan fell back, Lee pursued him in a relentless attempt to destroy the Union army. By the end of the week, McClellan, who always insisted that he was outnumbered and would not conduct offensive operations, had withdrawn to a defensive stance at Harrison's Landing on the James River. Although Lee lost twenty thousand men to McClellan's fifteen thousand, the Southern commander had seized the initiative and thwarted the Union's attempt to take Richmond.

Completely out of patience with McClellan's indecisive maneuvers, Lincoln now brought Halleck back to Washington as general in chief. He also put General John Pope in command of a new army composed of the remnants of the Union forces that had tried to destroy Jackson in the Shenandoah Valley.

The second Battle of Bull Run

McClellan was to join his forces with those of Pope for a new offensive against Richmond, but the two Union commanders were unable to work in harmony. McClellan for a long time stolidly refused to move.

While the Union forces slowly regrouped, Lee once more took advantage of the enemy's delay. Leaving a contingent to keep an eye on McClellan, Lee and Jackson engaged Pope on the old battlefield at Bull Run on August 28 and 29. Spectacularly outfought, Pope was driven back to Washington, whereupon Lincoln fired him and recalled McClellan to defend the Union capital.

Because of the genius of such commanders as Lee and Jackson, the Confederacy, which had been weakening in the spring of 1862, was on the offensive again by autumn.

Antietam

In September of 1862, a few weeks after the second Battle of Bull Run, Lee decided to strike the Union army in its own territory. He took his army across the Potomac River into Maryland for an invasion of Pennsylvania. He knew that McClellan and the Army of the Potomac were coming up from Washington, but he also needed to deal with the garrison of ten thousand federal troops at nearby Harpers Ferry. With his usual boldness, Lee divided his forces. He occupied Hagerstown, Maryland, and the South Mountain passes with half his men, and sent the other half under Stonewall Jackson to take Harpers Ferry.

Unfortunately for Lee a copy of his orders was lost and, as luck would have it, fell into the hands of McClellan who by now was flanked by the two halves of Lee's army. Even then, the

President Lincoln and General McClellan meet at Antietam in 1862.

Northern general did not move quickly to force Lee into combat, and Stonewall Jackson captured Harpers Ferry and its entire garrison.

McClellan finally met Lee on September 17 on the high ground above Antietam Creek near Sharpsburg, Maryland, in what was perhaps the bloodiest single day's battle of the entire war. McClellan had almost eighty-seven thousand men, and he lost nearly thirteen thousand. Lee lost at least ten thousand of his forty thousand troops. The fight was a draw tactically, but strategically a Confederate defeat. Lee's plans to invade the North were shattered and he was forced to withdraw back into Virginia.

The Emancipation Proclamation

The president had always believed the war was to save the Union, not to free the slaves. He was against emancipation without compensating slaveholders and devising a plan to colonize the freed blacks outside the United States. For some time he believed that Northern opinion in general and border state opinion in particular supported this point of view. Yet he never lost sight of the fact that he was fighting a war with the backing of two diverse groups: the pro-Union people who were against abolition, and the radical antislavery people who saw the war as a means of bringing about emancipation.

However, when the tide of battle seemed to be going against the North in the fall of 1862, Lincoln realized that he might have to turn the war into more than a struggle for the preservation of the Union. If the North was to win, it needed a lofty cause to rally a new wave of support. Lincoln decided to declare that the

▲ *"Grand Sweepstakes for 1862, Won by the Celebrated Horse Emancipation."*

◀ *"Lincoln signing the Emancipation, a Southern view." (The Metropolitan Museum of Art, Harris Brisbune Dick Fund, 1938)*

Union was waging a fight for human freedom, a fight against slavery. He feared that unless he did so, Congress would take control of the war out of his hands and Europe might throw its power on the side of the South.

Lincoln maneuvered cautiously until he believed most areas of Northern opinion would support such a policy. In April the Congress abolished slavery in the District of Columbia and in June it abolished it in the territories. In July 1862 the president accepted the Second Confiscation Act, which provided that slaves of those in rebellion were free, and he decided to make his own move. Secretary of State Seward, however, urged him not to issue a proclamation until the North had achieved a military victory. The president agreed to wait, and success soon came at Antietam. On September 22, 1862, Lincoln issued a preliminary emancipation proclamation, together with the announcement that a final proclamation would be forthcoming on January 1, 1863, "unless the Confederacy surrendered."

The initial significance of the proclamation was limited. Lincoln demanded that all the seceded states return to the Union by January 1863, or else face the following consequences:

> I do order and declare that all persons held as slaves within said designated States and parts of States are, and henceforward shall be free; and that the Executive Government of the United States, including the military and naval authorities hereof, will recognize and maintain the freedom of said persons.

With these words the president asserted freedom for slaves in areas not under the control of the federal government. However, he said nothing about emancipating slaves in those border states that remained in the Union, since abolition there would have alienated these slave states from the Union.

The proclamation was basically a military measure to create confusion in the Confederacy. Though the slaves were not actually freed by the Emancipation Proclamation, it somewhat pacified the Radicals, gained the admiration of antislavery people in England, provided an important source of volunteers for the Union cause, and made certain that slavery would not survive the war if the North was victorious.

BLACKS IN THE WAR

Following the Emancipation Proclamation, the United States armed forces began to enlist freed

Emancipation Proclamation Defended

"Thank God for what is already done, and let us all take heart as we go forward to uphold this great edict! For myself, I accept the Proclamation without note or comment. It is enough for me, that, in the exercise of the War Power, it strikes at the origin and mainspring of this Rebellion; for I have never concealed the conviction that it matters little where we strike Slavery, provided only that we strike sincerely and in earnest. So is it all connected, that the whole must suffer with every part. . . ."

Charles Sumner,
1863

Emancipation Proclamation Attacked

"The President has at last weakly yielded to the 'pressure' put upon him about which he has so bitterly complained, and issued his proclamation of negro emancipation . . . he has no constitutional power to issue this proclamation—none whatever. . . .

Nobody need argue with us that he has the power under military law. Military law does not destroy the fundamental civil law. In war, as in peace, the Constitution is 'the supreme law of the land.'

The government, then, by the act of the President, is in rebellion and the war is reduced to a contest for subjugation. . . ."

The Chicago *Times*,
1863

An 1865 photograph of "Company E, Fourth U.S. Colored Infantry." About one hundred fifty thousand blacks served in the Union army during the Civil War.

blacks with the president's encouragement. A May 1863 directive from the War Department called for the raising of black troops all over the country. Soon there were fourteen such regiments in the field. By the fall of 1864, there were one-hundred-fifty thousand in the Union forces, most of them from the South.

Many Northern black men hesitated to join the army since they were barred from becoming officers and were kept segregated. But some agreed with Frederick Douglass, who argued that wearing the American uniform was a step toward real citizenship.

The battle record of black troops was outstanding. They participated in some five hundred engagements and received twenty-two Congressional Medals of Honor. Thirty-eight thousand of them died while fighting for the North.

Although blacks accounted for about ten percent of the total enlistments in Union forces, the Confederacy could not bring itself to enlist slaves until a month before the war ended. Instead, slaves were sometimes impressed into labor battalions in war-related industries.

1863–1865: The War Grinds to an End

The Confederacy had passed its high-water mark. After the Battle of Antietam and the Emancipation Proclamation, the Southern tide began to recede in the West as well as the East. From then on, the South remained on the defensive, and would never again come as close to victory as it had in the early autumn of 1862.

As long as reunification remained the single issue, there existed the possibility of a negotiated peace between the North and the South. Because of the Emancipation Proclamation, however, the war would have to be fought to a finish. The South would not negotiate the end of slavery. And so the country was committed to an exhausting all-out war.

As the first step toward the final defeat of the South, Lincoln again reshuffled his military commanders. McClellan was out of favor with many in the North because of his opposition to the Emancipation Proclamation. Disgusted by McClellan's military sluggishness and his failure to exploit his victories, Lincoln replaced him with Major General Ambrose E. Burnside, who, ironically, had refused the post twice before on the grounds that he was unqualified. General Buell, a friend of McClellan's who shared his sentiments about slavery, was replaced in the West by Major General William S. Rosecrans.

NORTHERN AND SOUTHERN OFFENSIVES

Lincoln expected his new commanders to gain a victory without delay, but he was not immediately satisfied.

In the Western theater, Rosecrans advanced against Confederate General Braxton Bragg's Army of Tennessee. From December 30 to January 2 their armies fought ferociously southeast of Nashville. Bragg was forced to retreat, but he left Rosecrans' army so mangled and disorganized that it could not resume an offensive for several months. Grant, too, was stymied in his attempt to capture Vicksburg, Mississippi.

In the Eastern theater, Burnside decided to undertake an unprecedented winter campaign against Richmond. He met Lee at Fredericksburg, Virginia in December, and flung his armies at him in a series of hopeless, bloody attacks. Lee repulsed him with ease, inflicting twelve thousand Union casualties in the process. Lincoln then replaced Burnside, at the general's own request, with "Fighting Joe" Hooker, a favorite of the Radicals.

While Union forces reorganized in the Western theater, Hooker made ready for a new offensive in the East with his Army of the Potomac. But when he attacked Lee and Jackson at Fredericksburg and Chancellorsville in Virginia in early May 1863, he was brutally defeated in three days of savage fighting. It was a spectacular victory for the South, dimmed only by the death of Stonewall Jackson. The beloved division commander had been shot by mistake by his own men as he was reconnoitering between the lines during the night of May 2.

Heartened by the success at Chancellorsville, Davis and Lee decided on one more attempt to invade the North. A victory in Pennsylvania would put the major cities of Philadelphia and Washington in direct peril, and Lee's army badly needed the food in the barns and warehouses of Pennsylvania. He wanted to capture a Northern city to counter what he believed was the inevitable fall of Vicksburg in the West. He also hoped that such a victory might tip sentiment toward peace among the war-weary Northerners.

Early in June, Lee crossed the Blue Ridge Mountains and headed for the Potomac. Hooker followed him, constantly maneuvering to stay between the capital and Lee. On June 28 Lee's entire army was in Pennsylvania, and the Army of the Potomac was positioned near Frederick, Maryland. At this crucial hour, Hooker requested additional men and supplies, but Lincoln refused to send them on the grounds that Hooker had shown at Chancellorsville that he did not know how to use his resources. Angered and in disfavor, Hooker resigned. He was replaced by General George Gordon Meade. On July 1, 1863, Lee and Meade clashed at Gettysburg, Pennsylvania, beginning the largest battle of the war.

For three days the Confederate Army piled assault after assault on Union forces. Losses on both sides were enormous. Although the Union army was on the brink of defeat, Lee's mutilated and outnumbered forces no longer had the strength to deliver the final blow. On the third day, when Lee rammed fifteen thousand men under Major General George Pickett against the Union center column, the Union repelled the attack, destroying Lee's capacity for any further offensive action. The next day the Confederates began retreating to Virginia. By the middle of July they were back in the lower part of the Shenandoah Valley.

In the Battle of Gettysburg, some twenty-three thousand troops were lost on both sides, more than twenty-five percent of all the men engaged in the combat. Much to Lincoln's dismay, Meade did not pursue Lee and make military capital of the opportunity presented to him, but his encounter with Lee showed decisively that the South had insufficient resources to mount an effective offensive.

The final Confederate attempt to invade the North had failed. The North learned of Lee's retreat at the same time that it learned of Grant's capture of Vicksburg—a tremendous lift for Union morale.

GRANT BECOMES SUPREME COMMANDER

Grant was unable to attack Vicksburg from the Mississippi River, so he marched his army down the marshy western bank and crossed the river thirty miles below Vicksburg. On the drier but rough terrain of the east bank, Grant cleared an approach to the city by taking Jackson, the capital of Mississippi, on May 14. This action forced the Southern troops defending Vicksburg under John C. Pemberton to withdraw into its center. Unable to take the city itself by force, Grant laid siege to it for six weeks until Pemberton, recognizing the hopelessness of his position, surrendered his fortress and his thirty thousand men on July 4.

Grant's capture of Vicksburg was even more significant than the Union victory at Gettysburg. The federal government now had control of the Mississippi River all the way to the Gulf Coast, and the Southern states west of the Mississippi River were detached from the rest of the Confederacy. The effect of the successes at Vicksburg and Gettysburg was to reduce the South to defensive warfare.

In September Confederate forces under General Braxton Bragg were defeated at Chicamauga in northern Georgia. And in late November Grant had assumed firm federal control of Tennessee. In March 1864 Lincoln appointed Grant as general in chief of the Union armies, with Halleck as chief of staff, and sent him to Chattanooga with reinforcements.

At this time Grant was a militarily appropriate and politically popular choice, for the general had demonstrated at Vicksburg that Northern resources, applied relentlessly, would bring victory. Grant plowed through the kind of obstacles that had stopped the more cautious McClellan. With Grant, the president had found a general who would bring the war to an end in one year. Willing to pay any price for a victory which might spare the country another

"The Old Bull Dog on the Right Track" shows General Grant as a bull dog about to attack a kennel marked Richmond, while General McClellan urges caution. ▼

▲
Columbia, South Carolina after it was devastated by General Sherman's troops.

year of war, Grant battled the South relentlessly in his final offensives.

Grant's main objective was the defeat of the two major Confederate forces: Lee's army in Virginia and General Joseph E. Johnston's forces in Georgia. Grant's commander of the Union forces in the West, Major General William Tecumseh Sherman, led a strong force against Johnston near Dalton, Georgia. Sherman managed to take Dalton, but at the cost of tremendous casualties.

Meanwhile, Grant led his army against Lee's near the Rapidan River in Virginia. They fought without a halt for more than a month. Their engagements, among the hardest fought in American history, included the Battle of Cold Harbor. Grant seemed to be alone in his conviction that a general assault against the Confederate line at Cold Harbor was feasible; his subordinates felt it would be almost hopeless. Quietly, before the battle, they pinned on their shirts scraps of paper bearing their names, and then they charged the enemy. In less than ten minutes five thousand Union troops were dead. Doggedly, Grant refused to ask for a temporary truce to care for the wounded; they lay suffering for days until they finally died where they had fallen. Grant had lost fifty-five thousand men. The repercussions were widespread in the North. Politicians and newspapers assailed the commander as "Butcher" Grant.

THE WAR ENDS

Having gained a foothold in Georgia, Sherman was ordered to march across the state, destroying Atlanta's resources and cutting off more of the West. After fighting all summer against Southern delaying tactics, Sherman occupied Atlanta on September 2. As he moved across Georgia toward Savannah, Sherman devastated everything that lay in his path. His harsh, scorched-earth measures caused widespread civilian misery and contributed to the buildup of a lasting Southern hatred for Sherman and the North.

Savannah fell on December 20. By the beginning of 1865 the Confederacy consisted of little more than the Carolinas and the southern half of Virginia. In February 1865 Sherman moved across the Carolinas. Confederate resources were so low by this time that General Johnston admitted: "I can do no more than annoy him." Union forces moved into North Carolina and by the end of March were in Goldsboro, 160 miles south of Richmond.

The days of the Confederacy were numbered. A Union calvary corps moved down from Tennessee, captured Montgomery, and destroyed the munitions works at Selma, Alabama, on April 2,

1865. An amphibious expedition sealed off Wilmington, North Carolina, the last seaport held by the South. In desperation, Lee attacked Grant in an effort to disable his opponent long enough for his own forces to break away and consolidate with Johnston's. But on April 1, 1865, Grant's troops fragmented Lee's right flank in a battle at Five Forks. Lee was forced at last to evacuate Richmond.

With the occupation of Richmond by the North, the South's final hour had come. Most Southerners no longer cared to continue the struggle. The price was too high and the cause was lost. Loyalty to Robert E. Lee seemed to be the only unifying force left in the Confederacy. One of Lee's staff is said to have exclaimed, "Country be damned! There is no Country. There has been no Country, general, for a year or more. You are the Country for these men. They have fought for you. If you demand the sacrifice, there are still thousands of us who would die for you." Lee did not demand the sacrifice.

On April 9, in the McLean farmhouse at Appomattox Court House in southern Virginia, General Lee surrendered his army to Grant. The two generals arranged the terms of surrender: Confederate soldiers were to be paroled and public property and war materials surrendered. Officers were allowed to keep their side arms, and all men who owned a horse or a mule could "keep them to work their little farms."

Johnston surrendered to Sherman a few days later. By early June President Davis and a few Confederate officials had been arrested in Georgia and imprisoned in Fort Monroe. The remaining vestiges of Southern resistance had been obliterated.

The Election of 1864

As the conflict drew to a close, Northern politics reflected the tensions that had built up during the war. In the war-weary Union, Lincoln could please hardly anyone. He had offended moderates by the Emancipation Proclamation and the Radicals blamed him for inefficiency and Republican losses in the congressional elections of 1862. Union war casualties had upset everyone.

Yet the nation's economy was in a boom period, stimulated by government purchases of war materials. Crops were good and prices were high. The General Price Index had risen seventy-nine percent since 1860. But the Northern economy had been industrialized before the war began and would probably have progressed without it. The stepped-up pace brought on by war tended to disturb the normal flow of investments and prevent innovations in industry. There was much war profiteering and speculation, highly resented by many businessmen and all farmers. A labor shortage on the farms impeded agricultural growth, causing a rise in food costs for the industrial workers that was not equaled by increased wages.

Thousands looked for solutions to their problems in the growing peace movement. On the other hand, many antislavery Republicans were adamantly against any compromise with the South.

THE UNION PARTY

Lincoln won the Republican nomination in the 1864 presidential election over the protests of some factions of his own party. He had doubts that he would be reelected, but not that he was the best-qualified person to meet the current crises. Coolly and shrewdly he devoted himself to obtaining the nomination, using as his primary weapon skillful control of the patronage.

Lincoln's supporters dominated the Republican convention in Baltimore and he was nomi-

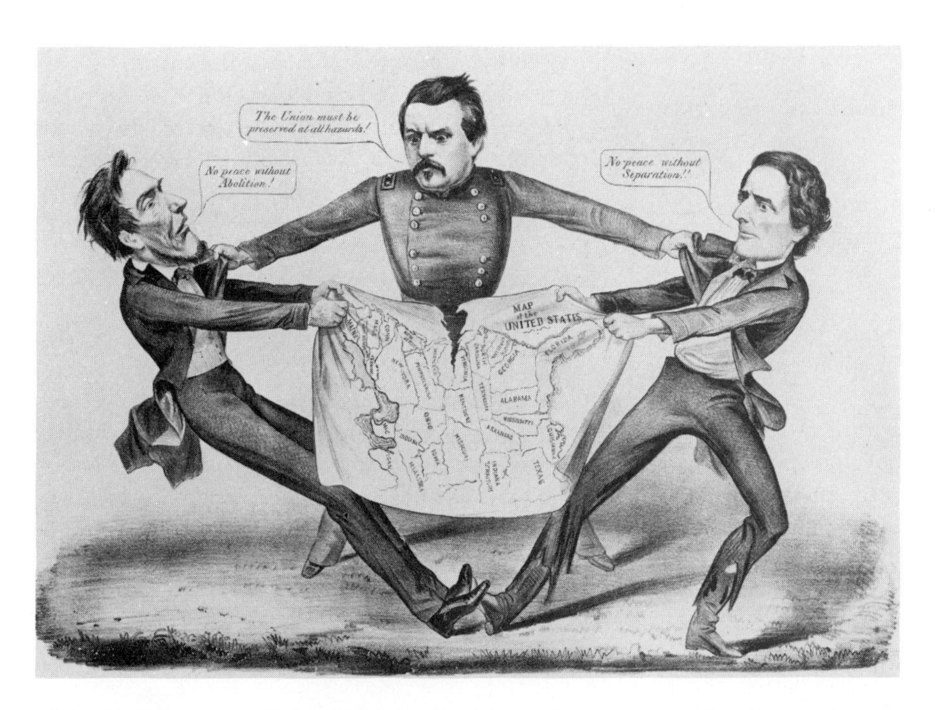

"The True Issue," or "That's What's the Matter," a cartoon of the election of 1864. McClellan, the Democratic candidate, tries to prevent Abraham Lincoln, the Republican incumbent, and Jefferson Davis, president of the Confederacy, from tearing a map of the United States in two.

nated unanimously. He further demonstrated his control when the convention nominated Andrew Johnson of Tennessee, a member of the prowar faction of the Democratic party, as its vice-presidential candidate. The Republicans also wooed war Democrats by changing their name to the Union party. Their platform denounced slavery and declared it a cause of the war, issued a call for a united front in the prosecution of the war, promised protection for black soldiers, and encouraged immigration. Quoting a remark made by Lincoln, the Union party appealed to voters with the slogan, "Don't swap horses in the middle of the river."

THE DEMOCRATIC PLATFORM

Sentiment for peace in the country was becoming so pronounced that the Democrats put off their convention during the summer of 1864 while C. L. Vallandigham led demonstrations for peace in the Midwest. It soon became apparent, however, that force alone would make the South accept a peace based on the abolition of slavery and the restoration of the Union.

To please the regular Democrats, the party's presidential nomination went to General McClellan, the cautious but popular war hero. To appease the peace faction, the Democrats adopted a platform which condemned the war as a failure and called for an armistice that would permit peace negotiations based on a restored union of all the states. The Democratic platform excluded emancipation as a condition for peace and assumed that peace would be easily negotiated. McClellan repudiated the platform, however, and ran as a war leader, attacking the Lincoln administration for inefficiency and charging that it had failed to prosecute the war successfully.

LINCOLN WINS

On August 23 Lincoln pessimistically remarked: "This morning as for some days past, it seems probable that this Administration will not be re-elected." But the peace movement and the Radicals had no effective candidates, and McClellan had to share the war vote with the incumbent president. Despite his gloomy outlook, Lincoln had no intention of withdrawing from the race, and his prospects soon looked brighter.

With Sherman's occupation of Atlanta early in September, spirits in the North were raised, and the tide began to turn toward the Republicans. The Radicals now joined with the president. In November Lincoln won, polling fifty-five percent of the popular vote of the dismembered Union and carrying the electoral college by 212 votes to 21. Congress also went again to the Republicans. Lincoln's reelection assured that the war would not end until the Union was restored and slavery was abolished.

LINCOLN'S ASSASSINATION

On April 9, 1865, with Lee's surrender to Grant at Appomattox Court House in Virginia, the restoration of the Union was no longer in doubt. But the North's triumph was shadowed by the tragedy that struck on Good Friday, April 14. On that night, while attending a performance of the play *Our American Cousin* at Ford's

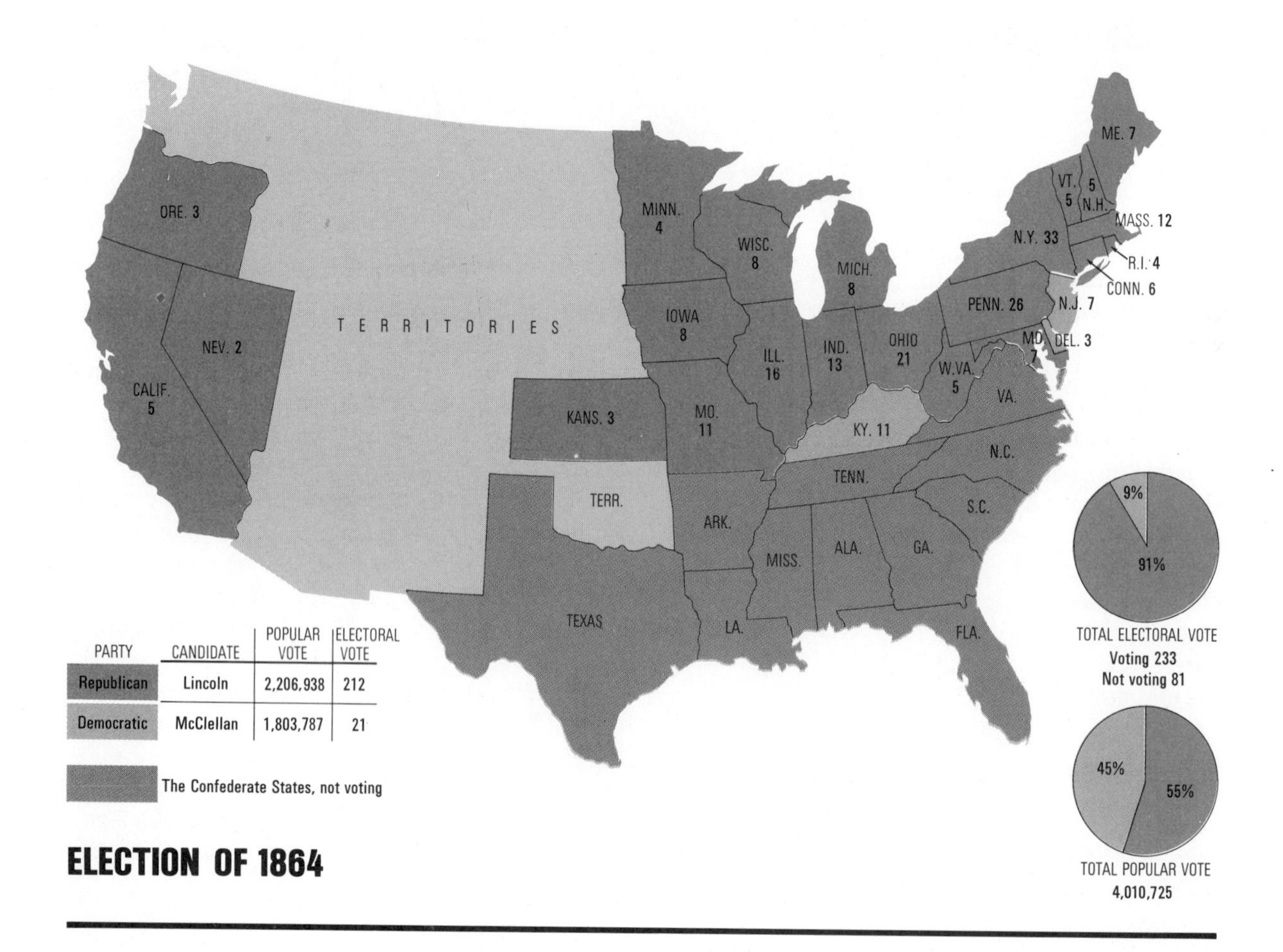

PARTY	CANDIDATE	POPULAR VOTE	ELECTORAL VOTE
Republican	Lincoln	2,206,938	212
Democratic	McClellan	1,803,787	21

ELECTION OF 1864

Theatre in Washington, Lincoln was shot by a proslavery fanatic, John Wilkes Booth. Booth entered the presidential box and shot Lincoln in the head. He then sprang to the stage of the theater, crying "*Sic Semper Tyrannis!* The South is avenged!" and escaped. Lincoln was quickly carried across the street to a private home, where he died the next morning. A few days later Booth was overtaken and shot in a barn in Virginia.

Lincoln's assassination greatly diminished hopes for an early reconciliation of the North with the South. It not only deprived the nation of a great leader, but it also deprived the South of a compassionate friend. His instructions to Grant had been to arrange surrender "on the most liberal and honorable terms." In his second Inaugural Address, he had called on the North to act "with malice towards none, with charity for all."

Readings

GENERAL WORKS

Catton, Bruce, *Centennial History of the War*, Vols. I–III. Garden City, N.Y.: Doubleday, 1961–1965.

Cole, Arthur C., *The Irrepressible Conflict 1860–1865*. New York: Reprint House International, 1960.

Donald, David (Ed.), *Why the North Won the Civil War*. New York: Macmillan, 1960.

Eaton, Clement, *A History of the Southern Confederacy*. New York: Macmillan, 1954.

Leech, Margaret, *Reveille in Washington, 1860–1865*. New York: Grosset & Dunlap, 1941.

Nevins, Allan, *The War for the Union*, Vols. I–III. New York: Scribner's, 1959–1970.

Randall, James G., and David Donald, *The Civil War and Reconstruction*. Boston: Heath, 1961.

Vandiver, Frank E., *Their Tattered Flags: The Epic of the Confederacy*. New York: Harper Magazine Press, 1970.

Williams, Kenneth P., *Lincoln Finds a General: A Military History of the Civil War*, Vols. I–IV. New York: Macmillan, 1949.

SPECIAL STUDIES

Andreano, Ralph (Ed.), *The Economic Impact of the American Civil War*. Cambridge, Mass.: Schenkman, 1967.

Current, Richard N., *The Lincoln Nobody Knows*. New York: McGraw-Hill, 1958.

Donald, David, *Lincoln Reconsidered*. New York: Random House, 1956.

Franklin, John H., *The Emancipation Proclamation*. Garden City, N.Y.: Doubleday, 1963.

Frederickson, George M., *The Inner Civil War: Northern Intellectuals and the Crisis of the Union*. New York: Harper & Row, 1965.

Hammond, Bray, *Sovereignty and an Empty Purse: Banks and Politics in the Civil War*. Princeton, N.J.: Princeton University Press, 1970.

McPherson, James M., *The Struggle for Equality: Abolitionists and the Negro in the Civil War and Reconstruction*. Princeton, N.J.: Princeton University Press, 1964.

Owsley, Frank L., *King Cotton Diplomacy*. Chicago: University of Chicago Press, 1959.

Randall, James G., *Constitutional Problems under Lincoln*. Urbana: University of Illinois Press, 1964.

Wiley, Bell I., *The Life of Billy Yank*. Indianapolis, Ind.: Bobbs-Merrill, 1952.

Wiley, Bell I., *The Life of Johnny Reb*. Indianapolis, Ind.: Bobbs-Merrill, 1943.

Williams, T. Harry., *Lincoln and the Radicals*. Madison: University of Wisconsin Press, 1941.

PRIMARY SOURCES

Chestnut, Mary B., *A Diary from Dixie*. Boston: Houghton Mifflin, 1949.

Commager, Henry S. (Ed.), *The Blue and the Gray: The Story of the Civil War as Told by Participants*, Vols. I–II. Indianapolis, Ind.: Bobbs-Merrill, 1950.

Grant, Ulysses S., *The Personal Memoirs of U. S. Grant*. New York: Grosset & Dunlap, 1962.

McPherson, James M. (Ed.), *The Negro's Civil War.* New York: Pantheon, 1965.

Melville, Herman, *Battle-Pieces and Other Aspects of the War.* New York: T. Yoseloff, 1963.

Stephens, Alexander H., *Recollections.* New York: Doubleday, 1910.

BIOGRAPHIES

Dowdey, Clifford, *Lee.* Boston: Little, Brown, 1965.

Duberman, Martin, *Charles Francis Adams.* Boston: Houghton Mifflin, 1961.

Mitgang, Herbert, *The Fiery Trial: A Life of Lincoln.* New York: Viking Press, 1974.

Randall, James G., *Lincoln, the President: Springfield to Gettysburg,* Vols. I–IV. New York: Dodd, Mead, 1946–1955.

Sandburg, Carl, *Abraham Lincoln: The War Years,* Vols. I–IV. New York: Harcourt, Brace, 1939.

Strode, Hudson, *Jefferson Davis,* Vols. I–IV. New York: Harcourt, Brace, 1955–1966.

FICTION

Cable, George W., *Dr. Sevier.* Upper Saddle River, N.J.: Gregg, 1970.

Crane, Stephen, *The Red Badge of Courage.* New York: Macmillan, 1966. (Paper: Collier)

DeForest, John, *Miss Ravenal's Conversion.* New York: Holt, Rinehart & Winston, 1955.

Lancaster, Bruce, *For Us The Living.* New York: Stokes, 1940.

Shaara, Michael, *The Killer Angels: A Novel About the Four Days at Gettysburg.* New York: McKay, 1974.

Richmond, Virginia, after the Civil War. ▶

16
Reconstructing the Union

Under the pressure of federal bayonets, urged on by the misdirected sympathies of the world in behalf of the enslaved African, the people of Mississippi have abolished the institution of slavery. . . . We must now meet the question as it is, and not as we would like to have it. . . . The negro is free, whether we like it or not. . . . To be free, however, does not make him a citizen, or entitle him to social or political equality with the white man. But the constitution and justice do entitle him to protection and security in his person and property, both real and personal.

The Black Code of Mississippi

Although the Civil War had preserved the Union and abolished slavery its conclusion left a nation still bitter and divided. Of the issues remaining to be resolved, none was more critical than the need to restore the Union without sacrificing the newly won freedom of the ex-slaves.

In the North a great and violent debate developed over the nature of the settlement to be imposed on the defeated South. This debate, which largely determined the character of the postwar period, also contained power struggles between the legislative and executive branches of government and between a triumphant Republican party and a slowly reviving Democratic party.

In the South the war and the abolition of slavery had left a society in disarray. During the Reconstruction period lingering Southern bitterness against the North was only compounded by the determination of many Northerners to decide the shape of the South's postwar political and economic structure.

Presidential Reconstruction Plans

At the war's end the South was in ruins. Charleston and Richmond had been almost completely leveled. Entire sections of Atlanta, Mobile, Vicksburg, and Galveston lay in ashes. In the fall of 1865 a Northern visitor to Columbia, South Carolina, described it as "a wilderness of ruins. . . . not a store, office, or shop escaped." An Atlantan returning home after the war wrote, "Hell has laid her egg, and right here it hatched." Nor did the countryside escape unscathed. Sherman's armies cut a vicious swath through Georgia and the Carolinas on their march from Atlanta, leaving a charred and withered wasteland in their wake. Transportation, always inadequate in the South, was a hopeless shambles after the war. Roads were impassable, channels were unnavigable, bridges were burned, and wagons, horses, and steamboats had all but disappeared. Immediate prospects for Southern education were equally dismal. Countless schools had been destroyed and many teachers who had gone off to war would never return home to teach.

Yet the damage to the South was more than physical. The war and runaway inflation had closed banks and driven businesses into bankruptcy. More important, the abolition of slavery, in depriving the South of its unpaid labor force, delivered a blow to the region's economy from which it would not recover for many years. Even plantation owners who could afford to pay for laborers were often hard pressed to find ex-slaves willing to work for their former masters. More terrifying still were the persistent rumors that the victorious North intended to carve up Southern plantations and distribute the land among the newly freed blacks. If all this were not enough, Southern whites saw the freedom of their ex-slaves as a threat of unknown proportions to the future social and political order of the South.

LINCOLN'S RECONSTRUCTION PLANS

"Reconstruction is more difficult and dangerous than construction or destruction," President Lincoln had once remarked, "The bag is filled. It must be tied and tied securely." Lincoln at first believed he had two priorities: reconciling the white South and protecting the rights of black people. But he soon realized that his first consideration was to reunite the country. Therefore his primary goal for the postwar period was to have the Southern states resume their normal position in the Union. He believed that since secession was an illegal act, the Confederate states had in fact never really left the Union. All that was necessary was to remove the illegitimate rebel authorities and replace them with new and loyal state governments.

More than a year before the war ended Lincoln began to lay plans for the orderly reconstruction of the Union. On December 8, 1863, as Arkansas was preparing to surrender to Union forces, Lincoln issued his proclamation of Amnesty and Reconstruction. Known as the Ten Percent Plan, the president's Reconstruction blueprint stipulated that:

1. All high civilian and military officials of the Confederacy would be permanently barred from participating in the political process as punishment for their disloyalty to the Union;
2. Any citizen of a Confederate state would be granted amnesty and given back all property lost in the war (except slaves) upon agreeing to obey the Constitution and all laws of the Union;
3. When ten percent of those who had voted in the 1860 presidential election had taken this oath and sworn allegiance to the Union, that state would be allowed to write a new constitution, elect new state officials, and reassume its place in the Union.

Lincoln's plan was generous and was intended to make it as easy as possible for the former Confederate states to resume proper "practical relations" with the Union. He was willing to accept a pledge of future loyalty and overlook the past. He did not anticipate that blacks would help form the new governments, and his plan contained no protection for them beyond their emancipation. Yet he publicly stated in early 1865 that he wished the suffrage would be extended to very intelligent blacks and to "those who serve our cause as soldiers."

Many Republicans in Congress found Lincoln's plan far too lenient. A highly vocal and influential minority in the president's own party, the Radical Republicans, loudly opposed Lincoln's plan. The lines began to be drawn for a battle that would continue long after Lincoln's death, a battle that would shape the character of the Reconstruction period.

The battle over the shape of Reconstruction was also a struggle for power between the executive and legislative branches of government. During the course of the war Lincoln had enormously strengthened the presidency by assuming certain extraordinary powers at the expense of Congress. With the conclusion of the conflict, Congress no longer felt so inhibited and began to reassert its constitutional equality. The development of Reconstruction legislation provided the battleground for the struggle between the president and the Congress, with even moderate Republicans holding that such legislation was a congressional prerogative.

In March 1864 Congress introduced the Wade-Davis bill to counter Lincoln's Ten Percent Plan. The bill was much harsher than Lincoln's plan. It required that fifty percent of a state's citizens swear allegiance to the Union before it could be readmitted. It also limited political participation to those who had been loyal to the Union during the war, and required that new state constitutions repudiate all debts contracted by the Confederacy and deny the vote to all ex-Confederate officials. Like Lincoln's Ten Percent Plan it did not provide for the freedmen to participate in the process. The bill was passed by both houses of Congress in July but Lincoln, recognizing that it would exclude the vast majority of Southerners from the political process, let it die by a pocket veto.

Congress was enraged and reacted by issuing the Wade-Davis Manifesto, censuring the president and accusing him of an "outrage on the legislative authority." It further charged that the president was trying to gain Southern support for the upcoming national election. In fact, Lincoln sincerely believed that as president he had authority to carry out his Reconstruction plan without congressional interference. Reconstruction, he argued, was but another stage of the war that was being properly waged under the president's war powers.

The rift between Lincoln and Congress continued to widen. Under the Ten Percent Plan new state governments had been established in Tennessee, Arkansas, Virginia, and Louisiana even before the war ended. But despite the fact that the states had met the president's Reconstruction terms, Congress stubbornly refused to seat their newly elected congressional delegations.

On January 31, 1865 Congress also passed the Thirteenth Amendment to the Constitution, prohibiting slavery or involuntary servitude in the United States, except as punishment for a crime. This was the first time the federal government had undertaken a nationwide reform in the area of domestic institutions. The amendment also removed the doubts as to whether Lincoln's Emancipation Proclamation had been constitutional.

PRESIDENT ANDREW JOHNSON

In April 1865, when an assassin's bullet ended Abraham Lincoln's dream of restoring the Union, Vice-President Andrew Johnson inherited the complex problems of Reconstruction along with the presidency.

Johnson was of humble origins. He was born in Raleigh, North Carolina, in 1808, and apprenticed to a tailor in his youth. When he was eighteen he accompanied his widowed mother to Tennessee. Although he had no formal education, Johnson taught himself to read and his wife later instructed him in the basics of arithmetic and writing. Gradually his lot began to improve. His political career began in 1835 when he was elected to the Tennessee legislature as a Jacksonian Democrat. Eight years later he successfully ran for the House of Representatives. After ten years as a congressman and two terms as governor of Tennessee, Johnson was elected to the United States Senate in 1857.

Johnson opposed secession and continued to sit in the Senate even after his state had withdrawn from the Union. For this action he became a hero to many Northerners and his loyalty did not go unrewarded. When Tennessee fell to Union forces in 1862, Lincoln appointed him military governor of the state. Two years later, to demonstrate the nonpartisan character of the war effort and to attract Democratic support for the ticket, Lincoln selected Johnson as his running mate. Five months after the election Andrew Johnson was president.

Because Johnson detested the wealthy Southern aristocracy, the Radical Republicans at first thought they had an ally in the White House. "By the gods," exclaimed Senator Benjamin F. Wade, "there will be no trouble now in running this government!" Their optimism was short-lived, however. Johnson was no Radical, but a Democrat who represented the interests of the small farmer. His hatred of the old-line Southern ruling class was a poor boy's hatred of privilege. He wasted no love on black people and had little interest in racial equality. His opposition to secession had largely reflected his reverence for the Constitution, a copy of which he even requested to have placed in his coffin.

The Republicans in Congress found themselves at odds with the new president almost immediately. Johnson, a courageous but rigid man, felt strongly that the Constitution gave Congress no right to dictate the terms by which the Confederate states could rejoin the Union. But unlike Lincoln, who argued that the Southern states had never left the Union, Johnson was a states' rights advocate who believed that neither Congress nor any other branch of the federal government had a constitutional right to interfere with the internal politics of the states.

The new president decided to deal with Reconstruction himself and actively carried out his policy for seven months while Congress was not in session. He recognized the new state governments of Louisiana, Arkansas, Virginia, and his home state of Tennessee under Lincoln's Ten Percent Plan. This done, he issued his own Proclamation of Amnesty and Pardon on May 29, 1865. It was similar to Lincoln's plan in that it offered to pardon former Confederates who would pledge their loyalty to the Union. But it excluded his old enemies, the big planters: those with property worth more than $20,000

Ex-slaves arriving at a "contraband camp." ▲

had to petition the president himself for forgiveness.

During the next two months Johnson issued proclamations to all Southern states not already restored to the Union under the Ten Percent Plan. They provided for presidential appointment of a provisional governor in each state, for elections of delegates to state constitutional conventions, and for the reorganization of the state governments. Johnson also made it clear that before a state could be restored to the Union it had to nullify its ordinance of secession, ratify the Thirteenth Amendment to the Constitution abolishing slavery, and repudiate the Confederate debt.

Johnson's plan resembled Lincoln's but, unlike Lincoln, Johnson did not understand how delicately he must maneuver to make it work. Lincoln had believed that the South should be put in a position not of deciding on terms but of accepting them as a consequence of defeat. He had also believed that the terms should be acceptable to Congress and to the people of the North after the sacrifices of the war years. The North wanted to know that slavery was dead and that the power of the former slaveholders was at an end.

Johnson's enforcement of his Reconstruction policy was not reassuring on these grounds. Mississippi refused to ratify the Thirteenth Amendment and Alabama refused to ratify part of it. South Carolina and Mississippi refused to repudiate their Confederate debts. Seeing that the president would not force compliance with even such minimal demands, the South moved to place restrictions on black people as well.

THE FREEDMEN

Although the war had freed the blacks from slavery, the racial equality promised by the Radicals proved to be so much empty rhetoric. In both Lincoln's and Johnson's plans for Reconstruction, the welfare of the black freedmen had taken a backseat to the reunification of the nation. Some Radical Republicans' commitment to racial equality, though sincere, was subordinate to their struggle for power with the president and their desire to achieve Republican dominance in the South. Indeed, in all the power struggles during the Reconstruction period—between Congress and the president, between Radicals and moderates, between Democrats and Republicans, and between North and South—the freedmen were often the pawns.

By the war's end former slaves with no place to go were crowding into shantytowns often built by the Union army. So intolerable were conditions in these "contraband camps" that in 1865 alone an estimated one hundred thousand blacks reportedly died from starvation and disease. In March 1865 the Union government passed an act establishing the Freedmen's Bureau to supervise the transition from slavery to freedom. The bureau began by distributing food to prevent starvation.

One of the brightest hopes for the freedmen was the act's provision to distribute confiscated Southern land to them. According to the provision, the land was to be rented for three years and then sold to the holder at its 1860 appraised value. The black dream of "forty acres and a mule" was never realized though. The proposal immediately became bogged down in Reconstruction politics and ran counter to the firmly held American belief in the sanctity of property. Congress did open up some forty-six million acres of federal lands in the South for distribution to the freedmen, but the land cost $1.25 per acre and was so undesirable that few black homesteaders were interested. Good land would have been available only if it had been taken from former Confederates under the Confiscation Act of 1862. But once these people had been pardoned under Lincoln's and Johnson's Reconstruction plans their land was no longer subject to confiscation.

In the absence of a unified Northern policy on the rights of the freedmen, the defeated Confederate states began enacting measures designed to keep the ex-slaves in a position of economic, social, and political inferiority. Collectively called the "Black Codes," these measures had been passed in 1865 and 1866 to keep blacks in a position little better than they had been in as slaves. In most states they were prohibited from holding skilled jobs, to protect white workers. In South Carolina blacks were allowed to work only as farm laborers or servants. In Mississippi they were prevented from owning land. In Louisiana they could not sell, barter, or exchange merchandise. In most Southern states blacks could not vote, hold office, testify against white people, serve on juries, or bear arms. Of all the Black Codes, the most repressive were the vagrancy laws, which permitted unemployed black people to be arrested and fined. Thus, anyone who could not pay the fine could be hired out to white employers, their wages going to pay the fine. Some states even provided that black people who jumped their labor contracts could be dragged back by white "negro catchers" who would be paid by the mile for their effort.

The Southern states also refused to grant blacks the right to vote. Johnson had suggested to the South that Northern advocates of black suffrage would be disarmed if blacks who could read, write, and had some real estate were enfranchised. But he did not order it done, and suffrage was restricted to white people. Southerners could point to the fact that blacks did not vote in most Northern states either.

Congressional Reconstruction Plans

By the end of 1865 every former Confederate state except Texas had generally met the terms of either the Ten Percent Plan or Johnson's plan. Most had accepted the Thirteenth Amendment, and all had organized new state governments and elected new senators and representatives. When Congress met in December, the new Southern congressmen arrived in Washington with the support of President Johnson. But Congress rebuffed them. The process had happened too fast, and the North did not find the terms of reconciliation acceptable.

REPUBLICAN VIEWS ON RECONSTRUCTION

The Republicans were already enraged by the Black Codes and by the South's reluctance to repudiate their ordinances of secession. Now they were further angered to find that the

Southern congressional delegation included many top-ranking former Confederates. Georgia, for example, had sent Confederate vice-president Alexander H. Stephens to the Senate. The Republicans were also disturbed because the almost exclusively Democratic delegation threatened their own majority in Congress.

Congress flatly refused to seat the newly elected delegations in what amounted to a rejection of both Lincoln's and Johnson's Reconstruction formulas. The effort to develop an acceptable Reconstruction plan would have to begin all over again. This time Congress was determined to take the initiative.

Congress immediately appointed a Joint Committee on Reconstruction. But most politicians were not sure what specific policy they should adopt toward the South.

The Radical Republican minority viewed the war as a struggle to rid the South of slavery. Consequently they believed that the victorious North had an obligation to enforce the principles of racial equality by changing the entire power structure in the South. Black suffrage, declared Representative Thaddeus Stevens of Pennsylvania, "should be our great aim." And to accomplish this he felt there should be far-reaching economic changes: "The whole fabric of Southern society *must* be changed," Stevens declared. Such a policy was legitimate because the Confederate states had indeed seceded from the Union, given up their constitutional rights as states, and should be treated as "conquered provinces." Stevens proposed to confiscate the land of all former slaveholders, carve it up, and distribute some of it to the ex-slaves and sell the rest. Revenue from sales could go toward reducing the national debt and toward starting a pension system for Union veterans and their families. "This must be done," said Stevens, "even though it drive [the South's] nobility into exile. . . . It is far easier and more beneficial to exile seventy thousand proud, bloated, and defiant rebels, than to expatriate four millions of laborers, native to the soil and loyal to the Government."

Senator Charles Sumner was more interested in a political revolution. The freedmen should be made citizens, should use all facilities freely, and public education should not be segregated. Blacks should have full rights in the courts to bring a case, to be a witness, or to be a juror. They should vote and hold office. Having the vote would help ensure their economic equality.

The Republican majority in Congress, however, did not hold such strong views on remaking Southern society. But they disliked Johnson's policy because it did not require a strong enough guarantee of Southern loyalty and gave no protection to black people. Although they did not believe in racial equality, they were infuriated by the virtual reenslavement created by the Black Codes.

Yet the Republicans were not entirely concerned about the plight of the freedmen. Well aware that if left to its own devices the South would rapidly become a Democratic stronghold, most Republicans hoped their plans would enable the party to maintain a strong influence in the former Confederate states. They feared that excluding blacks from the vote might result in a coalition of former rebels and Northern antiwar Democrats controlling the country. Commitment to black suffrage was thus maintained on partisan as well as on idealistic grounds.

THE FOURTEENTH AMENDMENT

To protect the rights of blacks while the Reconstruction debate raged on, Congress voted in 1866 to continue and broaden the powers of the Freedmen's Bureau. At first vetoed by Johnson, who considered it a violation of the states' right to control their own internal affairs, the bill was passed into law several months later over a second presidential veto. The bureau was authorized to supervise labor relations between blacks and their employers and to arrange court reviews of disputes that arose.

One of the great successes of the expanded bureau was the encouragement of black education. The bureau coordinated the supply of school buildings and teachers. Under its auspices, Atlanta University, Fisk University, and Howard University were established. Black response to these new educational opportunities was enthusiastic. In 1866 a Freedmen's Bureau study found that black children were attending school more regularly than whites.

In 1866, when Johnson vetoed the bill to continue the Freedmen's Bureau, Congress reacted by drawing up a new Civil Rights Act which guaranteed citizenship to blacks and prohibited discrimination against citizens on the grounds of race or color. Johnson again exercised his veto, this time making the politically foolish mistake of crudely insulting the congressional leadership. This action cost him the support of many moderate Republicans who had formerly opposed the Radicals. The moderates now realized that congressional prerogatives had to be protected against "Sir Veto." The resulting congressional solidarity against Johnson made it possible for the Civil Rights Act to be passed over his veto.

Faced with a hostile president and a recalcitrant South, Congress sought to give the new Civil Rights Act constitutional protection by incorporating its provisions into the Fourteenth Amendment. In doing so, they were also guarding against its annulment by a future Congress or by the Supreme Court. The Fourteenth Amendment amounted to a new congressional plan for Reconstruction. It was the moderate Republicans' final effort to find a solution that would be acceptable to the South and that would at the same time guarantee the rights of the freedmen.

The Fourteenth Amendment clearly defined American citizenship for the first time. In an effort to prevent a state from denying political rights to any citizen, it declared that anyone born or naturalized in the United States was a citizen. It also stipulated that no state could deny any citizen equal protection of the laws or deprive him or her of life, liberty, or property without due process of law. Although not directly conferring suffrage on every citizen, it declared that if a state denied the vote to any of its citizens, that state's representation in Congress and in the Electoral College would be proportionately reduced. Finally, the Fourteenth Amendment disqualified from federal office all those who had at one time pledged loyalty to the Constitution and then had broken that oath to support the Confederacy. Such persons could hold office only if pardoned by two-thirds of the Congress.

From the congressional point of view the Fourteenth Amendment was a fairly lenient proposal and represented an opportunity for compromise with the White House. It did not force the South to enfranchise the freedmen (as long as the states were willing to give up seats in Congress), nor did it try to legislate the freedmen's economic independence at the expense of Southern whites. But it did affirm the constitutional rights of black people and brought them under federal jurisdiction. It avoided the problem of black suffrage nationwide and at the same time kept former Confederates out of national office. It stated the terms of reunion and asked the South to accept them.

Had President Johnson been willing to accept the Fourteenth Amendment and to warn the South to accept it or face harsher terms from an angry Republican Congress, the travail of Reconstruction would have been over. But Johnson was no longer in touch with political reality. He believed that the Southern states were already reconstructed—that they were valid states—and that the Congress operating without them was not a legitimate Congress. He overlooked the fact that the South had lost the Civil War and that the North was in a position to dictate its own terms. The president advised the South to reject the amendment and to rely on a Republican defeat in the congressional elections of that year.

The lines of opposition were clearly drawn and the president, misjudging public opinion, decided to make the Fourteenth Amendment the major campaign issue. Laying his prestige on the line, Johnson embarked on a nationwide tour, campaigning hard for candidates who opposed the amendment. His two-fisted speaking style proved to be highly inflammatory in many parts of the country. When hecklers hurled insults at him, he responded in kind with his choicest homespun Tennessee epithets. The tour was a dismal failure. And when efforts to register black voters in Memphis and New Orleans resulted in race riots, the riots were unjustly blamed on Johnson's failure to support the amendment. The country's mood was against him and his position. The election gave the Republicans an even larger congressional majority, large enough to override any presidential veto.

Even with the overwhelming Republican victory, ten of the eleven Southern states followed the president's advice and rejected the amendment. Furious at continuing Southern defiance, the new veto-proof Congress was now in a position to enforce its will. Moderate and Radical Republicans were united in their stand to dictate terms to the defeated states.

RADICAL RECONSTRUCTION

The first Reconstruction Act, passed by Congress in March 1867 over Johnson's veto (and supplemented by three further Reconstruction Acts in 1867 and 1868), declared all existing state governments in the South to be illegal. This move allowed Congress to create new Southern state governments. It also avoided the delicate constitutional issue of states' rights. Since no state governments legally existed, their rights could hardly be violated.

Ten Southern states (excluding Tennessee) were divided into five military districts under the control of the United States Army. The major

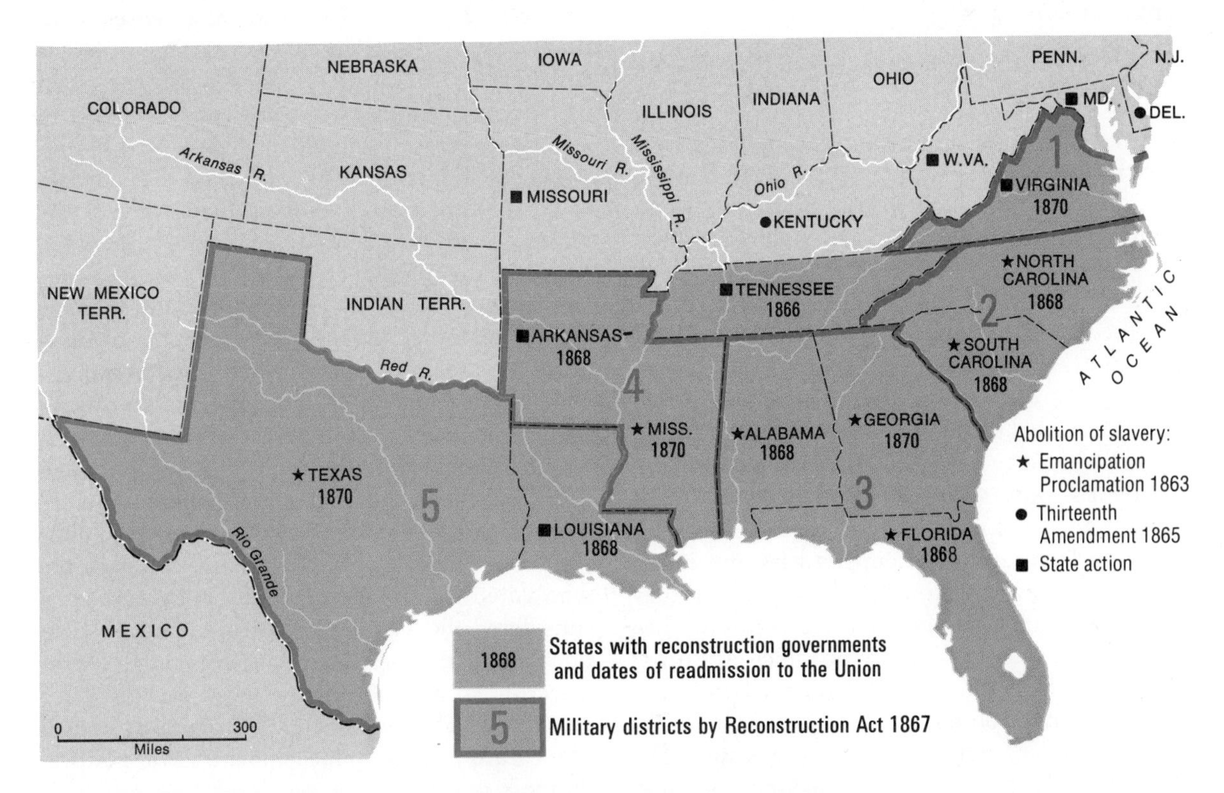

RECONSTRUCTION OF THE SOUTH • 1865 TO 1877

general in each district was to supervise the registration of all male citizens without regard to color, except for those former public officeholders disenfranchised by their participation in the rebellion. This new electorate would then choose delegates to state constitutional conventions and members of new state governments. The act further stipulated that each new state constitution had to provide for black suffrage and that each state had to ratify the Fourteenth Amendment. Once a state had met all of these conditions, Congress would readmit it to the Union and military occupation would end.

By June 1868 all states except Mississippi, Texas, and Virginia had fulfilled these terms and Congress had seated their delegations. Georgia was removed temporarily for expelling black members from its legislature, and was readmitted in 1870 with the three other recalcitrant Southern states.

IMPEACHMENT

The Radicals were fully aware that military Reconstruction was an extreme solution and they feared that the president or the Supreme Court would try to overturn it. A case challenging the constitutionality of the Reconstruction Act soon appeared on the Supreme Court docket. However the Court declined to lock horns with Congress and refused to hear the case.

Congress did not expect the president to share the Court's reluctance for battle. Accordingly, it passed two bills in 1867 that limited the president's power to obstruct its plan. The Army Appropriations Act limited his control of the army by preventing him from issuing military orders except through the general of the army who could not be removed without the Senate's consent. The Tenure of Office Act prohibited him from removing federal officials without the Senate's consent.

The president refused to bow to measures he considered unconstitutional. Believing the Supreme Court would overturn the Tenure of Office Act, Johnson tested it in February 1868 by removing the only Radical member of his cabinet, Secretary of War Edwin M. Stanton. The struggle between Congress and the president had now reached the point of no return. Within a few days the House of Representatives voted to impeach Johnson for his deliberate violation of a federal law.

For the first time in American history the United States Senate held an impeachment trial of a president. The trial, presided over by Chief Justice Salmon P. Chase, was a heated and bitter affair, lasting more than two months. Wild charges were hurled against Johnson, including one that suggested his complicity in the assassination of former president Lincoln.

The trial itself focused on the question of what constituted an impeachable offense. Johnson's lawyers argued that the Constitution called for impeachment only in cases of "high crimes and misdemeanors" (or criminal offenses) and that none of the charges against the president could be so characterized. If a president could be removed simply for being unacceptable to Congress, executive independence would be destroyed. The prosecution contended that officials could be impeached for other than criminal offenses, such as actions or even intentions "against the public interest." It was the only way to get rid of an incompetent officeholder. If the Senate had upheld the prosecution's argument, it would have established a precedent for using impeachment as a means of expressing "no confidence" in an official. But the argument was defeated. When the count was finally taken, the prosecution failed by one vote to muster the two-thirds majority needed to remove Johnson from office. The seven Republican senators who voted to clear Johnson did so because they considered the Tenure of Office Act unconstitutional, and the president therefore innocent of the criminal offense they believed necessary for conviction. The outcome of the trial discouraged the future use of impeachment as a political weapon.

Although allowed to finish his term, the beleaguered president was unable to secure the

"The Smelling Committee," an 1868 cartoon, comments on the Radical Republicans' effort to impeach President Andrew Johnson.

Democratic nomination in 1868. He returned to Tennessee where he failed in a number of attempts for election to local offices. In 1874 he was elected again to the United States Senate from Tennessee. He died the following year.

THE SOUTH UNDER RADICAL RECONSTRUCTION

Although it did not live up to Radical hopes Reconstruction did have some successes. The Southern constitutional conventions produced documents that were distinct improvements over those they replaced. They provided for more equitable apportionment of representation; they often included recognition of women's rights and penal code reform; and they made many appointive offices elective. State-supported education began to close the educational gap between the South and the rest of the nation. And the reorganized governments encouraged and supported the development of new industry.

As noted, Radical Reconstruction deprived large numbers of Southern whites of their right to participate in the political process and hold public office. Although the number of disenfranchised whites has often been exaggerated (in fact the number never exceeded one hundred fifty thousand), the fact remains that Northerners played an inordinately large role in Southern politics during the Reconstruction era. In 1869 "carpetbaggers," as these Northerners came to be called, occupied four Southern governors' mansions, held ten Southern senate seats, and represented twenty Southern congressional districts. The carpetbaggers have often been painted

Hiram R. Revels of Mississippi (left) was the first black person to sit in the United States Senate. The other men in this engraving were Congressmen in 1872.

as immoral Northern opportunists who moved to the South merely to plunder it. Although many of them were indeed primarily interested in power and wealth, many others were idealistic reformers who went south to work for racial equality.

As bitterly as Southerners resented the presence of the carpetbaggers, they hated native Southerners who collaborated with the Reconstruction regimes even more. "Scalawags," as these collaborators were called, were regarded by their fellow Southerners as unprincipled individuals who had sold out to the enemy in order to advance their own interests. This view neglected the fact that many so-called scalawags had opposed secession and the Confederacy from the beginning, while a few were genuinely devoted to achieving equality for the black freedmen.

Under Radical Reconstruction Southern blacks began to take part in the political process. Although it was never as large a part as many have claimed, it was significant in the political plans of the Republican party. In 1868 seven hundred thousand blacks voted for Grant, contributing heavily to his three-hundred-ten-thousand vote margin. Once the Republicans realized how important the black vote would be to them they took steps to protect it. Shortly after the election they proposed the Fifteenth Amendment, stating that the right of citizens to vote "shall not be denied or abridged by the United States or by any State on account of race, color, or previous condition of servitude." By March 1870 the Fifteenth Amendment had been ratified by three-quarters of the states and had become part of the United States Constitution.

Blacks also began to serve in public office. Between 1868 and 1875 two blacks served in the Senate and fourteen in the House of Representatives. A black man, Jonathan Jasper Wright, was appointed to the Supreme Court of South Carolina. Yet for the most part black officeholders served at the state and local level and, considering the proportion of blacks living in the South, their participation in Southern politics must be considered extremely limited. They were a majority in only one state constitutional convention (South Carolina) and were never a majority in both houses of any state legislature. They never elected a state governor. They never pressed for desegregated schools and seldom raised the question of land confiscation.

Some historians have alleged that Reconstruction failed to create a new South because of the large-scale corruption, extravagance, and waste in Reconstruction governments which plunged the Southern states into debt. Corruption did exist. In South Carolina the legislature voted to reimburse one of its members for the $1000 he lost betting on the horses, and payments were made for at least three times as many militia as were actually serving in the state force. In Louisiana the annual $100,000 cost of running the state government skyrocketed to $1 million under Reconstruction. Public funds were commonly squandered on furniture, homes, jewelry, and even liquor for public officials. Yet corruption was widespread throughout the country at this time and the level of corruption in the Reconstruction governments was probably no greater than in other sections of the country.

THE END OF RECONSTRUCTION

From the very beginning of Reconstruction Southerners were bitterly resentful of their exclusion from politics, of the presence of carpetbaggers, and of the attempt to elevate the blacks and, in general, alter the political and social fabric of the South. Southern resentment of the Radical governments hardened their attitude toward the freedmen and led to even greater discrimination.

White Southerners found two ways of combating carpetbag rule, the threat of the black vote, and the creation in several states of militia made up primarily of blacks. In states like Virginia, Tennessee, and North Carolina, large white majorities were able to control their government through elections. In other states, however, white citizens resorted to economic pressure and terrorism. Thousands of white Southerners banded together in secret organizations such as the White Brotherhood, the Knights of the White Camelia, and the Ku Klux Klan. Best known of all the societies, the Klan was based mainly in the deep South. It was dedicated to driving blacks out of Southern politics, ending Reconstruction, and restoring white supremacy. Wrapping themselves in sheets to resemble the ghosts of dead Confederate soldiers, Klan members roamed the countryside burning crosses and terrorizing blacks as well as whites committed to registering black voters. They also killed and injured a large number of people. The Klan's actions were directly responsible for the congressional Enforcement Acts of 1870 to 1871 which placed elections under federal jurisdiction, gave the president the right to suspend habeas corpus and declare martial law, and imposed fines and sentences on those convicted of interfering with any citizen's right to vote. But most Southern judges were white, and few people indicted under these acts were convicted. By the end of the 1860s many criminals were operating under cover of the Klan, and its activities became so outrageous that its own leader denounced the organization and ordered it disbanded in 1869.

Now many Southerners began to take more direct action against the regimes that were denying them control of their own internal affairs. In 1871 the president had to send reinforcements to South Carolina to quell a rebellion against the Reconstruction government there. Organizations such as the South Carolina Redshirts continued to terrorize blacks, even more openly

The plight of black people after the Civil War is depicted in this 1870 engraving.

This cartoon of the 1870s shows the dilemma of the freed blacks. Many who left the South after the Civil War found they were not particularly welcome in the North.

than the Klan had done. Other groups, such as the Rifle Clubs and the White Leagues, used whatever force was necessary to ensure election victories. Violence and economic pressure began scaring blacks away from the polls and welded the South into a solidly Democratic voting bloc for nearly a century.

While the South was growing more determined to run its own political affairs, the North was losing interest in enforcing Reconstruction policies. It was also less willing to bear the cost of defending the freedmen and of maintaining Republican regimes and an army in the South. The Northern business community wanted stability in the South to restore normal cotton production and trade. The Republicans in the South could not accomplish this but the white Southerners could. The Civil War was fading into memory and sectional hatred between North and South was declining.

Republican politicians were also beginning to realize that they could win national elections by carrying the North and West alone and that the Southern black vote was expendable. Reconstruction was now considered largely a failure in both North and South, and as the 1872 presidential election drew near, Republicans wished to get rid of a political liability. These factors were all reflected in the Radicals' waning influence in the Republican party and in Congress. By 1872 the Freedmen's Bureau had expired and a more moderate Congress was willing to pass an Amnesty Act restoring voting and officeholding privileges to almost all white Southerners.

One by one the Reconstruction regimes began to topple. By the end of 1875 only Louisiana, Florida, and South Carolina still had Reconstruction governments. One year later a disputed presidential election was settled by a compromise that brought Reconstruction to an end. The last federal forces were withdrawn from the South in April 1877.

As extreme as Radical Reconstruction seemed at the time, it did not go far enough to change the basic structure of Southern life. Blacks had been unable to achieve economic independence, and so were unable to retain their political equality when Reconstruction ended. The machinery established to protect their right to vote proved inadequate. All that remained as a positive, enduring legacy of Reconstruction were the Fourteenth and Fifteenth Amendments to the Constitution.

THE 1868 ELECTION

In 1868 the Democrats nominated Horatio Seymour as their presidential candidate. A former governor of New York, Seymour enjoyed the support of Southern whites and many moderates because he opposed Radical Reconstruction as unconstitutional and the embodiment of "military despotism and Negro supremacy."

Seymour's Republican opponent was General Ulysses S. Grant, "the saviour of the Union," an extremely popular war hero with few known political views. Grant had been courted by the Democrats but had finally been drawn into the Republican camp in the controversy over military Reconstruction. In 1868 the Republicans continued to seek the support of Northern manufacturing interests by adopting a platform which supported a high tariff and encouraged cheap labor through a liberal immigration policy.

The Democrats appealed to Western farmers and other indebted voters with a "cheap money" platform. During the war Congress had issued a large amount of paper money that was not backed by gold. Greenbacks, as the new paper money was called, had less value than money with gold behind it. At the end of the war Congress gradually began withdrawing the greenbacks from circulation. Debtors—Western bankers, farmers, and railroad promoters—favored keeping the greenbacks in circulation so that they could repay their debts with cheap money. Creditors—largely Eastern bankers and financiers—wanted to receive full value for the money they had lent and consequently favored

"The Republican Platform, or the Political Mountebank" is a political cartoon from the election of 1868. U. S. Grant, the Republican candidate, balances himself on a narrow platform supported by the anti-slavery crusader Horace Greeley on one end and a black man on the other. His balancing rod, labeled "U.S. Treasury" spews greenbacks out one end and gold coins out the other.

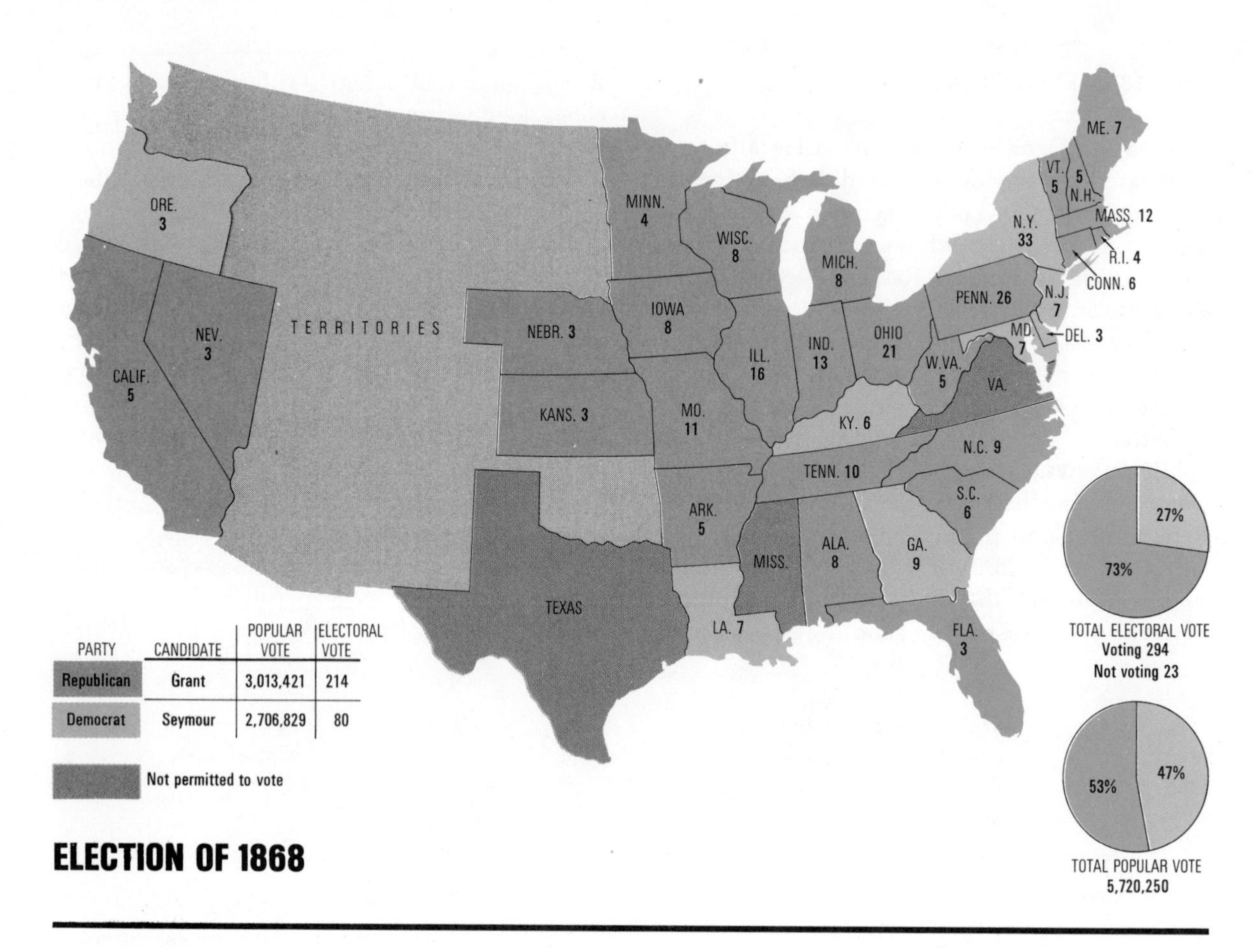

PARTY	CANDIDATE	POPULAR VOTE	ELECTORAL VOTE
Republican	Grant	3,013,421	214
Democrat	Seymour	2,706,829	80

ELECTION OF 1868

withdrawing the greenbacks from circulation. The Democratic platform of 1868 supported the continued circulation of greenbacks.

Despite these clear economic differences between the parties, the decisive issue in the campaign proved to be the war that had ended three years earlier. The Republicans, resorting to a tactic that came to be known as "waving the bloody shirt," presented themselves as the party that had saved the Union and the Democrats as the party of rebellion. Grant's candidacy reinforced the images and, although the popular vote was close, the Republicans won 214 of the 294 electoral votes.

Grant's Presidency

A former general with limited political experience, Grant believed that the president's primary duty was to execute the will of Congress. Those with hopes that he would be a firm and wise leader who would control the Radicals and raise the tone of public life were doomed to disappointment. Grant ran the presidency along military lines, issuing commands and discouraging debate of the issues. At the same time, his lack of political experience and receptivity to flattery made him an easy target of self-seeking politicians and businessmen.

When he did undertake an act on his own initiative the results were very uneven. The appointment of his cabinet is a good example. While some of his advisers were competent, his secretary of the navy's only qualification was wealth and the secretary of the army was one of Grant's old war cronies. The "Kitchen Cabinet," Grant's White House staff of advisers which also controlled federal patronage appointments, was dominated by old army colleagues with no political experience who dispensed jobs to friends, relatives, and those with the money to pay for their positions.

ECONOMIC POLICIES

One of the central domestic issues facing Grant was the need to formulate a policy concerning the greenbacks. Grant wanted to please the Eastern financiers who had supported him, but feared that retiring the greenbacks would alienate those in debt. The president finally settled on a compromise that would leave the greenbacks in circulation but made it possible to back them with gold in the future. Congress supported him and enacted the plan. Because the compromise was not especially popular with the large mass of voters, Grant supported the highly popular congressional measures aimed at eliminating the wartime income tax and excise duties.

Another economic issue Grant faced involved the high tariff Congress had enacted as an emergency measure during the war. When the war ended manufacturing and industrial interests favored retaining the duties to maintain high prices on domestic goods and keep out foreign competitive products. These interests had strongly supported Grant in the election and their lobbyists had little trouble convincing him that the high tariff should be retained. Grant's own economic adviser, David A. Wells, supported by consumers and farmers opposed the high tariff. Wells claimed that it tended to encourage monopolies and merely enriched the Eastern industrialists at the expense of many consumers, especially Western farmers. The president ignored Wells' opinions, and supported the protectionists in Congress, who raised duties on many products in 1870.

CORRUPTION IN WASHINGTON

The major issue of Grant's administration was misconduct in the federal government. During the eight years of Grant's presidency, corruption and scandal infiltrated and finally rocked the highest levels of government. Holders of high political office used their power and influence to amass personal fortunes at the expense of the voters who elected them. Other public officials

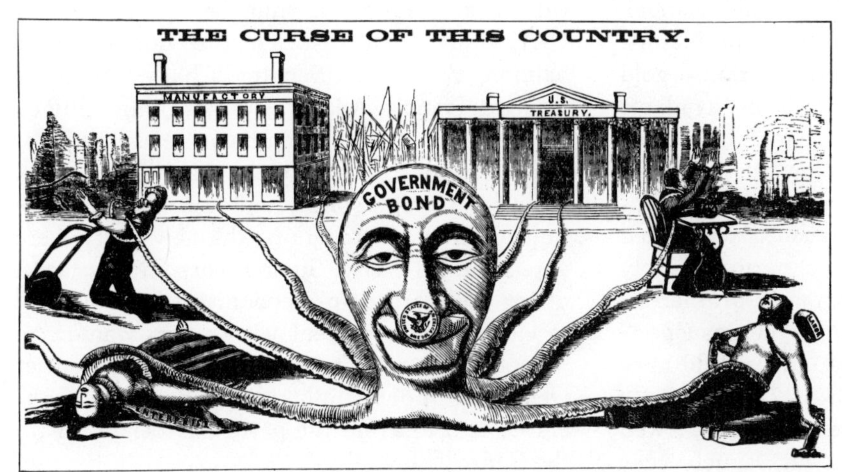

In this pro-greenback cartoon of the 1870s a gold-nosed government octopus is shown strangling workers, farmers, and small businessmen.

were naive victims of businessmen who exploited them and their offices. The result was a great loss of public confidence in government. The corruption of the Grant years would probably have existed no matter who was in the presidency since it was largely the result of the relaxed moral vigilance that followed the Civil War. Both the North and the South had fought and suffered for a generation on behalf of cherished ideals. As the war ended Americans were weary of the struggle and looked forward to leading more comfortable lives. At the same time, the opportunities for achieving such comfort were more available. Industrialization and the war itself had created a wealthy class of industrialists and businessmen. Americans worshipped wealth as never before and the acquisition of material possessions became an obsession.

In this new climate many politicians were unable to resist bribes for favors they could dispense freely. Many others, including Grant himself, did not intentionally abuse their offices or gain personally from corruption, but were unwitting accomplices in scandal because of their naivety and negligence. Infatuated by the startling successes of American business and possessing only a limited understanding of the complex postwar economic situation. Grant allowed incompetence and corruption to infest and ultimately erode his entire administration.

The largest incident of corruption during Grant's first term was the Fisk-Gould scandal. Jay Gould and Jim Fisk, two bold speculators, conceived a plan to corner the nation's gold supply. They would buy up all the available gold, hold it until its price soared, and then dump it on the market, reaping an enormous profit. The plan would work only if the government could somehow be persuaded or tricked into withholding from sale its normal supply of gold. Working through Grant's brother-in-law, Gould managed to convince the unsuspecting president that withholding gold would raise the price of bullion and indirectly raise the price of American farm commodities in Europe. Awed by Gould's wealth, the president vaguely consented to a plan he did not really understand. Gould and Fisk begged, borrowed, and bought all the gold they could. The gigantic gamble came to a head on "Black Friday," September 24, 1869. There was a panic at the New York Stock Exchange because the price of gold had soared so high that gold supplies were insufficient for the conduct of ordinary trading. Finally realizing what was happening, the president released $4 million in gold to stabilize the market. But his action came too late to avoid serious damage to the business community.

That same year Grant was duped again, this time by a group of American fortune hunters who wished to exploit the economic potential of the Dominican Republic. The speculators managed to convince Grant that the island was of strategic importance to the United States and should be annexed. Annexation would lead to enormous business profits. Only the Senate's opposition, led by Charles Sumner of Massachusetts, prevented the annexation proposal from going through.

THE 1872 ELECTION: A NEW PARTY

Toward the end of Grant's first term a group of disillusioned Republicans and Democrats formed the Liberal Republican party. Angered by Radical Reconstruction, scandal, and Grant's lack of interest in civil service reform to end corruption in government, the new party's members included an impressive number of reformers: Carl Schurz, Chief Justice of the Supreme Court Salmon P. Chase, Senator Charles Sumner, Charles Francis Adams (son of John Quincy Adams), and several prominent newspaper editors including Horace Greeley of the New York *Tribune.* Though solidly united in their opposition to Grant, members of the new party were agreed on little else. Some favored a low tariff, others were ardent protectionists. Some wanted to circulate more greenbacks, others wanted all greenbacks withdrawn. Some of the former Democrats opposed military Reconstruction, others wanted to avoid the party's association with the Confederacy.

▲ *A particularly cruel Thomas Nast cartoon of the election of 1872 shows Greeley being carried away under a satirical rendition of his* New York Tribune *banner.*

When it came time to nominate a presidential candidate and formulate a platform, the results reflected the party's internal conflicts. While the platform demanded amnesty for all former Confederates and the withdrawal of troops from the South, it also approved Radical Reconstruction. On the tariff and greenback issues the Liberal Republicans were unable to reach agreement and took no stand at all. The platform did, however, state strong support for civil service reform.

When the Liberal Republicans nominated Horace Greeley to oppose Grant in the 1872 election, they ensured their own defeat. Though admired and well known as a newspaper editor and greatly respected for his years of crusading against slavery, Greeley was also widely regarded as an eccentric. Given to erratic and untempered enthusiasms, Greeley had taken up every fad of the past few decades from vegetarianism to spiritualism. He had been denounced as an atheist, and as a free lover. Despite all of this, however, the Democrats realized that their only hope of unseating Grant was to align themselves with the Liberal Republicans. When the Democrats announced their endorsement of Greeley, the Republicans were overjoyed to learn that their only opposition would be a candidate that many people regarded as a crackpot.

In contrast to the Liberal Republican and Democratic confusion, the regular Republican party stood on its record of high tariffs and Radical Reconstruction. Industrialists and bankers poured large sums of money into Grant's campaign.

Although he ran a surprisingly good campaign, Greeley carried only two Southern states and four border states. Many Democrats, remembering Greeley's flinty attacks against the South over slavery, stayed home on Election Day, and Grant won by a larger margin than he had before. Devastated by his loss and by the recent death of his wife, Greeley died three weeks after the election. The Liberal Republican movement, lacking a party structure, disintegrated.

MORE SCANDALS

During Grant's second term scandals involving the government continued to erupt on an even greater scale. There was corruption in the Bureau of Indian Affairs and in the Treasury Department. One of the worst scandals was the Crédit Mobilier affair, which involved both Grant's previous vice-president, Schuyler Colfax, and his current vice-president, Henry Wilson. In 1867 the Crédit Mobilier, a construction company formed to assist in building the transcontinental railroad, virtually gave away stock in the company to congressmen and other high government officials. The bribes were given to prevent investigation of the company's fraudulent drain of profits from construction contracts. The New York *Sun* exposed the bribes in 1872, and a subsequent congressional investigation found that both vice-presidents and a number of influential congressmen had been among the recipients. One of the implicated congressmen freely voiced his regret that the bribe "was no larger."

As scandals continued to unfold, it became increasingly difficult to shock a public that had grown used to corruption in government. One, the "Whiskey Ring" conspiracy, involved hundreds of distillers who bribed internal revenue officials to falsify reports that defrauded the government out of millions of dollars in excise tax revenue. When Grant's own private secretary, General Orville Babcock, was exposed as one of the conspirators, Grant unquestioningly defended him and even sent a written character deposition to his trial. Babcock was acquitted and the President allowed him quietly to resign.

Corruption was not confined to the federal government, either. Politics in large cities began to be dominated by political machines that maintained power by giving and taking bribes in return for favors. Perhaps the most notorious example was New York's Tweed Ring led by William Tweed, boss of the Democratic Tammany Hall machine. In 1869 bribery reached new heights when Tweed managed to bribe the New York State legislature into passing a new charter which entrenched the Tweed Ring in power. Maintaining its power through graft and intimidation, the Tweed Ring was finally exposed in 1871. Tweed and many of his coconspirators were sent to prison.

THE PANIC OF 1873

A nation racked by scandal also went through a disastrous economic decline during Grant's second term. Since 1850 the economy of the North and West had grown steadily. During the boom years following the Civil War the growth rate had accelerated: thousands of new businesses were started and railroads were built to link the various regions of an expanding economy. By 1871, however, the economy had clearly overextended itself. Expansion had occurred too rapidly and the new businesses and railroads found themselves without the markets they needed to survive. Rapid expansion had also caused imports to outstrip exports, creating a drain on the nation's gold reserves. These factors combined to create a severe decline in the economy. By 1872 over four thousand businesses had failed. In September 1873 the foremost banking firm in America, Jay Cooke and Company, declared bankruptcy. Its failure triggered a chain reaction of additional business failures. By the end of the year more than five thousand commercial firms and nearly ninety railroads had failed. One-half million workers were soon out of jobs. The hard times that began in 1873 were to continue until almost the end of the decade.

THE ELECTION OF 1876

The scandals of the Grant years had cost the Republicans control of the House of Representatives in the 1874 elections. President Grant's popularity had also been badly eroded by cor-

"Panic, as a Health Officer, Sweeping the Garbage out of Wall Street," comments on the causes of the Panic of 1873.

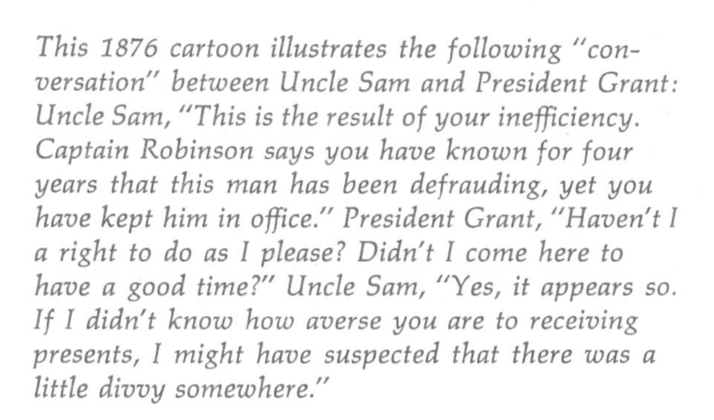
This 1876 cartoon illustrates the following "conversation" between Uncle Sam and President Grant: Uncle Sam, "This is the result of your inefficiency. Captain Robinson says you have known for four years that this man has been defrauding, yet you have kept him in office." President Grant, "Haven't I a right to do as I please? Didn't I come here to have a good time?" Uncle Sam, "Yes, it appears so. If I didn't know how averse you are to receiving presents, I might have suspected that there was a little divvy somewhere."

ruption (now known as "Grantism") and the depression, but many Republicans still supported him and wanted him in 1876 for a third term. The president's supporters, known as the "Stalwarts," were opposed by the "Halfbreeds," Republicans who claimed to be reformers although they had remained loyal to the party in 1872. At the Republican convention the Halfbreeds supported the nomination of Speaker of the House James G. Blaine of Maine. Blaine, however, had been accused of dispensing favors to several railroads. In the end the Republicans

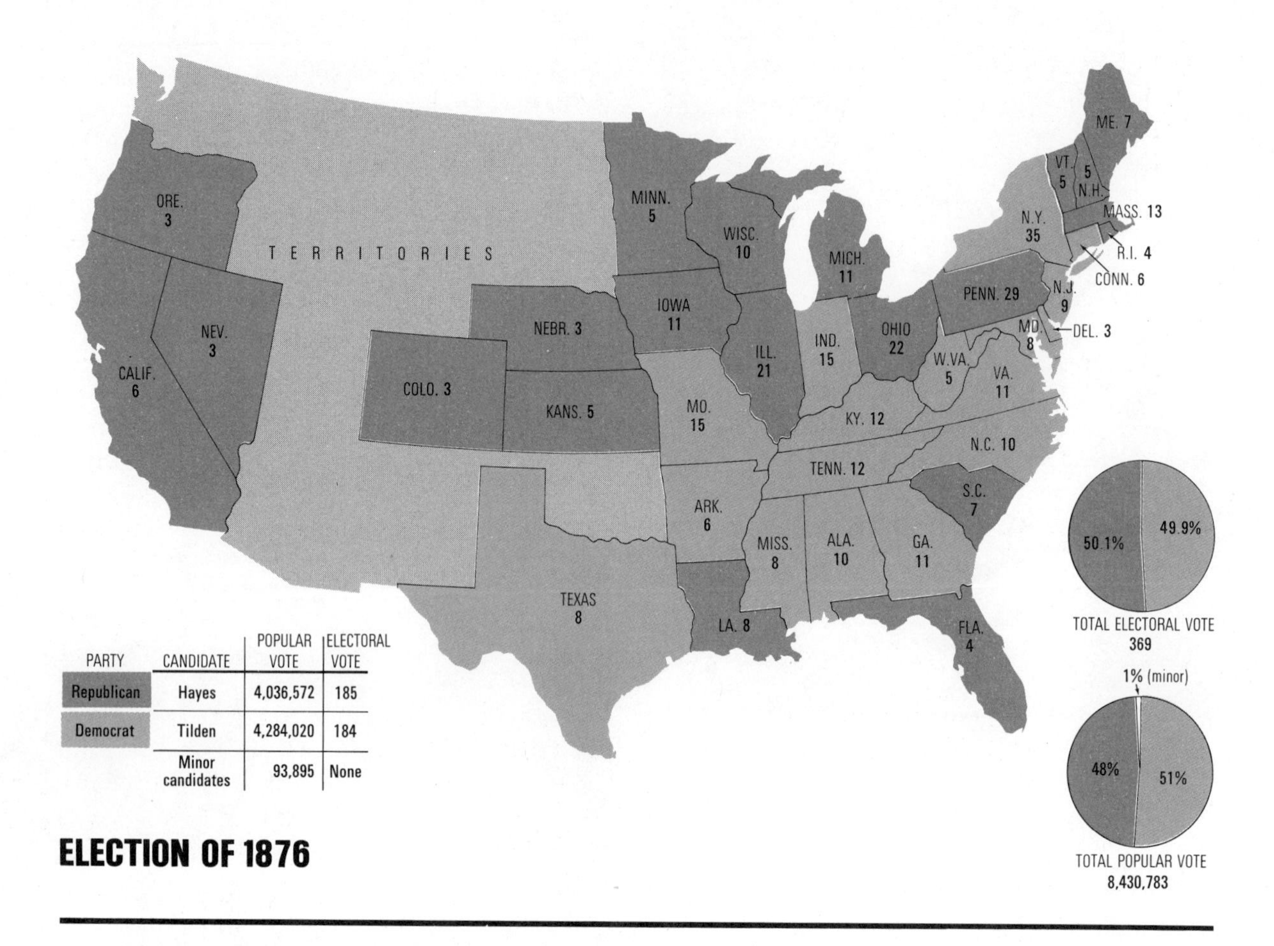

PARTY	CANDIDATE	POPULAR VOTE	ELECTORAL VOTE
Republican	Hayes	4,036,572	185
Democrat	Tilden	4,284,020	184
	Minor candidates	93,895	None

ELECTION OF 1876

voted to avoid all taint of scandal and nominated the untarnished, if undramatic, Rutherford B. Hayes, three times governor of Ohio.

The Democrats, also reacting against corruption in government, nominated Governor Samuel Tilden of New York. A conservative corporation lawyer and millionaire, Tilden had been instrumental in breaking up the Tweed Ring and exposing another scandal, the New York State Canal Ring.

No clear issues divided the candidates. Both called for an end to Reconstruction (still in force in three Southern states), both avoided a stand on the tariff issue, and both called for civil service reform to end corruption in government. In the absence of substantive issues, the Republicans again "waved the bloody shirt." "Soldiers," a prominent Republican told a rally of Union War veterans, "every scar you have on your heroic bodies was given you by a Democrat." In response, Democratic speakers branded the Republicans as the party of lawlessness and corruption.

On the morning after the election the outcome was still undecided. Although Tilden had carried four Northern states as well as the solid South, and had a popular majority of two hundred thousand votes, the returns from Florida, South Carolina, Louisiana, and one electoral vote from Oregon were still in dispute. Nevertheless, Tilden needed only one of the twenty outstanding electoral votes to win, and it seemed that a

Democrat would soon occupy the White House for the first time since 1856. The real winner remains unknown since both Republican and Democratic election supervisors in the disputed states filed returns claiming that their candidate had won.

To solve a dilemma for which there was no remedy provided by the Constitution, Congress appointed a commission to investigate the disputed returns and award them to the rightful winner. The commission was initially made up of seven Democrats, seven Republicans, and one Independent, but at the last minute the Independent was disqualified and replaced by a Republican. In a straight party vote the commission awarded all of the disputed electoral returns, and therefore the presidency, to Hayes. But it took further negotiation and compromise before Hayes could take office.

Although they had lost the battle for the disputed presidency, the Democrats still had a high card left to play. The Republicans feared that the Democrats would stage a filibuster in the Senate and prevent the commission from reporting its findings. Using a threat of a filibuster as leverage, the Democrats secured a Republican promise to, among other things, remove all remaining federal troops from the South.

The Republicans had more than the presidency at stake. They knew that when the Reconstruction governments fell they could no longer count on the Southern black vote, and the South would be lost to the Democrats. They therefore welcomed the opportunity to attract white Southerners to the Republican camp. They were willing to agree not only to end the military occupation of the South, but to other Democratic demands as well. They would return control of federal patronage in the South to Southerners, work for federal support for the Texas and Pacific Railroad, and include at least one Southerner in Hayes' new cabinet. In return for these additional concessions, the Democrats agreed to support the election of a Republican Speaker of the House, even though they controlled the chamber. Now Hayes moved into the White House without opposition. And the last federal troops were withdrawn from the South in April 1877. The Democrats, however, did not elect a Republican Speaker, and Hayes was not able to provide the promised railroad funds.

The South After Reconstruction

With the end of Reconstruction control of Southern politics was returned to Southerners. State governments fell into the hands of the old planter aristocracy and the equally-conservative new business class, called the "Bourbons" after the French royal house. The new ruling elite immediately took steps to ensure its continued political, social, and economic dominance.

Within twenty years after the end of Reconstruction had deprived blacks of Radical Republican protection, Southern state governments acted to ensure the segregation of the races. They were aided by the United States Supreme Court. In 1883 the Supreme Court declared unconstitutional an 1875 Civil Rights Act which had guaranteed all citizens "full and equal enjoyment" of public places. The Court's opinion declared that Congress had no jurisdiction over discrimination by private individuals and private organizations. In its 1896 decision (*Plessy* v. *Ferguson*) the Court further declared that railroad cars could be segregated as long as blacks were provided with "separate but equal" facilities. This decision also provided the constitutional rationale for segregated schools for the next fifty years.

Plessy *v.* Ferguson

"A statute which implies merely a legal distinction between the white and colored races . . . has no tendency to destroy the legal equality of the two races, or reestablish a state of involuntary servitude. . . .

Laws permitting, and even requiring, their separation in places where they are liable to be brought into contact do not necessarily imply the inferiority of either race to the other, and have been generally, if not universally, recognized as within the competency of the state legislatures in the exercise of their police power. The most common instance of this is connected with the establishment of separate schools for white and colored children, which has been held to be a valid exercise of the legislative power even by courts of states where the political rights of the colored race have been longest and most earnestly enforced. . . .

If the two races are to meet upon terms of social equality, it must be the result of natural affinities, a mutual appreciation of each other's merits and a voluntary consent of individuals. . . . If one race be inferior to the other socially, the Constitution of the United States cannot put them upon the same plane. . . ."

The United States Supreme Court,
1896

Plessy *v.* Ferguson: *Dissenting Opinion*

"Every one knows that the statute in question had its origin in the purpose, not so much to exclude white persons from railroad cars occupied by blacks, as to exclude colored people from coaches occupied by or assigned to white persons. . . . The fundamental objection, therefore, to the statute is that it interferes with the personal freedom of citizens. . . . If a white man and a black man choose to occupy the same public conveyance on a public highway, it is their right to do so, and no government, proceeding alone on grounds of race, can prevent it without infringing the personal liberty of each. . . .

In the view of the Constitution, in the eye of the law, there is in this country no superior, dominant, ruling class of citizens. There is no caste here. Our Constitution is color-blind, and neither knows nor tolerates classes among citizens. In respect of civil rights, all citizens are equal before the law. The humblest is the peer of the most powerful. The law regards man as man, and takes no account of his surroundings or of his color when his civil rights as guaranteed by the supreme law of the land are involved. . . ."

Justice John Marshall Harlan,
1896

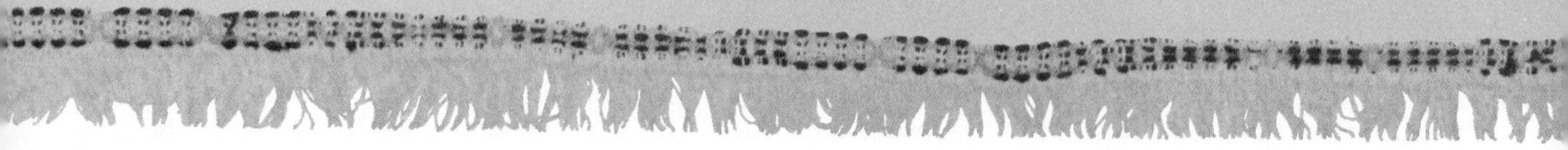

One of the leaders of the Populist party, John Painter, and his family and friends pose outside Painter's house in Broken Bow, Nebraska.

Although the planters and the Bourbons believed in segregation and the doctrine of white supremacy, they made no immediate attempt to deprive blacks of their right to vote. Recognizing that the black vote could help them, the Bourbons shrewdly courted black support to offset the opposition of poor whites to the dominance of the new Southern aristocracy.

In the late 1880s and early 1890s, however, a severe agricultural depression changed the Bourbon strategy by triggering the emergence of a new political movement. Poor whites realized that they and poor blacks were equally victimized by the economic control of the Bourbon group. Under the banner of the Populist party, a coalition of poor blacks and poor whites developed throughout the South.

Conservative white Democrats in the South were understandably alarmed by the emergence of Populism since it threatened to undermine their dominance in Southern politics. The Bourbons and the planters therefore began appealing to white Populists on the basis of race, calling for unity against the blacks. Their pleas were heeded and a new coalition by Bourbons and poor farmers developed, dedicated to white supremacy.

Now that the black vote was no longer useful to them, Southern Democrats moved to disenfranchise their former slaves. Southern legislatures enacted a host of technical qualifications for voting. The new requirements were designed to prevent blacks from voting without violating the Fifteenth Amendment, which prohibited disenfranchisement based on race. Several states required the payment of poll taxes, which most black people could not afford. Other states enacted "grandfather clauses," guaranteeing the right to vote only to those whose ancestors had voted before the Civil War. In 1898 the Supreme Court upheld these requirements. In *Williams* v. *Mississippi* the Court declared that since these laws did not "on their face discriminate between the races," they did not violate the Fifteenth Amendment, and were therefore legal.

The new Bourbon strategy had worked. Poor whites had been drawn into the Bourbon camp by the call for white unity and blacks had been deprived of the right to vote. Those whites who did not cooperate were kept away from the polls by the same technical restrictions used against the blacks. The populist movement collapsed. The new coalition in control of Southern politics would ensure the outcome of elections for years to come.

AGRICULTURE

Black people's economic situation was no better than their political situation. The South's postwar agricultural system victimized poor whites and poor blacks alike. During Reconstruction plantation owners without money could not pay wages to their newly freed slaves. Poor farmers therefore became tenants on small plots on the old plantations. The planters paid no wages and the tenants paid no rent. Each agreed to share the profits of the forthcoming crop. The plantation owner provided food, seed, tools, and animals to the tenant farmer, commonly called a sharecropper. When the crop came in, the sharecropper would usually receive one-half of the profit, and the landowner the other half.

Many plantation owners had been so devastated by the war and the conditions it produced that they could not even afford to pay for the sharecropper's supplies. They would often turn to the local merchant for help and both planter and sharecropper often became indebted to the merchant who would demand that the most marketable crop—cotton—be planted. Although the crop-lien system, as it came to be known, revived Southern agriculture, it also kept the South a one-crop economy and prevented the introduction of technological advances in farming. It also kept thousands of sharecroppers living in submarginal economic conditions.

With much of the fruits of their labor going to the plantation owner and the local merchant, sharecroppers were barely able to eke out a living. Black sharecroppers, who comprised nearly seventy-five percent of the black population, were little better off than they had been as slaves.

As a result, many blacks felt that it was more realistic and more important for them to seek economic security than political equality. They called for an emphasis on manual labor, vocational education, and subsistence farming. In 1895 the distinguished black educator, Booker T. Washington, suggested exactly that in a speech delivered in Atlanta that became known as the Atlanta Compromise. "The wisest among my race," said Washington, "understand that the agitation of questions of social equality is the extremest folly. . . . It is important and right that all privileges of the law be ours, but it is vastly more important that we be prepared for the exercises of these privileges. The opportunity to earn a dollar in a factory just now is worth infinitely more than the opportunity to spend a dollar in an opera-house." Many whites applauded and wholeheartedly supported the concept embodied in the Atlanta Compromise.

Yet many blacks were not willing to wait for political equality in order to achieve economic security. There were many, in fact, who thought that one was not possible without the other. In 1903 W. E. B. Du Bois, the first black to receive a Ph.D. from Harvard, asked, "Are we going to induce the best class of Negroes to take less and less interest in government, and to give up their daily right to take such an interest, without a protest? . . . Daily the Negro is coming more and more to look upon law and justice, not as protecting safeguards, but as sources of humiliation and oppression."

Interpreting Reconstruction

It was not until the 1890s that the first important historical perspectives on Reconstruction appeared. In *Reconstruction, Political and Economic,* William A. Dunning argued that Reconstruction had deprived Southern whites of their rightful control of Southern life and had given it to ignorant freedmen and unscrupulous carpetbaggers and scalawags. Central to Dunning's interpretation was his belief, much in vogue at that time, in the biological inferiority of blacks.

By the 1930s a new school of historians had emerged which rejected Dunning's perspective. Historians such as Francis B. Simkins, Robert Woody, and C. Vann Woodward contended that blacks had played a relatively minor role in Reconstruction politics. Corruption under Radical Reconstruction regimes was no worse than in the North at the same time and was less prevalent than in the Southern Bourbon regimes that followed. The real struggle of Reconstruction, these Revisionist historians claimed, was the economic conflict between the business and financial interests of the North represented by the Radicals and the old agrarian interests of the South.

In the 1950s a third historical interpretation of Reconstruction developed. This Neo-revisionist interpretation emphasized the moral issue of racial equality as the central theme of the Reconstruction struggle. Its proponents included R. P. Sharkey, Eric L. McKitrick, LaWanda and John Cox, and Kenneth M. Stampp. In general they held that the Reconstruction era was a tragedy. McKitrick argued that Reconstruction was a failure because efforts to achieve racial equality created intense hostility in the minds of the white South. Stampp, on the other hand, maintained that if the white South had been forced to accept racial equality long enough, it would ultimately have acquiesced in it. In part, following this same line of argument, the Coxes stressed that the major flaw of Reconstruction policy was the failure to give the freedmen land.

Readings

GENERAL WORKS

Buck, Paul H., *The Road to Reunion, 1865–1900.* Boston: Little, Brown, 1937.

Cash, Wilbur J., *The Mind of the South.* New York: Knopf, 1960.

Cruden, Robert, *The Negro in Reconstruction.* Englewood Cliffs, N.J.: Prentice-Hall, 1969.

Donald, David, *The Politics of Reconstruction.* Baton Rouge: Louisiana State University Press, 1965.

Du Bois, William E. B., *Black Reconstruction in America, 1860–1880.* New York: Atheneum, 1969.

Franklin, John H., *Reconstruction After the Civil War.* Chicago: University of Chicago Press, 1961.

Patrick, Rembert W., *The Reconstruction of the Nation.* New York: Oxford University Press, 1967.

Randall, James G., and David Donald, *The Civil War and Reconstruction.* Boston: Heath, 1961.

Stampp, Kenneth M., *The Era of Reconstruction 1865–1877.* New York: Knopf, 1965.

Trefousse, Hans L., *The Radical Republicans: Lincoln's Vanguard for Racial Justice.* New York: Knopf, 1969.

SPECIAL STUDIES

Bentley, G. R., *A History of the Freedmen's Bureau.* New York: Octagon, 1970.

Cox, La Wanda, and John H. Cox, *Politics, Principle and Prejudice, 1865–66.* New York: Free Press, 1963.

Gillette, William, *The Right to Vote: Politics and the Passage of the Fifteenth Amendment.* Baltimore: Johns Hopkins Press, 1965.

James, Joseph B., *The Framing of the Fourteenth Amendment.* Urbana: University of Illinois Press, 1956.

Logan, Rayford W., *The Negro in American Life and Thought: The Nadir 1877–1901.* New York: Macmillan, 1965.

McKitrick, Eric L., *Andrew Johnson and Reconstruction.* Chicago: University of Chicago Press, 1960.

McPherson, James M., *The Struggle for Equality: Abolitionists and the Negro in the Civil War and Reconstruction.* Princeton, N.J.: Princeton University Press, 1964.

Meier, August, *Negro Thought in America, 1880–1915: Racial Ideologies in the Age of Booker T. Washington.* Ann Arbor: University of Michigan Press, 1963. (Paper)

Nolen, Claude H., *The Negro's Image in the South: The Anatomy of White Supremacy.* Lexington: University Press of Kentucky, 1967. (Paper)

Trelease, Allen W., *The White Terror: The Ku Klux Klan Conspiracy and Southern Reconstruction,* Kenneth B. Clark (Ed.). New York: Harper & Row, 1971.

Wharton, Vernon L., *The Negro in Mississippi, 1865–1869.* New York: Harper & Row, 1965.

Williamson, Joel, *After Slavery: The Negro in South Carolina During Reconstruction, 1861–1877.* Chapel Hill: University of North Carolina Press, 1965.

Woodward, C. Vann, *Reunion and Reaction: The Compromise of 1877 and the End of Reconstruction.* Boston: Little, Brown, 1966.

Woodward, C. Vann, *The Strange Career of Jim Crow.* New York: Oxford University Press, 1966.

PRIMARY SOURCES

Current, Richard N. (Ed.), *Reconstruction, 1865–1877.* Englewood Cliffs, N.J.: Prentice-Hall, 1965.

Meier, August, *Negro Thought in America, 1880–1915.* Ann Arbor: University of Michigan Press, 1963.

Reid, Whitelaw, *After the War: A Tour of the Southern States, 1865–1866.* New York: Harper & Row, 1965.

Shenton, James P., *The Reconstruction, A Documentary History: 1865–1877.* New York: Putnam, 1963.

Turner, Arlin (Ed.), *The Negro Question: A Selection of the Writings on Civil Rights in the South by George W. Cable.* Garden City, N.Y.: Doubleday, 1958.

Washington, Booker T., *Up from Slavery.* New York: Bantam, 1970.

BIOGRAPHIES

Brodie, Fawn M., *Thaddeus Stevens: Scourge of the South.* New York: Norton, 1959.

Donald, David, *Charles Sumner and the Rights of Man.* New York: Knopf, 1970.

Hesseltine, William B., *Ulysses S. Grant: Politician.* New York: Ungar, 1957.

Lomask, Milton, *Andrew Johnson: President on Trial.* New York: Farrar, Straus & Giroux, 1960.

McFeely, William S., *Yankee Stepfather: General O. O. Howard and the Freedmen.* New Haven, Conn.: Yale University Press, 1968.

Van Deusen, Glyndon, *Horace Greeley: Nineteenth-Century Crusader.* Philadelphia: University of Pennsylvania Press, 1953.

FICTION

Faulkner, William, *Go Down, Moses.* New York: Random House, 1942.

Faulkner, William, *The Hamlet.* New York: Random House, 1940.

APPENDIX

Further Readings

CHAPTER 1

Beer, George L., *The Old Colonial System*, 2 volumes. Gloucester, Mass.: Peter Smith; Beer, George L., *The Origins of The British Colonial System*. Gloucester, Mass.: Peter Smith; Brandon, William, *The American Heritage Book of Indians*. New York: Dell, 1961; Byrne, M. St. Clare, *Elizabethan Life in Town and Country*. New York: Barnes & Noble, 1961; Enterline, James Robert, *Viking America: The Norse Crossings and their Legacy*. New York: Doubleday, 1972; Horgan, Paul, *Conquistadors in North American History*. New York: Farrar, Straus and Giroux, 1936. (Paper: Fawcett, 1969); Mason, J. Alden, *The Ancient Civilization of Peru*. Baltimore: Penguin, 1957; Notestein, Wallace, *The English People on the Eve of Colonization*. New York: Harper & Row Torchbooks, 1954; Parry, J. H., *The Spanish Seaborne Empire*. New York: Knopf, 1966; Reynolds, Robert L., *Europe Emerges: Transition Toward an Industrial World-Wide Society*. Madison, Wis.: University of Wisconsin Press, 1961.

CHAPTER 2

Greven, Philip J., Jr., *Four Generations: Population, Land and Family in Colonial Andover, Massachusetts*. New York: Cornell University Press, 1970. (Paper); Lankgord, John (Ed.), *Captain John Smith's America: Selections from his Writings*. New York: Harper & Row, 1967; Leach, Douglas E., *Flintlock and Tomahawk: New England in King Philip's War*. New York: Norton, 1966. (Paper); Lockridge, Kenneth A., *New England Town: The First Hundred Years*. New York: Norton, 1970; Middleton, Arthur Pierce, *Tobacco Coast: A Maritime History of Chesapeake Bay in the Colonial Era*. George Carrington Mason (Ed.), Newport News, Va.: Mariners' Museum, 1953; Morgan, Edmund S., *Visible Saints*. New York: New York University Press, 1963. (Paper: Cornell University Press, 1970); Nettels, Curtis P., *The Roots of American Civilization*. New York: Appleton-Century-Crofts, 1963; Powell, Sumner C., *Puritan Village: The Formation of a New England Town*. Middletown, Conn.: Wesleyan University Press, 1963. (Paper); Rutman, Darrett B., *American Puritanism: Faith and Practice*. Philadelphia: Lippincott, 1970. (Paper); Rutman, Darrett B., *Winthrop's Boston: A Portrait of a Puritan Town, 1630–1649*. New York: Norton, 1965. (Paper); Smith, Bradford, *Captain John Smith*. Philadelphia: Lippincott, 1953; Wertenbaker, T. J., *The First Americans*. New York: Macmillan, 1927; Willison, George E., *Behold Virginia*. New York: Harcourt Brace Jovanovich, 1951.

CHAPTER 3

Bailyn, Bernard, *Education in the Forming of American Society: Needs and Opportunities for Study*. Chapel Hill: University of North Carolina Press, 1960. (Paper: Random House, 1962); Bonomi, Patricia U., *Factious People: Politics and Society in Colonial New York*. New York: Columbia University Press, 1971. (Paper); Bridenbaugh, Carl, *The Colonial Craftsman*. Chicago: University of Chicago Press, 1950; Bushman, Richard L., *From Puritan to Yankee: Character and Social Order in Connecticut, 1690–1765*. Cambridge, Mass.: Harvard University Press, 1967 (Paper: Norton, 1970); Craven, Wesley F., *White, Red and Black: The Seventeenth Century Virginian*. Charlottesville: University Press of Virginia, 1971; Cunliffe, Marcus, *The Literature of the United States*. Baltimore: Penguin, 1954; Curtin, Philip D., *Atlantic Slave Trade: A Census*. Madison: University of Wisconsin Press, 1969. (Paper); Franklin, John H., *From Slavery to Freedom: A History of Negro Americans*.

New York: Random, 1969. (Paper); Hall, M. G., L. H. Leder, and M. G. Kammen (Eds.), *The Glorious Revolution in America: Documents on the Colonial Crisis of 1689.* Chapel Hill: University of North Carolina Press, 1964; Hindle, Brook, *The Pursuit of Science in Revolutionary America, 1735–1789.* Chapel Hill: University of North Carolina Press, 1956; Meier, August, and Elliot Rudwick, *From Plantation to Ghetto.* New York: Hill & Wang, 1970. (Paper); Merritt, R. L., *Symbols of American Community, 1735–1775.* New Haven, Conn.: Yale University Press, 1966; Mullin, Gerald W., *Flight and Rebellion: Slave Resistance in Eighteenth Century Virginia.* New York: Oxford University Press, 1972. (Paper).

CHAPTER 4

Bowen, Catherine D., *John Adams and the American Revolution.* New York: Grosset & Dunlap, 1957. (Paper); Dickerson, Oliver M., *The Navigation Acts and the American Revolution.* New York: Octagon, 1974; Fithian, Philip V., *Journal and Letters of Philip V. Fithian, 1773–1774: A Plantation Tutor at the Old Dominion.* Charlottesville: University Press of Virginia, 1968; Ketchum, Richard M. and American Heritage Editors, *The World of George Washington.* New York: McGraw-Hill, 1974; Labaree, Leonard Woods, *Royal Government in America.* New Haven: Yale University Press, 1930; Morison, Samuel E., *John Paul Jones: A Sailor's Biography.* Boston: Little, Brown, 1959; Namier, Lewis B., *England in the Age of the American Revolution.* New York: St. Martin's Press, 1961; Nash, Gary B., *Quakers and Politics: Pennsylvania, 1681–1726.* Princeton, N.J.: Princeton University Press, 1968; Trevelyan, George O., *The American Revolution,* Richard B. Morris, (Ed.). New York: David McKay, 1964; Washington, George, *Journal of Major George Washington,* James R. Short and Thaddeus W. Tate, Jr., (Eds.). Charlottesville: University Press of Virginia, 1963.

CHAPTER 5

Chinard, Gilbert, *Thomas Jefferson: The Apostle of Americanism.* Ann Arbor: University of Michigan Press, 1957; Dodge, Ernest S., *New England and the South Seas.* Cambridge, Mass.: Harvard University Press, 1965; Ketchum, Richard M., *The Winter Soldiers.* Garden City, N.Y.: Doubleday, 1973; Nevins, Allan, *American States During and After the Revolution, 1775–1798.* Clifton, N.J.: Kelley; Whitaker, Arthur P., *The Spanish-American Frontier: 1783–1795; The Westward Movement and the Spanish Retreat in the Mississippi Valley.* Boston: Houghton Mifflin, 1927 (Paper: University of Nebraska Press, 1969).

CHAPTER 6

Ammon, Harry, *The Genet Mission.* New York: Norton, 1973. (Paper); Beard, Charles A., *Economic Interpretation of the Constitution of the United States.* New York: Free Press, 1965 (Paper); Boorstein, Daniel J., *Lost World of Thomas Jefferson.* Gloucester, Mass.: Peter Smith, 1960. (Paper); Bowers, Claude G., *Jefferson and Hamilton.* Boston: Houghton Mifflin, 1925; Boyd, Julian P., *Number Seven: Alexander Hamilton's Secret Attempts to Control American Foreign Policy.* Princeton, N.J.: Princeton University Press, 1964; Brown, Robert E., *Charles Beard and the Constitution.* New York: Norton, 1965. (Paper); Buel, Richard, *Securing the Revolution: Ideology in American Politics 1789–1815.* New York: Cornell University Press, 1972. (Paper); Clarfield, Gerald H., *Timothy Pickering and American Diplomacy, 1795–1800.* Columbia: University of Missouri Press, 1969; Cooke, Jacob E., (Ed.), *The Reports of Alexander Hamilton.* New York: Harper & Row, 1964; Farrand, Max, *Framing of the Constitution of the United States.* New Haven, Conn.: Yale University Press, 1913. (Paper); Goebel, Julius, Jr., *History of the Supreme Court, Vol. I: Antecedents and Beginnings to 1800.* Roberts, Roy (Ed.). New York: Macmillan, 1971; Hazen, Charles D., *Contemporary American Opinion of the French Revolution.* Baltimore: Johns Hopkins Press, 1897; Hills, Peter P., *William Vans Murray, Federalist Diplomat: The Shaping of Peace with France.* New York: Syracuse University Press, 1971; Koch, Adrienne, *Philosophy of Thomas Jefferson.* New York: Quadrangle, 1964. (Paper); Lycan, Gilbert L., *Alexander Hamilton and American Foreign Policy: A Design for Greatness.* Oklahoma: University of Oklahoma Press, 1970. Lynd, Staughton (Ed.), *Class Conflict, Slavery and the United States Constitution: Ten Essays.* New York: Bobbs-Merrill, 1967. (Paper); Miller, John C., *Crisis in Freedom.* Boston: Little, Brown, 1964; McLaughlin, Andrew C., *Confederation and the Constitution 1783–1789.* Gloucester, Mass.: Peter Smith, 1905; Murphy, William, *The Triumph of Nationalism: State Sovereignty, the Founding Fathers, and the Making of the Constitution.* New York: Quadrangle, 1968; Rutland, Robert A., *Ordeal of the Constitution: The Antifederalists and the Ratification Struggle of 1787–1788.* Norman: University of Oklahoma Press, 1966; Smith, Charles P., *James Wilson, Founding Father: 1742–1798.* Westport, Conn.: Greenwood, 1973; Stourzh, Gerald, *Alexander Hamilton and the Idea of Republican Government.* California: Stanford University Press, 1970; Warren, C., *The Making of the Constitution.* Boston: Little, Brown, 1928; Whitaker, Arthur P., *The Mississippi Question, 1795–1803.* Gloucester, Mass.: Peter Smith, 1962; White, Leonard, *The Federalists: A Study in Administrative History.* New York: Macmillan, 1945; Wright, Benjamin

F., *Consensus and Continuity, 1776–1787.* New York: Norton, 1967. (Paper).

CHAPTER 7

Bowers, Claude G., *Jefferson in Power.* Boston: Houghton Mifflin, 1936; Brant, Irving, *The Fourth President: The Life of James Madison.* New York: Bobbs-Merrill; Brodie, Fawn M., *Thomas Jefferson: An Intimate History.* New York: Norton, 1974; Corwin, Edward, *John Marshall and the Constitution.* New Haven, Conn.: Yale University Press, 1919; Cunliffe, Marcus, *The Nation Takes Shape: 1789–1837.* Chicago: University of Chicago Press, 1959; Engelman, F. L., *The Peace of Christmas Eve.* New York: Harcourt Brace Jovanovich, 1962; Kirk, Russell, *Randolph of Roanoke: A Study in Conservative Thought.* Chicago: University of Chicago Press, 1951; Rich, E. E., *The Fur Trade and the Northwest to 1857.* Buffalo, New York: McClelland & Stewart, 1967; Schachner, Nathan, *Thomas Jefferson: A Biography,* Vols. I–II. New York: Appleton-Century-Crofts, 1951; VanEvery, Dale, *Ark of Empire, The American Frontier, 1784–1803.* New York: Morrow, 1963.

CHAPTER 8

Bruchey, Stuart, *The Roots of American Economic Growth, 1607–1861.* New York: Harper & Row, 1965; Cresson, William P., *James Monroe.* Chapel Hill: University of North Carolina Press, 1946; Faulkner, Harold U., *American Economic History.* New York: Harper & Row, 1960; Shannon, Fred A., *America's Economic Growth.* New York: Macmillan, 1951.

CHAPTER 9

Brown, Norman D., *Daniel Webster and the Politics of Availability.* Athens, Georgia: University of Georgia Press, 1969; Mudge, Eugene T., *The Social Philosophy of John Taylor of Caroline.* New York: Columbia University Press, 1939.

CHAPTER 10

McGrane, Reginald C., *The Panic of 1837.* Chicago: University of Chicago Press, 1924; Pessen, Edward (Ed.), *New Perspectives on Jacksonian Parties and Politics.* Boston: Allyn & Bacon, 1969; Wiltse, Charles M., *The New Nation, 1800–1845.* New York: Hill & Wang, 1961.

CHAPTER 11

Aptheker, Herbert, *American Negro Slave Revolts.* New York: Columbia University Press, 1943; Aptheker, Herbert (Ed.), *A Documentary History of the Negro People in the United States.* New York: Citadel Press, 1910; Berlin, Ira, *Slaves Without Masters: The Free Negro in the Antebellum South.* New York: Pantheon, 1974; Conrad, Alfred H., and John R. Meyer, *The Economics of Slavery and Other Studies in Econometric History.* Chicago: Aldine, 1964; Craven, Avery O., *Edmund Ruffin, Southerner.* New York: Appleton, 1932; Curti, Merle, *The Making of an American Community: A Case Study of Democracy in a Frontier County.* Stanford, Calif.: Stanford University Press, 1959. (Paper); Fishel, Leslie H., Jr., and Benjamin Quarles, *The Black American: A Documentary History.* Glenview, Illinois: Scott-Foresman, 1970. (Paper); Fogel, Robert W., *Railroads and American Economic Growth.* Baltimore: Johns Hopkins Press, 1964; Gara, Larry, *The Liberty Line: The Legend of The Underground Railroad.* Lexington: University Press of Kentucky, 1967. (Paper); Gray, Lewis C., *History of Agriculture in the Southern United States to 1860, Vols. I–II.* Washington, D.C.: Carnegie Institution, 1933; Handlin, Oscar, *Boston's Immigrants: A Study of Acculturation.* Cambridge, Mass.: Harvard University Press, 1959; Jordan, Winthrop, *The White Man's Burden.* New York: Oxford University Press, 1974. (Paper); Knights, Peter R., *The Plain People of Boston, 1830–1860: A Study in City Growth.* New York: Oxford University Press, 1973. (Paper); Lane, Ann J. (Ed.), *The Debate Over Slavery: Stanley Elkins and his Critics.* Urbana: University of Illinois Press, 1971. (Paper); Litwack, Leon F., *North of Slavery: The Negro in the Free States, 1790–1860.* Chicago: University of Chicago Press, 1961. (Paper); Mitchell, Broadus, *William Gregg, Factory Master of the Old South.* Chapel Hill: University of North Carolina Press, 1928; Neu, Irene D., *Erastus Corning, Merchant and Financier.* Ithaca, N.Y.: Cornell University Press, 1960; Pelling, Henry, *American Labor.* Chicago: University of Chicago Press, 1960; Smith, Henry N., *Virgin Land.* Cambridge, Mass.: Harvard University Press, 1950; Starobin, Robert, *Industrial Slavery in the Old South.* New York: Oxford University Press, 1970. (Paper); Sydnor, Charles S., *The Development of Southern Sectionalism.* Baton Rouge: Louisiana State University Press, 1948; Weinstein, Allen, and Frank O. Gatell (Eds.), *American Negro Slavery: A Modern Reader,* New York: Oxford University Press, 1973.

CHAPTER 12

Barnes, Gilbert H., *The Anti-Slavery Impulse, 1830–1844.* Gloucester, Mass.: Peter Smith, 1933. (Paper: Harcourt Brace Jovanovich, 1964); Cover, Robert, *Justice Accused: Anti-Slavery and the Judicial Process.* New Haven, Conn.: Yale University Press, 1975; Gusfield, Joseph R., *Symbolic Crusade: Status Politics and the American Temperance Movement.* Urbana: University of Illinois Press, 1966. (Paper); Howe, D. W., *The Unitarian Conscience: Harvard Moral Philosophy, 1805–1861.* Cambridge, Mass.: Harvard University Press, 1970; Katz, Michael B., *The Irony of Early School Reform: Education Innovation in Mid-Nineteenth Century Massachusetts.* Cambridge, Mass.: Harvard University Press, 1968. (Paper: Beacon Press, 1970); Muncy, Raymond Lee, *Sex and Marriage in Utopian Communities: 19th Century America.* Bloomington: Indiana University Press, 1973. (Paper: Penguin, 1974); Osterweis, Rolin G., *Romanticism and Nationalism in the Old South.* Gloucester, Mass.: Peter Smith. (Paper: Louisiana State University Press, 1967); Rudolph, Frederick, *The American College and University.* New York: Knopf, 1967; Scott, Anne F., *The Southern Lady: From Pedestal to Politics, 1830–1930.* Chicago: University of Chicago Press, 1970. (Paper); Sorin, Gerald, *Abolitionism: A New Perspective.* New York: Praeger, 1972. (Paper); Sweet, William W., *The Story of Religion in America.* New York: Harper, 1930; Taylor, William B., *Cavalier and Yankee.* New York: Braziller, 1961; Thomas, Benjamin P., *Theodore Weld: Crusader for Freedom.* New Brunswick, N.J.: Rutgers University Press, 1950; Van Doren, Mark, *Nathaniel Hawthorne.* New York: William Sloane, 1949.

CHAPTER 13

Connor, Seymour V. and Odie B. Faulk, *North America Divided: The Mexican War, 1846–1848.* New York: Oxford University Press, 1971; Hawgood, John A., *America's Western Frontiers.* New York: Knopf, 1967; Rayback, Joseph G., *Free Soil: The Election of 1848.* Lexington: University Press of Kentucky, 1970.

CHAPTER 14

Alexander, Thomas B., *Sectional Stress and Party Strength: A Computer Analysis of Roll-Call Voting Patterns in the United States House of Representatives, 1836–1860.* Nashville, Tennessee: Vanderbilt University Press, 1967; Blue, Frederick J., *The Free Soilers: Third Party Politics, 1848–54.* Urbana: University of Illinois Press, 1973; Boyer, Richard O., *The Legend of John Brown: A Biography and a History.* New York: Knopf, 1973; Campbell, Stanley W., *Slave Catchers: Enforcement of the Fugitive Slave Law, 1850–1860.* Chapel Hill: University of North Carolina Press, 1970. (Paper: Norton, 1972); Davis, David B., *The Slave Power Conspiracy and the Paranoid Style.* Baton Rouge: Louisiana State University Press, 1970; Isely, Jeter A., *Horace Greeley and the Republican Party, 1853–1861.* New York: Octagon, 1965; Luebke, Frederick C. (Ed.), *Ethnic Voters and the Election of Lincoln.* Lincoln: University of Nebraska Press, 1971; Nevins, Allan, and M. H. Thomas (Eds.), *The Diary of George Templeton Strong,* Vols. I–IV. New York: Macmillan, 1952; Potter, David M., *The South and the Concurrent Majority,* Fehrenbacher, Don E., and Degler, Carl N. (Eds.). Baton Rouge: Louisiana State University Press, 1972; Pressly, Thomas J., *Americans Interpret Their Civil War.* New York: Free Press, 1965. (Paper); Silbey, Joel, *The Shrine of Party: Congressional Voting Behavior 1841–1852.* Pittsburgh, Penn.: University of Pittsburgh Press, 1967; Simms, H. Henry, *A Decade of Sectional Controversy.* Chapel Hill: University of North Carolina Press, 1942.

CHAPTER 15

Andrews, J. Cutler, *The South Reports the Civil War.* Princeton, N.J.: Princeton University Press, 1970; Connelly, Thomas L., and Archer Jones, *The Politics of Command: Factions and Ideas in Confederate Strategy.* Baton Rouge: Louisiana State University Press, 1973; Coulter, E. Merton, *The Confederate States of America, 1861–1865.* Baton Rouge: Louisiana State University Press, 1950; Durden, Robert F., *The Gray and the Black: The Confederate Debate on Emancipation.* Baton Rouge: Louisiana State University Press, 1972; Gerteis, Louis S., *From Contraband to Freedman: Federal Policy Toward Southern Blacks, 1861–1865.* Westport, Conn.: Greenwood, 1973; Kirwan, Albert D. (Ed.), *The Confederacy.* New York: Meridian, 1959; Myers, Robert M. (Ed.), *The Children of Pride: A True Story of Georgia and the Civil War.* New Haven, Conn.: Yale University Press, 1972; Nichols, Roy F., *The Stakes of Power.* New York: Hill & Wang, 1961; Niven, John, *Gideon Welles.* New York: Oxford University Press, 1973; Roland, Charles P., *The Confederacy.* Chicago: University of Chicago Press, 1960; Tredway, G. R., *Democratic Opposition to the Lincoln Administration in Indiana.* Indianapolis: Indiana Historical Bureau, 1973; Turner, Justin G., and Linda L. Turner (Eds.), *Mary Todd Lincoln: Her Life and Letters.* New York: Knopf, 1972; Voegeli, V. Jacque, *Free but Not Equal: The Midwest and the Negro During the Civil War.* Chicago: University of Chicago Press, 1967. (Paper).

CHAPTER 16

Abbott, Martin L., *The Freedman's Bureau in South Carolina, 1865–1872.* Chapel Hill: University of North Carolina Press, 1967; Brandfon, Robert, *Cotton Kingdom of the New South: A History of the Yazoo Mississippi Delta from Reconstruction to the Twentieth Century.* Cambridge, Mass.: Harvard University Press, 1967; Brock, William R., *An American Crisis.* New York: St. Martin's, 1963; Carpenter, John A., *Sword and Olive Branch: Oliver Otis Howard.* Pittsburgh, Penn.: University of Pittsburgh Press, 1964; Current, Richard N.,

Three Carpetbag Governors. Baton Rouge: Louisiana State University Press, 1968; Dorris, Jonathan D., *Pardon and Amnesty under Lincoln and Johnson.* Chapel Hill: University of North Carolina Press, 1953; Dunning, W. A., *Reconstruction, Political and Economic, 1865–1877.* New York: Harper & Row, 1968; Friedman, Lawrence J., *The White Savage: Racial Fantasies in the Postbellum South.* Englewood Cliffs, N.J.: Prentice-Hall, 1970. (Paper); Harris, William C., *Presidential Reconstruction in Mississippi.* Baton Rouge: Louisiana State University Press, 1967; Hesseltine, William B., *Lincoln's Plan of Reconstruction.* New York: Quadrangle, 1967. (Paper); Hyman, Harold M. (Ed.), *New Frontiers of the American Reconstruction.* Urbana: University of Illinois Press, 1966; Kirwan, Albert D., *The Revolt of the Rednecks: Mississippi Politics, 1876–1925.* Gloucester, Mass.: Peter Smith, 1964; Mantell, Martin E., *Johnson, Grant, and the Politics of Reconstruction.* New York: Columbia University Press, 1973; Mohr, James C., *The Radical Republicans and Reform in New York during Reconstruction.* Ithaca, N.Y.: Cornell University Press, 1973; Montgomery, David, *Beyond Equality.* New York: Knopf, 1967; Osterweis, Rollin G., *The Myth of the Lost Cause, 1865–1900.* Hamden, Conn.: Shoe String, 1973; Perman, Michael, *Reunion Without Compromise: The South and Reconstruction, 1865–1868.* New York: Cambridge University Press, 1973; Polakoff, Keith Ian, *The Politics of Inertia: The Election of 1876 and the End of Reconstruction.* Baton Rouge: Louisiana State University Press, 1973; Rose, Willie Lee, *Rehearsal for Reconstruction: A Historical and Contemporary Reader.* New York: Random, 1964. (Paper); Simkins, Francis B., and Robert H. Woody, *South Carolina during Reconstruction.* Gloucester, Mass.: Peter Smith, 1932; Tang, Anthony M., *Economic Development in the Southern Piedmont, 1860–1950.* Chapel Hill: University of North Carolina Press, 1958; Tindall, George B., *South Carolina Negroes, 1877–1900.* Columbia: University of South Carolina Press, 1970; Williamson, Joel R. (Ed.), *The Origins of Segregation.* Lexington, Mass.: Heath, 1968. (Paper).

CHAPTER 17

Bogue, Allan G., *From Prairie to Cornbelt: Farming on the Illinois and Iowa Prairies in the Nineteenth Century.* Chicago: University of Chicago Press, 1963; Bogue, Allan G., *Money at Interest: The Farm Mortgage on the Middle Border.* New York: Russell, 1968; Durham, Philip, and Everett L. Jones, *The Negro Cowboys.* New York: Dodd, 1965. (Paper); Lamar, Howard R., *The Far Southwest, 1846–1912: A Territorial History.* New York: Norton, 1970. (Paper); Priest, Loring Benson, *Uncle Sam's Stepchildren: The Reformation of United States Indian Policy, 1865–1887.* New York: Octagon, 1969; Roe, Frank G., *The Indians and the Horse.* Norman: University of Oklahoma Press, 1955; Skaggs, Jimmy M., *The Cattle-Training Industry: Between Supply and Demand, 1866–1890.* Lawrence: University Press of Kansas, 1973; Taft, Robert, *Artists and Illustrators of the Old West 1850–1900.* New York: Scribner's, 1953; Webb, Walter P., *The Great Frontier.* Austin: University of Texas Press, 1964; Wilkins, Thurman, *Clarence King.* New York: Macmillan, 1958.

CHAPTER 18

Diamond, Sigmund, *The Reputation of the American Businessman.* Gloucester, Mass.: Peter Smith, 1955; Dorfman, Joseph, *The Economic Mind in American Civilization, 1606–1933.* 5 volumes. Clifton, N.J.: Kelley, 1946–59; Doster, James F., *Railroads in Alabama Politics, 1875–1914.* University: University of Alabama Press, 1957; Holbrook, Stewart H., *The Age of the Moguls.* Garden City, N.Y.: Doubleday, 1953; Lane, W. J., *Commodore Vanderbilt: An Epic of the Steam Age.* New York: Knopf, 1942; Miller, William (Ed.), *Men in Business.* Cambridge, Mass.: Harvard University Press, 1952. (Paper); North, Douglass C., *Growth and Welfare in the American Past: A New Economic History.* Englewood Cliffs, N.J.: Prentice-Hall, 1966. (Paper); Oliver, John W., *History of American Technology.* New York: Ronald Press, 1956; Stover, John F., *American Railroads.* Chicago: University of Chicago Press, 1961; Stover, John F., *The Railroads of the South, 1865–1900.* Chapel Hill: University of North Carolina Press, 1955; Taylor, George R., and Irene D. Neu, *The American Railroad Network, 1861–1890.* Cambridge, Mass.: Harvard University Press, 1956; Williamson, Harold F., and Arnold M. Daum, *The American Petroleum Industry: Age of Illumination, 1859–1899.* Evanston, Ill.: Northwestern University Press, 1959; Wyllie, Irvin G., *The Self-Made Man in America.* New York: Free Press, 1966. (Paper).

CHAPTER 19

Barth, Gunther, *Bitter Strength: A History of the Chinese in the United States, 1850–1870.* Cambridge, Mass.: Harvard University Press, 1964; Bruce, Robert V., *Eighteen Seventy-Seven: Year of Violence.* New York: Watts, 1959. (Paper); Dulles, Foster Rhea, *Labor in America: A History.* New York: Crowell, 1966; Foner, Philip, *History of the Labor Movement in the United States.* 4 volumes. New York: International Publishing Company, 1947–1965; Furnas, J. C., *The Americans: A Social History of the U.S., 1587–1914.* 2 volumes. New York: Putnam, 1971; Ginger, Ray, *Altgeld's America: The Lincoln Ideal Vs. Changing Realities.* New York: Watts, 1965. (Paper); Glazer, Nathan, *American Judaism.* Chicago: University of Chicago

Press, 1972. (Paper); Green, Constance M., *American Cities in the Building of the Nation.* Tuckahoe, N.Y.: De Graff, 1957; Grob, Gerald, *Workers and Utopia: A Study of Idealogical Conflict in the American Labor Movement, 1865–1900.* New York: Quadrangle, 1969. (Paper); Hawes, Joseph M., *Children in Urban Society: Juvenile Delinquency in Nineteenth-Century America.* New York: Oxford University Press, 1971; Hibben, Paxton, *Henry Ward Beecher, An American Portrait.* New York: Doran, 1927; Huggins, Nathan, *Protestants Against Poverty: Boston's Charities.* Westport, Conn.: Greenwood, 1970; Jones, Maldwyn A., *American Immigration.* Chicago: University of Chicago Press, 1960; Kirkland, Edward C., *The Age of Enterprise: A Social History of Industrial America.* New York: Harper & Row, 1961; Linn, James W., *Jane Addams: A Biography.* Westport, Conn.: Greenwood, 1968; McAvoy, Thomas T., *The Great Crisis in American Catholic History, 1895–1900.* Chicago: Regnery, 1957; McLaurin, M. A., *Paternalism and Protest: Southern Cotton Mill Workers and Organized Labor, 1875–1905.* Westport, Conn.: Negro University Press, 1971; Mumford, Lewis, *The Culture of Cities.* New York: Harcourt, Brace, 1938; Rayback, Joseph G., *A History of American Labor.* New York: Macmillan, 1959; Rosenblum, Gerald, *Immigrant Workers: Their Impact on American Labor Radicalism.* New York: Basic, 1972; Ware, Norman J., *The Labor Movement in the United States, 1860–1895.* Gloucester, Mass.: Peter Smith, 1959; Weber, Max, *The City.* New York: Macmillan, 1958.

CHAPTER 20

Burchard, John E., and Albert Bush-Brown, *The Architecture of America.* Boston: Little, Brown, 1961; Case, Robert O., and Victoria Case, *We Called it Culture: The Story of Chautauqua.* Garden City, N.Y.: Doubleday, 1948; Condit, Care W., *The Rise of the Skyscraper.* Chicago: University of Chicago Press, 1952; Goodrich, Lloyd, *Winslow Homer.* Greenwich, Conn.: New York Graphics Society, 1973; Morgan, Arthur E., *Edward Bellamy.* New York: Columbia University Press, 1944; Wisbey, Herbert A., *Soldiers Without Swords: A History of the Salvation Army in the United States.* New York: Macmillan, 1955.

CHAPTER 21

Buck, Solon J., *The Granger Movement.* Lincoln: University of Nebraska Press, 1963; Davison, Kenneth E., *The Presidency of Rutherford B. Hayes.* Westport, Conn.: Greenwood, 1972; Edmonds, Helen, *The Negro and Fusion Politics in North Carolina, 1894–1901.* New York: Russell, 1973; Faulkner, Harold U., *Politics, Reform and Expansion.* New York: Harper & Row, 1959; Ginger, Ray, *Age of Excess: The United States from 1877–1914.* New York: Macmillan, 1965. (Paper); Glad, Paul, *The Trumpet Soundeth: William Jennings Bryan and his Democracy, 1896–1912.* Gloucester, Mass.: Peter Smith, 1960; Hackney, Sheldon, *Populism to Progressivism in Alabama.* Princeton, N.J.: Princeton University Press, 1969; Hirshson, Stanley P., *Farewell to the Bloody Shirt: Northern Republicans and the Southern Negro, 1877–1893.* New York: Quadrangle, 1968. (Paper); Keller, Morton, *The Art and Politics of Thomas Nast.* New York: Oxford University Press, 1968; Knoles, George H., *The Presidential Campaign and Election of 1892.* New York: AMS Press, 1972; Koening, Louis W., *Bryan: A Political Biography of William Jennings Bryan.* New York: Putnam, 1971; Leech, Margaret, *In the Days of McKinley.* New York: Harper, 1959; Logan, Rayford, *The Betrayal of the Negro: From Rutherford B. Hayes to Woodrow Wilson.* New York: Macmillan, 1965. (Paper); McKenna, George, *American Populism.* New York: Putnam, 1974. (Paper); McSeveney, Samuel T., *The Politics of Depression: Political Behavior in the Northeast, 1893–1896.* New York: Oxford University Press, 1972; Merrill, Horace S., *Bourbon Leader: Grover Cleveland and the Democratic Party.* Boston, Mass.: Little, Brown, 1965. (Paper); Parsons, Stanley B., *The Populist Context: Rural Versus Urban Power on a Great Plains Frontier.* Westport, Conn.: Greenwood, 1973; Pollack, Norman, *The Populist Mind.* New York: Bobbs-Merrill, 1967. (Paper); Simkins, Francis B., *Pitchfork Ben Tillman: South Carolinian.* Baton Rouge: Louisiana State University Press, 1967. (Paper); Welch, Richard E., Jr., *George Frisbie Hoar and the Half-Breed Republicans.* Cambridge, Mass.: Harvard University Press, 1971; Williams, T. Harry, *Romance and Realism in Southern Politics.* Baton Rouge: Louisiana State University Press, 1966. (Paper).

CHAPTER 22

Allen, Douglas, *Frederic Remington and the Spanish-American War.* New York: Crown, 1971; Calvert, Peter, *The Mexican Revolution 1910–1914: The Diplomacy of Anglo-American Conflict.* New York: Cambridge University Press, 1968; Challenner, Richard D., *Admirals, Generals and American Foreign Policy, 1898–1914.* Princeton, N.J.: Princeton University Press, 1973; Dulles, Foster R., *The Imperial Years.* New York: Apollo, 1960. Freidel, Frank, *The Splendid Little War.* Boston: Little, Brown, 1958; Grieb, Kenneth J., *The United States and Huerta.* Lincoln, N. B.: University of Nebraska Press, 1969; Herman, S. R., *Eleven Against War: Studies in American Internationalist Thought, 1898–1921.* Stanford, Calif.: Hoover Institution Press, 1969. (Paper); McCormick, Thomas J., *China Market.* New York: Quadrangle, 1970. (Paper); Millis, Walter, *The Martial Spirit.* Boston: Houghton Mifflin, 1931; Nevins, Allan, *Hamilton Fish*, Vols. I–II. New York: Ungar, 1957; Pratt, Julius W., *America's Colonial Experiment*. Gloucester, Mass.: Peter Smith, 1964; Roosevelt, Theodore, *The Rough Riders*. New York: New American Library, 1961; Schirmer, D. B., *Republic or Empire: American Resistance to the Philippine War*. Cambridge, Mass.: Schenkman, 1972; Schmidt, Hans R., *The United States Occupation of Haiti, 1915–1934*. Brunswick, N.J.: Rutgers University Press, 1971; Scholes, Walter V., and Mary V. Scholes, *The Foreign Policies of the Taft Administration*. Columbia, Mo.: University of Missouri Press, 1970; Sprout, Harold, and Margaret Sprout, *The Rise of American Naval Power*. Princeton, N.J.: Princeton University Press, 1943; Strong, Josiah, *Our Country*. Cambridge, Mass.: Harvard University Press, 1963; Trani, Eugene P., *The Treaty of Portsmouth: An Adventure in American Diplomacy*. Lexington, Ky.: University Press of Kentucky, 1969; White, John A., *The Diplomacy of the Russo-Japanese War*. Princeton, N.J.: Princeton University Press, 1964.

CHAPTER 23

Aaron, Daniel, *Men of Good Hope*. New York: Oxford University Press, 1951; Anderson, Donald F., *William Howard Taft: A Conservative's Conception of the Presidency*. Ithaca, N.Y.: Cornell University Press, 1973; Bailey, Hugh C., *Liberalism in the New South: Southern Social Reformers and the Progressive Movement*. Coral Gables, Fla.: University of Miami Press, 1969; Braeman, John, *Albert J. Beveridge: American Nationalist*. Chicago: University of Chicago Press, 1971; Brandeis, Louis D., *Letters of Louis D. Brandeis*, 3 Volumes. Melvin I. Urofsky and D. W. Levy (Eds.). Albany: State University of New York Press, 1972; Burton, David H., *Theodore Roosevelt*. Boston, Mass.: Twayne, 1973; Chrislock, Carl H., *The Progressive Era in Minnesota, 1899–1918*. St. Paul: Minnesota Historical Society, 1971; Goldman, Eric F., *Rendezvous with Destiny*. New York: Random House, 1956; Hoover, Herbert, *The Ordeal of Woodrow Wilson*. New York: McGraw-Hill, 1958; Kaplan, Justin, *Lincoln Steffens*. New York: Simon & Schuster, 1974; Kennedy, David M., *Birth Control in America: The Career of Margaret Sanger*. New Haven, Conn.: Yale University Press, 1970. (Paper); Kerr, K. Austin, *American Railroad Politics, 1914–1920*. Pittsburgh: University of Pittsburgh Press, 1968; Kraditor, Aileen S., *The Ideas of the Woman Suffrage Movement, 1890–1920*. Garden City, N.Y.: Doubleday, 1971. (Paper); Lasch, Christopher, *The New Radicalism in America*. New York: Knopf, 1965; Laslett, James, *Labor and the Left: A Study of Socialist and Radical Influences in the American Labor Movement*. New York: Basic, 1970; Leopold, Richard, *Elihu Root and the Conservative Tradition*. Boston: Little, Brown, 1954; Lowitt, Richard, *George W. Norris: The Making of a Progressive, 1861–1912*. Syracuse, N.Y.: Syracuse University Press, 1963; Lubove, Roy, *The Professional Altruist: The Emergence of Social Work as a Career*. New York: Atheneum, 1969. (Paper); Mann, Arthur, *Yankee Reformers in the Urban Age*. New York: Harper & Row, 1966; Manners, William, *TR and Will*. New York: Harcourt, Brace, 1969; Marchand, C. Roland, *The American Peace Movement and Social Reform, 1898–1918*. Princeton, N.J.: Princeton University Press, 1973; Martin, Albro, *Enterprise Denied: Origins of the Decline of American Railroads, 1897–1917*. New York: Columbia University Press, 1971; Maxwell, Robert S., *La Follette and the Rise of the Progressives in Wisconsin*. Madison: State Historical Society of Wisconsin, 1956; Mowry, George E., *The California Progressives*. Chicago: Quadrangle, 1963; Noble, David W., *The Paradox of Progressive Thought*. Minneapolis: University of Minnesota Press, 1958; Olin, Spencer C., Jr., *California's Prodigal Son: Hiram Johnson and the Progressives*. Berkeley: University of California Press, 1968; Parris, Guichard and Lester Brooks, *Blacks in the City: A History of the National Urban League*. Boston, Mass.: Little, Brown, 1971; Penick, James, Jr., *Progressive Politics and Conservation: The Ballinger-Pinchot Affair*. Chicago: University of Chicago Press, 1968; Pinkett, Harold T., *Gifford Pinchot: Private and Public Forester*. Urbana: University of Illinois Press, 1970; Quandt, Jean B., *From the Small Town to the Great Community: The Social Thought of Progressive Intellectuals*. New Brunswick, N.J.: Rutgers University Press, 1970; Roosevelt, Nicholas, *Theodore Roosevelt: The Man as I Knew Him*. New York: Dodd, Mead, 1967; Trattner, Walter I., *Crusade for the Children*. New York: Quadrangle, 1970; Urofsky, Melvin I., *Big Steel and the Wilson Administration: A Study in Business-Government Relations*. Columbus: Ohio State University Press, 1969; Weinberg, Arthur, and Leila Weinberg (Eds.), *The Muckrakers*. New York: Putnam, 1964; Wiebe, Robert H., *Businessmen and Reform*. Cambridge, Mass.: Harvard University Press, 1962; Wiebe, Robert H., *The Search for Order, 1877–1920*. New York: Hill & Wang, 1967. (Paper); Wilson, Woodrow, *The New Freedom*. Englewood Cliffs, N.J.: Prentice-Hall, 1961.

CHAPTER 24

Baruch, Bernard M., *American Industry in War*. New York: Prentice-Hall, 1941; Birdsall, Paul, *Versailles Twenty Years After*. Hamden, Conn.: Shoestring Press, 1962; Blakey, George T., *Historians on the Homefront: American Propagandists for the Great War*. Lexington: University Press of Kentucky, 1970; Cuff, Robert D., *The War Industries Board: Business-Government Relations During World War I*. Baltimore: Johns-Hopkins,

1973; Gregory, Ross, *Walter Hines Page: Ambassador to the Court of St. James.* Lexington: University Press of Kentucky, 1970; Kennan, George F., *The Decision to Intervene.* Princeton, N.J.: Princeton University Press, 1958; Kennan, George F., *Russia Leaves the War.* Princeton, N.J.: Princeton University Press, 1956; Lodge, Henry C., *The Senate and the League of Nations.* New York: Scribner's, 1925; Marshall, S.L.A., *The American Heritage History of World War I.* New York: American Heritage, 1964; Mock, James R., and Cedric Larson, *Words that Won the War.* Princeton, N.J.: Princeton University Press, 1939; Paxson, Frederick L., *American Democracy and the World War,* Vols. I–IV. New York: Cooper Square Publishers, 1966; Pershing, John J., *My Experiences in the World War,* Vols. I–II. New York: Stokes, 1931; Peterson, Horace C., and Gilbert C. Fite: *Opponents of War: 1917–1918.* Seattle: University of Washington Press, 1968. (Paper); Simpson, Colin, *The Lusitania.* New York: Ballantine, 1974. (Paper); Stallings, Laurence, *The Doughboys.* New York: Harper & Row, 1963; Tansill, Charles C., *America Goes to War.* Boston: Little, Brown, 1938; Tillman, Seth P., *Anglo-American Relations at the Paris Peace Conference of 1919.* Princeton, N.J.: Princeton University Press, 1961; Thompson, John M., *Russia, Bolshevism, and the Versailles Peace.* Princeton, N.J.: Princeton University Press, 1966; Tulchin, Joseph S., *The Aftermath of War: World War I and United States Policy Toward Latin America.* N.Y.: New York University Press, 1971.

CHAPTER 25

Ashby, Leroy, *The Spearless Leader: Senator Borah and the Progressive Movement in the 1920s.* Urbana: University of Illinois Press, 1972; Bagby, Wesley, *The Road to Normalcy.* Baltimore: Johns Hopkins Press, 1962; Cronon, E. D., *Black Moses.* Madison: University of Wisconsin Press, 1955; Divine, Robert A., *American Immigration Policy, 1924–1952.* New Haven, Conn.: Yale University Press, 1957; Downes, Randolph C., *The Rise of Warren Gamaliel Harding: 1865–1920.* Columbus: Ohio State University Press, 1970; Gustin, Lawrence R., *Billy Durant: The Creator of General Motors.* Grand Rapids, Mich.: Eerdmans, 1973; Hale, Nathan G., Jr., *Freud and the Americans: The Origin and Foundation of the Psychoanalytic Movement in America, 1876–1917.* New York: Oxford University Press, 1971; Handlin, Oscar, *Al Smith and His America.* Boston: Little, Brown, 1958; Harbaugh, William H., *Lawyer's Lawyer: The Life of John W. Davis.* New York: Oxford University Press, 1973; Hicks, John D., and Theodore Saloutos, *Twentieth Century Populism: Agricultural Discontent in the Middle West, 1900–1939.* Lincoln: University of Nebraska Press, 1964; Huggins, Nathan I., *Harlem Renaissance.* New York: Oxford University Press, 1973. (Paper); Jackson, Kenneth T., *The Ku Klux Klan in the City, 1915–1930.* Richard C. Wade (Ed.). New York: Oxford University Press, 1967. (Paper); Johnson, Donald, *The Challenge to American Freedoms.* Lexington: University of Kentucky Press, 1963; Joughin, Louis, and Edmund M. Morgan, *The Legacy of Sacco and Vanzetti.* Chicago: Quadrangle, 1964; Lemons, J. Stanley, *The Woman Citizen: Social Feminism in the 1920s.* Urbana: University of Illinois Press, 1973; Levine, Lawrence W., *Defender of the Faith: William Jennings Bryan, The Last Decade, 1915–1925.* New York: Oxford University Press, 1965; Levy, Eugene, *James Weldon Johnson: Black Leader, Black Voice.* John H. Franklin (Ed.). Chicago: University of Chicago Press, 1973; Moore, Edmund A., *A Catholic Runs for President: The Campaign of 1928.* Gloucester, Mass.: Peter Smith; Quint, Howard H., and Robert H. Ferrell (Eds.), *The Talkative President: The Off-the-Record Press Conferences of Calvin Coolidge.* Amherst: University of Massachusetts Press, 1964; Rice, Arnold S., *The Ku Klux Klan in American Politics.* New York: Haskell, 1972; Schriftgiesser, Karl, *This Was Normalcy.* Boston: Little, Brown, 1948; Sherman, Richard B., *The Republican Party and Black America: From McKinley to Hoover, 1896–1933.* Charlottesville: University Press of Virginia, 1973; Sinclair, Andrew, *The Available Man: The Life Behind the Masks of Warren Gamaliel Harding.* New York: Quadrangle, 1969. (Paper); Tuttle, William M., Jr., *Race Riot: Chicago in the Red Summer of 1919.* New York: Atheneum, 1970. (Paper); Vincent, Theodore G., *Black Power and the Garvey Movement.* Palo Alto, Calif.: Ramparts, 1972. (Paper); Wik, Reynold M., *Henry Ford and Grass-Roots America.* Ann Arbor, Mich.: University of Michigan Press, 1972.

CHAPTER 26

Arnold, Thurman, *The Folklore of Capitalism.* New Haven, Conn.: Yale University Press, 1937; Blum, John M., *Roosevelt and Morgenthau.* Boston, Mass.: Houghton Mifflin, 1972. (Paper); Bunche, Ralph J., *The Political Status of the Negro in the Age of FDR.* Dewey W. Grantham (Ed.). Chicago: University of Chicago Press, 1973; Daniels, Roger, *The Bonus March: An Episode of the Great Depression.* Westport, Conn.: Greenwood, 1971; Douglas, Paul H., *In the Fullness of Time: The Memoirs of Paul H. Douglas.* New York: Harcourt Brace Jovanovich, 1972; Draper, Theodore, *The Roots of American Communism.* New York: Viking, 1957; Ekirch, Arthur A., Jr., *Ideologies and Utopias: New Deal and American Thought.* New York: Quadrangle, 1971. (Paper); Freidel, Frank (Ed.), *The New Deal and the American People.* Englewood Cliffs, N.J.: Prentice-Hall, 1964; Gould, Jean, and Lorena Hickok, *Walter Reuther: Labor's Rugged Individualist.* New York: Dodd, 1971;

Greer, Thomas H., *What Roosevelt Thought: The Social and Political Ideas of Franklin D. Roosevelt.* East Lansing: Michigan State University Press, 1958; Hollingsworth, Harold M. (Ed.), *Essays on the New Deal.* Austin: University of Texas Press, 1969; Ickes, Harold L., *The Secret Diary of Harold L. Ickes,* Vols. I–III. New York: Simon & Schuster, 1953–54; Jackson, Robert H., *The Struggle for Judicial Supremacy.* New York: Random House, 1941; Josephson, Matthew: *The Money Lords: The Great Finance Capitalists, 1925–1950.* New York: Weybright, 1972; Kennedy, Susan E., *The Banking Crisis of 1933.* Lexington: University Press of Kentucky, 1973; Koskoff, David E., *Joseph P. Kennedy: A Life and Times.* Englewood Cliffs, N.J.: Prentice-Hall, 1974; Lash, Joseph P., *Eleanor and Franklin.* New York: New American Library, 1973. (Paper); Lash, Joseph P., *Eleanor: The Years Alone.* New York: Norton, 1972; McCoy, Donald R., *Landon of Kansas.* Lincoln: University of Nebraska Press, 1966; McCraw, Thomas K., *TVA and the Power Fight, 1933–1939.* Philadelphia: Lippincott, 1971. (Paper); Marcus, Sheldon, *Father Coughlin: The Tumultuous Life of the Priest of the Little Flower.* Boston: Little, Brown, 1973; Millis, Henry A., and Emily C. Brown, *From the Wagner Act to Taft-Hartley.* Chicago: University of Chicago Press, 1950; Parrish, Michael E., *Securities Regulations and the New Deal.* New Haven, Conn.: Yale University Press, 1970; Patterson, James T., *The New Deal and the States: Federalism in Transition.* Princeton, N.J.: Princeton University Press, 1969; Perkins, Dexter, *The New Age of Franklin Roosevelt.* Chicago: University of Chicago Press, 1957; Perkins, Van L., *Crisis in Agriculture: The Agricultural Adjustment Administration and the New Deal.* Berkeley: University of California Press, 1969; Phillips, Cabel, *From the Crash to the Blitz: 1929–1939.* New York: Macmillan, 1969; Pusey, Merlo J., *Charles Evans Hughes,* Vols. I–III. New York: Columbia University Press, 1951; Schapsmeier, Edward L., and Frederick S. Schapsmeier, *Henry A. Wallace of Iowa: The Agrarian Years, 1910–1940.* Ames: Iowa State University Press, 1969; Sherwood, Robert E., *Roosevelt and Hopkins.* New York: Harper & Row, 1950; Stave, Bruce M., *The New Deal and the Last Hurrah: Pittsburgh Machine Politics.* Pittsburgh: University of Pittsburgh Press, 1970; Stein, Herbert, *The Fiscal Revolution in America, 1931–1962.* Chicago: University of Chicago Press, 1969. (Paper); Stein, Walter J., *California and the Dust Bowl Migration: Contributions in American History.* Westport, Conn.: Greenwood, 1973; Sternsher, Bernard, *The Negro in Depression and War: Prelude to Revolution.* New York: Watts, 1969. (Paper); Stott, William, *Documentary Expression and Thirties America.* New York: Oxford University Press, 1973; Tugwell, Rexford, *In Search of Roosevelt.* Cambridge, Mass.: Harvard University Press, 1972; Wecter, Dixon, *The Age of the Great Depression.* New York: Macmillan, 1948; Wolfskill, George, *The Revolt of the Conservatives.* Boston: Houghton Mifflin, 1962.

CHAPTER 27

Baker, Leonard, *Roosevelt and Pearl Harbor.* New York: Macmillan, 1970; Barnard, Ellsworth, *Wendell Wilkie: Fighter for Freedom.* Amherst: University of Massachusetts Press, (Paper); Bishop, James, *FDR's Last Year, April 1944–April 1945.* New York: Morrow, 1974; Blum, John M., *From the Diaries of Henry Morgenthau,* Vols. I–II. Boston: Houghton Mifflin, 1959–67; Bowles, Chester, *Promises to Keep: My Years in Public Life, 1941–1969.* New York: Harper & Row, 1972. (Paper); Bradley, Omar N., *A Soldier's Story.* New York: Popular Library, 1970; Buckley, Thomas H., *The United States and the Washington Conference, 1921–1922.* Knoxville: University of Tennessee Press, 1970; Calcott, Wilfrid H., *The Western Hemisphere: Its Influence on United States Policies to the End of World War II.* Austin: University of Texas Press, 1968; Chatfield, Charles, *For Peace and Justice: Pacifism in America, 1914–1941.* Knoxville: University of Tennessee Press, 1971; Cole, Wayne S., *Charles A. Lindbergh and the Battle Against American Intervention in World War II.* New York: Harcourt Brace Jovanovich, 1974; Current, Richard N., *Secretary Stimson: A Study in Statecraft.* Hamden, Conn.: Shoe String, 1970; Dalfiume, Richard M., *Desegregation of the United States Armed Forces: Fighting on Two Fronts, 1939–1953.* Columbia: University of Missouri Press, 1969; DeConde, Alexander (Ed.), *Isolation and Security: Ideas and Interests in Twentieth Century American Foreign Policy.* Durham, N.C.: Duke University Press, 1957; Dulles, Foster R., *America's Rise to World Power.* New York: Harper & Row, 1955; Eisenhower, Dwight D., *Crusade in Europe.* Garden City, N.Y.: Doubleday, 1948; Farnsworth, Beatrice, *William C. Bullitt and the Soviet Union.* Bloomington: Indiana University Press, 1967; Gardner, Lloyd, *Economic Aspects of New Deal Diplomacy.* Madison: University of Wisconsin Press, 1964; Goodman, Jack (Ed.), *While You Were Gone: A Report on Wartime Life in the United States.* New York: Simon & Schuster, 1946; Grew, Joseph C., *Turbulent Era,* Vols. I–II. Freeport, N.Y.: Books for Libraries, 1970; Heinrichs, Waldo H., *American Ambassador: Joseph C. Grew.* Boston: Little, Brown, 1966; Hull, Cordell, *Memoirs,* Vols. I–II. New York: Macmillan, 1948; Iriye, Akira, *After Imperialism: The Search for a New Order in the Far East, 1921–1931.* Cambridge, Mass.: Harvard University Press, 1965; Kimball, Warren F., *The Most Unsordid Act: Lend-Lease, 1939–1941.* Baltimore: Johns-Hopkins, 1969; MacArthur, Douglas, *Reminiscences.* New York: McGraw-Hill, 1964; Maddox, Robert J., *William E. Borah and*

American Foreign Policy. Baton Rouge: Louisiana State University Press, 1969; Morison, Samuel E., *The Two-Ocean War.* Boston: Little, Brown, 1963; Neumann, William L., *America Encounters Japan: From Perry to MacArthur.* Baltimore: Johns Hopkins, 1969. (Paper); Nevins, Allan, *The New Deal and World Affairs.* New York: United States Publishers Association, 1970; Nevins, Allan, *The United States in a Chaotic World: Chronicle of International Affairs 1918–1933.* New York: United States Publishers Association, 1970; O'Connor, Raymond G., *Diplomacy for Victory: FDR and Unconditional Surrender.* New York: Norton, 1971. (Paper); Polenberg, Richard, *War and Society: The United States, 1941–1945.* Philadelphia: Lippincott, 1972. (Paper); Smith, Richard Harris, *OSS: The Secret History of America's First Intelligence Agency.* Berkeley: University of California Press, 1972; Smith, Robert F., The *United States and Revolutionary Nationalism in Mexico, 1916–1932.* Chicago: University of Chicago Press, 1972; Snell, John L. (Ed.), *The Meaning of Yalta.* Baton Rouge: Louisiana State University Press, 1956; Stimson, Henry L., and McGeorge Bundy, *On Active Service in Peace and War.* New York: Harper & Row, 1948; tenBroek, Jacobus, et al., *Prejudice, War and The Constitution: Causes and Consequences of the Evacuation of the Japanese Americans in World War II.* Berkeley: University of California Press, 1954. (Paper); Thorne, Christopher, *The Limits of Foreign Policy: The West, the League, and the Far Eastern Crisis of 1931–1933.* New York: Putnam, 1973. (Paper); Traina, Richard P., *American Diplomacy and the Spanish Civil War.* Bloomington: Indiana University Press, 1968; United States, Bureau of the Budget Committee on Records of War Administration, *The United States at War.* New York: Da Capo, 1972; Varg, Paul, *The Closing of the Door: Sino-American Relations, 1936–1946.* East Lansing: Michigan State University Press, 1973; Wilson, Theodore A., *The First Summit: Roosevelt and Churchill at Placentia Bay, 1941.* Boston: Houghton Mifflin, 1969; Wood, Bryce, *The Making of the Good Neighbor Policy.* New York: Columbia University Press, 1961.

CHAPTER 28

Aron, Raymond, *The Imperial Republic: The United States and the World, 1945–1973.* Englewood Cliffs, N.J.: Prentice-Hall, 1974; Agar, Herbert, *The Price of Power: America Since 1945.* Chicago: University of Chicago Press, 1957; Beal, John R., *Marshall in China,* Garden City, N.Y.: Doubleday, 1970; Brown, Seyom, *The Faces of Power: Constancy and Change in U.S. Foreign Policy from Truman to Johnson.* New York: Columbia University Press, 1968; Caridi, Ronald J., *The Korean War and American Politics: The Republican Party as a Case History.* Philadelphia: University of Pennsylvania Press, 1969; Davis, K. S., *The Politics of Honor.* New York: Putnam, 1967; Divine, Robert A., *Second Chance: The Triumph of Internationalism in America During World War II.* New York: Atheneum, 1971. (Paper); Fairbank, John K., *The United States and China.* New York: Viking, 1971; Ferrell, Robert H., *George C. Marshall.* New York: Cooper Square, 1966; Freeland, Richard M., *The Truman Doctrine and the Origins of McCarthyism, 1946–1948.* New York: Knopf, 1972; Gardner, Lloyd C., *Architects of Illusion: Men and Ideas in American Foreign Policy, 1941–1949.* New York: Watts, 1972. (Paper); Glick, Edward B., *Soldiers, Scholars and Society: The Social Impact of the American Military.* Pacific Palisades, California: Goodyear, 1971; Goldman, Eric F., *The Crucial Decade.* New York: Knopf, 1956; Graebner, Norman A., *Cold War Diplomacy: American Foreign Policy, 1945–1960.* New York: Reinhold, 1962. (Paper); Griffith, Robert, *The Politics of Fear: Joseph B. McCarthy and the Senate.* Lexington: University Press of Kentucky, 1971. (Paper); Gunther, John, *Inside U.S.A.* New York: Harper & Row, 1951; Harper, Alan D., *The Politics of Loyalty.* Westport, Conn.: Greenwood, 1969; Kennan, George F., *American Diplomacy 1900–1950.* Chicago: University of Chicago Press, 1951; Kolko, Gabriel, *The Roots of American Foreign Policy: An Analysis of Power and Purpose.* Boston: Beacon Press, 1969. (Paper); Kolko, Joyce, and Gabriel Kolko, *The Limits of Power: The World and United States Foreign Policy, 1945–1954.* New York: Harper & Row, 1972. (Paper); Kuklick, Bruce, *American Policy and the Division of Germany: The Clash with Russia Over Reparations.* Ithaca, N.Y.: Cornell University Press, 1972; Maddox, Robert J., *The New Left and the Origins of the Cold War.* Princeton, N.J.: Princeton University Press, 1974; Markowitz, Norman D., *The Rise and Fall of the People's Century: Henry A. Wallace and American Liberalism, 1941–1948.* New York: Free Press, 1973; Matusow, Allen J., *Farm Policies and Politics in the Truman Years.* Cambridge, Mass.: Harvard University Press, 1967; Mee, Charles L., Jr., *Meeting at Potsdam.* New York: Evans, 1975; Murphy, Robert, *Diplomat Among Warriors.* Garden City, N.Y.: Doubleday, 1964; Neumann, William L., *After Victory.* New York: Harper & Row, 1967; Reischauer, Edward O., *The United States and Japan.* Cambridge, Mass.: Harvard University Press, 1965; Rose, Lisle A., *After Yalta: American Political Culture and the Cold War.* New York: Scribner, 1973; Snell, John L., *Wartime Origins of the East-West Dilemma Over Germany.* New Orleans: Hauser Press, 1959; Spanier, John, *American Foreign Policy Since World War II.* New York: Praeger, 1968; Spanier, J. W., *The Truman-MacArthur Controversy and the Korean War.* Cambridge, Mass.: Harvard University Press, 1959; Steel, Ronald, *Pax Americana.* New York: Viking Press, 1970. (Paper); Steinberg, Alfred, *Sam Rayburn: A Bi-*

ography. New York: Hawthorn, 1975; Theoharis, Athan, *Seeds of Repression: Harry S Truman and the Origins of McCarthyism.* New York: Quadrangle, 1971; Truman, Margaret, *Harry S Truman.* New York: Morrow, 1973; Tucker, Robert W., *The Radical Left and American Foreign Policy.* Baltimore: Johns Hopkins, 1971. (Paper); Ulam, Adam B., *The Rivals: America and Russia Since World War II.* New York: Viking Press, 1972. (Paper); Zink, Harold, *The United States in Germany.* Princeton, N.J.: Van Nostrand, 1957.

CHAPTER 29

Adams, Sherman, *Firsthand Report.* New York: Harper & Row, 1961; Adams, Walter, and Horace M. Gray, *Monopoly in America: The Government as Promoter.* New York: Macmillan, 1955; Albertson, Dean (Ed.), *Eisenhower as President.* New York: Hill & Wang, 1963; Baldwin, D. A., *Economic Development and American Foreign Policy.* Chicago: University of Chicago Press, 1966; Bell, Daniel, *The End of Ideology.* New York: Macmillan, 1960; Benson, Ezra T., *Crossfire: The Eight Years with Eisenhower.* Garden City, N.Y.: Doubleday, 1962; Bickel, A. M., *The Supreme Court and the Idea of Progress.* New York: Harper & Row, 1970. (Paper); Blaustein, Albert P., and Clarence C. Ferguson, Jr., *Desegregation and the Law: The Meaning and Effect of the School Segregation Cases.* New Brunswick, N.J.: Rutgers University Press, 1957; Chandler, A. D., Jr. (Ed.), *The Papers of Dwight David Eisenhower: The War Years.* 5 volumes. Alfred D. Chandler Jr., and Stephen Ambrose (Eds.) Baltimore: Johns Hopkins, 1970; Childs, Marquis, *Eisenhower: Captive Hero.* New York: Harcourt Brace, 1958; Clark, Thomas D., *The Emerging South.* New York: Oxford University Press, 1968; Cox, Archibald, *The Warren Court: Constitutional Decision as an Instrument of Reform.* Cambridge, Mass.: Harvard University Press, 1968; Dalfiume, Richard M., *Desegregation of the United States Armed Forces: Fighting on Two Fronts, 1939–1953.* Columbia: University of Missouri Press, 1969; Dozer, Donald M., *Are We Good Neighbors? Three Decades of Inter-American Relations, 1930–1960.* Gainesville: University of Florida Press, 1959; Eden, Anthony, *Full Circle: The Memoirs of Anthony Eden.* Boston: Houghton Mifflin, 1960; Frier, D. A., *Conflict of Interest in the Eisenhower Administration.* Ames: Iowa State University Press, 1969; Galbraith, John K., *The Affluent Society.* Boston: Houghton Mifflin, 1969; Gerson, Louis L., *John Foster Dulles.* New York: Cooper Square, 1967; Goold-Adams, Richard, *John Foster Dulles: A Reappraisal.* New York: Appleton-Century-Crofts, 1962; Johnson, Walter, and Carol Evans (Eds.), *Papers of Adlai E. Stevenson.* Vols. 1–3. Boston: Little, Brown, 1972–1973; Key, V. O., Jr., *The Responsible Electorate: Rationality in Presidential Voting, 1936–1960.* Cambridge, Mass.: Harvard University Press, 1966; Larson, Arthur, *Eisenhower: The President Nobody Knew.* New York: Scribner, 1968; Miller, Loren, *The Petitioners.* New York: Pantheon, 1956; Mills, C. Wright, *The Power Elite.* New York: Oxford University Press, 1959. (Paper); Mills, C. Wright, *White Collar: American Middle Classes.* New York: Oxford University Press, 1956; Mowry, George E., *Another Look at the Twentieth Century South.* Baton Rouge: Louisiana State University Press, 1972; Noble, Bernard G., *Christian A. Herter.* New York: Cooper Square, 1970; Osgood, Robert E., *Alliances and American Foreign Policy.* Baltimore: Johns Hopkins, 1968. (Paper); Pusey, Merlo J., *Eisenhower: The President.* New York: Macmillan, 1956; Rovere, Richard, *The Eisenhower Years: Affairs of State.* New York: Farrar, Straus, 1956; Soth, Lauren, *Farm Trouble in an Age of Plenty.* Princeton, N.J.: Princeton University Press, 1957; Spanier, John, *American Foreign Policy Since World War II.* New York: Praeger, 1973; Tindall, George B., *The Disruption of the Solid South.* New York: Norton, 1972. (Paper); Trebing, Harry M. (Ed.), *The Corporation in the American Economy.* New York: Watts, 1970. (Paper); Widick, B. J., *Labor Today.* Boston: Houghton Mifflin, 1964.

CHAPTER 30

Allison, Graham T., *Essence of Decision: Explaining the Cuban Missile Crisis.* Boston: Little, Brown, 1971. (Paper); Anderson, Patrick, *The President's Men.* Garden City, N.Y.: Doubleday, 1968; Anderson, Walt (Ed.), *The Age of Protest.* Pacific Palisades, California: Goodyear, 1969. (Paper); Baldwin, James, *The Fire Next Time.* New York: Dial, 1963; Baldwin, James, *Nobody Knows My Name.* New York: Dial, 1961; Barnet, Richard, *The Roots of War: The Men and Institutions Behind U.S. Foreign Policy.* New York: Penguin, 1973. (Paper); Belin, David, *November Twenty Second: You Are the Jury.* New York: Quadrangle, 1973; Bell, Daniel, and Irving Kristol (Eds.), *Confrontation: The Student Rebellion and the Universities.* New York: Basic Books, 1969; Bishop, James A., *The Days of Martin Luther King, Jr.* New York: Putnam, 1971; Burns, James M., *The Deadlock of Democracy.* Englewood Cliffs, N.J.: Prentice-Hall, 1963; Chester, Lewis, et al., *An American Melodrama: The Presidential Campaign of 1968.* New York: Viking Press, 1969; Cooper, Chester L., *The Lost Crusade: The U.S. in Vietnam.* New York: Dodd, Mead, 1970; Donald, Aida DiPace (Ed.), *John F. Kennedy and the New Frontier.* New York: Hill & Wang, 1966; Douglas, Paul, *America in the Market Place: Trade, Tariffs and the Balance of Payments.* New York: Holt, Rinehart & Winston, 1966; Draper, Theodore, *Abuse of Power.* New York: Viking Press, 1967; Epstein, Edward J., *Inquest.* New York: Viking, 1966; Faber, Harold

(Ed.), *The Road to the White House.* New York: McGraw-Hill, 1965; Fifield, Russell H., *Americans in Southeast Asia: The Roots of Commitment.* New York: Crowell, 1973; Fuchs, Lawrence H., *John F. Kennedy and American Catholicism.* New York: Meredith Press, 1967; Galloway, John, *The Gulf of Tonkin Resolution.* Cranbury, N.J.: Fairleigh Dickinson, 1970; Gardner, John W. (Ed.), *To Turn the Tide.* New York: Harper & Row, 1962; Goldman, Peter, *The Death and Life of Malcolm X.* New York: Harper & Row, 1974. (Paper); Graff, Henry, *The Tuesday Cabinet: Deliberation and Decision on Peace and War under Lyndon B. Johnson.* Englewood Cliffs, N.J.: Prentice-Hall, 1970; Graham, Hugh D., and Ted R. Gurr, *A History of Violence in America: Historical and Comparative Perspectives.* New York: Praeger, 1969; Hayden, Tom, *Rebellion and Repression.* New York: World Publishing Company, 1969; Heller, Walter, *New Dimensions of Political Economy.* Cambridge, Mass.: Harvard University Press, 1969; Hilsman, Roger, *To Move a Nation.* Garden City, N.Y.: Doubleday, 1967; Hilsman, Roger, and R. C. Good (Eds.), *Foreign Policy in the Sixties.* Baltimore: Johns Hopkins Press, 1965; Lowenthal, Abraham F., *The Dominican Intervention.* Cambridge, Mass.: Harvard University Press, 1972; Kennedy, Rose Fitzgerald, *Times to Remember.* Garden City, N.Y.: Doubleday, 1974; Martin, John B., *Overtaken by Events.* Garden City, N.Y.: Doubleday, 1966; Miller, Herman P., *Rich Man, Poor Man.* New York: Crowell, 1971. (Paper: Apollo, 1971); Mitgang, Herbert (Ed.), *America at Random.* New York: Putnam, 1970. (Paper); Moulton, Harland B., *From Superiority to Parity: The United States and the Strategic Arms Race, 1961–1971.* Westport, Conn.: Greenwood, 1973; Muse, Benjamin, *The American Negro Revolution: From Non-violence to Black Power, 1963–1967.* Bloomington: Indiana University Press, 1968. (Paper: Citadel, 1970); New York Times Editors, *Report of the National Advisory Commission on Civil Disorders.* New York: Dutton, 1968; Power, Thomas, *The War at Home.* New York: Grossman, 1973; Quinn, Edward G., and Paul J. Dolan (Eds.), *The Sense of the Sixties.* New York: Free Press, 1968. (Paper); Reedy, George E., *The Twilight of the Presidency.* New York: New American Library, 1971. (Paper); Reich, Charles, *The Greening of America: How the Youth Revolution is Trying to Make America Liveable.* New York: Random, 1970. (Paper: Bantam, 1971); Rogers, William D., *The Twilight Struggle: The Alliance for Progress and the Politics of Development in Latin America.* New York: Random House, 1967; Roszak, Theodore, *The Making of a Counter-Culture.* Garden City, N.Y.: Doubleday, 1969. (Paper); Ruiz, Ramon E., *Cuba: The Making of a Revolution.* Amherst: University of Massachusetts Press, 1968. (Paper: Norton, 1970); Schwartz, Urs, *American Strategy: A New Perspective.* Garden City, N.Y.: Doubleday, 1966; Sidey, Hugh, *John F. Kennedy, President.* New York: Atheneum, 1963–64; Vanden Heuvel, William, and M. Gwirtzman, *On His Own: Robert F. Kennedy, 1964–1968.* Garden City, N.Y.: Doubleday, 1970; Waskow, Arthur I., *From Race Riot to Sit-in.* Garden City, N.Y.: Doubleday, 1966; Waxman, Chaim, *Poverty: Power and Politics.* New York: Grosset & Dunlop, 1968. (Paper); Whalen, Richard J., *The Founding Father: The Story of Joseph P. Kennedy.* New York: New American Library, 1964; White, William S., *The Professional: Lyndon B. Johnson.* Boston: Houghton Mifflin, 1964.

CHAPTER 31

Ahlstrom, Sidney, *A Religious History of the American People.* New Haven, Conn.: Yale University Press, 1974. (Paper); Barber, Richard J., *American Corporation: Its Power, Its Money, Its Politics.* New York: Dutton, 1970. (Paper); Barnet, Richard J., and Ronald Muller, *Global Reach: The Power of the Multinational Corporations.* New York: Simon & Schuster, 1974; Bird, Caroline, *Born Female.* New York: McKay, 1974. (Paper); Boorstin, Daniel J., *The Americans: The Democratic Experience.* New York: Random House, 1973; Burke, Vincent J., and Vee Burke, *Nixon's Good Deed: Welfare Reform.* New York: Columbia University Press, 1974; Cochran, Thomas C., *Business in American Life: A History.* New York: McGraw-Hill, 1974. (Paper); Cochran, Thomas C., *Social Change in America: The Twentieth Century.* New York: Harper & Row, 1972. (Paper); Cogley, John, *Catholic America.* New York: Dial, 1973. (Paper: Doubleday, 1974); Cohen, Richard M., and Jules Witcover, *A Heartbeat Away.* New York: Bantam, 1974. (Paper); Davies, Peter, *The Truth About Kent State: A Challenge to the American Conscience.* New York: Farrar, Straus & Giroux, 1973. (Paper); Decter, Midge, *The New Chastity and Other Arguments Against Women's Liberation.* New York: Coward, 1972. (Paper: Putnam, 1974); Degler, Carl, *Out of Our Past: The Forces That Shaped Modern America.* New York: Harper & Row, 1970. (Paper); Deloria, Vine, Jr., *We Talk, You Listen.* New York: Macmillan, 1970. (Paper: Dell, 1974); Dorson, Richard M., *America in Legend: Folklore from the Colonial Period to the Present.* New York: Pantheon, 1973. (Paper); Ellison, Mary, *The Black Experience: American Blacks, 1865–1972.* New York: Barnes & Noble, 1974; Fairman, Charles, *History of the Supreme Court* (Vol. 5): *Reconstruction and Reunion, 1864–1888.* New York: Macmillan, 1971; Friedan, Betty, *The Feminine Mystique.* New York: Norton, 1974. (Paper); Goldwater, Barry, *The Conscience of a Majority.* New York: Pocket Books, 1971. (Paper); Graubard, Stephen R., *Kissinger, Portrait of a Mind.* New York: Norton, 1974. (Paper); Hahn, Emily, *Once Upon a Pedestal: An Informal History of Women's Lib.* New York: Crowell,

1974; Handlin, Oscar, and Mary Handlin, *Facing Life: Youth and the Family in American History.* Boston: Little, Brown, 1972. (Paper); Hart, Gary W., *Right From the Start.* New York: Quadrangle, 1973; Hoffman, Paul, *The New Nixon.* New York: Tower, 1970; Hofstadter, Richard, *Anti-Intellectualism in American Life.* New York: Knopf, 1963; Hofstadter, Richard, *The Progressive Historians.* New York: Knopf, 1968. (Paper: Random, 1970); Kendrick, Alexander, *The Wound Within: America in the Vietnam Years, 1945–1974.* Boston: Little, Brown, 1974; McCloskey, Robert G., *The Modern Supreme Court.* Cambridge, Mass.: Harvard University Press, 1972. (Paper); Magruder, Jeb S., *An American Life.* New York: Atheneum, 1974; Manchester, William, *The Glory and the Dream: A Narrative History of America, 1932–1972.* Boston: Little, Brown, 1974; Mann, Arthur, et al., *History and the Role of the City in American Life.* Indianapolis: Indiana Historical Society, 1972; Marty, Martin E., *Righteous Empire: The Protestant Experience in America.* New York: Dial, 1970. (Paper); Millet, Kate, *Sexual Politics.* New York: Avon, 1973. (Paper); Myers, Margaret G., *A Financial History of the United States.* New York: Columbia University Press, 1970. (Paper); Packard, Vance, *A Nation of Strangers.* New York: McKay, 1972. (Paper: Pocket Books, 1974); Sale, Kirkpatrick, *SDS: Ten Years Toward a Revolution.* New York: Random, 1973; Schlesinger, Arthur M., Jr., *The Imperial Presidency.* Boston: Houghton Mifflin, 1973; Schlesinger, Arthur M., Jr., and F. L. Israel, *History of American Presidential Elections.* New York: McGraw-Hill, 1971; Sinclair, Andrew, *The Emancipation of the American Woman.* New York: Harper & Row, 1970; Smith, Page, *Daughters of the Promised Land: Women in American History.* Boston: Little, Brown, 1970. (Paper); Sochen, June, *Movers and Shakers: American Women Thinkers and Activists, 1900–1970.* New York: Quadrangle, 1973. (Paper); Spencer, Robert F., et al., *The Native Americans.* New York: Harper & Row, 1965; Sussman, Barry, *The Great Cover-up: Nixon and the Scandal of Watergate.* New York: Crowell, 1974; Ware, Cellestine, *Woman Power.* New York: Tower, 1970. (Paper); Washburn, Wilcomb E., *Red Man's Land: White Man's Law.* New York: Scribner, 1971. (Paper); Witcover, Jules, *The Resurrection of Richard Nixon.* New York: Putnam, 1970; Zaretsky, Irving I., and Mark P. Leone (Eds.), *Religious Movements in Contemporary America.* Princeton, N.J.: Princeton University Press, 1974.

The Declaration of Independence

When in the Course of human events, it becomes necessary for one people to dissolve the political bands which have connected them with another, and to assume among the Powers of the earth, the separate and equal station to which the Laws of Nature and of Nature's God entitle them, a decent respect to the opinions of mankind requires that they should declare the causes which impel them to the separation.

We hold these truths to be self-evident, that all men are created equal, that they are endowed by their Creator with certain unalienable Rights, that among these are Life, Liberty and the pursuit of Happiness. That to secure these rights, Governments are instituted among Men, deriving their just powers from the consent of the governed, That whenever any Form of Government becomes destructive of these ends, it is the Right of the People to alter or to abolish it, and to institute new Government, laying its foundation on such principles and organizing its powers in such form, as to them shall seem most likely to effect their Safety and Happiness. Prudence, indeed, will dictate that Governments long established should not be changed for light and transient causes; and accordingly all experience hath shown, that mankind are more disposed to suffer, while evils are sufferable, than to right themselves by abolishing the forms to which they are accustomed. But when a long train of abuses and usurpations, pursuing invariably the same Object evinces a design to reduce them under absolute Despotism, it is their right, it is their duty, to throw off such Government, and to provide new Guards for their future security.—Such has been the patient sufferance of these Colonies; and such is now the necessity which constrains them to alter their former Systems of Government. The history of the present King of Great Britain is a history of repeated injuries and usurpations, all having in direct object the establishment of an absolute Tyranny over these States. To prove this, let Facts be submitted to a candid world.

He has refused his Assent to Laws, the most wholesome and necessary for the public good.

He has forbidden his Governors to pass Laws of immediate and pressing importance, unless suspended in their operation till his Assent should be obtained; and when so suspended, he has utterly neglected to attend to them.

He has refused to pass other Laws for the accommodation of large districts of people, unless those people would relinquish the right of Representation in the Legislature, a right inestimable to them and formidable to tyrants only.

He has called together legislative bodies at places unusual, uncomfortable, and distant from the depository of their public Records, for the sole purpose of fatiguing them into compliance with his measures.

He has dissolved Representative Houses repeatedly, for opposing with manly firmness his invasions on the rights of the people.

He has refused for a long time, after such dissolutions, to cause others to be elected; whereby the Legislative Powers, incapable of Annihilation, have returned to the People at large for their exercise; the State remaining in the mean time exposed to all the dangers of invasion from without, and convulsions within.

He has endeavoured to prevent the population of these States; for that purpose obstructing the Laws of Naturalization of Foreigners; refusing to pass others to encourage their migration hither, and raising the conditions of new Appropriations of Lands.

He has obstructed the Administration of Justice, by refusing his Assent to Laws for establishing Judiciary powers.

He has made Judges dependent on his Will alone, for the tenure of their offices, and the amount and payment of their salaries.

He has erected a multitude of New Offices, and sent hither swarms of Officers to harass our People, and eat out their substance.

He has kept among us in times of peace, Standing Armies without the Consent of our legislature.

He has affected to render the Military independent of and superior to the Civil power.

He has combined with others to subject us to a jurisdiction foreign to our constitution, and unacknowledged by our laws; giving his Assent to their acts of pretended Legislation:

For quartering large bodies of armed troops among us:

For protecting them, by a mock Trial, from punishment for any Murders which they should commit on the Inhabitants of these States:

For cutting off our Trade with all parts of the world:

For imposing taxes on us without our Consent:

For depriving us in many cases, of the benefits of Trial by Jury:

For transporting us beyond Seas to be tried for pretended offences:

For abolishing the free System of English Laws in a neighbouring Province, establishing therein an Arbitrary government, and enlarging its Boundaries so as to render it at once an example and fit instrument for introducing the same absolute rule into these Colonies:

For taking away our Charters, abolishing our most valuable Laws, and altering fundamentally the Forms of our Governments:

For suspending our own Legislature, and declaring themselves invested with Power to legislate for us in all cases whatsoever.

He has abdicated Government here, by declaring us out of his Protection and waging War against us.

He has plundered our seas, ravaged our Coasts, burnt our towns, and destroyed the lives of our people.

He is at this time transporting large Armies of foreign Mercenaries to compleat the works of death, desolation and tyranny, already begun with circumstances of Cruelty & perfidy scarcely paralleled in the most barbarous ages, and totally unworthy the Head of a civilized nation.

He has constrained our fellow Citizens taken Captive on the high Seas to bear Arms against their Country, to become the executioners of their friends and Brethren, or to fall themselves by their Hands.

He has excited domestic insurrections amongst us, and has endeavoured to bring on the inhabitants of our frontiers, the merciless Indian Savages, whose known rule of warfare, is an undistinguished destruction of all ages, sexes and conditions.

In every stage of these Oppressions We have Petitioned for Redress in the most humble terms: Our repeated Petitions have been answered only by repeated injury. A Prince, whose character is thus marked by every act which may define a Tyrant, is unfit to be the ruler of a free People.

Nor have We been wanting in attention to our British brethren. We have warned them from time to time of attempts by their legislature to extend an unwarrantable jurisdiction over us. We have reminded them of the circumstances of our emigration and settlement here. We have appealed to their native justice and magnanimity, and we have conjured them by the ties of our common kindred to disavow these usurpations, which, would inevitably interrupt our connections and correspondence. They too have been deaf to the voice of justice and of consanguinity. We must, therefore, acquiesce in the necessity, which denounces our Separation, and hold them, as we hold the rest of mankind, Enemies in War, in Peace Friends.

We, therefore, the Representatives of the united States of America, in General Congress, Assembled, appealing to the Supreme Judge of the world for the rectitude of our intentions, do, in the Name, and by Authority of the good People of these Colonies, solemnly publish and declare, That these United Colonies are, and of Right ought to be Free and Independent States; that they are Absolved from all Allegiance to the British Crown, and that all political connection between them and the State of Great Britain, is and ought to be totally dissolved; and that as Free and Independent States, they have full Power to levy War, conclude Peace, contract Alliances, establish Commerce, and to do all other Acts and Things which Independent States may of right do. And for the support of this Declaration, with a firm reliance on the protection of divine Providence, we mutually pledge to each other our Lives, our Fortunes and our sacred Honor.

The Constitution of the United States

We the people of the United States, in Order to form a more perfect Union, establish Justice, insure domestic Tranquility, provide for the common defence, promote the general Welfare, and secure the Blessings of Liberty to ourselves and our Posterity, do ordain and establish this CONSTITUTION for the United States of America.

ARTICLE I

Section 1. All legislative Powers herein granted shall be vested in a Congress of the United States, which shall consist of a Senate and House of Representatives.

Section 2. The House of Representatives shall be composed of Members chosen every second Year by the People of the several States, and the Electors in each State shall have the Qualifications requisite for Electors of the most numerous Branch of the State Legislature.

No Person shall be a Representative who shall not have attained to the Age of twenty-five Years, and been seven Years a Citizen of the United States, and who shall not, when elected, be an Inhabitant of that State in which he shall be chosen.

Representatives and direct Taxes shall be apportioned among the several States which may be included within this Union, according to their respective Numbers, which shall be determined by adding to the whole Number of free Persons, including those bound to Service for a Term of Years, and excluding Indians not taxed, three fifths of all other Persons. The actual Enumeration shall be made within three Years after the first Meeting of the Congress of the United States, and within every subsequent Term of ten Years, in such Manner as they shall by Law direct. The Number of Representatives shall not exceed one for every thirty Thousand, but each State shall have at Least one Representative; and until such enumeration shall be made, the State of New Hampshire shall be entitled to chuse three, Massachusetts eight, Rhode-Island and Providence Plantations one, Connecticut five, New-York six, New Jersey four, Pennsylvania eight, Delaware one, Maryland six, Virginia ten, North Carolina five, South Carolina five, and Georgia three.

When vacancies happen in the Representation from any State, the Executive Authority thereof shall issue Writs of Election to fill such Vacancies.

The House of Representatives shall chuse their Speaker and other Officers; and shall have the sole Power of Impeachment.

Section 3. The Senate of the United States shall be composed of two Senators from each State, chosen by the Legislature thereof, for six Years; and each Senator shall have one Vote.

Immediately after they shall be assembled in Consequence of the first Election, they shall be divided as equally as may be into three Classes. The Seats of the Senators of the first Class shall be vacated at the Expiration of the second Year, of the second Class at the Expiration of the fourth Year, and of the third Class at the Expiration of the sixth Year, so that one-third may be chosen every second Year; and if Vacancies happen by Resignation, or otherwise, during the Recess of the Legislature of any State, the Executive thereof may make temporary Appointments until the next Meeting of the Legislature, which shall then fill such Vacancies.

No Person shall be a Senator who shall not have attained to the Age of thirty Years, and been nine Years a Citizen of the United States, and who shall not, when elected, be an Inhabitant of that State in which he shall be chosen.

The Vice President of the United States shall be President of the Senate, but shall have no vote, unless they be equally divided.

The Senate shall chuse their other Officers, and also a President pro tempore, in the absence of the Vice President, or when he shall exercise the Office of the President of the United States.

The Senate shall have the sole Power to try all Impeachments. When sitting for that purpose, they shall be on Oath or Affirmation. When the President of the United States is tried, the Chief Justice shall preside: And no person shall be convicted without the Concurrence of two thirds of the Members present.

Judgment in Cases of Impeachment shall not extend further than to removal from Office, and disqualification to hold and enjoy any Office of honor, Trust, or Profit under the United States: but the Party convicted shall nevertheless be liable and subject to Indictment, Trial, Judgment, and Punishment, according to Law.

Section 4. The Times, Places and Manner of holding Elections for Senators and Representatives, shall be prescribed in each state by the Legislature thereof; but the Congress may at any time by Law make or alter such Regulations, except as to the Places of Chusing Senators.

The Congress shall assemble at least once in every Year, and such Meeting shall be on the first Monday in December, unless they shall by Law appoint a different Day.

Section 5. Each House shall be the Judge of the Elections, Returns and Qualifications of its own Members, and a Majority of each shall constitute a Quorum to do Business; but a smaller number may adjourn from day to day, and may be authorized to compel the Attendance of absent Members, in such Manner, and under such Penalties, as each House may provide.

Each House may determine the Rules of its Proceedings, punish its Members for disorderly Behaviour, and, with the Concurrence of two thirds, expel a Member.

Each House shall keep a Journal of its Proceedings, and from time to time publish the same, excepting such Parts as may in their Judgment require Secrecy; and the Yeas and Nays of the Members of either House on any question shall, at the Desire of one fifth of those Present, be entered on the Journal.

Neither House, during the Session of Congress, shall, without the Consent of the other, adjourn for more than three days, nor to any other Place than that in which the two Houses shall be sitting.

Section 6. The Senators and Representatives shall receive a Compensation for their Services, to be ascertained by Law, and paid out of the Treasury of the United States. They shall in all Cases, except Treason, Felony, and Breach of the Peace, be privileged from Arrest during their Attendance at the Session of their respective Houses, and in going to and returning from the same; and for any Speech or Debate in either House, they shall not be questioned in any other Place.

No Senator or Representative shall, during the Time for which he was elected, be appointed to any civil Office under the Authority of the United States, which shall have been created, or the Emoluments whereof shall have been increased, during such time; and no Person holding any Office under the United States shall be a Member of either House during his continuance in Office.

Section 7. All Bills for raising Revenue shall originate in the House of Representatives; but the Senate may propose or concur with Amendments as on other Bills.

Every Bill which shall have passed the House of Representatives and the Senate, shall, before it become a Law, be presented to the President of the United States; If he approve he shall sign it, but if not he shall return it, with his Objections, to that House in which it shall have originated, who shall enter the Objections at large on their Journal, and proceed to reconsider it. If after such Reconsideration two thirds of that House shall agree to pass the Bill, it shall be sent, together with the Objections, to the other House, by which it shall likewise be reconsidered, and if approved by two thirds of that House, it shall become a Law. But in all such Cases the Votes of both Houses shall be determined by Yeas and Nays, and the Names of the Persons voting for and against the Bill shall be entered on the Journal of each House respectively. If any Bill shall not be returned by the President within ten Days (Sundays excepted) after it shall have been presented to him, the Same shall be a Law, in like Manner as if he had signed it, unless the Congress by their Adjournment prevent its Return, in which Case it shall not be a Law.

Every Order, Resolution, or Vote to which the Concurrence of the Senate and House of Representatives may be necessary (except on a question of Adjournment) shall be presented to the President of the United States; and before the Same shall take Effect, shall be approved by him, or being disapproved by him, shall be repassed by two thirds of the Senate and House of Representatives, according to the Rules and Limitations prescribed in the Case of a Bill.

Section 8. The Congress shall have Power To lay and collect Taxes, Duties, Imposts and Excises, to pay the Debts and provide for the common Defence and general Welfare of the United States; but all Duties, Imposts and Excises shall be uniform throughout the United States;

To borrow money on the credit of the United States;

To regulate Commerce with foreign Nations, and among the several States, and with the Indian Tribes;

To establish an uniform Rule of Naturalization, and uniform Laws on the subject of Bankruptcies throughout the United States;

To coin Money, regulate the Value thereof, and of foreign Coin, and fix the Standard of Weights and Measures;

To provide for the Punishment of counterfeiting the Securities and current Coin of the United States;

To establish Post Offices and post Roads;

To promote the Progress of Science and useful Arts, by securing for limited Times to Authors and Inventors the exclusive Right to their respective Writings and Discoveries;

To constitute Tribunals inferior to the Supreme Court;

To define and punish Piracies and Felonies committed on the high Seas, and Offenses against the Law of Nations;

To declare War, grant Letters of Marque and Reprisal, and make Rules concerning Captures on Land and Water;

To raise and support Armies, but no Appropriation of Money to that Use shall be for a longer Term than two Years;

To provide and maintain a Navy;

To make Rules for the Government and Regulation of the land and naval forces;

To provide for calling forth the Militia to execute the Laws of the Union, suppress Insurrections and repel Invasions;

To provide for organizing, arming, and disciplining the Militia, and for governing such Part of them as may be employed in the Service of the United States, reserving to the States respectively, the Appointment of the Officers, and the Authority of training the Militia according to the discipline prescribed by Congress;

To exercise exclusive Legislation in all Cases whatsoever, over such District (not exceeding ten Miles square) as may, by Cession of particular States, and the acceptance of Congress, become the Seat of Government of the United States, and to exercise like Authority over all Places purchased by the Consent of the Legislature of the State in which the Same shall be, for the Erection of Forts, Magazines, Arsenals, dock-Yards, and other needful Buildings;—And

To make all Laws which shall be necessary and proper for carrying into Execution the foregoing Powers, and all other Powers vested by this Constitution in the Government of the United States, or in any Department or Officer thereof.

Section 9. The Migration or Importation of such Persons as any of the States now existing shall think proper to admit, shall not be prohibited by the Congress prior to the Year one thousand eight hundred and eight, but a tax or duty may be imposed on such Importation, not exceeding ten dollars for each Person.

The privilege of the Writ of Habeas Corpus shall not be suspended, unless when in Cases of Rebellion or Invasion the public Safety may require it.

No Bill of Attainder or ex post facto Law shall be passed.

No Capitation, or other direct, Tax shall be laid unless in Proportion to the Census or Enumeration herein before directed to be taken.

No Tax or Duty shall be laid on Articles exported from any State.

No Preference shall be given by any Regulation of Revenue to the Ports of one State over those of another: nor shall Vessels bound to, or from, one State, be obliged to enter, clear, or pay Duties in another.

No Money shall be drawn from the Treasury, but in Consequence of Appropriations made by Law; and a regular Statement and Account of the Receipts and Expenditures of all public Money shall be published from time to time.

No Title of Nobility shall be granted by the United States: And no Person holding any Office of Profit or Trust under them, shall, without the Consent of the Congress, accept of any present, Emolument, Office, or

Title, of any kind whatever, from any King, Prince, or foreign State.

Section 10. No State shall enter into any Treaty, Alliance, or Confederation; grant Letters of Marque and Reprisal; coin Money; emit Bills of Credit; make any Thing but gold and silver Coin a Tender in Payment of Debts; pass any Bill of Attainder, ex post facto Law, or Law impairing the Obligation of Contracts, or grant any Title of Nobility.

No state shall, without the Consent of the Congress, lay any Imposts or Duties on Imports or Exports, except what may be absolutely necessary for executing its inspection Laws: and the net Produce of all Duties and Imposts, laid by any State on Imports or Exports, shall be for the Use of the Treasury of the United States; and all such Laws shall be subject to the Revision and Control of the Congress.

No State shall, without the Consent of Congress, lay any duty of Tonnage, keep Troops, or Ships of War in time of Peace, enter into any Agreement or Compact with another State, or with a foreign Power, or engage in War, unless actually invaded, or in such imminent Danger as will not admit of delay.

ARTICLE II

Section 1. The executive Power shall be vested in a President of the United States of America. He shall hold his Office during the Term of four Years, and, together with the Vice President, chosen for the same Term, be elected, as follows:

Each State shall appoint, in such Manner as the Legislature thereof may direct, a Number of Electors, equal to the whole Number of Senators and Representatives to which the State may be entitled in the Congress: but no Senator or Representative, or Person holding an Office of Trust or Profit under the United States, shall be appointed an Elector.

The Electors shall meet in their respective States, and vote by Ballot for two Persons, of whom one at least shall not be an Inhabitant of the same State with themselves. And they shall make a List of all the Persons voted for, and of the Number of Votes for each; which List they shall sign and certify, and transmit sealed to the Seat of the Government of the United States, directed to the President of the Senate. The President of the Senate shall, in the Presence of the Senate and House of Representatives, open all the Certificates, and the Votes shall then be counted. The Person having the greatest Number of Votes shall be the President, if such Number be a Majority of the whole Number of Electors appointed; and if there be more than one who have such Majority, and have an equal Number of Votes, then the House of Representatives shall immediately chuse by Ballot one of them for President; and if no Person have a Majority, then from the five highest on the List the said House shall in like Manner chuse the President. But in chusing the President, the Votes shall be taken by States, the Representation from each State having one Vote; a quorum for this Purpose shall consist of a Member or Members from two-thirds of the States, and a Majority of all the States shall be necessary to a Choice. In every Case, after the Choice of the President, the Person having the greatest Number of Votes of the Electors shall be the Vice President. But if there should remain two or more who have equal votes, the Senate shall chuse from them by Ballot the Vice President.

The Congress may determine the Time of chusing the Electors, and the Day on which they shall give their Votes; which Day shall be the same throughout the United States.

No person except a natural-born Citizen, or a Citizen of the United States, at the time of the Adoption of this Constitution, shall be eligible to the Office of President; neither shall any Person be eligible to that Office who shall not have attained to the Age of thirty-five Years, and been fourteen Years a Resident within the United States.

In Case of the Removal of the President from Office, or of his Death, Resignation, or Inability to discharge the Powers and Duties of the said Office, the same shall devolve on the Vice President, and the Congress may by Law provide for the Case of Removal, Death, Resignation, or Inability, both of the President and Vice President, declaring what Officer shall then act as President, and such Officer shall act accordingly, until the Disability be removed, or a President shall be elected.

The President shall, at stated Times, receive for his Services a Compensation, which shall neither be increased nor diminished during the Period for which he shall have been elected, and he shall not receive within that Period any other Emolument from the United States, or any of them.

Before he enter on the Execution of his Office, he shall take the following Oath or Affirmation:—"I do solemnly swear (or affirm) that I will faithfully execute the Office of President of the United States, and will, to the best of my Ability, preserve, protect, and defend the Constitution of the United States."

Section 2. The President shall be Commander in Chief of the Army and Navy of the United States, and of the Militia of the several States, when called into the actual Service of the United States; he may require the Opinion, in writing, of the principal Officer in each of the executive Departments, upon any subject relating to the Duties of their respective Offices, and he shall have Power to Grant Reprieves and Pardons for Offences against the United States, except in Cases of Impeachment.

He shall have Power, by and with the Advice and Consent of the Senate, to make Treaties, provided two thirds of the Senators present concur; and he shall nominate, and by and with the Advice and Consent of the Senate, shall appoint Ambassadors, other public Ministers and Consuls, Judges of the supreme Court, and all other Officers of the United States, whose Appointments are not herein otherwise provided for, and which shall be established by Law: but the Congress may by Law vest the Appointment of such inferior Officers, as they think proper, in the President alone, in the Courts of Law, or in the Heads of Departments.

The President shall have Power to fill up all Vacancies that may happen during the Recess of the Senate, by granting Commissions which shall expire at the End of their next Session.

Section 3. He shall from time to time give to the Congress Information of the State of the Union, and recommend to their Consideration such Measures as he shall judge necessary and expedient; he may, on extraordinary occasions, convene both Houses, or either of them, and in Case of Disagreement between them, with respect to the Time of Adjournment, he may adjourn them to such Time as he shall think proper; he shall receive Ambassadors and other public Ministers; he shall take Care that the Laws be faithfully executed, and shall Commission all the Officers of the United States.

Section 4. The President, Vice President and all civil Officers of the United States, shall be removed from Office on Impeachment for, and Conviction of, Treason, Bribery, or other high Crimes and Misdemeanors.

ARTICLE III

Section 1. The judicial Power of the United States, shall be vested in one supreme Court, and in such inferior Courts as the Congress may from time to time ordain and establish. The Judges, both of the supreme and inferior Courts, shall hold their Offices during good Behaviour, and shall, at stated Times, receive for their Services, a Compensation, which shall not be diminished during their Continuance in Office.

Section 2. The judicial Power shall extend to all Cases, in Law and Equity, arising under this Constitution, the Laws of the United States, and Treaties made, or which shall be made, under their Authority;—to all Cases affecting Ambassadors, other public Ministers and Consuls;—to all Cases of admiralty and maritime Jurisdiction;—to Controversies to which the United States shall be a Party;—to Controversies between two or more States;—between a State and Citizens of another State;—between Citizens of the same State claiming Lands under Grants of different States, and between a State, or the Citizens thereof, and foreign States, Citizens or Subjects.

In all Cases affecting Ambassadors, other public Ministers and Consuls, and those in which a State shall be Party, the supreme Court shall have original Jurisdiction. In all the other Cases before mentioned, the supreme Court shall have appellate Jurisdiction, both as to Law and Fact, with such Exceptions, and under such Regulations as the Congress shall make.

The trial of all Crimes, except in Cases of Impeachment, shall be by Jury; and such Trial shall be held in the State where the said Crimes shall have been committed; but when not committed within any State, the Trial shall be at such Place or Places as the Congress may by Law have directed.

Section 3. Treason against the United States, shall consist only in levying War against them, or in adhering to their Enemies, giving them Aid and Comfort. No Person shall be convicted of Treason unless on the Testimony of two Witnesses to the same overt Act, or on Confession in open Court.

The Congress shall have power to declare the Punishment of Treason, but no Attainder of Treason shall work Corruption of Blood, or Forfeiture except during the Life of the Person attainted.

ARTICLE IV

Section 1. Full Faith and Credit shall be given in each State to the public Acts, Records, and judicial Proceedings of every other State. And the Congress may by general Laws prescribe the Manner in which such Acts, Records and Proceedings shall be proved, and the Effect thereof.

Section 2. The Citizens of each State shall be entitled to all Privileges and Immunities of Citizens in the several States.

A Person charged in any State with Treason, Felony, or other Crime, who shall flee from Justice, and be found in another State, shall on demand of the executive Authority of the State from which he fled, be delivered up, to be removed to the State having Jurisdiction of the crime.

No Person held to Service or Labour in one State, under the Laws thereof, escaping into another, shall, in Consequence of any Law or Regulation therein, be discharged from such Service or Labour, but shall be delivered up on Claim of the Party to whom such Service or Labour may be due.

Section 3. New States may be admitted by the Congress into this Union; but no new State shall be formed or erected within the Jurisdiction of any other State; nor any State be formed by the Junction of two or more States, or parts of States, without the Consent of the Legislatures of the States concerned as well as of the Congress.

The Congress shall have Power to dispose of and make all needful Rules and Regulations respecting the Territory or other Property belonging to the United States; and nothing in this Constitution shall be so construed as to Prejudice any Claims of the United States, or of any particular State.

Section 4. The United States shall guarantee to every State in this Union a Republican Form of Government, and shall protect each of them against Invasion; and on Application of the Legislature, or of the Executive (when the Legislature cannot be convened) against domestic Violence.

ARTICLE V

The Congress, whenever two thirds of both Houses shall deem it necessary, shall propose Amendments to this Constitution, or, on the Application of the Legislatures of two thirds of the several States, shall call a Convention for proposing Amendments, which, in either Case, shall be valid to all Intents and Purposes, as part of this Constitution, when ratified by the Legislatures of three fourths of the several States, or by Conventions in three fourths thereof, as the one or the other Mode of Ratification may be proposed by the Congress; Provided that no Amendment which may be made prior to the Year One thousand eight hundred and eight shall in any Manner affect the first and fourth Clauses in the Ninth Section of the first Article; and that no State, without its Consent, shall be deprived of its equal Suffrage in the Senate.

ARTICLE VI

All Debts contracted and Engagements entered into, before the Adoption of this Constitution, shall be as valid against the United States under this Constitution, as under the Confederation.

This Constitution, and the Laws of the United States which shall be made in Pursuance thereof; and all Treaties made, or which shall be made, under the Authority of the United States, shall be the supreme Law of the Land; and the Judges in every State shall be bound thereby, any Thing in the Constitution or Laws of any State to the Contrary notwithstanding.

The Senators and Representatives before mentioned, and the Members of the several State Legislatures, and all executive and judicial Officers, both of the United States and of the several States, shall be bound by Oath or Affirmation to support this Constitution; but no religious Test shall ever be required as a qualification to any Office or public Trust under the United States.

ARTICLE VII

The Ratification of the Conventions of nine States shall be sufficient for the Establishment of this Constitution between the States so ratifying the same.

Done in Convention by the Unanimous Consent of the States present the Seventeenth Day of September in the Year of our Lord one thousand seven hundred and Eighty seven, and of the Independence of the United States of America the Twelfth. In Witness whereof We have hereunto subscribed our Names.

Articles in Addition to, and Amendment of, the Constitution of the United States of America, Proposed by Congress, and Ratified by the Legislatures of the Several States, Pursuant to the Fifth Article of the Original Constitution.

AMENDMENT I [1791]

Congress shall make no law respecting an establishment of religion, or prohibiting the free exercise thereof; or abridging the freedom of speech, or of the press; or the right of the people peaceably to assemble, and to petition the Government for a redress of grievances.

AMENDMENT II [1791]

A well regulated Militia, being necessary to the security of a free State, the right of the people to keep and bear Arms, shall not be infringed.

AMENDMENT III [1791]

No Soldier shall, in time of peace, be quartered in any house, without the consent of the Owner, nor in time of war, but in a manner to be prescribed by law.

AMENDMENT IV [1791]

The right of the people to be secure in their persons, houses, papers, and effects, against unreasonable searches and seizures, shall not be violated, and no Warrants shall issue, but upon probable cause, supported by Oath or affirmation, and particularly describing the place to be searched, and the persons or things to be seized.

AMENDMENT V [1791]

No person shall be held to answer for a capital or otherwise infamous crime, unless on a presentment or indictment of a Grand Jury, except in cases arising in the land or naval forces, or in the Militia, when in actual service in time of War or public danger; nor shall any person be subject for the same offence to be twice put in jeopardy of life or limb; nor shall be compelled in any criminal case to be a witness against himself, nor be deprived of life, liberty, or property, without due process of law; nor shall private property be taken for public use, without just compensation.

AMENDMENT VI [1791]

In all criminal prosecutions, the accused shall enjoy the right to a speedy and public trial, by an impartial jury of the State and district wherein the crime shall have been committed, which district shall have been previously ascertained by law, and to be informed of the nature and cause of the accusation; to be confronted with the witnesses against him; to have compulsory process for obtaining witnesses in his favor, and to have the Assistance of Counsel for his defence.

AMENDMENT VII [1791]

In Suits at common law, where the value in controversy shall exceed twenty dollars, the right of trial by jury shall be preserved, and no fact tried by a jury, shall be otherwise re-examined in any Court of the United States, than according to the rules of the common law.

AMENDMENT VIII [1791]

Excessive bail shall not be required, nor excessive fines imposed, nor cruel and unusual punishments inflicted.

AMENDMENT IX [1791]

The enumeration in the Constitution, of certain rights, shall not be construed to deny or disparage others retained by the people.

AMENDMENT X [1791]

The powers not delegated to the United States by the Constitution, nor prohibited by it to the States, are reserved to the States respectively, or to the people.

AMENDMENT XI [1798]

The Judicial power of the United States shall not be construed to extend to any suit in law or equity, commenced or prosecuted against one of the United States by Citizens of another State, or by Citizens or Subjects of any Foreign State.

AMENDMENT XII [1804]

The Electors shall meet in their respective States and vote by ballot for President and Vice President, one of whom, at least, shall not be an inhabitant of the same States with themselves; they shall name in their ballots the person voted for as President, and in distinct ballots the person voted for as Vice-President, and they shall make distinct lists of all persons voted for as President, and of all persons voted for as Vice-President, and of the number of votes for each, which lists they shall sign and certify, and transmit sealed to the seat of the government of the United States, directed to the President of the Senate;—The President of the Senate shall, in the presence of the Senate and House of Representatives, open all the certificates and the votes shall then be counted;—The person having the greatest number of votes for President, shall be the President, if such number be a majority of the whole number of Electors appointed; and if no person have such majority, then from the persons having the highest numbers not exceeding three on the list of those voted for as President, the House of Representatives shall choose immediately, by ballot, the President. But in choosing the President, the votes shall be taken by states, the representation from each state having one vote; a quorum for this purpose shall consist of a member or members from two-thirds of the states, and a majority of all the states shall be necessary to a choice. And if the House of Representatives shall not choose a President whenever the right of choice shall devolve upon them, before the fourth day of March next following, then the Vice-President shall act as President, as in the case of the death or other constitutional disability of the President.—The person having the greatest number of votes as Vice-President, shall be the Vice-President, if such number be a majority of the whole number of Electors appointed, and if no person have a majority, then from the two highest numbers on the list, the Senate shall choose the Vice-President; a quorum for the purpose shall consist of two-thirds of the whole number of Senators, and a majority of the whole number shall be necessary to a choice. But no person constitutionally ineligible to the office of President shall be eligible to that of Vice-President of the United States.

AMENDMENT XIII [1865]

Section 1. Neither slavery nor involuntary servitude, except as a punishment for crime whereof the party shall have been duly convicted, shall exist within the United States, or any place subject to their jurisdiction.

Section 2. Congress shall have power to enforce this article by appropriate legislation.

AMENDMENT XIV [1868]

Section 1. All persons born or naturalized in the United States, and subject to the jurisdiction thereof, are citizens of the United States and of the State wherein they reside. No State shall make or enforce any law which shall abridge the privileges or immunities of citizens of the United States; nor shall any State deprive any person of life, liberty, or property, without due process of law; nor deny to any person within its jurisdiction the equal protection of the laws.

Section 2. Representatives shall be apportioned among the several States according to their respective numbers, counting the whole number of persons in each State, excluding Indians not taxed. But when the right to vote at any election for the choice of electors for President and Vice President of the United States, Representatives in Congress, the Executive and Judicial officers of a State, or the members of the Legislature thereof, is denied to any of the male inhabitants of such State, being twenty-one years of age, and citizens of the United States, or in any way abridged, except for participation in rebellion, or other crime, the basis of representation therein shall be reduced in the proportion which the number of such male citizens shall bear to the whole number of male citizens twenty-one years of age in such State.

Section 3. No person shall be a Senator or Representative in Congress, or elector of President and Vice President, or hold any office, civil or military, under the United States, or under any State, who, having previously taken an oath, as a member of Congress, or as an officer of the United States, or as a member of any State legislature, or as an executive or judicial officer of any State, to support the Constitution of the United States, shall have engaged in insurrection or rebellion against the same, or given aid or comfort to the enemies thereof. But Congress may by a vote of two-thirds of each House, remove such disability.

Section 4. The validity of the public debt of the United States, authorized by law, including debts incurred for payment of pensions and bounties for services in suppressing insurrection or rebellion, shall not be questioned. But neither the United States nor any State shall assume or pay any debt or obligation incurred in aid of insurrection or rebellion against the United States, or any claim for the loss or emancipation of any slave; but all such debts, obligations, and claims shall be held illegal and void.

Section 5. The Congress shall have the power to enforce, by appropriate legislation, the provisions of this article.

AMENDMENT XV [1870]

Section 1. The right of citizens of the United States to vote shall not be denied or abridged by the United States or by any State on account of race, color, or previous condition of servitude—

Section 2. The Congress shall have power to enforce this article by appropriate legislation.

AMENDMENT XVI [1913]

The Congress shall have power to lay and collect taxes on incomes, from whatever source derived, without apportionment among the several States, and without regard to any census or enumeration.

AMENDMENT XVII [1913]

The Senate of the United States shall be composed of two Senators from each State, elected by the people thereof, for six years; and each Senator shall have one vote. The electors in each State shall have the qualifications requisite for electors of the most numerous branch of the State legislatures.

When vacancies happen in the representation of any State in the Senate, the executive authority of such State shall issue writs of election to fill such vacancies: *Provided,* That the legislature of any State may empower the executive thereof to make temporary appointments until the people fill the vacancies by election as the legislature may direct.

This amendment shall not be so construed as to affect the election or term of any Senator chosen before it becomes valid as part of the Constitution.

AMENDMENT XVIII [1919]

Section 1. After one year from the ratification of this article the manufacture, sale, or transportation of intoxicating liquors within, the importation thereof into, or the exportation thereof from the United States and all territory subject to the jurisdiction thereof for beverage purposes is hereby prohibited.

Section 2. The Congress and the several States shall have concurrent power to enforce this article by appropriate legislation.

Section 3. This article shall be inoperative unless it shall have been ratified as an amendment to the Constitution by the legislatures of the several States, as provided in the Constitution, within seven years from the date of the submission hereof to the States by the Congress.

AMENDMENT XIX [1920]

The right of citizens of the United States to vote shall not be denied or abridged by the United States or by any State on account of sex.

Congress shall have power to enforce this article by appropriate legislation.

AMENDMENT XX [1933]

Section 1. The terms of the President and Vice President shall end at noon on the 20th day of January, and the terms of Senators and Representatives at noon on the 3d day of January, of the years in which such terms would have ended if this article had not been ratified; and the terms of their successors shall then begin.

Section 2. The Congress shall assemble at least once in every year, and such meeting shall begin at noon on the 3d day of January, unless they shall by law appoint a different day.

Section 3. If, at the time fixed for the beginning of the term of the President, the President elect shall have died, the Vice President elect shall become President. If a President shall not have been chosen before the time fixed for the beginning of his term, or if the President elect shall have failed to qualify, then the Vice President elect shall act as President until a President shall have qualified; and the Congress may by law provide for the case wherein neither a President elect nor a Vice President elect shall have qualified, declaring who shall then act as President, or the manner in which one who is to act shall be selected, and such person shall act accordingly until a President or Vice President shall have qualified.

Section 4. The Congress may by law provide for the case of the death of any of the persons from whom the House of Representatives may choose a President whenever the right of choice shall have devolved upon them, and for the case of the death of any of the persons from whom the Senate may choose a Vice President whenever the right of choice shall have devolved upon them.

Section 5. Sections 1 and 2 shall take effect on the 15th day of October following the ratification of this article.

Section 6. This article shall be inoperative unless it shall have been ratified as an amendment to the Constitution by the legislatures of three-fourths of the several States within seven years from the date of its submission.

AMENDMENT XXI [1933]

Section 1. The eighteenth article of amendment to the Constitution of the United States is hereby repealed.

Section 2. The transportation or importation into any State, Territory, or possession of the United States for delivery or use therein of intoxicating liquors, in violation of the laws thereof, is hereby prohibited.

Section 3. This article shall be inoperative unless it shall have been ratified as an amendment to the Constitution by conventions in the several States, as provided in the Constitution, within seven years from the date of the submission hereof to the States by the Congress.

AMENDMENT XXII [1951]

No person shall be elected to the office of the President more than twice, and no person who has held the office of President, or acted as President, for more than two years of a term to which some other person was elected President shall be elected to the office of the President more than once.

But this Article shall not apply to any person holding the office of President when this Article was proposed by the Congress, and shall not prevent any person who may be holding the office of President, or acting as President, during the term within which this Article becomes operative from holding the office of President or acting as President during the remainder of such term.

AMENDMENT XXIII [1961]

Section 1. The District constituting the seat of Government of the United States shall appoint in such manner as the Congress may direct:

A number of electors of President and Vice President equal to the whole number of Senators and Representatives in Congress to which the District would be entitled if it were a State, but in no event more than the least populous State; they shall be in addition to those appointed by the States, but they shall be considered, for the purposes of the election of President and Vice President, to be electors appointed by a State; and they shall meet in the District and perform such duties as provided by the twelfth article of amendment.

Section 2. The Congress shall have power to enforce this article by appropriate legislation.

AMENDMENT XXIV [1964]

Section 1. The right of citizens of the United States to vote in any primary or other election for President or Vice President, for electors for President or Vice President, or for Senator or Representative in Congress, shall not be denied or abridged by the United States or any State by reason of failure to pay any poll tax or other tax.

Section 2. The Congress shall have the power to enforce this article by appropriate legislation.

AMENDMENT XXV [1967]

Section 1. In case of the removal of the President from office or his death or resignation, the Vice President shall become President.

Section 2. Whenever there is a vacancy in the office of the Vice President, the President shall nominate a Vice President who shall take the office upon confirmation by a majority vote of both houses of Congress.

Section 3. Whenever the President transmits to the President pro tempore of the Senate and the Speaker of the House of Representatives his written declaration that he is unable to discharge the powers and duties of his office, and until he transmits to them a written declaration to the contrary, such powers and duties shall be discharged by the Vice President as Acting President.

Section 4. Whenever the Vice President and a majority of either the principal officers of the executive departments, or of such other body as Congress may by law provide, transmit to the President pro tempore of the Senate and the Speaker of the House of Representatives their written declaration that the President is unable to discharge the powers and duties of his office, the Vice President shall immediately assume the powers and duties of the office as Acting President.

Thereafter, when the President transmits to the President pro tempore of the Senate and the Speaker of the House of Representatives his written declaration that no inability exists, he shall resume the powers and duties of his office unless the Vice President and a majority of either the principal officers of the executive departments, or of such other body as Congress may by law provide, transmit within four days to the President pro tempore of the Senate and the Speaker of the House of Representatives their written declaration that the President is unable to discharge the powers and duties of his office. Thereupon Congress shall decide the issue, assembling within 48 hours for that purpose if not in session. If the Congress, within 21 days after receipt of the latter written declaration, or, if Congress is not in session, within 21 days after Congress is required to assemble, determines by two-thirds vote of both houses that the President is unable to discharge the powers and duties of his office, the Vice President shall continue to discharge the same as Acting President; otherwise, the President shall resume the powers and duties of his office.

AMENDMENT XXVI [1971]

Section 1. The right of citizens of the United States, who are 18 years of age or older, to vote shall not be denied or abridged by the United States or any state on account of age.

Section 2. The Congress shall have the power to enforce this article by appropriate legislation.

Presidential Elections

Year	*Candidates*	*Party*	*Popular Vote*	*Electoral Vote*
1789	**George Washington**			69
	John Adams			34
	Others			35
1792	**George Washington**			132
	John Adams			77
	George Clinton			50
	Others			5
1796	**John Adams**	Federalist		71
	Thomas Jefferson	Democratic-Republican		68
	Thomas Pinckney	Federalist		59
	Aaron Burr	Democratic-Republican		30
	Others			48
1800	**Thomas Jefferson**	Democratic-Republican		73
	Aaron Burr	Democratic-Republican		73
	John Adams	Federalist		65
	Charles C. Pinckney	Federalist		64

Year	*Candidates*	*Party*	*Popular Vote*	*Electoral Vote*
1804	**Thomas Jefferson**	Democratic-Republican		162
	Charles C. Pinckney	Federalist		14
1808	**James Madison**	Democratic-Republican		122
	Charles C. Pinckney	Federalist		47
	George Clinton	Independent-Republican		6
1812	**James Madison**	Democratic-Republican		128
	DeWitt Clinton	Federalist		89
1816	**James Monroe**	Democratic-Republican		183
	Rufus King	Federalist		34
1820	**James Monroe**	Democratic-Republican		231
	John Quincy Adams	Independent-Republican		1
1824	**John Quincy Adams**	Democratic-Republican	108,740	84
	Andrew Jackson	Democratic-Republican	153,544	99
	Henry Clay	Democratic-Republican	47,136	37
	William H. Crawford	Democratic-Republican	46,618	41
1828	**Andrew Jackson**	Democratic	647,231	178
	John Quincy Adams	National Republican	509,097	83
1832	**Andrew Jackson**	Democratic	687,502	219
	Henry Clay	National Republican	530,189	49
	William Wirt	Anti-Masonic	33,108	7
	John Floyd	National Republican		11
1836	**Martin Van Buren**	Democratic	761,549	170
	William H. Harrison	Whig	549,567	73
	Hugh L. White	Whig	145,396	26
	Daniel Webster	Whig	41,287	14
1840	**William H. Harrison**	Whig	1,275,017	234
	(**John Tyler,** 1841)			
	Martin Van Buren	Democratic	1,128,702	60
1844	**James K. Polk**	Democratic	1,337,243	170
	Henry Clay	Whig	1,299,068	105
	James G. Birney	Liberty	62,300	
1848	**Zachary Taylor**	Whig	1,360,101	163
	(**Millard Fillmore,** 1850)			
	Lewis Cass	Democratic	1,220,544	127
	Martin Van Buren	Free Soil	291,263	
1852	**Franklin Pierce**	Democratic	1,601,474	254
	Winfield Scott	Whig	1,386,578	42
1856	**James Buchanan**	Democratic	1,838,169	174
	John C. Frémont	Republican	1,335,264	114
	Millard Fillmore	American	874,534	8
1860	**Abraham Lincoln**	Republican	1,865,593	180
	Stephen A. Douglas	Democratic	1,382,713	12
	John C. Breckinridge	Democratic	848,356	72
	John Bell	Constitutional Union	592,906	39

Year	Candidates	Party	Popular Vote	Electoral Vote
1864	**Abraham Lincoln** (**Andrew Johnson,** 1865)	Republican	2,206,938	212
	George B. McClellan	Democratic	1,803,787	21
1868	**Ulysses S. Grant**	Republican	3,013,421	214
	Horatio Seymour	Democratic	2,706,829	80
1872	**Ulysses S. Grant**	Republican	3,596,745	286
	Horace Greeley	Democratic	2,843,446	66
1876	**Rutherford B. Hayes**	Republican	4,036,572	185
	Samuel J. Tilden	Democratic	4,284,020	184
1880	**James A. Garfield** (**Chester A. Arthur,** 1881)	Republican	4,449,053	214
	Winfield S. Hancock	Democratic	4,442,035	155
	James B. Weaver	Greenback-Labor	308,578	
1884	**Grover Cleveland**	Democratic	4,874,986	219
	James G. Blaine	Republican	4,851,981	182
	Benjamin F. Butler	Greenback-Labor	175,370	
1888	**Benjamin Harrison**	Republican	5,444,337	233
	Grover Cleveland	Democratic	5,540,050	168
1892	**Grover Cleveland**	Democratic	5,554,414	277
	Benjamin Harrison	Republican	5,190,802	145
	James B. Weaver	People's	1,027,329	22
1896	**William McKinley**	Republican	7,035,638	271
	William J. Bryan	Democratic; Populist	6,467,946	176
1900	**William McKinley** (**Theodore Roosevelt,** 1901)	Republican	7,219,530	292
	William J. Bryan	Democratic; Populist	6,356,734	155
1904	**Theodore Roosevelt**	Republican	7,628,834	336
	Alton B. Parker	Democratic	5,084,401	140
	Eugene V. Debs	Socialist	402,460	
1908	**William H. Taft**	Republican	7,679,006	321
	William J. Bryan	Democratic	6,409,106	162
	Eugene V. Debs	Socialist	420,820	
1912	**Woodrow Wilson**	Democratic	6,286,820	435
	Theodore Roosevelt	Progressive	4,126,020	88
	William H. Taft	Republican	3,483,922	8
	Eugene V. Debs	Socialist	897,011	
1916	**Woodrow Wilson**	Democratic	9,129,606	277
	Charles E. Hughes	Republican	8,538,221	254
1920	**Warren G. Harding** (**Calvin Coolidge,** 1923)	Republican	16,152,200	404
	James M. Cox	Democratic	9,147,353	127
	Eugene V. Debs	Socialist	919,799	

Year	*Candidates*	*Party*	*Popular Vote*	*Electoral Vote*
1924	**Calvin Coolidge**	Republican	15,725,016	382
	John W. Davis	Democratic	8,385,586	136
	Robert M. LaFollette	Progressive	4,822,856	13
1928	**Herbert C. Hoover**	Republican	21,392,190	444
	Alfred E. Smith	Democratic	15,016,443	87
1932	**Franklin D. Roosevelt**	Democratic	22,809,638	472
	Herbert C. Hoover	Republican	15,758,901	59
	Norman Thomas	Socialist	881,951	
1936	**Franklin D. Roosevelt**	Democratic	27,751,612	523
	Alfred M. Landon	Republican	16,681,913	8
	William Lemke	Union	891,858	
1940	**Franklin D. Roosevelt**	Democratic	27,243,466	449
	Wendell L. Willkie	Republican	22,304,755	82
1944	**Franklin D. Roosevelt** (**Harry S Truman,** 1945)	Democratic	25,602,505	432
	Thomas E. Dewey	Republican	22,006,278	99
1948	**Harry S Truman**	Democratic	24,105,812	303
	Thomas E. Dewey	Republican	21,970,065	189
	J. Strom Thurmond	States' Rights	1,169,063	39
	Henry A. Wallace	Progressive	1,157,172	
1952	**Dwight D. Eisenhower**	Republican	33,936,234	442
	Adlai E. Stevenson	Democratic	27,314,992	89
1956	**Dwight D. Eisenhower**	Republican	35,590,472	457
	Adlai E. Stevenson	Democratic	26,022,752	73
1960	**John F. Kennedy** (**Lyndon B. Johnson,** 1963)	Democratic	34,227,096	303
	Richard M. Nixon	Republican	34,108,546	219
1964	**Lyndon B. Johnson**	Democratic	43,126,233	486
	Barry M. Goldwater	Republican	27,174,989	52
1968	**Richard M. Nixon**	Republican	31,783,783	301
	Hubert H. Humphrey	Democratic	31,271,839	191
	George C. Wallace	Amer. Independent	9,899,557	46
1972	**Richard M. Nixon** (**Gerald R. Ford,** 1974)	Republican	47,169,911	521
	George S. McGovern	Democratic	29,170,383	17

Date of Statehood

Delaware	December 7, 1787	Michigan	January 16, 1837
Pennsylvania	December 12, 1787	Florida	March 3, 1845
New Jersey	December 18, 1787	Texas	December 29, 1845
Georgia	January 2, 1788	Iowa	December 28, 1846
Connecticut	January 9, 1788	Wisconsin	May 29, 1848
Massachusetts	February 6, 1788	California	September 9, 1850
Maryland	April 28, 1788	Minnesota	May 11, 1858
South Carolina	May 23, 1788	Oregon	February 14, 1859
New Hampshire	June 21, 1788	Kansas	January 29, 1861
Virginia	June 25, 1788	West Virginia	June 19, 1863
New York	July 26, 1788	Nevada	October 31, 1864
North Carolina	November 21, 1789	Nebraska	March 1, 1867
Rhode Island	May 29, 1790	Colorado	August 1, 1876
Vermont	March 4, 1791	North Dakota	November 2, 1889
Kentucky	June 1, 1792	South Dakota	November 2, 1889
Tennessee	June 1, 1796	Montana	November 8, 1889
Ohio	March 1, 1803	Washington	November 11, 1889
Louisiana	April 30, 1812	Idaho	July 3, 1890
Indiana	December 11, 1816	Wyoming	July 10, 1890
Mississippi	December 10, 1817	Utah	January 4, 1896
Illinois	December 3, 1818	Oklahoma	November 16, 1907
Alabama	December 14, 1819	New Mexico	January 6, 1912
Maine	March 15, 1820	Arizona	February 14, 1912
Missouri	August 10, 1821	Alaska	January 3, 1959
Arkansas	June 15, 1836	Hawaii	August 21, 1959

Population of the United States

1790	3,929,214
1800	5,308,483
1810	7,239,881
1820	9,638,453
1830	12,860,692
1840	17,063,353
1850	23,191,876
1860	31,443,321
1870	38,558,371
1880	50,155,783
1890	62,947,714
1900	75,994,575
1910	91,972,266
1920	105,710,620
1930	122,775,046
1940	131,669,275
1950	150,697,361
1960	179,323,175
1970	204,765,770

Chief Justices of the United States Supreme Court

John Jay, N.Y. 1789–1795
John Rutledge, S.C. 1795
Oliver Ellsworth, Conn. 1795–1799
John Marshall, Va. 1801–1835
Roger B. Taney, Md. 1836–1864
Salmon P. Chase, Ohio 1864–1873
Morrison R. Waite, Ohio 1874–1888
Melville W. Fuller, Ill. 1888–1910
Edward D. White, La. 1910–1921
William H. Taft, Ohio 1921–1930
Charles E. Hughes, N.Y. 1930–1941
Harlan F. Stone, N.Y. 1941–1946
Fred M. Vinson, Ky. 1946–1953
Earl Warren, Calif. 1953–1969
Warren E. Burger, Minn. 1969–

Presidents, Vice-Presidents, and Cabinet Members

President		Vice-President		Secretary of State		Secretary of Treasury		Secretary of War	
1. George Washington	1789	John Adams	1789	T. Jefferson	1789	Alex. Hamilton	1789	Henry Knox	1789
Federalist				E. Randolph	1794	Oliver Wolcott	1795	T. Pickering	1795
				T. Pickering	1795			Jas. McHenry	1796
2. John Adams	1797	Thomas Jefferson	1797	T. Pickering	1797	Oliver Wolcott	1797	Jas. McHenry	1797
Federalist				John Marshall	1800	Samuel Dexter	1801	John Marshall	1800
								Samuel Dexter	1800
								R. Griswold	1801
3. Thomas Jefferson	1801	Aaron Burr	1801	James Madison	1801	Samuel Dexter	1801	H. Dearborn	1801
Republican		George Clinton	1805			Albert Gallatin	1801		
4. James Madison	1809	George Clinton	1809	Robert Smith	1809	Albert Gallatin	1809	Wm. Eustis	1809
Republican		Elbridge Gerry	1813	James Monroe	1811	G. W. Campbell	1814	J. Armstrong	1813
						A. J. Dallas	1814	James Monroe	1814
						W. H. Crawford	1816	W. H. Crawford	1815
5. James Monroe	1817	D. D. Tompkins	1817	J. Q. Adams	1817	W. H. Crawford	1817	Isaac Shelby	1817
Republican								Geo. Graham	1817
								J. C. Calhoun	1817
6. John Quincy Adams	1825	John C. Calhoun	1825	Henry Clay	1825	Richard Rush	1825	Jas. Barbour	1825
Nat'l Republican								Peter B. Porter	1828
7. Andrew Jackson	1829	John C. Calhoun	1829	M. Van Buren	1829	Sam D. Ingham	1820	John H. Eaton	1829
Democrat		Martin Van Buren	1833	E. Livingston	1831	Louis McLane	1831	Lewis Cass	1831
				Louis McLane	1833	W. J. Duane	1833	B. F. Butler	1837
				John Forsyth	1834	Roger B. Taney	1833		
						Levi Woodbury	1834		
8. Martin Van Buren	1837	Richard M. Johnson	1837	John Forsyth	1837	Levi Woodbury	1837	Joel R. Poinsett	1837
Democratic									
9. William H. Harrison	1841	John Tyler	1841	Daniel Webster	1841	Thos. Ewing	1841	John Bell	1841
Whig									
10. John Tyler	1841			Daniel Webster	1841	Thos. Ewing	1841	John Bell	1841
Whig and Democrat				Hugh S. Legare	1843	Walter Forward	1841	John McLean	1841
				Abel P. Upshur	1843	John C. Spencer	1843	J. C. Spencer	1841
				John C. Calhoun	1844	Geo. M. Bibb	1844	Jas. M. Porter	1843
								Wm. Wilkins	1844
11. James K. Polk,	1845	George M. Dallas	1845	James Buchanan	1845	Robt. J. Walker	1845	Wm. L. Marcy	1845
Democrat									
12. Zachary Taylor	1849	Millard Fillmore	1849	John M. Clayton	1849	Wm. M. Meredith	1849	G. W. Crawford	1849
Whig									
13. Millard Fillmore	1850			Daniel Webster	1850	Thomas Corwin	1850	C. M. Conrad	1850
Whig				Edward Everett	1852				
14. Franklin Pierce	1853	William R. D. King	1853	W. L. Marcy	1853	James Guthrie	1853	Jefferson Davis	1853
Democratic									

Attorney General		Postmaster General*		Secretary of Navy		Secretary of Interior		Secretary of Agriculture	Other Members
E. Randolph Wm. Bradford Charles Lee	1789 1794 1795	Samuel Osgood Tim Pickering Jos. Habersham	1789 1791 1795						
Charles Lee Theo. Parsons	1797 1801	Jos. Habersham	1797	Benj. Stoddert	1798				
Levi Lincoln Robert Smith J. Breckinridge C. A. Rodney	1801 1805 1805 1807	Jos. Habersham Gideon Granger	1801 1801	Benj. Stoddert Robert Smith J. Crownin-shield	1801 1801 1805				
C. A. Rodney Wm. Pinkney Richard Rush	1809 1811 1814	Gideon Granger R. J. Meigs, Jr.	1809 1814	Paul Hamilton William Jones B. W. Crownin-shield	1809 1813 1814				
Richard Rush William Wirt	1817 1817	R. J. Meigs, Jr. John McLean	1817 1823	B. W. Crownin-shield S. Thompson S. L. Southard	1817 1818 1823				
William Wirt	1825	John McLean	1825	S. L. Southard	1825				
John M. Berrien Roger B. Taney B. F. Butler	1829 1831 1833	Wm. T. Barry Amos Kendall	1829 1835	John Branch Levi Woodbury M. Dickerson	1829 1831 1834				
B. F. Butler Felix Grundy H. D. Gilpin	1837 1838 1840	Amos Kendall John M. Niles	1837 1840	M. Dickerson J. K. Paulding	1837 1838				
J. J. Crittenden	1841	Francis Granger	1841	G. E. Badger	1841				
J. J. Crittenden Hugh S. Legare John Nelson	1841 1841 1843	Francis Granger C. A. Wickliffe	1841 1841	G. E. Badger Abel Upshur D. Henshaw T. W. Gilmer John Y. Mason	1841 1841 1843 1844 1844				
John Y. Mason Nathan Clifford Isaac Toucey	1845 1846 1848	Cave Johnson	1845	George Bancroft John Y. Mason	1845 1846				
Reverdy Johnson	1849	Jacob Collamer	1849	Wm. B. Preston	1849	Thomas Ewing	1849		
J. J. Crittenden	1850	Nathan K. Hall S. D. Hubbard	1850 1852	W. A. Graham J. P. Kennedy	1850 1852	A. H. Stuart	1850		
Caleb Cushing	1853	J. Campbell	1853	J. C. Dobbin	1853	R. McClelland	1853		

*Not in Cabinet until 1829.

Presidents, Vice-Presidents, and Cabinet Members (Continued)

President		Vice-President		Secretary of State		Secretary of Treasury		Secretary of War	
15. James Buchanan Democratic	1857	John C. Breckinridge	1857	Lewis Cass J. S. Black	1857 1860	Howell Cobb Philip F. Thomas John A. Dix	1857 1860 1861	John B. Floyd Joseph Holt	1857 1861
16. Abraham Lincoln Republican	1861	Hannibal Hamlin Andrew Johnson	1861 1865	W. H. Seward	1861	Salmon P. Chase W. P. Fessenden Hugh McCulloch	1861 1864 1865	S. Cameron E. M. Stanton	1861 1862
17. Andrew Johnson Unionist	1865			Wm. H. Seward	1865	Hugh McCulloch	1865	E. M. Stanton U. S. Grant L. Thomas J. M. Schofield	1865 1867 1868 1868
18. Ulysses S. Grant Republican	1869	Schuyler Colfax Henry Wilson	1869 1873	E. B. Washburne Hamilton Fish	1869 1869	Geo. S. Boutwell W. A. Richardson Benj. H. Bristow Lot M. Morrill	1869 1873 1874 1876	J. A. Rawlins W. T. Sherman W. W. Belknap Alphonso Taft J. D. Cameron	1869 1869 1869 1876 1876
19. Rutherford B. Hayes Republican	1877	William A. Wheeler	1877	W. M. Evarts	1877	John Sherman	1877	G. W. McCrary Alex. Ramsey	1877 1879
20. James A. Garfield Republican	1881	Chester A. Arthur	1881	James G. Blaine	1881	Wm. Windom	1881	R. T. Lincoln	1881
21. Chester A. Arthur Republican	1881			F. T. Frelinghuysen	1881	Chas. J. Folger W. Q. Gresham Hugh McCulloch	1881 1884 1884	R. T. Lincoln	1881
22. Grover Cleveland Democratic	1885	T. A. Hendricks	1885	Thos. F. Bayard	1885	Daniel Manning Chas. S. Fairchild	1885 1887	W. C. Endicott	1885
23. Benjamin Harrison Republican	1889	Levi P. Morton	1889	James G. Blaine John W. Foster	1889 1892	Wm. Windom Charles Foster	1889 1891	R. Proctor S. B. Elkins	1889 1891
24. Grover Cleveland Democratic	1893	Adlai E. Stevenson	1893	W. Q. Gresham Richard Olney	1893 1895	John G. Carlisle	1893	D. S. Lamont	1893
25. William McKinley Republican	1897	Garret A. Hobart Theodore Roosevelt	1897 1901	John Sherman Wm. R. Day John Hay	1897 1897 1898	Lyman J. Gage	1897	R. A. Alger Elihu Root	1897 1899
26. Theodore Roosevelt Republican	1901	Chas. W. Fairbanks	1905	John Hay Elihu Root Robert Bacon	1901 1905 1909	Lyman J. Gage Leslie M. Shaw G. B. Cortelyou	1901 1902 1907	Elihu Root Wm. H. Taft Luke E. Wright	1901 1904 1908
27. William H. Taft Republican	1909	James S. Sherman	1909	P. C. Knox	1909	F. MacVeagh	1909	J. M. Dickenson H. L. Stimson	1909 1911
28. Woodrow Wilson Democratic	1913	Thomas R. Marshall	1913	Wm. J. Bryan Robert Lansing Bainbridge Colby	1913 1915 1920	W. G. McAdoo Carter Glass D. F. Houston	1913 1918 1920	L. M. Garrison N. D. Baker	1913 1916
29. Warren G. Harding Republican	1921	Calvin Coolidge	1921	Chas. E. Hughes	1921	Andrew W. Mellon	1921	John W. Weeks	1921

Attorney General	Postmaster General	Secretary of Navy	Secretary of Interior	Secretary of Agriculture
J. S. Black 1857 Edw. M. Stanton 1860	A. V. Brown 1857 Joseph Holt 1859	Isaac Toucey 1857	J. Thompson 1857	Cabinet status since 1889.
Edward Bates 1861 Titian J. Coffey 1863 James Speed 1864	Horatio King 1861 M. Blair 1861 Wm. Dennison 1864	Gideon Welles 1861	Caleb B. Smith 1861 John P. Usher 1863	
James Speed 1865 Henry Stanbery 1866 Wm. M. Evarts 1868	Wm. Dennison 1865 A. W.Randall 1866	Gideon Welles 1865	John P. Usher 1865 James Harlan 1865 O. H. Browning 1866	
E. R. Hoar 1869 A. T. Ackerman 1870 G. H. Williams 1871 Edw. Pierrepont 1875 Alphonso Taft 1876	J. A. J. Creswell 1869 J. W. Marshall 1874 Marshall Jewell 1874 Jas. N. Tyner 1876	A. E. Borie 1869 G. M. Robeson 1869	Jacob D. Cox 1869 C. Delano 1870 Z. Chandler 1875	
Chas. Devens 1877	David M. Key 1877 H. Maynard 1880	R. W. Thompson 1877 N. Goff, Jr. 1881	Carl Schurz 1877	
W. MacVeagh 1881	T. L. James 1881	W. H. Hunt 1881	S. J. Kirkwood 1881	
B. H. Brewster 1881	T. O. Howe 1881 W. Q. Gresham 1883 Frank Hatton 1884	W. E. Chandler 1881	H. M. Teller 1881	
A. H. Garland 1885	Wm. F. Vilas 1885 D. M. Dickinson 1888	W. C. Whitney 1885	L. Q. C. Lamar 1885 Wm. F. Vilas 1888	N. J. Colman 1889
W. H. H. Miller 1889	J. Wanamaker 1889	Benj. F. Tracy 1889	John W. Noble 1889	J. M. Rusk 1889
R. Olney 1893 J. Harmon 1895	W. S. Bissell 1893 W. L. Wilson 1895	Hilary A. Herbert	Hoke Smith 1893 D. R. Francis 1896	J. S. Morton 1893
J. McKenna 1897 J. W. Griggs 1897 P. C. Knox 1901	James A. Gary 1897 Chas. E. Smith 1898	John D. Long 1897	C. N. Bliss 1897 E. A. Hitchcock 1899	James Wilson 1897
P. C. Knox 1901 W. H. Moody 1904 C. J. Bonaparte 1907	Chas. E. Smith 1901 H. C. Payne 1902 R. J. Wynne 1904 G. B. Cortelyou 1905 G. von L. Meyer 1907	John D. Long 1901 W. H. Moody 1902 Paul Morton 1904 C. J. Bonaparte 1905 V. H. Metcalf 1907 T. H. Newberry 1908	E. A. Hitchcock 1901 J. R. Garfield 1907	James Wilson 1901
G. W. Wickersham 1909	F. H. Hitchcock 1909	G. von L. Meyer 1909	R. A. Ballinger 1909 W. L. Fisher 1911	James Wilson 1909
J. C. McReynolds 1913 T. W. Gregory 1914 A. M. Palmer 1919	A. S. Burleson 1913	J. Daniels 1913	F. K. Lane 1913 J. B. Payne 1920	D. F. Houston 1913 E. T. Meredith 1920
H. M. Daugherty 1921	Will H. Hays 1921 Hubert Work 1922 Harry S. New 1923	Edwin Denby 1921	Albert B. Fall 1921 Hubert Work 1923	H. C. Wallace 1921

Other Members

Secretary of Commerce and Labor	
G. B. Cortelyou	1903
Victor H. Metcalf	1904
O. S. Straus	1907
Chas. Nagel	1909
(Department divided, 1913)	

Secretary of Commerce	
W. C. Redfield	1913
J. W. Alexander	1919
H. C. Hoover	1921
H. C. Hoover	1925
W. F. Whiting	1928
R. P. Lamont	1929
R. D. Chapin	1932
D. C. Roper	1933
H. L. Hopkins	1939
Jesse Jones	1940
Henry A. Wallace	1945
W. Averell Harriman	1946
Charles W. Sawyer	1948
Sinclair Weeks	1953
Lewis L. Strauss	1958
Frederick H. Mueller	1959
Luther H. Hodges	1961
J. Thomas Connor	1964
A. B. Trowbridge	1967
C. R. Smith	1968
Maurice H. Stans	1969
P. G. Peterson	1972
F. B. Dent	1973
R. C. B. Morton	1975

Secretary of Labor	
W. B. Wilson	1913
J. J. Davis	1921
W. N. Doak	1930
Frances Perkins	1933
L. B. Schwellenbach	1945
M. J. Tobin	1948
M. P. Durkin	1953
James P. Mitchell	1953
Arthur J. Goldberg	1961
W. Willard Wirtz	1962
George P. Shultz	1969
James D. Hodgson	1970
P. J. Brennan	1973
John Dunlop	1975

Secretary of Defense	
James V. Forrestal	1947
Louis A. Johnson	1949
George C. Marshall	1950
Robert A. Lovett	1951
Charles E. Wison	1953
Neil McElroy	1957
Thomas Gates	1960
Robert S. McNamara	1961

Presidents, Vice-Presidents, and Cabinet Members (Continued)

President		Vice-President		Secretary of State		Secretary of Treasury		Secretary of War*	
30. Calvin Coolidge Republican	1923	Charles G. Dawes	1925	Chas. E. Hughes Frank B. Kellogg	1923 1925	Andrew W. Mellon	1923	John W. Weeks Dwight F. Davis	1923 1925
31. Herbert Hoover Republican	1929	Charles Curtis	1929	H. L. Stimson	1929	Andrew W. Mellon Ogden L. Mills	1929 1932	James W. Good P. J. Hurley	1929 1929
32. Franklin D. Roosevelt Democratic	1933	John Nance Garner Henry A. Wallace Harry S Truman	1933 1941 1945	Cordell Hull E. R. Stettinius, Jr.	1933 1944	Wm. H. Woodin H. Morgenthau, Jr.	1933 1934	Geo. H. Dern H. A. Woodring H. L. Stimson	1933 1936 1940
33. Harry S Truman Democratic	1945	Alben W. Barkley	1949	James F. Byrnes Geo. C. Marshall Dean G. Acheson	1945 1947 1949	Fred M. Vinson John W. Snyder	1945 1946	Robt. H. Patterson K. C. Royall	1945 1947
34. Dwight D. Eisenhower Republican	1953	Richard M. Nixon	1953	John Foster Dulles Christian Herter	1953 1959	Geo. C. Humphrey Robt. B. Anderson	1953 1957		
35. John F. Kennedy Democratic	1961	Lyndon B. Johnson	1961	Dean Rusk	1961	C. Douglas Dillon	1961		
36. Lyndon B. Johnson Democratic	1963	Hubert H. Humphrey	1965			Henry H. Fowler	1965		
37. Richard M. Nixon Republican	1969	Spiro T. Agnew Gerald R. Ford	1969 1973	William P. Rogers Henry A. Kissinger	1969 1973	David M. Kennedy John B. Connally George P. Schultz	1969 1970 1972		
38. Gerald R. Ford	1974	Nelson A. Rockefeller	1974			William E. Simon	1974		

*Lost Cabinet status in 1947.

Attorney General		Postmaster General**		Secretary of Navy†		Secretary of Interior		Secretary of Agriculture	
H. M. Daugherty	1923	Harry S. New	1923	Edwin Denby	1923	Hubert Work	1923	H. M. Gore	1924
Harlan F. Stone	1924			C. D. Wilbur	1924	Roy O. West	1928	W. M. Jardine	1925
John G. Sargent	1925								
Wm. D. Mitchell	1929	W. F. Brown	1929	C. F. Adams	1929	Ray L. Wilbur	1929	A. M. Hyde	1929
H. S. Cummings	1933	James A. Farley	1933	C. A. Swanson	1933	Harold L. Ickes	1933	H. A. Wallace	1933
Frank Murphy	1939	F. C. Walker	1940	Chas. Edison	1940			C. R. Wickard	1940
Robt. H. Jackson	1940			Frank Knox	1940				
Francis Biddle	1941			J. V. Forrestal	1944				
Tom C. Clark	1945	R. E. Hannegan	1945	J. V. Forrestal	1945	Harold L. Ickes	1945	C. P. Anderson	1945
J. H. McGrath	1949	J. L. Donaldson	1947			Julius A. Krug	1946	C. F. Brannan	1948
J. P. McGranery	1952					O. L. Chapman	1951		
H. Brownell, Jr.	1953	A. E. Summerfield	1953			Douglas McKay	1953	Ezra T. Benson	1953
Wm. P. Rogers	1957					Fred Seaton	1956		
Robt. F. Kennedy	1961	J. Edward Day	1961			S. L. Udall	1961	O. L. Freeman	1961
		J. A. Gronouski	1963						
N. deB. Katzenbach	1965	L. F. O'Brien	1965						
Ramsey Clark	1967	W. M. Watson	1968						
John N. Mitchell	1969	W. M. Blount	1969			W. J. Hickel	1969	C. M. Hardin	1969
R. G. Kliendienst	1972					R. C. B. Morton	1971	Earl L. Butz	1971
E. L. Richardson	1973								
William B. Saxbe	1973								
Edward Levi	1975								

Other Members

Secretary of Defense (Cont.)

Clark M. Clifford	1968
Melvin R. Laird	1969
Elliott L. Richardson	1973
James R. Schlesinger	1973

Secretary of Health, Education, and Welfare

Oveta Culp Hobby	1953
Marion B. Folsom	1955
Arthur S. Flemming	1958
Abraham A. Ribicoff	1961
A. J. Celebrezze	1962
John W. Gardner	1965
Wilbur J. Cohen	1968
Robert H. Finch	1969
Elliott L. Richardson	1970
C. W. Weinberger	1973
David Mathews	1975

Secretary of Housing and Urban Development

Robert C. Weaver	1966
George W. Romney	1969
James T. Lynn	1973
Carla A. Hills	1975

Secretary of Transportation

Alan S. Boyd	1967
John A. Volpe	1969
C. S. Brinegar	1973
Wm. T. Coleman, Jr.	1975

**Lost Cabinet status in 1971.
†Lost Cabinet status in 1947.

PHOTO CREDITS

Addison Gallery of American Art, Phillips Academy, Andover, Mass.: 641

American Antiquarian Society: 93, 121, 142, 148, 181 bottom, 280 top, 292, 376 bottom, 758 bottom

American Museum of Natural History: 14

The Bettmann Archive: 21, 89, 181 top, 240, 243, 250, 254, 315, 363 right, 376 top, 392, 408 right, 471, 516, 545 right, 557, 622, 626, 633 bottom, 689, 766, 769, 783

Black Star (Fenno Jacobs): 899

Herbert Block from *The Herblock Book* (Beacon Press, 1952): 897

Collection of Boatmen's National Bank of St. Louis: 319

Boston Museum of Fine Arts: 104

The Boston Public Library, Print Department: 129, 137, 141, 147, 154, 158, 306, 335, 339, 340, 415 bottom, 426, 432, 444, 446, 450, 460, 464, 466, 474, 478, 480, 493, 499, 500, 514 top, 518, 521, 535, 539, 554, 627 top

Brown Brothers: 195 top, 216, 356 bottom, 396, 398, 399, 436 bottom, 437 bottom, 442, 481, 489, 491, 505, 580, 589, 607 bottom, 610, 615, 618, 627 bottom, 629, 631 top, 638, 644, 653, 659, 675, 703, 729, 741, 743, 749, 760, 776, 782, 788, 816, 817, 823, 907

Chicago Historical Society: 367

Geoffrey Clements, Staten Island, N.Y.: 323, 327

State Historical Society of Colorado: 564

Culver Pictures: 17, 46, 59, 156, 175, 242, 317, 346, 379, 408 left, 413, 461, 490, 541, 545 left, 555 left, 592, 594, 597, 603, 605, 607 top, 651, 669, 687, 706 bottom, 711, 725, 739, 742, 745, 752, 763, 767, 772, 797, 809, 812, 814, 815, 818, 906, 909

Daily Mail, November 17, 1939: 871

DeCapo Press (Eugene Lyons, *The Life and Death of Sacco and Vanzetti*, 1970): 801

Denver Public Library, Western History Department: 239, 574

Courtesy of the Essex Institute, Salem, Mass.: 95

Fruitlands Museum, Harvard, Mass.: 411

The Granger Collection, N.Y.: 125, 227

Harvard University: 324 and 400 (Houghton Library), 562 top (Peabody Museum), 168 (Portrait Collection, Bequest of Ward Nicolas Boylston, 1828)

Holt, Rinehart & Winston (*New History of the U.S.*): 187

Honolulu Academy of Arts: 363 left

Illinois State Historical Library, Springfield: 525

Illustrated Newspapers Group, *The Illustrated London News*, 8/9/1866: 386

Dorreen Labby: 953

The Latter Day Saints, Church of Jesus Christ: 440

Library of Congress: 57, 78, 113, 351, 356 top, 412, 415 top, 430, 495, 504, 513, 537, 562 bottom, 575 top, 579 top & middle, 580, 623, 625, 631 bottom, 635 bottom, 673, 684, 695, 837

Stefan Lorant, *The New World*: 1, 4, 11, 35 top

Macmillan Co. (*Robert M. LaFollette*, 1953; courtesy Boston Public Library): 732

Magnum Photos (Lessing): 951

Mariners Museum, Newport News, Va.: 211, 281

The Maryland Historical Society, Baltimore: 266

The Metropolitan Museum of Art: 73 (Gift of Edgar William and Bernice Chrysler Garbisch, 1963), 132 (Bequest of Charles Allen Munn, 1924), 133 (Arthur H. Hearn Fund, 1950, courtesy of Association of American Artists), 145 (Bequest of Charles Allen Munn, 1924), 280 bottom (Gift of Mrs. John Sylvester, 1936), 437, 514 bottom (Harris Brisbane Dick Fund, 1938), 661 (Wolfe Fund, 1906)

The University of Michigan at Ann Arbor, Engineering-Transportation Library: 361

Missouri Historical Society: 237, 301

University of Missouri at Columbia, Western Historical Manuscripts Collection: 570

Montana Historical Society, Helena: 575 bottom

NASA: 71

The National Archives: 70 (Bureau of Indian Affairs), 519 (U.S. Signal Corps), 778 (U.S. Signal Corps), 781 (165-WW-480D-1), 786 (U.S. Signal Corps), 885 top (80-G-164070)

National Gallery of Art, Index of American Design, Washington, D.C.: 582

Nebraska State Historical Society, Lincoln: 549, 579 bottom (both Solomon D. Butcher Collection)

The New Brunswick Museum, courtesy Webster Collection of Pictorial Canadiana: 112

New Hampshire Historical Society, Concord: 457

Museum of the City of New York: 389, 423 (H. T. Peters Collection), 633 top and 635 top (Jacob A. Riis Collection)

New York Graphic Society, Greenwich, Conn.: 364

The New York Historical Society: 195 bottom, 207, 245, 255, 265, 284, 304, 348, 371, 434, 456, 503, 658, 683, 839

New York News, Inc., *The News*: 666 bottom

The New York Public Library, Astor Lenox & Tilden Foundation: 258, 279, 302, 355, 357, 403, 656, 706, 709, 718; I. N. Phelps Stokes Collection, Prints Division: 27, 60, 80, 91, 107, 116, 183, 203, 270, 276 top; Rare Book Division: 7, 8, 32, 35 bottom, 101, 338 left, 455, 538; Manuscript and Archives Division: 441; Schomberg Collection: 536, 666 top

The New York State Library, Albany: 224, 225

Nosta Glaser, Philadelphia (*engraved America*, 1970): 2, 36, 58, 78, 80, 188, 223, 233, 292 bottom

The Old Print Shop, N. Y. C.: 271, 298

The Peabody Museum of Salem: 10, 31, 49, 69, 75, 149, 179, 259, 267, 281, 291, 369, 436 top and middle, 510

Penn Community Services: 555 right

The Historical Society of Pennsylvania: 153, 161, 253, 295

The Philadelphia Museum of Art: 103 (Mr. & Mrs. Wharton Sinkler Collection), 662 (Given by Mrs. Thomas Eakins & Miss Mary A. Williams)

The Pierpont Morgan Library: 601

Plimoth Plantation, Plymouth, Mass.: 24, 47

Public Archives of Canada: 117

Scribner Art Files: 808

Simon & Schuster (Roger Butterfield, *The American Past*, 1957): 543 (*The New York Tribune*), 670 bottom (Interstate Commerce Commission), 679 (*Evening Telegraph*), 719 (*The New York Sun*), 748 and 873 (courtesy, *Chicago Tribune*), 750 (The Art Young Estate), 832 (*Collier's*), 835 (Media General, Inc.)

Smithsonian Institution: 276 bottom, 384, 385, 405, 569, 571

The St. Louis Art Museum: 404

Stock Boston: 987, 994, 1000

Sy Seidman: 473, 529

Tennessee State Library and Archives, Nashville, Andrew Jackson Papers, Manuscripts Section: 337

Time Life Picture Agency, Mark Kauffman (*Time, Inc.*): 920

United Nations: 916

United Press International: 667, 712, 714, 744, 758 top, 771, 799, 830 bottom, 833, 842, 845, 854, 856 top, 865, 866, 869, 874, 878, 881, 885 bottom, 890, 892, 900, 903, 918, 924, 927, 929, 935, 940, 942, 943, 948, 950, 957, 966, 967 top, 970, 975, 981, 991, 993, 1004, 1005, 1006, 1007, 1010, 1014, 1015, 1017

"Verdict" January 22, 1900: 670 top

Virginia Museum of Fine Arts: 185

The Walters Art Gallery, Baltimore: 437 middle

Wide World: 724, 825, 830 top, 856 bottom, 859, 896 top and bottom, 913, 939, 962, 963, 967 bottom, 973, 984

The Henry Francis de Pont Winterthur Museum: 200

State Historical Society of Wisconsin, Madison: 737, 807

Woolaroc Museum, Bartlesville, Oklahoma: 326

Yale University Art Gallery: 277 (The Mabel Brady Garvan Collection)

INDEX

INDEX

B

C

D

F

K

M

O

P

T

U